The later Anglo-Saxon settlement at Bishopstone: a downland manor in the making

by Gabor Thomas

The later Anglo-Saxon settlement at Bishopstone: a downland manor in the making

by Gabor Thomas

with contributions by

Marion M Archibald, Steven Ashby,
Nancy Beavan Athfield, Rachel Ballantyne, Luke Barber,
Martin Bell, Mike Bispham, John Blair, Mykhailo Buzinny,
Gordon T Cook, David Defries, Pieter M Grootes, Ben Jervis,
Lynne Keys, Mary Lewis, Peter Marshall, Robert Neal,
Patrick Ottaway, Ben Pears, Kristopher Poole,
Thomas Pickles, Johannes van der Plicht,
Rebecca Reynolds, Louise C D Schoss,
Elizabeth Somerville

CBA Research Report 163
Council for British Archaeology
2010

Published in 2010 by the Council for British Archaeology
St Mary's House, 66 Bootham, York, YO30 7BZ

British Library cataloguing in Publication Data
A catalogue record for this book is available from the British Library
ISBN 978 1 902771 83 0

Typeset by Archétype Informatique, www.archetype-it.com
Cover designed by BP Design, York
Printed by Information Press, Eynsham, Oxon

Front cover: Conjectural reconstruction of Bishopstone courtyard range; view of excavation in progress
Back cover: Anglo-Saxon grave marker; burial row exposed in 2005; iron strap from ironwork hoard

Contents

List of figures

List of tables

List of colour plates (between pages 86 and 87)

List of contributors

Dr Marion M Archibald, formerly Department of Coins and Medals, British Museum

Dr Steven Ashby, Department of Archaeology, University of York, The King's Manor, York, Y01 7EP

Dr Nancy Beavan Athfield, Rafter Radiocarbon Laboratory, Institute of Geological and Nuclear Sciences, Box 31 312, Lower Hutt, New Zealand

Dr Rachel M Ballantyne, English Heritage, 24 Brooklands Avenue, Cambridge, CB2 2BU

Luke Barber, Sussex Archaeological Society, Barbican House Museum, 169 High Street, Lewes, East Sussex, BN7 1YE

Prof Martin Bell, Department of Archaeology, University of Reading, Whiteknights, Reading, RG6 6AB

Mike Bispham, 2 Cornerways, Well Lane, St Margaret's-at-Cliffe, Kent, CT15 6AA

Prof John Blair, The Queen's College, University of Oxford, Oxford, OX1 4AW

Dr Mykhailo Buzinny, The Marzeev Institute of Hygiene and Medical Ecology, 02094, Popudrenko str. 50, Kiev, Ukraine

Prof Gordon T Cook, SUERC, Rankine Avenue, Scottish Enterprise Technology Park, East Kilbride, G75 0QF

Dr David Defries, Department of History, University of Tennessee, 915 Volunteer Blvd., 6th Floor Dunford Hall, Knoxville, TN 37996-4065

Dr Pieter M Grootes, Leibiniz Labor für Altersbestimmung und Isopenforschung, Christian-Albrechts-Universität, Kiel, Germany

Ben Jervis, Department of Archaeology, University of Southampton, Highfield, Southampton, SO17 1BJ

Lynne Keys, 267 Weedington Road, London, NW5 4PR

Dr Mary Lewis, Department of Archaeology, University of Reading, Whiteknights, Reading, RG6 6AB

Dr Peter Marshall, Chronologies, 25 Onslow Road, Sheffield, S11 7AF

Robert Neal, 1 Thrush Close, Booker, High Wycombe, HP12 4RJ

Dr Patrick Ottaway, Archaeological Consultant, Tower House, Fishergate, York, YO10 4UA

Dr Ben Pears, Department of Archaeology, University of Exeter, Laver Building, North Park Road, Exeter, EX4 4QE

Dr Thomas Pickles, St Catherine's College, University of Oxford, Oxford, OX1 3UJ

Johannes van der Plicht, Centre for Isotope Research, University of Groningen, Nijenborgh 4, NL 9747, AG Groningen, The Netherlands

Kristopher Poole, Department of Archaeology, University of Nottingham, University Park, Archaeology and Classics Building, Nottingham, NG7 2RD

Rebbeca Reynolds, Department of Archaeology, University of Nottingham, University Park, Archaeology and Classics Building, Nottingham, NG7 2RD

Louise C D Schoss, Department of Anthropology, University of Kent, Canterbury, Kent, CT2 7NZ

Dr Elizabeth Somerville, Department of Biology and Environmental Science, School of Life Sciences, University of Sussex, Falmer, Brighton, BN1 9QG

Dr Gabor Thomas, Department of Archaeology, University of Reading, Whiteknights, Reading, RG6 6AB

Acknowledgements

The research upon which this report is based has relied upon the support and goodwill of nearly an entire community, including residents both within and without the historic core of Bishopstone. Over the past eight years the author has also been based in three different institutions, a journey which has allowed him to draw upon the input, advice, and expertise of many colleagues. It is hoped that this opening statement will provide some justification for the extensive list which now follows.

It is appropriate to commence at the beginning – the circle of friends and colleagues who helped to turn the Bishopstone excavations from the kernel of an idea into reality. I am deeply indebted to my former colleagues at the Sussex Archaeological Society, including those sitting on its Research and Editorial Committees in the three years of my tenure – in particular John Manley, John Bleach, Martin Brown, Peter Drewett, Sue Hamilton, and Chris Greatorex. Additionally, Pamela Combes and Christopher Whittick helped to develop the academic focus of the research and provided a fount of practical and moral support throughout the excavations: they will be only too aware of the gaps and deficiencies in this report, most gaping of all a synthesis of the medieval documentary archive for the manor of Bishopstone which deserves a volume of its own. The inaugural season of fieldwork at Norton went ahead with the permission and goodwill of the Collinsons of Norton Farm and the Tattershalls of Old Farm Cottages.

The audacious plan to dig up Bishopstone village green could not have happened without the kind permission of the then landowner John Willett, who has since generosity bequeathed the land to the parish council. Two individuals proved to be vital publicists for the project: Phillip Pople, the unofficial village historian whose work and publications have done much to instil a sense of place within the community, and the late Revd John Lloyd-Jones whose wisdom and infectious enthusiasm enlisted support from many quarters of the parish. Ultimately it was those living on the fringes of the village green who endured the sharp-end of the disruptions brought by a large-scale excavation: to tolerate our presence would have been nothing less than saintly, but all went beyond the call of duty to make us feel welcome. Karen Rayner and Tim Wilson of the Old School Cottage came to the rescue on innumerable occasions with tools and other logistical support and kindly gave us the run of the 'Walled Garden' for storage, whilst Peter and Janet Wright of Eadric Cottage assisted in our improvised system of turf removal and provided refreshments when most needed. From a personal perspective, I should like to register especial thanks to Dawn Lowe-Watson of Rose Cottage whose generosity and companionship will always be remembered with warm affection. Other local residents who deserve thanks for various forms of help and assistance include: Freyja Bailey-Barker, Ed and Biddy Jarzembowski, Kenneth Jones, Bob Moore, Richard and Die Morton, Gladys Pople, Peter Sinclair, Jeanie Sorrell, Roy Stratford, Linda Wallraven, and Jeff White.

Whilst many individuals passed through the excavations, the ultimate success of this research is attributable to a core group of staff and volunteers who undertook the majority of the digging, recording and analysis in the field. I owe a special debt of gratitude to the following individuals who applied themselves to the task of supervising with courage, humour and conviction: Ian Allison, Julie Bates, Rosie Cummings, Jack Feintuck, Kevin Fromings, Peter Ginn, Ben Jervis, Alex Langlands, Rufus Mitcheson, Owen O'Donnell, Leonie Pett, Simon Roffey, Dave Staunton, Martin Tkalez, Rob Wallace, and Liz Wilson. The Sussex Archaeological Society has amongst its membership a group of talented field technicians who brought comradeship and good humour to each of the excavations seasons: Darren and Lorna Hilborn, Tom Harrison, Bev Kerr, John Platt, and Matt Williams. Support of various forms was provided by the local commercial unit, Archaeology South-East, through the kind offices of Luke Barber, Neil and Fiona Griffin, and David Rudling.

The final two excavation seasons were conducted while the author was based in Classical and Archaeological Studies at the University of Kent. Three people in particular deserve mention for smoothing the transition to my first academic appointment and for encouraging me to continue with the excavations: Anthony Ward, Ellen Swift, and Steven Willis. Scott Legge in the Department of Anthropology enthusiastically took up the challenge of overseeing the study of the human remains, completed by his student, Louise Schoss, for an MSc dissertation. Analytical work on other aspects of the Bishopstone archive was also completed at Kent as part of undergraduate dissertations. I should like to thank Nigel Simpson and Lee Cunningham for help digitising plans and sections, Emily Bird and Jerry Cummings for cataloguing the ironwork and the loomweights respectively, and Mike Bispham for masterminding the analysis of the daub.

The bulk of this report in its current form was written after the author's move to the Department of Archaeology of the University Reading in 2007. It has benefited incalculably from the input of many of my current colleagues whose collective expertise has touched nearly all aspects of the analysis and interpretation. I owe a special debt of gratitude to Grenville Astill for providing critical feedback on several chapters and for supporting a case for research leave granted in my first academic year, to Mary Lewis for making improvements to the bone report, and to Martin Bell for contributing his piece on sea-level change. I should also like to thank the following who took time out of their busy schedules to provide technical input or else critical feedback on individual chapters: Richard Bradley, Hella Eckardt, Mike Fulford, Roberta Gilchrist, Rob Hosfield, Alexandra Knox, Margaret Mathews, Gundula Müldner, and Aleks Pluskowski.

Many colleagues working outside my own institutional sphere have provided intellectual input and ideas assimilated into the body of this report. John Blair has been an unfailing source of encouragement since the project's inception: he has added academic vigour to the final report not only through his own authorial contributions but also through his insights and observations on the archaeology both on site and during the post-excavation programme. I should also like to thank the following for useful discussions both on and off site: David Defries, Simon Draper, Mark Gardiner, Richard Gem, Helena Hamerow, the late Simon Jennings, David Martin, Andrew Reynolds, and Gareth Williams. Also deserving warm acknowledgment are the many individuals who provided expert guidance on various aspects of the post-excavation analysis whether in their capacity as professional consultants or as staff within the university sector. My special thanks to James Rackham and the team at the Environmental Archaeology Consultancy for devising an affordable strategy for analysing the plant biota assemblages and to Mike Allen and Rachel Ballantyne for seeing this analysis through to completion. Liz Barham, James Hales, and Patrick Ottaway provided advice on the storage and conservation of the ironwork, Naomi Sykes on the analysis of the faunal remains, Duncan Brown on the pottery, and Peter Marshall on the radiocarbon dating. For producing specialist reports in a timely and professional manner I should like to thank Marion Archibald, Steven Ashby, Luke Barber, Ben Jervis, Lynne Keys, Patrick Ottaway, Kris Poole, Rebecca Reynolds, and Liz Somerville. Graphics and illustrations were kindly provided by Rob Batchelor, Tyler Bell, Penny Copeland, Andy Gammon, Mark Gridley, Sue Rowland, and David Williams. Thanks are also due to an anonymous reviewer whose comments have helped to tighten up several aspects of the final report, especially those chapters discussing the buildings and other structural evidence.

The final expression of gratitude is reserved for my mother who has been an unfailing source of support and encouragement throughout my career in archaeology. I dedicate this report to her.

This research has been supported by grants from the British Academy, the Society of the Antiquaries of London, the Royal Archaeological Institute, the Council for British Archaeology, the Sussex Archaeological Society, the Society for Medieval Archaeology, the Robert Kiln Charitable Trust, and the Marc Fitch Fund.

Summary

The East Sussex village of Bishopstone, situated in a stretch of coastal downland in the lower reaches of the valley of the River Ouse, has entered archaeological orthodoxy as a classic example of a 'Middle Saxon Shift'. Today's settlement, a thin scatter of houses huddled around one of the county's finest pre-Conquest churches, lies along the axis of a valley which winds past the hamlet of Norton up towards the escarpment of the South Downs. Both are overlooked by the dramatic chalk promontory of Rookery Hill where rescue excavations in the early 1970s uncovered an 'antecedent' settlement pattern stretching back deep into prehistory. Habitation on this long-established site came to an abrupt end with the desertion of a sprawling settlement and associated burial ground established in the early Anglo-Saxon period. The current excavations, run between 2002 and 2005 under the auspices of the Sussex Archaeological Society and subsequently the University of Kent, were launched to investigate the transition between these two distinct phases of human habitation – the antecedent and the medieval – with an explicit focus on the origins of Bishopstone village. This report provides a comprehensive analysis, interpretation and academic contextualisation of the archaeological discoveries brought to light by that excavation, the first to sample a later Anglo-Saxon rural settlement in East Sussex on an extensive scale.

The target of the investigations was the village green, an area of 1800m² lying on the north side of the churchyard, under which was preserved a dense swathe of later Anglo-Saxon (8th- to late 10th-/early 11th-century) habitation. This took the form of a planned complex of timber 'halls', some with evidence for repairs and rebuilds, accompanied by a notable diversity of 'service structures' including one and possibly two latrines, and a unique survival in the form of a 1.8m-deep cellar surmounted by a tall, timber superstructure interpreted as a tower. A marked characteristic of the occupation was a zoned concentration of pits filled with large volumes of domestic rubbish, cess, and burnt structural remains. These contexts produced large volumes of artefacts, including no less than half a metric tonne of walling daub, and rich bioarchaeological data, the analysis of which has allowed the economy, culture, and living conditions of the Anglo-Saxon settlement to be examined. Domestic occupation encroached upon the outer portion of a pre-Conquest cemetery comprising 43 inhumations representing a mixed population, the majority buried clothed and in shrouds. These individuals displayed a range of pathologies including a high number of bone fractures, perhaps sustained through working in close proximity to farm animals, which might suggest that the excavated portion of the cemetery was reserved for estate workers.

In the absence of refined stratigraphic phasing, radiocarbon dating of human burials and articulated animal deposits proved crucially important for establishing a basic chronological framework for the settlement sequence. The results pushed the inception of the occupation back into the 8th century, considerably earlier than the oldest datable artefact, and determined that burial within the sampled portion of the pre-Conquest cemetery commenced during the later 7th or early 8th century and terminated in the decades around AD 900 when it was encroached upon by domestic occupation. The fact that these unexpectedly early dates conflict with recognised pottery chronologies has important implications for the dating of other later Anglo-Saxon settlements in the Sussex region.

Contextualisation of the archaeological discoveries made at Bishopstone was gained by integrating the results of geoarchaeological work in and around Bishopstone, enabling a reconstruction of dynamic changes to the coastal environment in the early medieval period, and a wide-ranging historical analysis including a re-examination of an 11th-century hagiographical source, the *Historia translationis sanctae Lewinnae*. The latter provides a possible context for linking the rebuilding of St Andrew's church to an act of saintly enshrinement towards the end of the 10th century; a fresh interpretation of the pre-Conquest phases of the church fabric is offered in support of this hypothesis.

The analytical sections of the report interrogate different classes of archaeological information – the built environment, the health and diet of the human population, personal possessions, and economic and craft activities – in order to elucidate the socio-economic conditions of the settlement. These various archaeological signatures allow Bishopstone to be situated within the context of an increasingly stable and hierarchical settlement pattern – an estate-centre complex where surplus generated from a resource-rich rich hinterland was channelled into lifestyles and activities expressive of the ideology and aspirations of a later Anglo-Saxon land-owning elite. This basic characterisation is enriched by alternative forms of analysis designed to bring deeper insights into daily life on later Anglo-Saxon settlements. Consideration is given to evidence for domestic rituals in the form of 'termination deposits' placed in abandoned structures and the possibility that the regulated approach to the disposal of human and domestic waste implied by Bishopstone's unusually high pit density may be related to its elevated social status.

The opportunity is taken to evaluate this archaeological visualisation against a historically derived settlement-narrative commencing with the foundation of an Anglo-Saxon minster at Bishopstone during the later 7th century and progressing to a period, from about AD 800, when the estate came under the 'direct lordship' of South Saxon bishops. Examination of the interplay between these different disciplinary perspectives is used to highlight the complexities and challenges of integrating archaeological and historical evidence in reconstructions of Anglo-Saxon life in the dynamic period of social change characterising the three centuries before the Norman Conquest.

The perception that the early medieval settlement sequence unearthed at Bishopstone subscribes to the paradigm of a 'Middle Saxon Shift' is finally brought under critical scrutiny. An evaluation of archaeological discoveries and metal-detected finds made elsewhere in the Bishopstone valley suggests that the emergence of the medieval settlement pattern could have followed a more complex course than a simple move from Rookery Hill to the site of the present-day village, a conclusion which has wider implications for understanding the dynamics of early medieval settlement in the chalklands of southern England.

Sommaire

Le village de Bishopstone se situe dans les collines côtières de l'East Sussex sur la partie inferieure de la rivière Ouse. Il est entré dans le canon archéologique comme un exemple classique du 'changement de l'époque saxonne moyenne'. Le village actuel, formé de maisons groupées autour d'une des plus belles églises du comté datant d'avant la conquête normande, suit les contours d'une vallée qui serpente vers les hauteurs des South Downs en passant á coté du hameau de Norton. Le promontoire spectaculaire de Rookery Hill, site de fouilles de sauvetage du début des années 1970, surplombe ces deux habitats. Ces fouilles ont révélé les traces d'un habitat étendu remontant loin dans la préhistoire. L'habitat prit fin de façon abrupte : en effet il fut abandonné, tout comme son cimetière établi au début de l'époque anglo-saxonne. Des fouilles récentes, entreprises entre 2002 et 2005 sous les auspices de la Sussex Archaeological Society puis de l'Université du Kent, ont été conduites dans le but d'examiner la transition entre ces deux phases distinctes d'habitation — c'est-à-dire l'habitat antérieur et le village médiéval — avec pour question centrale les origines du village de Bishopstone. Les résultats des fouilles archéologiques, les premières à avoir été conduites de manière extensive sur un habitat rural anglo-saxon tardif dans l'East Sussex, sont présentées dans ce rapport sous forme d'analyse détaillée, de mise en valeur et de mise en contexte

Les recherches se sont concentrées sur le terrain communal (*village green*), une surface de 1800m^2 située au nord du cimetière recouvrant une zone d'occupation dense datant de la période Anglo-Saxonne tardive 8ème–fin 10ème/début 11ème siècle apr. J.-C.). Il s'agit d'un complexe planifié de bâtiments en bois (*halls*), dont certains ont été réparés ou reconstruits, accompagnes de 'structures annexes' y compris une ou peut-être deux latrines et d'une structure unique formée par une cave profonde de 1,8m surmontée d'une superstructure en bois

haute, peut-être une tour. L'occupation se caractérise tout particulièrement par l'agencement en zone de fosses remplies d'abondants déchets domestiques, d'excréments et de vestiges brulés. Ces contextes on fourni un mobilier important, tel qu'une demie tonne de torchis ; l'analyse des données biologiques a permis de mieux cerner l'économie, la culture et les conditions de vie de l'habitat anglo-saxon. La zone d'occupation domestique a empiété sur la partie extérieure d'un cimetière datant d'avant la conquête normande qui contenait 43 inhumations, la plupart habillées et enveloppées dans linceuls. Ces individus, appartenant a une population mixte, souffraient d'une série de conditions pathologiques, y compris de nombreuses fractures peut-être survenues lors du maniement du bétail ; ceci pourrait suggérer la présence d'ouvriers agricoles dans cette partie du cimetière.

Vu le manque de données stratigraphiques, la datation par radiocarbone de sépultures humaines et d'ossements d'animaux articulés s'est révélée d'importance primordiale pour la mise en place d'un cadre chronologique pour les différentes phases de l'établissement. Elle a permis de faire remonter son origine au 8ème siècle apr. J.-C., donc bien avant le mobilier le plus ancien, et a démontré que les sépultures dans la partie fouillée du cimetière antérieur à la conquête normande s'échelonnent entre la fin du 7ème ou le début du 8ème siècle apr. J.-C. et les décennies autour de l'an 900 apr. J.-C., époque à laquelle l'habitat domestique gagna du terrain sur le cimetière. Des répercussions importantes pour la chronologie des établissements anglo-saxons tardifs du Sussex sont à prévoir étant donné la datation précoce et surprenante des vestiges qui est en désaccord avec la chronologie établie basée sur la céramique,

Les résultats de recherches géoarchéologiques à Bishopstone et dans ses environs ont permis de replacer les découvertes archéologiques dans leur contexte et de reconstruire les dynamiques du milieu côtier pendant le Haut Moyen-âge. Une analyse poussée des sources historiques, y compris le réexamen d'un texte hagiographique du 11ème siècle, l'*Historia translationis sanctae Lewinnae*, a également été entreprise. Ce document fournit un contexte probable pour la reconstruction de l'église de St Andrew, comme sanctuaire établi vers la fin du 10ème siècle apr. J.-C ; une nouvelle interprétation des phases antérieures à la conquête normande est proposée pour étayer cette hypothèse.

Le rapport contient une série d'analyses menées sur diverses catégories de données archéologiques — le bâti, la santé et l'alimentation de la population, les objets personnels, l'économie et l'artisanat — visant à mettre en valeur les conditions socio-économiques de l'habitat. Ces diverses signatures archéologiques permettent de situer Bishopstone dans un contexte marqué de plus en plus par une forme d'habitat stable : un complexe au centre d'un domaine bénéficiant du surplus produit par un arrière-pays riche en ressources, ce qui lui permit de diriger ces ressources vers un mode de vie reflétant l'idéologie et les aspirations des propriétaires terriens de l'époque anglo-saxonne tardive. A cette caractérisation de base viennent s'ajouter d'autres formes d'analyse cherchant à approfondir notre connaissance du quotidien anglo-saxon. On considère ainsi le rituel domestique sous forme de 'dépôts de fermeture' placés dans des structures abandonnées ainsi que la possibilité que l'attitude réglementée envers le

traitement des résidus domestiques et humains, attestée par la grande densité des fosses-dépotoir de Bishopstone, soit due a son rang social élevé.

La mise en valeur archéologique donne l'occasion de confronter cette dernière à une séquence basée sur les sources historiques qui débute avec la fondation de l'église (*minster*) anglo-saxonne de Bishopstone vers la fin du 7ème siècle apr. J.-C. et qui progresse, à partir d'environ 800 apr. J.-C., vers un domaine sous le contrôle direct des évêques du Sud saxon. Un examen des relations entre ces perspectives diverses permet de mettre l'accent sur les difficultés et la complexité d'une intégration entre les documents archéologiques et historiques dans le but de reconstruire un mode de vie anglo-saxon à une époque qui vécut de profondes transformations sociales pendant les trois siècles antérieurs à la conquête normande.

Enfin la séquence découverte à Bishopstone et sa conformité au concept du 'changement de l'époque saxonne moyenne' sont soumises à un examen critique. Une évaluation d'objets récupérés par détecteurs de métaux et d'autres trouvailles faites ailleurs dans la vallée de Bishopstone permet de suggérer que l'origine de la trame de l'habitat a suivi une trajectoire plus complexe qu'un simple déplacement depuis Rookery Hill vers le village actuel. Cette conclusion est riche de conséquences pour la compréhension des dynamiques de l'habitat haut-moyenâgeux sur le sol calcaire de l'Angleterre du sud.

Zusammenfassung

Das Dorf Bishopstone (East Sussex) liegt in einer Hügellandschaft im unteren Bereich des Ousetals in der Nähe der Küste Südenglands. Bishopstone ist in die archäologische Orthodoxie eingetreten, da es ein klassisches Beispiel der 'mittelangelsächsischen Veränderung' darstellt. Die heutige Siedlung, eine wenig dichte Konzentration von Häuser rund um eine der schönsten Kirchen der vor-Normannischen Zeit des Bezirks, liegt in einem Tal, dass dem Weiler Norton vorbeiführt und die Höhen der South Downs erreicht. Der eindrucksvolle Sporn von Rookery Hill liegt oberhalb; dort haben Notausgrabungen anfangs der 1970er Jahren Spuren einer älteren Besiedlung, die weit in die Vorgeschichte zurückgeht, freigelegt. Die Belegung dieser langdauernden Wohnstätte kam zu einem abrupten Ende: die ausgedehnte Siedlung und das Gräberfeld, dass in frühsächsischer Zeit entstand, wurden aufgelassen. Neuere Ausgrabungen, die zuerst die Sussex Archaeological Society und dann die Universität Kent zwischen 2002 und 2005 durchgeführt haben, hatten das Ziel den Übergang zwischen den beiden Siedlungsphasen — die ältere Siedlung und das mittelalterliche Dorf — mit

besonderer Berücksichtigung des Ursprungs von Bishopstone zu untersuchen. Der vorliegende Bericht enthält umfassende Analysen, Auswertungen und Besprechungen des Kontexts des archäologischen Befundes, der erste der in großem Maßstab auf einer spätangellsächsischen Siedlung in East Sussex ausgegraben wurde.

Der Schwerpunkt der Untersuchungen war der Dorfplatz (*village green*), ein Areal von 1800m² auf der nördlichen Seite des Friedhofs, unter dem eine dicht belegte Siedlung der spätangelsächsischen Zeit (8. bis 10. oder anfangs 11. Jahrhundert) erhalten war. Es handelt sich um einen geplanten Komplex von Holzgebäuden (*halls*), die teilweise repariert oder wiedererrichtet wurden; dabei gab es auch zahlreiche und vielfältige Nebengebäude oder 'Dienststrukturen', wie zum Beispiel eine oder zwei Latrinen und einen 1,8m tiefen Keller mit einem hohen Obergeschoss aus Holz, der als Turm interpretiert wird. Bemerkenswert war die Zonierung der Gruben, die mit grossen Mengen von Abfall, Exkrementen und abgebrannten Resten von Strukturen gefüllt waren. Von diesen Gruben wurde eine eindrückliche Zahl von Artefakten, wie zum Beispiel eine halbe Tonne Hüttenlehm, sowie eine reichliche Sammlung von archäobiologischen Daten geborgen; dadurch konnten die Wirtschaft, die Kultur und die Lebensbedingungen der angelsächsischen Siedlung untersucht werden. Die Siedlungsfläche dehnte sich über den äußeren Teil eines vor-Normannischen Friedhofs aus; dieser enthielt 43 Bestattungen. Die Bevölkerung war gemischt und die meisten Leichen waren bekleidet, und trugen ein Leichentuch. Die Bestimmung einer Reihe von pathologischen Beschwerden, wie zahlreiche Knochenbrüche die vielleicht im Umgang mit Vieh erlitten wurden, lässt es vermuten, dass dieser Teil des Gräberfeldes für Landarbeiter bestimmt war.

Da keine stratigraphische Angaben vorlagen, war die ^{14}C Altersbestimmung von Bestattungen und Tierknochen noch im Skelettverband äußerst wichtig für die Festlegung eines chronologischen Rahmens. Die Resultate haben den Beginn der Belegung ins 8. Jahrhundert zurückgeschoben, also wesentlich früher als die ältesten datierbaren Artefakte und haben festgelegt, dass die Bestattungen im ausgegrabenen Teil des vor-Normannischen Gräberfeldes im späten 7. oder frühen 8. Jahrhundert einsetzten und um 900 zu Ende kamen, als die Siedlung sich darüber ausdehnte. Diese Altersbestimmungen sind überraschend früh und widersprechen die traditionelle Chronologie, die auf der Basis der Keramikfunde ruht, und hat besondere Bedeutung für die Datierung der angelsächsischen Besiedlung der Gegend Sussex.

Geoarchäologische Prospektionen in der Nähe von Bishopstone wurden in die Forschung integriert und haben es ermöglicht, den Befund von Bishopstone in Kontext zu bringen und die Veränderungen in der küstlichen Umgebung im Frühmittelalter auszuwerten, zusammen mit einer ausführlichen Untersuchung von einer hagiographischen Quelle des 11. Jahrhunderts, die *Historia translationis sanctae Lewinnae*. Diese Quelle liefert ein potentieller Kontext für die Umbruchphase im späten 10. Jahrhundert der Kirche St Andrew, vielleicht als Heiligenschrein; eine neue Interpretation der vor-Normannischen Phasen des Gebäudes wird hier vorgestellt.

Der analytische Teil des Berichts enthält die verschiedenen Datenkategorien — die bebaute Umgebung, die Gesundheit und Ernährung der Bevölkerung, persönliche Gegenstände, Wirtschaft und Handwerk — die die sozial-wirtschaftlichen Bedingungen in der Siedlung ins Licht bringen. Diese verschiedenen archäologischen Kennzeichen zeigen, dass Bishopstone zu einem mehr und mehr stabilen und hierarchischen Besiedlungschema gehörte — ein Landesbesitz wo der Überschuss von einem reichen Hinterland in das tägliche Leben, die Ideologie und die Aspirationen einer spätsächsischen Elite übermittelt wurde. Andere Auswertungen, die versuchen die Lebensbedingungen auf spätsächsischen Siedlungen in schärferen Fokus zu bringen, ergänzen diese Charakterisierung. Man betrachtet zum Beispiel eine Form Haushaltsritual, die sogenannten 'Schlussdeponierungen', die in verlassenen Gebäuden gefunden wurden. Es ist auch möglich, dass die besonders dichte Verbreitung der Abfallsgruben, die einem geregelten Verhalten gegenüber der Müllentsorgung entspricht, in Zusammenhang mit der hohen sozialen Stellung der Siedlung steht.

Das archäologische Bild wird auch mit der historisch übermittelten Darstellung der Siedlung verglichen; diese beginnt mit der Gründung im späten 7. Jahrhundert eines angelsächsischen Münsters in Bishopstone und führt, ab ungefähr 800, in einen Zeitraum in welchem der Landesbesitz unter 'direkter Herrschaft' der Südsächsischen Bischöfe kam. Die Verhältnisse zwischen diesen verschiedenen fachlichen Perspektiven werden untersucht und die Ergebnisse ausgewertet, um die Komplexität und die Aufforderungen einer Integrierung der archäologischen und historischen Daten deutlich zu machen; diese Fragestellungen betreffen die Schilderung angelsächsischer Lebensbedingungen in einem dynamischen Zeitraum in welchem, in den drei Jahrhundert vor der Normannischen Eroberung, grundsätzliche soziale Änderungen stattfanden.

Inwieweit die frühmittelalterliche Siedlungsfolge von Bishopstone das Modell der 'mittelsächsischen Veränderung' folgt wird schliesslich kritisch untersucht. Eine Auswertung von archäologischen Befunden und Fundstücken, die mit Metalldetektoren entdeckt wurden, in der Umgebung von Bishopstone lässt darauf schliessen, dass der Ursprung der mittelalterlichen Besiedlung etwas komplizierter war als eine einfache Verlagerung von Rookery Hill zum heutigen Dorf. Diese Schlussfolgerung hat weitere und wichtige Folgen für unser Verständnis der wechselnden Verhältnissen in der frühmittelalterlichen Besiedlung der Südenglischen Kreidelandschaft.

1 Introduction

1.1 Background and research context

The Bishopstone excavations emerged from humble beginnings: a small-scale archaeological evaluation undertaken in the summer of 2001 in pasture fringing the outlying hamlet of Norton. Designed to harness the voluntary input of fieldwork-active members of the author's then new employer, the Sussex Archaeological Society, the evaluation's modest aim was to confirm the date and identity of a complex of earthworks recorded as a 'shrunken medieval settlement' on the County Sites and Monuments Record (SMR no. 6066). On investigation, one of these supposed medieval 'house-platforms' turned into a well-preserved complex of middle Iron Age occupation whose rarity in a South Downs context prompted a larger-scale excavation the following summer (Seager Thomas 2005a).

It was this (in the end, fortuitously) misidentified prehistoric survival which led to the author's first encounter with St Andrew's church – one of the finest examples of pre-Conquest ecclesiastical architecture in Sussex. The impression made by this evocative structure, deepened by its stunning downland backdrop, initiated a quest to establish a broader archaeological context for the church. A cursory search in the collections of Barbican House Library, Lewes, soon established that the same block of downland harboured a buried, yet no less significant portal reaching back into the early historic past: the early Anglo-Saxon settlement and associated cemetery excavated some 30 years previously on a dramatic chalk ridge known as Rookery Hill which offers stunning panoramic views of the coastline and of Bishopstone village nestled in the valley below (Bell 1977; Plate 1).

These two key witnesses to Bishopstone's Anglo-Saxon past established the immediate context for the current project, one of the primary aims of which was to resolve some of the issues and ambiguities prompted by the discoveries made on Rookery Hill. In the published report, a narrative of shifting settlement is presented in a form clearly influenced by the sequence which had been recently proposed for the abandoned early Anglo-Saxon settlement excavated at Church Down, Chalton (Hants) (Cunliffe 1972). (See Figure 1.1 for the location of key sites mentioned in the discussion.) Under this view, the Anglo-Saxon occupation at Rookery Hill ended at some point during the 6th century (as estimated by the latest datable grave-goods in the cemetery), after which settlement migrated down into the valley below. This relocation culminated in the establishment of the site of the present-day village as the principal focus within the valley, a process linked to the acqui-

sition of the Bishopstone estate by the South Saxon bishopric *c* AD 800 (as informed by two relevant pre-Conquest charters) and the supposed date of construction of St Andrew's church (Bell 1977, 240–1; Haselgrove 1977, 248).

Whilst on the surface the evidence appeared to support the view that Bishopstone constituted a classic case of 'a Middle Saxon Shift' – the model later developed by archaeologists to explain similar desertions (Arnold and Wardle 1981) – the picture was not so straightforward. The report had to concede that on the basis of the interpretative model presented there appeared to be a niggling chronological gap of some 200 years separating the abandonment of the early Anglo-Saxon precursor and the foundation of its permanent, valley-bottom successor (Bell 1977, 241, 248). Fundamental questions thus remained unanswered. Was there really a genuine gap in the settlement record and, if so, where was the intermediary mid Saxon settlement located? Alternatively, contrary to the historically and architecturally informed village genesis, could it be that St Andrew's was implanted in a pre-existing settlement focus established by earlier generations, perhaps even that which had turned its back (for reasons unknown) on the ancestral settlement of Rookery Hill?

The stage was thus set for a new chapter of research in which the spotlight would be firmly trained on Bishopstone village, with an explicit focus on dating its inception and recovering the archaeological character of its embryonic phases. At the commencement of the excavations, it was already clear that the gap in the settlement sequence was perhaps more apparent than real. Archaeologists' understanding of the early medieval rural landscape has developed considerably since the pioneering days of the Rookery Hill campaign when the number of excavated sites existing nationally was meagre if not minuscule. Since then, the study of Anglo-Saxon settlements has grown from relative obscurity into a vibrant field of research buoyed by a considerably expanded corpus of published sites and a proliferating range of approaches with which to gather, analyse, and interpret settlement data as a mirror on contemporary society (Brown and Foard 1998; Hamerow 2002; Reynolds 2003).

Much of the recent fieldwork examining the origins of villages and open fields has focused on the Midlands and East Anglia (Rippon 2008). Yet turn the clock back to the 1970s and early 1980s, and the chalklands of southern England enjoyed similar prominence thanks to the Anglo-Saxon occupation brought to light by such major excavations as Rookery Hill, Bishopstone, and its Hampshire

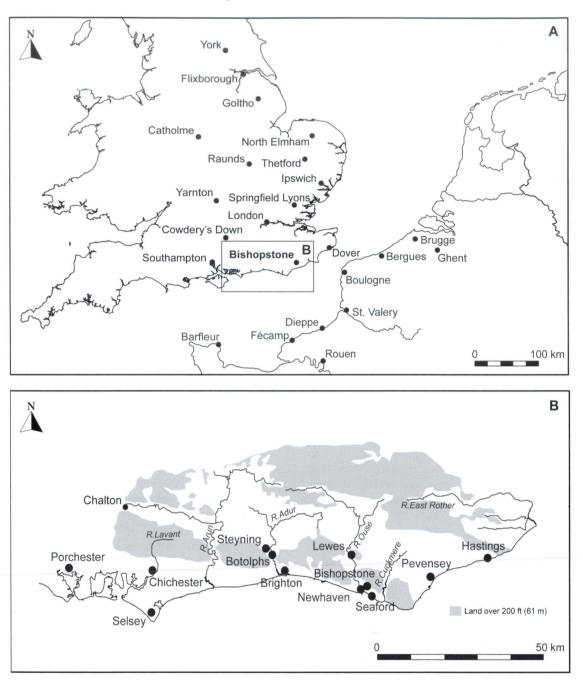

Fig 1.1 Locations of key sites and places mentioned in the text

counterparts of Chalton and Cowdery's Down (Bell 1977; Millett and James 1983; Hughes 1984). The discovery of these long-deserted downland communities provided an important key for unlocking what has since been recognised as a major reorientation in settlement patterns over the final quarter of the first millennium. Encapsulating what Hamerow (1991, 16) has called 'a crucial change from fluid to essentially stable communities', this transition established the framework for the medieval and modern landscape across most of lowland England including areas lying beyond the broad swathe of the country characterised by nucleated villages and open fields. Understanding the timing, mechanisms,

and causal factors behind this transition as played out in different parts of the English countryside remains a pre-eminent topic of research amongst archaeologists and landscape historians (Williamson 2003; Jones and Page 2006; Rippon 2008).

The original model developed to account for settlement desertions of the type demonstrated at Rookery Hill – the 'Middle Saxon Shift' (Arnold and Wardle 1981) – has not been immune to the critical scrutiny of more recent scholarship. One of the major objections is that it paints too simplistic a picture in its environmentally deterministic narrative of an abrupt settlement drift from the light soils of the downland plateau to the heavy soils of surrounding valleys. As revealed by a growing corpus of 5th- to 7th-century settlements located in either valleys adjacent to the chalk or in the so-called scarpfoot zone of the South Downs, this is a false impression connected to issues of site visibility (Welch 1985, 21–2; Lewis 1994, 187–8; Gardiner 2003, 152; Draper 2006, 96; Rippon 2007). As excavations at Botolphs in the Adur valley of West Sussex have demonstrated, evidence for early Anglo-Saxon habitation may lie hidden beneath occupied village cores or else accumulations of hillwash (Gardiner 1990). Armed with this critical awareness, it is no longer safe to assume that settlements like Bishopstone, which became permanent fixtures in the medieval landscape, were necessarily recent establishments when recorded in Domesday Book at the end of the Anglo-Saxon period (Lewis 1994, 187–8; Rippon 2007, 119).

A further argument supporting the view that such desertions reflect more of a gradual thinning out, as opposed to dramatic depopulation of the downland plateau, derives from large-scale excavations at Mucking (Essex) in the 1980s. Mucking's sprawling occupation sequence indicates that some early Anglo-Saxon settlements shared a tendency with early medieval counterparts on the Germanic continent to migrate across the landscape over time leaving a trail of spatially distinct phases (Hamerow 1991). This new perspective on the fluidity of early Anglo-Saxon settlements raised the prospect that the seemingly abrupt desertions encountered in downland regions might be a product of partial excavation. Indeed, the Anglo-Saxon occupation excavated on Rookery Hill has itself been re-evaluated in precisely these terms following the redating of an isolated post-in-trench building located on the southern periphery of the excavations to the 7th–8th centuries (Gardiner 2003, 153).

The understanding derived from studies both within and without downland regions of southern England indicated that there was much still to learn about the fluid geography underpinning the development of Anglo-Saxon communities such as Bishopstone. Yet it remained the case that with one or two notable exceptions, very few opportunities had been taken to deploy an explicitly archaeological methodology to track the evolution of downland settlement patterns across the crucial period of transition, broadly speaking the 7th to the 11th centuries. An attempt had been made to situate the 6th- to 8th-century occupation excavated at Church Down, Chalton, into a longer chronological framework, partly through fieldwalking and partly through targeting the origins of the medieval settlement pattern through the excavations at Manor Farm (within the inhabited core of Chalton village). Regrettably the goals of this ambitious programme of research remain unpublished and consequently unrealised (though see Hughes 1984 for some provisional conclusions).

The Bishopstone project was thus initiated to provide a modern platform from which to re-examine

the questions of when and in what form stable components of the medieval settlement pattern first emerged in the chalklands of southern England. Studies addressing the same theme in other parts of England showed that the whole problem required a distinctive methodological approach that had been largely neglected in Sussex and neighbouring southern counties since the golden age of Rookery Hill and other large-scale downland excavations. Influential in the design and conception of the Bishopstone project were programmes of university-led research then nearing completion at Shapwick (Somerset) and Whittlewood (Northants) – both inspired by the pioneering work at Wharram Percy (North Yorks) (Jones and Page 2006; Gerrard and Aston 2007). Undertaken respectively at parish and multi-parish scales of analysis, these multidisciplinary projects demonstrated how archaeological evidence recovered from still-inhabited village cores (through targeted excavation and test-pitting) could contribute crucial evidence for reconstructing settlement histories and thus help to unlock the mechanisms and chronology of village formation. More locally, inspiration was provided by Mark Gardiner's work in the Adur valley at Botolphs, an exercise in settlement-core excavation specifically designed to contextualise new evidence for the Anglo-Saxon origins of Steyning recovered from several commercially funded interventions within the town (Gardiner 1990). This integrated approach, also taking in the results of small-scale interventions at Old Erringham in the 1970s, allowed Gardiner to generate a diachronic model explaining the origins of the medieval settlement pattern in Steyning's hinterland (partly based upon the construction of a ceramic chronology), which he linked to the emergence of stable church/manor nuclei around the year AD 1000 (Gardiner 2003).

The role of church/high-status nuclei in the wider story of the genesis of medieval settlement patterns appeared to be particularly pertinent to Bishopstone as a case study, given the prominence of St Andrew's as a physical and contextual backdrop to the excavations and its widespread though not necessarily universal acceptance as a pre-Viking minster (Kelly 1998, 58–65; Combes 2002, see below). The initiation of the Bishopstone project coincided with a growing consensus amongst archaeologists that aristocratic and/or minster complexes dating to the 8th and 9th centuries were responsible for initiating at least a proportion of the new generation of Anglo-Saxon settlements established on permanent sites that would later emerge as medieval villages (Brown and Foard 1998, 75–80; Draper 2006, 103–05; Gerrard and Aston 2007, 976–8; Rippon 2008; Audouy and Chapman 2009, 51–7). This view is at variance with the thrust of earlier scholarship which, in explaining the same developments, laid emphasis on the rise of local lordship in the final two centuries of the Anglo-Saxon era when the English countryside fell under the full impetus of 'manorialisation' (Harvey 1989; Morris 1989, 227–75; Saunders 2000). Work in currently occupied rural settlements has provided crucial markers for pinning down this earlier chronology. For example, a significant number of the medieval settlements sampled under the banner of the Whittlewood project produced ceramic evidence for Mid Saxon origins in close proximity to parish churches (Jones and Page 2006). Larger-scale excavation within such extant settlements as Cottenham (Cambs) (Mortimer 2000); Raunds (Northants) (Audouy and Chapman 2009); and Lower Slaughter (Glos) (Kenyon and Watts 2006) has also served to establish a mid-9th century or earlier origin for these places, several in the form of high-status enclosures (for wider discussion see Brown and Foard 1998; Rippon 2008, 261–5).

This earlier chronology, which derives additional support from the recognition that the excavated repertoire of 7th- to 9th-century settlements displays evidence for the structured planning previously seen as an intrinsic characteristic of medieval village plans (Reynolds 2003; 2005), provides an important new dimension to understanding the impact of socio-economic change on the Mid Saxon countryside. In particular, transformations witnessed in the rural settlement record can now be interpreted more directly as but one strand in a whole suite of inter-related developments – agricultural intensification, the rise of kingdoms and with them the establishment of *wics*, monastic establishments, and secular estate centres sustained by rural surpluses – together characterising a period of economic growth which has gained the label 'the long eighth century' (Hamerow 2002; Reynolds 2003; 2005; Rippon 2008, 261–8).

Fortunately, a number of southern English sites could be called upon to help contextualise the physical form and character of any embryonic nucleus likely to be unearthed at Bishopstone. Clear evidence for later Anglo-Saxon seigneurial planning had previously been gained by excavations at the Hampshire sites of Portchester Castle (Cunliffe 1976), Faccombe Netherton (Fairbrother 1990), Brighton Hill South (Fasham and Keevil 1995), and Trowbridge (Wilts) (Graham and Davies 1993). It remained to be seen how closely Bishopstone might resemble these regional comparanda and indeed a wider repertoire of sites providing insights into the physical nature and culture of Anglo-Saxon aristocratic residences as gleaned by excavations at Raunds (Northants) (Audouy and Chapman 2009); Goltho (Lincs) (Beresford 1987); Flixborough (Lincs) (Loveluck 2007); and Springfield Lyons (Essex) (Tyler and Major 2005).

At the outset of the Bishopstone excavations, there was thus a reasonable expectation that targetable spaces flanking the churchyard might produce traces of Anglo-Saxon occupation (how well preserved remained to be determined) approximating to an embryonic settlement complex of potential high-status character. Yet, as we shall see presently, there was still considerable flexibility of interpretation within this fairly loose characterisation. It

was clear that any archaeological evidence brought forth would be coloured by notions of the historical origins and status of St Andrews. But there was no clear consensus on this issue, with scholarly opinion dividing along lines very similar to the debate surrounding the origins of Shapwick (Somerset) (Gerrard and Aston 2007, 26–30).

The estate that would emerge as the 25-hide Domesday manor of Bishopstone first enters the historical record *c* AD 800 as a holding of the South Saxon bishops under the earlier topographic name *denu-tūn* 'valley farm/estate', a descriptor of the meandering valley stretching from the headlands of Rookery and Hawth Hills in the south towards the escarpment of the South Downs in the north passing the site of the modern-day village and its satellite of Norton en route (see Blair and Pickles, Chapter 3.1). The contentious issue concerned the extent to which a Christian presence at Bishopstone could be pushed back beyond this historical horizon. Depending on which view is preferred, a Christian presence at Bishopstone (and, by implication, any associated settlement) emerged *c* AD 800 as a proprietorial establishment of the South Saxon bishopric (Gem 1993, 45), or alternatively, in the decades after the conversion of the South Saxon kingdom in the 660s, as an independent minster community perhaps, as Kelly has speculated, established as a daughter house of the royal minster of Beddingham from which the Anglo-Saxon estate of Bishopstone was evidently detached (Kelly 1998, 58–65; Combes 2002).

The aspiration at the start of the excavation was that archaeology might offer a new way of seeing Bishopstone's pre-Conquest development independent of previous readings based upon historical and topographical evidence. In this sense, the Bishopstone project keyed into a broader discussion linked to the disputed characterisation of later Anglo-Saxon settlements such as Flixborough and Brandon (Suffolk), regarded by some as poorly documented monastic establishments and by others as secular estate complexes (Loveluck 2001; Blair 2005, 204–12). Lying at the heart of this debate is how successfully signatures derived from the archaeological record (whether relating to portable material culture, the built environment, dietary, and other lifestyle indicators) can be mapped on to narrow, historically defined conceptualisations of settlement character. Some archaeologists have claimed that any attempt to categorise excavated sites in these terms is futile because lifestyles expressed at the upper echelons of the settlement hierarchy, whether secular or ecclesiastical, might be expected to leave behind broadly analogous footprints in the archaeological record and furthermore that the two modes of existence may have intersected on certain hybrid classes of settlement containing both a religious and a secular component (Hines 1997, 390–1; Pestell 2004, 59–64; Loveluck 2007, 145).

In a period with as many ambiguities and uncertainties as that popularly known as the 'Dark Ages', it seems unlikely that a clear interdisciplinary consensus will emerge on how to interpret poorly documented sites in the category of Flixborough and Brandon. Nonetheless, it can be argued that by bringing into focus the tensions lying at the interface of conceptualisations drawn respectively from textual and physical sources, these difficult questions on site character encourage exactly the kind of dialogue which defines medieval archaeology as a discipline (Austin and Thomas 1990; Andrén 1998; Moreland 2001). A multi-vocal dialogue, not only between archaeologists and historians but also between specialists working in different fields of archaeology, forms a strand running through the chapters of this report. Rather than being air-brushed out, differences of opinion and contrasting viewpoints have been deliberately included precisely because they highlight the challenges and nuances of attempting to piece together a picture of Bishopstone's pre-Conquest origins as a multi-disciplinary endeavour.

1.2 Methodology

Like most research excavations, the Bishopstone project evolved organically in response to changing aims, priorities, and circumstances. The deployment of geophysics and test-pitting in and around Bishopstone village in the project's inaugural year, 2002, was initially intended as one component of a broader inter-disciplinary survey integrating field-walking, geoarchaeological study, and documentary research (Thomas *et al* 2002). The ultimate decision to narrow the focus to open-area excavations on the village green rested on the quality of archaeology brought to light by the test-pits which demonstrated that the churchyard was surrounded (at least on its northern and western sides) by a dense swathe of pre-Conquest occupation, seemingly undisturbed by medieval and later activity. The prospect of uncovering a substantial, well-preserved portion of Bishopstone's early nucleus proved too tantalising an opportunity to ignore, given the ambiguities surrounding the origins of the village (including the disputed ancestry of St Andrew's church) and the paucity of later Anglo-Saxon settlements excavated on an informative scale nationally, let alone locally.

The 2003–2005 excavations comprised three six-week campaigns undertaken each summer between early August and mid September. Each season was run as a training excavation open to members of the public enrolled on a week-long programme of archaeological instruction (one of the principal sources of funding for the excavations) and more experienced volunteers drawn from the membership of the Sussex Archaeological Society. Staffing comprised the Director accompanied by eight student supervisors (including individuals respectively responsible for finds and environmental processing), the core team including undergraduates and recent graduates from the Institute of Archae-ology, University College London. In any one week, the total number of participants (including staff) on the excavation ranged between 30 and 60.

In the spirit of large-scale research excavations, each campaign had to strike a sometimes difficult balance between meeting the archaeological objectives of the excavation and providing supervised instruction for trainees and volunteers. The latter were encouraged to play an active role in all aspects of site recording including the completion of pro forma context sheets, drawn sections, and plans. Whilst the speed of the recording suffered as a result of this inclusive approach, site records were checked on a regular basis to ensure consistency and quality of data entry.

The excavation proceeded along the following lines each year. Initially the turf was removed mechanically for storage and reinstatement at the end of the excavation. The results of test-pitting in 2002 showed that the thin topsoil covering the chalk did not preserve any meaningful spatial patterning in the distribution of artefacts, nearly all of which were intermingled at the base of the worm-sorted horizon. This provided the justification for mechanically stripping the topsoil with a JCB, fitted with a toothless bucket. The remaining overburden was hand-excavated with mattock and trowel and the surface of the chalk carefully cleaned to reveal cut archaeological features which were usually clearly distinguishable as soil marks (Plate 2). This level was planned at 1:20 and photographed and then individual contexts were excavated according to a pre-defined strategy. Due to the fact that most cut features formed stratigraphically discrete components, sections were in most cases established on an arbitrary basis: half-sections in the case of pits and postholes and quadrants in the case of the cellar of Structure W; the excavation of wall-trenches followed rather different lines (see below).

To maximise the recovery of artefactual and eco-factual evidence and to provide spatial control, the following sampling strategy was adopted. All cut features were subjected to total excavation. All pit and grave fills were passed through a 6mm sieve, and sampled for on-site flotation at a standard volume of 30 litres. Environmental samples were also taken from wall-trenches and postholes on a selective basis. Spoil heaps were metal-detected on a daily basis and the position of all stratified artefacts, other than pottery, quernstones, and animal bone, was recorded three-dimensionally.

Some experimentation was attempted to maximise the structural information recovered from the wall-trenches of buildings. Drawing upon the methodology employed at Cowdery's Down (Millett and James 1983), a portion of the southern wall of Structure C was excavated as a series of spits in 2003, the surface of each being planned at a detailed scale of 1:10 in the hope that the patterning of stone inclusions might reveal silt-rich post-ghosts. Unfortunately this time-consuming process failed to produce any meaningful results and was abandoned thereafter. For the remainder of the structures, longitudinal sections were established along wall-trenches, their length being broken by transverse sections positioned either arbitrarily or, when discernable, with respect to notable concentrations of packing material associated with entrances. As a general rule, post-ghosts were seldom visible in the excavated fills of the wall-trenches and this has militated against the level of structural interpretation possible where such distinctions are more visible, most notably at Cowdery's Down and at Yeavering (Northumberland).

Chalkland sites in the Cowdery's Down category enjoying a good level of structural detail share a particular combination of cultural and post-depositional circumstances (Millett and James 1983, 200–1, fig 66). Results are best when: 1) plough damage is reduced (eg protection under dumped or redeposited soil); 2) the chalk is capped by a thin covering of clay-with-flints; and 3) on abandonment the posts are burnt leaving the buried portion of the post to rot *in situ*. This combination leads to the creation of a sharply defined post-ghost (comprising a mixture of brown soil and charcoal) clearly distinguishable from the surrounding bedrock and chalk packing material. In stark contrast, most of the excavated area at Bishopstone displayed a classic rendzina soil profile showing that the chalk spur had suffered the usual affects of natural erosional processes exacerbated by ploughing and/or kitchen-garden activity (Bell 1977, 6). Truncation was most severe at the southern, upslope portion of the excavation where some of the wall-trenches were as little as 50mm deep. Survival was generally better at the opposite end of the excavation thanks to the accumulation of colluvium which survived to a maximum depth of 300mm, but only in defined areas, as for example the eastern end of Structure C. Except for the timber superstructure of cellared building W, there is no clear evidence to suggest that any of the Bishopstone buildings were burnt *in situ*.

1.3   Layout of this volume

Chapter 2 provides the essential preliminary of documenting the major geomorphic changes which shaped the coastline and environment surrounding Bishopstone over the first millennium AD, with a particular focus on the shifting dynamic of the outlet of the River Ouse. Chapter 3 presents a historical interpretation of pre-Conquest Bishopstone derived from the concept that the settlement originated as an Anglo-Saxon minster. Three strands are woven into this synthesis: firstly, charter and place-name evidence; secondly, information buried within an 11th-century hagiographical source, Drogo's *Historia translationis sanctae Lewinnae* (to be consulted alongside a commentary and edited extracts of the same text appearing as Appendix 1); and thirdly, a new interpretation of the pre-Conquest constructional development of St Andrew's church.

Chapter 4 presents the settlement remains under two categories, the built environment and non-structural features, and Chapter 5 examines the cemetery, including an osteological study of the human remains, with a grave catalogue appearing as Appendix 3. Material culture assemblages and economic resources are covered in Chapters 6 and 7 respectively.

Chapter 8 provides more in-depth analysis and interpretation of the archaeological remains commencing with the buildings, their constructional characteristics, function, and status. This is followed by the construction of a chronological framework, in which evidence for site phasing and the results of radiocarbon dating are integrated to help understand the layout and spatial development of the Anglo-Saxon settlement.

Chapter 9 assesses the excavated evidence under a series of themes characterising the current academic thrust of Anglo-Saxon settlement studies by which Bishopstone is situated in its national context. Whereas the first theme probes the potential meanings behind the settlement's high pit density as a particular strategy for disposing of human and domestic waste, the second explores the significance of Bishopstone's pre-Conquest cemetery within the wider context of the origins of churchyard burial. The third deploys Bishopstone as a case-study for examining inter-disciplinary tensions surrounding the characterisation of high-status settlements of the later Anglo-Saxon period, whilst the fourth reflects upon evidence for continuity and change in the economy of coastal communities in the second half of the first millennium AD.

Chapter 10 draws together some concluding remarks on the local settlement pattern. Bishopstone, as an example of a 'Middle Saxon Shift', is brought under critical scrutiny and finally various scenarios are presented for the abandonment of the excavated complex during the late 10th or 11th century.

1.4   Terminology

The period spanned by the excavated occupation sequence – the 8th to the 11th centuries AD – straddles two of the conventional period divisions applied to Anglo-Saxon England: mid Saxon (*c* 650–*c* 850), and late Saxon (*c* 850–*c* 1066). To avoid the use of the rather cumbersome conflation mid-to-late Saxon, the alternative label 'later Anglo-Saxon' has been adopted; this is used throughout except in parts of the discussion where it is possible to speak in chronological terms sufficiently refined to distinguish between 'mid' and 'late' (see Reynolds 1999, 23–4).

2   Landscape and environmental context

The stretch of Sussex coastline embracing the estuary of the River Ouse was subject to dynamic changes during the first millennium AD. The purpose of this chapter is to reconstruct as far as possible those changes and to understand their immediate impact on the environment surrounding the excavated settlement at Bishopstone. To enable this process of reconstruction, the opportunity is taken to integrate the results of a number of recent geoarchaeological studies undertaken within the lower reaches of the valley of the River Ouse, including the reclaimed tidal inlet sitting astride Bishopstone village.

2.1   Site location

The site of the excavations occupies a small parcel of downland forming the northern half of a westward-projecting spur of Upper Chalk, surmounted by the parish church at a height of 25m OD (TQ 547 010). Measuring some 2500m² in extent and functioning as a village green, the land is bounded to the west and east by houses (the Old School House and Eadric House respectively), to the south by the churchyard, and to the north by a steep, artificially accentuated scarp (since 1950 covered by trees and flora) which descends into a narrow tributary of the Bishopstone valley (Plate 1; Fig 2.1A). The village green is known locally as 'the Egg', seemingly a modern corruption of an older version – 'Hagg' – and named after a property recorded as 'Hage' house and croft in the Bishopstone Court Rolls for 1646.[1] Admittedly a late piece of evidence, it is tempting to ascribe the name's formation to the Anglo-Saxon period given the use of [OE] 'haga' as a generic term for enclosure (for either a homestead or a piece of land) as attested in pre-Conquest charter bounds (Blair 1991, 46; Hooke 1998, 154–7).

The valley within which Bishopstone sits forms one branch of an extensive dry-valley system etched into the southern dipslope of the South Downs between the valleys of the Rivers Ouse and Cuckmere (British Geological Survey Sheet 334 Eastbourne). At Poverty Bottom, the valley assumes a strongly asymmetrical profile, its steep western side contrasting markedly with the gently inclined eastern slopes on which are located Bishopstone village and its northern satellite of Norton. Below Bishopstone, the floor of the valley expands to encompass a broad floodplain incised with an extensive network of artificial drainage channels, which feed into a small central stream emerging at a pond to the north-west of the village (Plate 3; Fig 2.1B). The mouth of this valley is guarded majestically by two prominent, south-facing ridges

– Rookery and Hawth Hills – both ending abruptly in palaeoclifflines, which extend back inside the valley as prominent landscape features. This high ground overlooks a narrow strip of reclaimed saltmarsh formerly within the tidal basin of the Ouse estuary. Today, protected by a substantial shingle barrier and coastal defences, it is traversed by the A259 and the portion of the south-coast railway connecting the towns of Newhaven and Seaford (Plate 4; Fig 2.2).

A key to understanding how human settlement in and around Bishopstone has evolved over the past 10,000 years is the changing geomorphology and environment of the coastline. Before being reclaimed and stabilised in relatively recent times, the seasonally inundated coastal wetlands fringing the contours of the chalk would have been highly prized for their rich biodiversity and varied resources encompassing summer grazing, salt, fuel, and thatch, and a wide range of edible fauna (Rippon 2000, 21). During phases of climatic amelioration and marine regression experienced in many coastal regions of north-west Europe in the Roman and Anglo-Saxon periods these unstable environments were progressively tamed. This process usually commenced with relatively minor modifications which served to extend seasonal windows of exploitation, but subsequently progressed to much more elaborate sea-defence/drainage schemes which allowed permanent reclamation and settlement. Artificially reclaimed wetlands were at constant risk of inundation and, accordingly, their long-term development is interspersed by periods of transgression, when they returned to their natural, semi-aquatic state (ibid, 46–53).

Under the population expansion of the later Anglo-Saxon period, England's coastal wetlands experienced one of their most intensive periods of reclamation (Brooks 1988; Rippon 2000, 39–53). Too small to sustain wholly marshland communities like those on neighbouring Romney Marsh, the exploitation of the tidal basin of the Ouse estuary will have fallen to those communities located, like Bishopstone, on its dryland margins. Consequently, the exploitation of marshland habitat leaves a particularly strong imprint in the historical sources relating to Bishopstone as surveyed by Haselgrove in the Rookery Hill excavation report (Haselgrove 1977, 243–4). The evolution of Bishopstone's wetlands thus deserves close attention as a powerful force over the economy of Anglo-Saxon Bishopstone and the daily lives of its inhabitants. This necessitates examining the general picture in the Lower Ouse valley as a prelude to a more specific consideration of the Bishopstone valley itself.

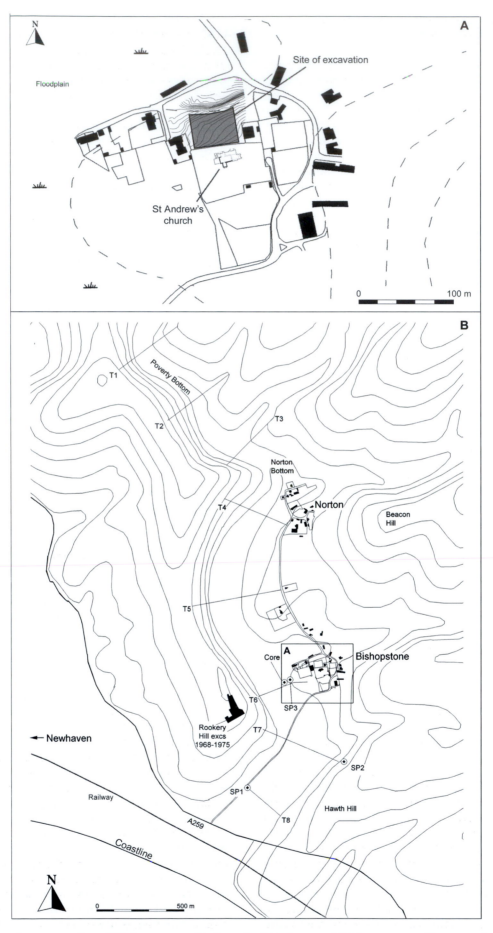

Fig 2.1   The local topography of Bishopstone: A) the inhabited core of Bishopstone village; and B) Bishopstone valley showing the locations of geoarchaeological transects, cores, and soil-pits

2.2 The wider context: geomorphology of the Lower Ouse valley

A generalised geomorphology of the Lower Ouse has been proposed on the basis of a previous palaeoenvironmental study (Burrin and Jones 1991). This has since been supplemented by geoarchaeological analysis of borehole data and palaeoenvironmental reconnaissance undertaken in advance of the creation of a wetland nature reserve on former agricultural land on the eastern fringe of Newhaven, known as the Ouse Estuary Project (Bates 1998; Archaeology South-East 2000; Jarzembowski 2003). This work showed that the depth of Holocene sedimentation to the east of Newhaven extends down to 35m below OD in places (Bates 1998, 33): a similar depth to that encountered in the valley-mouth transects involved in Burrin and Jones's earlier study (1991, 225–30).

These studies are in general agreement that the Holocene sedimentary sequence comprises four depositionary phases: 1) a lower stratum of Pleistocene sands and gravels deposited under periglacial conditions; 2) a lower complex of interbedded silts and clays with organic/peat horizons deposited in low-energy 'perimarine' conditions between *c* 9000 BP and *c* 2400 BP; 3) high-energy shingle deposits forming a barrier breach across the mouth of the estuary (originally dated by Burrin and Jones to *c* 2000 BP); 4) estuarine clays and silts laid down in a low-energy 'back-barrier' environment. The upper portion of this final phase, representing sedimentation stretching back over the last two millennia, has been divided into two lithostratigraphical units: a lower grey 'alluvium', rich in the estuarine species *Scrobicularia plana* (Peppery Furrow Shell), and an upper brown alluvium, indicative of soil formation accompanying land reclamation (Jarzembowski 2003, 40).

The principal geomorphic influence driving first millennium and later developments to the coastline was the formation (and periodic breaching) of a shingle bar between the two chalk headlands of Castle Hill, Newhaven, and Seaford Head, through the action of longshore drift (Castleden 1996; Rippon 2000, 30–2). The Ouse represents a classic case of this geomorphic process but its effects were felt by all of Sussex's major rivers including the Arun, the Adur, and the Rother (Castleden 1996; Woodcock 2003). As the spit grew, the mouth of the Ouse was deflected progressively eastwards, from a hypothetical original outfall below Castle Hill, Newhaven, towards the opposing headland of Seaford Head (Plate 4). Cut off from the open sea, the landward side of the estuary was transformed into a back-barrier saltmarsh environment, offering opportunities for land reclamation when conditions were favourable (Fig 2.2).

This process of barrier formation can now be fitted into a tighter chronological framework thanks to three recent radiocarbon dates, which can be added to two previously submitted samples taken from a buried wave-cut platform exposed beneath the fossil cliff at Rookery Hill (Hedges *et al* 1991; Higham *et al* 2007). The earliest of the two dates from the latter site (Fig 2.2, no. 1) indicates that the platform was subject to fully marine conditions in later prehistory (2710±90 BP: cal 500–100 BC; OxA-2149), a period when the Ouse and the neighbouring Bishopstone inlet were permanently flooded by sea-water to form an open estuary. The new dating evidence confirms that within a few hundred years the formation of a shingle bar had begun to take effect. A sample of the brackish water species *Scrobicularia plana*, taken at the north-east end of the Newhaven levels (Fig 2.2, no. 2), shows that estuarine saltmarsh had started to form within the valley of the Ouse by the early Roman period (2324 ± 22 BP: cal 115 BC–AD 91; OxA-12138) (Higham *et al* 2007). The physical remnant of this early barrier may be represented by a beach-gravel deposit encountered by Archaeology South-East (2000) in the levels directly to the south of Rookery Hill (Fig 2.2, no. 3); a suggestion which receives support from a sample of the marine species *Mytilus edulis*, dated firmly within the earlier part of the Roman period (2232 ± 29 BP: cal 6 BC–AD 218; OxA-15813).

These new dates support the theory that the Roman-period bar (located in close proximity to the present shingle beach) must have subsequently migrated southwards, perhaps by as much as 200m, to account for the deflection of the River Ouse to its eventual medieval outfall at Seaford (Castleden 1996, 24). This new barrier would have encouraged a general eastward expansion of the back-barrier saltmarsh formerly confined to the west of Rookery Hill. That this was indeed the case has been confirmed by two samples of *Scrobicularia plana* dated to the early Anglo-Saxon period (5th–7th centuries AD); one recovered from silty clays deposited on top of the wave-cut platform below Rookery Hill (Hedges *et al* 1991) (Fig 2.2, no. 4) and the other from the alluvial margins adjacent to Bishopstone village (Higham *et al* 2007) (Fig 2.2, no. 5).

Many uncertainties surround the precise morphology of the post-Roman shingle spit and the rate of its accretion, although it has been estimated through analogy with the historically attested barrier growth across the mouth of the Adur that the 4km separating Castle Hill and Seaford Head could have been bridged in as little as 200 years (Castleden 1996, 27). Otherwise, the extent of shingle spit formation at the end of the first millennium has been calibrated with respect to the rapid rise of Seaford as an urban and mercantile centre after the Norman Conquest (Gardiner 1995). The presumption has been that the port of medieval Seaford (a member of the Cinque Port Confederation since the early 13th century) developed in response to the stabilisation of a semi-permanent outfall immediately below Hawk's Brow, on the western edge of Seaford Head (Castleden 1996, 24). However, as the later history of the barrier would show in a succession of temporary breaches (Brandon 1971), it would be

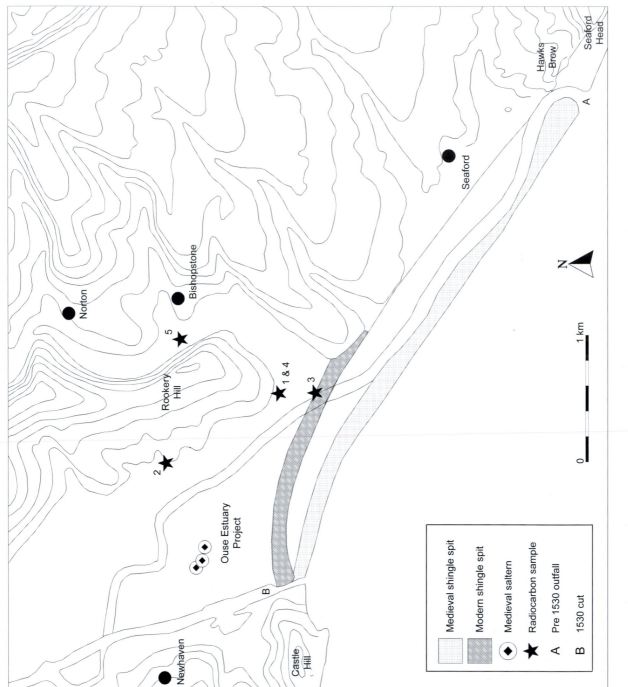

Fig 2.2 The medieval course of the River Ouse in relation to the modern coastline showing the location of radiocarbon-dated geoarchaeological samples and medieval saltern mounds discovered in reclaimed land to the east of Newhaven (after Castleden 1996, fig 7 with modifications)

unsafe to conclude that the point of the medieval outfall was necessarily fixed this far eastward by AD 1066.

The process of longshore drift responsible for Seaford's short heyday as a Cinque Port contributed to its ultimate demise by choking its harbour with shingle. These factors, combined with the onset of deteriorating climatic conditions at the end of the 13th century, led to the Lower Ouse valley being beset by an extended period of seasonal flooding, which continued well into the post-medieval era (Brandon 1971). A short-lived reprieve was bought with the cutting of a new outlet for the River Ouse at Newhaven in 1539, allowing a new phase of reclamation to take place, as indicated by such evidence as the field name 'Newlands' portrayed on a map of 1620 of the Lower Ouse Navigation (Brandon 1971, fig 3). This measure was only temporarily successful however and the cycle of eastwards deflection and periodic breaching began anew; the Newhaven outfall was only finally stabilised at the end of the 19th century, with the construction of major sea defences including a substantial breakwater below Castle Hill. Today the effects of longshore drift still have to be countered by the artificial nourishment of beach shingle (Castleden 1996, 24).

2.3 Localised sequence in the Bishopstone valley

The current excavations have inspired three programmes of palaeoenvironmental investigation which enable a long-term perspective to be gained on landscape changes within the Bishopstone valley. Sadly, it is of great regret that the most ambitious was cut short by the early death of Dr Simon Jennings, a leading specialist in the coastal geomorphology of southern England (eg Jennings and Smyth 1987; Jennings *et al* 1993). The remaining two studies were submitted as dissertations by students enrolled on the MSc in Geoarchaeology at the University of Reading (Pears 2002; Neal 2008). Their work, although lacking an absolute chronological framework, has enabled the sedimentary sequence within the valley to be established in relative terms, partly with reference to the broader Lower Ouse valley sequence outlined above. In both cases sedimentary and molluscan analysis has provided a basis for reconstructing the environmental history of the valley. This has elucidated changing patterns of land-use stretching as far back as the Neolithic, complementing the picture provided by the lynchet section investigated as part of the Rookery Hill excavations (Bell 1977, 251–66). Here, the opportunity is taken to summarise the main conclusions of their work, paying particular attention to results most germane to the post-Roman landscape and its exploitation.

The earlier of the two studies (Pears 2002) analysed one hundred core samples taken from eight transects spaced at 500m intervals along the valley from Poverty Bottom in the north, to its entrance between Rookery and Hawth Hills in the south (Fig 2.1B, T1–T8). Coring was supplemented by the excavation of two soil pits on alignment with T7 and T8 in order to determine sedimentary sequences at the intersection between slope deposits and the floodplain near the mouth of the valley (Fig 2.1B, SP1 and 2). The coring showed that the sedimentary history of the valley embraces two distinct units: a relatively shallow 'inland' sequence (1–2m deep) comprising a lower unit of periglacial melt-water deposits overlain by colluvial hill-wash (silty-clay with unsorted flint and chalk inclusions); and a much deeper 'perimarine' unit (10m+) dominated by fine-grained estuarine silts and silty sands. The transition between the two occurs between T3 and T4, some 800m north-west of Bishopstone church and 2km inland from the current shoreline (Fig 2.3). The division of the latter into an upper horizon of brown/orange silts and a lower one of grey silt matches the lithostratigraphic units identified in the Newhaven levels by Jarzembowski (2003).

The study showed that the substantial accumulation of colluvium found in the upper reaches of the valley thinned progressively towards its mouth; in the perimarine sector accumulations of 1–2m depth were restricted to the prominent lynchet banks located at the edge of the floodplain (Fig 2.3). The slice gained across the perimarine sector in T7 and T8, together with SP1 and SP2, defined an 'inter-depositionary' zone where valley-slope and perimarine sediments were interbedded. Micromorphogical analysis of these horizons showed a complex depositional relationship, including long periods of gradual merging and phases of slope erosion possibly linked to storm events (Pears 2002, 104–05). Analysis of colluvial deposits obtained from the excavated soil-pits revealed a sequence of changing land use which conforms closely to previous studies on the South Downs (eg Bell 1983; 1989). A sustained period of arable cultivation was inferred, stretching from the early Bronze Age through into the Romano-British period. This was followed by a broadly dated 'medieval' transition to open grassland with mollusc species (*Vertigo pygmaea*, *Cochlicopa* spp.) indicative of a closely grazed environment. A similar transition, though rather more closely dated to within the Anglo-Saxon period, was demonstrated by the excavation of a lynchet section on Rookery Hill (Bell 1977, 258). The sprawl of the Anglo-Saxon settlement excavated on Rookery Hill, which colonised former Romano-British field terraces, reinforces the impression of a major post-Roman transition in land use (Bell 1977, 238, 258).

The latter of the two studies (Neal 2008) was more locally focused, in order to refine the sedimentary sequence at the junction between the lower slopes of the chalk spur occupied by Bishopstone village and the adjoining floodplain (just to the north of T6); as such its conclusions are of particular relevance to the current excavations. The methodology involved

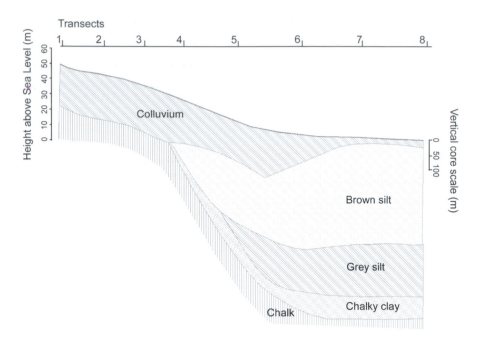

Fig 2.3   Longitudinal section of sediments within the Bishopstone valley (after Pears 2002, fig 19)

the excavation of a soil pit through a prominent bank marking the boundary between the spur and the relatively level alluvial sediments of the valley floor (Fig 2.1B, SP3; Fig 2.4A). The pit was dug to a depth of 1.6m below ground surface and below this the sequence was investigated by coring to a depth of 3.36m. A further core using a gouge auger was put down 30m to the west, to investigate the sedimentary sequence in the alluvial valley floor; this reached a depth of 7.20m below ground surface (Fig 2.4A).

The base of each sedimentary sequence was distinguished by a chalky mud attributed to Pleistocene erosion (Deposit I) (Fig 2.4). In the floodplain core this was overlain by a build-up of alluvial sediments in turn sealed, at a depth of 6.25m, by a dark greyish-brown silt containing flint inclusions (Deposit E) (Fig 2.4B). The remainder of the floodplain sequence above Deposit E demonstrated a further episode of alluvial deposition, which included a distinct organic horizon at 5.05m (Deposit D). Although it cannot be proved, the likelihood is that this corresponds to similar organic layers of Neolithic date encountered by the coring programme undertaken by Dr Simon Jennings in 2002, the significance of which is discussed below. This horizon was in turn overlain by further alluvial silts and clays (Deposits C–A) indicative of an extended period of sedimentation within a back-barrier saltmarsh environment.

In the soil pit sequence (Fig 2.4C), the Pleistocene mud was overlain at a depth of 2.8m by a dark grey silt containing frequent flecks of charcoal and therefore of likely anthropomorphic origin (Deposit G). This was in turn sealed by a sequence of stony, colluvial silts (Deposits F and E) followed by an alluvial sediment some 0.58m thick characterised

by the occurrence of the brackish water *Hydrobia ulvae* species (Deposit D). These saltmarsh silts were buried by a substantial deposition of colluvium, up to 1.45m thick, forming the main body of the valley-edge feature (Deposit C). This shows that this feature is in fact a lynchet at a field-boundary and not, as might otherwise be assumed on the basis of visual inspection, a continuation of a degraded former cliff which is particularly marked on the west sides of Hawth and Rookery Hills (Fig 2.5). The molluscan record for the colluvium was dominated by species indicative of mixed arable and grassland conditions, including *Trochulus* and *Candidula*. However, some of the clayier horizons of the colluvium produced significant quantities of *H. ulvae*, demonstrating the persistence of flooding events within the valley.

This discovery is a classic case of alluvial edge colluvial deposits (Bell and Walker 2005, fig 7.1) and a clear demonstration of the extent to which landscape topography can be modified locally by human agency. Furthermore, pottery recovered from the lynchet horizon allows this accumulation to be dated securely to the later Anglo-Saxon and Saxo-Norman periods.

2.4   Bishopstone valley sediments and sea-level relationships
by Martin Bell, Robert Neal, and Ben Pears

There has long been speculation as to whether the flat-floored Bishopstone valley, connected to the more deeply incised Ouse valley, formed an inlet of the sea and thus a suitable place for landing boats at the time of the prehistoric to early Anglo-Saxon activity on Rookery Hill and later Anglo-Saxon activity in

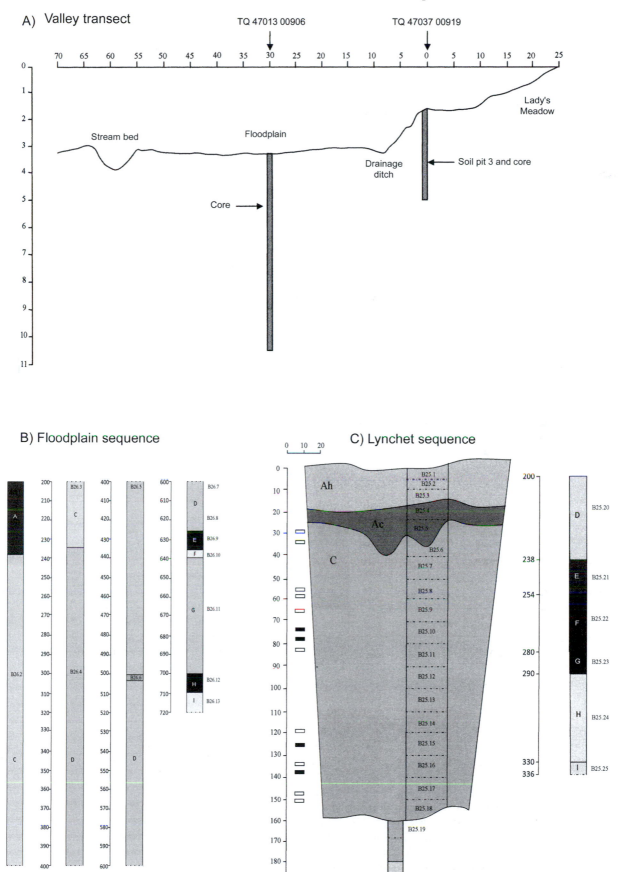

Fig 2.4   Location and profiles of core and soil-pit taken to the west of Bishopstone village (after Neal 2008, figs 10, 11 & 12 combined)

Fig 2.5   Prominent lynchet bank marking the junction between the lower slopes of the Bishopstone spur and the floor of the adjoining valley

Bishopstone village. Coring and test-pitting of the Bishopstone valley sediments by Pears (2002) and Neal (2008) has contributed to the resolution of this problem.

In soil pit 3 the top of the buried estuarine silts was at *c* 1.94m OD, which is very close to the general level of the adjoining (unburied) valley floor silts at *c* 2m (Figs 2.1B and 2.4A). This suggests that the valley has not been subject to subsequent saltmarsh deposition, and has thus been isolated from marine influence since the period when the later Saxon lynchet buried the estuarine silt edge. Marine influence may have been cut off by a precursor of the present shingle bar or as part of a later Saxon land claim. Haselgrove (1977) suggested that reclamation at Bishopstone had started by the later Saxon period because of the extent of meadow recorded in Domesday; he argued the hay crop is likely to have been protected from saline incursion. Parts of Romney Marsh were subject to later Saxon reclamation perhaps from the 9th century AD (Rippon 2000, 166). Four banks across the Bishopstone valley possibly relate to the history of land claim. The most landward is a short causeway carrying the access road to Bishopstone village from the base of Rookery Hill; it is possible, but uncertain, as to whether this also served as a reclamation bank. Between this causeway and the A259, a step in the level of the

valley floor down the axis of the valley shows that the eastern half was reclaimed before the western half of the valley, since the latter is higher and has been subject to saltmarsh accretion for longer. Two successive and much more substantial banks cross the mouth of the valley between Rookery Hill and Hawth Hill. Between these two, Google Earth shows a substantial meandering palaeochannel, which probably represents a former course of the River Ouse.

The surface of the sedimented valley floor at Bishopstone is about 2m OD. Mean High Water Spring Tide (MHWST) at Newhaven is 3.08m OD with a tidal amplitude of 6.1m. Saltmarsh would be expected to accumulate to about MHWST. The fact that this is 1m above the level of the Bishopstone valley supports the above argument that tidal influence has been excluded for a significant time. In the 20th century sea level rose at rates between 1–2mm per year; in the preceding two millennia rates were more like 0.5–1mm (Long and Roberts 1997). This suggests that the Bishopstone valley may have been cut off from regular marine influence for more than a millennium. If the coastal shingle barrier and sea defences were not there, the Bishopstone valley would today flood to a depth of 1m only at spring tides. However, one to two millennia ago, sea level is likely to have been 1–2m lower, so it is likely that the valley only flooded at extreme tides and would not have been suitable for the regular landing of boats.

The auger holes also contribute to an understanding of the earlier history of the Bishopstone valley. The more extensive survey by Pears (2002) showed that the valley contained about 5m of estuarine sediment (Fig 2.3). The original valley close to the village was U-shaped with steep sides and a level surface at –3m OD. A core by Neal beside the small stream in the valley centre demonstrated 7m of estuarine sediments down to –5m OD (Figs 2.1 and 2.4A and B). This probably represents an incised channel within the wider valley floor. Sea-level data for the area (Devoy 1982) indicates that marine influence is likely to have reached –5m OD in this channel around 5600 radiocarbon years BP. The valley floor as a whole at *c* –3m OD is likely to have been subject to marine influence by *c* 5000 radiocarbon years BP, thus at about the time when earlier Neolithic activity occurred on Rookery Hill (Bell 1977). A thin organic band occurred at about –3m in Neal's core. Organic bands within the Bishopstone valley alluvial sequence were also radiocarbon dated by the late Dr Simon Jennings to 4840 ± 40 BP: cal 3660–3520 BC (Beta-188375) and 4470 ± 40 BP: cal 3340–2930 BC (Beta-188376). Unfortunately, however, the location and height of the organic bands dated by Jennings is unknown due to his sad premature death. The dates are, however, strikingly close to that obtained for Neolithic activity on Rookery Hill (4460 ± 70 BP; HAR-1662), confirming that at the time of Neolithic activity, estuarine, probably saltmarsh, conditions prevailed in the valley with some probable reedswamp incursion in brief episodes of reduced marine influence. West of Rookery Hill, the much more deeply incised valley of the Ouse (down to -26m OD) will have been subject to marine inundation by about 8000 BP, judging by the sea-level curve (Devoy 1982). It is clear that marine influence continued in this area until the end of the Anglo-Saxon period because a cluster of saltern mounds broadly dated to the 12th century or possibly earlier (centred on TQ4550 0110) were found in advance of the Ouse Valley Project (Archaeology South East 2000) (Fig 2.2).

There is uncertainty as to what extent marine influence may have been moderated by the periodic growth and breaching of the shingle bars which are such a prominent feature of the Sussex coastal valleys today. However, organic stabilisation horizons, within the estuarine silts cored by Pears and Neal, were few and thin. This makes it probable that, for the duration of occupation on Rookery Hill, it was surrounded on three sides by estuarine saltmarsh, but it seems no longer to have been subject to accretion by the time the lynchet encroached over its edge at soil pit 3. A Saxon landing-place directly beside Bishopstone village seems unlikely. More probable is that maritime communication was maintained via a landing-place associated with a former easterly channel of the Ouse, 1km or so to the south-south-west of the village between Rookery and Hawth Hills.

2.5 Summary and conclusion

As a result of the various studies examined above, we have a relatively informed understanding of the sequence of landscape and land-use development in and around Bishopstone over the first millennium AD. Transitions are evident in three key zones, each contributing to the mixed resource profile characterising the economy of coastal downland communities: the chalk plateau, valley slopes, and the perimarine/inter-tidal zone. Bishopstone would appear to be no different from other locales examined in the South Downs which, as a result of soil erosion, witnessed a general downturn in the exploitation of the chalk plateau for arable cultivation after the Roman period (Bell 1983). The most conclusive evidence for this is provided by the results of the Rookery Hill excavation. Not only did Anglo-Saxon settlement features (such as Structure XLVIII) produce molluscan profiles indicative of closely grazed grassland, but the adjacent field system, which had seen continuous cultivation throughout the Iron Age and Roman periods, went out of use to be colonised by Anglo-Saxon buildings (Bell 1977, 239). All the indications are that Rookery Hill continued to be exploited as pasture following the final abandonment of the Anglo-Saxon settlement and we should expect the same from adjacent ridges; there is little reason to doubt that the foundations of the highly developed pastoral economy of the documented medieval period were laid down before the Norman Conquest (Haselgrove 1977, 249).

The long-term exploitation of the valley-slope sector is more difficult to gauge. The discovery of mid and late Iron Age occupation on the eastern edge of the hamlet of Norton, close to what would appear to be the surviving remnants of a contemporary field system, shows that arable cultivation extends at least as far back as later prehistory in some parts of the valley (Seager Thomas 2005a). However, as we have seen, the history of cultivation on the slopes of the spur below Bishopstone village appears to begin somewhat later, evidently being directly tied to the occupation of the later Anglo-Saxon settlement sampled during the current excavations. The discovery of a few highly abraded sherds of Romano-British pottery in the lynchet sequence is, however, suggestive of earlier episodes of cultivation in the general vicinity.

The predominant environment within the floodplain sector throughout the first millennium and beyond was estuarine mudflats and saltmarsh, which would have stabilised in response to the growth of the coastal spit on its eastwards journey towards Seaford Head. Historical sources show that by the end of the Anglo-Saxon period a proportion of this area, no doubt including the higher reaches of the valley, had been reclaimed for meadow. It may be noted that references to drainage features can be found in an Anglo-Saxon charter for the neighbouring parish of South Heighton, a detached portion of the original pre-Conquest estate of Bishopstone (S 869; Haselgrove 1977, 244; Kelly 1998, 65; Combes 2002; Chapter 3.1). In terms of landscape reconstruction, the greatest difficulty relates to pinpointing the precise location of the outfall of the River Ouse prior to its medieval-period breach below Seaford Head. The assumption has been that its medieval position may have been fixed by the Norman Conquest (Castleden 1996, 24), but the dynamics of spit formation would certainly allow for intermediate breaches in closer proximity to the entrance of the Bishopstone valley.

It must be assumed that the closest landing-place available to the later Anglo-Saxon settlement would have been located in the vicinity of this transitory outfall; any conception that craft could navigate directly up to the Bishopstone spur can now be safely dismissed on the basis of the sea-level and sedimentation evidence reviewed. This view is entirely consistent with excavated evidence, which shows that the range of imported commodities consumed by the later Anglo-Saxon community was very much defined by coastal trafficking, as opposed to cross-Channel trade (Chapter 9.4).

Note

1   East Sussex Record Office ACC 2327/1/2/1. I should like to thank Christopher Whittick for bringing this reference to my attention.

3 Historical synthesis

The following chapter integrates documentary, top-ographic, and toponymic sources to formulate an historical synthesis of Bishopstone's pre-Conquest development. It should be stressed that this is *an interpretation* only – albeit one which is derived from a sophisticated and nuanced appraisal of these sources in their national context – and the excavated evidence is reconcilable with alternative models (Chapter 9.3). It builds upon two previous studies conceptualising Bishopstone as an Anglo-Saxon minster: the first driven by an analysis of two relevant Anglo-Saxon charters in the Selsey archive (Kelly 1998, nos 14 and 15) and the second by local historical research (Combes 2002). The interpreta-tion offered below attempts to bring deeper meaning to this identification in two ways: first by revisiting the charter evidence in light of recent research on two relevant themes, the politics of Mercian involve-ment in the South Saxon kingdom, and place-name formations associated with pre-Conquest episcopal estates; and second by integrating the evidence of the *Historia translationis sanctae Lewinnae*, a hagio-graphical text composed around the year *c* 1060 in the Flemish monastery of St Winnoc in modern-day Bergues, Belgium.

The latter has been much discussed in a Sussex context, for the action of this mid-11th-century narrative account of relic theft is purportedly set in the vicinity of Seaford harbour. Whilst medieval hag-iography should never be taken at face value, a new appraisal by David Defries, incorporating re-edited extracts from the text previously published in 1886 (Appendix 1), suggests that the narrative incorpo-rates genuine topographical detail. This increases the probability that its first-hand informant, Balger, was indeed recalling events enacted in the Bishop-stone stretch of the Sussex coastline. With the general location of the narrative authenticated, a new case is presented for identifying Lewinna's shrine with St Andrew's church, Bishopstone. Further inter-rogation of the narrative is used to offer a fresh perspective on the constructional history of the church in its pre-Conquest phases as a setting for a minor saint's cult, arguably one of the most vividly documented in late Anglo-Saxon England.

3.1 Bishopstone and *Deantone*: the estate and the church under the Mercian kings and South Saxon bishops
by John Blair and Thomas Pickles

Two linked memoranda in the Selsey archive, dated 801 and 825, constitute the fundamental documentary evidence for the Anglo-Saxon origins of Bishopstone, but it is superficially a complication that they are concerned with a place called Denton (spelt as both *Deantone* and *Dentone*).[1] The purpose of this contri-bution is to show that this Denton is undoubtedly Bishopstone, and to suggest contexts both for the early estate and for the change of its name between the 820s and its next recorded appearance in 1086.

Both memoranda survive only as 14th-century cartulary copies, but specialists, including their latest editor Susan Kelly, consider them basically authentic. The first is a record of a synod at Chelsea, whereby Coenwulf, king of the Mercians (796–821), restored land at *Dentone* to Wehthun, bishop of Selsey (787x809–805x811). The second is a record of a synod at *Clofesho* settling, in the bishop's favour, a dispute about land at *Deantone* between Beornwulf, king of the Mercians (823–25) and Cynred, bishop of Selsey (816x824–839x845). Since these documents are of crucial importance for present purposes, but are less than crystal-clear in their formulation, the key passages require close attention:

801 ... *orta est aliqua dissencio ... de terra illius predicti episcopi, id est in Dentone .xxv. Dicebat rex ut rectius attingere deberet at monasterium in Beadynghomm; dicebat episcopus quod eius ante-cessoribus dudum datum fuerat ad ecclesiam que est in Seleseghe.*

(... a dispute has arisen ... concerning land of that said bishop, namely in Denton '25'. The king said that it should more properly pertain to the minster of Beddingham; the bishop said that it was given by his predecessors some time ago to the church that is in Selsey.)

825 ... *episcopus Australium Saxonum Coenredus [for Cynredus] fuit spoliatus de aliqua parte terre illius .xxv. ecclesie quod [for que²] vocitatur Deantone, quod [for quam] Plegheardus abbas dudum tradidit ad sedem episcopalem que est in Seleseghe cum corpore suo, quod [for quam] ei rex Offa ante condonerat et conscripserat de hereditate ecclesie Bedingehommes quam ipse sibi adquisi-erat in hereditatem propriam.*

(... Cynred, bishop of the South Saxons, was despoiled of a certain part of the land of that '25' church which is called Denton, which abbot Plegheard handed over some time ago, with his body, to the episcopal seat which is in Selsey, [and] which King Offa had previously presented and granted in writing to him [Plegheard] out of the inheritance of Beddingham church which he had himself acquired as his personal inheritance.)

Together these documents establish certain basic facts. Sometime prior to King Offa's reign, a minster had been founded at Beddingham; Offa had acquired control over Beddingham and granted part of its land to an abbot named Plegheard; Plegheard had then granted this land to the episcopal seat at Selsey. However, the two accounts leave significant room for interpretation over the way in which Offa acquired control over Beddingham and over the nature of the land at issue.

When the 825 text describes Offa's control of Beddingham, it states that he had acquired it (presumably with all its assets) *in hereditatem propriam*. How could Offa of Mercia, an alien and invading king in Sussex, have had 'personal inheritance' there? Alex Burghart has recently suggested one solution in his reassessment of political and territorial power during the 'Mercian Supremacy', and his observations are worth quoting:

This was written more than fifty years after Offa is likely to have 'inherited' the estates and it is possible that the scribe of 825 was simply making assumptions. However, the bishops of the South Saxons appear to have had Offa's charter to Plegheard and it may have been this document which stated that he had inherited the land. It might also be the case that by 'inheritance' the scribe meant that he had lawfully acquired Beddingham, but, if so, it is a slightly odd way of putting it. It is thus possible that Beddingham had actually been Æthelbald's [king of the Mercians 716–57], for Offa is known to have claimed his lands. It is a general assumption that kings did not hold estates in other kings' kingdoms, but it must be remembered that much of the 8th century was a time of multiple kingship and that just as two kings of Kent could both hold land in the same region of Kent, it may have been possible for a king of the Mercians and the kings of the South Saxons to hold land in the same region of Sussex.[3]

There is, however, no independent evidence that Æthelbald of Mercia had monastic property in Sussex.[4] An alternative explanation would be that the phrase 'personal inheritance' reflects the complex and ambiguous rights associated with bookland: lands granted by charter (*boc*) for the foundation of religious communities.[5] Our earliest surviving charters stress two principal rights associated with such grants of land. Firstly, they were made in perpetuity – *ius perpetuum* – in contrast to land which kings granted only for the recipient's lifetime or period in office. This principle would have protected the monastery against possible revocation after the death of its first founder or ruler. Secondly, such land was granted to an individual to dispose of freely in whatever way they should choose. This may have been because hereditary land was subject to partible inheritance and the claims of a wider kin-group: the principle would have helped to indemnify the monastery against future claims from the relatives of its founder or first ruler. If

this analysis of the charters is accurate, such land was not – strictly speaking – hereditary: it was not inherited but acquired and therefore was not subject to the conventions of partible inheritance. However, because such land was granted to an individual in perpetuity and to dispose of freely, it could come to be thought of as hereditary land. Bede, in complaining that such grants were being made for the foundation of 'false' monasteries, describes the land as granted in hereditary right (*ius hereditarium*) by royal edicts.[6] Consequently, the phrase *in hereditatem propriam* may simply mean that Offa had acquired the bookland owned by Beddingham minster with its distinctive rights, even if he had done this by expropriation after his victory over the South Saxon kings in the 770s.

Further ambiguities are presented by the texts' descriptions of the land that was the subject of the dispute. To remove first a surface confusion: the numeral '25', so oddly positioned in both texts, is clearly a copyist's interpolation designed (in our view truthfully) to equate this property with Domesday Book's 25 hides at Bishopstone.[7] Both texts agree that land in *Dentone/Deantone* was at issue – presumably originally *denu-tūn* 'valley farm/estate'. Since both suggest that the minster at Beddingham formerly owned the land under discussion, we can safely assume that they deal with the same land (Fig 3.1). The 801 text refers, in rather vague terms, to land of the bishopric, 'that is in *Denu-tūn*'. The formulation of 825 is even less clear, and open to two alternative interpretations. The reading 'a certain part – called *Denu-tūn* – of the land of that church [ie Selsey]' is superficially attractive, but compromised by the lack of any prior reference to Selsey or its church. The reading 'a certain part of the land of *Denu-tūn* church' makes better sense of the grammar, especially coming from a rather clumsy Latinist whose mind may have been distracted by the connection of this land with the minster at Beddingham. Even if this reading is accepted, it is not clear whether Beddingham and Selsey owned merely 'a certain part of the land of *Denu-tūn* church' or *Denu-tūn* church itself, since the sub-clauses concerning Offa and Plegheard could refer to either phrase. Indeed, the language used to describe *Denu-tūn* in both texts would be consistent with either interpretation. The property is called *terra* in 801, *villa* in a confirmation that King Coenwulf issued there in 821x3,[8] and either *terra* or *terra* and *ecclesia* in 825. *Prima facie* this might seem to suggest that the 801 and 821x3 texts refer to land whereas the 825 text refers to land and to a separate church. Yet the 801 and 821x3 texts could have been describing a church with its endowment, in other words a minster: by the early 9th century, minsters were increasingly conceived and written about as financial assets rather than religious institutions.[9] Nor need *ecclesia* imply a *mere* church as distinct from a minster: in these texts, for instance, Beddingham minster is variously called *monasterium* and *ecclesia*, while *ecclesia* is used in 801 for

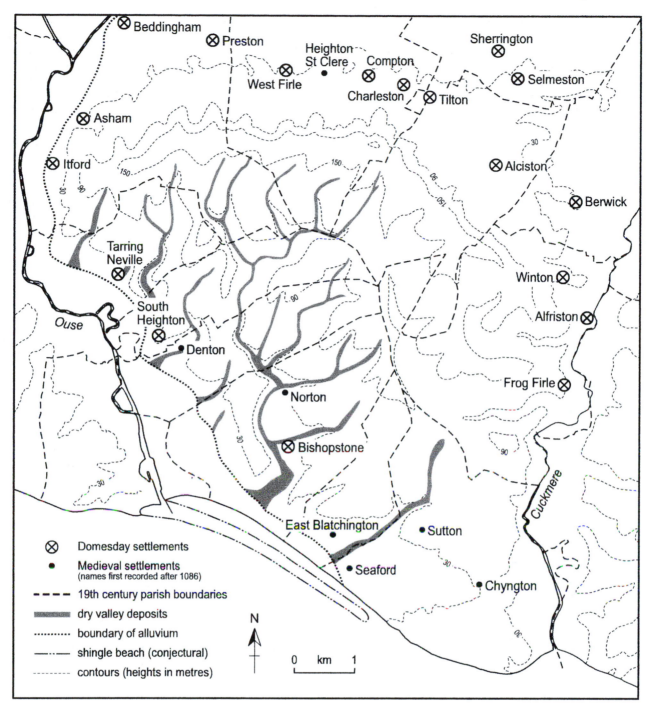

Fig 3.1 Location of Bishopstone in relation to neighbouring Domesday settlements within the block of downland between the Rivers Ouse and Cuckmere

the episcopal seat itself. Given these ambiguities, there seem to be two possibilities:

1 The sub-clauses concerning Offa and Plegheard in 825 refer only to 'a certain part of the land of *Denu-tūn*'. King Offa thus acquired control over Beddingham minster and granted to Plegheard a portion of its land in *Denu-tūn*. Plegheard could, then, have been abbot of a community at *Denu-tūn* or of another community. Plegheard then granted this portion of land to Selsey. On

this reading it remains unclear whether Beddingham ever controlled *Denu-tūn* church, whether *Denu-tūn* church existed when the 801 and 821x823 texts were written, and whether *Denu-tūn* church was at this stage granted to Selsey.

2 Alternatively, the sub-clauses concerning Offa and Plegheard in 825 refer to *Denu-tūn* church. Thus Beddingham minster originally owned *Denu-tun* church and its lands. Beddingham could have established a dependent minster

on outlying land in *Denu-tūn* or have acquired control over a formerly independent minster. Offa had acquired Beddingham and granted *Denu-tūn* church and its lands to Plegheard. Plegheard could have been abbot of *Denu-tūn* itself or of another community. Plegheard then granted *Denu-tūn* church and its lands to Selsey. However, Selsey had been despoiled of part of those lands.

With all this in mind, we may turn to further onomastic, topographical, archaeological, and parochial evidence. Beddingham parish sits at the northernmost edge of a block of contiguous parishes running south-eastwards to the sea: Tarring Neville, South Heighton, Denton, Bishopstone, East Blatchington, and Sutton (Fig 3.1). The name Denton – from *denu-tūn* 'valley estate/farm'[10] – presumably referred to the valley running southwards via Poverty Bottom, Norton Bottom, Norton, and Bishopstone to the harbour, and within which Bishopstone is the focal settlement.[11] During the 7th to 9th centuries such names, combining a topographical element with a habitative one, may have been coined to describe a geographical feature along with a settlement within that feature.[12] Like this *denu-tūn*, they could also be used to describe an estate, which might include a large swathe of territory and other subsidiary settlements. Indeed, *Denu-tūn* is very likely to have been the name for an estate covering much, or all, of this valley. The place-names Sutton (near Seaford) and Norton were presumably originally named as the South and North *tūnas* (farms in this instance) within this valley estate, although they are first recorded only in the 13th century.[13] South Heighton, OE *heah-tūn* 'high farm', could also have been named as the settlement within this estate which was furthest up the valley, though of course the name could simply refer to its elevation.[14] In her recent demonstration that Bishopstone church had a mother-parish comparable to that of other former minsters, Pam Combes makes the important observation that it received a pension and mortuary dues from South Heighton parish, which is separated from Bishopstone parish by Denton.[15] The implication – that both South Heighton and Denton were once part of a larger Bishopstone parish – is consistent with the argument for a larger Denton estate equivalent to that parish. Put together, this evidence suggests a Denton estate once running from South Heighton down the valley to Sutton.

It can therefore be concluded that if the 825 text does refer to *Denu-tūn* church, this was almost certainly the church at the place now called Bishopstone. This conclusion is of course strongly reinforced by the other evidence – the church building, the 'Eadric' sundial, the excavated cemetery and structures, the small-finds – discussed elsewhere in this volume.

By the 1080s, the episcopal seat had been moved from Selsey to Chichester. Domesday Book reveals that the bishop of Chichester held a 25-hide estate at Bishopstone, nine hides of which were held from the bishop by three men named Godfrey, Harold, and Richard.[16] Although Domesday mentions South Heighton as a separate holding, it fails to mention Norton, East Blatchington, or Sutton, suggesting that they were at this stage part of the Bishopstone estate. Our texts concerning the history of *Denu-tūn* are preserved in the 14th-century Chichester cartulary as part of the see's claims to Bishopstone and – as noted above – the numeral 25 is inserted in both texts, probably as an attempt to reinforce the identification between *Denu-tūn* and Bishopstone. Given this later information, the second of the two interpretations proposed above seems by far the more likely: Beddingham minster owned *Denu-tūn* church and its lands, probably stretching from South Heighton down to Sutton; when King Offa acquired control over Beddingham, he granted *Denu-tūn* church and its lands to Plegheard; Plegheard in turn granted them to Selsey; Selsey retained control over the church and its lands into the 11th century and beyond, but on at least two occasions it was despoiled of part of those lands.

Quite where the disputed land lay is not clear, but South Heighton is a possible candidate. As noted above, the fact that Bishopstone church had parochial jurisdiction over South Heighton church suggests a territorial connection between the two. In an apparently authentic charter of 988, Æthelred II confirmed an exchange by which Æthelgar, abbot of the New Minster at Winchester and bishop of Selsey, received seven hides at *Heantun* – probably South Heighton – from Ælfric, ealdorman of Hampshire, in return for land near the river Lambourne in Berkshire.[17] Æthelgar may have acquired South Heighton in his capacity either as abbot of New Minster or as bishop of Selsey: although in 1086 it seems to have been in lay hands, it subsequently belonged to New Minster and continued to until the Dissolution.[18] If South Heighton was the land in *Denu-tūn* that was disputed in 801 and 825, it apparently again passed out of the see of Selsey's hands, was re-acquired by Æthelgar as bishop of Selsey, but ultimately passed to his community at New Minster.

Of course, this leaves us with an important question: when and why was a new place-name coined to describe the church and the estate? The early 9th-century texts refer to the church and its lands as *Denu-tūn*: at that stage a whole range of circumstances may be envisaged, and it is impossible to distinguish between them. *Denu-tūn* could have been the name of the estate only, not of any settlements within it: its application to modern Denton may have been a later effect of the reorganisation of the estate into discrete units. *Denu-tūn* could have been the name for the estate and for the place now called Denton, perhaps because it was then the estate centre. Both Bishopstone and the estate might then have been renamed during some subsequent estate reorganisation that transferred the estate centre to Bishopstone. *Denu-tūn* could have been the name for the estate and for the place now called Bishopstone, and only applied to the place now called Denton after the name Bishopstone was coined. In all these cases, *Denu-tūn* church may have been a shorthand way of referring to the only important church on the estate.

Whatever the original circumstances, at some point between the early 9th and 11th centuries *Denu-tūn* church and its estate became known as *Biscopes-tūn*, 'the *tūn* of the bishop'. A straightforward explanation would be that the advent of a new owner simply occasioned the coining of a new place-name describing him. However, if Bishopstone is considered alongside other places called *biscopes-tūn*, *muneca-tūn* and *prēosta-tūn*, it becomes possible to suggest a more precise context.[19]

Such names are part of a wider group known as 'X's *tūn*' place-names, in which the name of an individual is combined with *tūn*. 'X's *tūn*' names are associated with the process by which the large royal and ecclesiastical estates of the 7th and 8th centuries were carved up into smaller units and granted out to new owners in the 9th, 10th, and 11th centuries, either on lease or as permanent holdings. In a significant number of cases, the personal name in an 'X's *tūn*' place-name can be connected with a recipient mentioned in a surviving 10th-century charter or an individual holding the place in Domesday Book.[20] Place-names like *biscopes-tūn* are evidently products of this process, but appear to denote all or part of an estate permanently set aside for the use of a person holding an official position, or a group of people holding land on quasi-official terms.

During the 7th and 8th centuries, narrative sources and charters suggest a close connection between episcopal and abbatial power, one which makes it unlikely that a distinction was drawn between the property of a bishop or abbot and the property of monks and priests within a community.[21] Episcopal churches and private estate churches seem to have been rare in pre-Viking England; to exert their authority within their dioceses and elsewhere, bishops tended to found minsters.[22] As far as we can see, the property granted to religious communities was considered the property of an individual bishop/abbot/abbess, to hold in perpetuity and to grant to his/her successor.[23] At this stage, it seems likely that estates were worked *en bloc* for the needs of the community and its head.

However, during the later 8th century and into the 9th century, parallel Frankish and Anglo-Saxon reform movements promoted the principle that episcopal and clerical property should be distinguished, resulting in the establishment of separate endowments for the common needs of monks or of clergy.[24] From the 9th century onwards charters survive for a range of clerical communities that include clauses setting land aside for the needs of the clergy, either for their work or for their refectory.[25] To judge from individual cases, the place-name forms *biscopes-tūn*, *muneca-tūn* and

prēosta-tūn were coined when kings and bishops expropriated and reorganised minster estates: they set aside all of the estate, or a portion of it, for the use of a bishop or as part of a common endowment for monks and clergy. An analogy for this process can be found in the expropriation and reorganisation of the estate at Bampton, Oxfordshire in the 10th century: it seems that it was carefully carved up into four discrete zones comprising royal demesne, bookland (including the endowments of the focal minster), comital land to be held by earls during their time in office, and ministerial land to be held by other royal officials.[26] The ecclesiastical focus at *Denu-tūn* may therefore have been renamed *Biscopes-tūn* not just because it came into episcopal ownership, but because it formed part of the episcopal holdings that were set aside for the personal use of the bishop, rather than that of the monks or clergy in his cathedral, or the clergy serving the churches on his estates.

Like Bishopstone itself, a number of other *biscopes-tūn* place-names are likely to have formed after royal or episcopal expropriation of minsters in the 8th, 9th, or 10th century. Sometime during the 8th century, the bishops of Worcester established a minster on their estate at Stratford.[27] A document of 1016 reveals Bishop Leofsige leasing one hide of land on this Stratford estate to his *minister* Godric: although the land is called *Biscopes-dūn* in the charter, it is likely that there were two concurrent names, *Biscopes-tūn* for a settlement within the estate and *Biscopes-dūn* for the estate as a whole.[28] Ripon minster in North Yorkshire seems to have come under archiepiscopal control in the 9th or 10th century.[29] During the late 10th to early 11th century, Archbishops Oswald and Wulfstan undertook to restore and reorganise the estates.[30] Wulfstan himself wrote a description of the estate into the York Gospels *c* 1020, which reveals two places in it known as *biscopes-tūn* and *muneca-tūn* along with various parcels of *prēosta-land*.[31] Reculver minster in Kent similarly came under archiepiscopal control in the 10th century, so that sometime between 1020 and 1038 Archbishop Æthelnoth was able to loan land in the estate to two of his *ministri*.[32] It is tempting to connect this lease with the place known as *biscopes-tūn*, first recorded in 1310, though the link is impossible to prove.[33] Ramsbury in Wiltshire may have been a minster before it became the seat of a bishop in 909; the great hundredal estate there included a place called *biscopes-tūn*, recorded in the 12th century, and another called *prēosta-tūn*, recorded in the 13th.[34] Finally, the great Winchester episcopal estate of Downton and Ebbesborne in Wiltshire was apparently subjected to royal lordship in the 10th century, so that parts of the estate were granted to royal *ministri*; this had the effect of isolating the episcopal demesne at Downton from an outlying portion of episcopal land, which became known as *biscopes-tūn*.[35]

All these places provide useful parallels for the

process by which *Denu-tūn* church and its estate became known as *Biscopes-tūn*. Possibly the whole estate was set aside for the personal use of the bishop. However, given that the name *Biscopes-tūn* became attached only to one parish within the estate, it may be that only Bishopstone and its parish were set aside in this way. If so, it is unclear how they would have differed from other parts of the estate. One interpretation would be that Bishopstone became an episcopal settlement, a precursor for the later medieval episcopal palace. Another might be that Bishopstone constituted the demesne portion of the estate, worked directly for the bishop. Alternatively, by analogy with Bishopton near Stratford-upon-Avon and, just possibly, with Bishopstone near Reculver, this could have been the portion that the bishop used as loanland for his *ministri*. Indeed, the three men holding hides from the bishop in 1086 might have been just such figures and could on that interpretation have been holding nine hides of land in Bishopstone parish.

Bishopstone emerges as a minster in the second rank of Anglo-Saxon ecclesiastical centres in Sussex: less important than the major early churches at Bosham and Selsey (both in West Sussex), but comparable to the other small minsters that are so unusually numerous in the Sussex coastal plain.[36] It is one of only three Sussex minsters known to have had their own saints, and the only one in East Sussex. It is just possible – though this is a shaky step indeed – that the apparent Kentish context of St Lewinna's later hagiography (see Chapter 3.2 below) hints at origins at a time when King Ecgberht of Kent (664–73) was a powerful figure in south-eastern England and was being advised by St Wilfrid[37] – in other words slightly before the 'official' conversion of Sussex under the native king Æthelwealh. Alternatively, it could be classed with those West Sussex minsters, such as Wittering, Ferring, and Henfield, which are documented as the modest foundations of early 8th-century thegnly families and which also came under episcopal control.[38] By Offa's time, at least, it seems to have been dependent on Beddingham, though that could be more a reflection of recent fortunes than of initial status. The dynamics apparent here are familiar from the fortunes of many other formerly independent minsters during the century after 750: manipulation in the portfolios of investment-building priest-abbots; annexation to episcopal sees; appropriation as *villae* where kings resided and issued charters.[39]

Bishopstone's monastic character, and its evolution into a royal and then episcopal estate centre through the 9th to 11th centuries, are basic to any interpretation of the settlement that developed next to the church during the same period. The general context of secularisation means, however, that that settlement itself need not have been essentially ecclesiastical: residence by priests, residence by secular tenants or dependents, and residence by the bishop himself, are all options open for consideration.

3.2   Bishopstone, its minster and its saint: the evidence of Drogo's *Historia translationis sanctae Lewinnae*
by John Blair

The hagiographer Drogo of Bergues wrote his *Historia translationis sanctae Lewinnae uirginis et martiris* in about 1060. Its tale of how Balger, a monk of the abbey of Saint-Winnoc at Bergues in Flanders, stole the relics of St Leofwynn ('Lewinna') from a Sussex minster in 1058, is one of the classic narratives of medieval 'holy theft';[40] it has also been much discussed in a Sussex context, not least in attempts to identify the minster. The story must, however, be revisited here. In its vivid and anecdotal detail, it gives a rare description of how the cult of a minor local saint could be presented and promoted in late 10th- and 11th-century England. It is also possible, by considering the topographical clues more carefully, to identify the site of the cult, with near-certainty, as the surviving Anglo-Saxon church of Bishopstone. In his contribution to this volume (Appendix 1), David Defries discusses the *Historia* and its author in their literary and hagiographical context. This section therefore confines itself to the work's local importance: as evidence for the identity of Balger's minster, for the physical setting of its saint's shrine, and for hagiographical traditions of the saint herself.

Most late 11th- and 12th-century hagiographies of older saints have dubious value as evidence. It is therefore important to stress that the *Historia* comes at a very early stage in the hagiographical revival, pre-dating even the major works of Goscelin of Saint-Bertin, and long pre-dating the more fanciful productions of hack 12th-century hagiographers.[41] It is also a very detailed and immediate account, compiled (as the prefatory letter stresses) soon after the event on the sworn testimony of first-hand witnesses.

The community at Bergues – currently rebuilding their church and soon to embark on a fund-raising tour with the bones of their newly-acquired saint – will naturally have wanted to honour her with appropriate hagiography. As Defries shows, Drogo's account fits clearly into the recognised genre of *furta sacra* narratives; but there may also have been more specific reasons for creating a precise and factual account of recent events. To an extent, the abbot and monks must have been delighted when their brother Balger returned from a trip to England and explained how he had been blown fortuitously into Seaford harbour, had visited a nearby minster, and had helped himself to the bones of its wonder-working virgin martyr. But they must also surely have feared that the injured community would try to recover its saint, for instance by persuading King Edward or Earl Harold to complain to the Count of Flanders.[42] It was perhaps to forestall such action that Drogo set about composing a narrative that would be consistent with any testimony from the people whom Balger had met, but would also assert divine sanction for an episode that could scarcely be justified in any other way. The story was therefore written down in all its unheroic detail; it is hard to avoid picturing Balger squirming somewhat under his cross-examination, and only the conventional device of the saint's visionary appearance mitigates one's impression of a shifty opportunist.

There are thus strong grounds for trusting this text, and for taking at face value its unique and extraordinary account of how a minor religious community in mid-11th-century England regarded, displayed, and promoted its local saint.

Seaford and Bishopstone: the identity of St Andrew's minster

The action starts when Balger sets sail for England, where he is 'known alike to the king, the queen, and several magnates of the realm'. He wants to disembark at Dover, but the crew press on towards some further port to sell their merchandise. A storm breaks, and after much fear and danger the ship takes refuge in Seaford harbour. The next morning – Easter Sunday – Balger wants to hear mass; from the harbour he can see a minster 'nearly three leagues' away, and he sets off on foot with one companion. On the road he feels faint, bursts into a cold sweat, and has to sit down on a stone. As he rallies himself, a grey-haired but robust old man approaches, and Balger asks him, 'What minster is that, which relics do they have there, and in whose honour is it dedicated?' The man replies, 'You see St Andrew's minster, dedicated in his honour; St Lewinna, virgin and martyr, rests there in the body. Heavenly virtue shows through her daily the greatness of her merits.' Thus encouraged, Balger and his companion walk on to the minster.

Frustratingly the church itself is not named and, in Sussex, St Andrew was the most popular of all patron saints for minsters; a local peculiarity that may go back to Wilfrid's special devotion to him. It is even possible that the robust old man is conceived as Andrew himself, who in another Sussex hagiography, that of St Cuthman of Steyning, turns up to offer guidance at a stressful moment.[43] Previous speculation has identified Balger's minster with a variety of local churches, notably Beddingham, Lewes, and Alfriston.[44] But the grounds for concluding that Bishopstone is the place described are compelling.

Previous commentators have naturally looked for a church visible from Seaford harbour, nearly three leagues (which in medieval terminology often means miles) away, approachable on foot, and dedicated to St Andrew. But no church satisfies these conditions; in fact no church at all can be seen from modern Seaford harbour except Newhaven (St Michael) and Seaford itself (St Leonard), neither of which shows any sign of pre-Conquest importance. There is, however, a solution: that in the 1050s 'Seaford' did not yet refer specifically to the town which now bears

that name, sited half-way between the Ouse and Cuckmere estuaries, but more generally to a topographical feature spanning the Ouse estuary from modern Newhaven eastwards. Here the account of it in the *Historia* is worth close attention:

> The port is called *Seuordt*. Let nobody wonder that I describe the name of this port, passing over the others mentioned above: there is a good reason for this, as will be shown in what follows. The etymology of the name is indeed fitting: *Seuordh* in the vernacular, *maris uadum* in Latin. And indeed it is a ford, for it was a welcome ford for people disembarking (*uenientibus ad littus*). To describe it for those who do not know it, the entrance to this port is so narrow that two ships could scarcely enter it side-by-side. On either side two headlands raised to the sky descend into a sloping 'yoke' (*bini scopuli uersus caelum erecti decliue iugum demittunt*), on which every wave breaks when a stormy wind whips up the troubled sea. There no anchor restrains the ships, no rope checks their swaying, but standing stable on their own, they do not fear the east wind, nor the north, nor the south-west.

The language of this passage is strongly influenced by Virgil's description of Aeneas's arrival in Carthage (*Aeneid*, book I, lines 159–73). However, as David Defries points out (Appendix 1), Drogo uses Virgil not to produce a fictionalised description but to embellish a very realistic one, of a place that some of his Flemish audience would have known at first-hand. In fact, the specific landmarks of the two passages only have in common the paired *scopuli* and the safe haven: the sloping *iugum* between them at Seaford contrasts with an island at Carthage. Drogo's focus of interest is the ford or ridge, which has no Virgilian parallel, and it is evident that he was simply giving a familiar literary turn to what Balger described for him.

The *bini scopuli* can only be the twin cliffs of Newhaven Head and Seaford Head. These are 4km apart, but running between them is a long, narrow spit of mounded shingle created by the process of 'longshore drift' from west to east (see above, Chapter 2.1). This must have been Drogo's *maris uadum* or *decliue iugum*, and the gap two ships wide must have pierced through it. The name 'Seaford' means what it says – 'a ford in the sea' – and clearly refers to the shingle bar, which although natural would have reminded Anglo-Saxons of the embanked causeways to which they applied the word 'ford'.[45]

For Balger, then, the name described not a settlement but a geographical configuration: two cliffs defining the broad estuarine harbour of the Ouse and linked by a 'sea-ford'. His point of reference was the gap in the shingle bar – presumably where the Ouse, running close up against its landward side, would have incised a narrow outflow channel through the shingle. In the Middle Ages, as shown elsewhere in this volume, the bar was slightly further out to sea than today, with an outflow probably near Seaford

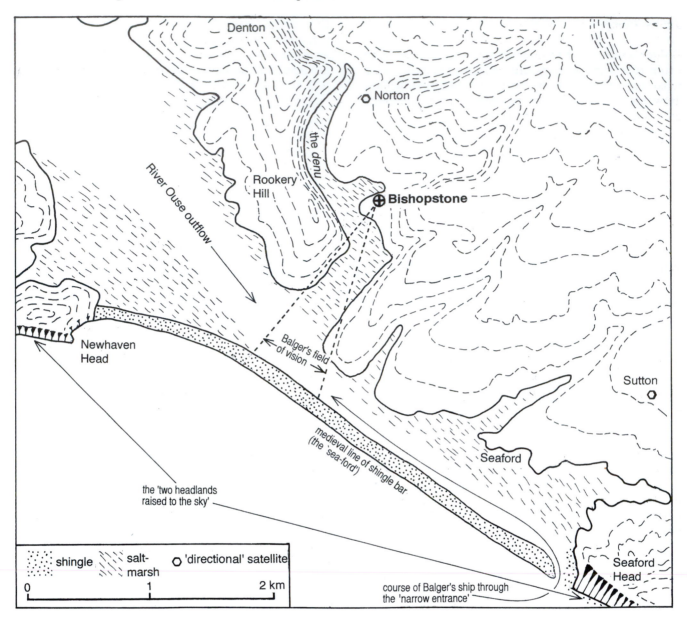

Fig 3.2   The environs of Bishopstone and Seaford harbour, illustrating the present interpretation of Balger's landing in 1058

Head (Fig 2.2). We can thus envisage Balger's ship passing behind the bar near Seaford and proceeding some 2km up-river, to a mooring opposite the Bishopstone inlet (Fig 3.2).

Bishopstone church can be seen up its little valley from a point somewhere near the present railway station: if Balger's ship was moored in this area, just inside the bar, he would have had a clear view of it, as Figure 3.2 illustrates. It is dedicated to St Andrew, was a significant ecclesiastical site, and even retains a pre-Conquest church building with a *porticus* that could have served as a shrine-chapel (below, Chapter 3.3). It would have been impossible for Balger to see any of the other local minsters without first climbing one of the headlands. The only remaining difficulty is that the church stands one mile, not three, from Balger's putative mooring. But medieval estimates of distance were often vague;

this one depends on Balger's memory, and in his fevered state as he walked from the harbour to the church he could have exaggerated it. Overall, the case for Bishopstone is as strong as it could reasonably be without the name actually appearing in the text.

One further consideration strengthens it still more. As discussed below, Drogo goes on to say that Lewinna's relics were translated into a raised shrine by Bishop Eadhelm of Selsey (?963–979x80). At this date, elevation was still exceptional for minor English saints, and the episode suggests high-level influence by someone connected to reforming circles, presumably Eadhelm himself. The explanation surely lies in the identity of Lewinna's minster with Bishopstone, an important manor and probably residence of the bishops of Selsey at this date.

The setting of the cult

Balger and his companion reach the minster, and after celebrating mass they inspect the building with eager admiration. They venerate Lewinna, 'holy virgin of God and martyr', and at this point comes a passage of remarkable general interest:

> Among other things they saw parchment sheets fixed to the wall (*scedas membranarum parieti affixas*), and that miracles which Almighty God had done through his saint were described in them. And because these were written in English, as is the custom among those people (*quia Anglice, uti apud ipsos mos habetur, scripte erant*), they could read nothing of them.

While English-language *miracula* pasted up near shrines are attested from the 14th century onwards, this is the sole piece of evidence that the practice existed by the mid-11th century. Indeed, *uti apud ipsos mos habetur* suggests that it was widespread, and to be contrasted with Flemish practice. As well as emphasising the precocious use of the written vernacular in late Anglo-Saxon England, the passage evokes a lost world of Old English local hagiography: conceivably it was from such *scedae membranarum* that 12th-century hagiographers pieced together some of the Latin *Vitae* that have come down to us.[46]

Asked to translate, one of the minster-priests explains: 'The virtues of this holy virgin, which almighty God has performed through her merits, are described here, so that they should not escape the notice of those coming after, and so that these things should remain among the people to her honour and veneration'. Then he explains every miracle: one man, long blind and needing to be led around, had his sight miraculously restored; a paralytic carried by others to the shrine walked home cured; a withered man crawled there but regained full health; yet another cripple came and was healed. In fact, anyone coming there with a disease or infirmity, however incurable, went away healthy and strong.

The Flemish visitors are impressed, and the unsubtle Balger wastes no time in taking the priest aside and making him an offer for some of the relics. The priest, outraged, rebukes this un-monastic behaviour in forthright terms. Balger turns red and back-tracks: it was, of course, just a joke. All he really wants, he says, is to hear mass and pray at his leisure. The priest replies that the church doors are open to all well-disposed people.

The scene is set for pure farce. Balger chants psalms in the church, but he glances furtively around and then starts to finger the reliquary containing Lewinna's bones (*loculum, in quo condita erat sancta Dei, manu attrectare*). One end of the reliquary is fixed with iron nails (*clavi ferrei scrinium eorum ossuum in uno fine sua arte tenebant*), some of which Balger prises out to open the box 'accidentally' (*casu*) from its end. Inside he sees the bones, wrapped in a red cloth (*rubeo palleo*). Taking fright, Balger replaces the panel and resumes his prayers. But the temptation to take the relics to a worthier setting grows on him – if only he can get permission from God and the saint! He keeps his vigil through the night.

Next day the churchwarden (*aedituus*) has to go out on the minster's business, and puts Balger in charge until evening. Left alone, he approaches the reliquary more boldly and tries to lift it up, but finds it rooted to the spot (*acsi terrae radicitus hereret*). After unsuccessful attempts, he tries a new approach: he hangs a strap (*corrigia*) around his neck and, putting both ends of it on the reliquary, offers his service to the saint and asks her to let herself be taken to a place of greater honour. Putting his trembling hand on the reliquary, he now finds that he can instantly move it. Asking the saint to promise that his 'faithful theft' (*fidele furtum*) will be pardoned, he continues his psalter and falls asleep; Lewinna appears in a dream and urges him to take her with him. Balger wakes with a start, thinking that the churchwarden has returned and caught him, but finding himself still alone he opens the reliquary, takes out the bones and wraps them in linen. In the process a few small bones drop out, and fall twice more despite his attempts to pick them up: a demonstration 'that she wanted something of her bodily relics to remain there, in the place where she had finished her life with the martyr's palm, and where her corpse was entrusted to the earth'.

The circumstantial detail of this narrative probably makes Lewinna's the best-recorded minor cult setting in late Anglo-Saxon England. The reliquary, held together with iron nails, was a wooden box. But Balger's strategem of opening the end rather than the lid suggests that it was not a simple flat-topped box, but perhaps – like many early medieval reliquaries – house-shaped with triangular panels in the ends of the roof. Even allowing for the miraculous element, it seems to have been relatively large and heavy. It stood on the floor or on a low plinth, since Balger could stand or stoop over it with a strap around his neck. Given Drogo's tendency to put a decorous gloss on rather sordid proceedings, one might conjecture that Balger did not merely 'place' the ends of the strap on the feretory to submit himself as Lewinna's serf, but tied them and braced it across his shoulders: in that case there were probably rings or handles of some kind. In fact, this sounds rather like the surviving 12th-century feretory of St Manchan at Boher (Co Offaly), which is a roof-shaped wooden box with metal appliqués, and has metal rings to take poles for carriage in procession.[47] Presumably the reliquary stood in some enclosed space (the surviving south or demolished north *porticus* of Bishopstone church?), where suppliants kneeling before it could read accounts in their own language of their predecessors' successful cures.

The relic-label: hagiography and history

Balger's flight with the relics, and adventurous voyage back to Bergues, provide more moments of comedy (notably an episode in which he lands to buy fish and gets left behind) but these need not detain us here. Safely installed in the monastery and examined more closely, the bones are found to be authenticated with three seals (*tribus sigillis signata*), and accompanied by a label (*cartula*) reading:

> This is the body of the glorious virgin Lewinna, who flourished, adorned with many virtues, under a king of the English called 'Eubertus' [presumably Ecgberht of Kent, 664–73], and afterwards in the time of the same king ended her life in martyrdom, in the lifetime of an archbishop named Theodore [of Canterbury, 669–90]. After many years had passed, by a revelation from God her corpse was raised from the ground by Bishop 'Edelmus' [Eadhelm of Selsey, ?963–979x80], with a great multitude of people standing around, and thus with due honour deposited inside the minster.

Authentication labels reported by relic-thieves must obviously be regarded with the severest suspicion. In this case, however, it is encouraging that the witness is relatively early – only a century after the purported date of the label – and that the label mentions a very obscure bishop of Selsey, whose name can scarcely have been familiar at Bergues. Hardly anything is known of Bishop Eadhelm, but the circumstances of his appointment to Selsey in (or perhaps shortly before) 963 show that he must have been in good standing with King Eadgar and his mentor Æthelwold of Winchester.[48] Two of the charters witnessed by Eadhelm are Eadgar's refoundation of Winchester New Minster (966), and the document in which Eadgar describes the replanning of the precincts of the three Winchester minsters (?970).[49] At this date the elevation of relics – certainly in minor minsters – was still abnormal in England:[50] it seems highly likely that Æthelwold's elevation of St Swithun's relics at Winchester in 971 was a direct inspiration for the episode at Bishopstone, which would thus be datable to between 971 and 980. This innovative liturgical project, at an old minster on one of the Selsey estates, may indicate that Eadhelm did not share Æthelwold's doctrinaire aversion to unreformed minsters of clergy; but another possible interpretation is that the minster was – without other surviving record and presumably briefly – actually reformed as a monastery of strict-living monks. Given that the sequence of excavated buildings north of the church ends at around this time, it is worth pondering whether Eadhelm may also have undertaken some physical replanning of the community's accommodation.

If the label can perhaps be accepted as an authentic late 10th-century product, the 7th-century events that it purports to describe are an entirely different matter. The references to Ecgberht and Theodore date Lewinna's putative martyrdom quite narrowly, to 669/73. This was precisely the period of the 'official' conversion of the South Saxons, with the baptism of

King Æthelwealh at the suggestion of King Wulfhere of Mercia (d 674/5).[51] St Wilfrid's adventures on the Sussex coast only a few years earlier suggest that the pagan South Saxons were eminently capable of creating martyrs.[52] But of course a fictional Sussex martyr would have been located at this date almost as a matter of course, and the reference to a 'revelation from God' – the standard vehicle for the 'invention' (in both senses of the word) of spurious relics – does not raise confidence.

On the other hand, a forger drawing on the obvious sources might have been more likely to say 'in the time of King Æthelwealh and Bishop Wilfrid', while a forger operating specifically in the late 10th-century monastic milieu of Æthelwold would have been more likely to align Lewinna westwards with Winchester than eastwards with Kent. There is some chance that this label, if not recording real history, does preserve a snippet of pre-Reform hagiography.

One clue may lead us in the right direction: this is not the only episode of innocent martyrdom associated with both King Ecgberht and Archbishop Theodore. The complex body of Kentish hagiography, known collectively as the 'Mildrith Legend', tells of the saintly young princes Æthelberht and Æthelred, who are murdered by Ecgberht's wicked counsellor and buried under the throne in the royal hall at Eastry. After a miraculous column of light reveals the grave, Theodore and others hold a council which recommends that the murdered princes' sister should receive a wergild.[53] The phrase used in the relic-label for Lewinna – that in Ecgbert's time she 'ended her life in martyrdom, in the lifetime of an archbishop named Theodore' – could reflect a parallel narrative with a different victim. No 'Lewinna' (presumably Leobwynn or Leofwynn) figures in the Kentish texts, and indeed names in *L-* are notably absent from that royal dynasty. On the other hand, the 'Mildrith Legend' material circulated widely in a variety of recensions, Old English as well as Latin. A possible explanation for Lewinna's Kentish context is that a lost version including her once circulated in Sussex: a version that the monks of Bergues, eager to disconnect Lewinna from her Sussex landscape and locate her in her new Flemish one, had no interest in preserving.[54]

3.3 The Anglo-Saxon church building
by John Blair

The core of Bishopstone parish church comprises the nave and south *porticus* of a small Anglo-Saxon church of 'cellular transverse' plan, apparently all of one phase (Fig 3.3). Originally surveyed and discussed by Walter Godfrey, the church was included in the Taylors' corpus with a preference for a pre-Viking date.[55] In 1982 Eric Fernie proposed a late date on the grounds of the church's 'long-and-short' quoining, whereas in 1993 Richard Gem reasserted the early one.[56] Opinion on whether this is a building of the 8th to 9th centuries, or of the

Fig 3.3   St Andrew's church, south elevation

10th to 11th, is therefore divided. Arguments for the early date – including Gem's – have rested partly on the sundial set in the south wall of the *porticus*, bearing the name +EADRIC and fret decoration, which current opinion assigns to the 9th century or earlier (Fig 3.4).[57]

In 2006, as described in an unpublished report by Guy Beresford, plaster-stripping revealed two early windows and facilitated examination of two that were already visible.[58] As well as augmenting the potentially datable features, this work had the important consequence of showing that the sundial is not *in situ*: it fills the blocking of a window in the south gable wall of the *porticus*. Beresford proposes, on the basis of a woodcut of 1856, that the sundial was re-set after that date from a position higher in the gable.[59] Whether or not this it true (and the woodcut is small, crude, and inaccurate), it now seems that the sundial cannot be used to date the building, though it may well be evidence for some earlier church associated with the cemetery revealed by the recent excavations. In the light both of these discoveries and of the archaeological project, the time is ripe for a reassessment of the building.

To take first its form and function, the most distinct-ive plan feature is the south *porticus* (Fig 3.3 and 3.8B). This now serves as an entrance porch, with a gabled 12th-century external doorway; another 12th-century doorway – off-centre – communicates between the *porticus* and the nave. It is impossible to be certain whether either or both of these doorway positions are early; on the whole it seems most likely that the outer doorway has been punched through a solid wall, but that the inner reflects an original

Fig 3.4   St Andrew's church, detail of sundial

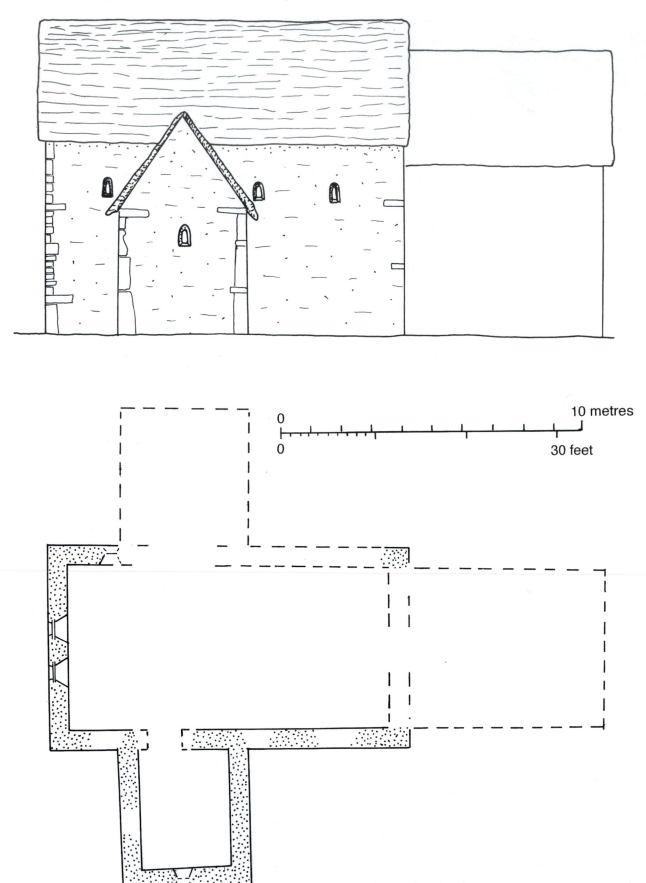

0   10 metres

0   30 feet

Fig 3.5   The first phase of St Andrew's church: interpretative plan and sketch of south elevation. The window in the porticus *wall is concealed externally by the sundial, but visible internally; the nave south windows are conjectural, though the westernmost mirrors the surviving one on the north side; the chancel is conjectural*

Fig 3.6   St Andrew's church: blocked window revealed in south wall of the porticus *following render stripping in 2006 (Christopher Whittick)*

doorway position communicating with the nave, its off-centre position suggesting that the *porticus* contained an altar or something similar against its east wall. The recently discovered window lit the *porticus* from its south gable wall. The existence of a matching north *porticus* can probably be assumed on grounds of symmetry, and large sandstone blocks reused in the footings and buttresses of the north aisle may derive from its quoins (Fig 3.5).

Nothing is known of the east *porticus*/chancel, though Godfrey cites an earlier statement that 'the foundations of the original Saxon chancel were discovered when the church was repaved'.[60] There is no evidence for any western *porticus*, even if one is theoretically possible.[61]

A peculiarity of the south *porticus* (and by implication of its lost pair, assuming that this existed), is that it is set slightly to the west of the mid-point of the nave (Fig 3.5). A recent discussion of the liturgical arrangements in this and comparable churches observes: 'The function of these *porticus* half-way down the nave is difficult to understand. They suggest that additional rooms were required for functions best kept away from the main space and not related to activity at the altar, such as for burial, or for relics'.[62] This was written without the St Leofwynn narrative in mind: in the light of it, it is worth suggesting the possibility that the reliquary

seen by Balger stood in one of the *porticus* with the 'parchment sheets' posted up on the walls around it (this chapter, 3.2 above). There is evidence that local saints' shrines often stood in north transepts or *porticus*.[63]

This configuration of *porticus* (Fig 3.5) could potentially have existed at any time in the mid to late Anglo-Saxon period: it occurs both at Ledsham (Yorks), which is certainly early within this range,[64] and at Bradford-on-Avon (below), which is certainly late. So it is unlikely that the building can be dated with any confidence on grounds of plan or liturgical layout: arguments about dating need to rely on visible architectural features, namely the windows and the quoins.

The two windows previously known are high in the west gable of the nave: 'each single-splayed opening, some 25cm wide, once contained a timber frame; the frame was 4 to 5cm thick and [was] let about 4cm into the plaster', the external jambs being of plastered flint rubble.[65] Nothing explicitly rules out an early date for wooden frames of this sort, but it remains the case that the known parallels – at Clapham, Hadstock, Witley, and Wootton Wawen – are all in the range c 980–1080.[66] Of the two newly discovered windows, that in the south wall of the *porticus* has flint-rubble internal reveals and no stone dressings; its outer face is hidden by the sundial, so it could be either single- or double-splayed (Fig 3.6). The other window is in the north wall of the nave, close to its west end and partly cut by the inserted arcade. As existing, it is single-splayed: internally, it has plastered rubble reveals and an arch of rough, squareish voussoirs (Fig 3.7A); externally, the well-squared ashlar of the opening is clearly Norman (Fig 3.7B). There are, however, signs of adaptation: photographs taken by Christopher Whittick before the recent re-plastering and painting show traces of a wider external opening, and what looks like a vertical break in the plaster on the internal reveals about two-thirds of the way towards the outer face (Fig 3.7A). While this evidence is hard to interpret, it tends to suggest either an originally double-splayed window – which would certainly be a late Anglo-Saxon feature rather than earlier – or a window with an in-set wooden frame like those in the west gable.

The remains of what looks like 'long-and-short' quoining are visible at three external corners of the nave (Figs 3.3 and 3.8): the south-west (two blocks, contiguous 'long'–'short', at ground level), the north-west (contiguous 'short'–'long'–'short' at a high level), and the south-east (two non-contiguous 'shorts'). The corners of the *porticus* are more intact (though the south-eastern is now a modern facsimile), and display a rather irregular version of the same technique consisting mainly of very large, megalithic 'longs' (Fig 3.8B). If this can be taken as true 'long-and-short' work, a mode of construction not reliably attested in England before the 10th-century Monastic Reform,[67] it would tend to suggest a date in the post-Viking rather than pre-

Fig 3.7   St Andrew's church: window revealed in arcade wall of northern aisle following render stripping in 2006. A) internal view; B) external view (Christopher Whittick)

Viking period. Taylor and Taylor observe that the quoins at Bishopstone 'show a method of construction peculiar to Sussex, or at least more common in that county than elsewhere', where the pillar-stones alternate not with uniform flat blocks but with blocks that run alternately into the two faces of the wall.[68] It is especially the pillar-like 'longs', set with the bedding running vertically, that links the Bishopstone masonry to 'long-and-short' technology, and the Sussex parallels adduced do all seem to be late.

Arguments for a pre-Viking date – which in any case are now weakened by the discovery that the sundial is not an integral feature – must reckon with this persuasive evidence of the quoins, reinforced by the more ambiguous evidence of the windows, weighing in favour of construction in the 10th or 11th century. It is therefore possible that the existing church was built at a time close to the translation of St Lewinna's relics in the 970s: could it even have been built for that event? A suggestive parallel in plan, and only slightly smaller in scale, is the lavish, shrine-like chapel at Bradford-on-Avon (Wilts), which may have been built after 1001, when the nuns of Shaftesbury fled there with the bones of Edward the Martyr (Fig 3.9).[69] At Bishopstone we may indeed have a rare survival: a building close to the architectural and liturgical ideas of the Reform, presumably mediated from the circle of Æthelwold of Winchester through Bishop Eadhelm (this chapter, 3.2 above).

Notes

1   Kelly, S E (ed), 1998 *Charters of Selsey: Anglo-Saxon charters* VI. Oxford: published for the British Academy by Oxford University Press, Nos 14 and 15 (= Sawyer, P H, 1968 *Anglo-Saxon charters: an annotated list and bibliography*. London: Royal Historical Society [hereafter 'S'], Nos 158 and 1435)

2   This emendation, like the others, is Kelly's. Since *terra, ecclesia,* and *pars* are all feminine nouns, it must be correct however the phrase is understood

3   Burghart, M A, 2007 The Mercian polity, 716–918. Unpublished King's College London PhD thesis, 67–8

4   We are grateful to Susan Kelly – who is sceptical on this point – for her comments

5   Wormald, C P, 1985 *Bede and the conversion of England: the charter evidence*. The Jarrow Lecture 1984, reprinted in C P Wormald, 2006 *The times of Bede.* Oxford: Blackwell, 135–66, at 153–8 and Wormald, C P, 2001 *On þa wæpnedhealfe*: kingship and royal property from Æthelwulf to Edward the Elder, in N J Higham

Fig 3.8   *St Andrew's church: Anglo-Saxon quoins. A) at north-west angle of Anglo-Saxon nave; B) southern elevation of the Anglo-Saxon porticus*

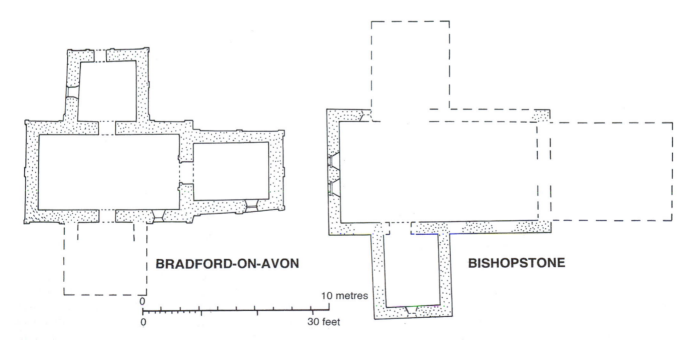

BRADFORD-ON-AVON

BISHOPSTONE

Fig 3.9   *The first phase of Bishopstone church compared with the late Anglo-Saxon chapel at Bradford-on-Avon*

& D H Hill (eds) 2001 *Edward the Elder, 899–924*. London: Routledge, 264–79, at 264–5

6   Bede, Epistola ad Ecgbertum Episcopum, cc 10–13, in C Plummer (ed) 1896, reprinted 1946 *Venerabilis Baedae opera historica*. Oxford: Clarendon, 413–17

7   As observed by Kelly (1998, 64)

8   'Acta sunt hec in villa que dicitur Deanitone' (Kelly 1998, No. 2 (= S 45))

9   Blair, J, 2005 *The church in Anglo-Saxon society*. Oxford: Oxford University Press, 129–30

10 Mawer, A, Stenton, F M, & Gover, J E B, 1930 *The place-names of Sussex*, II. Cambridge: Cambridge University Press, 365

11 It conforms very well to the definitions of *denu* in Gelling, M, & Cole, A, 2000 *The landscape of place-names*. Stamford: Shaun Tyas, 113–21

12 See Gelling & Cole, 2000, xvii for a useful discussion

13 Mawer *et al*, 1930, 364–5. See Cameron, K, 1977 *English place-names*. 3rd edn. London: BT Batsford, 142–3

14 Mawer *et al*, 1930, 363; 'south' was a later addition to distinguish it from Heighton Street in West Firle (*ibid*, 361)

15 Combes, P, 2002 Bishopstone: a Pre-Conquest Minster Church, *Sussex Archaeol Collect*, **140**, 49–56. See Greenway, D E (ed), 1991 *Fasti Ecclesiae Anglicanae 1066-1300: IV, Salisbury*. London: Institute of Historical Research, 34, and Mayr-Harting, H (ed), 1964 *The Acta of the Bishops of Chichester, 1075–1207*. Canterbury and York Society **56**. Torquay: Devonshire Press, no. 105

16 Domesday Book i, fo 16v

17 Miller, S (ed), 2000 *Charters of the New Minster, Winchester: Anglo-Saxon charters IX*. Oxford: Oxford University Press, no. 30 (= S 869)

18 Domesday Book i, fo 21v, and possibly the *Hectone* estates on 20r; Miller 2000, 143

19 See Pickles, T, 2009 *Biscopes-tûn, muneca-tūn and prēosta-tūn*: dating, significance and distribution, in E Quinton (ed) 2009 *The church in English place-names*, English Place-Name Society Extra Series, **IV**. Nottingham: English Place-Name Society, 39–108 for a comprehensive discussion of these names

20 Gelling, M, 1978 *Signposts to the past: place-names and the history of England*. London: Dent, 123–5, 180–5

21 Blair 2005, 65–78, 91–100; Wood, S, 2006 *The proprietary church in the medieval west*. Oxford: Oxford University Press, 30–1, 82–4

22 Blair 2005, 95–9 for Wilfrid as the prime example

23 Wormald 1985, *passim*; Wood 2006, 152–60

24 McKitterick, R, 1977 *The Frankish Church and the Carolingian reforms, 789–895*. London: Royal Historical Society, Ch 1–2; Wallace-Hadrill, J M, 1983 *The Frankish Church*. Oxford: Clarendon Press, 258–91; Claussen, M, 2004 *The reform of the Frankish Church: Chrodegang of Metz and the 'Regula Canonicorum' in the eighth century*. Cambridge: Cambridge University Press, esp 86–88, 94–103 on feasting and property arrangements; Brooks, N, 1984 *The early history of the Church of Canterbury: Christ Church from 597 to 1066*. Leicester: Leicester University Press, 132–42, 155–60

25 John, E, 1955 The division of the *mensa* in early English monasteries, *J Eccles Hist*, **6**, 142–55; Barrow, J, 1999 Cathedral clergy, in M Lapidge, J Blair, S Keynes, & D Scragg (eds) 1999 *The Blackwell encyclopaedia of Anglo-Saxon England*. Oxford: Blackwell, 84–7

26 Baxter, S, & Blair, J, 2005 Land tenure and royal patronage in the early English Kingdom: a model and a case study, *Anglo-Norman Studies*, **28**, 19–46

27 S 1252 for the charter recording Bishop Ecgwine of Worcester's acquisition of the estate, 699x717; S 198 for a grant of exemption in 844 to a minster founded on the estate

28 S 1388 for the lease; Gover, J E B, Mawer, A, & Stenton, F M, 1936 *The place-names of Warwickshire*. Cambridge: Cambridge University Press, 238 on the names

29 Pickles, 2009, 53–5

30 See Baxter, S, 2004 Archbishop Wulfstan and the administration of God's property, in M Townend (ed) *Wulfstan, Archbishop of York: the proceedings of the second Alcuin conference*. Turnhout: Brepols, 176–91

31 S 1461a; Smith, A H, 1961 *The place-names of the West Riding of Yorkshire*, **V**. English Place-Name Society 34. Cambridge: Cambridge University Press, 169

32 S 546 for a charter of disputed authenticity claiming that Reculver was granted to Christ Church, Canterbury in 949. See Gough, H, 1992 Eadred's charter of AD 949 and the extent of the monastic estate of Reculver, Kent, in N Ramsay, M Sparks, and T Tatton-Brown (eds) *St Dunstan: his life, times and cult*. Woodbridge: Boydell, 89–102 on the bounds of this charter and the extent of the estate; Brooks 1984, 203–06, 232–7, for a judicious discussion of the means by which Reculver passed to Christ Church

33 Wallenberg, J K, 1934 *The place-names of Kent*. Uppsala: Appelbergs boktryckeriaktiebolag, 512

34 Cramp, R (ed), 2007 *Corpus of Anglo-Saxon stone sculpture, VII, south-west England*. Oxford: Published for the British Academy by Oxford University Press, 228–9, Ramsbury 1, for sculpture dated to the 9th century and suggesting a possible pre-existing religious community; S 1451a, for the document recording the consecration of a bishop for Ramsbury; Gover, J E B, Mawer, A, & Stenton, F M, 1939 *The place-names of Wiltshire*. Cambridge: Cambridge University Press, 286, 291 for the place-names, recorded in 1186 and 1268 respectively

35 Pickles, 2009, 59–62

36 Blair, J, 1997 Saint Cuthman, Steyning and Bosham, *Sussex Archaeol Collect*, **135**, 173–92, at 173–4

37 Kirby, D P, 1991 *The earliest English kings.* London: Unwin Hyman, 43–4

38 Kelly 1998, lxv–lxviii

39 Blair 2005, 124–34, 323–9

40 Geary, P J, 1990 *Furta Sacra: thefts of relics in the central Middle Ages*, 2nd edn. Princeton: Princeton University Press, 63–5; Defries, D, below Appendix 1. I am very grateful to David Defries for discussions, and to Helen Gittos and Kanerva Heikkinen for their comments on this section

41 Campbell, J, 1986 Some twelfth-century views of the Anglo-Saxon past, repr in J Campbell 1986 *Essays in Anglo-Saxon history.* London: Hambledon Press, 209–28; Lapidge, M, & Love, R C, 2001 The Latin hagiography of England and Wales (600–1550), in G Philippart (ed) 2001 *Hagiographies*, III. Turnhout: Brepols, 203–325; Blair, J, 2002 A saint for every minster? Local cults in Anglo-Saxon England, in A Thacker & R Sharpe (eds) 2002 *Local saints and local churches in the early medieval west.* Oxford: Oxford University Press, 455–94

42 For relations see Campbell, J, 1986 England, Flanders, France and Germany in the reign of Ethelred II, in *Essays in Anglo-Saxon history*, 191–207; Lapidge, M, 1999 Flanders, in M Lapidge *et al* (ed) 1999 *The Blackwell encyclopaedia of Anglo-Saxon England.* Oxford: Blackwell, 186–7. David Defries suggests (pers comm): 'Saint-Winnoc may have used its influence to quash efforts by the English community to recover the saint. Between 1052 and 1065, the Godwines were powerful in England and enjoyed good relations with both Saint-Bertin, Saint-Winnoc's mother abbey, and Count Baldwin V of Flanders (r. 1030/35–67), who also had close ties with Saint-Winnoc. Either Saint-Bertin or Count Baldwin could have enlisted the Godwines' aid in preventing an attempt to recover the relics.'

43 Blair, J, 1997 St Cuthman, Steyning and Bosham, *Sussex Archaeol Collect*, **135**, 173–92, at 178–9, 192

44 Blaauw, W H, 1848 On the translation of St Lewinna from Seaford, in 1058, *Sussex Archaeol Collect*, **1**, 46–54 (perhaps Lewes); Stephens, G R, 1959 The burial-place of St Lewinna, *Medieval Stud*, **21**, 303–12 (probably Alfriston); Whatmore, L E, 1979 *St Lewinna: East Sussex martyr.* Pevensey, 43–53

45 See Blair, J, & Millard, A, 1992 An Anglo-Saxon landmark rediscovered, *Oxoniensia*, **57**, 342–8

46 For this argument see Blair 2002, 478–9

47 Harbison, P, 1999 *The golden age of Irish art: the medieval achievement, 600–1200.* London: Thames & Hudson, 276–96

48 For the context of this see Wormald, P, 2001 The strange affair of the Selsey bishopric, 953–63, in R Gameson & H Leyser (eds) 2001 *Belief and culture in the Middle Ages: studies presented to Henry Mayr-Harting.* Oxford: Oxford University Press, 128–41

49 Rumble, A R, 2002 *Property and piety in early medieval Winchester,* Winchester Studies **IV.3**. Oxford: Clarendon Press, No. IV, 95, No. VI, 138 (= Sawyer, P H, 1968 *Anglo-Saxon charters: an annotated list and bibliography.* London: Royal Historical Society, no. 745, 807)

50 Blair 2002, 486, 490–4

51 Bede, *Historia Ecclesiastica*, iv.13, in B Colgrave & R A B Mynors (eds) 1969 *Bede's ecclesiastical history of the English people.* Oxford: Clarendon Press, 370–7

52 Stephen of Ripon, *Vita Wilfridi*, c 13, in B Colgrave (ed) 1927 *The life of Bishop Wilfrid.* Cambridge: Cambridge University Press, 26–9

53 Rollason, D W, 1982 *The Mildrith legend: a study in early medieval hagiography in England.* Leicester: Leicester University Press, 78 etc

54 Drogo observes ('Historia translationis', Prologue, 7) that in his time there was little knowledge of her life or martyrdom 'either on account of the negligence of scribes or indeed because the writing perished'. Probably little can be made of this: if English-language texts had existed it is unlikely that the Flemish monks would have known them, or at least would have known how to read them, as the episode of the displayed miracle narratives illustrates

55 Godfrey, W H, 1948 The parish church of St Andrew, Bishopstone, *Sussex Archaeol Collect*, **87**, 164–83; Taylor, H M, & Taylor, J, 1965–78 *Anglo-Saxon architecture*, I–III. Cambridge: Cambridge University Press, I, 71–3. I am grateful to Helen Gittos and David Hinton for their comments on this section

56 Fernie, E, 1983 *The architecture of the Anglo-Saxons.* London: BT Batsford, 149; Gem, R, 1993 Architecture of the Anglo-Saxon church, 735 to 870, *J Brit Archaeol Ass*, **146**, 29–66, at p45

57 Tweddle, D, *et al*, 1995 *Corpus of Anglo-Saxon stone sculpture IV: south-east England.* Oxford: Published for the British Academy by Oxford University Press, 124–5 and ills 6–7

58 Beresford, G, 2007 The minster church of St Andrew, Bishopstone, and the probable onetime shrine of St Lewinna: a new interpretation following recent conservation, Unpubl report; consulted from the copy deposited by Bishopstone Parochial Church Council in East Sussex Record Office PAR 247/16/2/4

59 Beresford 2007, 20 and fig 13

60 Godfrey 1948, 171n

61 Gem 1993, 45, proposes that the windows in the west wall are 'at a level suggesting that they were originally placed above the roof of a west porticus'. But it seems doubtful that this conclusion can be drawn purely from the presence of gable-level windows: single windows in this position occur in the west walls of several late Anglo-Saxon churches

lacking further western adjuncts, for instance Barton-on-Humber, Haddiscoe Thorpe, and Witley (Taylor & Taylor 1965–78, I: 54, 272; II: 676–7)

62   Gittos, H, 2002a Sacred space in Anglo-Saxon England: liturgy, architecture and place, Unpublished Oxford University DPhil thesis, 151

63   Biddle, M, 1986 Archaeology, architecture and the cult of saints, in L A S Butler & R K Morris (eds) 1986 *The Anglo-Saxon church: papers on history, architecture, and archaeology in honour of Dr H M Taylor,* CBA Res Rep **60**, 1–31, at 11

64   Taylor & Taylor 1965–78, I: 378–84; Gem 1993, 46, 48–9

65   Beresford 2007, 15

66   Taylor & Taylor 1965–78, I: 274–5; II: 676–7; Rodwell, W, 1986 Anglo-Saxon church building: aspects of design and construction, in Butler & Morris (eds) 1986, 156–75, at 164; Bassett, S, 1988 *The Wootton Wawen Project: interim report 6.* Birmingham: School of History, University of Birmingham, 4–8

67   Fernie 1983, 144–5. The most recent discussion of this technology is Potter, J F, 2005 No stone unturned – a re-assessment of Anglo-Saxon long-and-short quoins and associated structures, *Archaeol J,* **162**, 177–214, but it is not primarily concerned with chronology and does not discuss Bishopstone

68   Taylor & Taylor 1965-78, I: 72

69   Fernie 1983, 149; Hinton, D A, forthcoming, Recent work at the chapel of St Laurence, Bradford-on-Avon, Wiltshire, *Archaeol J,* **166**

4 The settlement remains

The following chapter presents the main discoveries from the excavated settlement, commencing with structural features and progressing to remains which are non-structural in character. The decision to present the evidence in this form (as opposed to the conventional alternative of a phased narrative) has been dictated by the relatively compressed occupation sequence combined with the difficulties of site phasing, issues which are given full consideration in Chapter 8.3.

4.1 The buildings and structural evidence

The following structural catalogue is organised on the grounds of constructional technique and building typology. It commences with structures of 'posthole', through to 'post-in-trench' and 'aisled' construction, and ends with single structures of respectively 'cellared' and 'house-platform' construction. Within the most commonly occurring category, 'post-in-trench', coherent ground-plans (Structures C–M)

Fig 4.1   Location of structural features

Fig 4.2   Structure A, photo looking east

are presented first followed by 'Structural complex O', a palimpsest open to multiple interpretations. The sequence ends with isolated wall-trenches lacking post-depressions (Structures Q and R), which could equally represent buildings or parts of palisaded enclosures. Given these ambiguities, the total number of discrete 'buildings' represented within the structural record can only be expressed as a range of between 22 and 25. The location of these structures in relation to the overall site plan is shown in Figure 4.1.

Posthole

Structure A (Figs 4.2 and 4.3)

Exposed in 2005, this is the only building of exclusive posthole construction represented on the site, although it is open to question how many more might be represented amongst the plethora of unassigned postholes strewn across the excavated area (see below). Parts of the ground-plan (the western end and north-east corner) were obscured by later features.

The plan of this building comprised an outer pair

of walls set 3.40m apart with a third, longitudinal alignment set midway between them. There are some difficulties establishing the building's length as the poorly defined western end was obscured by later features. One possibility for a missing wall is a protuberance in the southern side of post-pit 2389 forming an alignment with posts 1215 and 1291; this would give an overall length of 10.24m and a length to width ration of 3:1.

The postholes forming the three wall alignments were either circular or sub-rectangular in shape and were generally small, with diameters ranging from 0.16m to 0.33m and depths from 0.08m to 0.46m. None contained packing and 2552 was the only example to display clear signs of a timber ghost, indicating a post of circular section, 0.18m in diameter with a tapering base. The fact that this was the deepest post by a considerable margin suggests that it might have been a jamb for an offset northern doorway, possibly paired with 2550; no evidence for an opposed entrance survived in the southern wall.

Interpretation

The construction of this building evidently called upon a fairly regular alignment of transversally paired posts, eight pairs of which can be recognised in the long walls. This regularity strongly suggests that wall-posts were connected by a tie beam spanning the width of the building. Variability in the positioning of posts in each of the wall alignments suggests a series of imperfectly aligned wall plates, as has been argued for slightly later buildings (Wrathmell 2002). The misalignment of the central posts with the transverse pairs of the outer walls makes most sense if they are interpreted as Sampson posts supporting a first floor. These would not need to be aligned with the exterior lines of posts if they supported a longitudinal plate which in turn supported the joists of an upper floor.

Structure B (Figs 4.4 and 4.5)

The ground plan of this east-west aligned building overlapped with post-in-trench Structures J and K, but a stratigraphic sequence could not be established. It comprised five pairs of transversally paired posts together with a short stretch of wall-trench (3157) defining a floor area of 5.80m by 4.10m.

The five postholes forming the southern wall (3158, 3021, 3023, 3025, and 3160) averaged 0.48m in diameter and displayed depths ranging from 0.12m to 0.25m. Their opposites (2037, 2155, 2159, 2120, and 2122) were smaller and shallower, averaging only 0.40m in diameter and 0.19m in depth. The section of wall-trench (3157), 0.30m wide and only 0.05m deep, linked the building's south-western corner with posthole 2021. There was no evidence for timber ghosts or packing material amongst any of these structural remnants.

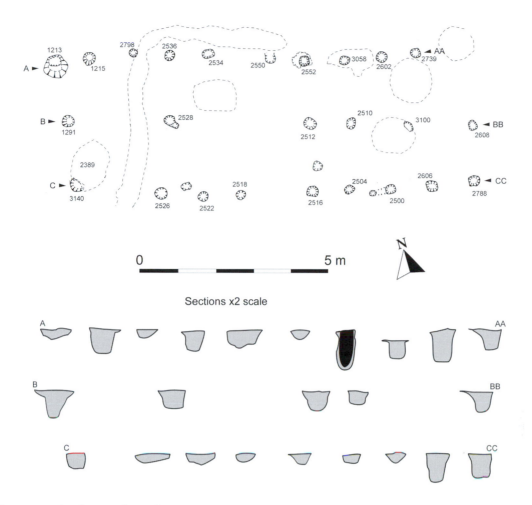

Fig 4.3 Structure A, plan and sections

Interpretation

Whilst substantially of posthole construction, this representative was of a very different character to Structure A. The postholes were larger and were less carefully aligned in each of the long walls. The one similarity is that the posts were clearly configured in pairs across the width of the building indicating that they most probably supported tie-beams on their heads. The imperfect alignment of the posts in each of the long walls is, as we have already seen with Structure A, a common feature of timber structures in the *earthfast* tradition (Wrathmell 2002).

Post-in-trench

Structure C (Figs 4.6 and 4.7)

This building, aligned east-west and measuring 8.50m by 4.00m internally, was excavated in the northern half of the 2003 excavation where an accumulation of colluvium afforded some protection against plough erosion.

Its two long walls were represented by continuous foundation trenches (93 and 166) whilst the remaining eastern end-wall (243) was defined by a

Fig 4.4 Structures B, J, and K, vertical photo

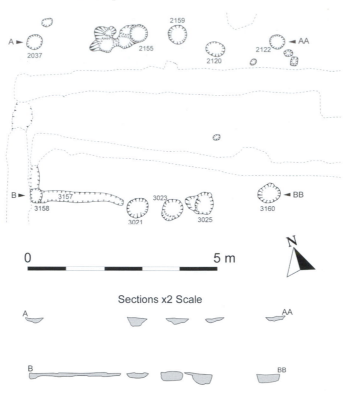

Fig 4.5   Structure B, plan and sections

discontinuous portion of trench and possibly a single rectangular posthole (481); the cut of its opposite end wall was less well-defined as a result of a coincident alignment with walls belonging to Structures E and F. The wall-trenches of the long walls displayed an average width of around 0.45m, whereas their depth ranged from a maximum of 0.50m in parts of the southern wall to a minimum of 0.30m at the western end of its opposite. A notable feature of the wall-trenches was their strongly asymmetrical profile with a straight vertical inside face, contrasting with a less regular sloping outer edge.

As probably the best preserved of the post-in-trench buildings from Bishopstone, an attempt was made to locate and define timber ghosts through detailed recording of the fill of the southern long wall (93). An initial plan of the soil-mark was produced at a scale of 1:10 and then a 2.5m-long portion was reduced in three 10cm spits, the surface of each being planned at 1:10. Unfortunately this time-consuming exercise did not yield definitive results; there was no indication in the soil matrix of a vertical horizon between an inner alignment of wall-posts, or outer trench packing (Gardiner 1990, 229), and the spatial patterning of flint and chalk did not reveal clear indications of silt-rich interstices interpretable as timber ghosts. The only pattern observed was a slight bias in the distribution of large nodular flints towards the inside edge of the trench. This location was shared by a cluster of four complete bun-shaped loom-weights found in the middle section of wall-trench 92 which could have similarly been used as packing material.

Constructional detail was otherwise provided by

rows of sub-rectangular post-depressions cut into the base of the wall-trenches; five and four respectively in the southern and northern long walls, and two and five respectively in the east and west end walls. Most were located hard up against the inner edge of the trench, but the opposed pairs (425/427 and 450/479) were positioned in the middle or towards the outer edges of the long walls. Depressions were more narrowly spaced in the west end wall and these were the only examples to register depths in excess of 0.30m; the north-west corner post (419) was cut by a substantial replacement (440) some 0.60m in depth.

Interpretation

The ground-plan of this building was relatively well preserved. The principal structural posts of the long walls appear to have been set hard up against the vertical inside edge of the construction trenches; flint packing was used to secure the posts in position. As far as can be reconstructed from the position of basal post-depressions, the structural timbers were spaced too irregularly and too far apart to suggest stave construction; the presence of the depressions themselves also argues against the use of buried sill-beams. The depth variation indicates that holes were dug to accommodate different lengths of timber, this being easier than chopping off excess sections. This evidence, combined with the presence of fragments of daub within the fill of the wall-trenches, points towards common-post construction with intervening wall panels of wattle and daub.

Fig 4.6 Structure C, photo looking south-east

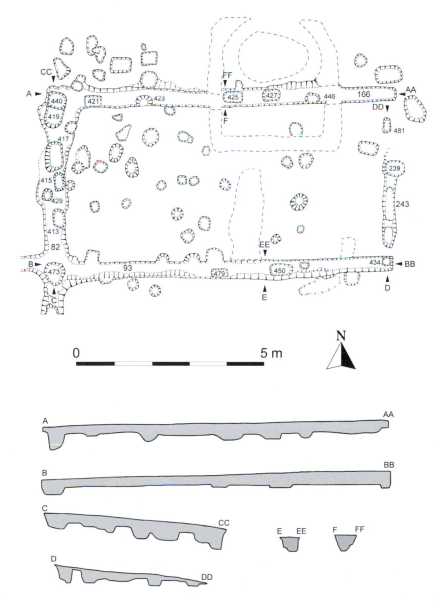

Fig 4.7 Structure C, plan and sections

In terms of layout, paired settings (425, 427, 450, 479) probably represent a cross-entry offset slightly to the west of the midpoint of the building. The fact that an original north-west corner post (419) had been replaced by a successor indicates that the building had been in use for some length of time (440).

Some of the rectangular postholes found on the north side of this building give the impression that they may be structurally related. An association may be suggested on the grounds that their form was quite distinct from the majority of the sub-circular postholes that littered the excavation, and the fact that they were aligned in parallel with the long axis of the building. It might be envisaged that their purpose was to buttress the side of the building, perhaps as a temporary repair.

Structure D (Figs 4.8 and 4.9)

The ground-plan of this north-south orientated building measured 3.80m wide and a maximum of 12.0m long internally. Whilst the footprint of the building was almost complete, definition of the northern end wall was lost where the building intersected with the course of Ditch 67. Due to the truncated ground-level and the homogeneous soil character, sections failed to establish with certainty the stratigraphic relationship between the two.

The internal space was divided between a main room measuring around 9m in length and a northern annexe, the two being separated by prominent gaps in the long-wall trenches (1199 and 1223) and a transverse partition wall (1295). The wall-trenches defining the southern compartment averaged 0.45m wide and 0.30m deep. Approximately 1.8m from the southern end of the building, each displayed a thickening corresponding to pairs of rectangular post-depressions. The settings within the western wall alignment (1387 and 1389) were deeper than their eastern counterparts and recut, indicating that the original posts (1383 and 1385) had been replaced. The trenches defining the main compartment of the building displayed a further three depressions but their presence may be purely incidental given the spread of postholes in this area.

The wall-trenches defining the northern annexe were on average about 0.1m narrower than their counterparts to the south and were also considerably shallower, registering a maximum depth of only 0.18m. Two rectangular post-depressions, one with a recut, were exhibited in the base of the partition wall (1295), with an additional rectangular example (1151) at the north-west corner of the building.

Interpretation

This was the only post-in-trench building from Bishopstone with surviving evidence for an internal partition. Access into the northern chamber may have been via a gap against the western wall or

Fig 4.8   Structure D, photo looking north, with Structure W in background

alternatively on a more central alignment corresponding to the rectangular post-settings within the partition wall-trench 1295.

Whilst the opposed breaches in the long walls could represent the location of a cross-entry, postholes 1383/1387 and 1385/1389 and their corresponding pairs in the east wall make best sense as door-posts given that their otherwise eccentric alignment with the wall trenches precludes an obvious structural function. On the other hand, the possibility that the breaches belong to different phase of construction cannot be ruled out.

As in the case of Structure B, structural information was limited by the fact that post-ghosts were absent from the fills of the wall-trenches. A slight protuberance in the outside edge of the southern end wall at its midpoint might be taken as evidence for a gabled roof, but the postholes represented within the footprint of the southern compartment may be coincidental given the wider scatter found externally.

Structure E (Fig 4.10)

This structure, on a north-south alignment, was defined by two parallel wall-trenches enclosing an

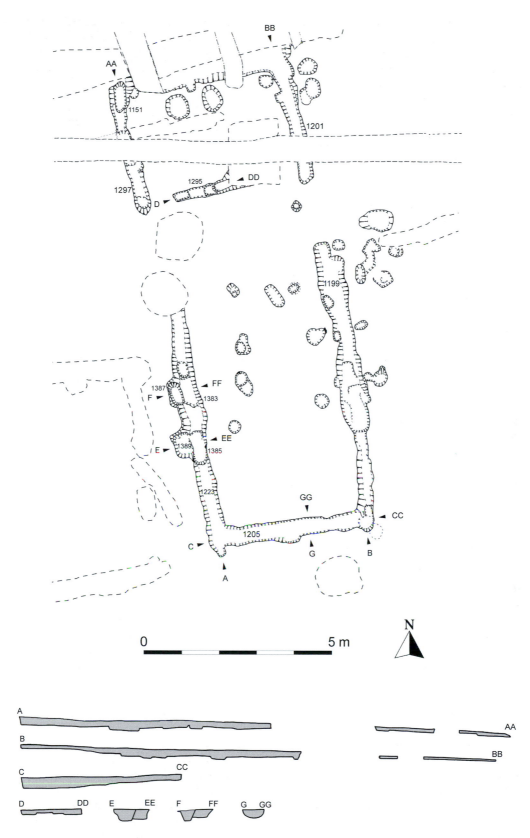

Fig 4.9 Structure D, plan and sections

area some 6.2m long and 3.7m wide; the floor-plan was bisected by the sewer trench. The alignment of its eastern wall was coincident with the western wall of a neighbouring and stratigraphically later

structure, F, and for this reason only a trace of the original cut survived in the base of the wall-trench of its successor. The northern end of the same wall was possibly marked by a step observed

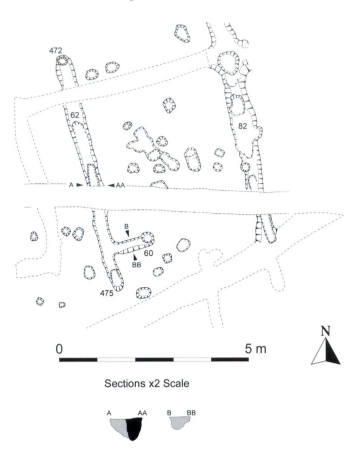

Fig 4.10   Structure E, plan and sections

in the outer edge of the western wall-trench of Structure C.

Whilst shallow and heavily truncated, the western wall-trench (62) exhibited some structural detail in the form of shallow post-settings at each terminal (472 and 475), the northern example of which was sub-circular and the southern sub-rectangular. The timber ghost of a rounded or squared post measuring 0.18m in diameter was also observed in the fill of the wall-trench at the point of intersection with the sewer trench. Extending into the interior of the footprint, about 0.9m from the southern terminal, was a short perpendicular section of wall-trench (60) which terminated in a circular post-setting.

A total of fourteen postholes were identified within the footprint of the building but there was nothing in their configuration to suggest that they were structurally integral to this building.

Interpretation

This structure represents the smaller end of the range of rectangular post-in-trench buildings excavated at Bishopstone and thus its function may have been ancillary. Very few structural inferences can be derived from the heavily truncated plan, other than the clear indication, based on the absence of end-wall foundations, that the weight of the roof was distributed along the side walls. The internally projecting portion of wall-trench is not easy to interpret; a partition seems unlikely given its proximity to the end wall of the building.

Structure F (Fig 4.11)

The principal structural evidence for this north-south orientated building was a pair of parallel wall-trenches set 4.5m apart (35 and 82/126). The western example was poorly defined as a result of superimposition with the eastern wall of Structure E and the western end wall of Structure C. Additionally there was no evidence for either of the end walls and consequently the length of the building could only be estimated to fall within the range of 8.5 to 9.5m.

In comparison with several of its counterparts constructed in the same style, the wall-trenches of this structure were notably broad, shallow, and irregular; the average recorded width was 0.67m and depth 0.20m. They also lacked the distinction of having vertically cut inside edges, but this may be a result of erosion. There were a number of features which could be interpreted as small post-settings exhibited in the base of the two wall-trenches, most falling within the confines of the eastern long-wall (126). Lending support to this interpretation is the fact that that the majority were located hard against

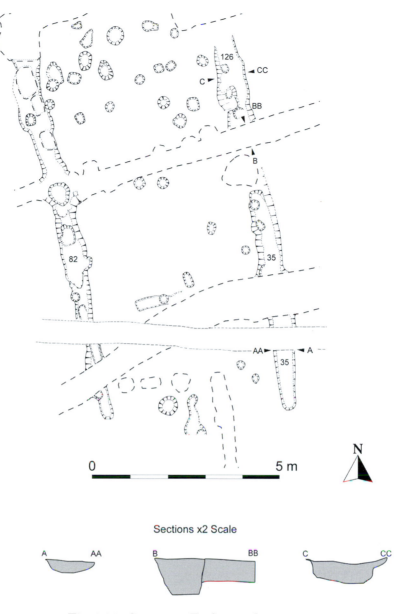

Sections x2 Scale

Fig 4.11 Structure F, plan and sections

the inside edge of the wall-trench; a more random distribution might be expected if they belonged to the disassociated scatter of postholes peppering this sector of the excavation.

Interpretation

Analysis of this building is impeded by poor preservation and a loss of definition resulting from the overlapping ground-plans of adjacent buildings. Whilst the width of its wall-trenches exceed that recorded for the majority of post-in-trench buildings from Bishopstone, other sites furnish wall foundations of comparable dimensions, for example Building S from North Elmham (Norfolk) (Wade-Martins 1980, 60, fig 78) and Building 1 from Springfield Lyons (Essex) (Tyler and Major 2005,

127, fig 69). A tentative case could be made for locating a cross-passage roughly in the centre of the building; one entrance represented by an interruption, at least 1.18m wide in the eastern wall-trench, and its opposite by a pair of substantial post-settings in wall-trench 35 spaced a similar distance apart.

The eastern wall of this building was cut by the southern long-wall of Structure B (93) establishing that it was the earlier of the two structures. Although it can only be conjectured, it may be the case that this building belonged to the same constructional phase as the latrine (Structure S) which was similarly truncated by Structure B.

Structure G (Fig 4.12)

Only a small portion of the ground-plan – too small

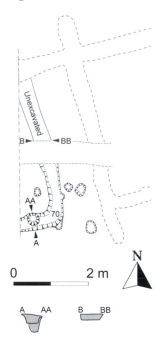

Fig 4.12   Structure G, plan and sections

to determine whether the building was of east-west or north-south orientation – was exposed at the western extremity of the 2003 excavation. It was also bisected by the east-west sewer trench and only the portion lying to the south of this modern intrusion was excavated. The excavated wall section (70) measured 0.35m wide and registered a maximum depth of 0.25m. A western return at the southern end of the trench contained a circular post-setting 0.30m in diameter cut hard against a vertical edge, indicating that the interior of the building lay beyond the confines of the excavation.

Interpretation

This fragment is clearly very similar in design and conception to the more complete post-in-trench buildings excavated at Bishopstone and its axis shows that it was evidently an integral part of the layout of the later Anglo-Saxon settlement complex.

Structure H (Fig 4.13)

The ground-plan of this north-south aligned building was incomplete and the location of its missing north and west walls can only be conjectured. The surviving portion was represented by one end wall, 1115/2073, and a long wall, 2075/2010, interrupted at its midpoint by a gap 0.50m wide.

The cut of the wall-trenches averaged 0.42m wide and varied in depth from 0.35m to only 0.20m at the northern end of the long wall. Three timber ghosts, each aligned on a basal post depression, were identified within the fill of the latter but, because they

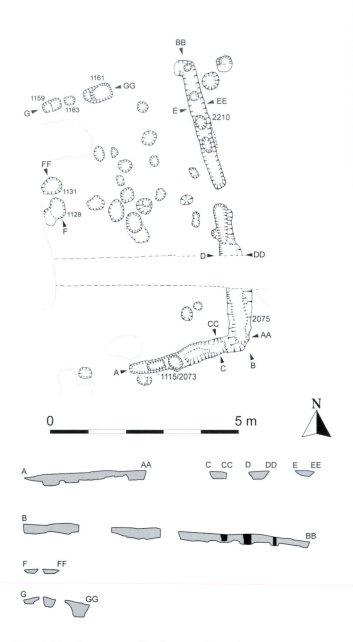

Fig 4.13   Structure H, plan and sections

were only observed in section, information on their shape was not forthcoming; their scantlings ranged from 0.10m to 0.22m. Four further post-depressions were located in the end wall-trench 1115/2073.

Eighteen postholes were located within the partial footprint defined by the two wall-trenches, but there was nothing in their configuration or spacing to suggest that they were structurally related.

Interpretation

It is likely that the missing east wall originally lay slightly beyond the tapering terminus of 1115/2073 which appears to have been truncated by the plough. It was plausibly on alignment with the pair of postholes 1129 and 1131, whereas the missing north wall could be represented by the row of three postholes 1159, 1161, and 1163. This would give internal measurements of 6.50m in length and approximately 3.70m in width. The most likely candidate for a doorway is the gap located centrally in the surviving eastern long wall.

The very narrow gap separating this building from Structure D, to its west, suggests that the two structures belong to different constructional phases; a proposition also indicated by a slight variance in alignment.

Structure I (Fig 4.14)

This fragmentary north-south aligned building exposed in 2005 was cut by later intrusions, including pit 2067 and the modern sewer trench. The extant portion, equating to the structure's southern end, comprised an end wall-trench (2055) and the stubs of a pair of contiguous long walls (2292 and 2053), set approximately 4.16m apart.

The trench averaged 0.40m in width and displayed a maximum depth of 0.18m in the southern end wall; this was reduced to the merest of shadows as the trenches progressed down the slope and no impression survived beyond the line of the sewer trench. The stub of the eastern end wall displayed two circular post-depressions (2862 and 2864), cut to depths of 0.20m and 0.07m respectively.

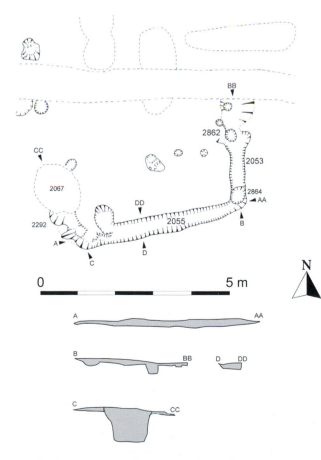

Fig 4.14   Structure I, plan and sections

Interpretation

This ground-plan is too attenuated to offer any detailed information on the building's structural characteristics. The narrow spacing between this and Structure H, to its west, suggests that they are likely to belong to different structural phases.

Structure J (Figs 4.4 and 4.15)

The ground-plan of this east-west aligned building, overlain by a successor, K, exhibited internal dimensions of 9.0m in length and 4.40m in width. It was constructed within the former limits of the pre-Conquest cemetery and accordingly its foundations cut two graves, 2792 and 2153. The plan was defined by three shallow wall-trenches, all heavily eroded, only the northern example of which (2013) was continuous for its entire length. Definition was poorest on the western side where all but a small northern section of the end wall (3170) had been obliterated by the corresponding wall of the successor building. There was no evidence for an opposite end wall, although pit 2578 may have removed all traces.

The wall-trenches of this building, averaging only 0.32m wide, were some of the narrowest recorded at Bishopstone; several sections were ploughed out and the maximum recorded depth was only 0.14m. Suffice it to say, structural information was minimal and restricted to four post-depressions, measuring between 0.12m and 0.27m in depth, in the base of the better-preserved long wall: a central pair (2714 and 2716) and a pair towards its eastern terminus (3174 and 3089).

Three short linear features and a smatter of postholes were located with the ground-plan of this building. It is quite possible that the two southern linear features represent truncated graves.

Interpretation

The level of erosion suffered by this building hinders structural interpretation. The pair of post-impressions (2714 and 2716) could be interpreted as evidence for a centrally located entrance in the northern wall.

Structure K (Plate 5; Figs 4.4 and 4.16)

The second post-in-trench building to occupy this site was on the same general east-west orientation but its long axis deviated slightly to the north of its predecessor. Its trenches cut a total of three graves (2233, 2186, and 3122), whereas each of the long walls was cut by a pit, 2578 on the south side and 2876 on the north.

Its long wall-trenches (2009 and 2167) were continuous and slightly bowed such that the internal width of the building at either end was around 0.30m

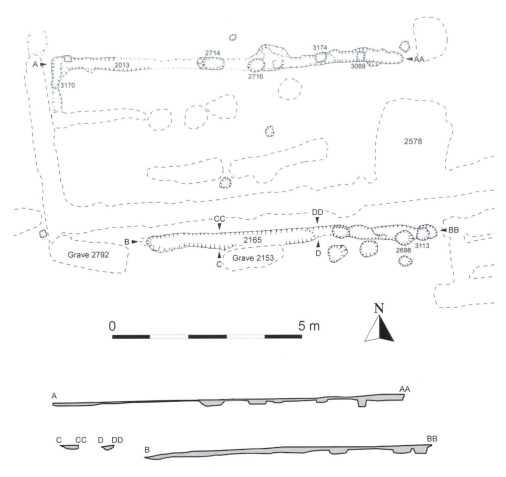

Fig 4.15   Structure J, plan and sections

narrower than the midpoint measurement of 5.52m; the internal length was 12.65m. Both the end walls (2011 and 2023) terminated short of the north wall leaving gaps 0.8m and 1.10m wide respectively; the shallowness of these trenches and their tendency to attenuate in the direction of the slope could account for these gaps.

All four wall-trenches displayed a consistent width of around 0.54m but there was a considerable variation in depth both between and within trenches. The two end walls were shallowest, 2011 penetrating to a maximum depth of 0.24m below the bedrock and 2023 to a depth of only 0.16m. The southern end wall displayed the greatest average depth of the four trenches, reaching a maximum of 0.32m, whilst its opposite ranged from between 0.12m and 0.18m.

As might be expected, the best structural information for this building was preserved in the more substantial long walls (2009 and 2167). Indirect evidence for structural timbers in trench 2009 took the form of three discrete clusters of sizeable flint nodules likely to represent packing around posts. Deeper post-settings were also present at each end of the trench.

Structural information from its southern opposite included rather more direct evidence in the form of a row of five timber ghosts at its western end recorded in section. The spacing between posts varied between 0.18m and 0.68m whereas the scantling of the timbers, as far as could be reconstructed from the section, varied between 0.12m to 0.30m; the easternmost post-ghost aligned with a depression which penetrated 0.18m below the base of the wall-trench. It seems implausible that slender, radially split planks, would have been identified using this method of recording; chunkier squared or sub-rectangular posts is in much better keeping with the evidence.

A further four sub-rectangular post-depressions were exhibited in the base of the trench (2983, 3128, 3129, and 3101), all located hard up against its inside edge.

Interpretation

Structure K was clearly an imposing structure and its prominent placement on top of the slope, potentially in close proximity to and in parallel alignment with the Anglo-Saxon church, reinforces the impression that it was a focal element of the settlement complex.

Again, structural details are in relatively short supply for this building and some speculation is required to flesh out the skeleton ground-plan. The

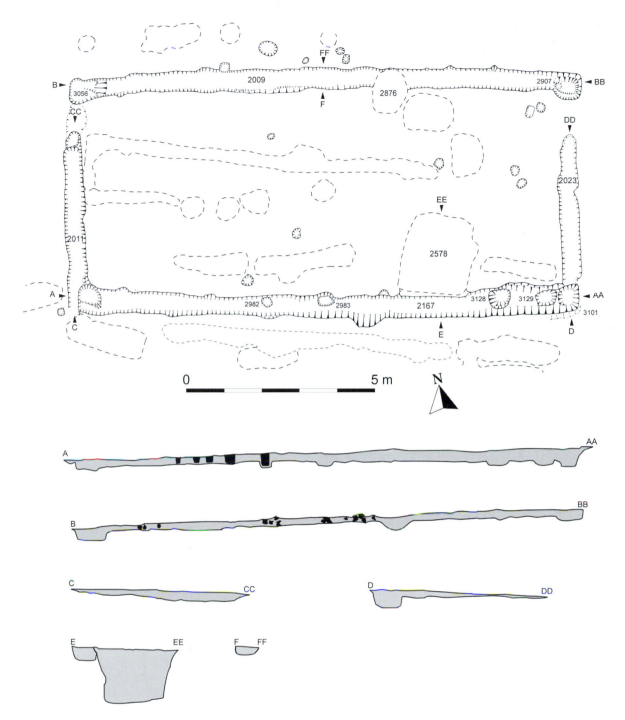

Fig 4.16 Structure K, plan and sections

first question concerns access arrangements. The possibility that the clusters of flint packing in wall 2009 may represent a northern entrance is strengthened by the parallel alignment of post-settings 2982 and 2983, indicating the by now familiar characteristic of cross-entry, on this occasion set at some distance to the west of the midpoint of the building.

Unlike many of the other post-in-trench buildings at Bishopstone, which appear to have been had their timbers salvaged on abandonment, at least part of the walling of this structure was evidently left *in situ*. The timber ghosts relating to this section of wall show that the posts were irregularly spaced, although some care was evidently taken to place them against the inside edge of the wall-trench to ensure a true alignment. Unfortunately, because equivalent evidence was lacking in the opposing long wall, it is impossible to know whether the posts were paired across the width of the building. The distinction between the depth of the long and end walls indicates that the weight of the roof was distributed on the former. The evidence is insufficient to distinguish clearly between a gabled and a hipped roof.

It is impossible to know whether the expansive floor area formed a large open hall or was instead compartmentalised; ephemeral evidence for internal partitions is unlikely to have survived the level of erosion experienced at this, the highest point of the village green.

Structure L (Fig 4.17)

This building was evidently orientated north-south but very little of the ground-plan survived intact and the extant portion was further truncated by the sewer trench. It comprised a pair of parallel wall-trenches originally set in the region of 3.80m apart: 2878/2047 located to the south of the sewer and 2268 to the north; the alignment of the former was possibly continued beyond the sewer by an elongated posthole 2309.

There was some disparity in the width of the two trenches, the western wall measuring 0.65m and its opposite only 0.46m. However, once the fill of the former trench was removed it was shown to be of two phases, as indicated by a longitudinally aligned step which defined an eastern trench only 0.26m wide and a parallel one some 0.40m wide. Although the two elements of the western wall were partially

superimposed, their chronological sequence could not be established in the uniform fill.

A particularly dense cluster of postholes was found to the north-west of the northern terminus of the building and it does not seem unreasonable to suggest that at least some of them were structurally related.

Interpretation

Very little structural detail can be derived from this very fragmentary and shadowy impression. There are two possible alignments for a northern end wall, one passing through postholes 2319, 2325, 2327, 2260, and 2252, and the other through 2331, 2337, and 2742. Its opposite might be represented by 2132, a circular posthole which occupies a central position on the conjectural alignment. On this interpretation the building would have measured in the range of 6.5m to 7.4m long internally placing its floor-plan well within the limits of the ubiquitous two-square module.

The evidence for a recut in the western wall, combined with the two post alignments for the northern wall, indicates that this building was either replaced on the same footprint or subject to a substantial repair during its lifetime.

Structure M (Figs 4.18 and 4.19)

The principal evidence for this building comprised two parallel east-west wall-trenches 2391 and 2442 located on a terrace towards the northern end of the 2005 excavation. A heavily truncated linear cut (2387/2598) is less certainly associated with this structure, but is included on the grounds that it could represent a further portion of the fragmented ground-plan. The east-west wall-trenches, both slightly

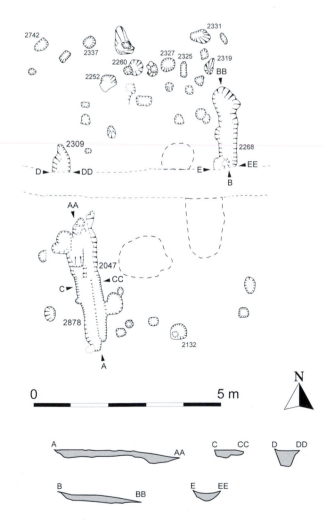

Fig 4.17   Structure L, plan and sections

Fig 4.18   Structure M, photo looking east

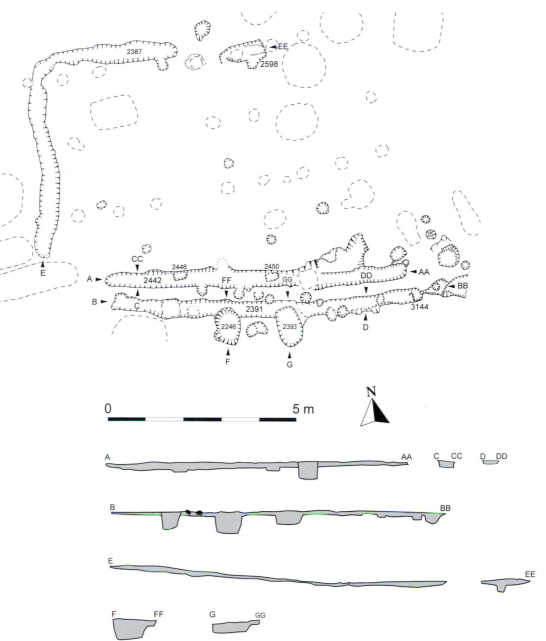

Fig 4.19   Structure M, plan and sections

bowed, could represent either two distinct constructional phases of a single building involving the total replacement of a long wall, or perhaps a sequence of two buildings occupying the same footprint.

The more southerly of the two trenches (2391) measured 8.13m in length and between 0.32m and 0.46m in width; it displayed a maximum depth of 0.14m. A sub-rectangular post-setting was cut 0.10m below the base of the trench at its eastern terminal. The fill of the trench was uniform and showed no signs of timber ghosts, although two large flints located at its western end could represent the remnants of post packing.

The trench cut two sub-rectangular pits (2246 and 2393) which, on the grounds of shared alignment and morphology, almost certainly represent a con-

temporary pair. For reasons discussed below, these could well be structurally associated with this phase of the building.

Wall-trench 2442 was marginally shorter than its neighbour, extending to a length of 8.0m. It was of a similar width, ranging between 0.35m and 0.44m, but was the deeper of the two trenches extending to a maximum depth of 0.24m. Its northern edge was cut on a vertical plane, against which was located a pair of sub-rectangular post-depressions (2446 and 2450). No timber impressions were visible in the fill of the trench.

Wall-trench 2387 commenced on a north-south alignment for a distance of 4.70m before turning a corner and extending for a further 3.30m on a perpendicular east-west bearing. The alignment of the latter section was continued by a further short length of trench (2598) separated from its neighbour by a gap of 0.92m. The cut was uniformly shallow, at no point breaching a depth greater than 0.12m, and structural information in the form of timber ghosts or post-depressions was absent. It superimposed the ground-plan of Structure A, in the process truncating three of its postholes.

Interpretation

Some speculation has to be exercised in reconstructing the ground-plan of what was originally an east-west building measuring at least 8m in length. The possibility cannot be ruled out that the missing side of the building, evidently located downslope of the extant long wall, failed to penetrate the subsoil or else has been truncated by the plough. Although the curving alignment of 2387/2598 is unusual, divorced from the extant long walls 2442/2391, it does stand in somewhat awkward isolation. One distinct possibility is that it served the function of an eaves-drip trench. The internal width of this hypothetical building extends to 5.60m when 2387/2598 is paired with wall-trench 2442 and rises to 6.30m when paired with 2391. On constructional grounds the narrower of the two possibilities is to be preferred.

This phase of the building may have had an entrance in its northern wall, if this is a correct reading of the 0.92m breach separating 2387 from its detached portion 2598. Evidence for a southern entrance, arguably of some pretention, proceeds from a possible interpretation of the oval cuts 2246 and 2393. These clearly formed a pair and were distinct from the morphological range of rubbish and cess pits found at Bishopstone; post-pits for a projecting porch would seem to be the most economical explanation.

Structure N (Fig 4.20)

This structure was represented by a pair of east-west aligned wall-trenches (2616 and 3037), which ran in parallel with the base of a negative lynchet exposed in the north-east sector of the 2005 excavation trench. The respective cuts, traced for a distance of 7.50m to a western terminus (their opposite ends extended beyond the limits of the excavation), truncated an alignment of three sub-rectangular pits: from west to east, 2618, 3086, and 3016. It proved impossible to establish a stratigraphic relationship between the two wall-trenches, which are here assumed to represent two different constructional phases of the same building.

2616 was the broader and deeper of the two trenches with an average width of 0.42m and an average depth of 0.12m, whereas 3037 averaged 0.32m in width and only 0.08m in depth. The only parts of the latter trench to extend below this depth were a pair of sub-rectangular post-settings at its

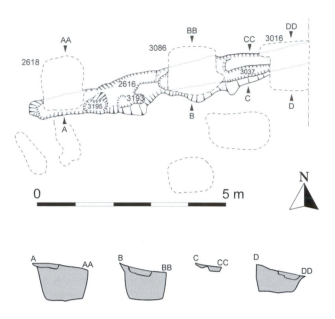

Fig 4.20   Structure N, plan and sections

western end (3193 and 3195) which penetrated to depths of 0.16m and 0.24m below the base of the cut respectively.

Interpretation

Fragmentary and poorly preserved, this ground-plan offers very little in the way of meaningful structural information. One can only speculate as to where the rest of the building originally stood, but it most probably extended across the terrace to the north of the negative lynchet in which case the gradient of the slope might explain why a northern wall no longer survives.

All that can be said with certainty is that the building appears to have been extensively renovated during its lifetime, as indicated by the rebuilding of what may putatively be regarded as its southern long wall.

Structural complex O (Figs 4.1, 4.21, and 4.22)

This heading relates to a group of wall-trenches and associated post-settings encountered on the south-east side of the village green in the 2003 and 2004 excavation trenches. As these features lay at the top of the slope they were severely truncated and the lack of superimposition meant that they could not be related stratigraphically. The wall-trench elements were uniformly shallow, none penetrating to a depth greater than 0.20m, and as a consequence post-impressions could not be distinguished in their fills. The only guide to the position of timbers was post-depressions. Indeed, alignments of isolated rectangular postholes represented in this area (eg 25, 283, 21) may represent plough-truncated remnants of former wall-trenches.

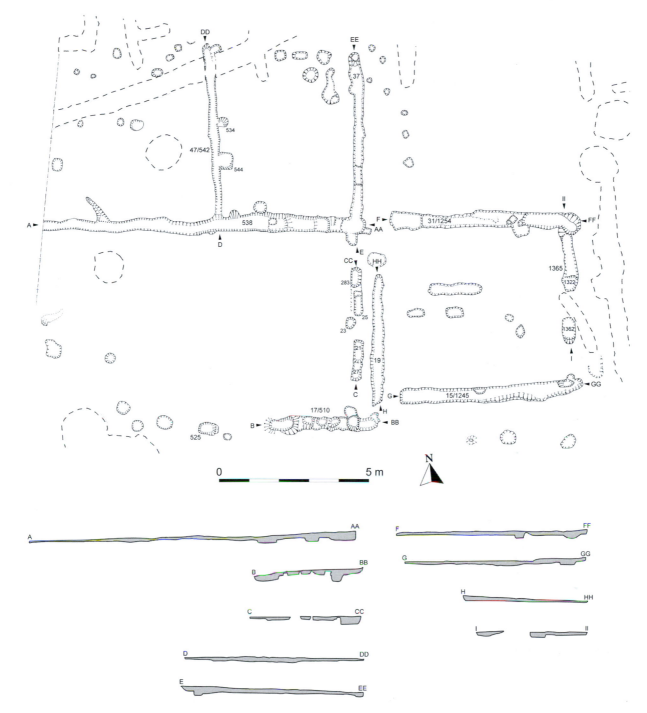

Fig 4.21 Structural complex O, plan and sections

As a result of these factors, it is safest to treat these features collectively and to test the combined evidence against different structural interpretations, the proviso being that it will be impossible to arrive at any one definitive conclusion (Fig 4.22).

Interpretation I (Fig 4.22A)

At one extreme the complex can be resolved into a sequence of three separate structures (1–3) occupying adjacent sites in different phases.

Structure O1 on a north-south alignment, was defined by a pair of trenches for its long walls (37 and 47/542) and by a row of three postholes for its northern end wall; the opposite end wall was coincident with the east-west wall-trench 538, giving internal dimensions of 5.60m by 4.60m. A possible doorway was represented by a pair of postholes (534 and 544) inset slightly from the edge of 47/542.

Structure O2 was located to the south-east of the first. Its north and south walls were defined by a pair of continuous wall-trenches (31/1254 and 15/1245), whereas its east wall comprised a discontinuous section (1365) with an aligned rectangular post-pit beyond (1362). A further north-south wall-trench

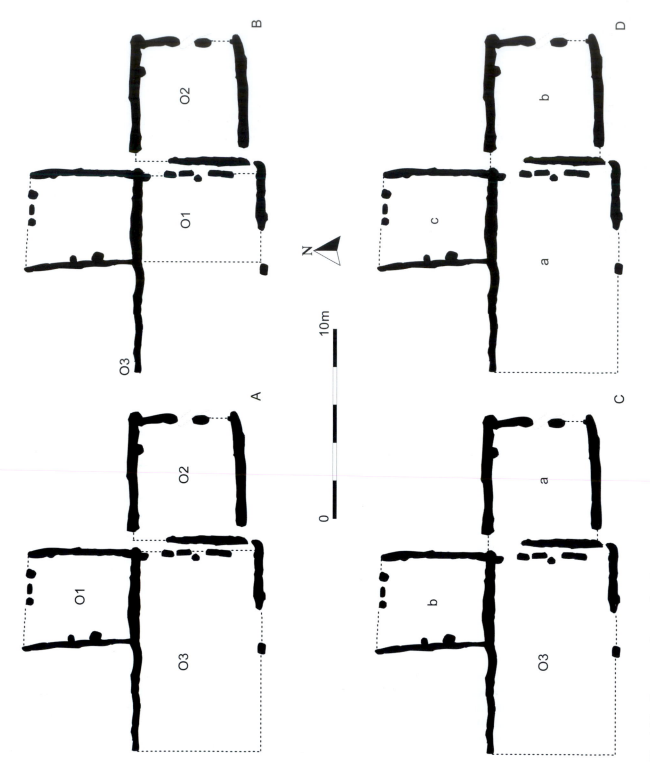

Fig 4.22   Structural complex O, interpretation plans

(19) could possibly be associated with this building on the grounds that breaks in the foundations do not necessarily represent gaps in the walls themselves. Whatever the case, it can be suggested that the building was nearly square in plan, measuring in the region of 5.30m to 5.60m east-west by 5.00m north-south. A possible doorway, represented by post-settings 1322 and 1362, was located roughly in the centre of the east wall.

The ground-plan of Structure O3, on axial alignment with the second, was incomplete and is assumed to have extended beyond the western limits of the excavation. Its north wall, represented by wall-trench 538, survived intact, meeting an eastern end wall marked by a row of four post-settings (from north to south 283, 25, 21 and 27). Only a 3.85m long portion of the southern long wall remained (17/510), although an isolated post-setting (525) could be regarded as a truncated continuation of the same alignment. If this reconstruction is accepted, then the building measured at least 10.45m in length and 5.90m in width.

Interpretation II (Fig 4.22B)

In this interpretation, Structure O1 is stretched on its long axis, so that its southern end wall coincides with wall-trench 17/510, and the southern half of its eastern long wall with post-settings 283–27, to give internal dimensions of 11.96m by 4.60m.

This scenario relegates Structure O3 to a single east-west linear feature, perhaps, like 259 (Structure Q) to its north, representing the line of a fence or a palisade.

Interpretation III (Fig 4.22C)

In this reading Structure O3 of 'Interpretation I' is retained, with one or other of the remaining structures forming an attached annexe: either an axially aligned eastern annexe (a), or a laterally projecting 'wing' (b). In the former case, an internal communicating doorway might be represented by the gap between rectangular post-settings 25 and 21, and in the latter by a pair of post-impressions in the base of 538.

Interpretation IV (Fig 4.22D)

At the other extreme all three structures are combined to form an elaborate three-celled plan, in effect a central 'hall' (a) with two attached annexes (b and c) recalling the plan of the hall at Bishops

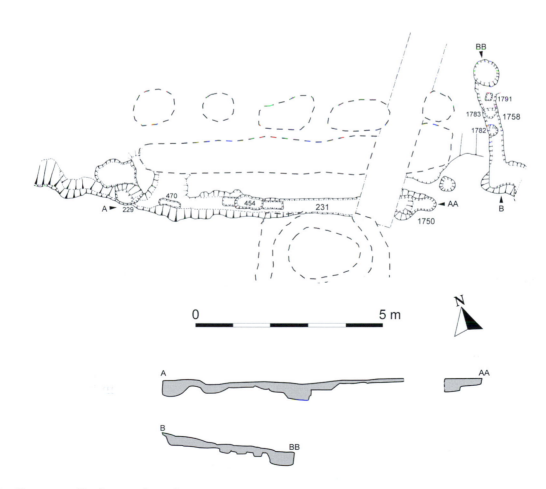

Fig 4.23 Structure P, plan and sections

Waltham (Hants), (Lewis 1985, 86, fig 4). This building may have been built to this plan in a single constructional phase, or alternatively the annexes could be regarded as secondary accretions. One piece of evidence which favours Interpretation IV over the others is the fact that the alignment of the component cells is strikingly similar, albeit within the standardised range of building alignments characterising the site plan (Chapter 8.4).

Structure P (Fig 4.23)

The incomplete ground-plan of this structure was represented by a single east-west aligned wall-trench (231/1750) discovered at the northern extremity of the 2003 excavation. There were problems defining this feature partly because it extended under the northern baulk of the excavation and partly because it ran along the base of the scarp of a negative lynchet; for these reasons it was not recognised as a discrete structural feature until the fill had been removed. The cut for the wall-trench measured just short of 8.0m in length and around 0.42m wide. Its base displayed two sub-rectangular post-depressions, the larger (454) measuring 0.30m deep and the smaller (470) only 0.12m.

Interpretation

The most likely scenario is that 231/1750 represents the long wall of an east-west aligned building and that its opposite wall, of which no obvious trace survives, was located down the slope to the north. 1758, a trench located to the north-east of 231/1750, could conceivably be associated with this building, although an objection to this hypothesis is that the two walls diverge from a perpendicular alignment. Traced for a distance of 2.80m, 1758 displayed three slight post-depressions in its base (1782, 1783, and 1791).

Structure Q (Fig 4.24)

The label 'building' should be used hesitantly in the description of what was no more than a single linear cut (259) on an east-west alignment. Its eastern terminus was located within a busy intersection formed by the overlapping ground-plans of Structures B, D, and E, whilst its opposing end lay beyond the confines of the excavation giving an exposed length of around 5.50m.

The cut shared a parallel alignment with the long axis of Structure B but was positioned slightly to the north, as indicated by a kink at the point of intersection with the south-west corner of that structure. It was also considerably shallower, nowhere exceeding 0.12m in depth, and lacked the post-impressions exhibited by more securely identified post-in-trench buildings.

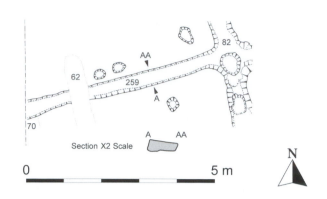

Fig 4.24   Structure Q, plan and sections

Interpretation

There are clearly problems identifying this feature as the portion of a post-in-trench building. Not least is the lack of a parallel wall – although, given the shallowness of the surviving cut, traces may not have survived if the opposite side of the building was located on sloping ground to the north. An alternative interpretation entertained in the discussion of Structures P and R is that it represents the foundation trench for a fence or palisade extending off the south-west corner of Structure C. Contiguous palisade alignments such as this are certainly found on other later Anglo-Saxon sites and a similar interpretation could be applied to other shallow trenches represented at Bishopstone (see 4.3 below).

Structure R (Fig 4.25)

This structure, not certainly a building, was represented by a single north-south linear feature (4000) which ran the full length of the 2005 extension trench for a distance of some 7.20m. The width of the cut varied from 0.55m to 0.62m and its maximum depth was 0.24m; no post-depressions were observed at its base.

Feature 4000 cut the northern external wall of aisled Structure V, indicating that it was stratigraphically the later of the two structures.

Interpretation

Two competing structural interpretations can be proposed for this length of wall-trench. The first is that it represents the long wall of a north-south aligned building with its opposite lying to the west beyond the limits of the excavation. The alternative, perhaps to be preferred in light of its shallow proportions and lack of post-depressions, is a timber palisade, as suggested for linear cut 259.

Structure S (Figs 4.26 and 4.27)

The ground-plan of this structure, cut by the

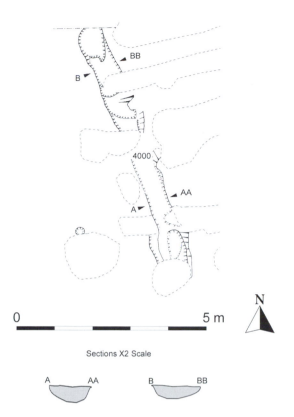

0   5 m

N

Sections X2 Scale

A   AA   B   BB

Fig 4.25   Structure R, plan and sections

southern long wall of Structure C and the single extant wall-trench of Structure Q, measured around 3.10m in length and 2.80m in width internally. It was defined by a continuous wall-trench forming three sides of a square with a curving northern end wall which enclosed an internal oval pit (271). The pit measured 1.90m × 1.30m in plan and 1.20m in depth, and was filled with two organic silty fills (63 and 65) each capped by a layer of chalk rubble (62 and 64). The cut of the wall-trench varied in width from 0.30m to 0.42m and registered a maximum depth of 0.34m at the eastern end of the southern wall (170/189), attenuating to a depth of 0.18m in the direction of the slope. The base of the southern end wall displayed two rectangular post-depressions (122 and 482) which penetrated to depths of 0.18m and 0.22m respectively.

Interpretation

Although resolution was lost at the point of inter-section with wall-trench 231, it is almost certain that the curved portions of the superstructure origi-nally formed a continuous apse, a feature evidently designed to enclose pit 271. Access was gained by an offset doorway in the southern wall. Faecal

Fig 4.26   Structure S, oblique photo

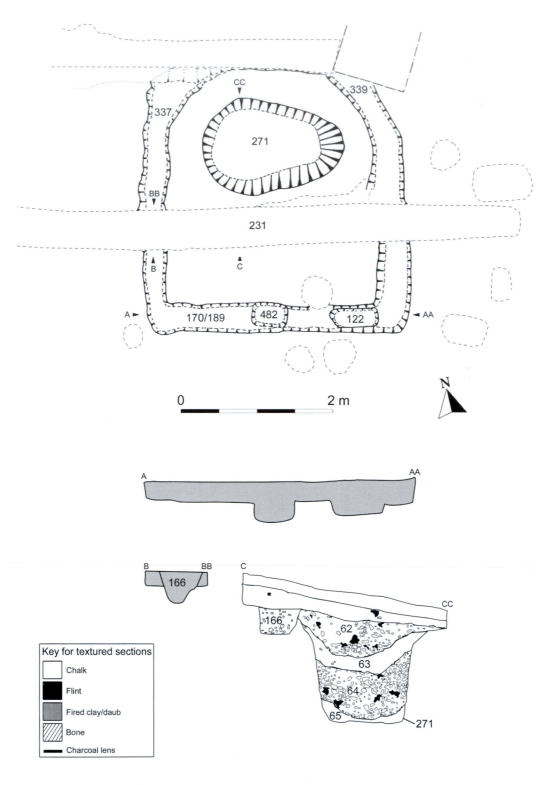

Fig 4.27   Structure S, plan and sections

matter was identified within the organic pit fills and this evidence combined with chalk capping layers, confirms that Structure S functioned as a latrine.

Structure T (Figs 4.28 and 4.29)

This structure, located a short distance beyond the south-east corner of Structure K, was defined by a shallow and heavily eroded U-shaped wall-trench, dug in two separate sections which overlapped at their curving southern termini (2678 and 2682). The gap at the open end of the 'U' measured approximately 0.60m, expanding to a width of 0.67m at the enclosed end. The eastern of the two trenches measured 3.50m in length and 0.38m in width and

Fig 4.28 Structure T, pre-excavation photo looking north, with east end of Structure K beyond

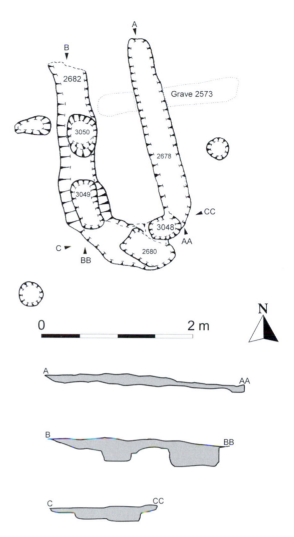

Fig 4.29 Structure T, plan and sections

displayed a single circular post-depression 0.19m deep at its southern terminus (3048). Its neighbour was 0.20m shorter, averaged 0.42m in width and included three sub-rectangular post-depressions (2680, 3049, and 3050), which ranged from 0.16m to 0.32m in depth.

Interpretation

This fact that this structure cut grave 2573 confirms that it post-dates the cemetery. Its western wall was on precise alignment with the end wall of Structure K and there is a distinct probability that the two structures belong to the same construction phase.

The ground-plan clearly denotes a narrow U-shaped building, measuring roughly 3.40m long and 0.60m wide internally with an opening at its northern end. Whilst very different in size and appearance from the main series of rectangular post-in-trench buildings from Bishopstone, it was evidently built using the same constructional

principles and must, by implication, have been roofed.

Aisled

Structure U (Fig 4.30)

This east-west aligned structure, measuring internally 7.00m wide and 9.30m long, occupied a flat terrace exposed at the northern end of the 2004 excavation. Its ground-plan comprised seven internal post-pits, three in pairs leaving a singleton at the north-west corner. These were set roughly 0.50m inside a pair of external walls represented by wall-trenches, the northern example of which had been reduced to a series of discontinuous depressions as a result of erosion. Two of the internal post-pits (1185 and 1336) intersected with other features. Whereas the former was clearly cut by pit 1193, the relationship between 1336 and the cut of the cellar (1167) was uncertain because the point of intersection was occupied by a silt-rich

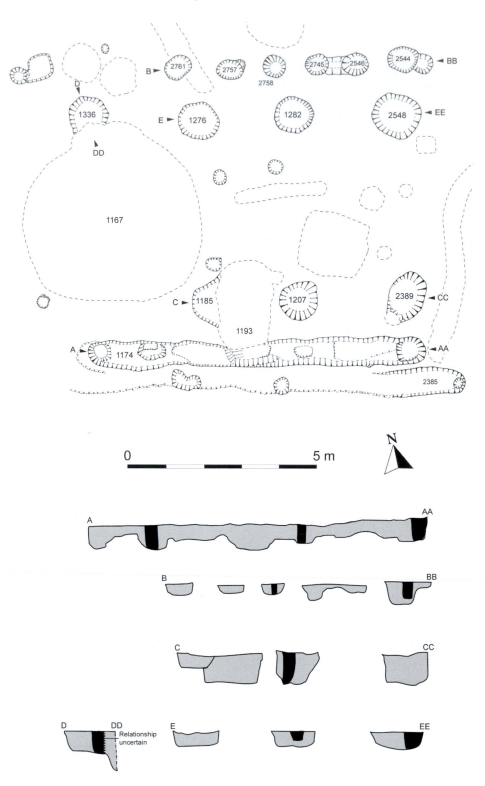

Fig 4.30 Structure U, plan and sections

timber ghost indistinguishable from the upper fill of the cellar.

The post-pits forming each arcade were set between 4.83m and 4.95m apart (measured centre to centre). The diameters of the post-pits ranged between 0.82m and 1.12m and their depths between 0.22m and 0.65m. Timber ghosts were recognised in the fills of 1207, 2548, and 1336. These indicated

that the posts were circular in section, around 0.30m diameter, and packed against the edge of the pit with coarse chalk rubble.

The external wall on the southern side comprised a substantial wall-trench (1174) measuring 8.90m in length and 0.70m in width. Its northern (inside) face was cut on a vertical plane and four post-depressions were located up against this edge. The fill of the trench was sectioned longitudinally, in the process revealing three possible post ghosts, all corresponding to basal depressions.

The severity of erosion on the northern side of the building was such that the opposite wall was reduced to a row of six post-depressions originally cut into the base of the trench. Their depth ranged between 0.24m and 0.43m and the fills of two examples (2544 and 2757) exhibited timber ghosts.

Interpretation

The ground-plan displays some idiosyncrasies which deserve comment. The most obvious is the missing pair for aisle post 1336. Unfortunately this cannot be blamed on cellar pit 1167 because the predicted position of the post (the regular spacing and alignment of the other posts allows its position to be pinpointed fairly accurately) lies to the south of the circumference of that feature. The most likely explanation is that this post was dug to a depth that has subsequently been swallowed up by erosion. Accepting this to be the case, then the building was divided into three equal bays of between 2.6m to 2.7m. There was no evidence for return bays at each end of the building, nor for external doorways or internal arrangements within the building.

The various elements of the ground-plan can be resolved into a so-called 'narrow-aisled' building: that is a structure in which the load-bearing aisle posts are set a short distance within external walls to protect them from the elements and thus prolong the life of the building (Chapter 8.1). Of significance is the fact that posts of the external walls fail to align with the internal aisle posts. This feature, shared by aisled buildings of later Anglo-Saxon date from Portchester (Building S15) and Faccombe Netherton (Building 11) (Cunliffe 1976, 41, fig 25; Fairbrother 1990, 116, fig 4.20), implies that each aisle formed a lean-to structure and that the roof of the nave must have been supported by the aisle posts alone.

Wall-trench 2385 – located just to the south of the main footprint – is almost certainly related to this building. Whilst it could have functioned as an eaves-drip trench, a more likely alternative, based on the assumption that the flimsy outer walls would have decayed more rapidly than the internal aisle posts, is that it represents a replacement for 1174.

Finally, some comment is required on the configuration of internal aisle posts of this building. On the basis of medieval exemplars, the two pairs of posts in the centre of the building, 1276/1185 and 1282/1207, could be regarded as settings for screens on either side of the cross-entry, perhaps to reduce draughts in the western and eastern halves.

Structure V (Figs 4.31 and 4.32)

The ground-plan of this building was exposed in two adjacent extension trenches excavated on the northern edge of the village green in 2004 and 2005 respectively. The complex array of structural

Fig 4.31   Structure V, vertical photo taken in 2004

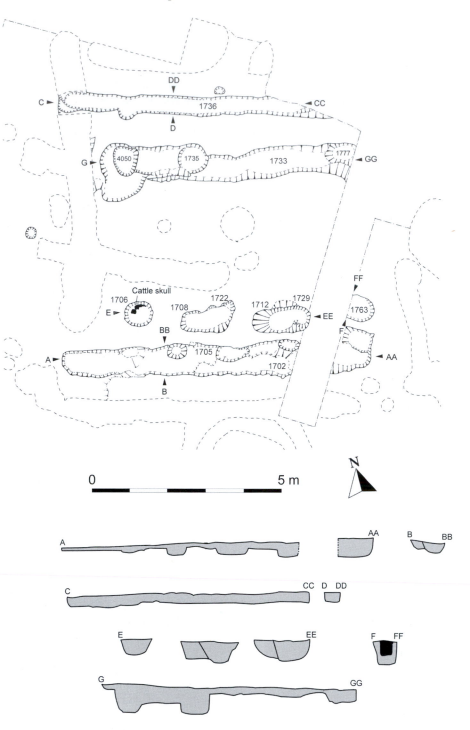

Fig 4.32   Structure V, plan and sections

elements found within this sector of the excavation is difficult to interpret and in all probability relates to more than one building (see Structure R). The best-fit for the majority of these features is an east-west aligned building of aisled construction, measuring internally 7.40m in length and 6.15m in width.

The internal elements of the plan comprised two alignments of pits spaced approximately 3.30m apart. The southern alignment consisted of four circular pits (1706, 1708, 1712, and 1763) two of which (1708 and 1712) were cut by larger and deeper oval replacements (1722 and 1729). The

original post-pits ranged between 0.60m and 0.85m in diameter and between 0.40m and 0.50m in depth. The opposing alignment comprised three pits only (1735, 1777, and 4050) set within a broad shallow trench (1733) which registered a maximum depth of 0.35m and an average width of 0.72m. Of the post-pits, only 1763 displayed clear signs of a timber ghost, indicating a post of circular cross-section measuring 0.22m in diameter. Of considerable interest were the mandible and articulated skull of two cattle placed at the base of the cut of pit 1706; the unfragmented condition of the bone indicated that this event occurred after the post had been removed on the building's abandonment.

The exterior of the building was defined by two parallel wall-trenches: 1702/1705 to the south and 1736 to the north. The former comprised two cuts on a convergent alignment; the innermost (1705) was about 0.50m in width and clearly truncated the northern edge of its neighbour (1702), some 100mm narrower in width. Whilst the two phases of wall were both about 0.20m in depth, 1705 was distinguished by having a row of five sub-rectangular post-depressions located against the inside edge of the cut. The northern wall-trench was of a single phase measuring 0.38m in width and on average 0.25m in depth; there were no apparent post-depressions in its base.

Interpretation

The smaller of the two 'narrow-aisled' structures at Bishopstone, this building evidently received substantial repairs during its lifetime as indicated by the replacement of two of its internal aisle posts and its southern exterior wall. As in the case of its larger counterpart, the ground-plan preserves no clues as to the position of entrances. The interior appears to have been divided into three bays, most probably with a return at the western end with a light west wall of which no trace survives.

Another distinguishing feature of Structure V is the use of a continuous trench for one alignment of arcade posts and discrete post-pits for the other, a combination exhibited by the 11th-century aisled building from Waltham Abbey, Essex (Huggins 1976).

Cellared

Structure W (Figs 4.8, 4.33–4.38)

The sub-circular soil-mark of what finally revealed itself to be a subterranean component of a timber superstructure was exposed at the northern end of the 2004 excavation trench (see Fig 4.8).

The pit had a near-circular opening some 4.80m in diameter and extending to a maximum depth of 1.80m, as measured from the northern edge of its base to the top of the bedrock. The upper section of the pit was flared and the chalk at this level presented a noticeably more fractured appearance than the squared vertical sides below (Figs 4.33 and 4.35). Whilst natural weathering may have contributed to this difference, there is a structural argument for this change in angle (see below). Incorporated within the northern side of the pit, some 0.55m above its base, was a flat-bottomed ledge, roughly D-shaped in plan with a neat, vertically cut inside edge (Figs 4.34 and 4.35). The latter descended into the base of the pit, a near square measuring 3.0m east-west by 2.60m to 2.80m north-south, with a level, worn surface. The

Fig 4.33   Structure W, vertical photo

primary evidence for a surmounting timber superstructure was a curved socket or niche cut into each of the pit's corners from top to base; in the case of the south-west corner, the socket extended for an additional 0.30m below the base of the pit as a tapering hole (1382) into which a hoard of iron objects had been tightly crammed (Figs 4.35 and 4.36). The diameter of the sockets, as measured at floor level, varied from between 0.51m to 0.60m; and the diametrically opposed north-west/south-east pairing was cut back further into the chalk than its counterpart.

Depositional history

On establishing that the pit was more than superficial depth, the strategy adopted for its excavation was the removal, by mattock and trowel, of diametrically opposed quadrants, with the north-west and south-east quadrants being removed first. For safety reasons, the upper stratigraphic horizon (context 1168) of each quadrant was stepped back by half a metre to allow excavation to proceed further.

The depositional sequence of the pit comprised three distinct stratigraphic phases, each separated by a clear interface (Figs 4.34 and 4.35). The latest was represented by a homogeneous brown silty-clay with unsorted stone inclusions (context 1168). This layer is almost certainly colluvial in origin (ie a downslope accumulation generated by tillage or kitchen garden activity), although it is impossible to ascertain whether it accumulated *in situ* or was dumped. Ceramic evidence, including sherds of multiple spouted pitchers, suggests that this terminal phase of infilling occurred within the later Anglo-Saxon period. This layer interfaced with a spread of flint nodules and animal bone, evidently dumped into the slumped upper surface of a series of loosely compacted chalk-rubble layers forming the intermediate horizon (grouped under a single context number, 1344). These were separated into distinct

Fig 4.34   Structure W, west-facing section showing step

– in some cases tipping – bands, distinguished by variable ratios of chalk to silt: whereas some bands were comprised almost entirely of randomly orientated chalk blocks (with a minor percentage of flint nodules), others took the form of finer-grained lenses. These layers were continuous across the full width of the pit suggesting that any internal structural elements had been removed prior to its infilling. Overall, the character of these deposits is consistent with several discrete episodes of dumping within quick succession. The sources appear to have been heterogeneous and included freshly dug chalk alongside secondary deposits derived from domestic occupation. The first 1.20m of infill appears to have been deposited at a rapid rate, as also indicated by conjoining sherds of pottery recovered from different levels; thereafter deposition slowed sufficiently for the sides of the pit to suffer from a limited amount of natural weathering, a process responsible for some of the finer-grained chalk seen in the upper levels. A range of domestic and other artefacts including pottery, ironwork, and animal bone (articulated and otherwise), was randomly distributed throughout this horizon.

The earliest horizon (1353) was represented by a thin continuous spread of charcoal deposited across the base of the pit, the charcoal being exclusively derived from the species oak (*Quercus* sp). There was no evidence for scorching on the surface of the underlying chalk, ruling out the possibility that this burning occurred *in situ*. Strewn throughout the charcoal layer was a selection of 47 iron objects. Although the objects were skewed spatially towards the south-west corner of the pit, it is impossible to establish whether or not they were originally derived from the same deposit as the hoard. However, differences in the size and range of the items found in the charcoal-spread and the hoard respectively (the former were generally much smaller and/or incomplete), combined with the fact that a miscellany of iron items were also found in the overlying chalk dumps, raises the possibility that the two are depositionally distinct.

Three radiocarbon dates were obtained from separate animal articulations recovered from the dumped infills of the cellar (context 1344; Table 8.3). Whilst one of the dates is a statistical outlier, there is sufficient agreement to indicate a late 9th- to early 10th-century *terminus ante quem* for the abandonment of the cellared structure.

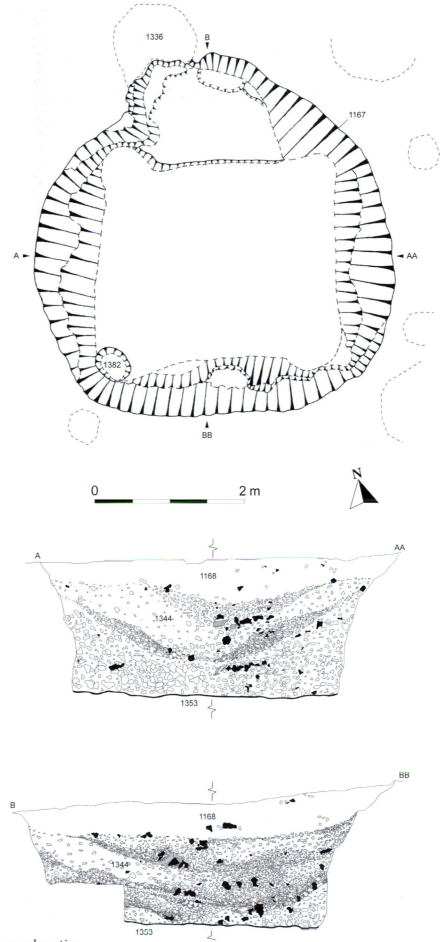

Fig 4.35   Structure W, plan and section

Fig 4.36   Structure W, view of iron hoard in situ (Scale = 300mm)

Platform

Structural complex X (Figs 4.37 and 4.38)

This is but a small portion of a more extensive array of structural features obliterated by the late-medieval quarry scarp at the northern edge of the village green (see Figure 2.1A).

The main component of the complex comprised an east-west aligned terrace, measuring 3.20m east-west and 1.56m north-south, cut into the gradient of the slope. The southern and eastern limits were defined by two irregular trenches (2823 and 3151) with rows of post-settings cut into their bases. The

longer of the two trenches (2823) contained a row of five post-settings (3153, 3186, 3149, 3146, and 3144), two sub-rectangular and three sub-circular, which varied in depth from 0.18m to 0.32m. The most notable in terms of its contents was 3146, which had been lined with a large ceramic vessel buried so that its rim was level with the surface of the chalk (Fig 4.37). The shorter section of trench (3151) contained three circular post-settings (3206, 3204, and 3210)

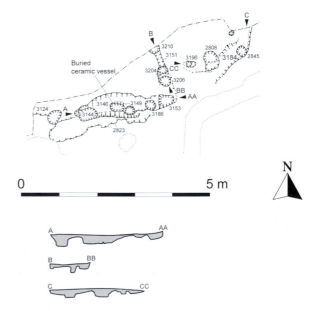

Fig 4.37   Structure X, view of ceramic container in situ (Scale = 150mm)

Fig 4.38   Structure X, plan and sections

the deepest of which penetrated 0.20m below the base of the cut.

Located some 0.50m to the east was the southern edge of a potential further platform defined by an indistinct cluster of postholes (2808, 3184) sited within a shallow cut.

Interpretation

Whilst the combination of a linear trench with basal post-depressions echoes the post-in-trench buildings represented at Bishopstone, the diminutive scale and irregular alignment of the 'walls' places this complex in a rather different structural category. The structural impressions appear to mark the southern boundary of one or possibly two platforms cut into the gradient of the slope.

The presence of a buried ceramic vessel within a post alignment is difficult to explain for it is stratigraphically contemporaneous with adjacent features. If this vessel functioned as a storage container then one would expect it to be obviously external or internal to a building.

4.2 Non-structural features

Pits

There were 78 pits of the Anglo-Saxon period represented within the area of the excavation, excluding the pit interpreted as a latrine associated with Structure S (Fig 4.27) and two late-medieval quarry pits located at the northern extremity of the village green where it ends abruptly in an artificial scarp

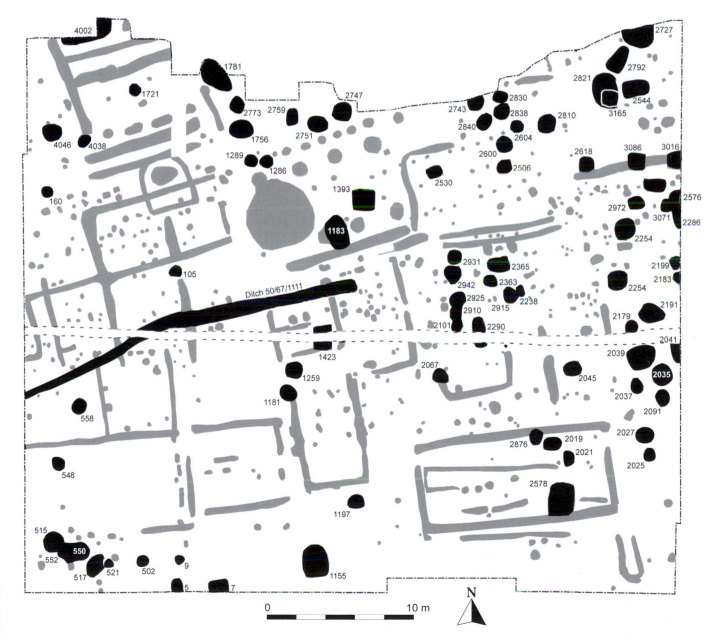

Fig 4.39 Location of non-structural features including pits and ditch 50/67/1111

Fig 4.40   Aerial view of eastern sector of excavation showing area of high pit density

Fig 4.41   Pit 1393 fully excavated

(Fig 2.1A). The distribution of pits was highly uneven; approaching 75% fell within the eastern half of the excavation, some forming dense and, in a few cases, intercutting clusters (Figs 4.39 and 4.40). Three further examples within the eastern sector area formed a distinct east-west pit alignment (see below). By comparison, the spread of pits in the western half of the excavation was much more diffuse, although there was a notable cluster in the extreme south-west corner.

Although lacking the deeper end of the range inter-

preted as wells, the morphology of the Bishopstone pits compares well with other later Anglo-Saxon settlements, including the locally excavated site of Market Field, Steyning, where a diversity of sub-square and sub-circular examples was excavated (Gardiner 1993). The following section describes a representative selection of pits under two main classes, sub-rectangular and sub-circular, a distinction of convenience which has been imposed on what in all respects represents a morphological continuum. Depositionary sequence and artefact taphonomy are then discussed in pursuit of establishing the function of the pits.

Sub-square

Two of a total of eight pits subscribing to this general morphology (1393 and 1423) were squared with vertically cut sides and flat bases (Figs 4.41 and 4.42). The obvious care taken in cutting these features suggests that they may have originally functioned as timber-lined storage pits, like those discovered at Portchester Castle and Hamwic retaining burnt linings and the impressions of corner stakes driven below their bases (Cunliffe 1976, 106, fig 81; 112, fig 88; Morton 1992, 45–6). No direct evidence for linings survived at Bishopstone, and in both cases the character of the fills is consistent with a depositionary 'afterlife' of rubbish and/or cess disposal. In the case of pit 1393 this included a solid amorphous mass of fired clay (1403) (Fig 4.42), the ultimate source of which may have been a kiln or hearth

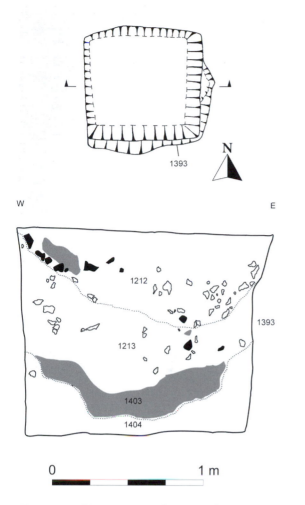
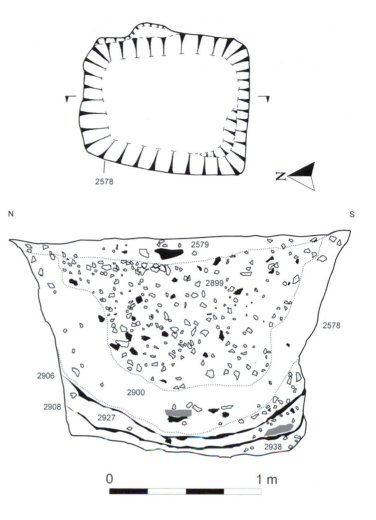

Fig 4.42   Pits 1393 and 2478, plans and sections

structure. Mineralised plants and fly puparia recovered from overlying fills indicate the presence of human cess and/or animal dung (Ballantyne, Chapter 7.3).

The remaining six pits falling within this general category (6, 1155, 2578, 2816, 3016, 3086) had sloping as opposed to vertical sides and more rounded corners. In spite of this morphological difference, the fill sequence of pit 2578 is also suggestive of a lining, the burnt remnants of which may be represented by a sequence of charcoal-rich basal layers (2906 and 2908) (Fig 4.42). These deposits were sealed by layers of a more heterogeneous character which, on the basis of palaeoenvironmental signature, included a constituent of cess and/or animal dung (Ballantyne, Chapter 7.3).

The final three pits in this category, 3016, and 3086, and 2618 formed an east-west alignment (Figs 4.43 and 4.44). The fact that they shared similar dimensions, morphology and orientation of axis strongly suggests that they were excavated in a contemporary episode, most probably around the turn of the 9th century on the grounds of a penny of King Alfred discovered in the primary fill of 3086 (see Archibald, Chapter 6.12). The fills of this same pit (the only one of the three subjected to

palaeoenvironmental analysis) generated charred cereal and indicators of human cess/animal dung. The significance of this pit boundary is discussed further in Chapter 9.1.

Sub-circular

This broad category embraced pits of the greatest depth and volume excavated at Bishopstone, but size and morphology was otherwise highly variable with neatly formed cylindrical examples at one end of the spectrum (eg 548, 2600, and 2035) and oval examples with sloping sides at the other (eg 1181 and 2025) (Figs 4.45 and 4.46). Registering 2.5m in depth and with a volume of about 7m³, 2039 was by far and away the largest of the pits excavated at Bishopstone and, by any estimation, must have involved considerable time and energy to dig (Fig 4.45). The remaining pits were of significantly smaller proportions, 0.70m being the mean depth and 1.10m the mean diameter.

Individually, pits of this general category displayed very different patterns of infilling (discussed further below), although some trends can be recognised amongst spatially-defined clusters. Thus 2039, 2041,

Fig 4.43   Pit alignment looking north

and 2035 shared a sequence marked by an initial phase of dumping (including dense concentrations of burnt daub and ash) followed by a sharp transition to a more passive depositionary environment involving the gradual accumulation of domestic waste in some instances including a contingent of cess (Fig 4.45). This same transition is also registered in the fragmentation pattern of pottery, with the largest sherds coming from basal fills of the pits (Jervis, Chapter 6.1).

A significant proportion of the sub-circular pits appear to have functioned as cesspits, at least for part of their depositionary cycles. Confirmation of this usage was provided by the identification of faecal waste including digested fish bone (Reynolds, Chapter 7.2) and mineralised plant biota (seeds from one or more edible plant taxon) sometimes preserved within larger cereal bran concretions derived from ingested bread flour (Ballantyne, Chapter 7.3). Pits with a cess constituent divide into a smaller group of five with a wide diversity of mineralised food seeds (548, 1259, 2035, 2039, and 2576), and a larger group of ten with a more restricted range. Of the former group, 2039 and 2576 have the strongest claim to have functioned as formal, incrementally filled latrines, both having fills rich in mineralised seeds interspersed with more sterile layers. Other attributes displayed by the same general range of pits included distinct concentrations of grassy materials, perhaps representing animal dung, or, given the context, the use of hay as a form of toilet paper (see Ballantyne, Chapter 7.3), and deposits of

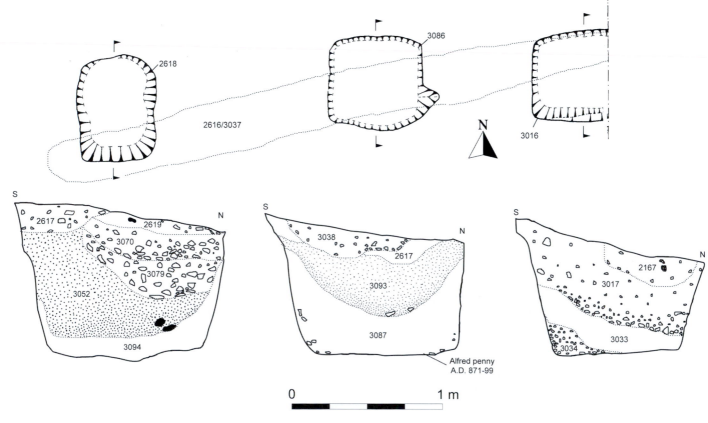

Fig 4.44   Pit alignment, plans and sections

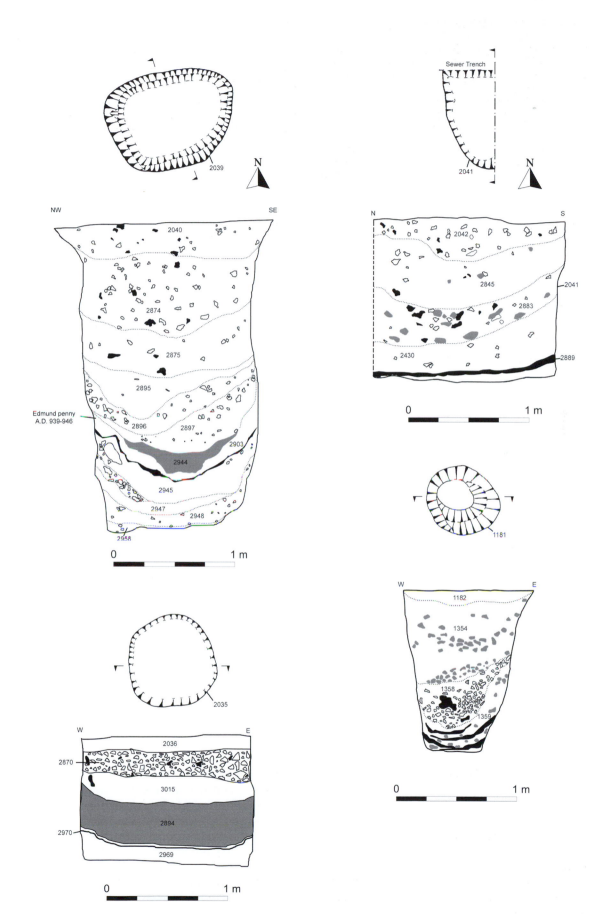

Fig 4.45   Sub-circular pits, select plans and sections

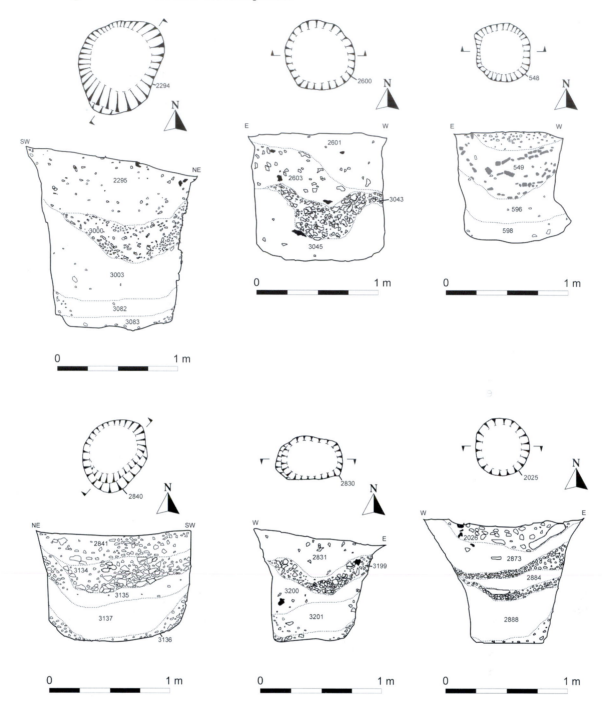

Fig 4.46 Sub-circular pits, select plans and sections

chalk rubble used as a capping with which to seal in noxious substances below (eg 2600, 2294, 2830, and 2025) (Fig 4.46).

Depositionary biography and function

Irrespective of morphology, most of the pits analysed from Bishopstone displayed complex biographies marked by sharp transitions in deposit formation processes and depositionary pathways. The implication that pits were backfilled with different types of refuse as required on an ad hoc basis (see Ballantyne, Chapter 7.3) accords with the findings from other Anglo-Saxon sites where pits have been the subject of detailed analyses, for example at Six Dials, Hamwic and Lake End, Dorney (Bucks) (Andrews 1997, 174–8; 184–7; Foreman *et al* 2002, 62–5). Enough research has now been undertaken to make quite clear that in most cases it is simplistic to use unitary labels such as 'rubbish' or 'cess' when describing pits in a later Anglo-Saxon context.

As to underlying causes, there is a distinct possibility that some of these transitory sequences may relate to the practice observed at medieval Winchester, whereby 'unlined cesspits seem to have been used for their original purpose only for the relatively short periods for which they remained sweet.

They seem then to have been filled with household and stable refuse and with the upcast from the new pits which replaced them' (Keene, 1982, 28). Yet, whilst the presence of cess and faecal matter as a component of primary fills suggests that many pits at Bishopstone are likely to have started life as latrines, this is by no means universal. For example pit 2039, one of a larger group of pits in which cess appears in the middle-fill horizons, only moved into its transitory cess phase after first receiving large dumps of primary rubbish (see Ballantyne, Chapter 7.3).

Analysis of faunal remains provides an additional insight into how daily activities and attitudes may have structured the depositionary profile of pits. It has been noted that some of the pit horizons containing mineralised cess (eg 271; Figs 4.26/7 and 1781; Fig 5.39) yielded a preponderance of smaller fish (particularly eel) and domesticated fowl to the exclusion of larger fish (eg cod, whiting, rays) and mammals (Reynolds, Chapter 7.2). This pattern appears to suggest that it was deemed appropriate to discard the lighter fraction of kitchen waste into open latrines whilst the remains of larger species (fish and mammals) were treated as general rubbish destined either for middens or pits which had passed out of their cess phase.

A rather different perspective on this subject was provided by land-snail and sedimentological analysis undertaken on two pit sequences as part of a University of Reading MSc Geoarchaeology dissertation (Neal 2008). The results from pit 2576 (Fig 4.39) showed the effects of changing depositional conditions on mollusc population, a sharp contrast being drawn between the primary erosion layers and overlying humic fills. Whereas the former contained species indicative of the habitat surrounding the pit (an open environment of short grassland), the latter attested to a wet and sheltered microhabitat rich in decaying organic matter colonised by the carnivorous species *Oxychilus cellarius*. Rather more distinctive was the molluscan record obtained from the burnt ash deposits from pit 2039 (Fig 4.45). This horizon contained mostly burnt specimens of molluscs native to both short-grazed grassland and freshwater habitats (*Hydrobia ulvae*). A mechanism proposed by Neal, which might explain the condition and source of these molluscs, is the burning of turf cut from surrounding pasture as a source of fuel, a hypothesis also entertained at Flixborough (Lincs), (Dobney *et al* 2007, 193–6). However, given the large volumes of burnt structural daub recovered from the same horizons, an alternative source might be thatched roofing which would have sustained its own living snail population whilst perhaps also incorporating a residual population inhabiting sedge cut as thatching material from the adjacent floodplain.

It is worth reflecting further on the distinctive ash/burning horizons shared by pits 2039, 2035, and 2041 which form a tight cluster beyond the north-east corner of Structure K. One can only speculate, but since much of this burning seems to be structural in character (large fragments of burnt daub, possible remnants of thatched roofing and/or internal hearth rake-out, etc), these pits were perhaps dug within a short period of each other following a substantial conflagration to facilitate the disposal of burnt debris from buildings. This real possibility serves as a reminder that the sequence of pit digging represented on settlements may provide its own perspective on site dynamics.

Boundary ditch

Only one unambiguous example of a boundary ditch – distinct from narrower linear features whose identity as either wooden fences or truncated post-in-trench buildings remains uncertain – was represented within the excavated area (50, 67, 1111). Following a general east-west alignment but with a slight north-to-south curvature, it spanned a distance of some 24m between the western limits and the midpoint of the excavation (Fig 4.39). The profile of the ditch, featuring slightly concave sides and a flat bottom, was fairly consistent along its length: its width increased west to east from a minimum of 0.45m to a maximum of 1.28m, narrowing back

Fig 4.47 View of boundary ditch looking west

down to 0.92m at its eastern terminal; depth also increased in the same direction from a minimum of 0.15m to a maximum of 0.35m (Fig 4.47).

The fill of the ditch, a mid greyish-brown silty-clay with chalk inclusions, was fairly uniform along its length and there was no evidence that this feature had been deliberately backfilled with dumps of domestic refuse or midden material as found on some Anglo-Saxon settlements such as Flixborough (Lincs), North Elmham (Norfolk), and Yarnton (Oxon) (Loveluck and Aitkinson 2007, 77–80; Wade-Martins 1980, 37–57; Hey 2004, 153–63). Whilst it should be remembered that only the lower portions of the ditch survive as a result of truncation, soil character and artefact taphonomy (above average levels of fragmentation and abrasion) combine to suggest that the preserved horizon represents natural erosional processes and silting. As experienced with the upper fills of some of the pits, this shallow remnant may have been contaminated by intrusive material only to comingle with residual artefacts introduced by natural silting; this heterogeneous mix obviously complicates the issue of dating.

For the reasons just given, any attempt to date the ditch on the grounds of a *terminus post quem* provided by pottery must proceed with due caution. The fill produced five sherds of later medieval sandy ware (Fabric 10) amongst a range of local course and sandy wares (1, 3, 11, 13, 14, 17, 22, and 26), all of which are represented in firmly stratified Anglo-Saxon contexts (see Jervis, Chapter 6.1). Whilst this former fabric could be regarded as contamina-

tion, the fact it accounts for as much as 16% of the total ditch assemblage could be taken as evidence for a genuinely post-Anglo-Saxon date. The same conclusion also receives tentative support from the fact that there is a greater diversity of Anglo-Saxon fabrics in the ditch than encountered in pits, a level of heterogeneity perhaps best explained if the pottery is residual.

Unfortunately stratigraphic phasing is unable to narrow the chronological parameters of the ditch. Although it intersected with the ground-plans of Structures D and F and the northern 'annexe' of Structural complex O, sections were rarely informative because of the shallowness of the features and the lack of soil contrast. The one exception to this rule was the intersection with wall-trench 35 (Structure F) which was clearly the earlier of the two features.

In reviewing the evidence, the impression given is that the ditch did not go out of use during the active life of the Anglo-Saxon settlement, a scenario which is highly likely to have produced dumps of domestic material from adjacent structures. Of course, this does not preclude the scenario whereby the ditch was cleaned out on a regular basis, delaying the process of infilling until after the settlement was abandoned. Yet this model of periodic maintenance must remain only an outside possibility given the lack of evidence for recutting or a later redefinition of the same boundary. When one takes into account the single stratigraphic relationship and the ceramic evidence, it is difficult to reject the conclusion that the ditch post-dates the Anglo-Saxon occupation.

5 The cemetery and human remains

One of the unexpected results of test-pitting in 2002 was the discovery of two human burials – both subsequently confirmed to be later Anglo-Saxon in date – beyond the boundary of St Andrew's churchyard: one to its north on the village green and the other (S280) in a plot of land abutting its western border (Figs 5.1 and 5.2). Over the course of the remaining three seasons' fieldwork this newly revealed zone of late Anglo-Saxon burials yielded 32 intact graves containing a total of 37 individuals.

This section comprises two components. The first commences with an examination of the archaeological evidence for the dating and layout of the cemetery and proceeds to a more detailed discussion of the burial rite represented at Bishopstone. The second reports on the osteological analysis of the human remains. Wider interpretation attempting to situate the burials within the spatial development of the settlement is reserved for Chapter 9.2.

5.1 Dating

A sample of seven burials from the excavated total was submitted for high-precision radiocarbon dating, providing a tightly defined chronological

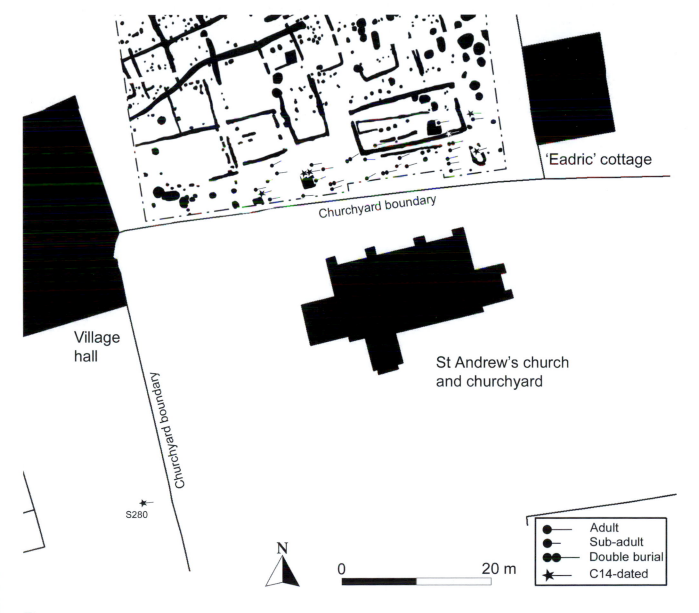

Fig 5.1 Plan of excavated burials

Fig 5.2   Burial 280 as excavated in a test pit in 2002

range spanning the 8th and 9th centuries (see Table 8.1). Bayesian modelling of the calibrated radiocarbon ages obtained from Bishopstone suggests that burial commenced no later than the final third of the 8th century with the possibility of a late 7th-century inception; none of the burials is likely to post-date AD 900 (Marshall *et al*, Chapter 8.2).

Although the general impression gained is that the chronology of the cemetery was relatively short, some time-depth is nevertheless indicated by two cases of intercutting burial (2004/2019 and 1317/1294), distinct from four cases of simultaneous double burial discussed below. Whatever the precise duration of burial activity (the statistical model suggests that the real figure falls somewhere between the outer limits of 40 to 220 years) it is clear that this part of the pre-Conquest cemetery was soon encroached upon by domestic occupation. A total of six burials covering the full spatial extent of the exposed cemetery (S280, S1105/1171, S1104, S2186, S3122, and S2573) were cut by settlement features – either pits or wall-trenches. Although none of these intercutting features is independently dated by scientific means, there is no indication that they post-date the late 8th- to 10th-century *floruit* of the settlement.

The same episode of encroachment also appears to

have been responsible for generating a pool of disarticulated human bone – in most cases amounting to single fragments contained within larger assemblages of domestic animal bone – subsequently diffused across a wide extent of the settlement. Whilst a proportion of the bone recovered from the upper fill of pits and wall-trenches may have been transported by comparatively recent ploughing and kitchen-garden activity, the best explanation for the more deeply stratified component (discounting the deliberate deposition of foetal remains) was the practice of redepositing surface middens into pits which seems to have produced a similar distribution pattern amongst encroached parts of Hamwic's cemeteries (Morton 1992, 42).

5.2   Cemetery layout and organisation

A major hindrance to the interpretation of spatial patterning within the cemetery is an uncertain number of missing graves. Most of the grave-cuts were eroded down to the truncated ground surface leaving the primary interments exposed to disturbance. With the exception of attrition caused by the encroachment of Anglo-Saxon occupation, it has to be

Fig 5.3 View of burials exposed in 2004

assumed that post-depositional ploughing/kitchen-garden activity will have obliterated the shallowest graves (Fig 5.3). The issue of the under-representation of graves comes immediately to the fore when attempting to reconstruct the original extent of the cemetery, for it is unclear whether its northern limits were marked by a boundary. In terms of spatial distribution, all intact burials were confined within a 9m-wide band to the north of the modern churchyard boundary; this zone could arguably be widened to 10m if the shallow rectangular cut 261 discovered within the footprint of Structural complex O represents an empty grave-cut (Fig 5.1).

An intriguing question is whether the burials originally extended up to the boundary marked by Ditch 67. This possibility would imply that a large swathe of the early cemetery located downslope of the zone of undisturbed graves has vanished (Fig 5.1). Such a proposition seems unlikely, however, given the arguments in favour of this ditch post-dating the later Anglo-Saxon occupation (see Chapter 4.2). Moreover, had this obtained, then we would expect to find indirect evidence in the form of distinct con-

centrations of human bone in intercutting features as demonstrated by pit 1155 and wall-trench 2067 located in the zone of intact burials. As we have seen, the character and condition of human bone yielded by the wider array of settlement features is rather more suggestive of incidental redeposition governed by site taphonomy and discard practices. There can be no certainty on this issue, but the balance of evidence suggests that the original northern limit of interment – marked or otherwise – was coincidental with the outermost of the intact burials.

It is possible to make further basic inferences on the spatial organisation of the pre-Conquest cemetery. If we are indeed looking at a primary phase of the churchyard (this is not the only explanation for these burials) then the span of date-ranges obtained, most notably three 'early' examples predating AD 780, might suggest that it had reached its maximum spatial extent at or soon after the point of inception. This is in accordance with the findings at Wharram Percy (North Yorks), where radiocarbon dating has forced a radical reversal of the view that the churchyard expanded steadily from an early core around the church (Mays *et al* 2007, 193–215, 327). It can also be said with certainty that the cemetery was planned, as indicated by the identification of burials aligned in north-south rows. The clearest example of one such row comprised a series of six burials: S2720, S2693, S2556, S2686, S2559/2924, and S3122 (not shown on plan; redeposited in wall-trench 2167), with the potential of a seventh if rectangular cut 2706 within the footprint of Structure K represents an empty grave (Figs 5.4 and 5.5). The extremities of further rows, on a skewed alignment to that just described, may be represented by three alignments of three graves: S1109, S87, and S86; S1104, S1105/1171, and S1294/1317; and S1103, S1108/1146, and S1102. The significance of single burials within this peripheral zone of interments is necessarily an open-ended question; some may represent the terminal graves of yet further rows especially if, as at Addingham (West Yorks), graves had a tendency to be spaced further apart and more irregularly at the extremity of rows (Adams 1996, 182). Alternatively, some of these graves may belong to later generations of 'overspill' when the rigid row structure of the cemetery had begun to break down, as documented at Raunds Furnells (Northants), (Boddington 1996, 53–7).

In light of the existence of row burials, the assumption must be that the graves were originally marked, although given the severity of ground-erosion it is hardly surprising that a small posthole located at the east (foot) end of S1102 represents the only, and by no means certain, evidence for a wooden marker (Fig 5.4). Evidence that later generations of Anglo-Saxon burial were marked more durably in stone exists in a previously unrecognised piece of pre-Conquest sculpture, now located in the porch of St Andrew's, closely comparable to the late Anglo-Saxon grave-markers represented at Old Minster, Winchester and more locally at Stedham (Sussex)

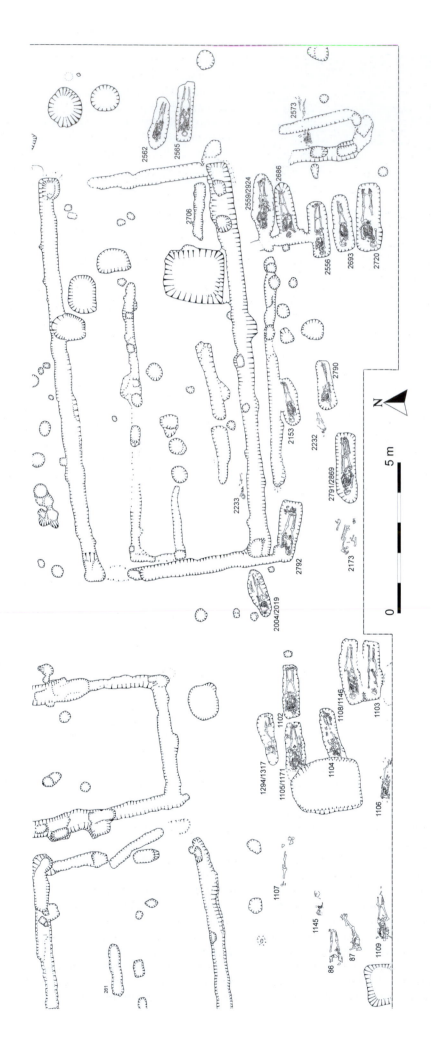

Fig 5.4 Detailed plan of excavated burials

Fig 5.5 Burial row exposed in 2005

(Tweddle *et al* 1995, 22–3; 194–5, ills 240–8; 337–8; ills 713–16) (Appendix 2).

5.3 Burial rite/grave structure

In so far as one is able to generalise, the standard rite practised at Bishopstone was that of extended supine burial with the head at the west end and with one or more arms folded across the pelvis. The one exception to this general rule was a non-adult burial of 1.5 years, S1145, placed on its left side with its legs in a flexed position (Figs 5.4 and 5.6).

Where they survived, graves were typically sub-rectangular with straight sides and with roughly squared or rounded ends. There was no evidence for the distinctive repertoire of grave elaboration/furniture (charcoal-/chest-burial or forms of stone containment) characterising some late Anglo-Saxon cemeteries, but then again, the burials could be deemed to be rather too early to display evidence of these traditions. On the basis of the evidence available, a mixture of coffined, shrouded and/or clothed burial should be envisaged with an emphasis on the latter. Such distinctions are barely percep-tible in the artefactual record: two copper-alloy belt-fittings were found in association with intercut-ting burials S2004/2019, but the tinned belt-chape (SF1) was almost certainly intrusive (Chapter 6.3),

and the copper-alloy buckle (SF2) is insufficiently diagnostic to rule out contamination. The same may be said of the iron nails recovered in association with burials S2565 (SF55–57) and S2573 (SF16–19 and 21), in the latter case alongside a U-shaped iron staple (SF20) which, if more securely strati-fied, would have genuine claim to be derived from a wooden coffin (Rodwell 2007, 22).

One would ordinarily turn to burial posture to provide indications of the mode of containment, but the severe post-depositional disturbance suffered by many of the burials places obvious limitations on this approach. On the other hand, amongst the more intact individuals, there are no classic cases of bone tumble (displacement of the vertebrae/ribcage and long bones) accepted as a diagnostic tool for the identification of coffined burial (Boddington 1996, 36, 47–8) (Fig 5.4). There are, however, several clear cases of 'parallel-sided' burial (eg S1102, S2153, S2562, and S2693) as defined under Boddington's criteria (1996, 35), but it is just as likely that these individuals were buried in shrouds as opposed to narrow coffins (Figs 5.4 and 5.7). Conversely, the comparatively splayed posture of S2720 gives the impression that this individual was interred clothed (Fig 5.4).

On balance, coffined burial would appear to be a minority rite in this portion of the pre-Conquest cemetery which, on the basis of its peripheral location,

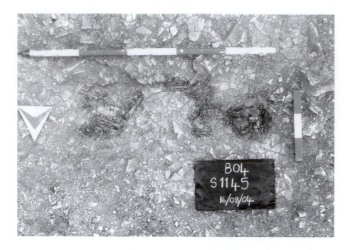

Fig 5.6   Sub-adult burial S1145 (Long scale = 1m)

may well have been dominated by poorer – and taking in recent studies on the social geography of Anglo-Saxon churchyards – socially marginal segments of Bishopstone's population (Lucy and Reynolds 2002, 16; Hadley and Buckberry 2005, 143–4).

Perhaps also carrying social connotations are four cases of simultaneous double burial which disrupt the simple uniformity in burial rite otherwise found at Bishopstone (Figs 5.4 and 5.8). These are discussed further below.

5.4   The human remains
by Louise Schoss and Mary Lewis

Introduction

This report examines a total of 43 inhumations recovered from the excavations. Of these, 32 were found in intact, the remainder being either partial articulations or perinates buried in pits (a burial catalogue appears as Appendix 3); the human bone assemblage also includes a spread of disarticulated bone from domestic contexts listed in the site archive. A single flexed inhumation radiocarbon-dated to the late Bronze Age (Appendix 7) was not included in this analysis nor was a single east-west burial (S280) found in a test-pit to the west of the churchyard in 2002, subsequently confirmed to be contemporaneous with the main concentration of later Anglo-Saxon burials.

This restricted sample of Bishopstone's early medieval population joins a significantly larger collection of burials (118 inhumations and 6 cremations) recovered from the cemetery attached to the early Anglo-Saxon settlement excavated on Rookery Hill (Bell 1977, 195). Regrettably, only a basic report on the human remains was completed at the time of the Rookery Hill excavations, so it has not been possible to make diachronic comparisons between the two Anglo-Saxon populations. This situation is being redressed by one of the authors (Schoss), currently engaged in the re-analysis of the original skeletal

archive held by Brighton and Hove Museum as part of a doctoral study at the University of Kent.

It hardly needs stating that it is impossible to make demographic generalisations based on such a small sample of Bishopstone's early medieval population. On the other hand, as one of the very few firmly-dated groups of later Saxon burials from Sussex, this modest collection at least permits a glimpse of the health and physical character of a rural community based in a coastal district of the South Saxon kingdom. This can be set against demographic trends derived from other parts of Anglo-Saxon England.

Condition of the skeletal material

The level of preservation of the remains will affect the amount of biological information that can be collected. For instance, extensive surface erosion can result in the loss of new bone deposits indicative of trauma or infection; fragmentation of the skull, pelvis, and long bones can limit recording of metrical data for age, sex, and stature estimates.

Three grades of preservation were assigned to the

Fig 5.7   Parallel-sided burial S2693

skeletons, reflecting the level of surface erosion, and post-mortem bone loss. Those in the first category (Grade 1) were almost complete, perhaps with the exception of a few smaller bones of the hands and feet, and had excellent surface preservation. Skeletons in the second category (Grade 2) suffered some degree of post-mortem damage, bone loss or fragmentation but were at least 50% complete, while those in the final category (Grade 3) were poorly preserved, with many skeletal elements missing, and poor surface preservation. Overall, the majority of individuals were quite poorly preserved (47.5%), although four adults and three children showed excellent levels of preservation (Table 5.1).

Table 5.1   Human skeletal remains: level of preservation

	Grade 1	Grade 2	Grade 3
Adult	4	12	18
Non-adult	3	2	1
Total	7	14	19
% sample	*17.5*	*35*	*47.5*

Fig 5.8   Double burial S2791/S2869

Demography of the sample

Sex estimations were attained using the methods described in Bass (1987) and based on the morphology of the skull and pelvis. Specific features on the skull and pelvis were considered in addition to measurements based on the size of the humerus, femur, and other bones, which have been found to be sexually dimorphic (Brothwell 1981). It is not yet possible to assign accurately a sex to non-adult remains, as the majority of features used in this estimation appear at puberty (Lewis 2007).

Methods used to determine age at death in adults are based on the morphological changes seen on the pelvis, ribs, and dentition during adulthood. Specific pathological changes relating to old age, such as degenerative joint disease and osteoporosis (or brittle-bone disease) can also provide a rough age estimate in the adult skeleton. Methods used, in order of preference, were the pubic symphysis (Brookes and Suchey 1990), pelvic auricular surfaces (Lovejoy *et al* 1985), late epiphyseal fusion (Scheuer and Black 2000), sternal rib ends (Iscan *et al* 1984, 1985) and molar attrition (Brothwell 1981). These methods were used to place a skeleton within the following age categories: 17–25 years, 26–35 years, 36–45 years, and 46+ years. After the age of 46 years, degenerative changes become too subjective to provide more precise ageing.

For the non-adults, age-at-death estimates were obtained using standards of development for the deciduous and permanent dentition published by Moorrees *et al* (1963a, 1963b) and tabulated by Smith (1991) and Lewis (1999). Where no teeth were present, diaphyseal lengths and skeletal maturation were used to assign an age (Ubelaker 1989). Age estimates for foetal and infant remains were derived from the British standards developed by Scheuer *et al* (1980) and adapted by Scheuer and Black (2000) based on diaphyseal lengths. Non-adults were divided into five age categories: perinate (<40 lunar weeks), infant (0–1 years), 1.0–2.5 years, 2.6–10.5 years, 10.6–17.0 years. The age and sex distribution of the sample is presented in Table 5.2.

A total of 43 inhumations comprised the current study sample, 28 adults, 9 non-adults, and 6 perinates, 5 of which were found within the settlement area. Of the 37 intact inhumations, 16 (43%) were female, 13 (35%) were male, and 1 adult individual could not be assigned a sex due to poor preservation. The majority of the female adults were aged between 26–35 years of age, with a more even spread of males and females in the mature age category. Ten adult individuals could not be aged due to poor preservation. The mortality peak at 26–35 years in females is often attributed to risk during successive childbirths; however, it may also be the result of bias in the current ageing techniques used in osteology (Chamberlain 2000). Of interest is the relatively high number of adolescents in the sample (4), because once they have survived the

Table 5.2 Human skeletal remains: demography of the sample

Age (years)	?Sex	Male	Female	Total individuals
Perinate				6
Infant (0.1–1.0)				1
1.1–2.5				1
2.6–10.5				3
10.6–17.0	2	1	1	4
17–25		1	1	2
26–35		2	6	8
36–45		1	3	4
46+		2	2	4
?Adult	1	6	3	10
Total	**3**	**13**	**16**	**43**

Table 5.3 Human skeletal remains: mean stature estimates (cm) from Anglo-Saxon cemeteries

Site	Males	Females	Source
Bishopstone	172	160	
Raunds Furnells, Northants	167	162	Powell, 1986
Empingham II, Rutland	174	164	Mays, 1996
Barton-on-Humber (Phase E), Lincs	169	161	Waldron, 2007

more hazardous childhood years, these individuals tend to survive and do not enter the archaeological record (Lewis 2007).

A young female (S2573) was excavated with foetal remains in her abdominal area. The remarkable find of such a tiny foetal radius indicates that the woman was carrying a 23-week-old foetus (full-term birth is generally at 38–40 weeks). It is unlikely that the pregnancy was related to her death in this instance, but the rare find of such tiny bones outlines the potential of careful excavation in identifying very young foetal remains on archaeological sites.

Anglo-Saxon cemeteries are notorious for their under-representation of infant remains (Lewis 2007). One explanation is that perinate and infant remains were given different burial locations to the older individuals in the community. Evidence for this may be found in the five foetal skeletons located in the chalk rubble dumps used to backfill the cellared component of Structure W (1344), and within three domestic pits (1344, 2645, and 3069). S1344 was estimated to be 36–37 weeks old at the time of their death; S2645 was of a similar age at 36 weeks, while S3069 was possibly full-term at 39–40 weeks. One of the pits contained two tiny perinates, both aged around 24 weeks, suggesting that they may have been miscarried twins.

Although it has often been suggested that the presence of full-term infants within domestic contexts indicates infanticide, the death of an infant is equally likely to have been the result of compli-

cations during childbirth, or a congenital deformity (Lewis and Gowland 2007). The presence of foetal remains in rubbish pits also has connotations as to the value that was placed on these individuals by their society. It is likely that all of the remains within the settlement area represent stillbirths, and as such were unlikely to have been considered 'members' of the community.

Metrical and non-metrical analysis

Studies of adult stature have shown variability according to geographical location, genetic and socio-economic factors, and have been shown to vary in archaeological populations from different periods. In fact, 90% of our attained adult height is determined by genetic factors, whereas 10% is influenced by the environment in which a person develops (Larsen 1997). Periods of malnutrition or disease in later adolescence can impact our final stature as adults, and hence, stature has been used as an indicator of overall population health (eg Roberts and Cox 2003). Adult stature was calculated according to Trotter's formulae (1970), using the left femur when intact. Eight males and ten females could be assigned a stature estimate, and averages for males and females were then compared to other data from later Anglo-Saxon populations (Table 5.3).

The Bishopstone males fall within the upper ranges of stature for men in the later Saxon period, while the females are among the shortest. What is clear is that stature between males and females during this period was sexually dimorphic, with women on average 90mm shorter than the males in the sites studied.

Health and disease

There are many pathological conditions that can be identified on the skeletons and teeth of past populations. Dental disease, osteoarthritis, trauma, and infections are among the most common. These and other conditions can provide information on population adaptation, diet, activity, treatment, hygiene, and levels of exposure to disease. However, the factors resulting in disease can only be understood within the cultural and biological context of that population. For example, a late Saxon population would have practised agriculture leaving them exposed to trauma through the use of farm equipment and close contact with livestock. In addition, for infectious diseases to be recognised on the skeleton, the individual has to be immunologically compromised enough to develop symptoms, whilst being healthy enough to survive the condition into its chronic stages (Ortner 1991). Hence, although the people of Bishopstone may well have been exposed to bouts of cholera, smallpox, the plague, whooping cough, and typhus, these conditions would kill the individual too quickly for traces to be evident on the skeleton.

Dental pathology

A total of 339 permanent teeth were available for examination (137 male; 154 female; 48 unknown sex). Of these, fifteen (4.4%) teeth were affected by caries, with females (8.4%) being significantly more prone to caries than the males (1.5%). One female (S2559) aged 46+ had a small abscess on the buccal side of her lower jaw. Four females and two males also had evidence for calculus (calcified plaque) on their teeth suggesting a high carbohydrate diet. There was one case of enamel hypoplasias in a 17–25 year old female (S2573). These pits and lines in the enamel suggest fever or malnutrition during childhood. Three individuals also had dental anomalies. Third molar agenesis was present in one woman (1146) who also had a super-numerary premolar, and one child (S2693) aged 10–12 years had a diastema (a gap between the maxillary central incisors) that would have been noticeable in life. Details of individual dental pathology are provided in the human remains catalogue (Appendix 3).

The average rate of caries in later Saxon populations is only slightly higher than at Bishopstone, at 4.8% (Freeth 2000), a decline from the Roman period, where caries rates were as high a 14.1% (Roberts and Cox 2003). In the 50 sites included in Roberts and Cox's analysis, the majority of those affected were women and this is reflected at Bishop-

stone. Moore and Corbett (1973) suggest that in the Anglo-Saxon period the only sweetener available to individuals was honey and fructose through the consumption of fruit, keeping levels of caries low.

Developmental anomalies

Abnormalities of growth and development, usually as the result of genetic disorders, trauma, or infection, can occur during foetal stages, or become apparent at birth or during childhood (Roberts and Manchester 2005). Most are asymptomatic in nature. Two cases of developmental abnormalities were identified in the Bishopstone sample. There was one case of sacralisation in a male (S1109), where the fifth lumbar vertebra of the spine develops sacral wings (alae) and fuses with the sacrum. When this defect only occurs on one side, spinal curvature can result, however in this case, the change was bilateral and probably went unnoticed by the individual. A more unusual developmental defect in the sternum occurred in a female (S1106) where one of the sternal segments present in childhood imperfectly fused with its counterpart below (Fig 5.9). The smooth, curvilinear nature of the lesion suggests a

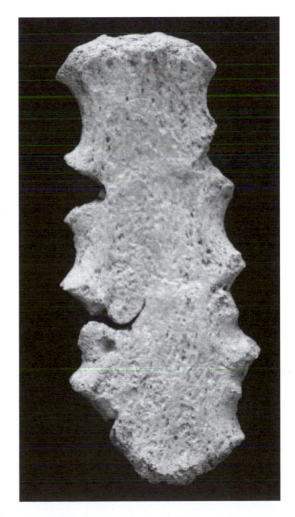

Fig 5.9 Probable congenital defect of the sternum in S1106 (M Lewis)

Table 5.4   Summary of the most severe cases of disease and trauma in the Bishopstone skeletons

Skeleton	Age and sex	Disease	Trauma
S86	Female, 36–45 yrs	Osteoarthritis of hands and spine	
S1102	Female, 26–35 yrs	Osteoarthritis of right wrist and elbow	Smith's fracture of the right radius. Compressed fractures of L4 and L5
S1103	Adult male	Healing bilateral periostitis on the tibiae and fibulae	
S1104	Adult male		Healed fracture of the right femur. Possible fracture with joint disease of the right distal phalanx of the first metatarsal (big toe)
S1105	Male, 46+ yrs	Severe osteoarthritis of hips, knee, hand, right ankle, and spine	Fractured fifth left metacarpal (little finger)
S1106	Female, 26–35 yrs	Osteoarthritis of the spine and right hand. Segment fusion developmental defect in the sternum	
S1108	Female, 26–35 yrs	Osteoarthritis of the lumbar spine. Healed bilateral periostitis of the tibiae and fibulae	
S1109	Adult male	Bilateral sacralisation of L5	
S1146	Male, 26–35 yrs		Healed oblique fracture of the right femur, with possible osteomyelitis
S1171	Adult female	Osteoarthritis of the elbows	Compressed fracture and fusion of two thoracic vertebrae
S1294	Adult female	Osteoarthritis and Schmorl's nodes in the spine. Severe osteoarthritis of the right hip	Possible 'stubbed' toe
S2004	Male, 17–25 yrs	Bilateral osteomyelitis of the tibiae	
S2019	Female, 26–35 yrs	Osteophytosis of the spine. Atrophied first rib?	
S2559	Female, 36–45 yrs	Osteoarthritis of the spine with osteophyte formation on the dens. Hand and left knee also affected	
S2562	Female, 36–45 yrs	Osteoarthritis of the spine and left hip	
S2565		Fusion of T9 and T10: possible underlying trauma	Possible compressed T10
S2720	Male, 26–35 yrs		Oblique fracture of left tibia

developmental problem rather than trauma. Finally, two non-metric traits were identified: S2556 had a supercondylar process on the right humerus and S2792, a mature female displayed a large occipital bun.

Joint disease

Osteoarthritis (arthritis) is recognisable as bony outgrowths (osteophytes) along the margins of the joints and spinal bodies, contour change, porosity, and polishing (eburnation) of the joint surfaces. It may occur as part of the normal ageing process, secondary to trauma, or as the result of mechanical stress or habitual use of the joint (Resnick 1995). Osteoarthritis was not uncommon in the early medieval period and has been attributed to the stresses and strains of agricultural work.

A total of 16 of the 28 adults (57%) had evidence for joint disease, with the majority of lesions in the lumbar and thoracic spine, followed by the wrist and hand, elbow, and knee. Eleven of the affected individuals were female. One individual, a 46+ year-old male (S2565), had fusion of the thoracic vertebrae (T9 and 10, and T12 and L1) with possible underlying trauma. Schmorl's nodes, or depressions in the body of the vertebrae, thought to be indicative of spinal pressure, were evident in four individuals (S1294, S87, S2019, and S1106). As a fairly elderly sample, this level of joint disease is not unexpected. Details of the lesions can be found in Table 5.4 and the human remains catalogue (Appendix 3). In the survey of joint disease in the Anglo-Saxon period by Roberts and Cox (2003, 195), males were more commonly affected than females, the opposite of the pattern seen in the small sample from Bishopstone. In addition, at Raunds Furnells, osteoarthritis of

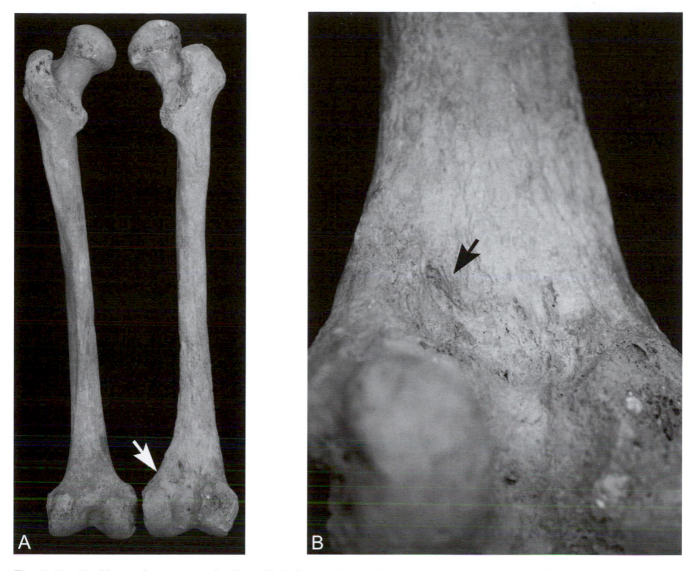

Fig 5.10 A) oblique fracture in the distal left femur shown from the posterior aspect in S1146; B) close-up of a draining sinus suggesting a secondary infection from an open fracture (M Lewis)

the wrist and hand was relatively uncommon, with the shoulder being the most severely affected joint after the spine (Powell 1996). This was also a trend noted at Barton-on-Humber (Waldron 2007).

Non-specific infection

Evidence for infection on the skeleton, as the result of inflammation or trauma to the sheath covering the bones (periostitis), can occur as new bone formation on the original bone surface. In severe cases, the infection may involve the bone, causing enlargement and constriction of the medullary cavity (osteitis), or result in an infection within the medullary cavity itself (osteomyelitis). The latter can be caused due to a blood-borne infection, especially in children when their bones are still growing and have a good blood supply, or as the direct spread of infection from an overlying lesion, or open fracture (Roberts and Manchester 2005). There were two cases of bilateral

periostitis, in an adult male (S1103) and adult female (S1108); both occurred in the lower legs and represent healed infections.

Probable secondary osteomyelitis from an open wound after fracture was identified in the femur of S1146; the infection had resulted in a bowed appearance to the bone, but the trauma itself appeared to be confined to the knee (Fig 5.10 A and B).

More unusually, a young male aged 17–25 years (S2004) had bilateral osteomyelitis of the tibiae. The whole of the left tibial shaft is enlarged (hypertrophic), but the right tibial lesions are mostly confined to the proximal end. The rest of the skeleton is too poorly preserved to track the extent of skeletal involvement, or determine an exact cause of the infection. However, that this infection was of long-standing duration is demonstrated by the distinct channel below the abscess (cloaca) on the anterior aspect of the right tibia, formed by the flow of pus down the bone. In life, this individual would have had obviously swollen legs, red and hot to the touch.

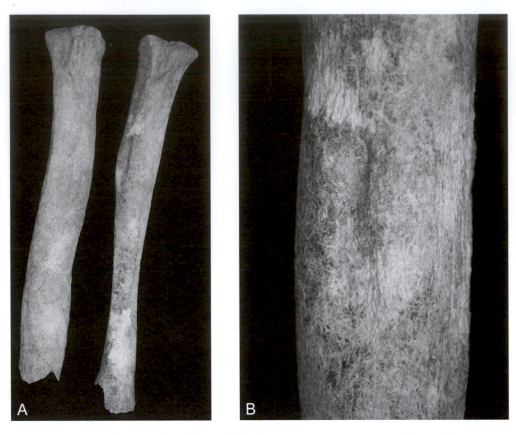

Fig 5.11 A) bilateral osteomyelitis of the tibiae of S2004, note greater extent of the enlargement on the right tibia; B) close-up of the draining sinus (cloaca) on the medial aspect of the left tibia (M Lewis)

Weeping sores would also have been evident on his legs, and he would probably have had difficulty walking (Fig 5.11 A and B). Osteomyelitis in juvenile remains is not that common, with only four other cases being identified in Anglo-Saxon populations. One of these was in a youth of similar age to S2004 who was excavated at Raunds Furnells; however, in this case the lesions were unilateral (Lewis 2002).

Trauma

There were eight cases of skeletal trauma in the Bish-opstone skeletons. There were two fractured femora and a fractured tibia, all in males (S1104, S1146, and S2720). All of these fractures were well-aligned suggesting that the men had sought treatment, and that the leg fractures had been reduced. There were also three cases of compressed fractures to the spine (S1102, S1171, and possibly S2565), this time mostly in the females. These often represent acute trauma due to a fall from a height, or may indicate a metabolic condition. S1102 also had a fracture of the right wrist (Smith's fracture), again indicative of a fall and potentially bone weakness as the result of osteoporosis. However, the spinal fractures did not show the classic 'cod-shaped' collapse expected in cases of brittle bone disease (Ortner 2003). In addition to the long bone fractures, those to the

hands and feet were also present, with a possible stubbed toe, a fractured right toe, and two fractured fifth fingers (MC5s). The fractured finger, combined with severe joint disease of the metacarpal heads ('knuckles') in S1105, suggests damage caused when the fist was clenched (Fig 5.12). With the exception of one fractured finger that occurred in the unstrati-fied material, all were in male individuals.

The crude prevalence rate for trauma in this sample is 22% (four males, three females, one unknown). At Raunds Furnells (Northants), it was much lower at 12% (Powell 1996), and in the late Saxon period at Barton-on-Humber (Lincs) it was between 9.8 and 16.5% (Waldron 2007, 86). The bones affected by trauma compare to those in the dataset of Anglo-Saxon skeletons compiled by Roberts and Cox (2003), although they found only four cases of fractured hands in a sample of 395 individuals. Foot and lower leg fractures are, however, more common for this period. As with Bishopstone, trauma in males in the Anglo-Saxon period is more common, and is likely to be the result of accidental injury during farming activi-ties, such as dealing with cattle and horse-drawn vehicles, and falling from horses (Roberts and Cox 2003, 203). The large number of fractures in such a small sample is notable, and could suggest that this contingent of Bishopstone's population may have suffered an arduous life.

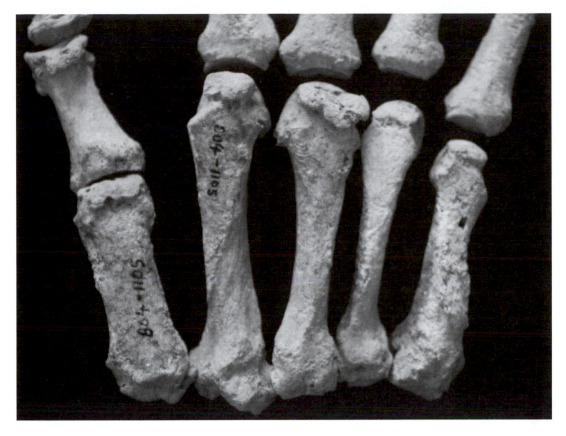

Fig 5.12   Oblique fracture of the fifth metacarpal and osteoarthritis of the metacarpal heads of S1105 (M Lewis)

The double burials

There were six cases of double burial at Bishopstone (Table 5.5, Figs 5.1, 5.4, and 5.8). Multiple burials are not unknown in Anglo-Saxon cemeteries and have been classified into several different types, including a cluster of individual burials, deliberately intercutting burials, and secondary burials deliberately inserted into pre-existing graves (Stoodley 2002). At Bishopstone, the archaeological evidence suggests that in at least four of the cases, the burials were made simultaneously, the bodies being placed one above the other. All of the bodies were laid out in a supine position, with the second burial placed so that the head, pelvis, and knees were in exact alignment with the underlying body. This type of body positioning suggests the bodies were wrapped, although there was no evidence for shroud or coffin pins. Two of the double burials were of mixed sex, and two involved individuals of the same sex, where an older male or female was buried with a younger male or female. Unlike the site of Empingham II (Crawford 2007), there were no cases of young children buried with adults.

The reason behind these burials, especially in sites where space was not at a premium, is uncertain. Crawford (2007) argues that simultaneous burials suggests that the deaths occurred at the same time, and perhaps indicate two close members of a family who may have succumbed to the same disease, or reflect a particular stress or tragic event within the community that could only be repaired by a multiple burial. At Bishopstone, in two cases, both individuals within the double graves showed some evidence of trauma or infection. S1105 had a fractured toe, while S1171 had a fractured spine; S1108 had bilateral infected legs, and S1146 had a fractured femur. Interestingly, although S2019 did not demonstrate any severe skeletal pathology, the accompanying burial, S2004, had severely infected legs. While these ailments were chronic and unlikely to have resulted in the deaths of the individuals, especially at the same time, most would have been visibly afflicted during their lives.

Conclusions

Analysis of this restricted number of burials from later Anglo-Saxon Bishopstone revealed a group of individuals with a fairly even demographic spread. The males were slightly taller than average but still within the height-range for the period, but the females were amongst the smallest women located from sites of this period. This difference between the men and women may be the result of genetic factors, illustrating a high level of sexual dimorphism, or may indicate something about the quality of the female

Table 5.5 Age and sex of individuals from double burials

Grave numbers	Body 1	Body 2	Type
S2004 over S2019	26–35, female	17–25, male	Intercutting
S1317 over S1294	Adult female	?adult	Intercutting
S1105 over S1171	?female	46+, male	Simultaneous
S1108 over S1146	26–35, male	26–35, female	Simultaneous
S2791 over S2869	?male	?male	Simultaneous
S2559 over S2924	16 years, female	46+, female	Simultaneous

diet and their exposure to stress during childhood. The cemetery and settlement excavations yielded several perinatal remains, one from the abdomen of a young woman, suggesting that miscarriages and death during pregnancy were not uncommon in this community.

There was a high level of bone fractures, infection, and osteoarthritis in these individuals. This perhaps reflects the hazards of agricultural intensification, with close proximity to animals and heavy equipment resulting in several accidents for both men and women. What is also clear is that fractures were being treated and set, in order to allow them to heal without deformity. Finally, analysis of the burials at Bishopstone has revealed several interesting funeral practices. Stillborn babies appear to have been disposed of in domestic pits, and more evidence has been provided for the nature of double burials in the Anglo-Saxon period, with the practice here confined to the adults, many of whom displayed pathology.

Plate 1   Bishopstone village from Rookery Hill: the 2004 excavation trench and spoil heap can be seen on the village green

Plate 2   Excavations in progress in 2003, as seen from the church tower showing freshly exposed archaeological features in front of the trowelling line

Plate 3 Lower reaches of the Bishopstone valley looking south-west towards Rookery Hill and Castle Hill, Newhaven, beyond: the floor of the valley is etched with a series of drainage channels and prominent lynchet banks can be seen at the bottom of its western slopes

Plate 4 The coastline as seen from Castle Hill, Newhaven, looking east towards Seaford Head in the far distance. The entrance to the Bishopstone valley is immediately behind the first string of houses in the middle distance

Plate 5   Looking south-east over the 2005 excavation trench with Structure K and the church in the background

Plate 6   Handled bowl in Fabric 1

Plate 7   Spouted pitcher sherds in Fabric 12

Plate 8   Main elements of the Bishopstone hoard recovered as a mass of conglomerated iron

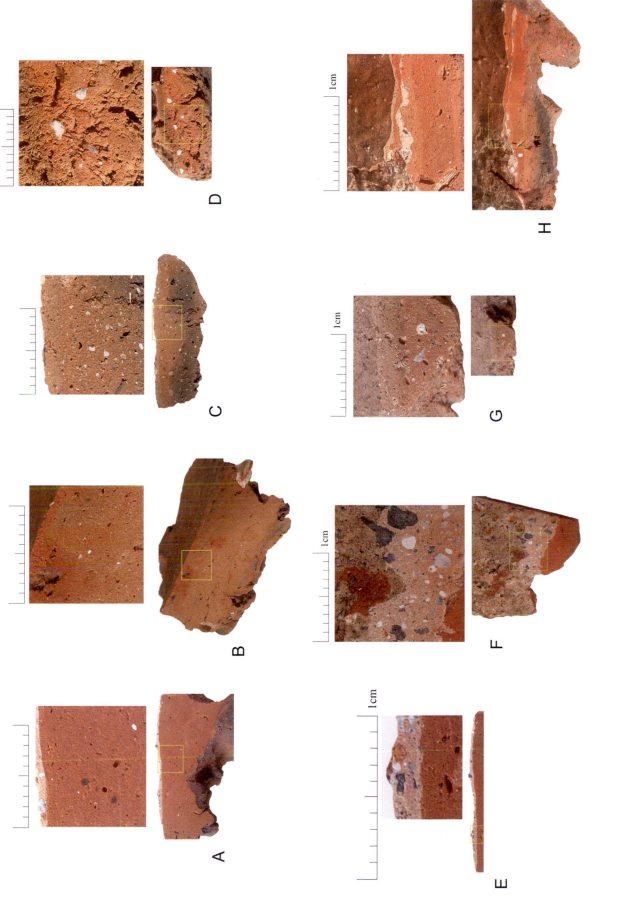

Plate 9   Compositional characteristics of structural daub: A–D; E–F) magnified views of lime wash; G) magnified view of clay skim; H) magnified view of multiple lime washes

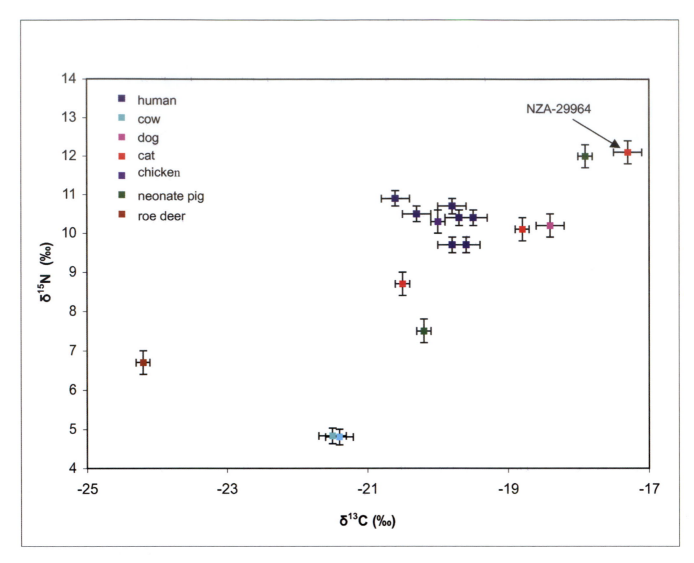

Plate 10 Human isotope data from Bishopstone in comparison with faunal values from the site

6 The artefacts

The bulk of this chapter is organised thematically according to broad functional groups (eg dress accessories, structural fittings) leaving only a small number of miscellaneous objects whose use is either unknown or unclassifiable under the existing scheme. Each of the functional headings is further subdivided into object categories (eg pins under dress accessories) comprising an introductory discussion followed by (in most cases) individual catalogue entries, the majority of which are illustrated. Only some object categories include a complete listing; others (eg knives) are accompanied by a select catalogue to economise on space. For the same reason, some of the more generic forms of domestic utensil (eg awls, shears) are reduced to a heading and a basic explanation which at the very least serves to preserve the functional spectrum embodied within the artefactual assemblage. Full listings of artefacts with accompanying descriptions are lodged with the site archive. Measurements given in catalogue entries are in grams and millimetres.

The iron hoard, discussion of which, along with the pottery, is accorded a separate section at the beginning of the chapter, contained a miscellany of tools, fittings, and equipment crosscutting the major classificatory divisions used to structure this chapter. For the sake of consistency, the individual items are included under the appropriate functional heading and cross-referenced numerically to a summarised list provided in the section dedicated to the hoard; for convenience, catalogue entries for these items are also marked with an asterisk.

6.1 Pottery
by Ben Jervis

Introduction

The pottery from Bishopstone is, by a considerable margin, the largest later Anglo-Saxon assemblage yet recovered from East Sussex. In addition to its size, two aspects of the Bishopstone pottery underline its importance as a crucial assemblage for understanding ceramic production in later Anglo-Saxon Sussex. First, it provides indirect evidence, in the form of misfired wasters, that a range of domestic coarsewares was produced at Bishopstone itself – one of the few securely located production sites in later Anglo-Saxon Sussex. Second, through associated radiocarbon dating, it provides a new fixed point for calibrating a key transition in the production of domestic coarsewares in Sussex, bringing greater precision to our understanding of the process by which mid Anglo-Saxon ceramic traditions came to be replaced by the more sophisticated industry which emerged during the late Anglo-Saxon period. On the basis of the above, no justification needs to be made for including a thorough analysis and appraisal of the ceramic evidence.

The assemblage under consideration comprises 9823 sherds, weighing 7697g with an Estimated Vessel Equivalent (EVE) figure, based on measurable rims, of 44.87. The first section of this report describes and quantifies the assemblage under local and non-local fabrics, followed by the various vessel forms exhibited within each of the two principal fabric categories. The alternative approach of considering all fabrics and forms in sequence has been avoided due to the fact that the distinction between 'local' and 'non-local' fabrics as defined in this study is reflected in clear morphological differences. Decoration, an attribute which transcends more localised distinctions observed in fabric-form combinations, receives separate treatment, as does the small quantity of imports present at the site, considered last.

Analysis includes an attempt to establish a site-based ceramic chronology for the settlement situated within sequences established through analysis of earlier pottery assemblages from Rookery Hill and Itford farm. Some consideration is also given to spatio-temporal patterns in the distribution of pottery. Finally, the assemblage is set within its broader regional context to explore patterns in ceramic production and consumption across the Sussex region between the later 7th and 11th centuries AD.

Methodology

The sherds were sorted into fabric and form types by the author and volunteers during the 2004 and 2005 excavation seasons. The fabric type series was developed initially by Duncan Brown with the author and volunteers, during the 2005 excavation season. Fabric identifications made under a x10 binocular microscope were subsequently refined by thin-section analysis carried out by the author at the University of Southampton (see Peacock 1969 for methodology). Petrological descriptions are included in Appendix 4. Fabric type sherds and thin-section slides have been deposited with the site archive. The 63 sequentially numbered fabrics identified in the field have inevitably been amalgamated into various groups. Broader categories have been created based on their characteristic inclusion (flint tempered ware) or on a more generic name relating to a distinctive feature (mainly on imports eg red painted ware).

Table 6.1 Quantification of the later Anglo-Saxon pottery fabrics from Bishopstone by sherd count, sherd weight (g), and Estimated Vessel Equivalent (EVE; based on rims)

Fabrics – ware types/nos		Sherd count	% Sherd count	Sherd weight	% Sherd weight	EVE	% EVE
Flint tempered ware							
	1	3687	38%	30199	39%	13.9	31%
	13	2279	23%	15083	20%	8.8	20%
	14	1978	20%	15613	20%	9.5	21%
	16	40	0%	505	1%	0.4	1%
	19	41	0%	767	1%	1.1	2%
	Total	**8025**	**82%**	**62167**	**81%**	**33.6**	**75%**
Sandy ware							
	2	101	1%	719	1%	0.3	1%
	3	916	9%	6049	8%	5.0	11%
	5	90	1%	598	1%	1.1	2%
	Total	**1107**	**11%**	**7366**	**10%**	**6.3**	**14%**
Chalk tempered ware							
	12	291	3%	4280	6%	1.7	4%
	35	1	0%	14	0%	0.0	0%
	Total	**292**	**3%**	**4294**	**6%**	**1.7**	**4%**
Wealden(?) coarseware							
	8	171	2%	1125	1%	0.8	2%
	44	30	0%	378	0%	0.5	1%
	Total	**201**	**2%**	**1503**	**2%**	**1.3**	**3%**
Shell tempered ware							
	52	32	0%	542	1%	1.4	3%
	Total	**32**	**0%**	**542**	**1%**	**1.4**	**3%**
Other coarseware							
	26	116	1%	736	1%	0.3	1%
	40	36	0%	302	0%	0.2	0%
	Total	**152**	**2%**	**1038**	**1%**	**0.5**	**1%**
Imported ware							
Glazed (63)		5	0%	12	0%	0.0	0%
Red painted blackware (32)		1	0%	18	0%	0.0	0%
Red painted ware (18)		8	0%	29	0%	0.1	0%
	Total	**14**	**0%**	**59**		**0.1**	**0%**
TOTAL		**9823**		**76969**		**44.9**	

Each vessel part is coded numerically with an alphabetical identifier; 'R' for rim, 'S' for spout, 'H' for handle, 'T' for body sherds, and 'B' for base. R1 therefore denotes a certain type of rim and H1 a certain type of handle. A full index of the codes used along with the database record is deposited with the archive.

The presence of fabrics and forms in each context is recorded by sherd count and sherd weight (grams). Rim percentage and diameter were also recorded and this has been used to quantify the assemblage by EVE (Orton *et al* 1993, 171).

Catalogue of fabrics and forms

The fabric type series established in the field has been refined by the author into eighteen fabrics divided into three categories: local wares, non-local English wares, and foreign imports. Many of the fabric types occur only in small numbers and most likely represent only one or two vessels. Where applicable, 'later Anglo-Saxon' has been adopted as a convenient label throughout this discussion but it is acknowledged that the currency of the Bish-

Table 6.2 Composition of the later Anglo-Saxon assemblage by vessel form and fabric, quantified by Estimated Vessel Equivalent (EVE, based on rims)

Fabric – ware type/no.	Jar	Bowl	Pitcher	Lamp	Unid.	Total fabric EVE
Flint tempered ware						
1	91%	7%			2%	13.9
13	96%				4%	8.8
14	94%	2%			4%	9.5
16	100%					0.4
19	26%	17%		57%		1.1
Total	**91%**	**4%**		**2%**	**3%**	**33.6**
Sandy ware						
2	83%				17%	0.3
3	92%		2%		6%	5.0
5	92%				8%	1.1
Total	**91%**				**7%**	**6.3**
Chalk tempered ware						
12	44%		49%		8%	1.7
Total	**44%**		**49%**		**8%**	**1.7**
Wealden(?) coarseware						
8	94%				6%	0.8
44	100%					0.5
Total	**96%**				**4%**	**1.3**
Shell tempered ware						
52	100%					1.4
Total	**100%**					**1.4**
Other coarseware						
26	57%		43%			0.3
40	100%					0.2
Total	**72%**		**28%**			**0.5**
Imported ware						
18 (red painted ware)	100%					0.1
Total	**100%**					**0.1**
Total vessel EVE	**40.2**	**1.3**	**1.1**	**0.6**	**1.6**	**44.9**
% of Total vessels	**90%**	**3%**	**2%**	**1%**	**4%**	

opstone pottery assemblage may overlap with the traditional period sub-divisions 'mid', 'late' (Anglo-Saxon), and 'Saxo-Norman'.

Local wares

The term 'local wares' is used to define fabrics that seem to be made from Ouse valley or Wealden Gault clays. Local wares are primarily flint tempered (see Table 6.1) and the inclusion of flint in pottery throughout Sussex and Hampshire makes petrological analysis of clay types a better means of distinguishing production sources (see Appendix 4).

The common vessel form is a jar with an everted rim and sagging base of a type common across southern England. Bowls are rare (Table 6.2) and one unusual example has a looped handle (Plate 6; Fig 6.5, no. 1) (see Jervis 2008). A spike lamp and a pedestal lamp are also present (Fig 6.3, nos 5 and 6).

All these fabrics were irregularly fired, with surface colours ranging from black through to red, although the majority are black or grey. This suggests that firing occurred in either a small bonfire or clamp kiln covered to produce a reducing atmosphere. The sandy wares are more commonly oxidised, suggesting they may have been fired in a more controlled manner, perhaps in a clamp kiln

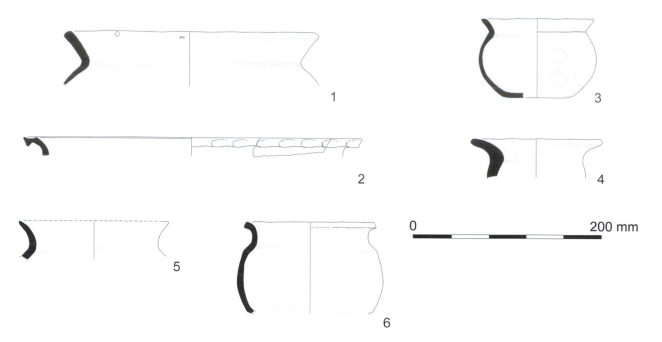

Fig 6.1 Pottery, jars in local fabrics: 1) Jar, Fabric 1, R1, context 6; 2) Jar, Fabric 5, R2 with thumb impressed decoration, context 2232; 3) Jar with stamped decoration, Fabric 19, R3, context 553; 4) Jar, Fabric 19, R4, context 1344; 5) Jar, Fabric 1, R4, context 2744; 6) Jar, Fabric 14, R5, context 1344

similar to those excavated at Chapel Street, Chichester (Down 1981, 138). The majority of local wares were handmade although there is some indication that some of the rims may have been finished on a turntable and some of the sandy fabrics appear to have been thrown on a wheel (Gardiner 1990, 252).

Local wares have been divided into two groups: flint tempered wares and sandy wares. These two groups are deemed to be local as they are quantitatively dominant (Tables 6.1 and 6.2) and therefore characterise the majority of the assemblage. A catalogue of local forms follows the catalogue of local fabrics.

Flint tempered wares (Fabrics 1, 13, 14, 16, and 19)

Flint tempering is common across Sussex and Hampshire, from Pevensey in the east (Lyne unpub) to Southampton in the west (Brown 1994). Based on evidence from Pevensey, Rookery Hill, Bishopstone, and Hassocks, the introduction of flint tempering in Sussex can be broadly attributed to the 7th century; dated assemblages from Portchester and Southampton suggest a slightly later, 8th-century adoption in Hampshire (Lyne 2000, 25). Flint tempered ware is the most common pottery type on the site, comprising 75% by EVE (Table 6.1). Five fabrics have been identified within this group.

Fabric 1 is the most common (Table 6.1). It is a hard, rough coarseware with an irregular fracture and surface colours ranging from red to black. Grey cores suggest partial reduction or a rapid firing. Flint inclusions range from 0.5–2mm in size (10%), chalk and shell of similar sizes comprise approximately 5% of the inclusions while iron oxide is present in the matrix. Jars with everted rims comprise 91% of vessel types by EVE. There is one bowl, an almost complete handled vessel (Plate 6; Fig 6.5, no. 1). Only one sherd is decorated, with an incised line around the neck.

Fabric 13 is very closely related to Fabric 1 but the inclusions are significantly smaller (0.5–1mm) and iron oxide does not appear to be present. This fabric comprises 20% of the assemblage by EVE (Table 6.1) and 96% of the identifiable vessels (EVE) are jars (Table 6.2). As with Fabric 1, vessels are predominantly plain, although two sherds exhibit incised lines on the body and two have thumb-impressed decoration, one on the rim and one on the body.

Fabric 14 is a hard, rough coarseware with an irregular fracture. Sherds have a grey core and surface resulting probably from reduction firing. Inclusions of flint are 0.5–2mm in size (20%) and chalk is 0.5–1mm (5%). Ten wasters from pit 1198 (Fig 6.8) included an R10 rim (the second most common rim form in this fabric) and nine associated body sherds, indicating that production occurred within the vicinity of the site. Fabric 14 constitutes 21% of the assemblage by EVE. Some 94% (EVE) of the vessels in this fabric are jars of a similar form to those in Fabrics 1 and 13. At least two bowls are present including three sherds from a simple sagging bowl with an upright rim (R9). Five sherds have thumb-impressed decoration, including the rim of a bowl.

Fabric 16 is a hard, abrasive, and coarse fabric with large inclusions, primarily angular flint, with chalk, shell, and other grits present in quantities below 5%. The fabric breaks with a hackly fracture and surfaces are pink/brown with a grey core. This fabric makes up less than 1% of the assemblage and jars are the only identifiable vessel form.

Fabric 19 is a black, soft fabric with an irregular fracture and large but sparse inclusions of sub-angular flint and chalk. Iron oxide is also present. Five sherds in this fabric are everted rims from jars, one of which is distinctively squat,

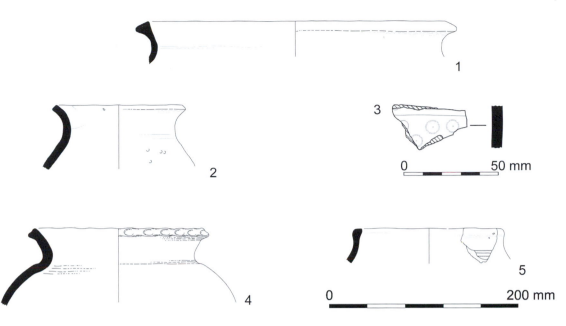

Fig 6.2 Pottery, jars in local and non-local fabrics: 1) Jar, Fabric 3, R7, context 2147; 2) Jar, Fabric 13, R10, context 549; 3) Jar with ring-dot stamped decoration, Fabric 8, context 3106; 4) Jar, Fabric 1, R10 with thumb impressed decoration, context 1404; 5) Jar, Fabric 14, R24, context 48

with a rim diameter of 180mm, and decorated with large circular stamps (Fig 6.1, no. 3). A similar stamp is known from Rookery Hill (Bell 1977, 231). A bowl with a beaded rim and a spiked lamp are also present (Fig 6.3, no. 5).

Sandy wares (Fabrics 2, 3, and 5)

Sandy wares make up 14% of the assemblage by EVE. Fabric 5 was produced on a wheel, which perhaps indicates a later date than Fabrics 2 and 3, although the latter may have been produced or finished on a turntable. The apparent use of a wheel or turntable, combined with oxidised surfaces, suggests that these fabrics represent a later stage of ceramic development than flint tempered wares, a transition which appears to have occurred over many parts of Sussex and Hampshire between the 10th and 12th centuries, in some cases in association with particular industries such as at Portchester and Michelmersh (Cunliffe 1976, 189; Gardiner 1990, 251–2; Brown and Mepham 2007).

Fabric 2 is generally black in colour with a bright orange core. Flint and chalk inclusions, present in an abundance of 5%, are between 0.5–2mm in size. The fabric is hard and rough and breaks with an irregular fracture. This fabric constitutes < 1% of the total assemblage by EVE and the only identifiable vessels are jars of a similar form to those in the flint tempered fabrics. No sherds are decorated.

Fabric 3 is a partially oxidised fabric with a red outer surface and a grey core. The fabric is hard with a rough feel and a fine fracture. Inclusions of flint (<5%) and chalk (<5%) are rare amidst a high quantity of sand. All inclusions are less than 1mm in size. It is possible that a turntable was used in the finishing of vessels in this fabric but they were not fully wheel-thrown. Thumbed decoration is present on five jar sherds. Three are thumbed around

the rim and two around the base. Stick-end decoration occurs on four body sherds. The fabric makes up 11% of the assemblage by EVE and 92% of vessels are jars. Three strap handles are present which may represent one or two handled jars similar to the kind known from Chichester (Down 1978, 349).

Fabric 5 has a very fine matrix. All of the inclusions (flint, chalk, and an iron-rich mineral) are present in less than 5% abundance and are less than 1mm in size. The fabric is hard and rough and breaks with a fine fracture. This fabric constitutes 2% of the assemblage by EVE. One sherd, an R2 rim, is decorated with an incised line.

Local forms

Jars (see Tables 6.3 and 6.4)

Jars with rounded, sagging bases and everted rims are the most common vessels on the site, making up

Table 6.3 Description and quantification of later Anglo-Saxon rim forms from Bishopstone (EVE, based on rims)

Rim type	EVE	% Jars
Simple everted, rounded profile	14.4	36%
Simple everted, squared profile	7.5	19%
Everted with thickening	5.3	13%
Everted with pronounced profile	4.5	11%
Upright	2.3	6%
Clubbed rim	2.6	7%
Bead rim	1.1	3%
Unidentified	2.5	6%
Total EVE	**40.2**	

Table 6.4   Quantification of rim forms by fabric type (EVE, based on rims)

Fabric	R1 Everted, externally thickened	R2 Everted with squared flange	R3 Upright, externally thickened and bevelled	R4 Everted, rounded	R5 Everted, rolled	R6 Upright, thickened	R9 Upright, squared	R10 Everted, squared profile
Flint tempered ware								
1	0.8	0.5	0.1	5.0	1.8	0.2	1.9	3.3
13	0.6	0.4		2.9	1.3	0.1	0.1	1.4
14	0.4	0.4	0.1	3.9	0.7	0.1	0.8	1.3
16				0.2				0.2
19		0.1		0.2				
Total	**1.8**	**1.3**	**0.2**	**12.2**	**3.8**	**0.3**	**2.9**	**6.2**
Sandy ware								
2	0.1			0.1	0.1			
3	0.4	0.7	0.3	1.1	0.2		0.2	1.0
5		0.4		0.1			0.1	0.1
Total	**0.6**	**1.1**	**0.3**	**1.2**	**0.3**		**0.2**	**1.0**
Chalk tempered ware								
12				0.6			1.1	
Total				**0.6**			**1.1**	
Wealden(?) coarseware								
8	0.1	0.2		0.2				0.2
44	0.1			0.2				
Total	**0.2**	**0.2**		**0.3**				**0.2**
Shell tempered ware								
52								
Total								
Other coarseware								
26				0.1				0.3
40		0.1		0.1				
Total		**0.1**		**0.1**				**0.3**
Imported ware								
18								
Total								
TOTAL EVE	**2.7**	**3.0**	**0.4**	**14.6**	**4.0**	**0.3**	**4.2**	**7.9**

R11 Upright, thickened with collar	R12 Everted, thickened, concave stepped	R13 Lamp rim	R14 Beaded rim	R24 R2 with internal lip	R27 Everted, rounded flange	R28 Upright, bevelled inwards	R29 Everted bead rim	Unid.	Total EVE
	0.2		0.1	0.1					13.9
	0.9		0.1		0.1	0.1	1.0		8.8
	0.2		0.1	0.1	0.2			1.2	9.5
									0.4
		0.6	0.2						1.1
	1.3	**0.6**	**0.3**	**0.2**	**0.2**	**0.1**	**1.0**	**1.2**	**33.6**
					0.1				0.3
	0.7			0.2	0.3			0.1	5.0
	0.3			0.1					1.1
	1.0			**0.3**	**0.3**			**0.1**	**6.3**
									1.7
									1.7
					0.1				0.8
	0.1					0.2			0.5
	0.1				**0.1**	**0.2**			**1.3**
								1.4	1.4
								1.4	**1.4**
									0.3
									0.2
									0.5
0.1									0.1
0.1									**0.1**
0.1	**2.3**	**0.6**	**0.3**	**0.5**	**0.8**	**0.3**	**1.0**	**2.8**	**44.9**

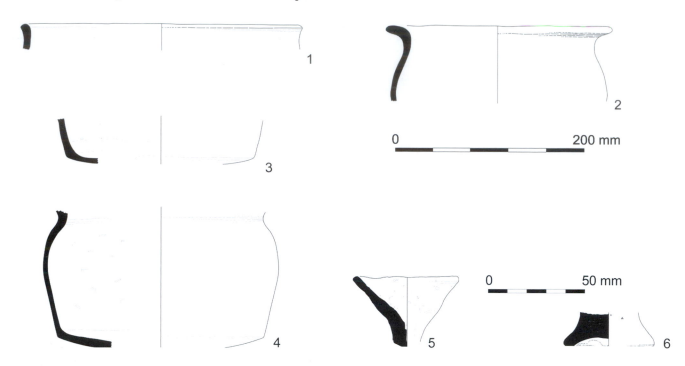

Fig 6.3   Pottery, jars, and lamps in local and non-local fabrics: 1) Jar, Fabric 14, R23, context 2674; 2) Jar, Fabric 8, R27, context 175; 3) Jar body and base profile, Fabric 14, context 2927; 4) Jar base, Fabric 13, context 2885; 5) Spiked lamp, Fabric 19, context 1288; 6) Pedestal lamp, Fabric 19, context 2760

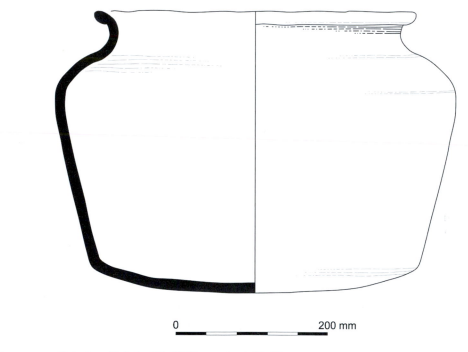

Fig 6.4   Pottery, complete jar, Fabric 13, R29, context 3148

91% of the assemblage by EVE (Table 6.2). These are common across southern England in the late Anglo-Saxon period, appearing as far west as Exeter (Allan 1984) and in Kent to the east (Dunning *et al* 1959, 32). There is little evidence of sooting or residues and therefore it is not possible to determine the function of these vessels. Barton (1979, 84) suggests that these vessels were used for cooking and storage

and that their purpose may have been related to their size. Vessels typically have a simple sagging base (Fig 6.3, no. 4; Fig 6.4).

The everted rims typically have a rounded (R4, Fig 6.1, no. 1, 36%) or squared (R10, Fig 6.2, no. 2, 19%) profile. Gardiner (1990, 251) suggests that at Botolphs, West Sussex, the squarer profile was most likely achieved using a turntable, and a similar

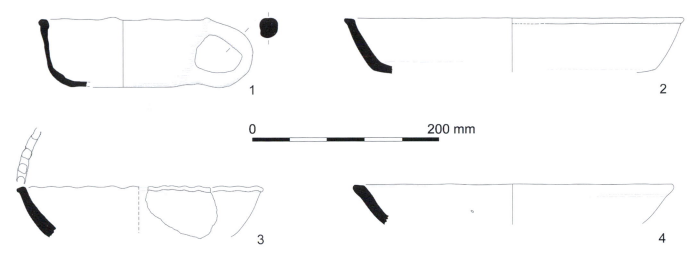

Fig 6.5 Pottery, bowls in local and non-local fabrics: 1) Handled bowl, Fabric 1, context 1260; 2) Bowl, Fabric 1, R9, context 2927; 3) Bowl, Fabric 14, R9, context 1224; 4) Bowl, Fabric 44, R28, context 36

conclusion has been reached at Chichester where it can be statistically demonstrated that there is a relationship between the presence of this kind of rim and the use of the turntable (Jervis 2009). R4 is more frequent than R10 in both the sandy and flint tempered wares. Both R4 and R10 have similar distributions by rim size. The mean rim size for R4 from the local wares is 179mm whilst for R10 it is 195mm. R4 has a mode of 150mm whilst R10 has a larger mode of 220mm. This perhaps demonstrates that the use of the turntable allowed the production of larger vessels. The remainder of the jar rims have variations on these forms, being externally thickened or having more pronounced profiles (Fig 6.1, no. 4; Fig 6.2, no. 1). Everted rims are typical of later Anglo-Saxon ceramic production across Sussex and southern England. They are less common in early Saxon assemblages such as at Rookery Hill, Bishopstone, where slightly inverted or straighter rims are more common (eg Bell 1977, 228).

Four jars, 7% by EVE, have more upright rim forms (Fig 6.2, no. 5). R9 occurs more commonly on non-local spouted pitchers and the form may be an imitation of this rim by local potters. Upright jar rims are present at Pevensey (Lyne unpub, 377) in sandy fabrics and at Chichester in small quantities (Jervis 2009); they are not present in the Adur valley (Gardiner 1993, 45). Other rim forms appearing in small quantities include versions of clubbed (squared) rims (Fig 6.1, no. 2) and a beaded rim appearing on a large jar (Fig 6.4). This vessel, in Fabric 14, was found sunken into the ground, possibly for use for cool storage or as a cistern (Chapter 4.1). This atypical rim could suggest that the vessel dates from a later phase of occupation on the site.

Bowls/dishes

There is one complete bowl in Fabric 1 with a simple straight rim and a rod handle (Plate 6; Fig 6.5, no. 1).

Recent research (Jervis 2008) indicates that this form is a comparative rarity in Anglo-Saxon England. Similar vessels are represented in the Midlands at Catholme (Staffs), (Vince 2002, 102–08) and more locally at Chichester (West Sussex), although the latter example is appreciably smaller than the bowl from Bishopstone (Dunning and Wilson 1953, 172).

Non-handled bowls in flint tempered Fabrics 1, 14, and 19 make up only 3% of the assemblage by EVE (Table 6.2). Most of the identifiable rims are upright and some are thumbed (Fig 6.5, no. 3); one bowl in Fabric 19 has a beaded rim. Similar vessels are known from Chichester where they are present in a much higher quantity (Jervis 2009). The rarity of bowls at Bishopstone suggests that wood, or other organic materials were more commonly used within this functional domain.

Lamps

Two lamps in Fabric 19 were identified (Fig 6.3, nos 5 and 6). No. 5 is a simple conical lamp with a spike, known alternatively as a suspension lamp (Vince and Jenner 1991, 34). No. 6 is a pedestal form with a shallow depression in the top, similar to examples from Chichester (Down 1978, fig 11.5, no. 85; Gardiner 1990, 252).

Non-local English wares and forms

Chalk tempered ware is the main fabric in this group, with some coarseware from the eastern Weald, as well as other shell and flint tempered wares.

Chalk tempered ware

Chalk tempered ware occurs in two variants at Bishopstone (Fabrics 12 and 35) and comprises 4% of the

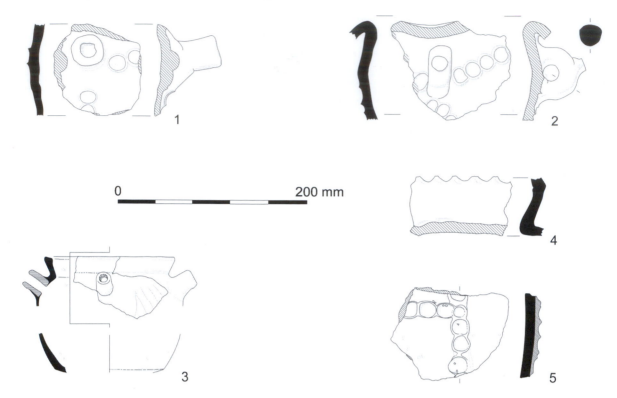

Fig 6.6   Pottery, spouted pitchers: 1) Chalk tempered spouted pitcher spout, Fabric 12, context 1347; 2) Chalk tempered spouted pitcher handle, Fabric 12, context 1179; 3) Spouted pitcher with incised decoration, Fabric 26, context 1344; 4) Thumbed rim (R9) from a chalk tempered spouted pitcher, Fabric 12, context 1179; 5) Thumb impressed applied strip decoration from a chalk tempered spouted pitcher, Fabric 12, context 1344

assemblage by EVE. The high limestone content could suggest a source in Hampshire, to the west, or near outcrops of Purbeck limestone located in the East Sussex Weald around Heathfield, Brightling, and Mountfield. The possibility cannot be ruled out that itinerant craft specialists produced this ware on site using imported clay or temper (Brown 1994, 144–5). Some support for this suggestion comes from a small number of cracked sherds and sagging rims that could be classed as wasters.

Fabric 12 is hard with an abrasive feel, hackly fracture, and grey colour with occasional orange/red surfaces. It is tempered with flint (flat splinters of 0.5–3mm comprising around 10% of the matrix) and chalk/limestone (flat splinters of 0.5–3mm comprising around 20%). Everted rim jars and pitchers are present, in approximately equal quantities (Table 6.2). They are often decorated with thumb impressions and have pie-crust rims. Pitchers are triple-spouted with straight (R9) rims and small loop handles that may have been used for suspension.

Fabric 35 is a hard fabric with a rough feel and irregular fracture, fired to a greyish orange colour and tempered with flint (flat splinters of 0.5–2mm in size, <5% of the matrix) and chalk (pieces 0.5–3mm in size forming approximately 5% of the matrix). No identifiable vessel forms are present. It comprises 0.01% of the assemblage by sherd count.

Cross-fitting sherds of Fabric 12 suggest that at least three pitchers are present in this fabric (Plate 7; Fig 6.6, nos 1–5). The chalk tempered tradition originated in the 8th century within the chalk downland of south Wiltshire and north Hampshire (Hodges 1981, 57), although the distribution of chalk tempered pitchers extends into Southampton (Brown 1994, 133), London (Vince and Jenner 1991, 72), and Sussex. A possible source of production in Sussex has been linked to the kiln evidence excavated in the Chapel Street area of Chichester (Down 1981, 184; Jervis 2005; 2009). Steyning has yielded vessels closely related to those from Chichester (Gardiner 1993, 41) although these products are thinner walled, more finely tempered and more highly oxidised than the Bishopstone examples, which are further set apart from West Sussex/Hampshire traditions by a lack of stamped decoration (Jervis 2009, 69). This latter distinction is perhaps not surprising, as stamping generally occurs to the west of the Adur valley in the late Saxon period (Cunliffe 1974). From a decorative point of view, the Bishopstone pitchers share a closer affinity with thumbed examples from London sourced to either Buckinghamshire or Berkshire (Vince and Jenner 1991, 70).

It is likely that the Bishopstone vessels were supplied from a more local source, perhaps based in the eastern half of Sussex, and given that the size of these vessels would have made them cumbersome to transport over land, perhaps using a coastal supply route. Unfortunately the ambiguity surrounding the identification of wasters in this fabric means that onsite production must remain only a tantalising possibility. The function of these vessels is unclear, although it has been suggested that they were used in the production of beer (Down 1981, 189). It should be noted that such vessels are much more strongly represented in towns than they are in rural locales, accounting for as much as 10% of the late Anglo-Saxon pottery assemblages from the urban centres of Southampton (Brown 1994, 139) and Chichester (Jervis 2009, table 8). This distinction may suggest a particular functional realm expressive of an urban, as opposed to a rural, lifestyle.

Wealden? coarsewares

Fabric 8 is black in colour, with occasional grey patches, hard and rough to feel, and with an irregular fracture. It is tempered with flint, ironstone, and possibly shell with pieces ranging from 0.5–2mm in size and each forming less than 5% of the matrix. This fabric constitutes 2% of the assemblage by EVE, all of the identifiable vessels being jars with everted rims. Two sherds are decorated with ring-and-dot stamps within a grid of incised lines (Fig 6.2, no. 3).

Sherds with a similar fabric/decoration combination have been identified at Sandtun (Cross *et al* 2001, 212), and at Pevensey Castle, East Sussex (Lyne unpub, 362). The Sandtun sherds were ascribed to a source in the eastern Weald based upon the similarity of the fabric to medieval pottery from Potter's Corner, Ashford (Cross *et al* 2001, 208–09); Bishopstone may thus mark the very western limits of this fabric's known distribution.

Fabric 44 this fabric is pink and grey in colour. A darker oxidised version is also present on the site. The fabric is hard and rough and breaks with an irregular fracture. Flint and chalk are present in small quantities (<5%) whilst an iron-rich mineral is marginally more common. The high iron content suggests a Wealden source. All of the inclusions are between 0.5–2mm in size. This fabric makes up 1% of the total assemblage by EVE and all of the identifiable vessels are jars with everted rims. One sherd is decorated with incised vertical lines.

Shell tempered ware

Shell tempering is fairly common in coastal districts of south-east England between the 7th and 9th centuries AD (Hodges 1981, 57), a pattern mirrored on the opposing side of the English Channel in Frisia (Stilke 1995, 11). It forms the largest group of pottery at the trading site at Sandtun, Kent (Cross *et al* 2001, 198) and is also present at Pevensey where oxidised shell tempered fabrics comprise the most abundant fabrics in later Anglo-Saxon contexts (Lyne unpub, 357). Shell tempered wares occur further west at Pagham, West Sussex (Gregory 1976, 215) and Hamwic where it comprises nearly 2% of the assemblage (Timby 1988, 87), although some of this material is likely to be imported (Worthington 1993). At Chichester, seemingly locally produced reduced shell tempered wares are present in chronologically early contexts (Jervis 2009, 71–2). It is largely absent from late Anglo-Saxon contexts in Southampton. The range of shell tempered ware at Bishopstone is restricted to a single fabric, 53, and it accounts for only 3% of the assemblage by EVE.

Fabric 53 is grey with inclusions of flint (0.5–2mm, 10% of the matrix) and shell (0.5–3mm, 30% of matrix). It is hard with an abrasive feel and irregular fracture. Two jars with everted rims are present in this fabric.

Non-local flint tempered ware

Fabric 40 is hard and rough to the touch, with a hackly fracture, and fired to various shades of grey. The main inclusions visible in the hand specimen is large splinters of flint (0.5–3 mm) in approximately 15% abundance. The fabric makes up <1% of the assemblage by EVE, and the only vessels represented are undecorated jars. The small quantity of this pottery suggests it is non-local. In thin section the matrix is particularly micaceous and this may suggest a Greensand source (see Appendix.4).

Chichester type

Fabric 26 is a soft, soapy fabric with flint, chalk, iron-rich, and shelly inclusions, all in quantities of around 5%. The inclusions appear unsorted, occurring in sizes between 0.5–3mm. The surface of the fabric is oxidised with a reduced core. This fabric is also known in small quantities from the Chichester Greyfriars site (Fabric 36, Jervis 2009). It is possible that it was produced in Chichester, although the small quantities present in the city perhaps suggest it was made elsewhere. The iron-rich matrix suggests it may have been produced from the Greensand or Gault clays, as is the case with a number of fabrics present in small quantities in Chichester (Jervis 2009, 64). The excavations produced one vessel, a small spouted pitcher around the size of a modern teapot, decorated with scoring (Fig 6.6, no. 3). The small size of this vessel may indicate that it was used as an item of tableware.

Decoration

It is useful to amalgamate the local and non-local wares in a discussion of decoration, partly because decoration is rare and partly because relevant themes apply to a wide geographical area. Thumb impressions are the most common decorative technique (present on 23 out of 61 decorated sherds), occurring on local wares, particularly around the rims of bowls and jars, and also on non-local wares, primarily the chalk tempered pitchers where they are present on the body as well as around the rim (Plate 7; Fig 6.6). This decoration is not present on local early Saxon pottery such as the assemblages from Rookery Hill (Bell 1977) and Botolphs (Gardiner 1990). Its presence in the destruction layers of the cellared structure suggests that the adoption of this decoration may date back to the 9th century, somewhat earlier than previously believed. This attribution does not contradict the supposition that the inspiration behind this decoration may be relief band amphora imported from the continent during the mid-Saxon period (Timby 1988, 91).

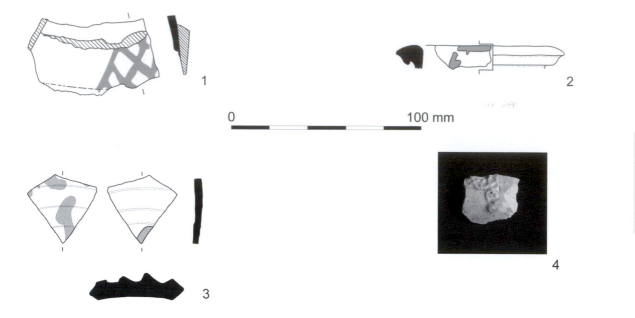

Fig 6.7   Pottery, imported wares: 1) Reduced north French red painted ware body sherd, Fabric 32, context 549; 2) Buff north French red painted ware jar, R11, Fabric 18, context 1764; 3) Buff north French red painted ware body sherd, Fabric 18, context 2068; 4) Southern English(?) glazed ware

The pie-crust rim form is common in Chichester from the 9th century, particularly on bowls and pitchers (eg Down 1978, 345) and also occurs in the Adur valley on similar vessels (Gardiner 1993, 40–1).

The second most common form of decoration is stick-end decoration (incised lines and dots), which occurs exclusively among the locally made flint tempered and sandy wares. This decorative technique is widespread in Sussex and Hampshire (eg Old Erringham: Holden 1976, 283; Hamwic: Timby 1988, 82–4; Botolphs: Gardiner 1990, 253) and was evidently long-lived, appearing on domestic and funerary pottery of the early Anglo-Saxon period up until the 11th century (Barton 1979, 81–98). The very strong prevalence of this technique in East Sussex may suggest that it was used as an alternative to stamping.

Stamping is restricted to one vessel in Fabric 19 and various sherds of Fabric 8. These stamps are distinct from those used in West Sussex and Hampshire where wheel and lattice stamps are common, particularly at Chichester (Cunliffe 1974, 132; Jervis 2005, 4–6). The circular stamp used to decorate Fabric 19 is similar to one used at Rookery Hill and may represent some chronological overlap in ceramic traditions between the two settlements.

Imported wares

Two types of imported pottery were recovered from the site, comprising five sherds apiece of red painted ware and glazed ware. Imported pottery of the later Anglo-Saxon period is rare in Sussex (Hurst 1980, 119)

and the low sherd-count at Bishopstone conforms to the small quantities recovered from Botolphs and Old Erringham, similarly located near to the mouth of an estuary (Holden 1976, 313; Gardiner 1990, 255).

Red painted ware

Fabric 18 is a hard, cream-coloured, wheel-thrown fabric decorated with lines of red paint that appear to have been applied with fingers (Fig 6.7, nos 2–3). Two variations of this fabric are represented amongst the total of five sherds implying the presence of at least two vessels (no cross-fits were observed). Judging by its small diameter, the one rim sherd represented in this fabric appears to be from a necked jar (Fig 6.7, no. 2).

The source of this type, also present at Botolphs and Pevensey Castle (Gardiner 1990, 255; Lyne unpub, 363), is either the Rhineland or northern France where red painted wares were produced between the 8th and 11th centuries and from the 9th century respectively (Kilmurry 1980, 188–9). At Chichester a sherd of red painted ware that was recovered from an 11th-century context has been ascribed to the Pingsdorf industry, whilst another vessel from the same town is believed to be French in origin (Hodges 1978, 352). At Portchester (Hants), red painted wares from both sources are present, whilst Southampton has only produced the French version (Brown 1994, 138). Although the small size and low quantity of the red painted sherds from Bishopstone makes it impossible to distinguish between these two sources with certainty, the collared rim perhaps tips the balance in favour of a north French origin (cf Lyne unpub, 365).

Fabric 32 is a wheel-thrown blackware with red painted lattice decoration represented by a single sherd (Fig 6.7, no. 1). This is possibly a north French blackware (cf Brown 1994, 138) and if so represents the only known example with red painted decoration from Sussex; the best parallels are otherwise from Sandtun in Kent (Cross et al 2001, 193).

Glazed ware (Fabric 63)

There were five pieces of glazed ware identified, seemingly from two vessels. One of three yellow-glazed sherds exhibits applied and rouletted decoration and one of two green-glazed fragments is rouletted with a line of squares (Fig 6.7, no. 4). The fine fabric and an absence of detailed work on late Anglo-Saxon glazed wares preclude close identification, especially when working with small body sherds. Three sources can be suggested: Stamford, 'Winchester', or northern France, all of which produced fine, quartz-rich, buff fabrics, similar to Fabric 63.

Glazed ware developed in northern France and Flanders in the 10th century. Both yellow- and green-glazed vessels were produced in this area, with similar rouletted decoration to that observed at Bishopstone. Winchester ware was first produced in the late 10th century for a variety of pitchers and serving vessels (Barclay and Biddle 1974, 139). The fabrics are primarily buff, sandy wares and glazes are yellow and dark olive green. The same tradition provides parallels for the distinctive crazing and rouletted decoration represented amongst the Bishopstone sherds (*ibid*, 141). On the basis of differences in form and decoration, Cunliffe (1976, 189) has proposed that the glazed ware from Portchester Castle (Hants) may have emanated from several small production centres rather than from the single centralised source of Winchester. The peak of glazed ware production at Stamford was the 11th to 13th centuries (Kilmurry 1980, 134). This, coupled with the distance from the production centre, makes it unlikely that any of the Bishopstone sherds is a Stamford product.

The glazed ware sherds from Bishopstone most probably originated from northern France or southern England. Whatever the case, the presence of glazed ware arguably attests to Bishopstone's higher than average status, for the consumption of this pottery was restricted to either rural settlements of thegnly character such as Portchester, or larger urban centres such as Exeter.

Chronology

Chronologies established for comparable sites in the Adur valley, themselves dated by comparison with more westerly groups from Medmerry, Pagham, and Chichester, initially suggested a 10th-century and later date for the Bishopstone pottery (Gardiner 1990, 251–3). One element which appeared to place Bishopstone on this chronological horizon was the occurrence of chalk tempered, spouted pitchers representing a variation on similar types of vessel made at Chapel Street, Chichester. Yet on the basis of radiocarbon dating it is now clear that occupation at Bishopstone almost certainly began in the 9th century, and very probably in the 8th, closing the chronological gap with the abandonment of the focus of early Anglo-Saxon occupation on Rookery Hill (Bell 1977). The following attempts to use seriation to construct a site-based relative ceramic sequence for Bishopstone, after which some consideration is given to the implications of the radiocarbon dates for ceramic chronologies in the Sussex region.

Seriation

The truncated nature of the features and the lack of stratigraphic relationships between them have made

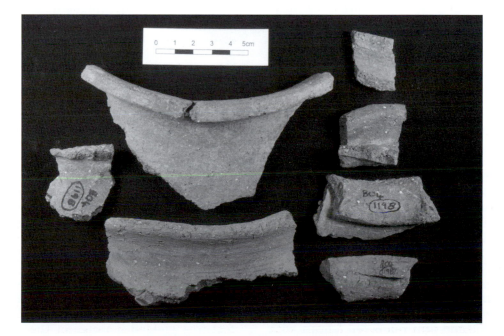

Fig 6.8   Pottery, Fabric 14 wasters

it difficult to create a pottery sequence. Seriation analysis has therefore been restricted to deeper sequences available for a select number of pits. In order to overcome some of the problems linked to seriation (Brainerd 1951, 303–4), a similar sampling method was used to that adopted at Hamwic (Cherry 1981). The twenty most pottery abundant, uncontaminated contexts by weight were selected. Only local coarsewares were present in sufficiently high quantities and accordingly the analysis was restricted to Fabrics 1, 14, and 13. Pottery assemblages from the 2004 and 2005 excavations were seriated separately in order to test the result. The ten most productive features from each season were then combined and seriated in order to iron out any inconsistencies in the sequencing over space. The seriation was carried out using the Bonn-Harris software suite.

All three attempts at seriation produced similar pottery sequences, whereby Fabric 1 is present throughout the occupation sequence. Its quantity in proportion to other fabrics does vary considerably however, being most abundant at the time of transition between the other fabrics. Fabric 14 (Fig 6.8) appears to predate Fabric 13. This sequence appears to correlate with stratigraphic relationships and the chronological implications of the proposed building typology. Pottery recovered from pits in the vicinity of aisled hall Structure V, for example, is placed last in the sequence. Although some localised patterns of this nature are apparent, the seriation does not suggest that the temporal distribution of pottery was strongly influenced by spatial patterns.

The apparent supersession of Fabric 14 by Fabric 13 offers an approximate tool for dating features, an observation which is tentatively supported by the higher proportion of wheel-finished rims in Fabric 13. The adoption of this technique cannot be established in precise chronological terms, although a 10th-century date is now preferred (Gardiner 1990; Jervis 2009) and it may be the case that the transition between the two fabrics occurred within the same century.

The pottery sequence in context

It is well established that the evolution of Anglo-Saxon ceramic traditions in southern England is punctuated by a transition from organic to flint tempering. Although there are slight regional variations in the timing of this transition, the consensus of academic opinion is that flint tempering emerged as an established – in many areas dominant – tradition between *c* AD 750 and 800 (Portchester: Cunliffe 1976; Hamwic: Hodges 1981, 56; Botolphs: Gardiner 1990, 245–6; Sandtun, Kent: Gardiner *et al* 2001, 223). The near ubiquity of flint tempered fabrics at Bishopstone places this assemblage firmly on the latter side of that transition. By contrast, the early Anglo-Saxon focus at Rookery Hill yielded a mixture of organic and flint tempered fabrics, with the latter type dated latest (Gardiner 1990, 245).

The two assemblages from the parish of Bishopstone would thus appear to support the suggestion that 'coarse flint tempered pottery increases during the 6th and 7th centuries and becomes predominant in the mid Anglo-Saxon period' (*ibid*, 245–6).

The dating of the sequence at Bishopstone to the 9th century and potentially earlier provides an opportunity to trace developments in the production of flint tempered pottery across the later Anglo-Saxon period from an East Sussex perspective. As Gardiner commented in his assessment of ceramic assemblages in the Adur valley (1990, 252–3), the longevity of this fabric type belies a sharp distinction in production techniques and morphology. On the one hand there are reduced handmade vessels, mostly small and globular in form with simple rims, which appear to define a mid Anglo-Saxon ceramic tradition stretching across much of Hampshire and Sussex. At Portchester this ceramic horizon occupies an intermediary position between organic tempered fabrics of the early Anglo-Saxon period and later wheel-thrown products, whilst at Market Field, Steyning, it constitutes the earliest significant phase of ceramic consumption on the site (Gardiner 1993, 253: fabrics CB, DI, DJ, and DC). On the basis of associated dating evidence at Hamwic and a sprinkling of sites in the far west of Sussex, such pottery is usually attributed to the 9th century with the acknowledgement that its origins may extend back into the 8th (Cunliffe 1976, 191).

On the other hand there are wares in the same general fabric type that attest to a more sophisticated mode of production. Predominantly oxidised, these vessels are either wheel-thrown or trued up on a turntable; they are generally larger than their handmade counterparts, and feature sagging bases and often strongly everted or 'developed' rims. They are also associated with a distinctive repertoire of decorative techniques ranging from thumbed rims, through to thumb-impressed strapping, stamping, stick-end decoration, and rouletting. In a Sussex context, pottery of this type is well represented on sites in the Adur valley and in Chichester, the latter including a kiln-site at Chapel Street. It would thus appear that Sussex to the west of the River Adur mirrored ceramic developments across the border in Hampshire where similar wheel-thrown industries (Portchester and Michelmersh) emerged during the late Anglo-Saxon period (Gardiner 1993, 41).

Radiocarbon dating at Bishopstone provides a new fixed point for the introduction of these later wares in the eastern half of Sussex. This analysis raises the possibility that previous commentators may have been unduly conservative in suggesting a mid-10th-century date. Several of the pits sampled at Bishopstone returned calibrated date ranges (at the 95% confidence level) which do not extend beyond AD 900 (eg 3055, 2255, 2948, 6, and 2877; see Marshall *et al*, Chapter 8.2). The same features yielded a range of the commonest local coarsewares in both flint tempered and sandy fabrics, some displaying morphological and decorative traits (eg large cooking pots with sagging bases, some with developed rims others with pie-crust decoration) which would normally be dated to the 10th to 11th centuries (see Gardiner 1990, 251–2). A key context in this regard comprises the rapidly deposited destruction layers of cellared structure W (1167, 1344, and 1353). These produced a large assemblage of pottery in a fresh condition, including spouted pitchers in non-local Fabrics 12 and 26 (both closely related to products from the Adur valley and Chichester) alongside a restricted range of local coarsewares. Taking into account marine reservoir effects and the results of statistical modelling, the three radiocarbon dates obtained suggest that these layers could not have been deposited much later than AD 900 (all samples were taken from animal articulations to rule out residual contamination: Marshall *et al*, Chapter 8.3). Armed with this new dating evidence it is difficult to dismiss the possibility that the inception of these ceramic types could extend back to the beginning of the 10th century and perhaps even earlier. A larger sample of radiocarbon dates derived from an expanded range of sites, both urban and rural, is required to test the veracity of this proposed re-dating and to establish to what extent it is representative of developments in Sussex as a whole. Given the primacy of pottery as a tool for dating later Anglo-Saxon settlements, however, the implications of this suggested early chronology can hardly be ignored.

Conclusions: production, tradition, and trade

Whilst the precise location of a pottery workshop remains to be determined, it can be safely asserted that Bishopstone was producing its own range of coarseware jars and bowls using local sources of clay (Fabrics 1, 13 and 14). It thus remains one of only a handful of rural production sites of the later Anglo-Saxon period in south-east England which can be confidently localised. The evidence is equivocal, but it remains a possibility that the Bishopstone potters also produced a more specialised range of spouted pitchers of a general type also made in late Anglo-Saxon Chichester.

It has been suggested that the coarsewares made at Bishopstone were either made from London Clay obtained from Newhaven or clay-with-flints obtained from surrounding downland (Appendix 4). This raises the prospect of a transition in patterns of clay procurement during the Anglo-Saxon period for it has been suggested that the pottery from Rookery Hill was predominantly made from clays obtained from the Low Weald, north of the downland escarpment (Bell 1977, 126). A later shift in procurement regime may also be indicated by the supersession of Fabric 14 by Fabric 13 observed in the ceramic sequence from Bishopstone village, the latter being made from clay with a notably higher sand con-

stituent. These shifts, accompanied by technological refinements which resulted in more sophisticated vessel and rim forms, must in some way be related to wider socio-economic change over the Anglo-Saxon period as otherwise documented locally by the settlement shift from Rookery Hill to the site of the present-day village (see Chapter 9.4).

When integrated with other sites, the evidence garnered from Bishopstone enhances the impression that pottery within the eastern half of the South Saxon kingdom was embedded in localised networks of production. During the period covered by Bishopstone's occupation, this region most probably comprised a patchwork of household-scale industries based within river valleys and/or adjacent territorial blocks carved out of the coastal plain (Van der Leeuw 1976, 394). This fragmented pattern may be responsible for some of the observed distinctions in the ceramic landscape of later Anglo-Saxon Sussex; for example, the fact that stamping is more common to the west of the Adur valley, whereas stick-end decoration is dominant to the east (Jervis 2005, 4–6). In this sense, the consumption of pottery may have contributed to perceptions of local and/or territorial identity reproduced through daily activities within the domestic sphere of settlements (Symonds 2003, 216). Conversely there was clearly some level of contact between various production centres; each follows a broadly similar trajectory of development down through the later Anglo-Saxon period expressed in a fairly coherent ceramic zone which subsumes much of Sussex and neighbouring parts of Hampshire (Jervis 2005).

Beyond the locally produced coarsewares, there are ceramic types which attest to Bishopstone's integration within wider spheres of economic interaction and regional supply networks. One such includes the large, chalk tempered pitchers. Whilst it has not been possible to define a precise source and supply chain for these vessels, it is tempting to attribute their popularisation (if not their manufacture) to the expanding industrial base of nascent urban centres such as Chichester. A further potential product from a source in the west of Sussex is the smaller pitcher in Fabric 26, which perhaps attests to the coastal trade evidenced particularly clearly in the quern assemblage (see Barber this Chapter, Section 6.8 below).

The low quantity of continental imports recovered from Bishopstone mirrors the situation at other coastal and estuarine sites in Sussex including Botolphs (Gardiner 1990), Steyning (Gardiner 1993), and Pevensey (Lyne unpub). This argues against such sites being direct participants in cross-channel trade, indeed communities such as Bishopstone were more probably the recipients of imported by-products trafficked along the coast whether from larger ports of trade such as Hamwic or smaller beach markets – precisely the kind of trafficking evoked by Balgar's voyage as recounted in Drogo's *Historia* (see Chapter 3.2 & Appendix 1, Hodges 1981, 100; Brown 2002, 22). Imported pottery at Bishopstone may therefore have more to do with accessibility rather than with elevated socio-economic status. Perhaps more directly expressive of social status is the late Anglo-Saxon glazed ware which does genuinely appear to be consumed by the more affluent sectors of the urban and rural populace.

6.2   The hoard of ironwork
by Gabor Thomas and Patrick Ottaway

Introduction

The iron hoard recovered from Bishopstone comprises a remarkable collection of 25 complete objects, including rare – and in the case of the large mounted lock case – unique forms (Table 6.5). Yet its significance extends well beyond the realms of artefact typology. Amongst a select group of iron hoards known from the period (tabulated below), Bishopstone is one of only two (with St Saviourgate, York) to have benefited from modern scientific excavation. This has allowed its uniquely informative archaeological context to be maximised to the full with the result that it is possible to see the hoard's deposition as one of a series of events linked to the abandonment and dismantling of the cellared building. Furthermore, the event under consideration can be fixed in absolute terms by a robust *terminus ante quem* provided by the radiocarbon dating of multiple animal articulations contained within dumps of chalk rubble by which the hoard was sealed (see Marshall *et al*, Chapter 8.2). This contextual framework has not only called into question the traditional dating schemes attached to contemporary iron artefacts but also provided a platform from which to reassess the nature and meaning of later Anglo-Saxon iron hoards in general. As these themes

Table 6.5   Concordance of the contents of the Bishopstone iron hoard

Object no. appearing in Thomas 2009a	Concordance	Object description	Functional category (as appearing in Finds chapter)
1	44	Draw knife	Domestic tools
2	46	Claw hammer	Domestic tools
3	87	Wool comb	Textile manufacture
4	76	Sickle	Agricultural tools
5	77	Plough share	Agricultural tools
6	42	Knife	Domestic tools
7	64	Clench bolt	Structural fittings
8	65	Clench bolt	Structural fittings
9	66	Staple	Structural fittings
10	68	Hinge pivot	Structural fittings
11	69	U-eyed hinge	Structural fittings
12	70	U-eyed hinge	Structural fittings
13	71	U-eyed hinge	Structural fittings
14	72	U-eyed hinge	Structural fittings
15	73	U-eyed hinge	Structural fittings
16	75	U-eyed hinge	Structural fittings
17	74	U-eyed hinge	Structural fittings
18*	–	Strap terminal	Domestic fittings
19*	–	Strap terminal	Domestic fittings
20	51	Chain link	Domestic fittings
21	59	Barrel padlock	Domestic fittings
22	60	Barrel padlock fin	Domestic fittings
23	60	Barrel padlock fin	Domestic fittings
24	63	Mounted lock	Domestic fittings
25	109	Buckle	Equestrian equipment
26	111	Horseshoe (fragment)	Equestrian equipment
27	110	Horseshoe	Equestrian equipment

* Mistakenly attributed to the hoard = uncatalogued site find

**Table 6.6 British later Anglo-Saxon (or equivalent) ironwork hoards:
approximate numbers of tools and other iron objects: type of container, if any**

Site name	Tools	Other	Container	Reference
Asby, Cumbria	18	*c* 85	none recorded	Edwards 2002
Bishopstone	7	19	none	Ottaway in Thomas 2009
Crayke, N Yorks	15	14	none	Sheppard 1939
Flixborough, Lincs	14	1	2 lead tanks	Ottaway 2009
Hurbuck, Co Durham	14	5	none recorded	Hodges 1905
Nazeing, Essex	15	2	none recorded	Morris 1983
Stidriggs, Dumfriesshire	14	7	lead tank	Unpublished, pers comm M Haines
Westley Waterless, Cambs	3	2+	lead tank	Fox 1930
York, St Saviourgate	8	22	iron cauldron and lead tank	Unpublished, excavated MAP Archaeological Consultancy

have been examined in detail elsewhere (Thomas 2008), only a summary of the main arguments and conclusions is included here for the sake of brevity. We may commence by reminding ourselves of the circumstances of the hoard's deposition.

Circumstances of deposition

The hoard was discovered tightly crammed in a sub-floor post-setting in the south-west corner of the cellared building (Fig 4.36). As many of the objects formed a corroded mass (Plate 8) it is difficult to reconstruct the exact order of deposition, but it appears that the first to be buried in the north-west half of the posthole were the bifurcated hinge (73) followed one of the clench bolts (64 or 65), the sickle (76), the draw knife (44), the buckle (108), and the complete horseshoe (110). On the south-east side of the posthole was the lock (63) within a mass of corroded objects including most of the other items and the remainder of the U-eyed hinges.

On this evidence, it would appear that the items were placed directly into the post-setting without a container, as sometimes found in association with other iron hoards of the later Anglo-Saxon period (Table 6.6); the tightly crammed disposition of the locks and hinges rules out the possibility that they were buried *in situ* attached to a wooden box.

As we have seen (Chapter 4.1), the deposition of the hoard was sandwiched between two linked events associated with the abandonment of the cellared building: 1) the dismantling of the timber superstructure, part of which had succumbed to fire (as evidenced by the layer of charcoal covering the floor of the cellar strewn with iron structural fittings); and 2) the deliberate and rapid backfilling of the redundant void with dumps of chalk rubble intermingled, on the basis of a rich assemblage of artefacts and animal bone, with tips of domestic refuse (Fig 4.35). There is no reason to suggest that any appreciable period separated these two episodes.

Conclusion on the typological dating of the hoard

Iron objects are not usually susceptible to close dating, although form and, where relevant, decoration do change over time. In the case of the Bishopstone hoard all the items conform to types which were current during the late Anglo-Saxon period. Without the scientific evidence, a mid-10th- to early 11th-century date might have been suggested for the assemblage on the basis that the most closely datable parallels – including those for the distinctive barrel padlock with its fins and the hinges – come from large urban centres, most notably Winchester and York. Yet the *terminus ante quem* derived from radiocarbon samples recovered from the dumps sealing the Bishopstone hoard indicates that currency of these types must extend back into the 9th century. This is an important reminder that chronologies largely derived from urban contexts may be skewed. Urban expansion in most parts of late Anglo-Saxon England was very much a 10th-century and later phenomenon, as critical scrutiny of archaeological evidence has shown (Astill 2000).

Interpretation and meaning: iron hoards in later Anglo-Saxon England

Given that the Bishopstone hoard was buried beneath nearly two metres of chalk rubble it is very difficult to sustain the view that this cache was intended for later recovery – a view which is commonly expressed in discussions of comparable depositions whether interpreted as collections of tools or scrap metal or combinations of the two (Leahy 2003, 169–70; Cowgill 2009). As we shall see presently, this simplistic argument ignores persistent patterns in the siting of the hoards (including examples deposited in obviously watery contexts), and the significance of an association with lead tanks, both of which arguably carry strong ritual connotations. Moreover, the Bishopstone hoard suggests that collections of iron tools might embody rites of votive deposition enacted within the sphere of settlements, a ritual domain that has become an established focus of scholarly attention in the prehistoric and Romano-British periods and indeed on the early medieval continent, but which remains understudied in an Anglo-Saxon context (Hamerow 2006).

In pursuing a ritual dimension to the hoards under review it is important to acknowledge that the establishment of Christianity in Anglo-Saxon England did not bring about a swift and wholesale end to pre-conversion beliefs and traditions (Pluskowksi and Patrick 2003). On the contrary, various studies have shown that material and symbolic expressions of popular devotion and superstitious belief rooted in the pre-Christian past were given new meaning and significance and thus a new lease of life within a Christianised Anglo-Saxon milieu (see Jolly 1985; Niles 1991; Hollis 2001; Webster 2003; Blair 2005, 166–81). With this foremost in our minds we may turn to an evaluation of the evidence.

Find contexts

A key reason why a ritual context needs to be seriously considered in interpreting such hoards is that three of the group – Hurbuck, Westley Waterless, and Nazeing – were deposited in unambiguously watery contexts, the first in the bank of a stream, the second in marshland beside the River Lea, and the third deep within waterlogged clay (Hodges 1905; Morgan 1861; Fox 1923, 300; Morris 1983, 27). The link between hoards and watery locales is most familiar in a prehistoric context (Bradley 1998), but it should not be forgotten that the votive deposition of objects – particularly weaponry – in rivers persisted throughout the Anglo-Saxon period and indeed beyond (Hines 1997, 380–1; Halsall 2000, 267–8). A striking demonstration of this persistence is provided by the extraordinarily rich concentration of votive deposits – including such iconic Anglo-Saxon finds as the Witham hanging-bowl and the Witham pins – found in association with a ladder of fenland causeways flanking a stretch of the River Witham east of Lincoln (Stocker and Everson 2003). This work has demonstrated that each of the causeways attracted a remarkably long sequence of votive activity, in several cases extending from the Bronze Age through until the 14th century. What is particularly instructive about this case-study is that it demonstrates that the onset of Christianity had no diminishing effect on these traditions. On the contrary, it would appear that one of the key factors instrumental in promoting continued cycles of votive deposition into the later Anglo-Saxon period and beyond was a network of early churches deliberately sited to exploit the strong cultic resonances emanating from this landscape.

But what of the remaining hoards? A clear answer to this question is barred by the ambiguity surrounding the find contexts of older finds such as Asby (Cumbria), Crayke (North Yorks), and Stidriggs (Dumfrieshire). On the other hand, it would appear to be the case that St Saviourgate in York, Flixborough, Asby, and Crayke were (in a similar fashion to Bishopstone) deposited within the bounds of a contemporary settlement (Adams 1990; Edwards 2002; see Thomas 2008 for a full discussion of find contexts). Moreover, an evaluation of available contextual information suggests that three (Bishopstone included) were concealed either within or in close proximity to buildings of potentially focal/symbolic importance. One might be inclined to explain these collections in more prosaic terms than their counterparts deposited in watery locales, but to do so would be to ignore mounting evidence that, in common with Romano-British and prehistoric forebears, settlements of the Anglo-Saxon period attracted their own repertoire of ritual enactments, a theme explored further below (Hamerow 2006). Finally, it should be noted that Anglo-Saxon settlements also produce evidence for the deliberate concealment of smaller collections of iron, as in the case of a plough share and cauldron chain buried in a pit at Flixborough (Lincs) (Ottaway 2009d) and the selection of iron tools and other metalworking detritus concealed in the upper fill of a sunken featured building at Bloodmoor Hill, Carlton Colville (Suffolk) (Lucy *et al* 2009, 65, 427–8). These Anglo-Saxon examples recall a similar class of deposit recognised on sites of Iron Age and Romano-British habitation (Hingley 2006).

Association with lead tanks

The recent publication of a hoard of carpenter's tools from Flixborough (Lincs), buried in two lead tanks placed one inside the other, has stimulated fresh debate on the significance of such vessels in later Anglo-Saxon England; as Table 6.6 shows, the Flixborough find joins three other iron hoards of the period buried in similar containers. As we shall see, the significance placed on these vessels as containers for iron hoards is tempered by divergent views on their function prior to deposition. Such tensions find clear expression in the relevant chapter of the Flixborough volume (Cowgill 2009; Ottaway 2009). Noting a parallel use of a Christian monogram on the iron bell and the outer of the two lead vessels (symbolism shared by a square example buried in Willingdon marsh, East Sussex), Ottaway (2009, 261) entertains the idea that the hoard is a product of a Christian ritual, its deposition perhaps being linked to the completion of a probable timber church constructed on a site some 50m distant – the excavated footprint of Building 1a (Phase 3a) with its associated cluster of inhumation burials. Although not stated explicitly by Ottaway, this theory is perfectly reconcilable with the view that in life such lead tanks played a liturgical role as baptismal vessels (Blair 2005, 461–2, note 161).

Cowgill (2009) on the other hand argues that such vessels provided fixed storage for dry goods, more particularly seed grain, possibly held in standard measures which could imply a connection with the collection and/or redistribution of food renders. Under this interpretation, the depositional association between the iron tools and the lead vessels becomes purely incidental; the latter is a convenient container for the former and, on account of the intrinsic functional and material value of buried items, it is surmised that the deposit was made with full intention of recovery. We shall avoid getting embroiled in the details surrounding this functional hypothesis, not least because for the purposes of our argument there is no reason why objects with *domestic* connotations should not have been implicated in ritualistic performances.

Part of Cowgill's argument rests on the assumption that such vessels were a relatively common adjunct to the domestic sphere of later Anglo-Saxon settlements, at least in those areas where lead was freely available. A reason advanced for their under-representation in the archaeological record is that examples without tool hoards will have gone unreported in antiquarian records: the implication here is that the strong association between lead tanks and iron hoards that we see today is more apparent than real (Cowgill 2009, 270). To back up her argument further, Cowgill draws attention to a distinct concentration of unaccompanied lead tanks produced by excavated later Anglo-Saxon settlements in north-east Lincolnshire. Again, these examples are interpreted as unintended losses concealed in convenient locations within centres of habitation.

One of the problems with this approach is that it fails to examine the tanks, their depositionary context, and their association with iron hoards in a long-term perspective, without which we are essentially blind to the temporal persistence which epitomises deeply embedded ritualistic traditions. To take the last strand of Cowgill's argument, it may be noted that the lead tanks from Riby and Bottesford were deposited in ditch termini, a boundary context well known for its ritual associations in prehistoric Britain whether in conjunction with ceremonial monuments or settlements (Hill 1995; Bradley 2005; Hingley 2006). A similar insight is gained when the correlation between lead tanks and iron hoards is examined in a broader chronological context. For precisely the same association can be found in late Roman Britain. This cultural domain provides its own category of lead tanks, several examples bearing Christian iconography encouraging the view that they functioned as baptismal vessels (Petts 2003). The find contexts of these tanks, showing an obvious predilection for watery locales, displays a strong overlap with that of contemporary pewter and iron hoards and there is at least one case of such a vessel with an internal collection of iron objects providing a direct analogy for our later Anglo-Saxon examples (Petts 3003, 112–13). Admittedly, this Roman background does not necessarily help us to probe the *contemporary* symbolic meanings held by these deposits in later Anglo-Saxon England. But it does suggest that the association seen during this period is more than simply fortuitous. Given the prominence of tools amongst such depositions, it is tempting to assign the ritual significance of this combination to the cosmological aura surrounding smiths and other skilled craftsmen as holders of 'reserved' knowledge (Hinton 2003).

Bishopstone and ritual life on Anglo-Saxon settlements

A framework for understanding the Bishopstone hoard as a deposit with potential ritual connotations may be developed further by considering some of the implications of Hamerow's recent study of 'special deposits' encountered on early Anglo-Saxon settlements (Hamerow 2006). One of the themes to emerge from her provisional investigation is a preponderance of so-called 'closure deposits'; that is burials of animals, humans, and manufactured objects in contexts suggestive of a ritualistic act connected with the abandonment of a given structure. This pattern presents something of a contrast with related practices in adjacent parts of the early medieval continent where votive items – most conspicuously gold-foil figures placed in the foundations of focal buildings – form the commonest class of ritual deposit observed on contemporary settlements.

In spite of this divergence with other parts of early medieval north-west Europe, the former category of special deposit has clear resonances with rites of ritually enacted closure found on settlements in prehistoric Britain which in their turn have influenced the interpretation of placed deposits discovered beneath the floors of superimposed house-sequences characteristic of late Norse farmsteads recently excavated on the Outer Hebrides (Parker Pearson *et al* 2004). The meaning behind these domestic concealments has been informed by ethnographic studies attesting situations where the lifecycle of houses and their occupants become metaphorically intertwined (Brück 1999a). In such cases, the death of the prominent member of a community may be accompanied by the ritual destruction of a house; in this way cycles of abandonment and construction witnessed in the built environment of a settlement may become synchronised with the multiple biographies of its inhabitants.

This cosmological perspective may have relevance to the Bishopstone hoard whose deposition appears, on the grounds of supporting contextual information, to have been intimately connected with the decommissioning of the cellar which marked its permanent resting place – the final stage in a process of the abandonment which eradicated all traces of an imposing multi-storeyed timber structure.

An examination of the contents of the hoard can help to bring deeper meaning to this interpretation. One of the most conspicuous elements within the collection is the elaborate series of hinges and the lock furniture, both of which are sufficiently robust to have come from sturdy doors, entirely appropriate to the category of timber construction with secure underground storage hypothesised from the excavated footprint. If some of the items were indeed derived from the superstructure itself, then the deposition of the hoard could be seen as symbolic reference to the 'death' of what appears on the basis of spatial relationships and architectural grounds to have been a structure of focal importance within the excavated settlement complex. Indeed, taken a step further, it is possible to see the hoard's contents as not just one but rather a series of interlinked metaphors designed to symbolise the status and role of Bishopstone as an estate centre (for further examination of this theme, see Thomas 2008).

As an envoi to this discussion, it should be noted that a proportion of the 50 or so articulated or semi-articulated animal burials recovered from the excavations might also be explained in similar ritualistic terms. Perhaps the strongest claim relates to three largely complete skeletons of a dog, a cat, and a sheep – all juveniles and evidently without butchery marks, deposited within the chalk rubble infill of the cellar (Poole, Chapter 7.1). The intriguing implication of these burials when considered alongside the iron hoard is that the dismantling of the Structure W was marked by multiple, perhaps mutually reinforcing, acts of ritual closure.

6.3   Personal accessories and jewellery
(Figs 6.9–6.13)
by Gabor Thomas, with contributions by Patrick Ottaway and Steven Ashby

Disc brooch (Fig 6.9, no. 1)

The brooch decorated with a backward-looking animal motif represents a well-known variant of the diminutive base-metal disc-brooch popularised in late Anglo-Saxon England under continental Carolingian influence. It is clear that several variations on this specific zoomorphic design existed, some forming localised workshop groups such as that identified in respect of a concentration of near identical brooches from East Anglia (Smedly and Owles 1965). More recent finds reinforce the distributional bias highlighted in this early study, but the spread is now more widely diffused across eastern England, extending as far north as York (Mainman and Rogers 2000, 2571, fig 1267, nos 10428–30) and as far south as Kent. The Bishopstone brooch adds to a sprinkling of finds from central and southern England including Winchester and Oxfordshire (Hinton 1990e, 636, no. 2010, fig 170, note 8).

The Bishopstone specimen belongs to the plainer end of the range for it lacks the beaded border and the level of zoomorphic detail distinguishing mainstream expressions of this brooch style. Its closest

parallel comes from Dunwich, Suffolk (Smedley and Owles 1965, 174, pl XXVg), but given the internal variations within the class combined with its expanded distribution, one cannot discount a more local source of manufacture, perhaps the temporary abode of an itinerant craftsman. Stratified archaeological discoveries from Coppergate, York, support the view that the fashion for such brooches centred on the 10th century (Mainman and Rogers 2000, 2571).

1 Copper-alloy disc brooch. Cast with integral pin-loop and catch on the reverse. The front is decorated with a plain border enclosing a central motif in the form of a stylised backward-looking animal shown in profile. The beast has gaping jaws and a stubby tail but is otherwise distinctly featureless.
D. 20, Th. 2.5. B02, unstratified subsoil find

Annular brooch (Fig 6.9, no. 2)

The plain annular brooch belongs to a standard medieval type introduced during the 12th and common well into the 14th century (Egan and Pritchard 1990, 248, no. 1307, fig 160). It forms one of a selection of medieval small finds from the excavations derived either from unstratified levels or from superficial features such as postholes which attest to continued activity on the north side of the church, albeit of a different order of intensity to pre-Conquest occupation.

2 Copper-alloy brooch. Comprising a plain annular frame with a constriction to which is attached a copper-alloy pin.
D. of hoop 20, Th. 1.5, L. of pin 21. B05, SF 244, context 2833

Pendant (Fig 6.9, no. 3)

This object represents something of an oddity in a southern English context if the identification argued here is accepted. The only obvious parallels for this piece belong to the distinctive class of Thor's hammer pendant popularised in Viking-period Scandinavia, but also represented in burials and hoards located in eastern and northern England (Graham-Campbell 1980a, 156, no. 524; Biddle and Kjølbe-Biddle 1992, 48–50; Margeson 1997, 14). The majority of the excavated examples known are made of silver, but cheaper-quality versions in base metals have been brought to light by metal-detecting in East Anglia and other regions of the English Danelaw (eg Pestell 2004, 70, plate 4). Quite how this example arrived in coastal Sussex is impossible to determine, but one possible mechanism could be the attested Viking raids along the south coast in the 9th century and subsequently in the late 10th to early 11th centuries (Graham-Campbell 1980, 26–35).

3 Copper-alloy pendant. T-shaped with a circular hole for suspension. The lateral portion has a slightly concave

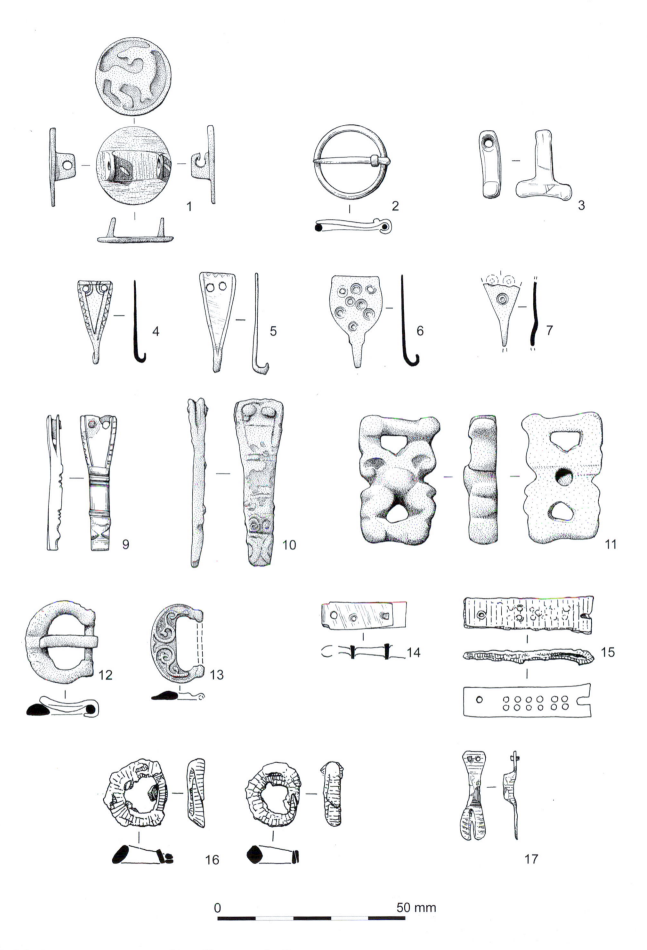

Fig 6.9 Dress accessories and jewellery, nos 1–17

bottom edge and appears to be crudely decorated with incised lines partly obscured by surface corrosion.
L. 19, W. 15, Th. 5. B05, no SF number, metal-detector find from spoil heap

Hooked-tags (Fig 6.9, nos 4–7)

The excavations yielded five hooked-tags, one of the commonest varieties of dress accessory in later Anglo-Saxon England (see Thomas 2009 for the latest discussion). There is some ambiguity as to their precise use; pairs found in coin-hoards indicate that one of their functions was to fasten purses, but the evidence from graves is more difficult to interpret and one recent commentator has questioned the orthodoxy that one of their main uses was to secure delicate items of costume such as garters (Owen-Crocker 2004, 154). After entering the repertoire in limited numbers during the 7th century, the incidence of hooked-tags increased during the 9th, after which they enjoyed widespread production until the end of the Anglo-Saxon era and possibly for a short period beyond. There is little chronological variation in form or decoration with the exception of fine-quality silver examples with nielloed decoration which appear to be restricted to the 9th and early 10th centuries, and rocker-engraving which is confined to the end of the series. The combination of circular and triangular hooked-tags in both copper-alloy and iron and with either simple incised or stamped decoration is typical of sites dating to between the 9th and 11th centuries; both Flixborough and Thetford provide comparable assemblages to Bishopstone (Thomas 2009; Goodall 1984).

4 Copper-alloy hooked-tag. With a triangular plate pierced with two attachment holes at the upper edge. The front surface is decorated with an incised double border along its tapering edges, the inner of which is plain, and the outer of which comprises a simple zigzag design. The inside line of the latter extends across the top edge of the plate where it intersects with paired concentric arcs forming a border for the attachment holes.
L. 22, W. 9, Th. 0.5. B03, SF1, unstratified metal-detector find from subsoil
5 Copper-alloy hooked-tag. With a triangular plate pieced with two attachment holes at the upper edge. The front surface is decorated along its tapering edges with an incised border whereas the top edge carries four V-shaped notches.
L. 26, W. 10, Th. 0.5. B05, SF121, unstratified metal-detector find from spoil heap
6 Copper-alloy hooked-tag. With a sub-circular plate squared off at the top edge pierced with a pair of attachment holes. The front surface is decorated with an asymmetrical arrangement of six punched ring-and-dots.
L. 23, W. 14, Th. 0.5. B04, SF139, context 1212
7 Copper-alloy hooked-tag. Fragment comprising hook and lower part of a triangular plate. The latter is decorated with a single centrally placed punched ring-and-dot.
L. 16, W. 9, Th. 0.4. B04, SF10, context 511
8 Iron hooked-tag (not illustrated). Triangular plate pierced twice for attachment. Top has four nicks cut into it.
L. 26, W. 10, Th. 2. B05, SF121, unstratified metal-detector find

Strap-ends (Fig 6.9, nos 9–10)

Bishopstone has produced two examples of a highly ubiquitous class of later Anglo-Saxon strap-end characterised by a split attachment end and an animal-head terminal, though the examples here also display the distinctive feature of a parallel-sided shaft (Thomas 2000; Thomas 2003a, Class B). This variant usually displays more restrained decoration than its popular, convex-sided counterpart; groups of transverse grooves or mouldings being a particular common treatment. The few examples of this type of strap-end bearing diagnostic animal ornament combined with stratified finds from Hamwic and Winchester, indicate a long currency stretching from the 8th century through until the 11th (Hinton 1990b; Thomas 2003a). In comparative terms this type is better represented in southern England than its convex-sided cousin, a distribution certainly skewed by multiple finds from Southampton, Winchester, and Canterbury which are likely to have been centres of manufacture (Hinton 1990b; 1996, 43, fig 17; Thomas 2000, 99–100). Strap-ends of this type are represented locally at Hamsey, the site of a possible pre-Conquest manorial complex located in the Ouse valley, north of Lewes (Thomas 2003b).

9 Copper-alloy strap-end. With a wedge-shaped split-end pierced by a pair of copper-alloy rivets for attachment and a parallel-sided shaft terminating in a stylised en-face animal head. The latter has lentoid eyes and a pair of arc-shaped incisions extending across the brow and snout; the ears are oval with lentoid incisions. The front surface of the split-end is decorated with incised outer borders. The object is complete, but detail is obscured by pitting and surface corrosion.
L. 45, W. 13, Th. 4.5. B05, SF15, context 2818
10 Copper-alloy strap-end. With a wedge-shaped split-end pierced by a pair of holes for attachment, the right-hand of which retains an iron rivet. The parallel-sided shaft terminates in a stylised en-face animal head featuring lentoid eyes and a squared-off snout. The front surface of the split-end is decorated with an incised and edge-nicked outer border whereas groups of transverse incisions mark the top and bottom of the shaft.
L. 35, W. 10, Th. 4. B05, SF249, unstratified metal-detector find

Buckles and strap-fittings (Fig 6.9, nos 11–17)

Object no. 11, whilst by no means expertly executed, represents an interesting addition to the morphological repertoire of minor objects decorated in the Winchester style (Wilson 1984, 154ff). Although highly stylised, the deployment of symmetrical plant-scroll issuing from a cat-like animal mask, with inhabiting creatures (if that is indeed the true identity of the opposing protrusions) executed in chunky openwork is an unmistakable Winchester-style combination. Crisper, more confidently executed versions of the same motif appear amongst the finer specimens of the series of tongue-shaped strap-ends from Winchester (Hinton 1990a), but it is usual (as here) to find it rendered in a more degenerate and visually compressed form (eg Kershaw 2008). Sussex represents something of a gap in the distribution of artefacts attributable to this 10th- to 11th-century artform, but this is almost certainly a reflection of the low densities of later Anglo-Saxon metalwork found in the county generally as opposed to a genuine regional difference in the popularity of the Winchester style (Thomas 2003b).

Unique to the corpus of Winchester-style metalwork, the function of the Bishopstone 'fitting' is less easy to establish than its art historical context. The closest morphological parallels of comparable date include a class of iron bridle-fitting represented at Coppergate, York, and indeed in the ferrous assemblage from Bishopstone itself (Ottaway 1992, 706, fig 307, no. 3849; see Ottaway, Chapter 6.5, no. 108). Copper-alloy strap-unions of not dissimilar form are also known from the immediate pre-Roman Iron Age in southern England (Hinton 1990d, 546, no. 1401, fig 63). It is equally plausible that the Bishopstone find functioned as a costume-fitting, perhaps as an accompaniment to a baldric.

The single copper-alloy buckle recovered from a surely stratified context, no. 12, with a loop of simple D-shaped form with a thickening for the pin, is a type manufactured throughout the Anglo-Saxon and medieval periods and is not therefore susceptible to close dating (Egan and Prichard 1990, 21–3; cf 89, fig 55, no. 392; Marzinzik 2003, 29–30). The remainder of the copper-alloy buckles and strap-fittings are all from unstratified contexts and belong to medieval types. Worthy of comment is the gilt example decorated with a foliate design, no. 13, with 12th- to 13th-century features comparable to the buckle recovered from a medieval settlement complex at Westbury-by-Shenley (Bucks) (Ivens *et al* 1995, 345, no. 56, fig 154.81).

Amongst the iron items within this functional category, there is a buckle which has a plated D-shaped frame, but no tongue surviving. It may, therefore, be an example of a belt-hasp, an object which joined one strap to another and is similar to a buckle but without a tongue. There are also three certain iron belt-hasps: no. 16 comprising two examples found fused together. All three are D-shaped, the curved side having a triangular cross-section. Surviving fragments of the fittings which attached them to a leather strap make it clear that there had not been a tongue. The discovery of two together may reveal that belt-hasps were usually used in pairs. Belt-hasps are probably identified as buckle frames in many cases, but there is another certain example from a late 11th- to 12th-context at Winchester (Hinton 1990c, 539–41, fig 143, 1350*)*.

No. 17 is a small plated fitting which was probably attached to a belt or strap, primarily for decorative purposes. It consists of a narrow raised component in the centre which probably had relief decoration on the surface, although this is now lost to corrosion.

This lies between two flat elements, essentially terminals. One is triangular and the other has convex sides and a central slot; on its surface are grooves in a chevron pattern. Fittings similar to this with opposed terminals either side of a raised component are not common in England but there are two from Coppergate, York, which exist as pairs riveted to each other and which originally gripped a leather strap (Ottaway 1992, 691–2, fig 299, 3795–6). However, on these objects the terminals are both triangular. In addition, there are two buckle-plates from Coppergate with the same basic design (*ibid*, 688, fig 296, 3746, 3759). Comparanda for these York objects have hitherto been found in areas of Viking settlement. They include a copper-alloy buckle-plate from Ardskinish, Colonsay (Grieg 1940, 61, fig 34), a copper-alloy fitting from Whitby (Peers and Radford 1943, fig 10, *4*) and a plated iron fitting from Dublin on display in the National Museum of Ireland. The Bishopstone object suggests that the basic design idea was not confined to the north and west of the British Isles.

11 Copper-alloy strap-fitting. Cast rectangular frame with a pair of attachment loops at the shorter sides. The swollen terminals of the latter conjoin with the exterior of a central motif executed in heavy relief with a pair of sub-triangular piercings. The design is centred on a stylised animal mask with a pair of curling foliate tendrils to one side and to the other a pair of indeterminate projections which could represent animal heads shown in profile.
L. 34, W. 21, Th. 9. B05, SF253, unstratified metal-detector find from spoil heap
12 Copper-alloy buckle-loop. Cast D-shaped loop with a thickened pin-rest opposing a constricted bar around which is secured a copper-alloy pin.
L. 19, W. 22, Th. 5. B05, SF206, context 2728
13 Gilt copper-alloy buckle-loop. D-shaped with a missing bar. The front surface is engraved with a delicate foliate design comprising looping plant tendrils, two of which terminate in trifoliate buds, reserved against a pointillé background.
L. 14, W. 21, Th. 2. B04, SF167, unstratified subsoil find
14 Copper-alloy belt-plate. Comprising a narrow sheet of metal folded over to create a housing for the missing buckle-loop. The plate is pierced by an axial alignment of three rivet holes, the outer pair of which retain their original copper-alloy rivets.
L. 23, W. 7, Th. 4. B05, SF2, context 2004
15 Iron buckle-plate, plated. Consists of two rectangular arms folded over the remains of a buckle at one end. Two rows of six indentations on the face of one arm. Pierced for attachment to a strap at the rear.
L. 68, W. 20, Th. 4. B04, SF157, context 1423
16 Iron belt-hasp. Two found fused together which had originally been held together by an iron fitting of which fragments survive. Both are D-shaped, the curved part has a triangular cross-section. Also both are flattened out on the straight side where there is a scarf weld. XRF shows they are tin-plated.
L. 34, W. 28, Th. 8. B04, SF154, context 1422
17 Iron strap-fitting. It has a raised area in the centre with terminals on either side. One is triangular and pierced twice, one rivet *in situ*. The other has convex sides and a central slot, at the head of which there was probably a rivet. Grooves in a chevron pattern. XRF shows this is tin-plated.
L. 47, W. 12, Th. 6. B04, SF15, context 1156

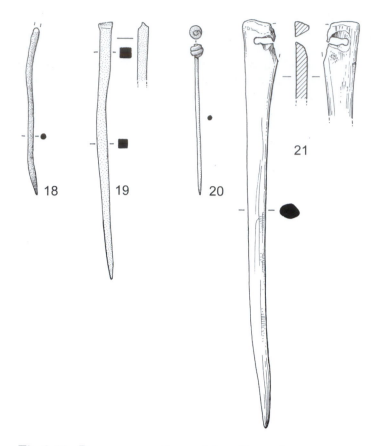
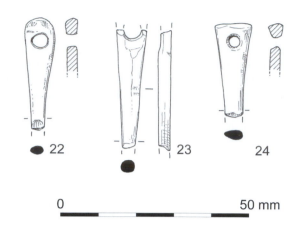

Fig 6.10   Dress accessories and jewellery, pins

Pins (Fig 6.10)

Copper-alloy pins (nos 18–20)

In spite of being a common form of later Anglo-Saxon dress accessory, there are at most only two copper-alloy pins represented at Bishopstone and both have missing heads. The first, no. 18, is more typical of pin-shafts of this period – with a collar at the top of the shaft. However the designation 'pin' can be applied only tentatively to no. 19 given that it is of square section; possible alternatives include a stylus or a nail. The remaining example, no. 20, with a twisted wire head, is considerably later for it belongs to a type mass-produced during the late medieval and post-medieval periods (cf Caple 1991; Egan and Pritchard 1990, 299–301, fig 200).

18 Copper-alloy pin-shaft. Of circular cross-section with a collar below the broken end.
L. 45, Th. 1.5. B05, SF113, context 2495
19 Copper-alloy ?pin-shaft. Of rectangular cross-section with the stub of a flattened projection at the head end.
L. 68, Th. 4. B04, SF131, context 1175
20 Copper-alloy pin. Composite with a straight shaft with an applied head of twisted flattened wire.
L. 40, Th. 3. B05, SF9, context 2001 (subsoil)

Bone pins (nos 21–4)

Pig fibulae pins are ubiquitous finds on later Anglo-

Saxon settlements. Amongst the four represented at Bishopstone, examples such as no. 21, with expanded triangular heads, would have served as dress pins; no. 22, of more slender proportions, could have functioned as a needle (MacGregor *et al* 1999, 1950–1, fig 909).

21 Complete but with a damaged head. Expanded head with a rectangular perforation, shank of oval section.
L. 108, Head W. 11, Th. 4. B04, SF137, context 1212
22 Head fragment. Expanded with circular perforation, shank of oval section.
L. 25, W. 10, Th. 4. B05, SF45, context 45
23 Head fragment, broken across perforation. Expanded head with circular perforation, shank of oval section.
L. 31, W. 8, Th. 4. B05, SF186, context 2647
24 Head fragment with circular perforation.
L. 30, W. 8, Th. 3. B05, SF63, context 2194

Finger rings (Fig 6.11)

Copper-alloy rings (nos 25–6)

Although not a common type, rings such as no. 25, featuring bevelled hoops with notched or punched decoration, are attested in stratified contexts securely dated to the late Anglo-Saxon period including 10th-century levels at Coppergate, York (Mainman and Rogers 2000, 2585, nos 10512, 10514, fig 1279). The plain example with twisted ends, no. 26, is a form commonly found on later Anglo-Saxon settlements,

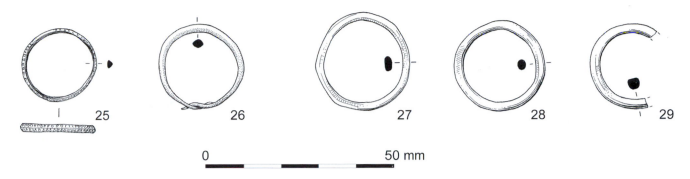

Fig 6.11 Dress accessories and jewellery, rings

particularly within urban environments as demonstrated by multiple finds from Coppergate, York, and Thetford (Mainman and Rogers 2000, 2583, no. 10499, fig 1278; EAA 22, 69, fig 110, nos 19 and 20). Whilst they are sometimes described as finger- or ear-rings, their use as suspension rings for tweezers and hones is also attested (Mainman and Rogers 2000, 2583).

25 Copper-alloy finger-ring. Comprising a hoop of triangular section with decoration either side of the medial apex comprising continuous rows of triangular notches.
D. 20, Th. 1. B05, SF102, context 2577
26 Copper-alloy ring. Plain band of circular section with tapering ends twisted over each other once to close the hoop.
D. 23, Th. 2. B05, SF128, context 3017

Bone finger rings (nos 27–9)

Somewhat surprisingly given the simplicity of their design, bone rings are a rarity on later Anglo-Saxon settlements so it is of interest that Bishopstone has produced three. One of the few places to supply parallels is Coppergate, York, where three plain examples were recovered from Period 5A (later 10th-century) deposits (MacGregor *et al* 1999, 1943, fig 903, no. 6802, 7698 and 7699). One further example, from a late 9th- or early 10th-century context, is recorded at Winchester (Biddle 1990d, 1136, no. 4391, fig 369). Given the rarity of the type, this distinctive element of Bishopstone's corpus of skeletal artefacts most likely denotes onsite manufacture.

27 Flattened section
D. 25, Th. 4. B05, SF81, context 2972
28 D. 24, Th. 2.5. B05, SF31; context 2873
29 Incomplete; D-shaped section.
D. 23, Th. 3. B05, SF39, context 2875

Bone combs (Fig 6.12, nos 30–3)
by Steven Ashby

No. 30 is a fragmentary bone-and-horn comb consisting of two straight strips of small mammal bone (split sheep ribs) fastened together with three sets of iron rivets, and decorated on both outer faces with cross-hatched decoration. Similar objects have frequently been referred to as 'riveted mounts'. Arthur MacGregor's detailed study of the collection from York (MacGregor *et al* 1999, 1952–4) demonstrated that these paired, rectangular strips of bone have a remarkably standardised morphology, and this also seems to be the case elsewhere in the British Isles. There seem to be two principal forms: a small type, measuring around 100mm in length, and secured with one iron rivet at each end; and a larger variant, around 150mm long, with an additional central rivet (see Biddle 1990b, 678–85 for a discussion). The present example clearly fits into the latter category.

Martin Biddle (1990b, 678–90) has suggested that 'riveted mounts' were the remains of bone-and-horn combs (being keratinaceous, horn is not well preserved in most sub-surface environments, leaving the more sturdy bone and iron components as the only surviving elements). The idea that these objects are the bone connecting plates/grips from combs with horn (or perhaps wooden) toothplates finds support from a number of pieces of evidence. First, several examples bear 'toothcuts' along their edges. Second, the few examples of connecting plates of this form that do preserve toothplates have toothplates of horn (see MacGregor 1985, 95). Third, the spacing of rivets (50mm or more) is too wide to secure toothplates of bone/antler (with the possible exception of the antler of the European elk *Alces alces*, which is not native to the British Isles, and for which there is no evidence of exploitation in early medieval England).

However, this explanation has not found widespread acceptance and MacGregor, in particular, has called for caution until further, more complete, examples are recorded (MacGregor *et al* 1999, 1952–4). Furthermore, the idea that these rather crude objects instead represent some form of industrial device has remained persistent. One suggestion is that they were used to secure antler blanks prior to toothcutting, thus facilitating the rapid, systematised production of large numbers of toothplates. This explanation is not satisfactory, as the iron rivet in the centre of the larger varieties would preclude easy insertion or removal of toothplates, and Biddle's suggestion is more parsimonious. A small number of decorated examples provide further support

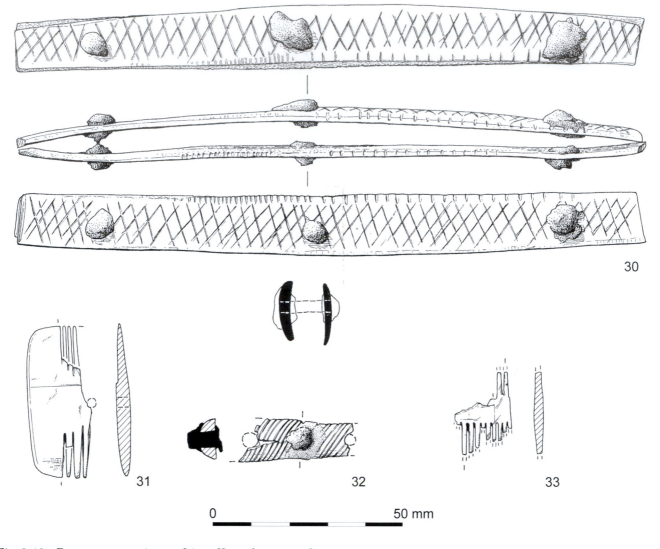

30

31   32   33

0 _____ 50 mm

Fig 6.12   Dress accessories and jewellery, bone combs

for 'riveted mounts' having some role in personal display, and it is difficult to conceive of the Bishopstone example in particular having a function in industry, rather than being used as a grooming implement and dress accessory.

A recent study of material from Viking Age and medieval northern Britain (Ashby 2006, 102; Ashby 2007, 2) took 'riveted mounts' as most likely to be the remains of bone-and-horn combs, and incorporated them into a typology of early medieval combs as 'Type 4'. Type 4 combs date to the period between the 10th and 12th centuries, and seem to be peculiar to the British Isles, with collections coming from the towns of Viking Age and late Saxon England (eg Mann 1982, 7–8; Biddle 1990b, 686–90; MacGregor *et al* 1999, 1952–4; Riddler 2004, 64). The Bishopstone example is thus unusual in that it is was found in a rural context. Moreover, it is a notable addition to the corpus, not only for its extensive decoration, but for the fact that its slightly curved back – which lacks toothcuts – might be taken to suggest that the comb was single-sided (that is to

say that the missing horn toothplate was equipped with teeth on only one edge). In this respect it is particularly interesting that the toothcuts visible on the extant connecting plates show a division into coarse and fine gauges. It seems that the comb was designed to fulfil the function of a double-sided comb, while adopting the profile of the single-sided variety.

Given that so few examples have been recorded with toothplates intact (see MacGregor 1985, 95), and that a number of the extant connecting plates lack toothcuts along either edge, it is difficult to comment on how many combs of this design may have been produced. Nonetheless, the Bishopstone example is interesting in that it may demonstrate that horn combs were being manufactured in a variety of forms, to suit a range of consumers, just as a number of designs of bone and antler composite combs seem to have been in circulation at any one time (Ashby 2006, 238–58). Nonetheless, Type 4's rather crude, standardised manufacture in easily available materials (postcranial bone and

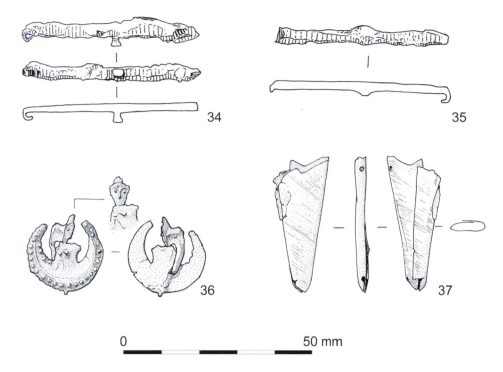

Fig 6.13 Dress accessories and jewellery, nos 34–7, various

horn rather than antler) and using only the most simple forms of ornament, is suggestive that these were combs for the less-discerning consumer. The presence of an example at Bishopstone is arguably suggestive of some level of contact with a larger town, perhaps Winchester or London.

Three other small fragments (nos 31–3) were recovered from the excavations, one from a single-sided and two from double-sided combs; all subscribe to standard early medieval types (see MacGregor 1980).

30 Fragmentary bone-and-horn comb consisting of two straight strips of small mammal bone (split sheep ribs) fastened together with three sets of iron rivets, and decorated on both outer faces with cross-hatched decoration. The rough knife/saw-cut ornament covers both faces, and is not disrupted by the presence of rivets, suggesting that decoration preceded final construction. Toothcuts are visible on one edge of both plates, and on each plate they are split into two gauges: a coarse gauge (*c* four teeth/10mm), and a finer gauge (*c* eight teeth/10mm).
L. 168, W. 16, Th. 10. B04, SF103, context 2947
31 Double-sided composite comb end plate fragment. Squared, teeth graduated in length towards end of plate, four teeth per 10mm.
L. 17, W. 40, Th. 4. B05, SF247, context 2389
32 Composite single-sided bone comb side plate, burnt and fragmentary. Tapered and of plano-convex section with central *in situ* iron rivet flanked by two further rivet holes at the broken edges. The front surface is decorated with a pattern of closely spaced diagonal lines running the full width of the plate.
L. 30, W. 12, Th. 4. Rivet spacing centre to centre: 1.3. B04, SF18, context 549
33 Double-sided composite comb toothplate fragment. Seven teeth per 10mm on one side; other side indeterminate.
L. 15, W. 21, Th. 2. B04, SF4, context 1111

Purse mounts (Fig 6.13, nos 34–5)

These two iron objects, both probably tin-plated with small loops at each end, are best interpreted as purse mounts. In use the purse bag hung from the end-loops and the purse was then suspended from the owner's belt by means of a short projection in the centre of the mount. In each case this is burred over at the top as if to retain a small ring or loop. There appear to be no similar objects from the later Anglo-Saxon period, although they are similar in conception to purse mounts of the early Anglo-Saxon period found, on occasions, in inhumation graves. Another object rather more similar in form to those from Bishopstone, but existing as an elongated lozenge shape rather than a strip comes from Yeavering (Hope-Taylor 1977, fig 87). In the medieval period the purse mount became a frame for the bag and usually had a swivel ring set in the top for attachment to the belt.

34 L. 92, W. at centre 5. B05, SF218, context 3166
35 Some indication on X-radiograph of grooves around one end.
L. 97, W. at centre 5. B05, SF220, context 3116

Pilgrim badge (Fig 6.13, no. 36)

No. 36 belongs to an established class of medieval pewter pilgrim badge depicting the Virgin and Child set within a crescent moon (Spencer 1998, 149–152, no. 159a). The shrine to which this imagery refers remains obscure, but may well have been that of Our Lady of Willesdon, as supported by the discovery of over 300 standardised finds from sites in and around medieval London. These archaeological discoveries, combined with other iconographic sources, suggest that her cult flourished for a brief period in the years around 1500. The Bishopstone find, alongside others from Salisbury and Canterbury, is one of only a handful of such badges to have been recovered outside the capital.

36 Pewter badge. Crescent-shaped with a laterally projecting pin on the reverse. The front of the badge is decorated with borders of raised pellets and a stylised human figure wearing a crown with the broken stub of a second figure to its left.
D. 20, Th. 2. B04, SF164, context 1162

Dagger chape (Fig 6.13, no. 37)

This object is representative of a common form of chape specifically used in association with leather dagger sheaths; finds from urban centres such as London and York indicate a 14th- to 15th-century date-range (Ward Perkins 1940, 281; Ottaway and Rogers 2002, 2904, fig 1478).

37 Tinned copper-alloy chape. Comprising a piece of sheet-metal folded over at the reverse and tapered to a point. The upper edge is damaged but appears to have been V-shaped; the preserved, left-hand portion retains a small attachment hole at the side in the fold of the metal.
L. 35, W. 13, Th. 3. B05, SF1, context 2004

6.4   Domestic tools and implements
by Patrick Ottaway and Luke Barber

Iron knives (Fig 6.14, nos 38–42)

There are thirteen tanged knives, most of them very typical in form for the later Anglo-Saxon period with representatives of the two main blade types identified at Anglo-Scandinavian York (Ottaway 1992, 561–72). In nine cases the form of the blade is clear. No. 38 has the angle-back blade seen on large single-bladed weapons or seaxes, but also common on small knives. It occurs, for example, on *c* 19% of knives from Anglo-Scandinavian contexts at 16–22 Coppergate, York (*ibid*, 562–4). On the Bishopstone example the back rises from the shoulder (*ibid*, Back Form A2). There is also a slightly larger knife with a similar angle-backed blade. There is a groove incised into the top of both blade faces of no. 38 and the other knife running between the angle and the shoulder. Such grooves can be seen on many Anglo-Saxon knives and they occur in various patterns, although one on each face is the commonest (*ibid*, 579–81); the knife in the hoard appears to have two on the same blade face.

Seven knives have blade backs which are straight before curving down to the tip. In four cases the back appears more or less horizontal when the blade is viewed in relation to a line passing from the tip of the blade to the tip of the tang. The exact form of no. 41 cannot be determined accurately because the

blade end is missing. This appears to have been a relatively large knife, as its blade is 20mm wide and as much as 138mm long with its end missing.

Blades of this basic form are by far the commonest in Anglo-Saxon contexts and those with a horizontal back are the commonest variant (*ibid*, 568–70; Back Form C1). However, those with a downward slope (*ibid*, 570; Back Form C3) are only common in contexts of the late Anglo-Saxon period and it has been suggested (*ibid*, 570) that these are heavily worn versions of knives with a horizontal back which were created as a result of changes in metallographic structure in the early 10th century. The introduction of a blade with a steel core as opposed to a steel edge may have allowed knives to be more heavily worn before being discarded.

Finally, no. 41 is also of interest because it has a preserved portion of a wooden handle encircled by four copper-alloy bands immediately behind the blade. This is not a common feature, the only known parallels coming from late 11th- to mid-13th-century contexts. In spite of these associations, there is no reason to doubt the existence of similar handles at an earlier period in light of the fact that the Bishopstone knife was recovered from a securely stratified context also yielding a 10th-century penny unlikely to have been discarded much later than *c* AD 960 (see Archibald, this chapter 6.12). A knife from an 11th- to 12th-century context at Winchester (Victoria Road site, Rees *et al* 2008, fig 175, 2244) had discs of horn between the non-ferrous discs on the handle. There is also another Winchester example with just the metal discs surviving (Crowder Terrace site, *ibid*, 319, 2273). Comparable examples from Goltho are dated 1000–1080 (Goodall 1987, fig 157, 64–5*)* and from London examples are dated to the early to mid-13th century (Cowgill *et al* 1987, fig 54, 15).

The following select catalogue follows the categories for blade back types as per Ottaway (1992, 561–72).

A2: back slopes upward from shoulder before sloping down to the tip

38 A groove is incised into top of both blade faces between angle and shoulder. Cutting edge is slightly convex. Tang largely missing.
L. 91; blade: L. 85, W. 15, Th. 3. B05, SF105, context 2577.
Illustrated

C1: back straight and horizontal before curving down to the tip

39 Blade and tang complete. Cutting edge slightly S-shaped.
L. 92; blade: L. 68, W. 10, Th. 4. B04, SF152, context 1184.
Illustrated
40 Blade and tang complete. Cutting edge straight before curving up to the tip which lies on blade mid-line. Remains of handle survive as mineralised wood on the tang.
L. 79; blade: L. 47, W. 10, Th. 2. B04, SF158, context 1435.
Illustrated

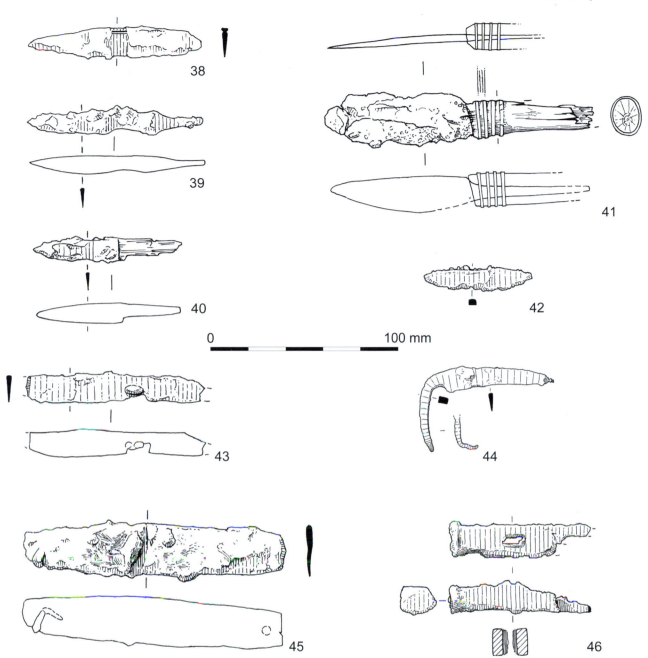

Fig 6.14   Domestic tools and implements, nos 38–46, various

C indeterminate: back straight before curving down to the tip

41 The end of the blade is missing. Tang is probably complete; the handle is missing but in the corrosion products, four non-ferrous discs set on the tang survive. L. 138, blade: L. 76, W. 20, Th. 4. B05, SF107, context 2386

Blade form indeterminate

42* Tang missing. Corrosion obscures form of the blade back. Cutting edge appears straight before curving up to the tip.
L. 77, W. 14, Th.5. Hoard no. 7

Pivoting knife (Fig 6.14, no. 43)

No. 43 is of usual Anglo-Saxon form with two blades, one on each side of a slightly off-centre pivot which is in a U-shaped area flanked by two inverted U-shaped notches between the cutting edges. When a blade was in use the notch on the opposite side of the pivot rested on a rivet which was also one of two holding the sides of the handle-cum-case together; this rivet counteracted the upward pressure on the blade's cutting edge (Ottaway 1992, 586–7, fig 243). These knives usually have one blade with an angle back, but the other can have a back which is either convex and curves down to the tip or is, as in the case of no. 43, slightly concave. The former is usual in the mid Anglo-Saxon period, but the latter becomes common in the later period as can be seen on three from York (*ibid*, 586–8, fig 244, 2976–8) and two from Thetford (Goodall and Ottaway 1993, 112–14, fig 127, *146*, fig 128, 152).

Pivoting knives appear to be an introduction of the mid Anglo-Saxon period and remained current in the later, but there are no examples securely datable to the post-Conquest medieval period. Their function is unknown, although Biddle (1990c) has suggested they were used by scribes. Except for two from a grave at Middle Harling, Norfolk (Margeson 1995, 79–80, fig 76, 4–5), they usually occur on occupation sites. They may have had some craft purpose, although a wide variation in size, *c* 100–180mm in length suggests there may have been more than one purpose.

43 The tips of both blades are missing. One has an angle back and the back of the other becomes slightly concave after a short step down from the central part.
L. 94, W. 16, Th. 4; angle-back blade: L. 36. B04, SF118, context 1296

Drawknives (Fig 6.14, nos 44–5)

Whilst of differing form, nos 44 and 45 both probably functioned as drawknives – a tool used for finishing objects by chamfering, rounding, trimming, and so forth. The example from the hoard shows signs of heavy use, leaving the blade asymmetrical. There is only one other known Anglo-Saxon parallel (similar tools were in use in the medieval and post-medieval periods) from Sandtun (Kent) (Wilson 1968, 148). However, shaves which have tanged U-shaped blades and were used in much the same way as a drawknife come from a mid Anglo-Saxon hoard at Flixborough (Ottaway 2009c) and an Anglo-Scandinavian context at 16–22 Coppergate, York (Ottaway 1992, 531–2, fig 206, 2259). The site find is flat and pierced at each end for attachment to a handle by means of nails. Comparable finds of the mid Anglo-Saxon period come, *inter alia*, from Butley Hill (Suffolk) (Fenwick 1984, 40, fig 4) and Riby (Lincs) (Ottaway 1994, 251–2, 257, illus 14, 22). There are also Anglo-Scandinavian (late 9th- to 10th-century) examples from 16–22 Coppergate, York (Ottaway 1992, 589, 2982) and Repton (Derbys), (unpublished, excavated by M Biddle and B Kjølbye-Biddle, sf 3331 and sf 5708).

44* Drawknife. Incomplete, one tang missing. The blade is worn asymmetrically, narrowing towards the missing tang. There is a slight step in the cutting edge below the surviving tang which is clenched at tip.
L. 117; blade: W. 19, Th. 6; tang: L. *c* 62. Iron hoard no. 1
45 In two pieces. A flat blade the back of which rises from each end to the centre. One end is rounded and the other straight. Pierced at each end, one hole has a small nail *in situ*.
L. 136, W. 26, Th. 4. B05, SF92, context 2945

Hammer (Fig 6.14, no. 46)

A versatile carpenter's tool, the principal function of the claws being to draw nails from wood during dismantling of furniture, structures, and other wooden objects; it could also be used by a farrier when extracting horseshoe nails. Although one would have thought this a useful item, only two others are known from later Anglo-Saxon contexts, both from Goltho (Goodall 1987, 177–8, *5–6*). Another from a late 11th-century context comes from Winchester (Goodall 1990a, 273, 276–7, fig 60, *400*).

46* Iron claw hammer head. In profile the rear is straight. The front is straight below the head before a slight triangular projection in the centre where the eye is located, and it then slopes inwards to the claw tips. Head is burred with use and one claw is missing. Eye is rectangular.
L. 101; claw: L. 25, W. 22, Th.17. Iron hoard no. 2

Wedges (not illustrated)

There are six small iron wedges which would have been used either for splitting timber during woodworking or to hold tool handles in place, as can be seen, for example, on a late Anglo-Saxon axe from London (Pritchard 1991, 135, fig 3.14, *26*). Wedges are common objects in Anglo-Saxon contexts, although their simple form means that they sometimes go unrecognised.

Awl (not illustrated)

This tool, of which only a single example is represented in the Bishopstone iron assemblage, might have been used for leatherworking or piercing tasks in other crafts such as woodworking.

Shears (not illustrated)

A single incomplete shears blade with a stub of tang was recovered from the excavation. This may have been used in a craft context for leatherworking or textile manufacture.

Hones and grinding stones (Fig 6.15, nos 47–50)
by Luke Barber

Fourteen hone fragments were recovered from the site, the majority of which are of Wealden sandstones. Two pebbles appear to have been utilised for sharpening or polishing (eg a Wealden sandstone example from lynchet 69) and at least one large (1514g) Wealden sandstone piece shows signs of having been used as a stationary sharpening stone judging by the wear on one of its faces (context 516). It is possible that pieces such as this utilised

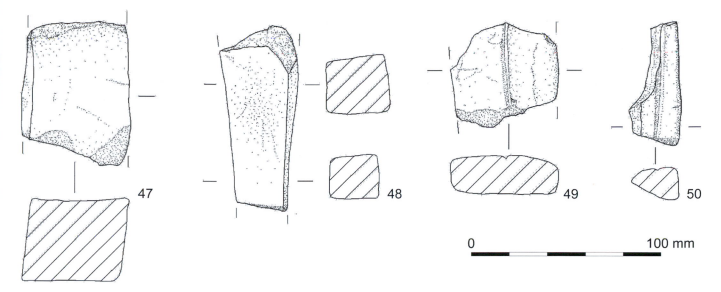

Fig 6.15 Domestic tools and implements, hones and grinding stones

ship's ballast to create sharpening stones and it is interesting to note the presence of a 356g block of Thanet-type sandstone in wall-trench 2443 which may have been intended for such use.

The remaining regional hone type consists of examples which have been deliberately shaped to form elongated tapering stones with square or rectangular sections. These are likely to have been made at the source of stone and traded as hones rather than created on site. Such stones are common in post-Conquest deposits in the region and the Wealden sandstone examples are thought to derive from the Hastings area (Barber forthcoming). Two of the most complete examples of this type are nos 47 and 48. An example in Thanet-type sandstone, no. 49, is only one of two from the site with sharpening grooves.

The only definite hones from outside the region consist of a D-sectioned stone fragment in schist probably from Devon/Cornwall (not illustrated) and no. 50 made from Norwegian ragstone. Norwegian ragstone hones first appear in 10th-century deposits in London though they become far more common after the Conquest (Pritchard 1991, 155).

47 Hone fragment; Wealden sandstone. Rectangular with parallel sides and a sub-square profile.
L. 76, W. 50, Th. 44. B05, context 2040
48 Hone fragment; Wealden sandstone. Of square section with a pronounced taper made concave through use.
L. 90, W. 28–40, Th. 22–30. B05, context 2911
49 Hone fragment; Thanet-type sandstone. Rectangular in section with slightly tapered sides and with a medial groove on one surface.
L. 54, W. 56, Th. 20. B03, context 89, unstratified subsoil find
50 Hone fragment; Norwegian ragstone. Irregular form with a sharpening groove on one surface.
L. 66, W. 24, Th. 16. B03, context 7

6.5 Domestic fixtures and fittings
by Patrick Ottaway

Chain link (Fig 6.16, no. 51)

Of the two discovered, the larger no. 51, from the hoard, is probably a link from a large chain of the sort that would be used to suspend a cauldron over the hearth. Links of similar basic form, albeit with a spirally twisted shank, were found in the complete cauldron chain of mid Anglo-Saxon date from Flixborough referred to above (Ottaway 2009a, sf7107).

51* Found fused to U-eyed hinge no. 12. A curved strip of square cross-section with a looped eye at each end, which face opposite ways.
L. 180, Th. 10; eyes: 27 × 24. Hoard no. 18

Pot hook (Fig 6.16, no. 52)

No. 52 was used to suspend a cooking vessel over a fire and originally hung at the end of a chain. There is a loop for attachment to the chain at the head of the shank. The hook is U-shaped and its tip is curved outwards. Similar, if slightly smaller, pot hooks are found in later Anglo-Saxon contexts elsewhere. Amongst thirteen mid Anglo-Saxon examples from Flixborough there is one (sf 3129) which has a hook closely comparable to no. 52 (Ottaway 2009a). Other examples of similar pot hooks from late Anglo-Saxon contexts include one from Coppergate, York (Ottaway 1992, 652, fig 277, 3565) and another from North Elmham (Norfolk) (Goodall 1980, 514, fig 267, 91). The excavations produced a second pot hook, though of considerably smaller dimensions (B04, SF48).

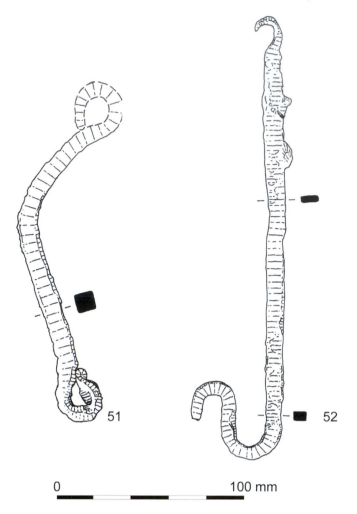

51   52

0   100 mm

Fig 6.16   Domestic fixtures and fittings, nos 51–2, chain link and pot hook

52 Looped at head of shank. Hook U-shaped and the tip recurved outwards.
L.232, T.10; hook: W.50. B04 SF27, context 1364

Casket fittings (Figs 6.17–18)

There is a range of what were probably iron casket or box fittings from the site existing as hinges and pierced strips and plates. They include, first of all, what is probably a more or less complete set of plated fittings from a casket which had itself not survived, no. 53, the lock and lock plate of which are described below. They are all heavily corroded and fragmented, and have been largely studied from X-radiograph. There are four small cross-shaped fittings, formed from two strips welded together. Three arms of the cross have, or in two cases had, rounded terminals. In addition there is a small drop handle with looped terminals each of which is linked to a tiny U-shaped fitting with pierced oval terminals by which the handle was fitted to the top of the casket. Other pieces include a strip which

narrows to a rounded terminal at one end and is broken at the other. Some of the other fragments are pierced.

The other small plated casket fittings represented at Bishopstone are common in late Anglo-Saxon and equivalent contexts and occur in a great diversity of forms. Tinned Y-shaped fittings such as nos 55 and 56 were probably fitted to the lid of a casket; they each have a loop by which they were linked to another strap set on the back of the casket. Similar objects occur in an Anglo-Scandinavian context at York (Ottaway 1992, 631, fig 255, 3393, and 3395) and in a late 11th- to 12th-century context at Winchester (Goodall 1990c, 788, fig 229, 2444).

Small hinge fittings (Fig 6.18, nos 54–6)

54 A U-shaped loop, one arm of which – now broken – widens and the other becomes a rounded terminal. Ends of both arms are pierced with rivets *in situ*, the heads on the inner side. Linked to a strip – incomplete – with D-shaped loop at head. XRF shows it is tin-plated.
L. 24; Strip: L. 27, W. 16. B05, SF123, context 2295
55 Y-shaped strap with curving arms of which the tip of one is missing, but the other is rounded and pierced. Pierced below the arms. There is a loop at the base which is linked to a strap with a loop at the head. This second strap is pierced at the base (and near loop?), rivet *in situ*. XRF shows it is tin-plated.
L. 41, W. (below arms) 11; second strap: L. 32, W. 10. B05, SF145, context 2295
56 Originally Y-shaped with a loop at base. The stem is pierced at the base of the arms. One arm is incomplete, the other is bent and damaged, but had a polygonal and pierced terminal. There are small V-shaped nicks in the edge on one face below the arms. XRF shows it is plated with tin-lead alloy.
L. 64, W. (at base of arms) 12. B05, SF238, context 2995

Bone casket mount (Fig 6.18, no. 57)

Bone mounts such as no. 57, a ubiquitous class of find on late Anglo-Saxon settlements, were used as decorative appliqués for wooden caskets. A fine selection of such mounts, including the rare survival of an array still attached to a casket lid have been produced by sites in Anglo-Scandinavian York (MacGregor *et al* 1999, 1954–60, fig 915).

57 Bone casket mount. A fragmentary piece of mammal rib decorated on both faces with a row of closely spaced ring-and-dots.
L. 40, W. 15, Th. 5. B04, SF2, context 501

Locks and key (Fig 6.18–6.20)

Key (no. 58)

The only key from the site is no. 58 which has a pear-shaped bow formed in one piece with a solid stem, the tip of which projects beyond the bit. This

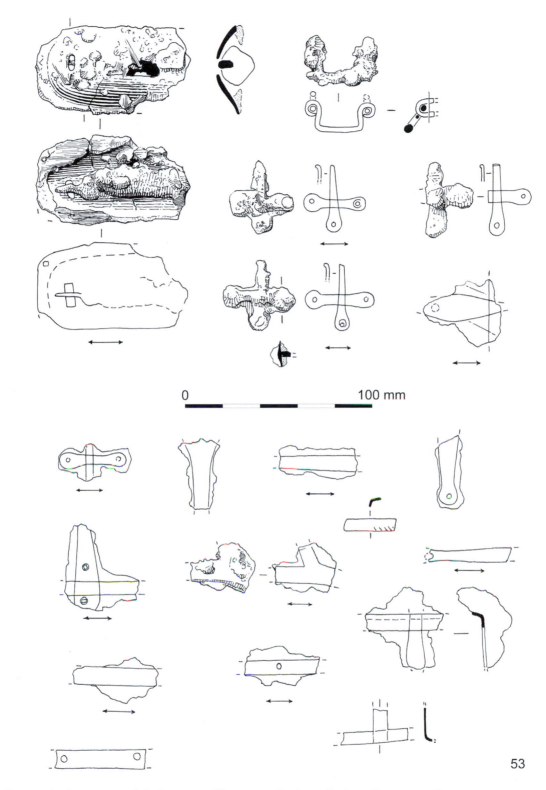

Fig 6.17   *Domestic fixtures and fittings, no. 53, composite iron fittings from a casket*

last feature and the fact that the bit probably curved over into two short prongs indicate that the key was used with a lock which had a bolt governed by leaf springs of the type exemplified by the large chest lock from the hoard. Locks of this type appear to be a development of the 9th century and remained current until the 11th. Similar keys to no. 58 come, for example, from 10th- to 11th-century contexts at

Winchester (Goodall 1990d, 1007, 1024–5, fig 325, *3731–8*).

58 Bow is pear-shaped and formed in one piece with a solid stem the tip of which projects beyond the bit. Bit has a cut in each side and the base is curved over into two prongs.
L. 90; bit: L. 9, bow: W. 29;. B05, SF52, unstratified metal-detector find from spoil heap

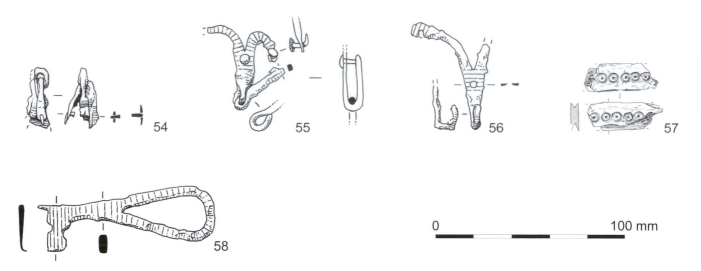

Fig 6.18   Domestic fixtures and fittings, nos 54–8, casket fittings and key

Barrel padlocks (Fig 6.19, nos 59–62)

The barrel padlocks from Bishopstone, of which there are three complete examples together with other fragments, display two diagnostically Anglo-Saxon features. First, the end plates are welded to the cylinder and project beyond it slightly, rather than being recessed into the cylinder as appears to have become standard in England by the later 11th century. Second, the free arm tube is welded directly on to the cylinder, rather than separated from it by a narrow plate. The full size-range is represented. No. 59 from the hoard is a relatively large example for the Anglo-Saxon period, the cylinder being 130mm long, whereas no. 62, at only 34mm long, is the smallest padlock of the later Anglo-Saxon period yet known. The context in which the large example was used was most probably either a large chest or a door fastened by a hasp and staple whilst the smaller may have been used in association with a delicate casket. A feature shared by the three examples, but seen most clearly on no. 59 from the hoard, is flanking spirally twisted strips, the function of which was to reinforce the cylinder. In the case of this last example, additional strength was provided by fins of elongated triangular form, the tips of which fit into holes in the end plates. Two other fins (no. 60) were found in the hoard, one of which was fused to the lock case (no. 63), and these are the right size to have come from this padlock. It would appear that they had been deliberately removed before deposition.

Anglo-Saxon padlocks were usually plated with brass or a similar copper alloy; it has not been tested in this case, although the X-radiograph suggests plating may survive. There is a fin of indeterminate form welded onto the free arm tube of no. 62. XRF analysis shows no. 62 is plated with a copper-tin alloy (probably a form of brass), as is usual on padlocks of the Anglo-Saxon period. Similar padlocks, with fins, have been found in contexts dated to the late 10th to 11th centuries from St Peter's, Northampton (Goodall *et al* 1979, 268–9, fig 116, 3) and Christchurch, Dorset (Goodall 1983, fig 34, 46). Two detached padlock fins come from mid- to late 10th-century contexts at Winchester (Goodall 1990d, 1001, 1008–9, fig 311, 3638–9).

59* Near complete. The end plates are roughly egg-shaped; they are welded/brazed to the end of the cylinder and project from it slightly. At the key-hole end there is a projection from the end plate with a recess to accommodate the mouth of free arm tube. Either side of the free arm tube a spirally twisted strip is welded on to the cylinder. In addition, an elongated triangular fin is set on one side of the cylinder with its tips fitted into holes in the end plates; originally there was clearly another opposite it and probably a third opposite the free arm tube so that the three were evenly spaced around the cylinder.
L. 130, W. (at key-hole end) 63, W. (cylinder) 43
60* (not illustrated). Fins probably from padlock 60, one of which was found fused to lock 63.
61 Bolt *in situ*. Case has five additional strips, probably spirally twisted, welded on to it, the tips of at least three of which are set in the end plates. XRF shows copper-tin alloy plating.
L. 34, W. 24. B04, SF23, context 1168
62 Bolt missing and both ends of case damaged. The case has three additional strips probably spirally twisted, welded on to it whose tips are set in the end plates. A fin of indeterminate form is welded onto the free arm tube.
L. 98, W. 31. B04, SF55, context 1344

Fixed locks (Figs 6.17, no. 53 and Fig 6.20, no. 63)

The lock in its case, no. 63 (Fig 6.20), recovered from the iron hoard, is a most remarkable object to which there appears to be nothing else exactly comparable from the Anglo-Saxon period. The case is almost semi-circular with a straight top. It bellies out to accommodate the mechanism within and has a flange around the edge through which it was nailed to the front of a chest. Some parts of the flange are missing, due largely to corrosion rather than the

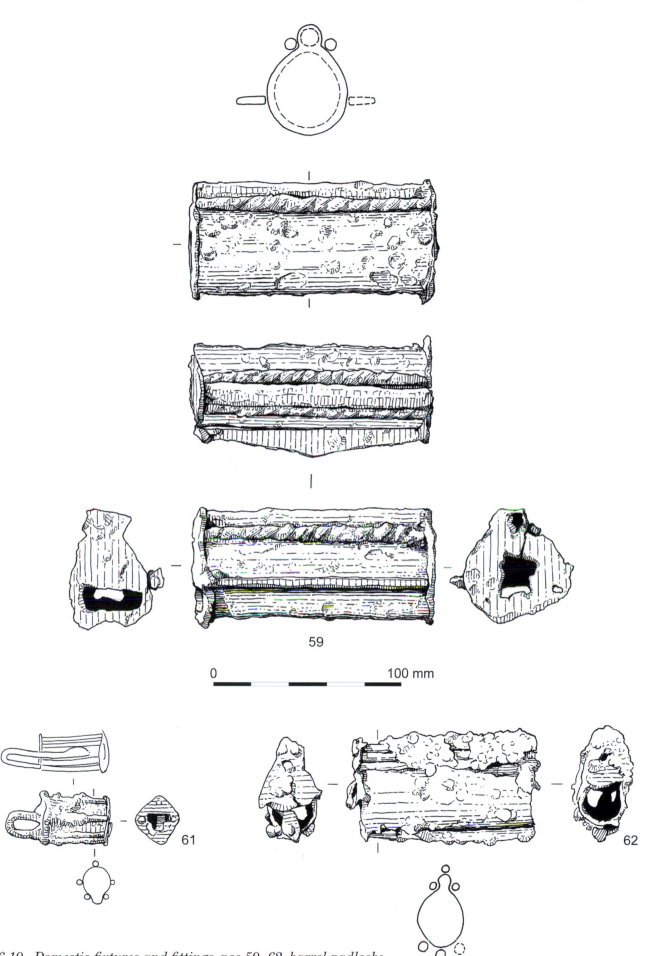

Fig 6.19 *Domestic fixtures and fittings, nos 59–62, barrel padlocks*

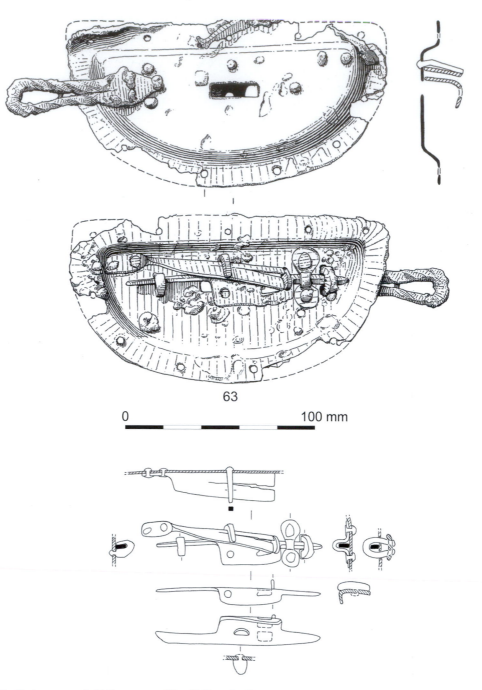

Fig 6.20   Domestic fixtures and fittings, no. 63, sliding lock

damage which might have occurred in removing it from a chest. The mechanism consists of a sliding bolt in the locked position, engaged in the staple of a stapled hasp. The bolt is governed by leaf springs set such that their faces lie in the horizontal plane and thus at 90° to the front of the chest. Operation of the lock required a key, firstly, with a bit pierced in the centre to fit over the short ward projecting from the underside of the bolt, and, secondly, teeth at the end of the bit capable of projecting through slots in the bolt, releasing the leaf springs and moving the bolt such that it disengaged from the hasp.

What is curious is that the staple is set *transversely* on the hasp such that the hasp lies in line with the

bolt. What one would expect is that the hasp would have had a staple set *in line* with its longer axis allowing the hasp to be fixed on the lid of the chest so that it could be raised and lowered as required for locking and unlocking. It is possible that the Bishopstone lock case was fitted on the chest such that the bolt moved up and down rather than from side to side. However, I know of no other example of a lock in which the bolt would have moved in this way. What is most likely is that there was a chain link (or links) attached to the hasp which was fitted to the lid of the chest allowing the lock to operate in the normal way.

Chest locks with bolts which are governed by leaf

springs, rather than a tumbler, are typically Anglo-Saxon. Much the most common type in England has springs which are set such that their faces lie in the vertical plane; the bolt is widened into a plate in the centre which has a ridge at one end to retain the springs in the locked position (Ottaway 1992, 660–2, fig 282). Locks of this type appear to become obsolete by the end of the 9th century. The mechanism in the Bishopstone lock is rather different because the spring faces lie horizontally. Locks of this type appear to be a development of the 9th century – perhaps they were seen as an improvement on the other style; they remained current until the 11th century to judge by the number of suitable keys, for example, from Winchester (Goodall 1990d, 1007, 1024–5, fig 325, *3731–8*). The only comparable lock from England, however, appears to be an example from a chest used as a coffin in the Cathedral Green cemetery at Winchester, dated to the late 9th century (*ibid*, 1016–17, *3686*).

The casket, no. 53 (Fig 6.17) of which the fittings were discussed above, also had a lock and lock plate with a bolt of a type held in place by a leaf spring. This was attached to the lock plate. The bolt consists of a central plate with an arm projecting from each end, although one is now largely missing. The plate faces lay in the same plane as the side of the casket – as opposed to being at right-angles to it as in the case of the bolt in the lock from the hoard. The bolt was held in place on the lock plate by small U-shaped staples which survive corroded to the arms. When locked, the spring, one end of which was fixed to the lock plate, pressed against a ridge at the end of the central plate whilst the arm projecting from this end engaged in the loop or staple of the hasp holding the lid closed. To unlock, an L-shaped key was inserted through the key hole in the lock plate and probably through a slot in the centre of the bolt (this is obscured by corrosion), and then twisted through 90° so that a tooth at the end of the bit engaged in the hole at the head of the central plate. Once engaged, the key was pulled back slightly to release the spring and the bolt could be slid back to free the hasp.

The lock plate was fitted to the front of the casket by nails through holes in a narrow flange around the edge. Otherwise it is curved in cross-section and would therefore have projected slightly from the face of the casket, but this was necessary to accommodate the lock mechanism and prevent it from interfering with the contents. In large chests the mechanism could usually be accommodated in the thickness of the wood. Like other fittings from the casket, the lock plate is plated. Locks of the type described here occur in a number of variants in terms of the form of the bolt. They appear to have been particularly characteristic of the 6th to 9th centuries in England and had become obsolete by the end of the 10th (Ottaway 1992, 660–2).

63* Lock case with bolt mechanism. The case is near semi-circular, the top being straight; around the sides a narrow flange (20mm wide) leaves the centre bellied out to accommodate the mechanism. The flange is pierced at least four times for attachment. A horizontal key hole lies near the centre and a vertical slot for the hasp (*in situ*) to the left. The mechanism consists of a bolt, the tip of which passes through the staple attached to the hasp. Near the centre the bolt is widened into a plate folded over at 90° to form a flange which is pierced, for the tip of a key, at the left-hand end (seen from rear); near the centre, projecting from the under side is a U-shaped ward. At the right-hand end of the flange a short strip has been welded to the bolt such as to act as a stop for the springs. The bolt is held in place at the right-hand end by a loop with pierced rounded terminals nailed to the case and at the left-hand end by a sort of plug set in the case with a narrow slot in it. A pair of leaf springs is held in place at the left-hand side above the bolt by a triangular terminal pierced twice and nailed to the case. Projecting from the case at a position about half way along the springs and above them is a strip which served to keep the springs in place. The ends of the springs rest on the stop as the lock is closed. The hasp has a looped head made from a spirally twisted strip, below which it widens into a plate in which the staple is set and then narrows to a recurved tip. The staple is set transversely to the hasp (instead of in line as is usual).
Case: L. 250, W. 130. Bolt: L. *c* 170. Springs: L. *c* 135. Hasp: L. 125, W. 29, Th. 8. Hoard no. 23

53 The lock consists of a central plate with an arm projecting from each end, one now largely missing, held in place on the lock plate by small U-shaped staples which survive corroded to the arms. The plate is pierced at one end and probably has a horizontal central slot for the key to pass through, although this is not clear due to corrosion. A leaf spring attached to the lock plate may also survive, although this is not clear either. The lock plate is broken at one end but the other is rounded. It is slightly curved in cross-section, and has a horizontal key-hole slot in the centre and a vertical slot for the hasp at the surviving end. In a narrow flange around the edge it is pierced at least four times for attachment to a box or casket. Plated, probably with tin.
L. 81, W. 46. B04, SF29 and 30, context 1364

6.6 Structural fittings and building materials (Figs 6.21–4)
by Patrick Ottaway

Clench bolts (Fig 6.21, nos 64–5)

Bishopstone produced seven examples of this common variety of late Anglo-Saxon structural fitting, including a pair from the iron hoard with all but one of the remainder coming from the charcoal deposit from the bottom of the cellared building. A clench bolt was used for joining overlapping timbers and consists of a nail-like component which, once it had passed through the timbers to be joined, had a small pierced plate, the rove, set over its tip.

The best known use for clench bolts in the Anglo-Saxon period is holding together the strakes of clinker-built ships. They occur on both maritime and inland occupation sites and a group of 55 was found in Anglo-Scandinavian contexts at 16–22 Coppergate, York (Ottaway 1992, 615–18). The Bishopstone examples are rather larger than most of those from Coppergate where only three were over 60mm in

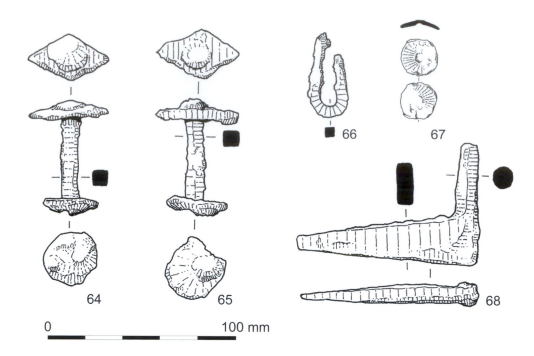

Fig 6.21　Structural fittings and building materials, nos 64–8, various

length. What this implies in terms of function is not clear, but clench bolts were not only used in ships, but also in doors, wagon bodies, and even coffins (Ottaway 1992).

64* Diamond-shaped rove.
L. 61; head: D. 30; shank: Th. 9; rove: 43 × 25
65* Diamond-shaped rove.
L. 58; head: D. 33; shank: Th. 10; rove: 43 × 26

Staples (Fig 6.21, no. 66)

Seven staples are represented in both U-shaped and rectangular forms. These would have been used for attaching iron fittings to wooden objects such as chests and doors.

66* U-shaped, one arm incomplete.
L. 45, W. 20, Th. 5

Nails (Fig 6.21, no. 67)

Around 135 nails were recovered from Anglo-Saxon contexts. They vary considerably in size from *c* 30mm to just over 100mm in length, although the majority appear to be 40–60mm long. More or less all the nails are, however, similar in form in having a roughly rounded, flattish head and a shank of rectangular cross-section with a wedge-shaped tip.

Amongst the more unusual representatives is no. 67, a plated nail head from which the shank is missing with two, or possibly three incised radial grooves. The plating of iron objects, including nails, with tin appears to be a development of the 8th century, but by the later 9th–10th centuries it seems to be widespread, largely, one presumes, for decorative purposes, but also for prevention of corrosion. Small dome-headed nails with plating similar to no. 67 are often not recognised unless ironwork is X-radiographed, but a number have been found at York (Ottaway 1992, 611–2).

67 Nail head with two or possibly three radial grooves visible on X-radiograph. Plated.
D. 38. B04, SF13, context 1344

Hinge pivots (Fig 6.21, no. 68)

Such items were used together with a U-eyed hinge (see below) for the suspension of a door. These are common artefacts in later Anglo-Saxon contexts. Four examples were recovered from the excavations; whilst all share the same basic L-shaped form, two examples (not illustrated) have shank tips bent over to make them more secure when in use.

68* Shank expands slightly in the centre, wedge-shaped tip.
Shank: L. 96, W. 25, Th. 8; guide arm: L. 65, Th. 12

U-eyed hinges (Figs 6.22 and 6.23, nos 69–75)

These robust U-eyed hinges comprise the largest and in many senses most distinct functional category in the Bishopstone hoard. They consist of a U-shaped eye with either two straps or a strap and a terminal which in three cases is bifurcated and decoratively scrolled. The straps and terminals gripped the

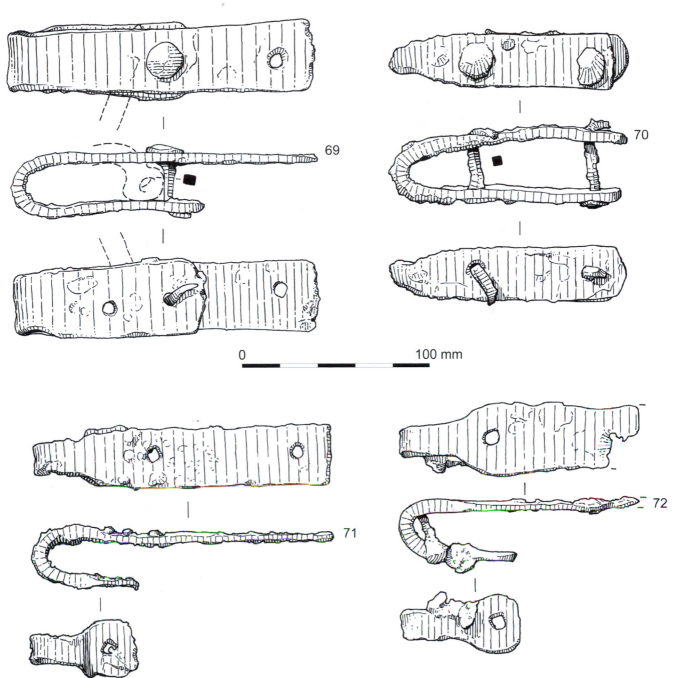

Fig 6.22   Structural fittings and building materials, nos 69–72, U-eyed hinges

wooden door of a building or item of furniture such as a cupboard, and the eye articulated on a hinge pivot. The Bishopstone group is fairly heterogeneous in that no two are exactly the same. However, nos 72 and 73, apparently found close together, differ only slightly in the length of the strap (155mm and 125mm) and probably came from the same door. They each have a strap pierced twice on one side of the eye, and a rounded and pierced terminal on the other. In both cases they would have gripped a piece of wood *c* 20mm thick.

These U-eyed hinges are typical artefacts of the late Anglo-Saxon and medieval periods, but none is known which can be dated before the mid-9th century. Doors in the mid Anglo-Saxon period were presumably hung in a way which did not use a U-eyed hinge and hinge pivot. Size must to some extent be related to function and it is reasonable to suppose that the Bishopstone hinges were large enough for the doors of a house rather than, for example, shutters or cupboards, even if they are not quite robust enough for a church door.

Straps with bifurcated and 'scrolled' ends of one sort and another are less common than those with plain straps, although two fine examples of the strap and terminal type, 195mm and 200mm long, with

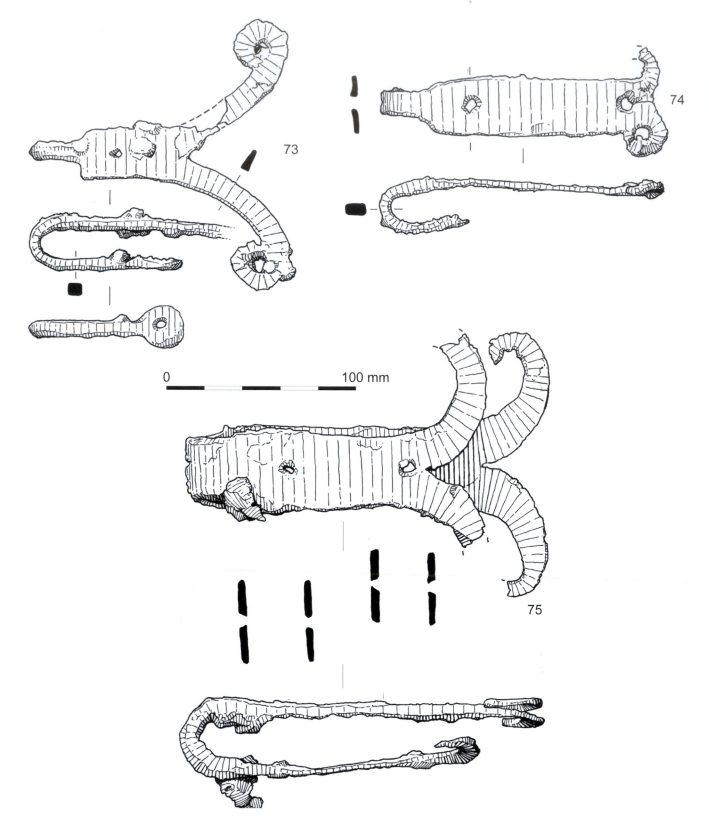

Fig 6.23   Structural fittings and building materials, nos 73–5, U-eyed hinges

arms similar to no. 74 in particular, come from early 11th-century contexts at 22 Piccadilly, York (Ottaway and Rogers 2002, 3010–11, figs 1556–7, *15341–2*) and another 11th-century pair (*c* 120mm long) was found in London *in situ* on a door recovered from demoli-

tion debris (Horsman *et al* 1988, fig 84; Pritchard 1991, 140–1, fig 3.20, *59–60*). Examples still survive on the 11th-century north door in the church at Hadstock (Essex) (Hewett 1978, 211–14; 1980, 21–2; Geddes 1982, 313) and can be seen in Anglo-Saxon illustrations (eg London, British Library, Cotton Caligula A. xiv fol 22 and Oxford, Bodleian Library, Junius II, p 66, showing Noah's Ark). Other illustrations show straps with two or more scrolls.

69* Straps of unequal length. The longer widens very slightly at the end. The shorter also widens slightly towards an end which is slightly rounded. Both straps pierced twice, one nail *in situ*.
Eye: Th. 6; straps: L. 165 and 103; W. 39 and 41; W. across the straps: 35

70* Straps of equal length. Both widen away from the eye and are then parallel-sided to the ends, one of which is rounded. Both pierced twice with nails *in situ*, set in same direction, clenched tips, one broken.
Eye: Th. 8; straps: L. 127, W. 29; W. across the straps: 39

71* Strap and terminal. As the strap widens away from the eye its sides are convex before becoming more or less parallel-sided up to a straight end. Pierced twice. Rounded terminal; pierced but the hole not in line with a hole in the strap.
Eye: Th. 6; strap arm: L. 155, W. 32; terminal arm: L. 57, W. 32; W. across strap and terminal: 32

72* Strap and terminal. As the strap widens away from the eye the sides are convex before becoming slightly concave in centre; end damaged. Pierced twice. Terminal is roughly rounded and pierced.
Eye: Th. 7; strap arm: L. 125, W. 38; terminal arm: L. 65, W. 28; W. across strap and terminal: 34

73* Strap with bifurcated end and terminal. Strap has straight shoulders, is then parallel sided before widening towards the end where it bifurcates into two recurving arms with closed loop terminals. Pierced once (?). The terminal is circular and pierced.
Eye: Th. 7; strap arm: L. *c* 140, W. across arms *c* 130; W. across the straps: 28

74* The surviving strap has a bifurcated end. As it widens from the eye the sides are convex before becoming more or less parallel-sided. At the end it bifurcates to form two small closed loops, one incomplete. The second strap or terminal is broken off.
Eye: Th. 6; strap: L. 151, W. 31, W. across loops 58; W. across the straps: 29

75* Two straps with bifurcated ends, one longer than the other. Both straps are at their widest around a piercing nearest the eye where sides are convex before converging slightly towards the ends which bifurcate to form extended recurved arms which narrow towards the tips. One arm of the longer strap is complete, although broken in the centre, the other arm is bent and the tip is missing. One arm of the shorter strap is now a stub and the end of the other is missing. The longer arm is pierced twice and the shorter arm pierced once but a second hole has been formed at the point where the arms divide.
Eye: Th. 7; straps: L. *c* 190 and 152, W. across arms of longer strap *c* 140; W across the straps: 38

6.7   An analysis of the structural daub
by Mike Bispham

Introduction

A staggering total of 500kg of structural daub was recovered from the excavations. Since an estimated 70% of this total bore wattle impressions and other structural detail, the daub can offer a rare glimpse of the materiality of the Anglo-Saxon built environment otherwise denied by the excavated

ground-level evidence. The study of this material formed the basis for an undergraduate dissertation in Classical and Archaeological Studies at the University of Kent, submitted in 2007. The first stage of the investigation involved the design and implementation of a strategy for cleaning, categorising, and sampling the daub. This was followed by a basic visual assessment leading on to targeted microscopic and compositional analysis using x-ray spectroscopy. Interpretation has been guided by previous analytical and experimental work on assemblages of comparable date, foremost amongst them being a study of the daub generated by various sites in mid Saxon London (Hughes 2004). Insights have also been gained from the author's own expertise as a professional carpenter specialising in the construction of bespoke buildings, extensions, and historical building renovation.

The taphonomy and character of the daub assemblage

The bulk of the daub recovered from the excavations was deposited in pits, including the large pit associated with Structure W. This general source yielded two distinct types of assemblage. First, primary dumps of daub present in dense concentrations, much of it in a 'fresh', unabraided condition, and second, smaller assemblages whose crushed and abraded condition suggests deposition via intermediary surface middens. The former assemblages were restricted to a small number of pits and formed either the dominant material category by volume or else defined depositionary horizons within longer infill sequences. It can be seen from Table 6.7 that the top ten most productive contexts with totals in excess of 8kg of daub yielded nearly 60% of the entire assemblage (daub was recovered from a total of 266 contexts) with a single pit context, 549, producing over 20% alone. Six of these contexts were fills of pits located in the western half of the excavation. It would appear that the key mechanism behind Bishopstone's superabundant total was the systematic dumping of fired daub in several discrete episodes.

Paradoxically structural features produced only comparatively small assemblages of daub, the typical yield for wall-trenches being only a few hundred grams; the only exception to this rule was the substantial southern wall of aisled Structure U which produced a total of 2.5kg. In all cases the crushed and abraded condition of the daub from these sources suggests that it forms a redeposited component.

It should be said from the outset that the preservation pathway affecting the survival of the daub is firing at a high temperature (say over 650°C) for a sustained period, conditions readily obtained during the burning of a timber building (Hughes 2004). It must be assumed that the preserved component represents only a fraction of the daub employed at any one time within the built environment of the

Table 6.7 Quantified daub assemblages from the ten most productive contexts

Context no.	Weight	Percentage
549	102,600	21
516	82,081	16.6
1364	20,700	4.2
1354	20,500	4.2
1168	12,700	2.5
1182	12,110	2.5
1344	11,650	2.4
1212	11,625	2.4
2255	8790	1.8
596	8550	1.8
Total	**291,036**	**59.4**

settlement, let alone for the entire duration of the occupation; most will have been reabsorbed back into the ground or else reused for new buildings. On estimates derived from other Anglo-Saxon daub assemblages, the Bishopstone collection (itself estimated to represent a wall coverage area of some 6.4m²) would only be sufficient to cover a single medium-sized building with ground-plan dimensions in the range of 10m by 5m (see Hughes 2004, 132–33, table 47).

In considering the implications of the unusually large assemblage of fired structural daub recovered from an Anglo-Saxon settlement like Bishopstone it has to be remembered that fire would have been an ever-present risk within such highly combustible environments; it may also be the case that the shells of abandoned buildings might have been deliberately burnt to help clear the ground whether for the construction of a replacement building or for some other use. On this basis, one might legitimately ask why it is that with the notable exception of Hamwic, other Anglo-Saxon settlements have not produced daub assemblages of comparable size to Bishopstone. One possibility is that Bishopstone's prominence may be related to the peculiarities of rubbish disposal practised by its inhabitants (see Chapter 9.1). The density of pits certainly plays a part; if pits are taken out of the equation, Bishopstone's total falls into line with the more modest assemblages (30kg or less) from sites such as Flixborough (Lincs), where rubbish was primary discarded in surface middens, a practice which militates against the survival of daub (Wastling 2009, 154–9).

But this does not of itself provide a satisfactory explanation, since not all sites with high pit densities have produced correspondingly large volumes of daub, as demonstrated by the situation in mid Saxon London (Hughes 2004). It seems inherently unlikely that the inhabitants of Anglo-Saxon Bishopstone were more assiduous than contemporaries in disposing of daub in pits. Taking into account the likelihood that the pits characterised by the highest volumes of daub belong to different stratigraphic phases, the evidence would instead appear to suggest that the occupation at Bishopstone was punctuated by repeated conflagrations, each producing substantial volumes of building detritus systematically dumped into pits.

Fabric (Plate 9, A–D)

Visual inspection showed that the daub was formed chiefly of clay usually transformed to a brick-red colour under oxidation. Whilst establishing a source for the clay lay outside the remit of the study, there is nothing in the composition of the daub to suggest that it was not local. Indeed, some 80% of the daub fragments examined contained small particles of chalk (confirmed by x-ray spectroscopic analysis), whilst splinters of flint were present in 5–10% of the assemblage.

As one might expect with such a sizeable assemblage, clear variations in fabric composition were noted, but the fact that this was apparent in individual contexts indicates that the likely cause was preparation of individual mixes as opposed to chronological trends in the way that daub was prepared. Four contrasting samples are here described to give a representative impression of the observed variation in fabric composition, as follows (Plate 9 A–D):

Fabric A (context 2894): a fine-grained clay, oxidised brick red, with very infrequent chalk particle inclusions. The matrix is tight, broken only by scattered small cavities that are visible in the enlargement. The cause of such pockets is difficult to establish. No fragments of organic matter were noted, and close examination failed to reveal identifiable impressions. Some cavities relate to folded air pockets which probably formed during the preparation processes. There were also several soft darkgrey particles, which appear to be charcoal based. Their tight fit indicates these fragments were embedded in their current state, and survived the baking event unaffected.
Fabric B (context 549): the matrix of this fabric was generally greyer in colour than Fabric A, but it contained a similarly low abundance of cavities. Darker red clay pellets, similar to that appearing in exterior washes, were also present as a minor constituent. Whether this material represents unmixed lumps of clay, or a pigmented wash that has penetrated into the matrix is unclear.
Fabric C (context 2044): a higher proportion of chalk was present in this fabric, evidenced both in the greater abundance of discrete particles and in the lighter colour of the matrix. The chalk grains seem more or less evenly graded from around 0.75mm down to invisible. Again, just a few small cavities were present, as were some unidentified grey particles.
Fabric D (context 2894): this fabric has a lower density than the others as a result of a comparatively high organic content. Some of this matter survives *in situ* as short lengths of chopped grass, both leaf and stalk of a largely regular length (between roughly 6mm and 10 mm), suggesting it was deliberately added to the clay. However, much of the original organic content has been burnt out to leave fossil voids.

Surface washes (Plate 9, E–H)

The flat surfaces of most of the larger fragments of daub were covered with exterior applications, one of the attributes suggestive that this material was used principally as walling for buildings as opposed to some other structural function such as kiln lining. These can be subdivided into either reddish clay skims or lime washes, although there are also a small number of fragments covered with what appears likely to be a mixture of the two, resulting in a brownish covering, as seen in Plate 9C. Whereas the purpose of the former was to patch cracks which would have appeared as the daub dried and to make repairs over the lifetime of the building (Wastling 2009, 156–7), the latter was applied as a form of weatherproofing. In addition to these structural purposes, small quantities of lime may have been used as an additive to the daub mix to improve its plasticity during application.

The composition of the limewashing varies somewhat, the main constituent being chalk particles roughly graded from a couple of millimeters in diameter down to those which are indiscernible under X20 magnification. Grey particles, assumed to be derived from charcoal, are often present. More rarely small particles of red matter are seen.

In some cases a cavity can be seen straddling the joint between the clay matrix and the surface wash demonstrating that the coat was applied whilst the daub was in a plastic state. This must have occurred within a few tens of minutes of the application of the daub, as it would have begun to harden very soon in all but the dampest weather conditions. Several fragments of daub displayed superimposed layers consistent with over-washing.

Structural impressions (Fig 6.24)

The wattle panels are formed of vertical 'staves' and horizontal 'withies', collectively termed the 'weave'. The mean diameter of the former is around 10–12mm, whereas the latter is in the region of 7–10mm; the wattle employed at Bishopstone is thus somewhat finer than that recorded from Flixborough (Lincs), which ranged between 15mm and 35mm and <10–20mm respectively (Wastling 2009, 157). There are almost no knots, forks, buds, or blemishes in the estimated 575m of impression-run, indicating that the wood was most likely coppiced during its first year of growth. A great many wattle impressions carry distinctive longitudinal striations probably relating to bark corrugations caused by shrinkage during drying – as observed by the writer in winter-cut first-year pollarded willow shoots.

The size of wall panels would appear to have been dictated by the length obtained by shoots coppiced in their first year of growth (as indicated by a lack of evidence for cleft wattles, offshoots, and a consistent diameter). This length would have varied according to agricultural practice and species. Coppices of established roots can provide faster than ordinary growth, and pollarded trunks are still more produc-

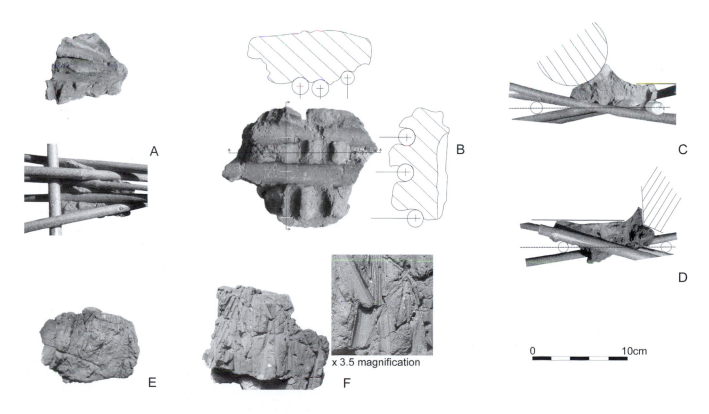

Fig 6.24 Structural characteristics of daub: A) typical weave pattern; B) anomalous criss-cross pattern; C) circular frame marking; D) squared frame marking; E) thatch impressions; F) thatch impressions

tive. The amount of usable material consistent with the diameters found in the Bishopstone daub varies from perhaps 2m in pollarded willow to around 1.25m in coppiced chestnut, birch, hazel, or ash.

Weave patterns

Some 7 to 10% of the assemblage carried impressions of both horizontal withies and vertical staves, most of which pass at right-angles to one-another. Rather anomalous are a few fragments where both vertical and horizontal members are arranged in parallel disposition: ie there is no apparent weave (Fig 6.24B).

Only a single piece of daub was sufficiently large to retain impressions of more than one stave, supplying a span of 102mm. However, estimations based upon the weave pattern and wattle diameter observed amongst the more informative daub fragments indicate a range of 100mm to 130mm. The daub averages around 60mm as measured from face to back encompassing within its width a central upright post and two passes of woven rod. This thickness is slightly greater than the 24mm to 45mm recorded at Flixborough (Wastling 2009, 157). Nonetheless, the dimensions are still consistent with light and economical work that played no role in the load-bearing capacity of the buildings.

Other structural impressions

Larger structural timbers from the host buildings are also preserved in the daub assemblage; this evidence attests to the use of both rounded and squared posts and/or split planking (Fig 6.24C and D). The former shows a particularly well-preserved impression of a rounded post, its curvature suggesting a diameter in the region of 60mm–100mm. This fragment also preserves a finished wall surface which has been curved outwards at the junction with the upright timber. Seen more widely amongst the daub assemblage, this feature suggests that it was common practice for the main structural timbers to be set slightly in front of the wattle panels, a technique of wall construction whereby prefabricated wattle panels were attached to the back of posts erected during the first stage of assembly (Hughes 2004, 131–2, fig 73).

Thatch

Many fragments of daub carry impressions made by small diameter stalks, often in close parallel disposition consistent with thatched roofing. One of the most revealing (shown in Fig 6.24F), also displays a number of angled surfaces typical of frame markings, suggesting that it might have been located at eaves-level where the wall surface would have met the overhanging thatch.

6.8   Cultivation, crop processing, and food procurement
by Patrick Ottaway, Luke Barber, and Gabor Thomas

Iron sickles (Fig 6.25, no. 76)

The sickle is a rare object for a later Anglo-Saxon or equivalent context in Britain, so it is of interest that Bishopstone has produced two, the most complete of which is no. 76 from the hoard. Sickles were presumably recycled when broken given their useful steel edges, but that these implements were occasionally thought of as suitable objects for a special deposit in the period is shown by there being one in each of the Viking graves at Hesket and Ormside in Cumbria (Cowen 1934, pl I, *9*, pl III, *5*; Edwards 1992, 45–6, fig 5.2).

76* Sickle. An incomplete curving blade widens away from the tang which is bent in centre and tapers to the tip where clenched. Mineralised wood remains survive on the tang.
L. *c* 325; blade: L. 205, W. 41, Th. 6. Hoard no. 4

Plough share (Fig 6.25, no. 77)

No. 77 would have been set on the wooden tip of an ard–type plough and would have sliced the soil in a horizontal plane, probably after it had been cut in a vertical plane by a coulter. Although it is hard to be certain, the Bishopstone example appears to shows no sign of use or damage. It is broadly similar to a small number of other plough shares from late Anglo-Saxon contexts in England at, for example, St Neots (Addyman 1973, 94, *30*) and Thetford (Goodall 1984, 81–2, *43*). In the context of the Bishopstone hoard it is of some interest that a plough share of mid Anglo-Saxon date was found at Flixborough (Lincs), where it had been carefully buried in a small pit with a second large and presumably valuable iron object, a cauldron chain. It seems clear that these objects had been deliberately deposited as a small hoard (Ottaway 2009b, sf 7110). A plough share was also found in a late Anglo-Saxon ironwork hoard at Westley Waterless (Cambs) (Fox 1923, 300).

77* Plough share. Curves slightly at the 'waist' and narrows to the tip which is thickened slightly. Flaps either side of the head to grip the wood of the plough, one flap longer than the other.
L. *c* 172, W. 77, W. (across flaps) 33, Th. 8. Hoard no. 5

Quernstones (Fig 6.26, nos 78–81)
by Luke Barber

Some 217 fragments of rotary quern were recovered from the excavations constituting 90.4% of the worked stone assemblage from the site (77% by weight due to the fragmentary nature of the lava querns). The fragmentary nature of the querns did not allow

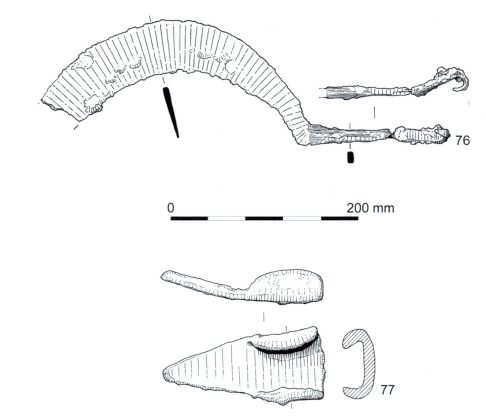

Fig 6.25 *Cultivation, crop processing and food procurement, nos 76–7, sickle and plough share*

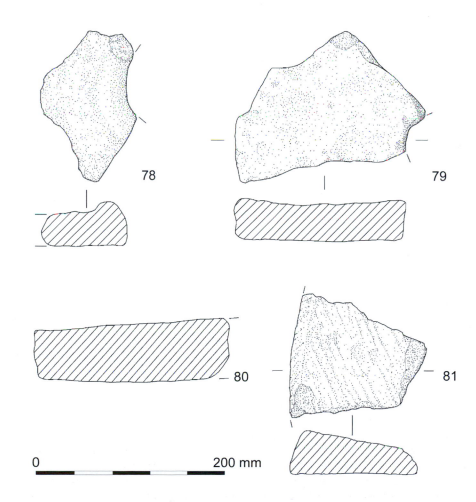

Fig 6.26 *Cultivation, crop processing and food procurement, nos 78–81, querns*

a reliable calculation of the minimum number of querns present. This fragmentation may in part be due to post-breakage burning as a number of pieces showed reddening on their broken edges suggesting some may have been reused for a time as hearth linings. Some were certainly reused as post-packing. The querns utilised three stone types: Ashdown sandstone from the Hastings area, Lower Greensand from the Lodsworth area of West Sussex, and German lava obtained either directly from the Rhineland or via a secondary market such as London. Of the quern assemblage the three types make up 6.9%, 9.7% and 83.4% respectively by count. However, due to the fragmentary nature of the lava, percentages based on weight are probably a more reliable indicator of the relative proportions: 19.2%, 32.2%, and 48.6% respectively. The wide dating of the ceramics makes it impossible to establish whether there is any chronological significance to the different sources of supply. Although the types often appear isolated in individual contexts there are a few deposits which contain two, or all three types mixed together (eg the demolition fills of cellared building W contained two or three different types).

Although the most abundant quern type, the fragmentary nature of the lava querns means most pieces are small with no diagnostic features. On the whole it was impossible to determine diameters or whether upper or lower stones were definitely represented, though variations in stone thickness may be an indicator. Five fragments had thicknesses of 35mm. These included no. 78, part of an upper stone with central collared hopper suggesting the thinner pieces are from upper stones. Six fragments had thicknesses between 40mm and 80mm and probably represent lower stones. Lava querns are common in the south-east during the later Saxon and medieval periods. In London they totally dominate the quern assemblages at this time (Pritchard 1991) and there is also evidence that there was a lava quern finishing workshop here (Freshwater 1996). These querns are also common in Sussex and Kent, with pre-12th-century examples having been recovered from Lewes (Barber in prep) and Sandtun (Riddler 2001) though they shared the market with other more local stone types.

The querns made from the Ashdown Beds sandstone are less fragmentary though only one, no. 79, provided an approximate diameter of 390mm. Pieces of at least four lower stones are present with edge thicknesses varying between 32mm and 40mm, increasing to 78mm thick adjacent to the spindle socket on at least one example (posthole 279). Two definite upper stone fragments were recovered which tended to be thinner, varying between 29mm and 45mm thick.

The Lower Greensand querns are similar to the Ashdown Beds examples – in generally being quite thick and crudely shaped. Only one approximate diameter was noted, this being a little over 400mm from a 50–60mm thick lower stone (no. 80). Four other fragments of lower stone were noted with thicknesses

varying between 57mm and 65mm. Two fragments of upper stone, including no. 81, were recovered with thicknesses varying between 24mm and 41mm. As with the lava querns, Lower Greensand examples are common in Sussex and are known from 12th-century deposits in Lewes (Barber in prep).

The querns are spread widely across the excavation area and as such do not suggest any specialised areas for processing. This is not surprising considering most were from secondary deposits in refuse pits, and more rarely reused as post-packing. The slight concentrations present are likely to be the result of the mechanics of secondary disposal, which will have altered the original distribution pattern. This is most notable with the largest feature concentration, the demolition layers of the cellared structure which contained two pieces of Ashdown Beds quern (2092g: an upper and lower stone possibly from the same quern), three fragments of Lower Greensand quern (594g: a minimum of one quern), and 28 pieces of lava quern (2534g: a minimum of one quern).

78 Quern fragment; lava (Mayen, Germany). Upper stone with fragment of central hopper.
L. 160, W. 95, Th. 35. B05, context 2900
79 Quern fragment; Ashdown Beds sandstone. Lower stone fragment.
Estimated total D. 390, Th. 38–42. B05, context 2895
80 Quern fragment; Lower Greensand. Lower stone fragment.
Estimated total D. 400, Th. 50–60. B05, context 2092
81 Quern fragment; Lower Greensand. Upper stone fragment.
L. 128, W. 144, Th. 41. B05, context 2895

Fish hooks (not illustrated)

Barbed fishing hooks are typical of the late Anglo-Saxon to early post-Conquest period. The head of no. 84 is flattened into the rounded terminal which is also typical of the period as can also be seen on examples from London (Pritchard 1991, 137–8, fig 3.17, *34, 37, 43*) and a collection from Yarmouth (Rogerson 1976, 166, fig 53).

Fish hooks are not common objects in later Anglo-Saxon or equivalent contexts, although there are six in all from 11th- to 12th-century contexts in London (Pritchard 1991, 137–8) and seven from Anglo-Scandinavian contexts at Coppergate, York (Ottaway 1992, 600–01). Of those in the latter group, four have barbed tips and four have looped terminals; they are all 55mm or more in length – although none in the London, Yarmouth, or York groups is as long as no. 83 except for one from London, with a looped terminal, which is over 120mm long. Whereas no. 83 was probably used for long-line fishing, the smaller hooks were probably used in association with a rod and line; a small hook like no. 84 was suitable for catching small fresh water species.

82 L. 60, hook: W.18. B04, SF49, context 1168
83 Head flattened into rounded terminal. Hook barbed.

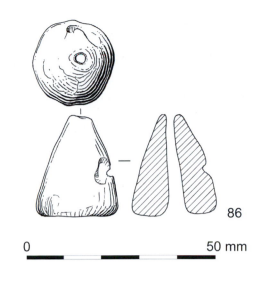

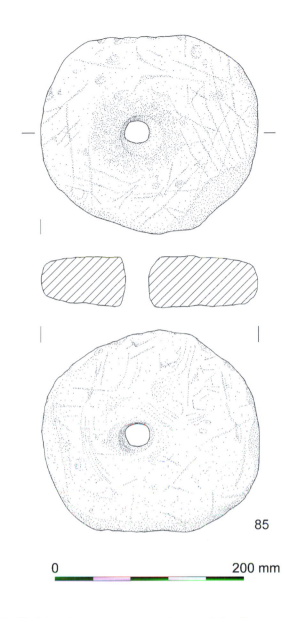

Fig 6.27 Cultivation, crop processing and food procurement, nos 85–6, fishing weights

L. 115, Th. 4; hook: W.31. B04, SF111, context 1344
84 Head missing, hook barbed.
L. 30. B05, SF11, context 2038

Fishing weights (Fig 6.27, nos 85–6)
by Gabor Thomas with Luke Barber

The exact function of no. 85, a large chalk disc with a central perforation, is uncertain, but a distinct possibility is that it served as net weight, a proposition supported by the discovery of an analogous example by a diver 400m off the coast at Seaford (Hutchinson 1994, 137–8, fig. 8.6a).

No. 86, a simple cone with a central perforation, represents a common category of lead find in later Anglo-Saxon and medieval contexts where they are usually interpreted as plumb bobs (cf Ottaway and Rogers 2002, 2705, fig 1317, no. 14512; Wastling 2009, 201, no. 2027). However, given Bishopstone's coastal location and a variety of other evidence attesting to

a maritime dimension, it is equally likely to have served as a fishing weight.

85 Large chalk disc with a centrally drilled hole which tapers outward to a maximum diameter of 35mm. Both surfaces of the disc have scratch marks though those on one side are notably more worn.
D. 210–30, Th. 50, Wt. 2,715g. B05, context 2884
86 Lead weight. Comprising a crudely cast cone with a central perforation.
Max D. 22, L. 26. B03, SF17, context 208

6.9 Textile manufacture and other crafts
by Gabor Thomas and Patrick Ottaway, with Lynne Keys

Wool comb (Fig 6.28, no. 87)
by Patrick Ottaway

A beautifully preserved example of a wool comb, no. 87, was discovered in the iron hoard. This is one of a

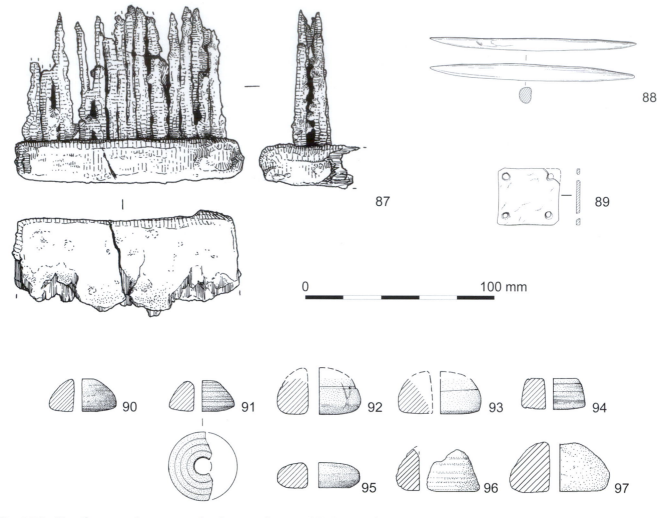

Fig 6.28   Textile manufacture and other crafts, nos 87–97, various

pair, which would have been held one in each hand, and used to straighten and align wool fibres, and remove foreign matter prior to spinning. A wooden board was made in one piece with the handle; the board was pierced for the teeth, usually in two rows, the holes staggered. Once the teeth were in place an iron sheet was wrapped around the board to strengthen it. The object's weak point was clearly in the wood at the junction of board and handle and the Bishopstone object joins a group of Anglo-Saxon wool combs which have suffered similar breakage. The earliest Anglo-Saxon wool combs known are a pair from a 7th-century grave at Lechlade (Glos) (Miles and Palmer 1986, 17). Other combs come from later Anglo-Saxon contexts including one from Coppergate, York with wool fibres still attached (Ottaway 1992, 538–40, fig 212, *2273*). Individual teeth are common finds from contexts of the 7th century onwards and there are a number from Bishopstone (see below); they may be distinguished from nail shanks by having pointed rather than wedge-shaped tips. The teeth in the Bishopstone wool comb are *c* 90mm long and so fall in the middle of the

usual range of *c* 70–110mm. The use of hand-held combs appears to have declined by the 13th century and combs with longer teeth set in permanent installations were preferred.

A further seventeen teeth from wool combs of the type found in the hoard were recovered, all but three from the destruction layers of cellared structure W. It is also possible that similar combs were used for flax processing. Most of the teeth have the characteristic stepped head which results from the way the teeth were severed from their parent iron bar during manufacture. A number are also slightly curved as a result of use. The length of the complete examples is 70mm–90mm, as would be expected; the teeth in the hoard comb are *c* 90mm long.

87* Wool comb. Exists as the remains of the wooden base from which the handle has snapped off. Around the base, except on the handle side, is wrapped iron sheeting, pierced for the comb teeth. The row nearest the handle had twelve teeth and the other fourteen, mostly complete, though a few broken. Teeth are rounded in cross-section and have pointed tips.
L. 120, W. 40, Th. 22; teeth: L. *c* 90. Hoard no. 3

Pin-beater (Fig 6.28, no. 88)

Along with loom-weights (see below), pin-beaters such as no. 88 represent a standard witness to the weaving of textiles on Anglo-Saxon settlements, although their frequency declines during the 10th and 11th centuries in response to new loom technology (Walton Rogers 1997, 1755–7, fig 815).

88 Pin-beater. Complete. Double-ended with circular cross-section.
L. 110, D. 9. B05, SF243; context 3166

Weaving tablet (Fig 6.28, no. 89)

Bone weaving tablets of square form such as no. 89 represent an established early medieval type whose use extended well beyond the confines of Anglo-Saxon England into Viking period Scandinavia and early Christian Britain and Ireland (MacGregor 1985; Walton Rogers 1997, 1786–7; Walton Rogers 2007, 35–6). In spite of this wide cultural domain, weaving tablets do not share the same ubiquity as other types of textile manufacturing implements such as pin-beaters. For example, they are absent from the site of Flixborough which has otherwise produced an extensive range of textile manufacturing paraphernalia, some evidently associated with the production of fine cloth (Walton Rogers 2009). One explanation for this paucity may be that weaving tablets were more commonly made of wood, a material attested by the complete weaving-tablet kit discovered in the Oseberg ship-burial from Norway (Walton Rogers 2007, 35).

89 Weaving tablet. Of square form with a circular hole in each corner; small fragment detached from one corner.
L. 33, W. 30, Th. 2. B04, SF71, context 1200

Spindle whorls (Fig 6.28, nos 90–7)

Stone identifications by Professor John Allen, University of Reading

All eight of the spindle whorls recovered from Bishopstone subscribe to common later Anglo-Saxon types as classified by Walton Rogers (1997). Fine encircling lines (and in some cases decorative grooves) indicate that all with the exception of no. 95 were made on a lathe; the latter is paralleled by an unturned example in the same material from Botolphs (Gardiner 1990, no. 66, fig 24). The spindle whorls made of Ferriginous cement stone are expertly crafted and provide a parallel for siltstone examples of comparable quality made at Sandtun (Kent) (Riddler 2001, 238–40). Whilst Bishopstone lacks evidence for onsite manufacture, such a scenario is highly plausible given the presence of a local outcrop of Ferriginous cement stone within the London Clay Formation at Castle Hill, Newhaven (Castleden 1996, 21–2, fig 6).

Given the continental source of its raw material, no. 97 made from Aubigny-type limestone is intriguing as these items were generally female personal belongings which tended to move with an individual. A Caen stone example has been noted from post-Conquest deposits in London where it is suggested it may have travelled with an individual from Normandy or, less interestingly, been shaped from a reused piece of imported building stone (Egan 1998, 258, no. 800). Considering the presence of a single fragment of Aubigny-type ashlar block at the current site in the same context, the latter possibility appears more likely.

90 Complete. Stone type uncertain but tests positive for carbonate; combined with relative density, the most likely candidate is chalk. Hemispherical, neatly made, encircling grooves on flat face, surface coloured graphite grey. Form A1.
D. 34, Th. 18; hole D. 8.5, Wt. 23g. B04, SF24, context 1344
91 Fragment (*c* 60% complete); Ferriginous cement stone, London Clay Formation. Hemispherical, neatly made, encircling grooves on flat face. Form A1.
D. 35, Th. 16; hole D. 8.5, Wt. 14g. B05, context 2895
92 Fragment (*c* 35% complete); Ferriginous cement stone, London Clay Formation.
Hemispherical, neatly made, lathe-turned grooves on flat face. Form A1.
D. 37+, Th. 20; hole D. 10, Wt.10g. B05, context 2040
93 Fragment (<15% complete); Chalk with black glauconitic grains. Hemispherical, neatly made, surface coloured graphite grey. Form A1.
D. 32+, Th. 18+, Wt. 6g. B04, SF174, context 518
94 Two fragments (< 10% complete); Ferriginous cement stone, London Clay Formation. Hemispherical, neatly made, lathe-turned grooves on flat face. Form A1.
D. 16+, Th. 16, Wt. 6g. B04, context 1364
95 Fragment (*c* 15% complete); Chalk. D-shaped section, crudely made. Form B2.
D. 27+, Th. 13; hole D. 10, Wt. 4g. B05, context 2036
96 Fragment (25% complete); Chalk. Hemispherical, lathe-turned with blackened exterior surface decorated with horizontal grooves. Form A1.
D. 26; Th. 20, Wt (complete) 40g. B03, context 132
97 Complete; Aubigny-type limestone. Hemispherical, lathe-turned. Form A1.
D. 48mm, Th. 23, Wt. 60g. B03, context 89, unstratified colluvium

Loomweights (Table 6.8; Fig 6.29, nos 98–103)

Some 36 nearly whole and fragmentary clay loomweights were recovered from the excavations, all conforming to the recognised late Anglo-Saxon 'bun-shaped' variety (Holden 1976, 310–11; Walton Rogers 2007, 30–3). It is apparent from the uniformity in fabric composition that the loomweights were made of local sources of clay containing a minor constituent of flint and chalk; variations in the proportions of these inclusions are minor and certainly not sufficient to warrant separation into discrete fabric types.

Most of the loomweights are featureless in terms of surface detail, but one fragment, no. 103,

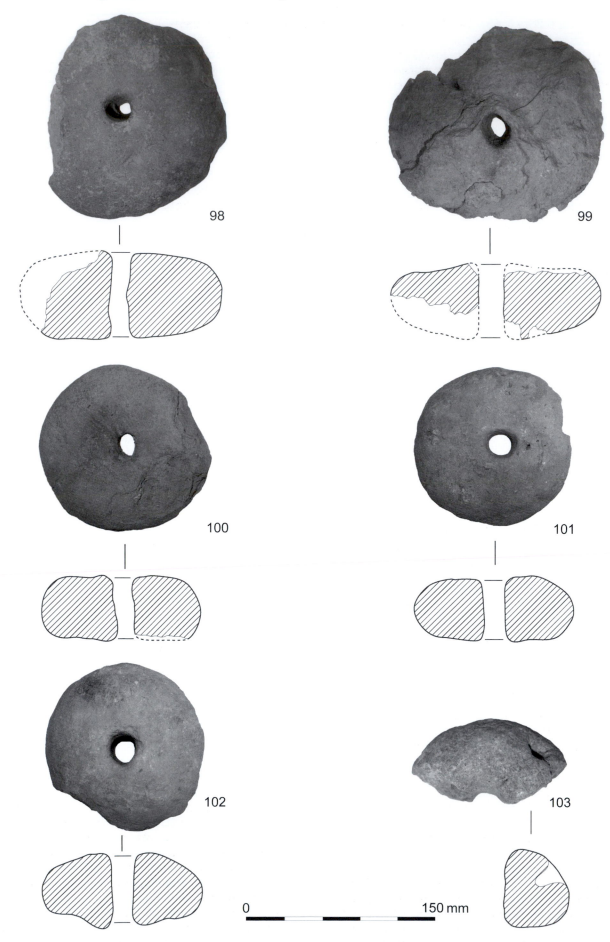

Fig 6.29   Textile manufacture and other crafts, nos 98–103, loomweights

Table 6.8 Attributes of catalogued loomweights

Cat. no.	Content	SF no.	Diameter/ width	Height	D. of perforation	Completeness	Weight (g)/ estimated total	Comment
98	B02 87	5	150	60	17	80%	1,145/1,430	Surfaces smooth and well preserved
99	B02 87	5	160	60	18	75%	840/1,120	Much of the surface has flaked away
100	B04 1198		140	40	13	95%	1,050/1,100	
101	B05 2908	54	126	45	18	95%	654/690	
102	B05 2875	61	130	45	21	95%	845/890	
103	B05 2896	47	110	60	20	35%	360/1,030	A finger hole is impressed into the surface

carries an impressed hole probably made with a finger. The metrology of the Bishopstone loomweights compares well with the assemblage from Old Erringham, West Sussex, where weights were between 532g and 1396g, and 109mm and 150mm diameter (Holden 1976, 315). The lowest estimable weight and diameter at Bishopstone is around 525g and 125mm and the highest 1430g and 160mm (no. 98). The spectrum represented at Bishopstone is consistent with the production of a standard range of domestic fabrics; there is a notable absence of the diminutive weights in the region of 200g and only 80mm diameter, associated with the production of fine cloth during certain phases of occupation at Flixborough (Lincs) (Walton Rogers 2009, 293).

In addition, a single chalk loomweight measuring 664g was recovered from pit 2931 (context 2932). The weight's form is that of a tapering ovoid with an 18mm diameter drilled hole near the upper, narrower end. Although a number of chalk weights from comparable sites of later Anglo-Saxon and medieval occupation have been interpreted as fishing weights (Riddler 2001, 250), the current example shows no sign of this usage and indeed there are wear grooves on both sides of the upper edge of the suspension hole consistent with repeated abrasion from a fine suspension thread.

A possible whalebone linen-smoothing board
(Fig 6.30, no. 104)

This forms one of five fragments of cetacean bone recovered from the excavations (see Poole, Chapter 7.1). It has been identified as a vertebra fragment from a medium-sized whale, and shows butchering marks on the surviving articular surface. This surface has been highly polished and displays a char-

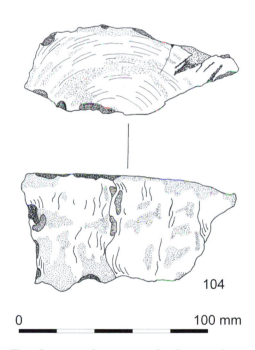

104

0   100 mm

Fig 6.30 Textile manufacture and other crafts, no. 104, polished whalebone vertebrae

acteristic wear pattern of closely spaced concentric striations which coincide with slight concavities.

The Bishopstone find represents an interesting addition to the more utilitarian range of whalebone artefacts used in Anglo-Saxon England, to be contrasted with this material's occasional use (sometimes as a substitute for walrus ivory) in the production of finely crafted liturgical objects such as the Franks Casket (Gardiner 1997). Waste from its use has been found from a range of mostly urban contexts, in the case of Ipswich and York alongside finished objects, including a comb and a sword pommel from the latter (MacGregor *et al* 1999, 1915).

Other finds of unmodified whalebone vertebra from Anglo-Saxon coastal settlements, including Hamwic and Sandtun (Kent), appear to have functioned somewhat differently to that from Bishopstone, for they bear cut-marks indicative of use as chopping boards or sawing blocks (Gardiner 1997, 189–92; Riddler 1998). Instead the surface patina and wear pattern of the Bishopstone find clearly indicates a process involving rotational rubbing or smoothing. One is here immediately reminded of the whalebone plaques found in Viking contexts interpreted as boards for smoothing linen cloth (Graham-Campbell 1980, 22–3, cat nos 90 and 91). These, and presumably commoner counterparts in wood, would have been used in association with 'stones' (whether of glass or naturally occurring pebbles) which occur fairly frequently on Anglo-Saxon and Anglo-Scandinavian settlements (Walton Rogers 2007, 39). The suggestion that the function of no. 104 was perhaps analogous to the whalebone plaques alluded to previously is strengthened by the fact that many of these plaques bear comparable polish-marks to the Bishopstone weight (Walton Rogers 1997, 1775–9, figs 826–8).

104 L. 115, W. 45, Th. 60. B05, SF48, context 2896

Ferrous metalworking (not illustrated)
(based on assessment by Lynne Keys)

The recovery of slag at Bishopstone contributes tangible evidence for the presence of a smith, also suggested by the excavation of the hoard of iron objects.. The majority of the 2.7kg recovered was undiagnostic smithing slag, but a hearth bottom was recovered from context 2553.

Non-ferrous metalworking (Fig 6.31, no. 105)
(based on assessment by Lynne Keys)

The evidence is exiguous, but one or two contexts provide hints that fine metalworking was taking place within the Anglo-Saxon settlement. Pit 548

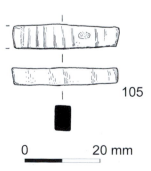

105

0   20 mm

Fig 6.31 Textile manufacture and other crafts, no. 105, copper-alloy ingot

produced a copper-alloy bar, no. 105, whose appearance is more suggestive of an ingot than of a finished object. Similarly, pit 1155 yielded a quantity of lead waste and runs.

105 Copper-alloy ingot. Rectangular-shaped bar, with rough, unworked surface finish.
L. 2.7, W. 5, Th. 4, Wt. 5g. B04, SF16, context 549

6.10 Horse equipment and riding gear
by Patrick Ottaway

Spur (Fig 6.32, no. 106)

No. 106 is very typical of spurs of the later Anglo-Saxon and equivalent periods as can be seen in spurs from York (Ottaway 1992, 698–701, eg fig 304, *3827*; also Waterman 1959, 104, fig 25, *8*) and Northampton (Goodall *et al* 1979, 273, fig 121, *120*).

106 Arms largely missing. Incised chevrons at the base of the goad. Goad expands towards the head, and was originally stepped in before the pointed tip. Incised groove(s) around the head. XRF shows this is tin-plated.
L. 103, Th. 9; goad: L. 25. B05, SF197, context 2774

Belt-slide (Fig 6.32, no. 107)

No. 107 was probably for the strap which attached a spur to the foot (Ottaway 1992, fig 305). It has a bilobate head which can also be seen on examples from York (Ottaway 1992, 689–90, fig 297, *3777, 3781, 3783*), Northampton (Goodall *et al* 1979, 273, fig 121, *121*), and Flaxengate, Lincoln (unpublished, sf no. Fe75, 2552). Surprisingly 107 is not plated with non-ferrous metal as is usual for these objects.

107 Head exists as two domed lobes, one arm is missing and the other is bent out of shape.
Head: L. 25, W. 16, Th. 8. B04, SF40, context 1776

Strap-joiner from bit (Fig 6.32, no. 108)

No. 108 is a double-eyed link which joined the snaffle of a bit to the bridle strap as can be seen by inspection of a complete bit from Winchester (Waterman 1959, 75, fig 8.2) and part of another bit from York (*ibid*, fig 8.1). A reconstruction of such a bit can be found in Ottaway and Rogers 2002 (fig 1525). The circular eye linked to the snaffle and the rectangular eye – in some cases a D-shaped eye – linked to the strap. Bits similar to those from Winchester and York noted above were widely used in England and northern Europe in the late Anglo-Saxon or equivalent periods, and links similar to no. 108 are common finds.

108 Composed of two eyes, one circular and the other D-shaped; a boss projects from the centre on one face.
L. 56, W. 36, Th. 10. B05, SF90, context 2211

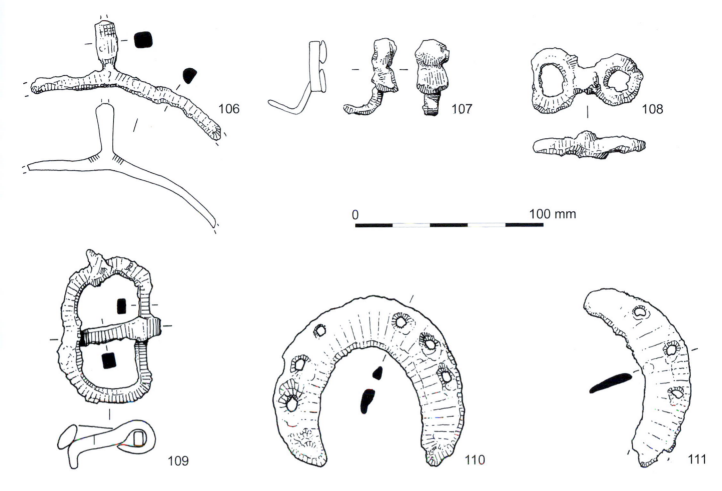

Fig 6.32   Horse equipment and riding gear, nos 106–11

Harness buckle (Fig 6.32, no. 109)

The size of no. 109 indicates that it was more likely used in association with horse harness, perhaps on the girth strap, than personal dress. The slightly kidney-shaped form of the frame can also be seen on a marginally smaller Anglo-Scandinavian buckle from Coppergate (Ottaway 1992, 684, fig 294, *3733*).

109* A slightly kidney-shaped frame. Tongue complete and tip lies under frame.
L. 77, W. 46; tongue L. 52.

Horseshoes (Fig 6.32, no. 110–11)

Both the horseshoes from the hoard, nos 110 and 111, are typically Anglo-Saxon. Compared to horseshoes of the later 11th to 12th centuries they have branches which are relatively wide and thin, a fairly smooth outer edge as opposed to a pronounced wavy edge, and countersunk holes but not of a pronounced and elongated form. The complete example (110) is more or less as long as it is wide which again is typical of the period. Although a fragment of a

horseshoe comes from a context thought to be mid Anglo-Saxon at Wicken Bonhunt (Essex) (excavations by A Rogerson and K Wade, sf 225), the use of horseshoes on any scale appears to begin in the late 9th century. Very similar horseshoes to the Bishopstone examples come from late Anglo-Saxon contexts at a number of sites including Coppergate, York (Ottaway 1992, 707–9, fig 308, *3852, 3854–6*) and Winchester (Goodall 1990e, 1054–5, 1057, fig 340, *3939–43*).

110* Complete. Branches narrow to inward facing tips which are rounded. Each has three countersunk holes.
L. 92, W. 105, Th. 6
111* Single branch. Narrows at the end which is rounded. Three slightly countersunk holes.
L. 100, W. 28, Th. 5

6.11 Miscellaneous objects
by Gabor Thomas

Copper-alloy binding-ring (Fig 6.33, no. 112)

A delicate binding-ring such as no. 112 could have been used in a range of domestic or personal

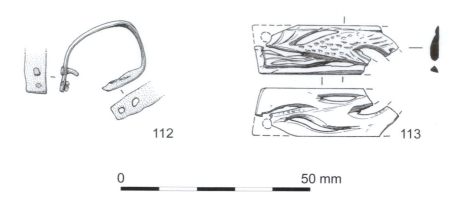

112

113

0   50 mm

Fig 6.33   Miscellaneous small finds, nos 112–13

contexts; a very similar example was found at Hamwic (Hinton 1996, 53, no. 32/4, fig 22).

112 Copper-alloy binding-ring. Comprising a flat, parallel-sided strip of metal bent into ring with a pair of attachment holes at one terminal and at the other a corresponding pair of small copper-alloy rivets with flat heads and shanks of square section.
D. approx 20; Th. 0.5. B04, SF7, context 596

Decorated bone mount (Fig 6.33, no. 113)

No. 113, a delicately carved bone mount, could have come from a casket although its function must remain uncertain given the lack of obvious signs of attachment. Rather more headway can be made with its ornament. The style and treatment of the beast bears some affinities with the zoomorphic content of Romanesque art expressed in a range of media, for example the winged creature depicted on a cast copper-alloy buckle found in the River Witham, near Lincoln (Zarnecki *et al* 1984, 252, no. 256); the zoomorphic designs carved on the reverse of the Lewis chessmen (*ibid*, 227, no. 212); and the animals appearing within the decorative borders of the Bayeux Tapestry (Wilson 1985). An openwork gilt copper-alloy mount recovered from an early 12th-century context at Goltho features a similar winged 'dragon' engaged in combat with a larger quadruped (Goodall 1987, 173, fig 153, no. 11). On this basis, a late 11th- to late 12th-century date seems most likely.

113 A sub-rectangular openwork plate, fragmentary with a damaged corner. The front is decorated with a sinuous zoomorphic motif shown in profile, of which the head section is missing, contained within a plain border. The beast has a long narrow body with speckled texturing which terminates in an outstretched three-toed hind leg and a textured flowing tail. A broken stub at the intersection between the tail and the body could represent the vestiges of a wing textured in a similar fashion to the tail.
L. 37, W. 13, Th. 2. B05, SF250, context 2100 (shallow feature with high probability of contamination)

6.12 Coins
by Marion M Archibald

Four Anglo-Saxon silver pennies were found in the excavation as isolated losses. All are corroded to some extent and, even with the help of x-rays, full identification can be difficult.

No particular significance should be attached to the fact that a coin of Berhtwulf of Mercia (no. 114) was found in Wessex as hoards and site finds both show that coins then circulated freely across boundaries (Metcalf 1998, 182). There may already have been a degree of political cooperation reflected in the types issued in common by the Mercian and West Saxon kings (Booth 1998, 65). The later coins show a typical local bias, all having been produced at mints south of the Thames. As most of the large hoards of this period have been found in the north-west and north-east, coins from the southern mints are less well represented in modern cabinets so it is not surprising that among the four coins here the Edward the Elder coin is of a rare moneyer apparently in an unrecorded variety and the Edmund find certainly of an unrecorded variety for the moneyer. On a non-urban site, four coins deposited between the mid-9th and mid-10th centuries is unusual and points to the settlement being of high status at that period. The absence of later Anglo-Saxon coins suggests that the status of the site had changed or that the coin-using area at that time has not been excavated.

114 Berhtwulf of Mercia, 840–52. Group II, *c* 848–*c* 850
Obv: [BERHTVVLF REX], HT ligulate
Rev: uncertain
Wt: 1.48g (severely corroded); Die axis: uncertain
Ref: North 1994, 418; Booth Group II, Bust F iii
B04, unstratified metal-detector find

The reign, types and bust variety are certain but the moneyer's name is not decipherable. The names of recorded moneyers in the type and other near contemporaries were tried but none fits comfortably and a 'new' moneyer would be possible. This coin is most likely to have been deposited before *c* AD 865.

115 Alfred, 871–99, Two line type, Four Part obverse division, *c* 880–*c* 890,
not mint-signed, but Canterbury style, moneyer Dudig
Obv: +ÆL FR ED RE
Rev: blank / DVDIG MON_ / blank
Wt: 1.55g (corroded) Die axis: 180°
Ref: North 1994, 635
B05, SF160, context 3087

Dudig is a prolific moneyer and hoards show that coins of this type remained in circulation into the reign of Edward the Elder and even early Athelstan. Although later survival remains possible, this coin is most likely to have been deposited before *c* 920.

116 132 3003
Edward the Elder, 899–924. HT1, Early II,
no mint signature but probably Canterbury, moneyer Ælfstan
Obv: EADWEARD REX
Rev: ∴ / ELFSTA / + + + / NMON
Wt: 0.59g (corroded, broken and incomplete); Die axis: 180°
Ref: North 1994, 649 but moneyer not listed; *CTCE* 184
B05, SF132, context 3003

The small flan of 20mm is indicative of the earlier period of the reign, but the inner circle diameter of 12mm is slightly wider than on the earliest issue so it belongs to the second phase of the coinage. The moneyer Ælfstan is not known for Alfred but worked prolifically during his reign for Archbishop Plegmund, presumptively at Canterbury. He is not among the moneyers of Edward the Elder rep-

resented in the Cuerdale hoard of *c* AD 905–10 although this is not necessarily chronologically significant. He is known for the reign only from a single coin in the British Museum from the Vatican hoard (1962-3-7-2) which is of type HP1 but the present coin appears to have a trefoil of pellets rather than a single pellet above and below the reverse inscription although, because of the condition of the coin, that is not quite certain. The evidence suggests that this coin was struck *c* AD 910. Theoretically it could have survived in circulation until the reform of *c* AD 973 but it is more likely that it was deposited before *c* AD 930.

117 Edmund, 939–46, HP1,
not mint signed but probably Winchester, moneyer Otic
Obv: +EADMUND REX
Rev: OTIC / + + + / MON ·
Wt: 1.29g (slight corrosion); Die axis: 0°
Ref: North 1994, 689; *CTCE* -.
B05, SF89, context 2903

The moneyer Otic was not previously recorded in the HP1 type. He was known without mint signature in HT1 for both Edmund and Eadred, in the Bust Crowned type for Athelstan on mint-signed coins at Winchester, and in HR3 for Eadwig also at Winchester. HP1 is essentially a southern type which is probably under-represented among surviving coins as most derive from hoards found outside the southern area so it is not surprising to that a find from Sussex is of a moneyer previously unrecorded in the type. This coin could have remained in circulation until the reform of the coinage *c* AD 973, but is more likely to have been deposited before *c* AD 960.

7   Economic resources

7.1   Mammal and bird remains
by Kristopher Poole

Some 28,135 fragments of animal bone were recovered from the excavations. In this report, the material is considered as a single-phase assemblage because the quantity of bone from phased features was too small to provide statistically reliable data for investigating temporal changes in animal exploitation (Table 7.2). Methods used for recording and analysis are listed in Appendix 5.

Taphonomy

The majority of bone (69%) was recovered from pits, some 11% of the assemblage coming from the fills of cellared Structure W, and the remaining 20% from assorted postholes, wall-trenches, ditches, and colluvial deposits. Bone was recovered through a combination of hand collection and sieving; whereas all deposits from pits and the cellared Structure W were sieved, material from more general spreads and layers was recovered by hand. Table 7.1 summarises taphonomic information for the total assemblage. Levels of gnawing were relatively low overall, with sheep/goat bones being the most frequently gnawed. The vast majority of gnawing was by dogs, although eight chicken and two goose bones had marks indicative of cat gnawing, and three other bones had been gnawed by rodents. Very few bones were burnt, and of the three main domesticates, cattle bones most frequently had butchery marks on them.

Species represented

In total, 6528 fragments (23.2%) could be identified to species (see Table 7.2), a relatively low figure due in large part to the effects of on-site sieving which boosted the recovery-rate of small undiagnostic fragments. The bones of domestic species dominate the assemblage, leaving a small yet diverse group of wild taxa, including roe deer, red deer, hare, badger,

and a wide range of wild birds. Where bones of sheep and goat could be distinguished morphologically, the majority were of sheep; on this basis it is assumed that the majority of bones broadly classifiable to the category 'sheep/goat' are from sheep. Measurements of pig teeth do not indicate the presence of wild boar in the Bishopstone assemblage, and so it is assumed that all of the pig remains are from domestic pigs. No galliform remains were identified as pheasant or guineafowl, unsurprising given their exotic status (Poole, forthcoming), and it is assumed that these all came from chickens.

Sheep, pig, and cattle

The relative frequencies of the three main domesticates demonstrate that sheep represent the most abundant species at 53.1%, followed by pig at 30.2%, and cattle at 16.7%.

Body-part patterns

Figures 7.1–7.3 show the total body-part data for cattle, sheep and pigs, respectively. All body-parts are present, suggesting that, in the main, complete animals were kept on, or brought to the site, with some variations. For cattle, horn cores and mandibles are the most frequently represented elements, although the main meat-bearing bones, such as the scapula, humerus, and pelvis are also well represented. It would seem likely that these remains originate from a range of activities, including primary butchery waste, craft working, kitchen, and table waste. The presence of so many horn cores, and patterns of butchery upon them may indicate a certain amount of hornworking being carried out on site (see Butchery section, below), although there were no concentrations of horn cores on the site.

In contrast, sheep horn cores are relatively poorly represented, although once again, the main meat-bearing elements are well represented compared to

Table 7.1   Taphonomic information for the Bishopstone animal bone

Species	% Gnawed	% Burnt	% Butchered	% Loose teeth
Sheep/goat	17.1%	2.8%	5.9%	28.0%
Pig	12.7%	1.8%	5.8%	24.1%
Cattle	14.3%	2.0%	15.5%	23.9%
TOTAL	**15.2%**	**2.3%**	**7.5%**	**26.1%**

Table 7.2 Number of Identified Specimens (NISP) per phase

Species	C8th–9th Pits	C9th Cellar destruction	C10th North-west area	C8th–LC10th Remaining bone	TOTAL
Sheep/goat	344	220	113	1601	2278
Sheep	102	42	30	388	562
Goat	1			13	14
Pig	251	181	104	1084	1620
Cattle	104	169	72	552	897
Horse	1	4	6	18	29
Dog	2	10	3	28	43
Cat	20	18	6	42	86
Red deer		2			2
Roe deer		6	3	8	17
Hare		3		11	14
Badger				1	1
Large whale		1	1		2
Medium whale				1	1
Whale		1		1	2
Galliform	133	25	25	441	624
Chicken/guinea fowl	23	4	2	81	110
Chicken/pheasant	14	5	2	43	64
Chicken	4		1	7	12
Anser/Branta sp.	4	2		29	35
Anser sp.	4			17	21
? Anser sp.	1	3		2	6
? Branta sp.		1		3	4
Mallard-size duck	9	3	2	22	36
Teal/garganey				2	2
Rock/stock dove				7	7
Wood pigeon				1	1
Sparrowhawk			2		2
Grey heron	2			1	3
Crane		1			1
Curlew			2	6	8
Golden plover				1	1
Oystercatcher				1	1
Dunlin				2	2
Cormorant				3	3
Herring gull				1	1
Common gull	1			2	3
Kittiwake				1	1
Raven				1	1
Crow	1				1
Crow/rook				2	2
Jackdaw/magpie				1	1
Tawny owl				1	1
Turdus sp.	2			4	6
Small passerine			1	12	13
Large mammal size	94	126	49	603	872
Medium mammal size	540	322	181	2568	3611
Small mammal size		2		4	6
Bird	122	18	12	336	488
Unidentified	2478	1520	840	11779	16617
TOTAL	**4257**	**2689**	**1457**	**19732**	**28135**

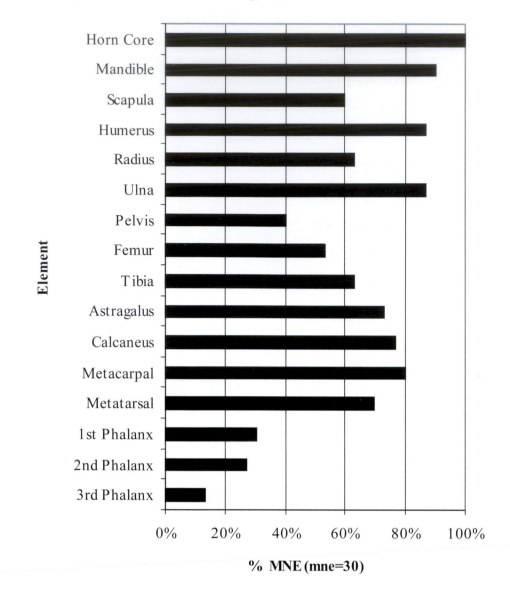

Fig 7.1   Minimum Number of Elements (MNE) for cattle

foot bones; in fact, humeri are the most numerous elements. The greater representation of the tibia to femur is likely because tibiae can be more easily identified than many other elements when fragmented. For pigs, both forelimbs and hindlimbs are well represented, although there is a slight under-representation of foot bones; perhaps at least some pigs were being brought to the site already partially butchered. Although spatial analysis was carried out, there was no evidence for concentrations of particular elements that might be indicative of specialised activity areas.

Butchery

As shown in Table 7.1, cattle remains were the most frequently butchered of the three main domesticates. The type of butchery mark also varied by species: Figure 7.4 shows that the majority of butchered

cattle bones were chopped, whereas for sheep, most butchered bones bore cut marks, with pigs having almost equal levels of chops and cuts. This is likely due to the practicalities of carcass division, the greater size of cattle requiring more use of cleavers. All stages of the butchery process are evident in this material. Transverse cut marks on the ventral surfaces of sheep atlas and axis vertebrae perhaps stem from slaughtering animals by slitting their throats, although they might also be related to carcass division (Landon 1996, 71–2). There are a number of marks resulting from division of the carcass, but there is little standardisation in the methods used to do so, with variation in the tool used, and location of the butchery marks on certain elements, even within the same species. Of particular interest are cattle atlas and axis vertebrae, and a pig atlas vertebra which had been chopped axially. Sagitally split vertebrae can be indicative of specialised butchery, with carcasses split longitudinally (O'Connor 1982, 16), but the very

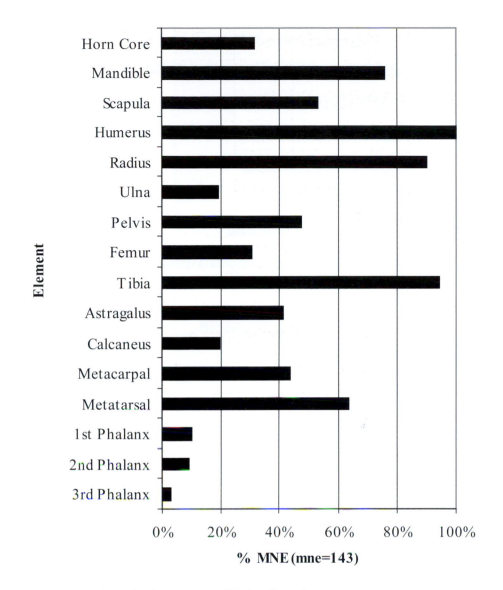

Fig 7.2 Minimum Number of Elements (MNE) for sheep/goat

small number at Bishopstone, along with lack of any other evidence for standardised butchery, indicate this probably was not the case here.

Chops on cattle mandibles indicate the possible extraction of tongue and jowls for consumption. Nine sheep and three pig frontals had been chopped in half along the midline, probably in order to remove the brain. Some of the cattle and sheep long bones and metapodia seem to have been exploited for marrow, having been chopped axially down the middle; a butchery type commonly found in Saxon period assemblages, including at Portchester (Grant 1976, 272). Various long bones of the three main domesticates also had scrapes and cuts on their shafts, possibly from deboning the meat for cooking and/or during consumption. Two pig scapulae seem to represent the remnants of preserved meat; one with its spinous process chopped off, and another with a meat hook mark in the blade, which suggests that it may have been suspended for smoking.

Ageing

Figures 7.5–7.7 and Tables 7.3–7.5 summarise the total ageing data for the three main domesticates. For cattle, a spread of ages is evident, with a peak at Stage C (6–18 months), and others at H (8–12 years) and J (12+ years). This fits with the fusion data, suggesting 62% of animals were still alive at 36–42 months. No neonatal mandibles or postcrania were present, suggesting cattle breeding was not taking place in the area excavated. Sheep also demonstrate a spread of ages, with one mandible at 0–1 month, and a small number of neonatal bones. Around 23.6% of sheep were killed within the first year of life, before a peak at 1–2 years (Stage D), and another at 3–4 years (Stage F), with a small proportion (10.1%) surviving beyond 4 years (Stage G). Epiphyseal fusion largely matches up with this picture.

Whilst cattle and sheep show a spread of ages,

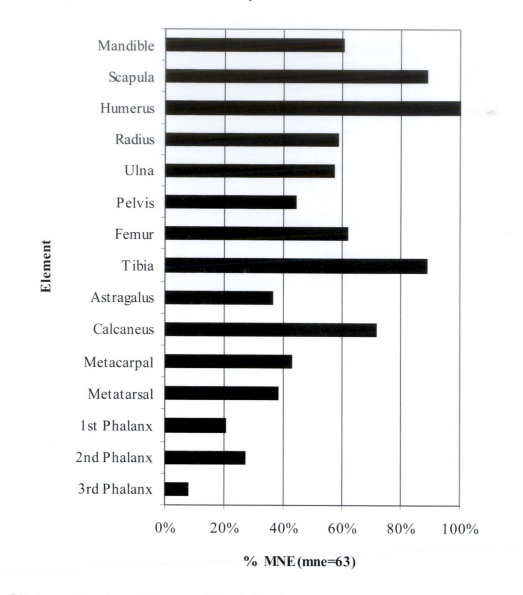

Fig 7.3   Minimum Number of Elements (MNE) for pigs

with slight peaks, the dental data for pigs hints at a much more selective culling pattern. A small number of pigs aged 0–2 months at death are present (including foetal and neonatal remains), with some also at Stages B and C (2–7 months and 7–14 months respectively), before a major peak at Stage D (14–21 months), in which over 40% of pigs were slaughtered. A further 21.7% were killed at 21–7 months (Stage E), but apart from a single fused distal radius and a fused proximal tibia (both of which usually fuse at 36–42 months), no animals appear to have been slaughtered above this age.

Sexing

Only five cattle pelves could be sexed on morphological grounds, all coming from females. Comparison of the size and shape of cattle metacarpals seems to indicate that ten are from females, three from males, and one possibly from a castrate. Of the sheep pelves

which could be sexed using the morphology of the medial acetabular wall, fifteen were male and nine female, with two possible castrates. Only five sheep horn cores could be sexed, two from males, three from females. Of the pig lower canines, both loose and still in the mandible, 49 were from females, 31 from males, a ratio of just over 1.5:1 females to males.

Metrics

No cattle long bones were complete enough to allow withers heights to be reconstructed, but greatest length measurements (GL) for cattle astragali range from 577–635mm, with a mean of 609mm (based on seventeen measureable astragali), which fits within the normal range for other Anglo-Saxon sites (Dobney *et al* 2007, 168). In contrast, sheep withers heights at Bishopstone range from 517–646mm, with a mean of 573mm (based on 80 measurements), and in general seem to have been smaller than at contemporary

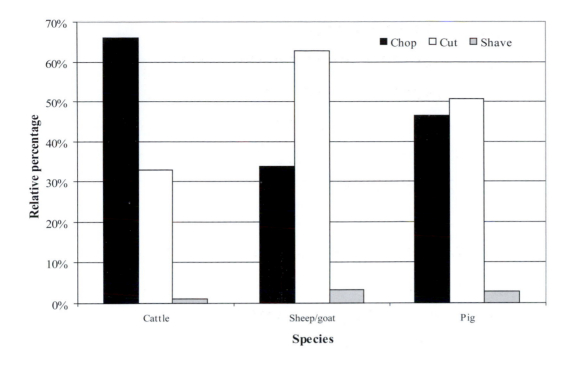

Fig 7.4   Differences in butchery types for the main domesticates

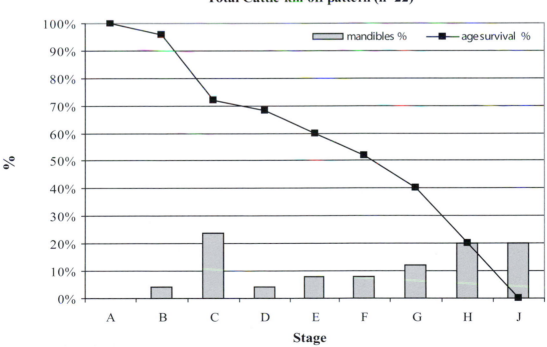

Fig 7.5   Dental ageing kill-off patterns for cattle

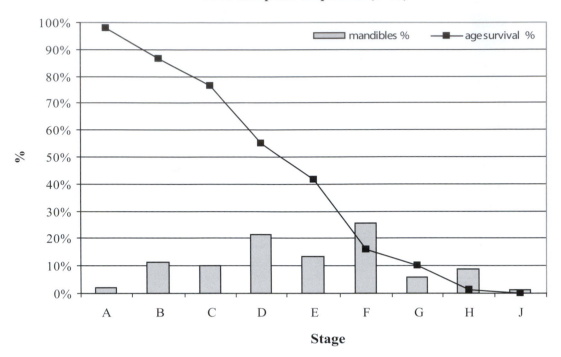

Fig 7.6   *Dental ageing kill-off patterns for sheep / goat*

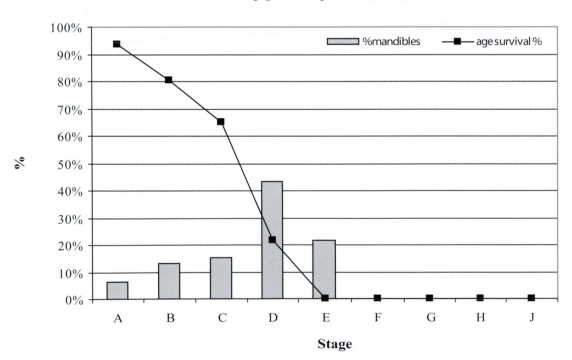

Fig 7.7   *Dental ageing kill-off patterns for pigs*

Table 7.3 Cattle epiphyseal fusion data

CATTLE	Element	F	UF	TOTAL	%F
7–15m	Scapula	19	1	20	
	Pelvis	6	0	6	
	P. Radius	21	0	21	
	TOTAL	**46**	**1**	**47**	**98%**
15–24m	Phalanx II	33	1	34	
	D. Humerus	21	1	22	
	Phalanx I	36	5	41	
	TOTAL	**90**	**7**	**97**	**93%**
24–36m	D. Tibia	16	3	19	
	D. Metapodial	49	9	58	
	Calcaneus	5	2	7	
	TOTAL	**70**	**14**	**84**	**83%**
36–48m	P. Femur	9	5	14	
	P. Humerus	6	5	11	
	D. Radius	6	3	9	
	P. Ulna	1	3	4	
	D. Femur	7	4	11	
	P. Tibia	5	1	6	
	TOTAL	**34**	**21**	**55**	**62%**

Table 7.4 Sheep epiphyseal fusion data

SHEEP	Element	F	UF	TOTAL	%F
3–10m	D. Humerus	88	15	103	
	P. Radius	65	8	73	
	Scapula	43	9	52	
	Pelvis	42	10	52	
	Phalanx I	49	9	58	
	Phalanx II	52	4	56	
	TOTAL	**339**	**55**	**394**	**86%**
15–24m	D. Tibia	51	19	70	
	D. Metapodial	40	54	94	
	TOTAL	**91**	**73**	**164**	**55%**
36–42m	Calcaneus	11	9	20	
	P. Femur	17	20	37	
	P. Humerus	8	18	24	
	D. Radius	15	12	27	
	P. Ulna	2	10	12	
	D. Femur	18	21	39	
	P. Tibia	7	22	29	
	TOTAL	**78**	**112**	**190**	**41%**

Table 7.5   Pig epiphyseal fusion data

PIG	Element	F	UF	TOTAL	%F
9–12m	Scapula	28	7	35	
	Pelvis	13	6	19	
	Phalanx II	65	22	87	
	TOTAL	**106**	**35**	**141**	**75%**
12–18m	Phalanx I	23	37	60	
	D. Metapodial	25	96	121	
	D. Humerus	29	11	40	
	P. Radius	37	5	42	
	TOTAL	**114**	**149**	**263**	**43%**
24–36m	D. Tibia	14	20	34	
	Calcaneus	3	19	22	
	TOTAL	**17**	**39**	**56**	**30%**
36–42m	P. Femur	0	18	18	
	P. Humerus	0	6	6	
	D. Radius	1	18	19	
	P. Ulna	0	7	7	
	D. Femur	0	32	32	
	P. Tibia	1	14	15	
	TOTAL	**2**	**95**	**97**	**2%**

sites (*ibid*, 172), with a wider range of sizes. Withers heights could be calculated for 21 pig bones, with a range of 630–739mm, and a mean of 681mm.

Pathology and non-metrics

'Penning elbow' was noted on five of 74 sheep humeri (6.8%) and four of 49 sheep radii (8.2%). Fourteen of 80 sheep mandibles (17.5%) had dental crowding. One sheep metacarpal had slight periostitis along the length of the shaft, and a sheep pelvis had eburnation in the acetabulum, possibly from osteoarthritis. For pigs, 23 of 61 mandibles (37.7%) had linear enamel hypoplasia, although in the majority of cases this was only of slight severity. One pig maxilla had periodontal disease in the area of the third molar, whilst a pig tibia had extensive bone growth, possibly cancerous in nature, towards the distal end. One cattle femoral head had eburnation, whilst two cattle metatarsals and one metacarpal had asymmetric condyles, a form of pathology apparently caused by use for traction (Bartosiewicz *et al* 1997). One cattle mandible had evidence of severe infection on both the left and right sides, in both cases originating around the third molar, with considerable resorption of the alveolar bone, and expansion of the diastema. In both cases, the infection also seems to have spread up the ascending ramus of the mandible.

As for non-metric traits, two of 27 (7.4%) cattle mandibles, and two of 55 (3.6%) sheep mandibles had congenitally absent second premolars, whilst only one of 85 (1.2%) sheep lower third molars had an underdeveloped third cusp. The position of the nutrient foramen on sheep femora was as follows: at the anterior proximal end on eight of 31 (25.8%) for which this trait was observable, two of 42 (4.8%) were on the midshaft posterior side, and three of 45 (6.7%) at the distal posterior end.

Other domestic mammals

A substantial number of the cat remains (as well as those of dog) are Associated Bone Groups (ABGs, see below), the majority of which were young or immature cats. One of these cats, aged between seven months and one year, recovered from the cellar of Structure W (context 1344), had an interesting dietary signature, indicating a strong marine component in its diet (see Marshall *et al* Chapter 8.2). The other two cat ABGs sampled also had significantly nitrogen-enriched diets, as one would expect of carnivores, but neither shows the striking pattern evident in the remaining cat from context 1344. Butchery indicative of skinning was noted on a disarticulated cat femur and mandible, as well as on a calcaneus, ulna, and tibia from three further ABGs. A cat humerus, again from the subterranean component of Structure W, had fractured just below halfway, but had completely healed except for a slight protrusion of bone where the fracture occurred, and the distal end is slightly displaced medially. Measurements of cat bones ruled out the possible presence of wild cats in the assemblage.

With the exception of three unfused disarticulated dog elements and three immature dog ABGs, all of the equid and dog bones were from mature animals. Two disarticulated dog bones were complete, allowing withers' heights to be calculated, of 534mm from a femur and 610mm from a humerus, whilst a tibia from a dog ABG in 1346B gave a height of 543mm. Only one horse bone, a metacarpal, was complete, giving a withers' height of 1436mm. One of the dog ABGs from the infill deposits of the cellar seems to have had major trauma to the right-hand side of its body – the humerus has a healed fracture at midshaft, with the distal end now at around a 45° angle, and the shaft is thickened, with the deltoid tuberosity being overdeveloped, perhaps to compensate for the injury. The right femur from this animal also seems to have been fractured just below midshaft, although unfortunately, the proximal end of the bone is missing, whilst the right tibia has a slight bony spur on the posterior side, about halfway down the shaft.

Shave marks on the lateral side of a horse metatarsal, near the distal end, and cut marks on a proximal metatarsal likely result from skinning, as does a shave mark on the lateral side of a dog 5th metacarpal. However, one horse metatarsal had been chopped through along the midline, in a similar fashion to that observed among the cattle and sheep metapodials, whilst another metatarsal had been chopped through mid-diaphysis. This raises the possibility that these remains represent human food waste, although it is also conceivable that the meat could have been fed to dogs.

Wild mammals

Table 7.6 presents body-part data for four of the wild mammals. Roe deer is the best represented of the four species, followed by hare, red deer, and badger. However, red deer is only represented by two very small fragments of antler, and this is in itself not good evidence for venison consumption. All bones of hare and the badger humerus had fused. Of the roe deer remains, the ABG is particularly interesting. These remains were recovered from a posthole and consist of a left frontal, six maxillary teeth, left mandible, left distal humerus, radius and ulna, right unfused distal radius epiphysis, carpals and left and right metacarpals, both unfused at the distal end. In the mandible, the dp4 was unworn, and the M1 was erupting, suggesting an animal less than two months of age. Roe deer tend to be born in May–June (Carter 2006, 51), indicating this animal was killed in late summer. None of the bones from this group had butchery marks. Butchery marks were found on a hare humerus, in the form of a horizontal cut mark on the posterior part of the proximal end, possibly from disarticulating the bones, or from defleshing. One roe deer radius had horizontal cut marks on the medial side of the distal end of the diaphysis.

Five fragments of whale bone were also present (identified through the assistance of Richard Sabin of the Natural History Museum), two of which were vertebrae fragments, in too poor a condition to

Table 7.6 Body-part representation for wild mammals

Element	Roe deer	Red deer	Hare	Badger
ABG	1			
Antler		2		
Skull			1	
Mandible			3	
Loose teeth	1			
Atlas/axis			1	
Scapula				
Humerus	3		1	1
Radius			1	
Ulna			1	
Pelvis				
Femur	1			
Tibia	2		1	
Astragalus			3	
Calcaneus	1		2	
Metacarpal	4			
Metatarsal	4		1	

attribute to species or size category. One vertebra came from a medium-sized whale, and the articular surface was highly polished, perhaps from use as a linen smoother (see Thomas, Chapter 6.9). A portion of mandible from a large whale, comparable with a sperm whale, bore a number of chop marks, and had been separated from the rest of the mandible at a point just below the ascending ramus. This was perhaps done in order to extract the tongue, which carries a considerable amount of meat, as suggested for whale mandibles from Flixborough (Dobney *et al* 2007, 199), although the bone itself may have been utilised as a raw material for carved objects (MacGregor 1985, 201).

Domestic birds

Chickens are overwhelmingly the best represented domestic bird in the Bishopstone assemblage, with very small goose and duck percentages in comparison. Overall, although the numbers of goose and duck bones are relatively small, there does not seem to be any obvious absence of elements. The large number of chicken remains made it possible to undertake statistical analysis of the body-parts present (Fig 7.8), and whilst some of the more fragile body parts, such as the scapula and pelvis, are noticeably under-represented, most parts of the body are present.

Table 7.7 Ageing data for domestic birds

Species	Fused	Unfused	Total	% Fused
Chicken	299	97	396	71.8%
Goose	29	2	31	82.6%
Duck	19	4	23	93.5%

Table 7.7 presents ageing data for the domestic birds. In all cases, the majority of bones had fused. It would seem that these birds were rarely being slaughtered before being used for eggs, suggesting these formed an important component of the diet for some of the inhabitants of Bishopstone. This is supported by the sexing data: 47.8% of femora have medullary bone representing hens in lay, whilst 7 of 34 tarsometatarsi have cock spurs or spur scars suggesting a hens-to-cockerel ratio of around 4:1. This would be consistent with a typical farmyard flock. Metrical analysis of the tarsometatarsi (Fig 7.9) has also identified a group of unfused tarsometatarsi which are very large, but have no spurs or spur scars. It may be that these represent caponised birds, or just young males. The isotopic data for one of the chicken Associated Bone Groups (an ABG being defined as the remains of an individual bird/animal found either in complete or partial articulation) provides useful information about husbandry of this species, with an elevated nitrogen value probably reflecting

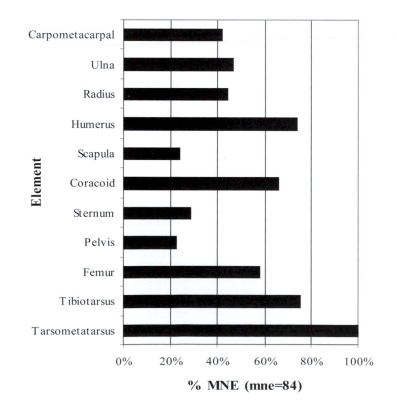

Fig 7.8   Chicken body-part patterns (% MNE)

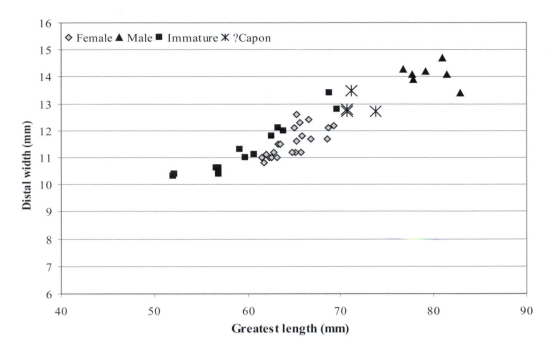

Fig 7.9 Scatterplot for chicken tarsometatarsi measurements of distal width against greatest length

an omnivorous diet comprising human food waste (see Marshall *et al*, Chapter 8.2).

Wild birds

Nineteen different wild bird species were recovered in total, with curlew and rock/stock dove the most frequent, followed by smaller proportions of other species. As one might expect, the range is dominated by waders and other species native to coastal and estuarine environments. However, not all of these species necessarily represent food remains; the status of sparrowhawk, raven, crow/rook, and jackdaw/magpie are uncertain, whilst tawny owl was present as an ABG. A possible interpretation of the sparrowhawks and corvids is that they were killed to protect animals, such as young lambs. This practice has been documented at Easton Lane, Winchester, where a late Anglo-Saxon pit located within a contemporary sheep enclosure yielded the bones of two young crows (Maltby 1989, 128).

Discussion

Socio-economic status

With the application of modern sampling regimes across a steadily expanding corpus of excavated later Anglo-Saxon settlements, zooarchaeological assemblages are increasingly being used as a tool for examining questions of site status and character complementing the picture provided by more tradi-

tional proxies including ornamental metalwork and domestic architecture (Ashby 2002; Albarella and Thomas 2002; Dobney *et al* 2007; Sykes 2007). In ideal circumstances such analysis should – in the words of Carver – help us determine 'whether we are in the presence of a homestead, a princely stronghold, a manor, fort or a town and its concomitant economy' (Carver 1994, 5). Yet recent comparative analysis of so-called 'zooarchaeological signatures' has demonstrated the considerable practical difficulties involved with overcoming problems of sample bias: how representative is an assemblage of the totality of the social make-up of a given settlement? Conversely, to what extent should we expect a given signature to relate to a single social scale given that excavated settlements and portions thereof, may embrace different social groups living in close proximity (Dobney *et al* 2007)? Furthermore, what allowance should be made for poorly phased assemblages such as Bishopstone which may mask transitions in social character and status of the type inferred from Flixborough's refined occupation sequence? On the other hand, comparative analysis of zooarchaeological profiles has highlighted significant distinctions between different categories of settlement (the most sharply drawn being between wics on the one hand and contemporary rural settlements on the other) suggesting that the data does indeed bear the imprint of contemporary trends in animal exploitation predicated on social difference.

Whilst acknowledging the interpretative limitations imposed by poor phasing, these recent approaches can be used to harness the interpretative potential of Bishopstone's zooarchaeological assemblage as a source for characterising the socio-economic identity of the settlement. Accordingly, the following examination focuses on three aspects of the faunal record with direct relevance to understanding the social connotations of the excavated settlement: animal husbandry, species representation, and finally, evidence for conspicuous consumption; the discussion concludes with evidence for social attitudes to animals followed by an evaluation of the meaning and significance of ABGs.

Animal husbandry

Age, metrical, and body-part analysis of the three major domesticates represents one of the established approaches by which zooarchaeological assemblages are used to infer socio-economic status (Ashby 2002; Crabtree 1990; DeFrance 2009). The dynamics of food production in Anglo-Saxon England were strongly influenced by social inequalities across the settlement hierarchy. Within the increasingly stratified society of the later Anglo-Saxon era, it is legitimate to make a broad distinction between 'producer' sites on the one hand, self-sufficient communities occupying the lower rungs of the settlement hierarchy, and 'consumer' sites on the other, places occupied by an elevated social contingent able to derive much of their dietary needs from food rents and renders supplied through a tributary system (Hagen 1995, 261–8).

Combined with other cultural factors (gender, ethnicity, etc) these social inequalities served to shape the nature of animal-human relationships (Fowler 2002, 2; Gumerman 1997, 114). Whereas the life of producers was dominated by the rearing of domestic stock, partly for internal consumption and partly for food payments, the emphasis at the other end of the social spectrum was on wild species, the procurement and consumption of which offered outlets for the expression of elite identity, as reflected in hunting and hawking which were subject to increasing formalisation over the final two centuries of the Anglo-Saxon era (Sykes 2005).

A synthesis of the available documentary sources, combined with place-name and topographic evidence encourages the view that Bishopstone fell into the former category: the head of a cohesive territory embracing dependent downland settlements which, through a process of estate fragmentation over the course of the 10th century, emerged as separate parishes – Sutton, Denton, South Heighton (Blair and Pickles, Chapter 3.1). One should therefore expect Bishopstone's zooarchaeological signature to embody aspects of elite-focused consumption.

On the other hand, the picture is complicated by the fact that in addition to operating as collection centres for food rents, high-status complexes (whether under the control of secular or ecclesiastical lords) also generated a proportion of their foodstuffs from the 'inland' of their estates (Faith

1997). As estate memoranda surviving from the end of the Anglo-Saxon period attest (Harvey 1993), lifestyles of consumption and production could thus be intertwined within the confines of a single excavated settlement. With the exception of the controlled provisioning possibly witnessed in mid Saxon wics (O'Connor 2001), one will rarely expect to encounter highly polarised assemblages during this period; it is rather the relative importance of onsite husbandry as against external provisioning that can provide an indication of socio-economic status.

At Bishopstone, sheep (perhaps with the occasional goat) seem to have been the most common species, with ageing data suggesting mixed usage for meat, dairy, and wool production, a conclusion backed by the substantial artefactual evidence for textile production recovered from the excavations (as reviewed in Chapter 6.9). However, given that nearly 85% of sheep were dead by the end of their fourth year, meat may have been the main aim. Such was also suggested for the 5th- to 8th-century phase at Portchester (Grant 1976, 277), where, in accordance with a wider Anglo-Saxon trend, there was an increase in the proportion of older sheep over the lifetime of the Anglo-Saxon occupation (Sykes 2006, 58–9). The presence of foetal/neonatal sheep implies some onsite husbandry, but the sexing data does not seem to indicate a typical breeding herd which implies some level of external resourcing whether in the form of food renders or direct provisioning from dependent farms located on outlying parts of the Bishopstone estate. The lack of a well-defined slaughter pattern may itself be indicative of multiple sources of supply (Huntley and Rackham 2007, 122) as might the observed diversity in the size of the animals which is consistent with a composite population drawn from multiple breeding flocks (O'Connor 2003, 84).

Species representation

Species representation has played a central role in recent studies attempting to link zooarchaeological signatures with the socio-economic status of later Anglo-Saxon settlements. Much of this work hinges on determining patterns in what might be called the 'social distribution' of different species, ie comparing the range and relative frequency of species across different social categories of settlement (Ashby 2002; Crabtree 1990; Sykes 2005). Care has to be taken in the interpretation of such evidence for, as Sykes (2005) has demonstrated, the role of certain species as status indicators was subject to dynamic change over the later Anglo-Saxon period.

Recent studies have shown that settlements with high-status attributes, whether secular or ecclesiastical, are proclaimed by a higher than average ratio of pig to the other main domesticates (20% or above by NISP) (Dobney *et al* 2007, 222–4; Sykes 2007; Poole, in prep). With a total of 30.2% (based on NISP), Bishopstone clearly falls into this elevated social category. Part of the reason why pigs are found in higher frequency on high-status sites may be related to their value as ideal food-rent animals (Sykes 2007, 42); unlike other domesticates valued for their secondary products, pigs also embodied the cult of meat consumption characterising an elite diet. Concurrently, deeper symbolic meanings may also have served to invest pork consumption with elite connotations. In the Anglo-Saxon period pigs were often driven into woodland to feed on acorns and beechmast where they may have interbred with native populations of wild boar (Albarella 2006). The popularity of pork consumption as a marker of elite status may therefore have been tied into the symbolic link made between domestic pig, wild boar, woodland and hunting (for example, Ervynck 2004, 219). In addition, perceptions may have been influenced by the high store placed on pork in contemporary medical tracts which drew upon a Greco-Roman inheritance extending back to Galen (*c* AD 130–200) (Hoffman 2008, 23).

In common with other high-status assemblages, Bishopstone also has elevated proportions of domestic birds, 13% overall, a total significantly above the national average (Poole in prep). Moreover, the comparatively high number of juvenile chickens – at 30% comparable to the late Anglo-Saxon phase of Eynsham Abbey (Mulville 2003, 355) and St Alban's Abbey (Serjeantson 2006, 137) – may suggest a dietary preference for the most palatable birds, alongside egg production.

The social implications of the wild bird taxa are not so clear-cut, for the wide diversity of species evidenced at Bishopstone almost certainly reflects the site's proximity to bird-rich coastal and estuarine habitats. Golden plover are ubiquitous on Anglo-Saxon settlements so cannot be used as markers of elevated social status (Sykes 2005, 98; Poole, in prep). More suggestive are the species heron and curlew, both strongly represented on high-status estate centres of the Anglo-Saxon period (Dobney and Jacques 2002, 14; Sykes 2005, 94; Poole, in prep).

The presence of a modest collection of whalebone at Bishopstone is also difficult to interpret in explicitly social terms. It has been suggested by Gardiner (1997) that the exploitation of cetaceans during the Anglo-Saxon period had yet to carry the elite associations which it was to enjoy in the 11th century when whale meat had become an established delicacy of the southern English nobility and when royal prerogative over stranded whales is first documented (Gardiner 1997, 174–5; Sabin *et al* 1999, 368). This view may require modification given that elite patronage very likely lies behind the seemingly systematic exploitation of bottlenose dolphins attested at Flixborough between the 8th and 10th centuries (Dobney *et al*, 2007, 240). On the other hand, the evidence from Bishopstone would appear to fit into a long-term picture of discrete beaching events documented locally in the small assemblages of whale bone recovered from late Iron Age and Romano-

British levels excavated on Rookery Hill; a pattern rather more suggestive of opportunism (Bell 1977, 135, 189).

In a period when hunting and hawking gained increasing prominence as markers of elite identity (Sykes 2007, 66), relatively high proportions of wild species (4% and above) can also be taken as a measure of elevated social status. Yet in spite of other status indicators, at Bishopstone such species comprise only 1% of the faunal assemblage. The observed contrast between a low percentage of wild mammal taxa on the one hand and the abundance of pig and domestic fowl on the other is, however, repeated on other settlements of the later Anglo-Saxon era. The closest correspondences are with North Elmham (Noddle 1980), Eynsham Abbey (Ayres *et al* 2003; Mulville 2003), and the suggested monastic phase at Flixborough (Dobney *et al* 2007) – sites of elevated social status where a significant ecclesiastical dimension has been inferred on the grounds of historical and/or archaeological evidence.

Given the suggested ecclesiastical context of these parallels, can Bishopstone's zooarchaeological signature be linked more directly to a monastic lifestyle? From a historical viewpoint, one might expect ecclesiastical communities of this period to display some marked differences from their secular counterparts if they were indeed (as others have argued) subject to dietary restrictions laid down by the rule of St Benedict – most obviously an emphasis on fish and fowl permitted as a red-meat substitute (Ervynck 1997; Harvey 2006, 215). Yet recent and ongoing syntheses across a growing number of high-status assemblages falling within the mid-9th to the mid-11th centuries, instead suggest that it is very hard to read distinctions between documented religious houses and secular estate complexes in the zooarchaeological record (Sykes 2007, 91, fig 84). Particularly surprising given the trajectory taken by monastic diet in the post-Conquest period (ibid 60, fig 58), is the fact that the similarity even extends to the consumption of fish for which there is plentiful evidence at Bishopstone (ibid 91, figs 58, 60, and 61; see Reynolds, Chapter 7.2). The challenge for zooarchaeologists working in this period is to refine further their ability to detect and attribute meaning to the subtle contrasts now emerging through the study of contemporary faunal assemblages, a prerequisite for which is a closer integration of bioarchaeological and cultural data in the process of site interpretation (for example, Dobney *et al* 2007; Loveluck 2007).

Conspicuous consumption

Feasting as a realm of elite culture is very well attested in Anglo-Saxon prose and textual sources, and periods of feasting and fasting were central parts of the agricultural cycle in Anglo-Saxon England (Hagen 1992; Pollington 2003). The social significance of communal eating has been much discussed

Table 7.8   Species present in context 2577

Species	NISP
Sheep/goat	123
Pig	56
Cattle	9
Roe deer	3
Galliform	11
Anser sp.	1
Anser/Branta sp.	2
Mallard	1
Branta sp.	1
Curlew	3
Cormorant	2
Heron	1
Oystercatcher	1
Large	12
Medium	68
Bird	9
Unidentified	300
TOTAL	**603**

within archaeology and anthropology (Jones 2007), with scholars recognising that it serves variously to express group identity and social position, and to create obligations. Yet archaeologists have found it difficult to distinguish what may be termed individual feasting events from more general indicators of conspicuous consumption defining broad phases of site activity, a problem recently acknowledged in a discussion of the faunal remains from Flixborough (Dobney *et al* 2007, 237).

With the development of more nuanced ways of reading zooarchaeological signatures, new evidence for feasting is emerging, complementing such well-known examples as the cattle skull 'stack' discovered against the wall of one of the 6th/7th-century buildings at Yeavering (Higgs and Jarman 1977), which finds later echoes in the cattle skull deposits buried in the vicinity of the great hall at Hofstaðir, Iceland (Lucas and McGovern 2007). One of these new insights is a bias in the representation of crania amongst deer assemblages from mid Saxon elite sites, a pattern correlated to venison redistribution at communal feasts (Sykes, forthcoming).

It is against this background that a distinctive faunal assemblage recovered from the upper fill of pit 2576 (context 2577) deserves attention as a possible feasting deposit (Table 7.8). It immediately stands out for a high concentration of wild species, at 5.1% well above the 1% site average, covering a diverse range including 3 curlew bones, 2 cormorant bones, 1 heron bone, 1 oystercatcher bone, 1 wild goose bone, as well as 3 roe deer elements (Thomas

1999). Other hallmarks include prime cuts of meat (in this case pork) (Albarella and Serjeantson 2002) and a complete lack of 'inedible' species such as cats, dogs and horses, indicating that the assemblage is exclusively food waste.

Evidence for social attitudes to animals

At Bishopstone, cats and dogs make up 1.6% and 0.8% of the total domestic mammal assemblage respectively, figures very much at the upper end of later Anglo-Saxon frequencies (Poole, in prep). The measured dog bones indicate the presence of large dogs by Anglo-Saxon standards, at least according to figures published by Harcourt (1974), with a stature comparable to that of a modern Alsatian (Clark 1998, 63). Given the evidence for dog gnawing on many of the bones, some of these animals may have lived in a semi-feral state, scavenging on middens.

Similarly, the age profiles of the cats indicate a largely feral population, some of which may have been exploited for their fur. The one possible exception is the cat from the infill of cellared Structure W whose isotopic signature shows a strong marine influence contrastingly markedly with the human remains which are otherwise accommodated within the normal terrestrial range (Marshall *et al*, Chapter 8.2). This dichotomy is difficult to explain, but evidence that the consumption of fish prior to AD 1000 was perhaps restricted to the higher echelons of Anglo-Saxon society (Barrett *et al* 2004), might suggest that the cat in question received favourable treatment. Alternatively, it is possible this signature was acquired as a result of scavenging fish from middens, but this would seem unlikely. Bone stable isotopes only provide an average of a human or animal's diet over long time spans, and cannot detect occasional consumption of certain foods such as fish in a largely land-based diet (Müldner and Richards 2006, 229). In other words, this cat would have had to be eating fish preferentially on a regular basis, and in large amounts for such a strong signature to occur. There has been some debate as to whether contemporary Anglo-Saxon attitudes to the animal world might allow for the keeping of pets (see, for example, Serpell and Paul 1994); a relationship with obvious status implications (Thomas 2005). It is difficult to verify such practices in the zooarchaeological record, but the period under review is not without hints including the diminutive skeletal remains of what have been interpreted as lap dogs recovered from late Saxon levels at Winchester (Bourdillon 2009).

Associated Bone Groups (ABGs)

A total of 43 ABGs were recovered during excavations, the species represented being cattle, sheep/goat, pig, cat, dog, roe deer, chicken, mallard, tawny owl, rock/stock dove, and *Turdus* species, with chicken and cats being by far the most common. Whilst ABGs are fairly common on settlements of the later Anglo-Saxon period (Poole, in prep), the number and variety from Bishopstone stands out in a national context providing an opportunity for a closer contextual analysis of the phenomenon across a spectrum of discrete deposits.

The ABGs from Bishopstone were recovered from a diversity of pits and the cellared component of Structure W. Most of the animals buried whole represent the smaller end of the species range, dog and cat, and birds (both domestic and wild). Only neonatal and juvenile specimens of sheep and pig are accorded similar treatment; adult cattle, sheep, and pig are represented exclusively by partial skeletons dominated by head and feet elements. Several of the ABGs displayed evidence for butchery indicating that they were exploited for meat and/or fur; cut marks were noted on one cat, three chicken skeletons, and a rock/stock dove.

From a traditional viewpoint all such deposits could be classed as the discarded remains of primary butchery waste. Whilst this may indeed provide an explanation for a proportion of the ABGs represented at Bishopstone, the possibility that some may be the result of domestic rituals also needs to be entertained, especially in the light of comparable evidence in the form of the iron hoard which has been interpreted in similar terms (Chapter 6.2). The strongest case for such an interpretation concerns those examples (detailed further below) apparently buried with care within a structure at the point of its abandonment. As shown by Hamerow's (2006) study of so-called 'special deposits' on early Anglo-Saxon settlements, the practice of burying partial or complete animals in abandoned structures, most conspicuously sunken-featured buildings, appears to have been a relatively widespread practice which endured into the 8th century and beyond (ie into the Christian era). Although the meaning of such 'termination deposits' remains obscure in an Anglo-Saxon context, there is good reason to believe that they represent a later echo of similar expressions of domestic ritual familiar in prehistoric and Romano-British contexts (see Chapter 6.2 for further discussion).

The most compelling example of an ABG meeting Hamerow's criteria for a 'termination deposit' concerns the skeletons of a cat, dog, and sheep – all immature and devoid of butchery marks – derived from one of the chalk rubble dumps (1344) of the cellared component of Structure W. This episode of dumping was immediately preceded by the deliberate dismantling of an overlying timber superstructure, culminating in the deposition of a hoard of iron objects in one of its post sockets. One can only speculate, but it may be that these multiple concealments shared the same symbolic meaning, one inextricably linked to the 'death' of a focal structure within the excavated settlement complex.

A second contender for a termination deposit relates to an association of cattle skulls – the mandible of an animal aged over twelve years and the articulated skull and mandible of a younger individual aged between six and eighteen months – buried at the base of one of the post-settings for aisled Structure V. This recalls the ox skull placed on the base of a sunken-featured building at Pennyland during the late 7th or 8th century, or, more specifically in relation to a ground-level structure, the cow and a fragment of ?boar skull placed in a pit located immediately next to the west entrance of Building C13 at Cowdery's Down (Hamerow 2006).

Conclusions

Discussion of the Bishopstone assemblage has highlighted some of the difficulties involved in using zooarchaeological signatures to characterise Anglo-Saxon settlements in social terms. Yet a contextualisation of the data has undoubtedly provided useful insights into the nature of occupation at this site. In terms of economic profile, the excavated settlement at Bishopstone can be characterised as both a consumer and a producer, meeting some of its own domestic needs but also drawing upon external resources in the form of food-renders either owed by subordinate peasants tied to the *inland* of the estate or perhaps dependent farms located further afield. Taken in combination, various elements of the zooarchaeological assemblage amplify the impression that there was an elite presence at Bishopstone, most notably the high proportions of pig and domestic bird remains and the presence of heron and curlew. Whether this presence constituted a secular or religious authority is impossible to answer on zooarchaeological grounds alone.

As well as revealing something of human social relationships, it has also been possible to explore the significance of animal species with little tangible economic role, namely cats and dogs. The complexities of these human-animal relationships are further evidenced by the probable use of animal carcasses as a part of termination deposits.

7.2 Fish remains
by Rebecca Reynolds

Introduction

The excavations at Bishopstone produced 2448 identified fish specimens covering seventeen taxa (Table 7.9). Whilst somewhat smaller than the later Anglo-Saxon assemblages from Flixborough and Sandtun (Kent) – at 6000 and 4000 respectively (Dobney *et al* 2007, 228–30; Hamilton-Dyer 2001), this is a significant total in a period when relatively few rural sites produce in excess of 50 specimens (Barrett *et al* 2004, 621; Dobney *et al* 2007, 228–34). Locally, Bishopstone's prominence is cast into strong relief by the very modest collection of fish bones recovered

Table 7.9　Quantification of all fish taxa by skeletal element present at Bishopstone

Sum over Qty	Element									
Taxon	cleithrum	dentary	denticle	other cranial	otolith	pre-maxilla	scale	urohyal	vertebrae	Total
Anguilla anguilla	12								559	571
Belone bellone									1	1
Conger conger	2	5		3		4		1	11	26
Clupea harrengus									706	706
Cyprinidae									5	5
Cyprinidae?									10	10
Dicentrachus labrax									1	1
Dicentrachus labrax?									4	4
Dicentrachus labrax / Perca fluviatilis				6		1			3	10
Gadidae		4		2		6			69	81
Gadus morhua	1	26		6		24			171	228
Pleuronectidae	11	2		6		4		3	205	231
Melanogrammus aeglefinus									2	2
Melanogrammus aeglefinus?									2	2
Merlangius merlangus	1	5		2		7			208	223
Platichthys flesus						1			1	2
Perca fluviatilis									2	2
Rajidae			57						64	121
Scombridae?									1	1
Salmonidae?									1	1
Scombrus scombrus		6				1			170	177
Scombrus scombrus-?									2	2
Trisopterus luscus					1					1
Triglidae				2						2
Trachurus trachurus							6		32	38
Unidentified		1			14				2	17
Total	**27**	**49**	**57**	**27**	**15**	**48**	**6**	**4**	**2232**	**2465**

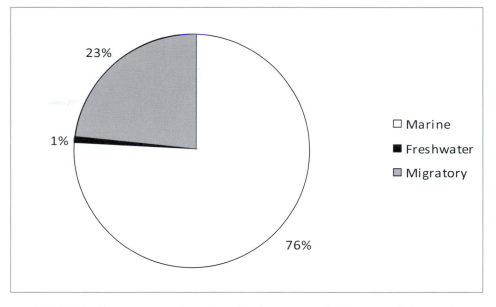

Fig 7.10 Percentages of marine, freshwater and migratory fish species

from the early Anglo-Saxon phase of Rookery Hill which is comparable to the low yields characterising the general run of early and mid Anglo-Saxon rural settlements (Jones 1977).

This study examines the evidence behind what appears to be a significant upturn in the exploitation of marine fish broadly concurrent with the growth of the excavated later Anglo-Saxon settlement. Themes addressed include procurement strategies and the likely role played by fish in the contemporary diet; comparisons are made with other Anglo-Saxon fish-bone assemblages in southern England and beyond to explore what implications this source of evidence might have for understanding the socio-economic character of the settlement. On a more localised scale, it is argued that the importance of the Bishopstone fish-bone assemblage lies in its ability to provide greater time-depth for exploring the emergence of marine fishing as a key component within the medieval economy of the lower Ouse Valley, a process otherwise only glimpsed at the end of the Anglo-Saxon period in Domesday herring renders (King 1962, 453–5; Gardiner 2000a, 82–3).

Methods

The material was examined as part of an undergraduate dissertation at the University of Nottingham (Reynolds 2008) and the recording methods reflect this research context. It should be noted, however, that specialist input and advice on sampling procedures and identifications were provided by Dr Heide Hüster-Plogmann, Dr Dirk Heindrich, and Dr James Barrett. The assemblage comprised a mixture of hand-collected, dry-sieved (10mm mesh), and wet-sieved (flotation samples) remains. As with

other elements of the bioarchaeological record from Bishopstone, the fish bone has been analysed as a broad, single-phase assemblage on account of the problems of site phasing.

In order to gauge rapidly the taxonomic composition of the assemblage, a select number of skeletal elements – pre-maxilla, cleithra, dentary, and vertebrae – were used to identify and quantify the species present. Where taxa were identified from other elements, their presence was noted but they were not included in calculations of relative frequencies. For instance one otolith was identified to species, although many more were noted. Similarly the presence of rajidae were noted from the large number of dermal denticles, as the rest of their bones rarely survive due to their cartilaginous skeleton, although a number of ossified vertebrae were recorded. The high number of calcified vertebrae of rajidae indicates fairly good preservation conditions.

Results

It is clear that marine taxa dominate the remains, the only freshwater species being a few cyprinid and perch (*Perca fluviatilis*) vertebrae (Fig 7.10). Migratory species are represented by eel (*Anguilla anguilla*) and a tentatively identified salmonid. Eel bones were the second most numerous after herring (*Clupea harengus*), although it should be noted that eel's NISP frequency is often inflated compared to other species because of the large number of identifiable elements in the eel skeleton. Other common species were Atlantic mackerel (*Scomber scrombrus*), flatfish (*Pleuronectidae*), whiting (*Merlangus merlangius*), and cod (*Gadus morhua*) (Table 7.9). The garfish (*Belone belone*) present may have been an

Fig 7.11   Cod and whiting vertebrae with a cod dentary and pre-maxilla

accidental catch with herring, as has been suggested for the presence of the same fish at late Anglo-Saxon deposits at Milk Street, London (Locker 1999). One vertebra was thought to belong to a member of the Scombridae family, possibly a tunny (*Thunnus* sp) of which some species may venture away from the Mediterranean during warm summers (Wheeler 1978).

Skeletal representation

The majority of the bones were vertebrae. No cranial bones of herring were found and, although these elements are very fragile, the large quantities of vertebrae belonging to the species suggests that the pattern is not a product of preservation bias; it is probable that the removal of heads took place at a processing site located in a seaward part of the Bishopstone estate (Serjeantson and Woolgar 2006, 116–17). The presence of cranial bones such as dentaries and pre-maxillas of cod, whiting, mackerel, and flatfish, indicate that fresh fish was being consumed on the settlement (Fig 7.11).

Spatial distribution

Fish remains were recovered from a wide array of features covering the full spatial extent of the occupation, though by far and away the most productive contexts were pit fills. Several pits produced assemblages dominated by significant quantities of eel and herring, often demonstrating strong evidence of digestion (Fig 7.12). In the case of pits 271, 1781, and 1181 this evidence tallies well with mineralised plant biota and insects indicative of their use as latrines (Ballantyne, Chapter 7.3). Other pits (eg 2039, 2294, 2576, 2678) were dominated by the larger fish such as cod, whiting, gadids, flatfish, and rays. A comparison with the spatial distribution of mammal and bird remains (Poole, Chapter 7.1) does not reveal any significant correlations other than the fact that larger fish bones appear to have been discarded in similar contexts to mammal bones; smaller fish bones clearly have a distinct depositionary pathway associated with the management and disposal of human excreta. Somewhat surprisingly, there is no depositionary association between fish and bird bones, a pattern which might be expected

Fig 7.12   Unidentifiable digested vertebrae under magnification

under the assumption that both are generated as kitchen/table refuse as opposed to preparatory processes involved with butchery; precisely the same situation was noted at Flixborough (Lincs) in those phases where the majority of the fish bone was recovered from communal refuse dumps (Phases 3b–6) (Dobney *et al* 2007, 74–5, fig 6.9 and 6.10). This could be taken as evidence that surface middens were periodically dumped into pits at Bishopstone, a practice also attested in the taphonomy of human bone and plant biota assemblages (see Chapters 5.2 and 7.3).

Fishing methods

All the species of fish identified could have been easily caught along the south-eastern coast and in the estuary of the River Ouse. Although there is no mention of eel fisheries at Bishopstone in Domesday Book, the fish would have been easily caught using baskets or traps when the elvers migrated upstream in February or when the adult eels returned to the sea for breeding in autumn after having spent a lifetime in freshwater (Wheeler 1969).

Though the spawning grounds of cod are located in the North Atlantic, they can often be found in the shallower waters of the southern North Sea and codlings may come inshore where they can be caught with a line (*ibid*, 275–6). Whiting, a smaller variety of the cod family, prefer shallower waters and thus were likely caught using a line and maybe even a net (Locker 1997). Herring, along with mackerel and horse mackerel, travel in shoals and would probably have been caught using a floating net (Locker 1987).

Some flatfish, such as flounder, will spend some time living in freshwater; others such as plaice will generally come inshore (Wheeler 1969, 535–6). These species were probably caught using shoreline 'kiddles' or 'sea hedges' which would trap the fish as they came inshore with the tide; a possible alternative, a 'sea hedge', would have employed nets and stakes configured to ensnare bottom swimming fish (Locker 1985).

Discussion

Species representation and temporal trends

As we have seen, one of the most distinctive aspects of Bishopstone as an Anglo-Saxon fish assemblage is the dominance of marine species (principally herring and cod) over migratory and freshwater species (Dobney *et al* 2007, 228–33). With the exception of other coastal settlements such as Sandtun, this pattern of fish consumption is relatively uncommon amongst rural sites of the later Anglo-Saxon period. As shown in Figure 7.13 most comparable assemblages from southern England come from late Saxon urban contexts which bear strong witness to a 'fish event horizon' in the years around AD 1000, when the harvesting of cod and herring was commercialised across many parts of Britain and northern Europe (Barrett *et al* 2004). Should Bishopstone be placed on this same horizon, given that its occupation extends into the 10th/early 11th centuries?

Unfortunately, because the assemblage is poorly phased, there can be no definitive answer to this

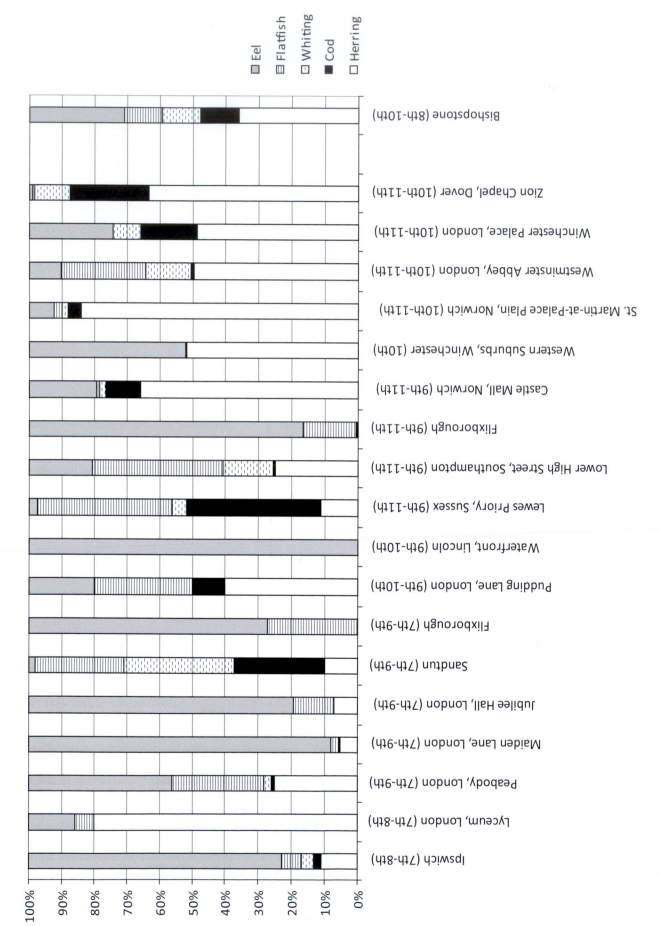

Fig 7.13   Relative frequencies of herring, cod, whiting, flatfish, and eel from different sites

question nor, by implication, to the not unreasonable suggestion that the majority of the marine fish may relate to the later phases of the occupation. The best evidence available for examining this issue comes from a small number of fish-producing contexts sampled by radiocarbon dating (Marshall *et al*, Chapter 8.2). Whilst the sample is too small to make site-wide generalisations, it is significant that pit 6, falling within the earlier end of the chronological range (cal AD 650–810 at 95% probability (SUERC-16015)), already displays a dominance of herring (Reynolds 2008, fig 3). Moreover, pits bearing marine-dominated fish-bone assemblages are widely diffused across the settlement, a fact which increases the probability that these features have a wide temporal distribution. This limited evidence can do no more than provide a hint of possible diachronic trends, but it does suggest that the exploitation of marine species on an organised scale was not confined to the end of the occupation sequence. On this basis, then, Bishopstone can be regarded as a site which predates the 'fish event horizon', probably by a significant margin. What implications does this have for the socio-economic status of the settlement?

Species representation and socio-economic status

Recent studies have shown that marine fish are consistently outnumbered by migratory and freshwater species on sites of the early to mid Saxon periods (mid-5th to mid-9th centuries). This pattern indicates that at this time the dominant strategy for procuring fish was the localised trapping of estuarine species (O'Sullivan 2003; Serjeantson and Woolgar 2006, 103; Sykes 2007, 57). Sites of the mid-9th to the mid-11th centuries demonstrate an across-the-board intensification in fishing including an increased abundance of marine species (especially herring), showing that this period laid the foundations for the commercial expansion in the marine fishing seen at the end of the first millennium AD (Sykes 2007, 57–8, fig 56–7). Analysis of the social distribution behind these figures indicates that outside urban centres, the most marked expressions of this trend are to be found on religious houses and elite settlements (Sykes 2007, 59–60, figs 58–61). The zooarchaeological data finds close accordance with the historically informed picture that these sectors of society were seeking to actively extend their control over fisheries and fish provisioning networks (Barrett *et al* 2004, 627; Serjeantson and Woolgar 2006, 103–04). Whilst the precise nature of dietary regimes within pre-Conquest monastic establishments remains unclear, the status accorded to fish under the rule of St Benedict (Magennis 1999) provides a clear rationale for understanding the role of religious establishments in this upturn. Yet the consumption of fish, most particularly herring, forms part of a broader social development which saw

the controlled exploitation of wild species emerge as an important marker of class identity amongst the burgeoning secular aristocracy – the thegnly sector – of late Anglo-Saxon England (Fleming 2001; Sykes 2007, 89–90).

It is important to proceed with caution in attaching social meanings to fish assemblages derived from coastal settlements, not least because such communities may have been involved with the provisioning of inland sites. Indeed, alongside acting as a seasonally occupied base for salt-processing and coastal trade, the excavated site of Sandtun, West Hythe, may well have served as a dependent fishery for the monastery of Lyminge, located some four miles inland, a suggestion strengthened by an impressive collection of marine-dominated fish bone generated by recent excavations targeting the mid-Saxon monastic complex (Hamilton-Dyer 2001; see also Barrett *et al* 2004, 627). However, the present assemblage embodies convincing evidence that Bishopstone was indeed a centre of consumption: abundant quantities of digested fish bone combined with skeletal representation data bearing witness to the eating of fresh and, perhaps in the case of the de-headed herring, processed fish (Barrett 1997; Serjeantson and Woolgar 2006, 117). On this basis, it seems likely that at least some members of Bishopstone's pre-Conquest population were consuming fish as part of a luxury diet.

One of the natural questions to emerge from this analysis is why little or no marine influence shows up in the isotopic signatures derived from the human population sampled at Bishopstone (see Marshall *et al*, Chapter 8.2). One possible explanation is that the consumption of fish amongst the wider Bishopstone community was subject to social restrictions. There are some indications that the excavated portion of the pre-Conquest cemetery may represent a socially-inferior element of the Anglo-Saxon population, for not only was it furthest away from the church, but it also contained a significant number of burials displaying trauma consistent with injuries sustained through heavy agricultural work (see Schoss and Lewis, Chapter 5.4). Of course, the only way one could hope to substantiate such a hypothesis is by sampling burials closer to the church where one might expect to find higher-status individuals who may have had access to marine fish as part of a diversified diet. On the other hand, it is tempting to view the cat with the elevated marine isotope signature (see previous section) as a proxy for fish consumption amongst this unseen portion of Bishopstone's population on the grounds that fish – fed or scavenged – must have comprised a regular component of its diet.

Conclusions

The Bishopstone assemblage sits astride two prominent markers casting historical light on the development of marine fishing in the South Saxon kingdom. The first appears in the conversion narrative of the South Saxon kingdom as related in Bede's *Life of St Wilfrid* in which the worldly bishop is said to have saved the people of Sussex from imminent starvation by teaching them how to fish in the sea so that 'they soon took three hundred fish of all kinds' (Kirby 1978, 168). The other takes the form of the substantial Domesday herring renders recorded for manors such as Ilford and Southease: a vivid indication of the importance which marine fishing had attained in the economy of the Lower Ouse valley by the end of the Anglo-Saxon period (King 1962, 453–55; Gardiner 2000, 82–3; Campbell 2002).

Whilst Bede's account may amount to little more than a narrative conceit (Kirby 1978, 168), the zooarchaeological record confirms that Anglo-Saxon communities did indeed start to exploit the bounty of the sea in earnest after the mid-7th century (Sykes 2007, 57). The current study suggests that the later Anglo-Saxon inhabitants of Bishopstone were very much active agents in the transition towards an increasingly marine-orientated fishing economy in the Ouse valley. Evidence for on-site consumption does not prove that this shift was necessarily connected with an elite presence at Bishopstone. On the other hand, marine-dominated rural assemblages predating the 'fish event horizon' (Barrett *et al* 2004) do derive mainly from the upper echelons of the settlement hierarchy, sites occupied by a late Saxon (lay and ecclesiastical) aristocracy increasingly preoccupied with exploring the opportunities which food and food procurement provided for symbolising rank and social exclusivity (Fleming 2001). Of course, this suggestion does not preclude the possibility that a proportion of Bishopstone's catch was diverted for sale at local markets for the purposes of income generation. Salt was required to preserve herring intended for onward sale: in the words of Campbell (2002, 9), 'the two form an umbilical relationship'. Domesday Book certainly refers to the existence of salt-pans in the locality, although somewhat upstream of Bishopstone at Beddingham and Rodmell (DB Sussex: folios 21 and 26v; King 1962, 455–7). However, the recent discovery of saltern mounds with 'Saxo-Norman' origins on land to the east of Newhaven – the first unequivocal archaeological evidence for salt-processing in the Lower Ouse valley – demonstrates that similar manorial appurtenances went unrecorded at Bishopstone (Archaeology South-East 2000; Chapter 2.2).

Acknowledgements

I am extremely grateful to both Dr James Barrett and Dr Heide Hüster-Plogmann for teaching me my first fish identification skills, as well as to Alison Locker and Sheila Hamilton-Dyer for providing me with their numerous reports. My supervisor, Dr Naomi Sykes, deserves special thanks for commenting on numerous drafts.

7.3   Charred and mineralised biota
by Rachel Ballantyne

Introduction

This report presents macro-botanical evidence for foodstuffs, activities, and deposition pathways at later Anglo-Saxon Bishopstone, with particular attention to the economic status and cultural identity of the inhabitants. Significant quantities of charred cereal grain and mineralised seeds of edible plants were recovered, but crop husbandry cannot be addressed in detail as there are very few arable weed seeds. Low to moderate quantities of mineralised arthropods and mammal droppings were also present.

The assemblage has few published comparanda, the majority being urban/proto-urban settlements such as sites in mid Saxon Southampton and London, and Anglo-Scandinavian York. The near absence of mineralised or waterlogged rural assemblages for this period has biased the range of comparable settlements and whilst charred assemblages occur widely, they are dominated by fuels and cereal processing waste. The incidence of mineralised remains is, however, an indicator of high concentrations of organic refuse, particularly formal latrines, which are characteristic of urban/proto-urban settings. The survival of rich mineralised plant remains at Bishopstone thus indicates similarities in living environment and intensity of activities to the settlements listed above.

Character of the assemblage

The richness and variability of charred and mineralised biota reflects the fact that all 92 fully analysed samples contain material from a wide variety of deposition pathways in secondary and tertiary contexts (Fig 7.14). There may also be some primary deposits, for example the direct use of pits as latrines. The complex range of pathways and lack of phasing means that very detailed spatial analyses cannot be justified. Only contexts with very distinctive compositions may be ascribed with any certainty to particular sources, for example:

- Contexts with high densities of very well-preserved charred biota are probably ash dumps relocated soon after charring (cf Hubbard and Clapham 1992)
- Contexts with a very wide range of mineralised seeds from plant foods are likely to represent human cess, perhaps from *in situ* latrines

These two assumptions are used below to explore refuse patterning across the settlement. Due to the probable lack of consistency in the representation of plants by mineralisation, including the effects of unspecialised processing of residues, even their basic statistics should be interpreted with caution (eg counts, numbers of taxa, and densities per litre of sediment).

Fig 7.14   Plan of all features with environmental bulk samples

Results

The fully analysed samples represent *c* 1800 litres of sediment from 82 contexts across 41 chalk-cut pits and one wall-trench. The average macrofossil counts per litre are 8.14 for charred plants, and 0.46 for mineralised plants (Fig 7.15). As there is no clear phasing on this densely occupied but short-lived settlement the results are subdivided below as cereals, probable food plants, other wild seeds, and other biota. Summaries of key components of the charred and mineralised assemblages are presented in Tables 7.10 and 7.11 respectively.

Cereals

Cereal grain is the predominant charred macrofossil in all samples. Remains of cereal chaff (glume bases, rachis internodes, and floret bases) and straw (culm nodes) are rare and usually co-occur with well-preserved grain; these were probably contaminants and never charred in any quantity. The charred wild seeds further support this interpretation, as they are infrequent and mostly grain-sized types difficult to remove during crop processing. In the samples with more than 50 charred plant macrofossils the charring of cleaned

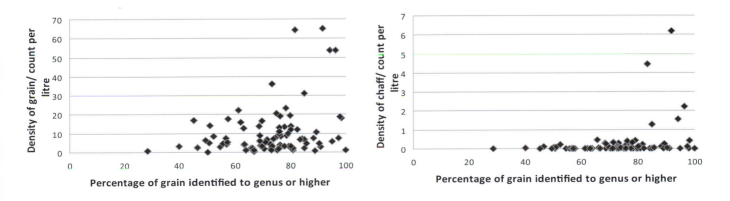

Fig 7.15   Charred grain preservation quality versus density for (a) grain (b) chaff

Table 7.10 Summary of charred plant remains from all 92 fully analysed samples

		Total count	% of total count	No. of contexts (overall 83 with charring)	No. of features (overall 41 with charring)
CEREAL GRAIN					
Cereal indet.	Indeterminate	3270	25.2	80	40
Triticum sp.	Wheat type	2959	22.8	77	39
Triticum aestivum sensu lato	Free-threshing wheat	2153	16.6	79	41
Hordeum vulgare sensu lato	Barley	2883	22.3	80	41
Triticum dicoccum / spelta	Hulled wheat	926	7.2	58	35
Avena sp.	Oats	597	4.6	61	35
Secale cereale	Rye	163	1.3	15	10
Total		**12951**	**100.0**		
CEREAL CHAFF					
Triticum dicoccum / spelta	Hulled wheat glume bases	111	79.3	28	20
Triticum aestivum sensu lato	Free-threshing wheat rachis internodes	21	15.0	11	9
Hordeum vulgare sensu lato	Barley rachis internodes	2	1.4	2	2
Avena sativa type	Oats floret base	6	4.3	4	3
Total		**140**	**100.0**		
CEREAL STRAW					
Cereal indet. culm node	Cereal straw-joint	27	19.3	14	10
ALL PROBABLE FOOD PLANTS					
Brassica / Sinapis sp.	Cabbage/Mustard seed	135	35.2	28	19
Vicia / Lathyrus / Pisum sp.	Large seeded legume [>4mm]	78	20.4	40	28
Pisum sativum	Pea	71	18.5	31	21
Vicia faba var. *minor*	Celtic bean	20	5.2	16	12
Rubus subgen. *rubus*	Blackberry seed	20	5.2	1	1
Papaver somniferum	Poppy seed	18	4.7	2	2
Malus / Pynls sp.	Apple/Pear seed	17	4.4	3	2
Linum usitatissimum	Flax seed	15	3.9	8	6
Corylus avellana	Hazelnut shell	11	2.9	8	5
Prunus domestica	Wild Plum stone	9	2.3	2	1
Prunus spinosa	Sloe stone	3	0.8	3	2
Prunus spp. fragments	Plum/Cherry/Sloe stone	2	0.5	2	2
Total		**75**	**100.0**		
SELECTED MOST FREQUENT ARABLE WEEDS					
Lolium spp.	Rye-grasses	307	27.7	45	29
large-seeded Poaceae indet.	Large-seeded grasses [>4mm]	181	16.4	45	26
Bromus spp,	Bromes	105	9.5	25	21
Sherardia arvenisi	Field Madder	73	6.6	4	4
Vicia / Lathyrus sp. [2–3mm]	Medium-seeded Vetch/Wild Pea	68	6.1	33	21
Atriplex patula / prostrata	Common/Garden Orache	34	3.1	16	11
Silene spp.	Campions	28	2.5	12	9
Galium aparine	Cleavers	27	2.4	18	9
small seeded *Rumex* spp.	small-seeded Docks [c 2mm]	21	1.9	14	12
Trifolium / Medicago sp.	Clovers/Medicks	19	1.7	12	9
Fallopia convolvulus	Black Bindweed	14	1.3	10	6
Malva sp.	Mallows	16	1.4	9	8
Total (all wild seeds)		**1107**	**100.0**		

Table 7.11 Summary of mineralised remains from all 92 fully analysed samples

		Total count	% of total count	No. of contexts (overall 57 with miner-alisation)	No. of features (overall 31 with miner-alisation)
ALL PROBABLE FOOD PLANTS					
Brassica / Sinapis sp.	Cabbage/Mustard seed	555	84.1	38	21
Papaver somniferum	Opium Poppy seed	20	3.0	7	6
Prunus domestica	Wild Plum stone	20	3.0	7	4
Ficus carica	Fig seed	17	2.6	5	3
Malus / Pyrus sp.	Wild/Cultivated Apple/Pear seed	9	1.4	8	5
cf. Malus sp.	Wild/Cultivated Apple seed	8	1.2	4	3
Vicia / Lathyrus / Pisum sp.	Large seeded legume [>4mm]	4	0.6	3	3
Prunus sp.	Sloe/Cherry/Plum stone frags.	4	0.6	4	2
Prunus spinosa	Sloe stone	4	0.6	2	2
Sambucus ebulus	Dwarf Elder seed	3	0.5	1	1
Prunus spinosa / avium	Sloe/Cherry stone	2	0.3	2	2
Prunus avium	Cherry stone	2	0.3	2	2
Vicia faba var. *minor*	Celtic Bean	2	0.3	2	2
Linum usitatissimum	Flax seed	2	0.3	2	2
Sambucus nigra	Elder seed	2	0.3	2	2
Papaver sp.	Poppy seed	2	0.3	1	1
Cereal indet.	Indeterminate grain	1	0.2	1	1
Lens culinaris	Lentil	1	0.2	1	1
Apium graveolens / nodiflorum	Celery/Fool's-water-cress seed	1	0.2	1	1
cf. Daucus carota	Wild/Cultivated Carrot seed	1	0.2	1	1
Total		**660**	**100.0**		
SELECTED MOST FREQUENT OTHER PLANTS					
Silene sp.	Campions	31	18.1	7	5
Agrostemma githago	Corncockle kernel	30	17.5	5	4
Lithospermum arvense	Corn Gromwell nutlet	22	12.9	11	10
Small seed indet.	Seed <3mm	15	8.8	10	10
Vicia / Lathyrus sp. [2–3mm]	Medium-seeded Vetch/Wild Pea	7	4.1	4	4
Atriplex prostrata / patula	Spear-leaved/Common Orache	6	3.5	6	6
small seeded *Rumex* spp.	small-seeded Docks [*c* 2mm]	4	2.3	3	3
Lithospermum arvense	Corn Gromwell kernel	4	2.3	3	3
Lamium album / purpureum	White/Red Dead-nettles	4	2.3	3	3
Total (an mineralised wild seeds)		**171**	**100.0**		
SELECTED MOST FREQUENT OTHER BIOTA					
Sphaeroceridae/Chloropidae indet. Type 1	Small Dung Fly/Frit Fly puparia	455	68.8	25	15
Sphaeroceridae/Chloropidae indet. Type 2	Small Dung Fly/Frit Fly puparia	81	12.3	11	6
Arvicola amphibius / Rattus rattus	Water Vole/Black Rat faeces	48	7.3	3	2
Cylindroiulus / Tachypodoiulu s / Blantulus sp. exoskeleton	Millipede exoskeleton		0.0	33	33
Calliphoridae indet.	Blow-fly puparia	23	3.5	11	8
Sphaeroceridae/Chloropidae indet. Type 3	Small Dung Fly/Frit Fly puparia	15	2.3	4	4
Oniscidea indet.	Woodlouse exoskeleton	12	1.8	13	6
cf. *Lepus europaeus* L.	Possible Hare dung pellets	11	1.7	1	1
Chloropidae indet.	Frit Fly puparia	9	1.4	3	3
Total (all quantified other biota)		**661**	**100**		

Fig 7.16   Distribution of charred cereals for all features with fully analysed samples

grain products is consistently indicated by grain: chaff ratios (Hillman 1981; 1984) and weed seed morphology (Jones 1984). These trends do not necessarily show an absence of cereal by-products at the settlement; rather, that only cleaned grain was frequently exposed to heat, perhaps in corn-drying or baking ovens.

Mineralised evidence for cereals is provided by bran impressions in the abundant amorphous calcium phosphate concretions, which probably reflect cess containing wholemeal flour. Although mineralised wild grass/rush stems are frequent, evidence of cereals is rare. There was a straw culm node in pit 2915, and one unidentifiable cereal grain in pit 1286. The contrast between rich charred cereals and the few mineralised examples shows that the charred grain represents a specific pathway generating refuse, and is not simply a subset of widespread uncharred cereal waste.

Wheat (*Triticum* sp) is the most abundant and frequent taxa and, of the grain identifiable beyond genus, two-thirds is free-threshing and one third hulled. The identification of wheat grain is notoriously difficult (Jones 1998), so identifications have only been attempted when there is very good preservation. Many of the hulled grains are comparable to spelt wheat (*Triticum spelta*); fairly elongate with flat ventral sides, slight dorsal ridges, and rounded apexes. All the well-preserved hulled wheat spikelet forks and glume bases are clearly of spelt wheat, so these grain identifications appear

confirmed. Free-threshing wheat rachis internodes are always hexaploid type when well-preserved, so the numerous very rounded wheat grains are probably from bread wheat (*Triticum aestivum sensu lato*).

Hulled six-row barley (*Hordeum vulgare*) has been identified from the high frequency of both hulled and twisted barley grains, although there is no well-preserved chaff for confirmation. Both rye (*Secale cereale*) and oats (*Avena* spp) are present in much lower quantities and contexts. The presence of cultivated oats (*Avena sativa*) is indicated by floret bases (chaff); wild oats cannot be fully excluded as they are common arable weeds and have seeds that are indistinguishable from cultivated forms.

Figure 7.16 illustrates the distribution of charred grain, showing that high-density remains are widespread and increase slightly towards the north-east. All samples contain grain from more than one cereal, raising the question of whether maslin crops (sown mixtures) are represented. Alternatively, the grain could just have been mixed during processing or at the later stage as ash. Since a number of features are dominated by one cereal type (Table 7.12), the late mixing of grain or ash is more plausible.

The number of 'pure' grain contexts for each cereal type mirrors their order of abundance in the overall assemblage. The example for oats is included for comparison, since this cereal never occurs as more than 61.5% of the grain in any context, perhaps suggest-

Table 7.12 Pit contexts dominated by one type of charred cereal grain

Pit cut number	Fill number	Sample number	Soil volume analysed/litres	% of all grain identified to genus or higher, after redistribution of counts for ambiguous wheat					Total grain identified to genus or higher		Total other indeterminate grains
				Barley	Hulled wheat	Free-threshing wheat	Rye	Oat	Ambiguous wheat grain	All other grain types	
[271]	(270)	<521>	30	86.7	1.4	1.8		10.1	3	316	91
[515]	(516)	<538>	5	96.6		2.3		1.1	3	262	60
[2294]	(3003)	<704>	5	97.8		1.1		1.1		92	2
[2363]	(2364)	<660>	5	5.0	88.5	3.5		3.0	89	299	27
	(2920)	<661>	4.5	4.4	84.4	9.9		1.3	101	228	14
		<662>	4.5	2.1	91.9	5.9			112	233	9
[2091]	(2858)	<625>	15.5	7.7		91.3		1.0	42	104	33
[2191]	(2192)	<642>	16	8.6		88.3		3.1	60	128	75
[2506]	(2501)	<705>	15	12.4	2.1	83.3	0.4	1.7	79	233	60
	(3056)	<708>	30	12.4		87.6			88	209	58
[2915]	(2916)	<659>	13.5	16.3	0.8	80.7		2.2	80	356	64
[2035]	(2969)	<685>	28.5	2.0		7.9	89.4	0.7	8	151	8
[2041]	(2885)	<632>	24.5	16.2	20.8	1.4		61.5	10	117	14

ing its use only within admixtures. The distribution of 'pure' grain contexts is marked. No pit with multiple samples is ever rich in more than one type of cereal, and most cases occur in the north-eastern area. Pits 2363 and 2915 lie very close to each other, as do pits 2041, 2035, and 2993; the purity of their contexts despite such proximity suggests these are specific dumps of ash, rather than tertiary deposits of surface refuse.

A radiocarbon date for spelt wheat chaff (spikelet forks and glume bases) from the basal layer of pit 2363 confirms that the rich spelt wheat grain in this pit is contemporary with the later Anglo-Saxon settlement. Calibration is based upon the IntCal04 curve (Reimer *et al* 2004), with data output from OxCal4 (Bronk Ramsey 2001; 2006):

Beta-256960   Measured 1240±40 BP δ^{13}C -26.9
Conventional 1210±40 BP
Calibration to 2 sigma (95.4% probability):
AD 687–895 (93.9%)   AD 925–937 (1.5%)

Assigning importance to the different cereal crops must be tentative since a quarter of the charred grain is unidentifiable and all represent their frequency of exposure to charring, rather than consumption. Free-threshing wheat and hulled six-row barley were processed in great quantity, with spelt wheat appearing to be a secondary crop. Oats were widespread but never numerous (some could also be weeds), and rye was a rarely charred crop. It should be noted that germinated grain is very rare, so there is no evidence for malting.

Probable food plants

The mineralised remains are dominated by seeds of edible plants (Table 7.11), as is common (Green 1984; Tomlinson and Hall 1996; Carruthers 2005). Charred food plants are surprisingly frequent, although they are far outnumbered by cereals and arable weeds (Table 7.10). When the values in Tables 7.10 and 7.11 are compared, only a few food plants are better represented when mineralised than charred. It is unclear how fruit seeds would become charred, although flax and legumes could sometimes be grain contaminants. A number of fills in pit 2039 show strong overlap between the charred and mineralised seeds of food plants, suggesting that proportions of both preservation pathways represent cooking or the part charring of mixed food waste.

Almost all the plant foods are types that could grow locally, both wild and cultivated. Seeds of cabbages/mustard (*Brassica*/*Sinapis* sp) are by far the most abundant and widespread; a mustard seed condiment is likely. Other evidence of condiments are poppy seed (*Papaver somniferum*), and one mineralised probable celery seed (*Apium graveolens*/*nodiflorum*). These three taxa are reported in mineralised and waterlogged cess for the middle to late Saxon periods onwards, with good examples at St Mary's Stadium, Southampton (Carruthers 2005; Clapham 2005), Anderson's Road, Southampton (Stevens 2006), Milk Street, London (Jones *et al* 1991), and Anglo-Scandinavian York (Kenward and Hall 1995). An early Saxon example at Abbots Worthy (Carruthers 1991) suggests these plants were consumed at more rural settlements than the archaeological record currently indicates.

Legumes are difficult to identify when only their gross morphology survives, as is common with both charring and mineralisation. Peas (*Pisum sativum*) are both abundant and widely distributed across the settlement. Celtic beans (*Vicia faba* var. *minor*), an early small broad bean, are less frequent but may be under-identified due to their tendency to fragment. Many pulses can only be attributed to 'large seeded legumes' but are likely to be one of these two cultivars. It is likely that legumes formed an important component of the diet, although they are not as numerous as at St Mary's Stadium, Southampton (Carruthers 2005, 162).

Flax seed (*Linum usitatissimum*) occurs in small quantities, and could have been grown for its oil, seed, or fibre. Mineralised fruit seeds tend to co-occur, particularly in pits 548, 558, 2039, and 2600. Wild plums (*Prunus domestica*), figs (*Ficus carica*), and apples/pears (*Malus*/*Pyrus* sp) are most frequent. The plum stones are all small, *c* 11mm long × 9mm wide × 6mm thick, which compares well to modern wild and feral types. A few very well-preserved apple/pear seeds are similar in shape and size to modern wild or feral apples (*Malus sylvestris*), but this cannot be confirmed from seeds alone. Many other wild fruits occur in only one or two pits, these are sloe (*Prunus spinosa*), wild cherry (*Prunus avium*), and elder (*Sambucus* spp). Sloe stones embedded in faecal concretions from Anglo-Scandinavian York show the consumption of fruits that today are considered too astringent (Tomlinson and Hall 1996), and the ingestion of fruit-stones.

When charred, gathered wild plant foods are also represented by hazelnut shells (*Corylus avellana*) in a number of contexts, and blackberry seeds (*Rubus* subgen. *rubus*) only in the fills of pit 2578. This one deposit appears to contain cooking or burnt kitchen refuse as, in addition to the blackberry seeds, there are low numbers of charred sloe stones, cabbage/ mustard seeds, and all the other food plants listed above.

Most of the fruit types are widespread and native to Britain, with evidence for use since prehistory (Greig 1991). However both cultivated plum and fig appear to be Roman introductions (van der Veen *et al* 2008; Greig 1991) and whilst plum is widely reported from then onwards, figs are rarely found between the Roman period and the 12th century (Dickson and Dickson 1996). These differing patterns may be linked to accessibility; plum became naturalised, whereas figs were probably always imported as dried fruits due to the dif-

Fig 7.17 Distribution of mineralised food plants and insects for all sampled features

ficulties of their cultivation in Britain, including absence of the gallwasp required for pollination (*ibid*). The presence of mineralised fig seeds in eastern pits 2576, 2039, and 2915 at Bishopstone therefore suggests trade connections.

Other post-Roman finds of fig are from Anglo-Scandinavian layers at Coppergate, York (Kenward and Hall 1995), Saxo-Norman Milk Street, London (Jones *et al* 1991), mid Saxon features at the Royal Opera House, London (Davis 2003) and Saxon mineralised faeces at West Heslerton (Carruthers 2005). There is always a possibility that low numbers of fig seeds on multi-phase excavations may represent Roman or medieval contaminants, but the tight dating at West Heslerton and Bishopstone suggests that figs were consumed.

Other wild seeds

Many of the other wild plant seeds are arable weeds, best represented by the charred assemblage. Multiple deposition pathways are suggested by the spatial distribution of mineralised plants, and their relationship to charred plants in the same contexts. Comparison of Figures 7.17 and 7.18 shows that, whilst diverse food seeds that may represent cess are widespread, mineralised grass/rush stems and diverse other wild seeds are confined to the central and eastern areas. Charred and mineralised food seeds often co-occur, suggesting a shared origin, but there is no such association between other wild seeds.

The mineralised 'arable weeds' seem to represent a different source to the identical examples charred as grain contaminants.

Charred seeds of wild plants are rare compared to grain and, like the chaff, are more abundant in contexts with dense cereal grain. The major wild taxa all have grain-sized seeds, such as darnel (*Lolium temulentum*), bromes (*Bromus* spp), and medium-seeded vetches/wild peas (*Vicia / Lathyrus* sp). Unless removed by hand, these seeds would either enter the flour or be re-sown with the next crop, making them troublesome arable weeds. Many less well-represented wild taxa also fit this category, such as black bindweed (*Fallopia convovulus*), corncockle (*Agrostemma githago*), cleavers (*Galium aparine*), and corn gromwell (*Lithospermum arvense*).

As the majority of crop weeds had been removed before charring, the surviving wild seeds are skewed heavily towards grain-sized types (Jones 1984). A few types are of note: weeds characteristic of arable on loamy calcareous soils include corn gromwell (*Lithospermum arvense*), field madder (*Sherardia arvensis*), and campions (*Silene* spp); this is consistent with the chalk downland (cf Wilson and King 2003). Other 'indicator' species include rare seeds of stinking mayweed (*Anthemis cotula*), which tends to thrive on heavy clay soils, and wetland plants such as meadow rue (*Thalictrum flavum*) and common spikerush (*Eleocharis palustris*), which suggest a proportion of crops grew on low-lying land that was seasonally damp to wet.

Although mineralised wild seeds are overall

Fig 7.18   Distribution of mineralised other wild seeds and grass items for all sampled features

far fewer than the charred cases, campions, corn-cockle, and corn gromwell are again frequent. The presence of intact large weed seeds is of interest as, if from cess, it is hard to imagine that flour products were the source (where they ought to have been milled). Perhaps these seeds were consumed with whole grain, such as in stews, or had been sieved/hand-cleaned from grain and then entered refuse either directly or after feeding to livestock. Other less frequent mineralised seeds of arable weeds are vetch/wild pea, small-seeded docks, and spear-leaved/common orache (*Atriplex patula / prostrata*).

With one exception, none of the charred wild seeds shows any association with particular cereals. Over half of the brome seeds listed in Table 7.10 (59 of the 105) are found with the nearly 'pure' spelt wheat grain in pit 2363, where they are comparable to soft/rye brome (*Bromus hordeaceus / secalinus*). An association between rye brome and spelt wheat was first noted in British prehistory by Helbaek (1953), and it frequently co-occurs with prehistoric hulled wheat in northern Europe; debate continues as to whether rye brome was originally a crop or a persistent weed (Schmidl *et al* 2007, 250). Charred assemblages from the late Bronze Age to late Roman periods in Britain have frequent soft/rye brome associated with emmer and spelt wheat, but after the 5th century their seeds occur sporadically and in very low amounts (data from Tomlinson and Hall 1996). It is therefore

striking to see the association between spelt wheat and soft/rye brome extending into the historical period at Bishopstone, as this implies some continuity in crop ecology, presumably due to husbandry.

A single, mineralised lentil (*Lens culinaris*) from pit 2035 is a rare early historic find. Most lentil remains in Britain are from Roman contexts (data in Tomlinson and Hall 1996), and occur in abundance only within imported grain at The Forum, London (Straker 1984) and Caerleon (Helbaek 1964). Later finds of lentils, usually single seeds, include those from later Anglo-Saxon phases at Milk Street, London (Jones *et al* 1991), Cottenham (Cambs) (Stevens in Mortimer 2000), Anderson's Road, Southampton (Stevens 2006), Yarnton (Oxon) (Stevens 2004), Burystead (Campbell and Robinson 2009), and Higham Ferrers (Northants) (Moffett 2007). It is unclear for all periods whether lentils were ever a food, rather than an arable weed, grain contaminant, or possibly a fodder crop (*ibid*, 175).

Diverse mineralised wild seeds are all found in the central and eastern excavation areas (Fig 7.18), which overlaps strongly with mineralised grass/rush stems and contrasts with the widespread distribution of possible cess and grain ash dumps. A few plant seeds also only occur mineralised and, whilst some can grow on arable land, they broadly characterise rough open ground and hedgerows: red/white deadnettle (*Lamium album / purpureum*), small nettle (*Urtica urens*), violet (*Viola* sp), garlic mustard

(*Alliaria petiolata*), dogwood (*Cornus sanguineus*), cut-leaved crane's bill (*Geranium dissectum*), fool's parsley (*Aethusa cynapium*), and hemp nettles (*Galeopsis* sp). The most plausible explanations are that these plants grew nearby, or they represent a gathered resource such as fodder, or they arrived via livestock dung. The association between mineralised grass/rush stems and wild seeds suggests that perhaps fodder or dung is most likely.

Other biota

All the mineralised invertebrates are types that could be expected to live within the pits themselves, and most are detritivores. Millipedes, woodlice, and pill bugs feed solely upon plant matter, so a significant proportion of the pit fills was probably dung and/or other plant materials akin to 'compost'. Table 7.11 almost certainly under-estimates the abundance of millipedes, as the many fragmented segments cannot easily be quantified to numbers of individuals. The remains of these creatures show no clear spatial patterning.

Larvae of lesser dung flies (*Sphaeroceridae*) and frit flies (*Chloropidae*) are known on decaying matter from both plants and animals, including manure, and many other frit fly larvae feed on living grasses. The sometimes very numerous puparia suggest decaying matter is their more likely source. Figure 7.17 illustrates that mineralised puparia are widespread but, when examined for each taxon this is only true for lesser dung/frit flies. Blow-fly larvae (*Calliphoridae*) usually feed on carrion or dung, and their puparia are found only in the central to eastern area: pits 1259, 1393, 2600, 3086, 2294, 2576, 2035, and 2039. The distribution for blow-fly larvae overlaps neatly with the distribution of mineralised grass/rush stems and other wild seeds in Figure 7.17, further suggesting cess and/or dung.

Mineralised rodent droppings are the correct size and shape for water vole (*Arvicola terrestris*), although black rat (*Rattus rattus*) cannot be fully excluded (Fig 7.19). Skeletal evidence is required for full identification, but the later Anglo-Saxon date makes water vole more probable (cf O'Connor 1992). One dropping is from pit 1393 and the rest are from layers 2945 and 2946 of pit 2039. There is no clear relationship between the incidence of faeces and other mineralised constituents of these pits. Although the droppings could be *in situ*, it is likely they represent surface debris. A number of fibrous dung pellets in pit 2578 are comparable to hare (*Lepus* sp), which is unusual upon a settlement, so this particular identification requires caution.

Depositionary pathways and feature function

There are no simple patterns in the distribution of charred and mineralised biota both within features and across the excavation area, except for the greater richness and diversity of remains in eastern pits. Traits linked to the charred and mineralised remains are outlined below, but as even basic statistical analyses are regarded as tenuous for the mineralised remains, cross-comparison between the two preservation types is largely qualitative.

Rapid dumps of grain ash

The strongest candidates are the 'pure' grain contexts listed in Table 7.13. Other contexts that may be ash dumps, due to high grain density and moderately good preservation, are pit fills (1156) [1155], (1354) [1181], (2038) [2037], (2854) [2041], (2577) [2576], (3069) [2646], and (3166) [3165]. When from pits with multiple samples the latter, less secure cases are middle to higher fills; in contrast, the more secure 'pure' grain contexts are basal to middle fills. The discrepancy may relate to greater disturbance and/or slower infilling of these upper layers.

Probable cess

The widest range of mineralised food seeds is in pit fills (596) [548], (1375) [1259], (2969) [2035], (2903) (2904) (2945) (2947) [2039], (2577) (2996) [2576]. When from pits with multiple samples, these tend to be middle fills, which may reflect geochemistry more than the original distribution of cess. Multiple food seeds, perhaps indicating cess in lower amounts are in pit fills (270) [271], (582) [517], (1184) [1183], (3045) [2600], (3137) [2840], (2916) [2915], (597) [558], (598) [548], (1288) [1286], (1431) [1393], (2874) (2875) (2897) (2948) (3009) [2039], (3006) [2576], (3201) [2830]; these are all basal or middle fills.

Fig 7.19   Mineralised water vole or rat droppings from pit [2039] (Scale = 4mm)

Redeposited surface debris

Both cases occur in pit [2039]; mineralised water vole/rat droppings in pit fills (2945) and (2946), and the identical charred and mineralised fly puparia in pit fills (2903) and (2904).

Fodder/dung/other materials

Diverse wild seeds with grass/rush stems are in (3137) [2840], (2916) [2915], (1375) [1259], (2969) [2035], (3003) [2294], (2577) (3006) [2576], (3087) [3086]. Many of these fills are also listed above as containing probable cess.

Food or cooking waste

Fills (2903) and (2904) of pit [2039] contain numerous charred and mineralised wild plum stones, suggesting a common source. Charred peas and beans are also abundant in the fill (2897) of the same pit. The charred hazelnut shell, fruit stones, and seeds in (2905/6/9) [2578] also suggest the presence of food waste in addition to grain ash.

Discussion

The strongest cases for incrementally filled formal cess pits or latrines are 2039 and 2576, which have fills rich in mineralised seeds interspersed with more sterile layers. Pit 2039 also has the strongest evidence for incorporation of other surface debris, such as cooking refuse or cess that accumulated above ground before redeposition into the pit. The most substantial tips of 'pure' grain ash are found in the both the basal and secondary fills of 2363 and 2506. All other pits with multiple samples contain one or two fills with strong characteristics, but with no clear patterning in terms of basal, secondary, or higher fills. Admixtures of cess with grassy materials (perhaps fodder or dung) indicate the locus for processing activities, surface refuse, or livestock lay towards the east.

The cross-cutting of pathways for charred and mineralised biota offers some opportunity to identify pit infilling episodes (see Chapter 9.1). Pits are notoriously difficult features to interpret, since there is always a tenuous link between their creation and subsequent fills. Many studies have relied on detailed taphonomic and contextual evidence from pits to identify their 'life-histories' (Hill 1995; Poole 1995; Piper and O'Connor 2001; Garrow *et al* 2005).

Interpretation

The following discussion returns to evidence for deposition pathways and activities at the settlement, before discussing the likely significance of grain processing at Bishopstone and, finally, the diet and identity of the inhabitants.

Pits – refuse and living environment

A wide range of material sources have been identified in the pits, but it is not clear whether they were dug specifically for refuse disposal; later medieval records do however describe such practices (Keene 1982, 27). The apparent lack of patterning will have been exacerbated by the decay of some original constituents, with slumping and compaction of fills. But the great variability across these fill sequences with multiple samples suggests that most pits were backfilled with different types of refuse as required ad hoc. Whilst some of the richest charred macrofossils indicate rapid deposition, two fills in pit 2039 include redeposited surface refuse that was already infested with fly larvae when partly charred. The increase in diversity of biota in the eastern area may reflect a locus for activities or refuse.

Similar very mixed results from pit fills occur at a number of large later Anglo-Saxon settlements, most notably at Hamwic (Carruthers 2005), Ludenwic (Davis 2003; Davis and de Moulins 1988) and Anglo-Scandinavian York (Kenward and Hall 1995). A complicating factor for identifying material sources is the possibility of pig waste, identified tentatively at both Hamwic (Buckland *et al* 1976) and York (Hall and Kenward 2000) from parasitic nematode eggs and related fauna of decaying faecal matter. Pigs could entangle material sources considerably by foraging widely on refuse and surface debris, including human faeces. The lack of waterlogged biota precludes detailed palaeoecological reconstruction at Bishopstone, but the mineralised blow-fly puparia suggest particularly fetid conditions in the eastern area, and clouds of dung/frit flies may have occurred during warmer months. Mineralised rodent droppings have also been noted at Hamwic (Carruthers 2005) and York (Hall and Kenward 2000).

Cereal processing and the economy

Although charred plant assemblages are found on both rural and proto-urban settlements during the later Anglo-Saxon periods, there are few examples with such abundant and well-preserved cereal grain. Most rural assemblages, even at relatively large settlements such as Higham Ferrers (Moffett 2007), Raunds Furnells (Campbell and Robinson 2009), and West Fen Road, Ely (Ballantyne 2005), do have numerous finds of charred grain but the finds are accompanied by other contexts rich in cereal chaff or a wide variety of wild seeds. At Bishopstone only grain-rich remains are present across all 192 assessed samples, and virtually all charred weed seeds are grain-sized. The assemblage is therefore dominated by a late stage of crop processing, most probably the oven drying of grain for granary storage or to facilitate milling (cf Moffett 1994, 61; Scott 1951).

One caveat to this explanation is that studies of *in situ* oven and kiln ash (Monk 1981; van der Veen 1989; Moffett 1994) show both grain and fuel are usually abundant, including numerous straw and chaff fragments from kindling. It is difficult to think of another process that would regularly produce abundant charred grain; perhaps the ovens at Bishopstone used wood kindling such as birch faggots, since charcoal is often abundant. If so, then cereal by-products such as straw or chaff may have been sufficiently limited as to discourage their use for fuel. This discussion is highly conjectural; however the absence of charred cereal by-products does suggest a separation between the processing of cleaned grain at Bishopstone and the original harvested sheaves.

The breadwheat, hulled six-row barley, rye, and oats at Bishopstone are commonly found in later Anglo-Saxon assemblages (Greig 1991; Tomlinson and Hall 1996). However, spelt wheat, which appears here to have been an important secondary crop, is rarely found in southern Britain after the Roman period. A few early Saxon assemblages displaying small amounts of spelt wheat chaff include West Stow (Murphy 1985), Higham Ferrers (Moffett 2007), and Yarnton (Stevens 2004). By the later Anglo-Saxon period, spelt wheat chaff occurs sporadically in very small amounts which do not show whether it was a crop or feral weed. Several glume bases have recently produced a late Saxon radiocarbon date at Stansted (Essex) (Carruthers 2008), and undated examples from later Anglo-Saxon settlements include Cottenham (Cambs) (Stevens in Mortimer 2000), Higham Ferrers (Moffett 2007), and Steyning (Hinton 1993). The spelt wheat chaff at Bishopstone is clearly from a crop due to its frequency and association with abundant well-preserved grain in pit 2363.

Two settlements with very good (numerous and radiocarbon dated) evidence for another hulled wheat, emmer (*Triticum dicoccum*), occur in the Thames valley at Lake End Road near Windsor, and Yarnton near Oxford (Pelling and Robinson 2000). The authors suggest that emmer may have been reintroduced for certain bread or beer types, as it is rarely found in Britain after the Iron Age. Spelt wheat is, however, a more complex case since it was the major crop of Iron Age and Roman southern Britain. The spelt wheat at Bishopstone may represent continued agricultural practices, or a reintroduction from the continent similar to the emmer wheat in the Thames valley.

There are known regional differences in the representation of cereals in the Saxon period, which can sometimes be linked to soil types; rye was of particular importance in the Brecklands (Murphy 1997). However, as noted by Green (1994, 85) and Rackham (1994, 129), there is far greater variation in charred cereals than might be expected between soil types and settlement forms, and a model based on these factors is over-simplistic. Such comparisons also assume that the importance of different cereals is reflected by the frequency of their charring at individual settlements, even with variation in activities. Due to this ambiguity, detailed comparisons of charred cereals between Bishopstone and nearby settlements cannot be justified; suffice to note that all taxa are shared with the exception of spelt wheat, and that rye was also rarely charred at Hamwic (Green 1994; Hunter 2005).

Plant foods – economy and status

Mineralised bran concretions show the frequent consumption of flour, most probably as bread. However it is not clear whether all the charred grain was intended for consumption by its processors, or was an intended surplus product. As the abundant charred grain surely represents accidents, the assemblage must represent a fraction of the original amounts dried before milling. Since the limits of the settlement remain undefined, it is impossible to distinguish whether the excavated area represents a zone dedicated to flour production, or a more widespread characteristic of the occupation. Any specialisation in grain processing would suggest that other members of the community also had specialised roles. The spelt wheat at Bishopstone, whether a continuation from the early Saxon period or reintroduced, reveals tastes that were increasingly rarefied due to the wider decline of this cereal across southern Britain.

All of the recovered legumes, fruits, nuts, and condiments are known from later Anglo-Saxon settlements with waterlogged or mineralised remains. The nearest similar assemblages are from Hamwic, particularly St Mary's Stadium (Carruthers 2005; Clapham 2005; Hunter 2005) and Anderson's Road (Stevens 2006). When ascribing status it is important to recognise that plant assemblages always favour certain pathways; at Bishopstone these are oven ash and tough seeds ingested in food. The absence of mineralised cess and refuse at most contemporary rural settlements surely reflects different structuring, probably the disposal of waste on surrounding land rather than formal latrines (cf Tomlinson and Hall 1996; Chapter 9.1). Bishopstone contains dense on-site accumulations of waste from a variety of sources consistent with a 'proto-urban' rather than rural lifestyle. This raises interesting questions about why refuse accumulated, the intensity of economic activity, and the density of habitation.

Steadily increasing, if still rare, finds of 'exotics' at rural settlements, such as figs at West Heslerton (Carruthers 2005, 162), show that dried fruits were traded more widely than previously thought. Medieval written sources further illustrate that later plant assemblages under-represent the range in diet (Green 1984; Greig 1996; Hagen 2006), as is likely for most periods. For example, direct biological evidence for leaf and root vegetables continues to be very rare. A simple shopping-list approach to assigning status by the presence of grape or fig seeds is thus highly flawed for this period.

A striking example of the role that deposition pathways play in shaping plant assemblages is the sparse charred evidence from the high-status settlement at Flixborough (Hall 2000; Dobney *et al* 2007). Despite an extensive sieving programme, very few charred cereals or arable weeds were recovered, and there was no mineralisation or waterlogging. The most frequently found items were plant stems and associated salt-marsh plants, perhaps from turves used as fuel. The lack of remains presents difficulties when contrasting this settlement to Bishopstone, since absence of evidence surely reflects an absence of suitable preservation pathways, rather than the original range of plant materials and activities.

As large midden deposits were present at Flixborough (Dobney *et al* 2007), it is also not possible to argue that refuse was systematically removed from the settlement area. Instead, it may be that the processing of cereals and cooking were juxtaposed with fires in a very different way to Bishopstone, a simple explanation being that large-scale drying of grain in ovens was absent. Although the lack of mineralised remains could reflect a lack of cess pits or dense organic pit fills, this cannot be substantiated due to the numerous geochemical variables involved. The strongest interpretation is, simply, that the differences in charred biota between Bishopstone and Flixborough serve to highlight socio-economic diversity during the later Anglo-Saxon period. Despite 'blanks' in both assemblages, each reveals a degree of specialisation in activities – at Bishopstone the processing of grain, and at Flixborough the use of estuarine turves as fuel. There would also appear to be no simple relationship between 'status' as indicated by settlement form and material culture, and 'lifestyle' as indicated by bioarchaeological remains and the treatment of refuse. The salient point is that, when addressing socio-economic questions, plant assemblages cannot be cross-compared in isolation from their archaeological context and associated material culture.

Conclusions

The charred and mineralised biota at Bishopstone are remarkably rich and the plant remains show that one facet of this settlement's character was as a specialised locus for grain processing. The settlement was densely occupied, generating refuse that both accumulated on the surface and was frequently buried in pits. Two formal, incrementally filled cess pits, 2039 and 2576, compound the sense that lifestyles were proto-urban, rather than rural. The consumption of dried figs indicates trade connections, but they represent a tiny proportion of the overwhelmingly local produce. These findings raise questions about the origin, identity, and status of the inhabitants that cannot be answered from botanical remains alone.

Acknowledgements

This work was partly funded by the Sato Project, Research Institute of Humanity and Nature (H-02, RIHN), Kyoto, Japan. I would also like to thank Paul Buckland, Alan Clapham, Henry Disney, Chris Stimpson, Phil Piper, and Terry O'Connor for their advice regarding identifications; Dawn Mooney for helping to quantify the wood charcoal; and Alan Clapham, Allan Hall, Chris Stevens, and Gabor Thomas for suggesting worthy comparanda. Finally, many thanks to my research supervisor, Martin Jones, and the Pitt-Rivers Lab members.

7.4   Marine molluscs
by Elizabeth M Somerville

Introduction

This report describes and discusses a sample of the rich marine mollusc assemblage recovered from the excavations. This sample is based on a selection of features,[1] mostly pits, providing a wide spatial and temporal spread of contexts. The assemblage is treated as effectively synchronous, and only passing mention is made of separate contexts and features, both of which are assumed to represent brief episodes within the occupation sequence. This assemblage is of some significance since excavated sites of this period with this amount of marine molluscs are rare in Sussex and beyond. Indeed, due to a lack of published assemblages, it is very difficult to make meaningful comparisons between Bishopstone and other contemporary sites in southern and eastern England. For this reason, this report restricts itself to assemblages of different dates – Roman, early Anglo-Saxon and medieval – local to Sussex to offer a diachronic perspective on mollusc exploitation at later Anglo-Saxon Bishopstone. A fuller appreciation of how this aspect of Bishopstone's economy fits into the regional and national context must await further publication and comparative research.

Results

Species representation

Tables 7.13 and 7.14 give the MNI and total weight of shell for the species found in the features analysed here. Table 7.13 shows the results for the species which were found in most of the features and in sufficient abundance for further analysis. Table 7.14 gives the data recorded for species found infrequently and in small numbers. The species found in the features selected for analysis were also found distributed across the rest of the site, and with the same split between frequent and infrequent species.

The four most common species from the features analysed are, in order of abundance (ie MNI): limpet (*Patella vulgata*), mussel (*Mytulis edulis*), oyster (*Ostrea edulis*), and winkle (*Littorina littorea*) – with mussel and oyster being recorded from every feature, although not from every context. Cockle (*Cerastoderma edule*) and carpet shell (*Tapes decussatus*) are found in the majority of contexts, but in much smaller numbers. All of these species are

Table 7.13 MNI and weight for species of marine mollusc found in the majority of features analysed

Feature	Oyster MNI	Oyster wt (g)	Cockle MNI	Cockle wt (g)	Mussel MNI	Mussel wt (g)	Winkle MNI	Winkle wt (g)	Limpet MNI	Limpet wt (g)	Carpet Shell MNI	Carpet Shell wt (g)
517	3	54.8			1	0.7			7	11.6		
1155	46	2017.6			18	214.8			2	10.2		
1167	199	5362.4	3	20.3	23	87.3	43	184.4	25	58.5	3	23.2
1197	7	144.4	1	0.7	1	0.8			2	5.9	1	0.8
1259	5	227	4	29.6	9	66.3	23	100.1	15	32.8	6	60.2
1756	6	171.5	1	1.5	3	6	3	8.6	1	1.6		
2035	11	346.8	10	39.8	14	7.2	13	45.3	9	18	1	5.7
2039	20	756.8	17	73.7	23	98.6	45	142	18	36.5	6	41
2576	20	568.1	13	53.4	224	1145.9	27	108.8	32	61.8	2	10.7
2578	26	894.6	3	14.5	10	33.8	37	134.6	13	49.7	5	43.8
3165	3	54	4	22.7	202	1430.4	76	352.5	551	678.3	6	44
2645	17	742.3	1	6	80	620.6	21	86.1	63	104.6	2	39.3
2771	2	30.4			2	3.3	2	7.5	1	6.3		
2838	2	51.6			13	102.4	27	121.2	9	18.7	2	24.5
4046	18	694.7	11	73	41	360.9	66	254.6	237	499.2	8	64.6
TOTAL	385	12117	67	335.2	664	4183.1	383	1545.7	984	1587.4	44	364.8
Meat weight est. (g)	2887.5 (wet weight)		117.64 (cooked weight)		2722.4 (wet weight)		386.83 (cooked weight)		2161.5		Not available	

Table 7.14 MNI and weight for species of marine mollusc found infrequently in the features analysed

Feature	Nucella lapillus		Paphia rhomboides		Buccimum undatum		Anomia ephippium		Littorina mariae		Chlamys varia		Acanthocardia sp		Scrobicularia plana	
	MNI	wt (g)	MNI	wt (g)	MNI	wt (g)	MNI	wt (g)	MNI	wt (g)	MNI	wt (g)	MNI	wt (g)	MNI	wt (g)
517																
1155					1	1.2	1	0.8								
1167					1	4	1	0.7	1	0.6						
1197							1	0.7			1	0.7				
1259																
1756																
2035																
2039					1	0.2							1	0.5	1	0.1
2576											1	0.1			18	18.1
2578					4	67.8										
3165	1	1.5			1	4.4							1	10.4		
2646			1	1.4												
2771																
2838																
4046																
TOTAL	1	1.5	1	1.4	8	77.6	3	2.2	1	0.6	2	0.8	2	10.9	19	18.2

edible (Mâitre-Allain 1991). Meat weight estimates are shown in Table 7.13 for the four most common species; these are discussed further in the sections on the individual species. However, it is notable that these calculations show that the amount of food from the marine molluscs is relatively small and also show that the yield from the larger oysters is about the same as that from the more numerous mussels. Also, by considering yield, the contribution of the most abundant species, limpets, is seen to be possibly less than that of oysters or mussels.

The species which were found infrequently are also edible (Mâitre-Allain 1991) except for the saddle oyster (*Anomia ephippium*) and the flat winkle (*L. mariae*), although the dog-whelk was exploited more for food in earlier prehistory (eg Andrews *et al* 1985). It should be noted that the first of these may be taken whilst gathering oysters and the other two may be taken whilst gathering winkles or limpets.

Today, all the species identified are known from the Channel coast of Sussex (Seaward 1982; Areas 14 and 15). Mussel, winkle, and limpet are typically found on the wave-cut chalk platforms along the Sussex coast. Mussel may also inhabit the sublittoral zone along with oyster, cockle, and carpet shell, and all of these may be gathered at low tide. It is possible that cockle and mussel would have been more tolerant of softer, muddier conditions than the oysters and carpet shell which prefer harder and sandier ground. Bell (1977, 285–7) suggests that any shingle bars along the coast would have made a good habitat for *Venerupis pullastra*, and this would also be true for the carpet shell. *Scrobicularia plana* is indicative of estuarine conditions which include deeper muds and its habitat may overlap with that of cockle (Fish and Fish 1989). Unfortunately, recent anthropogenic change of the coast near Bishopstone hampers any study of current distribution of marine molluscs.

Bell (1977, 240) noted a very similar range of species for the early Anglo-Saxon levels at Rookery Hill, although he did not find any specimens of

the carpet shell (*Tapes decussatus*). As discussed below, he found a different pattern of abundance amongst the exploited molluscs. Incidentally, Bell observes that the land snail *Helix aspersa* was found in the Roman and later levels and this species was also noted as frequently included with the marine shell in the material available for the current analysis.

Table 7.13 shows a slight tendency for the features with very high numbers of limpets, winkles, or mussels to have somewhat lower numbers of oysters. This is particularly notable for three pits: 4046 which has high numbers of winkles and limpets, with the majority of these in context 4054; 2576 which is dominated by mussels which are concentrated in context 2577; 3165 with high numbers of mussels, limpets, and winkles all concentrated in context 3166. However, the majority of features and contexts had low to moderate numbers of all the common species. In addition, it is notable that approximately half the oyster in this sample is derived from the infills of cellared Structure W.

Bivalves other than oysters

*Mussels (*Mytilus edulis*)*

There were a total of 31 mussels, combining right and left valves, whose length could be measured. The average length was 6.0cm, and the mode for length was 6.1–7.0cm (Fig 7.20). The distribution of lengths was markedly skewed, due to a number of very small valves primarily from one context (2577). Mussel fragments notoriously readily, as is evident from the fact that we are dealing here with measurements from 3.1% of the minimum number of valves from a total sample MNI of 659. Whilst sorting the material it was evident that the range of valve size was large, and this could represent the exploitation of mussel beds which were not

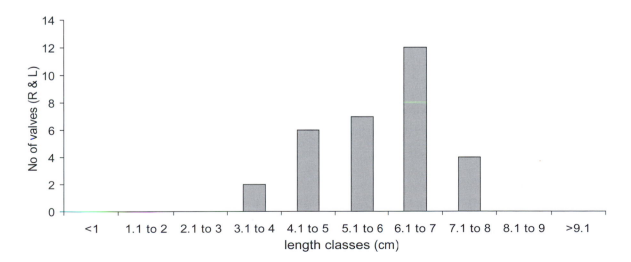

Fig 7.20 Length of mussel valves; data from left and right combined

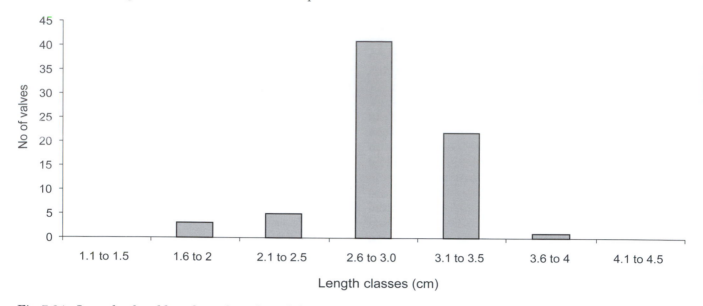

Fig 7.21   Length of cockle valves; data from left and right combined

regularly harvested. However, without being able to determine the size of valves for a larger proportion of the sample, this impression cannot be investigated further.

Bell (1977, 285–6) found that mussels massively dominated the Anglo-Saxon levels at Rookery Hill, accounting for just over 80% of the assemblage. In terms of abundance, the proportion of mussel in the sample analysed here is much lower at 26%. It is notable that mussel was ubiquitous, although the persistence throughout the sample could just reflect there being a background scatter of mussel shell in the settlement. Eight of the fifteen features analysed here have somewhat larger assemblages, in terms of MNI or shell weight or both, with two of the features (2756 and 3165) containing over two-thirds of the total. The meat weight estimate for mussel is based on the yield of a marketable mussel of 5cm in length (MacMillan 1990). Because of the fragmentation of the shell it was not considered appropriate to base an estimate on shell weight, as has been done for well-preserved shell from middens (eg Erlandson *et al* 1999).

Cockles (Cerastoderma edule*)*

There were a total of 72 measureable cockles, combining right and left valves. The average length was 2.9cm, and the mode for length was 2.6 to 3.0cm (Fig 7.21). The distribution of lengths shows an abrupt decline below this modal length, which may indicate some selectivity in harvesting. Survivorship of cockle is very much higher than mussel, with 52.2% of the expected number of valves being found whole, which may also indicate that the absence of smaller cockles is not because of poor survival of smaller shells.

The estimate of meat weight for the cockles is

based on Winder (1980), and is included here for comparison with the other abundant species.

Modern fishery practice (Hancock and Urquhart 1966) forbids the harvesting of cockles below 2.3cm in order to maintain a viable industry and the near absence of shells in this size range and smaller at Bishopstone would indicate that the exploitation of cockles was sustainable. However, the medieval levels at Lydd (Somerville, unpub data) produced vast quantities of cockles, including many which were very small (less than 2cm), and the average lengths for cockles of all periods at Lydd were smaller than those found here, ranging from 2.2 to 2.4cm. The medieval levels at Pevensey Castle (Somerville, unpub data) also produced a substantial quantity of cockle, and, although these did not include the very small valves found at Lydd, the average for the larger assemblages ranged from 2.3 to 2.5cm.

Cockles are commonly found in modest quantities on Sussex archaeological sites, and Bishopstone seems unremarkable in this respect. However, it is striking that Bell (1977, 285–6) found very few cockles in the Saxon levels at Rookery Hill.

*Carpet Shell (*Tapes decussatus*)*

A total of seventeen valves, combining right and left, were measured. The average length was 3.6cm, and the majority of shells were between 3.1 and 4.0cm in length. About 20% of the expected number of whole valves was found for this species. Although the numbers are low, the shells were found distributed across the site, occurring in nearly all the features sampled. It is possible that they were collected as dead shells and used rather than being harvested for food. Intriguingly, this species is not recorded at all at Rookery Hill (Bell 1977, 286), but the other common venerid clam from the Channel coast,

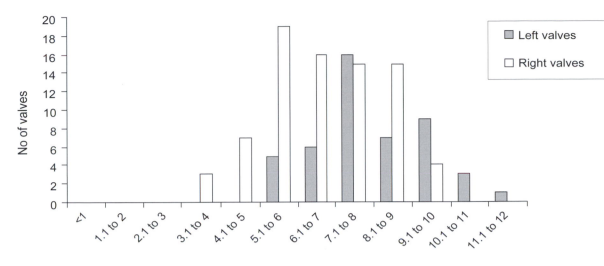

Fig 7.22   Length of oyster valves

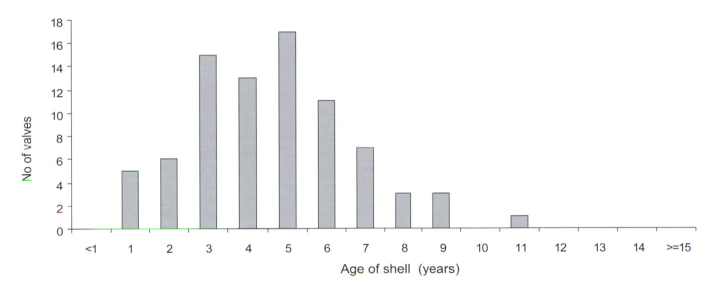

Fig 7.23   Age of oyster valves: data from right and left combined

Venerupis pullastra, was found. This species was noted at Bishopstone, although in very low numbers and not, as it happens, from the features analysed here.[2] One or other of these clams are often found in small numbers on Sussex sites of both the Roman and medieval period.

Oysters (Ostrea edulis)

There were a total of 126 whole valves (47 left and 79 right) and 389 umbos (181 left and 208 right) in the sample. Overall the survivorship of left valves is considerably lower, at 12.2%, than the survivorship of right valves, at 20.5%. The numbers of surviving valves permit the reporting of the analysis by side. The average length of left valves was 8.0cm (Fig 7.22). The distribution is slightly skewed, with the modal length being 7.1 to 8.0cm, but more valves

are above this length than are below it. The average length of right valves is 6.8cm which is above the modal length of 5.1 to 6.0cm, but here the distribution is also notably skewed towards longer lengths. It is notable that there are no left valves smaller than 5cm in length or right valves smaller than 3cm. The abrupt increase in the better preserved right valves at 5.1 to 6.0cm indicates that there may have been selectivity in harvesting.

The age of the oysters also showed a slightly skewed distribution (Fig 7.23). Not all the valves could be aged, and the data given here is for 81 valves where the growth lines at the umbo were clear.

There is a marked increase in the number of valves at three years that may reflect selectivity in the harvesting which, from modern data on farmed oysters, would match with the size distribution discussed above (Walne 1974). In this context, it is also worth noting that the recent oyster fisheries of

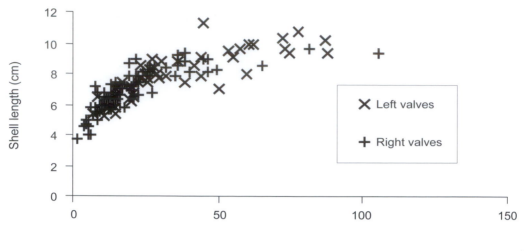

Fig 7.24　Oyster growth plotted as shell length against shell weight

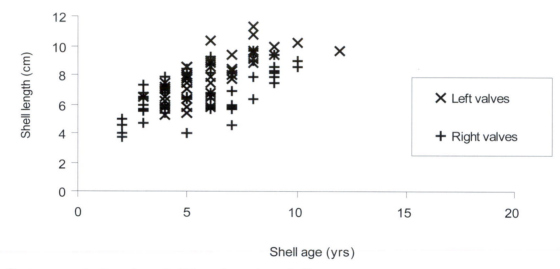

Fig 7.25　Oyster growth plotted as shell length against shell age

the southern English coast maintained a minimum diameter of 5cm for oysters taken from public grounds (Davidson 1976).

Thus the data on both size and age support the possibility that the oysters being harvested from the settlement at Bishopstone were being managed. The regular pattern of growth seen both in terms of shell length against shell weight (Fig 7.24) and shell length against age (Fig 7.25) is also consistent with this interpretation. Figure 7.24 also shows that there were very few oysters which had notably heavier than expected shells for their length. Such stunters (Cole 1956) are known from later medieval deposits in Sussex (eg Somerville 1996).

Winder (1992) gives an average size for oysters from Anglo-Saxon sites as 7.45cm for the length of left valves and 6.52cm for right valves. The overall average for her medieval sites was very similar, 7.5cm for left and 6.4cm for right valve length.

The Bishopstone oysters are slightly larger than Winder's average for Anglo-Saxon sites, and it is interesting to note that medieval assemblages from Sussex continue this disparity (Somerville, unpub data). Indeed, the Bishopstone oysters are closer to the average which Winder gives for Roman sites of 8.04cm for left and 7.15cm for right valve length, mirrored locally at Fishbourne (Somerville and Bonell 2006). Turning to a sample of medieval sites in Sussex, the Friary sites in Lewes (Somerville 1996) gave a range of 7.0 to 8.9cm for right valves and Pevensey a range of 6.3 to 6.8cm for right and 6.9 to 7.4cm for left valves from the medieval contexts (Somerville, unpublished data). Thus the Bishopstone oysters are of a size which is between that found for oysters from Roman sites and those found on medieval sites, giving the same pattern of change that Winder (1992) found for a larger geographic area.

The levels of the three infesting species (*P. ciliata*, *P. Hoplura*, and *C. celata*) which cause damage to the shell were quite low with 53.3% of right valves and 40% of left valves showing no trace of these species (Table 7.15). The rare cases of severe infestation

Table 7.15 The amount of infestation by species which damage the shell of oysters

Infestation category	Right valves		Left valves*	
	No	%	No	%
0 – no infestation	41	53.3	19	42.2
1 – slight traces	23	29.9	17	37.8
2 – up to 1/3 of shell affected	4	5.2	4	8.9
3 – between 1/3 and 2/3 of shell affected	7	9.1	3	6.7
4 – more than 2/3 of shell affected	2	2.6	2	4.4

*There were 2 whole valves which could not be scored for infestation due to surface wear

Table 7.16 Prevalence of infesting and epifaunal species on whole valves and umbos

Infesting or epifaunal species	Right valve		Right Umbo		Left Valve		Left Umbo	
	No	% of shells affected	No	% of shells affected	No	% of shells affected	No	% of shells affected
Polydora ciliata	23	29.9	57	27.4	20	44.4	38	21.0
Polydora hoplura	10	13	14	6.7	10	22.2	24	13.3
Cliona celata	4	5.2	1	0.5	2	4.4	12	6.6
Calcareous tube	8	10.4	14	6.7	9	20.0	21	11.6
Sand tube	0	0	1	0.5	8	17.8	22	12.2
Bryozoan	3	3.9	2	1.0	6	13.3	9	5.0
Piddock	1	1.3	0	0	1	2.2	0	0
Barnacle	2	2.6	0	0	0	0	0	0
Drillhole	1	1.3	5	2.4	0	0	3	1.7
Adhering shell	0	0	7	3.4	9	20.0	25	13.8

were attributable to *P. ciliata*. The majority of shells showing infestation were only lightly affected. Table 7.16 shows the numbers of affected shells and the prevalence both of these species and other epifauna for valves and umbos. Shells may have more than one infesting and/or epifaunal species but this has not been taken into account here. Left valves and umbos tend to have higher rates of both infesting and epifaunal species.

The amount of infestation is light, which resembles the situation at Fishbourne (Somerville and Bonell 2006), although very light levels of infestation were also seen in the earlier medieval contexts at Lydd (Somerville, unpublished data). Somewhat higher levels of infestation were found at the medieval Friary site in Lewes (Somerville 1996).

P. ciliata is the main infesting species of polychaete, with considerably lower levels of *P. hoplura* being present. The damaging boring sponge *C. celata* is quite rare. This pattern of infestation is also similar to Fishbourne (Somerville and Bonell 2006), and Lydd (Somerville, unpub data), and again contrasts with the situation at Lewes Friary (Somerville 1996) where *P. hoplura* was the most common species and levels of *C. celata* infestation were quite marked. The relative levels of the two polychaete species indicates that the Bishopstone oysters came from fairly shallow beds (Cole 1956; Smith 1987).

Table 7.16 also contains information about adhering shell, which is found predominantly on the left valves and umbos. This may represent the adherence of spat or it may reflect the condition of the ground on which the oysters were growing. Since the adhering shell appeared always to be oyster, the former explanation is the more likely. There were only two examples of conjoined shell in the sample, and this, together with the general shape of the oysters, indicates that the sample came from bottom-dwelling beds rather than reef formations.

If oysters were consumed raw, then we might see differential deposition of table and kitchen waste in a bias towards the cupped left-hand shells for table waste and the reverse for kitchen waste. There were eleven contexts in the sample which had ten or more whole valves plus sided umbos. Only one of these had a bias of more than 70% towards one side – the right – and another had a bias of just under 70% – again to the right. Hagen (1992) refers to oysters being taken out of their shells at the table, but it is unclear whether this was from a complete or already opened shell. There was no clear evidence in the form of notches for the method of opening the shells on the oysters in this sample.

The abundance of oyster at Bishopstone is 15%, which is nearly ten times greater than the abundance at Rookery Hill (Bell 1977, 285–7), although for both sites oyster is the third most common species. It is possible that there were changes in local availability between the earlier settlement at Rookery Hill and the later settlement at Bishopstone, and here further investigation of the development of the shingle bars along this part of the Sussex coast would be informative (see Jennings and Smyth 1990 for background). Changes in these bars would also affect the extent to which the valley leading up to Bishopstone was a marine inlet (see Chapter 2.2).

Gastropods

Winkles

Some 337 winkles could be measured for length. The average length was 26.4mm and the modal length for the sample was 26 to 30mm (Fig 7.26). The distribution was close to normal. The survivorship of winkles was very high for this

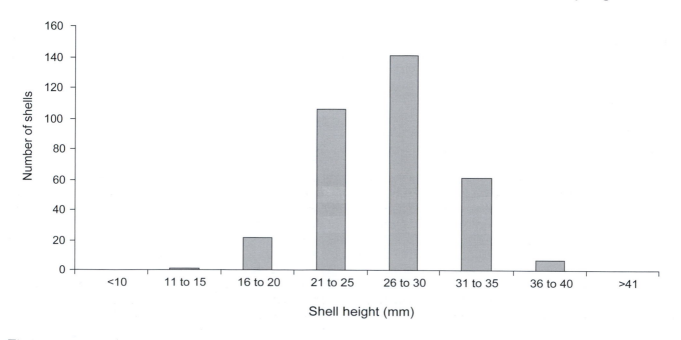

Fig 7.26   Height of winkles

sample at 88%. However, with hand collection of marine molluscs, it is possible that fragments of winkles would be lost, so this may inflate the survivorship.

Winkles are the second most abundant of the marine molluscs at Rookery Hill, comprising 14% of the total (Bell 1977, 285–7). At Bishopstone they are the fourth most abundant, but comprise very nearly the same relative abundance (14.9%). The abundance of winkles at both Rookery Hill and Bishopstone is not surprising given that both sites are near to a shore which had suitable habitat in the form of wave-cut platforms.

Bell does not give any information about the size of the winkles found, and neither does Winder (1980) for Saxon Southampton (Hamwic), where winkles were the second most abundant species after oysters. Winder's description of the wear on the Hamwic winkles implies a greater amount of attrition than was seen at Bishopstone, where wear on the apex was noted on 13% of the shells. Low levels of infestation by *P. ciliata* were seen on 23.2% of the winkles at Bishopstone, principally on the larger and presumably older shells. The mean height of infested shells was 31.1mm. Compared to other Sussex sites, the Bishopstone winkles are of a good size; those from medieval contexts in Pevensey Town were only 18mm in height, while the winkles from early medieval contexts at Pevensey Castle were 23mm (Somerville, unpub data). The small sample of winkles from Fishbourne Roman Palace averaged 24.1mm (Somerville and Bonell 2006).

Hagen (1992) describes winkles being taken out of their shells at table, so it is possible that the features which include higher numbers of this species (see Table 7.13) might contain table waste.

Limpets

Limpets were the most abundant marine mollusc at Bishopstone and 602 whole shells were measured. The survivorship of limpet was 61.2%, with most of the incomplete shell being represented by apices. This implies a degree of edge damage to the shells, which may have occurred on collection, although the shell was not examined in sufficient detail to see how it compared to the pattern of slight spalling reported by Evans (1983).

The average (modal) length of the limpets was only 27.4mm. The distribution of the data for length is close to normal, although with somewhat smaller shells than might be expected (Fig 7.27). This is very much smaller than the shell sizes reported from excavations in Scotland (Evans 1983), where the mean length is between 38 and 42mm. More locally, however, the size of the limpets from Bishopstone compares quite well with the size of the limpets from the medieval levels of Bullock Down (Cartwright 1982), where the modal length was 17mm and the range for length was from 10 to 26mm. Brief explo-

ration of the shore at nearby Cow Gap found only small limpets within this size range (Cartwright 1982).

Limpet shell morphology, particularly the ratio of height to length, is variable across the shore, with flatter limpets being more typical of the lower, less-exposed shore and more conical ones being found higher on the shore and in more exposed locations (Orton 1928; Moore 1934; Evans 1983). However, although this general relationship holds over a range of habitats and times, the exact proportions need to be established for each population and habitat (Bailey and Craighead 2003). Nonetheless, an examination of the distribution of the height to length ratio for the current sample (Fig 7.28) clearly indicates a unimodal distribution and therefore it is possible to suggest that the limpets all come from a similar habitat. Determining where this was likely to be on the shore would require actualistic investigation, but overall the limpets are flat rather than conical, although this observation has to be tempered by their small size (see Orton 1928).

The calculation of meat weight for limpets seems desirable given their abundance. They comprise 38.4% of the assemblage and are the most numerous of the marine molluscs. Unfortunately, a straightforward calculation using a published conversion for MNI to meat weight was not possible. Evans (1983) gives the conversion of meat to shell weight of 1:1.2 for limpet. Rather than calculate an average weight for a limpet shell in this sample, the survivorship of whole limpet shells (61.2%) was used to estimate the original total weight for the sample and this formed the basis for the calculation of meat weight of 2161.5g. This estimate would place limpets in the third rank in terms of meat yield from marine molluscs.

The abundance of limpets at Bishopstone is striking and contrasts with the much lower abundance, less than 1%, for the Saxon contexts at Rookery Hill (Bell 1977, 285–7), although they are more abundant in the earlier levels. As discussed by Cartwright (1982), limpets are not that common on Sussex medieval sites, nor have they been found in any abundance on Roman sites.

Conclusion

The marine molluscs from Bishopstone indicate that the inhabitants exploited a number of different ecological zones, ranging from the wave-cut platform (limpets and winkles) to the sublittoral (oysters and cockles). Although the most abundant mollusc harvested is limpet, calculations of yield indicate that either oysters or mussels should be regarded as contributing most to the diet. Although potentially informative, deductions from calculations of meat weight must be regarded as somewhat speculative; indeed Claassen (1998) regards them as extremely dubious.

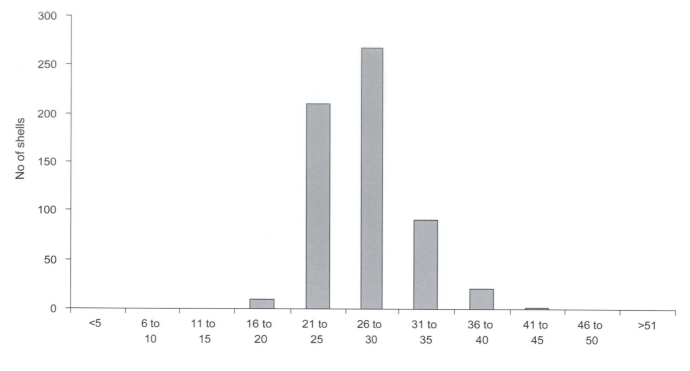

Fig 7.27   Length of limpets

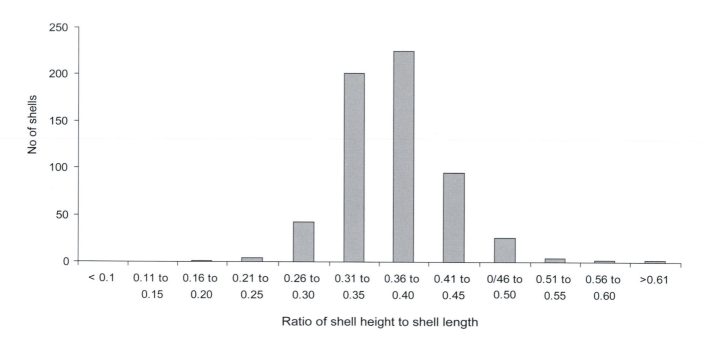

Fig 7.28   Distribution of shell height : shell length ratios for limpets

The oysters, winkles, and cockles from Bishopstone are of a good size. Only oysters can be compared against a contemporaneous average (from Winder 1992) and they do appear to be slightly above average size for southern England. Compared against a wider temporal framework, the oysters from Bishopstone are intermediate in size between those from Roman and medieval sites in Sussex.

In contrast, the limpets appear to be rather small, but this may be a local feature, as is shown by the similarly small size of the later medieval limpets from Bullock Down.

There are marked contrasts to the early Saxon site at Rookery Hill in terms of relative abundance. The exploitation of marine resources from Bishopstone appears to be more broadly spread over a number of common species but the exploitation pattern at Rookery Hill is focused on one species, mussels. This contrast, and the longer-term fluctuation in exploitation pattern at Rookery Hill, raises a question about whether the local environment was changing, possibly as a result of the dynamic nature of the coastal environment itself (Jennings and Smyth 1990).

Notes

1   The features selected for the sample analysed here are given in Tables 7.13 and 7.14. The individual contexts within these which contained shell are listed here in brackets after the feature number.
517 (518); 1155 (1156); 1167 (1168; 1342; 1344); 1197 (1198); 1259 (1364); 1756 (1757; 1776; 1778); 2035 (2036; 2827; 2870; 2894; 2969); 2039 (2040; 2874; 2875; 2895; 2896; 2897; 2898; 2944; 2946; 2947; 2948); 2576 (2577; 2995; 2996; 3006); 2578 (2579; 2899; 2900; 2906; 2908); 3165 (2646, 3166; 3176); 2646 (2647; 3055; 3069); 2771 (2772); 2838 (2839; 3188); 4046 (4047; 4054).

2   In addition, records for the whole site include infrequent finds of *Littorina obtutasta*, *Venerupis pullastra*, and *Pecten maximus*. The first of these is noted as occurring slightly further to the west along the Channel coast by Seaward (1982).
One of the specimens of *P. maximus* (context 2533) could have been worked. This was an umbo of the flat left valve lacking the 'ears' and the natural edge of the shell. Although the sculpturing of the shell is still sharp, the edge of the shell was smooth, and it is this smoothness, and the complete absence of the 'ears' which appears artificial, although there are no tool markings on the shell.

8   Reconstructing Bishopstone

This chapter commences with an in-depth reconstruction of the buildings and other structural features presented in Chapter 4, progressing through an examination of their constructional affinities, function, and status. It then attempts to situate the built environment within a chronological and spatial framework constructed with reference to radiocarbon dating, an assessment of site phasing, and a consideration of the evolving layout of the settlement.

8.1   The built environment

Introduction

The timber buildings excavated at Bishopstone, at least in the shadowy form usually recovered on dry rural sites, cannot match the vivid structural detail preserved at the settlements of Yeavering, and Cowdrey's Down, which have both helped to bring new understanding to the construction technology of Anglo-Saxon timber architecture. Yet Bishopstone has nevertheless produced an impressive range of complete and near complete ground-plans, some representing distinctive (in one case a unique) expressions of the contemporary built environment. In this sense, Bishopstone's structural record helps to bring to the fore the expanding diversity of building forms distinguishing the later Anglo-Saxon period from the comparative architectural homogeneity of the 5th to the 7th centuries (Hamerow 2002, 46–8; Reynolds 2003, 130–3; Loveluck 2007, 31–51). In this discussion, informed by comparative analysis across a spectrum of 8th- to 11th-century settlements, attention will first be given to the constructional characteristics of the buildings followed by a consideration of their possible functions; discussion will conclude by attempting to extrapolate aspects of settlement character and status from the built environment.

Constructional characteristics

Posthole structures

Structure A (Fig 4.3)

Of all the buildings represented on the excavations, Structure A shows the greatest affinity with the repertoire of halls of posthole construction recovered from the Rookery Hill settlement; indeed, such a building would not look out of place on innumerable 5th- to 7th-century Anglo-Saxon settlements

– Mucking (Essex), Chalton (Hants), West Stow (Suffolk), Catholme (Staffs), to quote some of the best-known examples. Its rectangular ground-plan is based on a multiple-square (3:1) module and its precise layout comprises posts paired transversely across the building – features which tally with a recurring range of structural attributes displayed by Anglo-Saxon timber buildings of this date. With an internal floor area of a little under 35m², this building also falls within the average size range of similar structures (see James *et al* 1984; Marshall and Marshall 1991).

The central alignment of posts is more difficult to parallel in this early period. Although the same layout appears amongst a selection of the 7th- to 9th-century buildings from Catholme (Losco-Bradley & Kinsley 2002, 87), it is attested at a later period amongst the 8th- to early 9th-century buildings at North Elmham (Structures S, Z1, and Z2: Wade-Martins 1980, 64–8, figs 82–3) and Higham Ferrers (Buildings 2664 and 2665: Hardy *et al* 2007, 32–5, figs 3.19 and 3.24) and locally, in the 10th century, at Market Field, Steyning (Building B: Gardiner 1993, 30–4, fig 9). In such cases the central posts are usually interpreted as supports for the roof, the assumption being that this role was shared between the wall-posts and a central ridge running from gable to gable (*ibid*, 33–4). An alternative possibility is that they were used to support the floor-joists of an upper storey.

As these later parallels suggest, caution must be exercised in attributing this building an 'early' date purely on the basis of building typology. Whilst this style of building is superseded by post-in-trench construction in some internal site sequences spanning the 5th to the 7th centuries (eg Chalton: Addyman and Leigh 1973, 7), it persisted throughout the later Anglo-Saxon period (and indeed beyond) in many parts of the country, as an alternative to post-in-trench construction, and the two traditions frequently appear side by side on any one site (eg Springfield Lyons, Essex: Tyler and Major 2005, 192–3; see Gardiner 1990, 242). Thus, there is certainly no need to view Structure A as an anachronism or to invent an otherwise silent phase of early Anglo-Saxon occupation on the village green to explain its existence. On the other hand, it is so far removed in design and conception from the mainstream repertoire of post-in-trench buildings at Bishopstone, that to deny it any chronological significance seems overly cautious. It seems relevant that this building was sited in one of the few parts of the excavation to produce intercutting pit sequences, suggestive of an extended occupation sequence. Whilst the evidence is far from conclusive, this building has greater claim than any other from Bishopstone to be regarded as a remnant of the earliest generations of the later Anglo-Saxon settlement. The diffuse spread of domestic pits returning radiocarbon date-ranges covering the earlier (8th- to 9th-century) part of the occupation sequence suggests that this building is unlikely to have existed in isolation and others in the same constructional style may be represented amongst the scatters of postholes found across the site.

Structure B (Fig 4.5)

Although Structure B belongs to the same general class as Structure A, there are some clear divergences in the construction. The most obvious disparity is the larger size of its postholes; those belonging to Structure A appear to have been cut only marginally larger than the scantling of the timbers. Whilst there are similarities in the way both buildings have posts which are paired transversely across the building, Structure B's posts are aligned much less regularly within each of the walls suggesting a different method of assembly; the likelihood is that the wall-plate was carried on top of the tie-beams (Dixon 2002, 94–5, fig 3.83C). This building also utilised a small length of wall-trench at its south-west corner; the combined use of both types of foundation within the footprint of the same building is widely attested amongst settlements of the later Anglo-Saxon period; see, for example, Building 4 at Springfield Lyons (Essex) (Tyler and Major 2005, 131, fig 73) and Building AS45 at Catholme (Losco-Bradley and Kinsley 2002, 72–3, fig 3.61).

The post-in-trench structures

Despite an under-representation of timber ghosts, some family traits of structural significance can be recognised across Bishopstone's post-in-trench buildings, which accord closely with evidence from other sites. The most obvious is the superficiality of the end-wall foundations in comparison to those of the long walls; in several cases they were absent altogether and in others they were defined by rows of postholes or discontinuous sections of wall-trench. As others have commented, the clear implication of this is that the weight of the roof was chiefly distributed along the long walls of such buildings with the end walls playing a minor or insignificant role.

Another recurrent feature, seen particularly clearly in Structure C (Fig 4.7), was the asymmetrical profile of the wall-trenches resulting from the considerable care taken to cut the inside edge on a vertical plane. This familiar trait, supposedly giving this construction technique an advantage over earth-fast buildings founded in individual postholes, has traditionally been interpreted as a method for accurately aligning posts within the wall-plate (Rahtz 1976, 84; Gardiner 1990, 243; Fairbrother 1990, 191).

That this was an important incentive is borne out by numerous cases of buildings at Bishopstone, and beyond, where posts (located either by timber ghosts or basal depressions) were clearly placed hard up against a straight vertical inner edge of the trench. Yet there are examples – Building 9 from Faccombe Netherton and Structure 2224 from Brighton Hill South (Hants) – where post positioning appears to have been more variable (Fairbrother 1990, 109–14, fig 4.15; Fasham and Keevil 1995, 85–8, fig 46). Mark Gardiner (forthcoming) has argued that a more satisfactory explanation for this characteristic profile may lie in a process of pre-assembly (termed longitudinal) whereby sections of wall-frame (comprising uprights, wall-plate, and perhaps wattling) were constructed on the ground beyond the footprint of the house (Meeson and Welch 1993, 13, fig 9). When each of the wall frames was raised into position, the feet of the posts would have slid down the outer sloping face of the trench and then been held firm against the flat inner edge with packing material, until the wall was finally stabilised with the erection of the opposite wall and the connecting tie-beams.

The majority of the buildings constructed in this style displayed basal post depressions. That the form of the depressions was invariably sub-rectangular provides indirect evidence that the structural posts were shaped as opposed to being in-the-round; the few surviving timber ghosts suggest that the posts were squared and considerably thicker than the radially split planks recorded at Botolphs (Sussex) (Gardiner 1990, 243). The substantial depth variation registered across basal depressions within individual buildings shows that their purpose was to accommodate irregularities in the lengths of the timber uprights, this being an easier technique than chopping off excess sections of post.

There can be little doubt that the majority of the post-in-trench buildings employed wattle and daub panelling for walling. The clearest evidence was the large quantity of structural daub recovered from the excavations, totalling a staggering half metric ton in weight (Chapter 6.7). A rather more circumstantial clue pointing in the same direction was the irregular spacing of posts within wall-trenches – as revealed, for example, by the timber ghosts preserved in the southern long wall of Structure K (Fig 4.16). There is no evidence for the alternative types of walling seen at other contemporary settlements such as stave or plank-on-end construction; the possibility of interrupted ground sills to support the wall-fill between structural uprights is a development generally attested at a later period in rural contexts (Meeson and Welch 1993).

Aisled structures (Figs 4.30 and 4.32)

A tradition of late Anglo-Saxon aisled construction first came to light some 30 years ago following the excavation of two aisled halls at Portchester Castle (Cunliffe 1976, 60; Rahtz 1976, 86–7; Beresford 1987,

64–7; Grenville 1997, 83–6). Since then the number of such buildings has increased steadily, although it appears nevertheless to have been a relatively minor tradition with seigniorial connotations. The advantages of this technique as a form of earth-fast construction were two-fold when viewed from a purely technological perspective: firstly, buildings with internal posts were able to span greater widths than those with load-bearing side walls which were necessarily constrained by the length of unsupported tie-beams; and secondly, placing the load-bearing posts inside the walls helped to extend the life of the building by reducing their exposure to damp in the soil and to the elements. The introduction of this new constructional technique, alongside stone footings (another innovation designed to increase the longevity of earth-fast buildings) and a mounting body of evidence for the refurbishment, repair, and replacement of buildings on fixed plots, all bear witness to the emergence of a stable settlement pattern and with it tighter control over social space and property units (Hamerow 2002; Reynolds 2003; Gardiner 2004, 357–8).

The expanding number of excavated case studies supports the theory that the aisled tradition emerged largely within a high-status social milieu in later Anglo-Saxon/Saxo-Norman England. Accordingly, a significant number of pre-Conquest aisled buildings form the 'hall' component of formally planned manorial ranges whether within axially aligned suites, as at Raunds Furnells, West Cotton, Goltho, and Faccombe Netherton (Audouy and Chapman 2009, 53–5, fig 4.2), or within courtyards as at Portchester (Cunliffe 1976, 123–6, fig 99). In cases of manorial compounds with a more diffuse layout, such as Ketton (Rutland) (Meadows 1998), the importance of the aisled hall is signalled both by its size in relation to adjacent buildings and its focal location, in this particular case dwarfing an adjacent contemporary stone church. Significantly, the aisled halls at Raunds Furnells, Faccombe Netherton, and Goltho are all superimposed by Norman and medieval successors demonstrating continuity in seigneurial role.

The relatively narrow social context surrounding the genesis of the tradition belies considerable diversity in design and constructional arrangements, although this is in part related to the fact that aisled construction was also used for ancillary buildings within manorial compounds, as in the case of the 'Eastern Range' of Goltho and the putative granary from West Cotton (Beresford 1987, 79–82, fig 86; Windell *et al* 1990, 24–5, fig 13b) (Table 8.1). A basic distinction can be made between one- and two-aisled structures. The former are evidently exclusive to the axially aligned domestic ranges at West Cotton, Raunds Furnells, and Goltho – although in all such cases the reconstruction is uncertain due to the ground-plans forming complex palimpsests (Audouy and Chapman 2009, 53–5). Moving on to genuine two-aisled buildings, a distinction exists between examples with aisles of a comparable width

to those found in high medieval buildings (Structure 16 at Portchester Castle at 2m; Cunliffe 1976, 44–8, fig 26) and a more populous group with comparatively narrow aisles of 1.5m and under, in some cases extending to as little as 0.3m (see Gardiner 2004, 352–8). At 0.65m and 0.45m respectively, Structures U and V from Bishopstone fall comfortably into the latter of the two categories.

As a group, these buildings display considerable variability in the width of the aisles and in the number and spacing of the arcades (Fig 8.1; Table 8.2). As exemplified by the 'Eastern Building' of the 11th-century manorial complex at Goltho (Beresford 1987, 79–81), the width of aisles and bays within the same building can also be highly irregular (Fig 8.1 C and E). Overall, the tendency is for close-set arcades within the region of 2.0m to 2.5m and both of the Bishopstone examples fall within this range. On sites with internal sequences of aisled buildings (Faccombe Netherton, Goltho) there is an increase in width of bays over time; only Building S15 at Portchester Castle, dated to the 10th century, with relatively wide bays of 4m, bucks the trend for what otherwise appears to be a general increase in spacing over the 10th to the 12th centuries (Fig 8.1A). This development looks ahead to the roomier bay arrangements found in medieval aisled halls, suggesting that there may be an evolutionary link between pre-Conquest aisled buildings as excavated and the earliest standing vernacular buildings of later medieval England (Fairbrother 1990, 186–7; Gardiner 2004, 356).

Fairbrother (1990, 92–3) has discussed the structural implications of narrow bay spacing and suggests that it denotes a rather different type of construction to fully bayed buildings of the medieval period. Given that the arcade posts of the earliest aisled structure from Faccombe Netherton were set into continuous trenches (comparable to the northern aisle of Bishopstone Structure V), he suggests that the arcades were constructed using longitudinal assembly as in a typical wall, commencing with the attachment of the arcade posts to an arcade plate, with the latter resting directly upon the former. This certainly seems like a plausible suggestion for the Bishopstone buildings which may have approximated to Fairbrother's interpretative reconstruction of Faccombe Netherton Building 2 (Fairbrother 1990, 91, fig 4.6).

There is no direct dating evidence for the Bishopstone aisled buildings. The construction of Structure U is provided with a late 9th- to early 10th-century *terminus post quem* from the radiocarbon assays from the infilling of the cellared Structure W which it superimposed. A rubbish/latrine pit located in close proximity to these buildings yielded a radiocarbon date of cal AD 890–1030 at 95% confidence (SUERC-16016), the latest in the series of scientific dates recovered from the occupation sequence. On this basis, an attribution of the mid to late 10th century for both buildings seems likely.

Table 8.1 Attributes of the excavated structures

Structure	Internal dimensions (m)	Floor area (m²)	Orientation	Construction method	Relationships
A	10.24 × 3.40	34.8	E–W	Individual posthole	Earlier than Structure M
B	5.80 × 4.10	23.78	E–W	Individual posthole	
C	8.50 × 4.00	34.0	E–W	Post-in-trench	Later than Structures F and S
D	12.00 × 3.80	45.60	N–S	Post-in-trench	
E	6.20 × 3.70	22.94	N–S	Post-in-trench	
F	8.50-9.50 × 4.50	>38.25	N–S	Post-in-trench	Earlier than Structures E and C
G	–	–	?	Post-in-trench	
H	6.50 × 3.70	24.1	N–S	Post-in-trench	
I	? × 4.16	-	N–S	Post-in-trench	
J	9.00 × 4.40	39.6	E–W	Post-in-trench	Earlier than Structure K
K	12.65 × 5.52	69.8	E–W	Post-in-trench	Later than Structure J
L	6.5-7.4 × 3.80	>24.7	N–S	Post-in-trench	
M	>8.20 × 5.60	>45.92	E–W	Post-in-trench	Later than Structure A
N	>7.50 × ?		E–W	Post-in-trench	
O	5.60 × 4.60 5.60 × 5.30 >10.45 × 5.90	25.76 29.7 >61.7	N–S E–W E–W	Post-in-trench Post-in-trench Post-in-trench	
P	>8.0m × ?	–	E–W	Post-in-trench	
Q	>5.50m × ?	–	E–W	Post-in-trench	
R	>7.20 × ?	–	N–S	Post-in-trench	
S	3.10 × 2.80	8.68	N–S	Post-in-trench	Earlier than Structure C
T	3.40 × 0.60	2.0	N–S	Post-in-trench	
U	9.30 × 7.00	65.1	E–W	Aisled	Later than Structure W
V	7.40 × 6.15	45.5	E–W	Aisled	
W	3.0 × 2.6-2.8	8.1	–	Cellared	Earlier than Structure U
X	> 3.20 × >1.56	–	E–W	Platform	

Table 8.2 Attributes of later Anglo-Saxon aisled buildings

Building	Dimensions	Aisle width (m)	Arcade spacing (m)	No. of bays	No. of aisles
Bishopstone U	9.3 × 7.0	0.45	2.65	3	2
Bishopstone V	7.4 × 6.15	0.65	1.8-2.0	3	2
Portchester S15	12.80 × 9.45	2	4	2	2
Portchester S16	10.06 × 9.14	1.5	2.5	2	2
Faccombe Netherton 2	12.8 × 8.55	1.6	1.6-1.75	5	2
Faccombe Netherton 11	18.3 × 7.3	0.3-1.8	2.6-3.0	5	2
Goltho, Period 5 Hall	12.6 × 6.6	1.8	2.6	3	1
Goltho, Period 5 Eastern Building	21.6 × 6.0	0.75	4.5-4.8	3	2
Raunds Furnells	16.0 × 10.5	2.3	3.2	3	1
Ketton	12.0 × 8.0	1.5	2.2	3	2

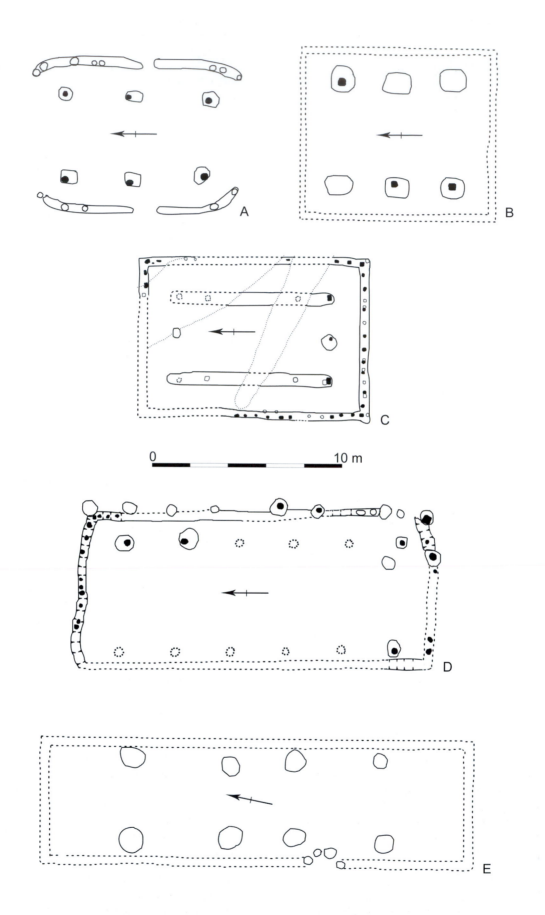

Fig 8.1   Anglo-Saxon aisled buildings: A) Portchester S15; B) Portchester S16 (after Cunliffe 1976, figs 25 and 26); C) Faccombe Netherton 2; D) Faccombe Netherton 11 (after Fairbrother 1990, figs 4.5 and 4.19); E) Goltho Eastern Building (after Beresford 1987, fig 86)

Cellared Structure W

A structural interpretation of this remarkable building – evidently unique to the corpus of later Anglo-Saxon rural settlements – has been laid out in detail elsewhere (Thomas 2008). On the basis of three structural inferences, it has been argued that the excavated footprint can be resolved into a timber tower raised above an internally accessed cellar with a broader lean-to structure at ground level. Rather than rehearse the argument in detail, the opportunity is here taken to address some anachronisms which have been pointed out since the reconstruction appeared in press (Thomas 2008, ill 8). Notwithstanding these criticisms, it should be stated that the basic form of the tower, as visualised, has been well received by scholars familiar with the technology of later Anglo-Saxon timber buildings. A highly distinctive addition to the repertoire of later Anglo-Saxon period timber buildings, the Bishopstone tower again emphasises the growing structural diversity distinguishing the built environment of the 8th to the 11th centuries from the rather more uniform structural traditions of the early Anglo-Saxon era (Hamerow 2002, 46–7; Reynolds 2003, 99).

The chief failing of the reconstruction as first published is that it relies too heavily on post-Conquest timber towers at Brookland (Kent) and Yarpole and Pembridge (Herefordshire) (Gravett 1975; Higham and Barker 1992, 254; Molyneux *et al* 2003), comparisons which introduce a series of anachronisms into the proposed design. The first and most blatant is the use of notched lap-joints in the diagonal bracing, a form of carpentry not attested until 1125 at the earliest (Goodburn 1992, 126–30; 1997; see Milne and Milne 1982, 109–11, fig 66 for a useful illustrated glossary of these terms). A more acceptable alternative in a pre-Conquest (*c* AD 900) context, is a tusk tenon extending through a loose mortice – this is the only form of jointing known from the period capable of sustaining the compression of the four canted corner posts and is present on dated timbers from the Tamworth water mill (Rahtz and Meeson 1992, 125–35, figs 83–4; Darah 2007, 62–3). In addition to providing structural stability at the core of the tower, these joints also would have served the horizontal beams supporting the floor joists suspended over the cellar.

The second anachronism is the lattice bracing shown on each face of the tower. Since this form of structural reinforcement is not attested directly in timber constructions of the pre-Conquest period (whether in buildings or in waterfront installations), one must be open to other possibilities, for example beams running diagonally in a horizontal plane between the posts. Whilst this needs to be entertained as an alternative, it should be stated that within the constricted confines of the structure concerned (recalling that the base dimensions are 2.60m by 2.80m), diagonal timbers would have seriously hindered movement within the tower and

thus limited its functional efficacy. The form of the bracing used must therefore remain an issue of uncertainty.

A third issue is the visualisation of the lower ground-level stage shown resting on solid sill-beams jointed to each of the corner uprights. On analogy with Building S15 from Portchester Castle it is perhaps better to envisage a lighter, lean-to structure (Cunliffe 1976, 41, fig 25). This broadly contemporary comparison – a rectangular hall with pairs of internal aisle posts which may be regarded as analogous to the four corner posts of the Bishopstone tower – demonstrates that the outer walls were of flimsy construction with rounded corners and with uprights bedded in shallow foundation trenches. On the basis that the latter are unlikely to have survived the severe ground-erosion suffered at Bishopstone, this seems like a more acceptable alternative.

Given the uncertainties involved with the type of bracing used on the tower, the decision has been taken not to publish an updated version of the original detailed reconstruction in this report but instead to modify the general view of the tower in its settlement context (originally appearing as ill 9, Thomas 2008) (see Fig 8.6).

House platform: Structural complex X

Whilst presenting only a partial view, the combination of features represented by Structural complex X displays certain affinities with the (12th- to 16th-century) farmstead excavated at Kiln Combe, near Eastbourne, one of very few sites to provide an insight into the character of medieval settlement on the chalk uplands of Sussex (Drewett and Freke 1982). In its earliest guise the farm comprised a series of terraces occupied by timber buildings, represented by shallow slots and postholes, some rebuilt in flint masonry in subsequent phases (*ibid*, 144–63, figs 73–4). In addition to serving as house platforms, some terraces of the more substantially excavated later medieval settlement were occupied by agricultural outbuildings and processing areas. Either of these scenarios is a possibility for the Bishopstone platform/s.

The significance of the buried ceramic vessel located at the edge of the Bishopstone platform is difficult to interpret (see Jervis, Chapter 6.1). Typologically it fits into a post-Saxo-Norman tradition, supporting the theory that the occupation represented by the platform complex is later than, and distinctive from, the main sequence of 8th- to 10th-century activity on the village green; this might well explain the noted structural affinities with the medieval farm at Kiln Combe. The same site provides an intriguing parallel for a buried ceramic vessel but in this instance its placement was clearly exterior to a building; the recovery of cereal grain from the contents of the vessel leading to the suggestion that it might have functioned as an animal feeder (Drewett and Freke 1982, 171, fig 89). A similar interpretation has been proposed for a small pit partially lined with slabs of ceramic vessel from the Saxo-Norman occupation at Botolphs (Gardiner 1990, 237, fig 14). The purpose of the Bishopstone vessel is more difficult to define both because it lacked a grain constituent and because it is neither unambiguously 'internal' nor 'external' to a building. Its function as a storage vessel must therefore remain untested.

The evidence provided by structural daub

The structural daub recovered from Bishopstone, weighing in at over 500kg, outstrips by a substantial margin any previous assemblage to have been generated by an Anglo-Saxon settlement. The assemblage as a whole receives fuller attention in Chapter 6.7 and the details discussed here are only those pertinent to the construction of the buildings. The condition of the daub varied considerably between contexts from large 'fresh' slabs to small weathered fragments. This differential fragmentation pattern of the daub indicates varied pathways of deposition from primary rubbish (literally burnt sections of wall dumped into pits) through to the reposition and reworking of midden material, and house and yard sweepings (see Chapter 6.7). Combined with its ubiquity, this varied taphonomic background reinforces the impression that daub was used as the primary walling material throughout Bishopstone's occupation sequence.

Over 70% of the material carried wattle impressions equating to a total of 575 metres of linear impression-run. The structural attributes of the daub are remarkably consistent. The impressions denote consistently clean and smooth hazel with almost no knots, forks, buds, or blemishes indicating that the wood was harvested within the first year of growth as part of managed coppice. The mean diameter of the rods or staves was around 10–12mm and the withies 7–10mm; longitudinal rods were spaced at regular intervals of between 0.10m and 0.13m. A few daub fragments displayed an anomalous pattern of rods and withies laid in parallel, but the majority of the larger pieces (7–10% of the assemblage) carried impressions of a criss-cross weave. Some fragments were marked with impressions from structural posts indicating both squared timber and timber in-the-round, with the former predominating; it was not possible to reconstruct the original dimensions of the posts. Several fragments, presumably originally located at the junction between the wall-plate and the eaves of the roof, bore impressions of straw thatch providing indirect evidence of roofing material. The exterior surface of a large percentage of the daub was covered with a layer of limewash waterproofing. Thin-section analysis revealed that the exterior weatherproofing on some walls had been reapplied on several occasions, probably on an annual basis.

Function

Rectangular buildings

Without the testimony of floor levels, hearths, and other superficial deposits, it is impossible to make any precise statements on the function of the rectangular post-in-trench buildings found at Bishopstone. On the other hand, from the wide range of sizes represented (Table 8.2), it is possible to draw the conclusion that the repertoire encapsulates a *multiplicity* of functions. This observation might seem self-evident but it argues against a scenario involving, for example, an agglomeration of separate household units, a possible social context lying behind the layout of enclosed domestic compounds at Catholme (Hamerow 2002, 126–7). It therefore has direct implications for characterising the type of settlement represented on Bishopstone village green (Chapter 9.3).

What other interpretations can be derived from the size and layout of timber buildings? Exploring this question is not as straightforward as one would like as a result of several incomplete or ambiguous building ground-plans, but some basic observations can nevertheless be made. The first relates to an ability to distinguish domestic accommodation from agricultural/ancillary functions. The 9th to 11th centuries represent a transitional period in terms of the way in which domestic houses were organised (Gardiner 2000b). On the one hand there is general evidence for an increasing use of partitions to divide up interior space, usually forming narrow annexes at the ends of the main room. On the other, particularly in relation to high-status complexes, functional rooms which would later come together under one roof with the emergence of the so-called 'Later Medieval Domestic Plan' were frequently disaggregated between physically separate and sometimes contiguous buildings, manifested in axial and courtyard ranges. What is uncertain, given these two parallel developments, is whether the function of the narrow annexes found in larger hall-type structures of the period was in any way analogous to the service rooms or chambers characterising medieval buildings. Whilst there is a possibility of some functional overlap, Gardiner has observed that the organising principle behind the layout of these earlier buildings was very different. In medieval buildings the cross-entry, always offset to one side of the building, marks an important structural and social division between hall and services, respectively the 'upper' and 'lower' end of the building (Gardiner 2000, 168–70). In the later Anglo-Saxon period the cross-entry perpetuated the long-established trend for being situated in the middle of the building and, because it was rarely marked by internal structural divisions, may not have drawn sharp functional distinctions within the internal use of space. Irrespective of the precise usage of end chambers in late Anglo-Saxon buildings, their presence can, however, be regarded as an important diagnostic tool for identifying domestic accommodation. Similarly, complexes forming courtyards or contiguous 'long-ranges' also imply a domestic role, at least for the focal building, which may further encapsulate a division between public and private space, as argued for long-ranges of the type defined at Raunds Furnells (Audouy and Chapman 2009, 54–5).

On the basis of the foregoing discussion, Structure D, with its clearly defined northern chamber, has good claim to represent domestic accommodation, offering a close parallel to the similarly juxtaposed hall with attached 'bower' represented in Period 5 of the manorial enclosure at Goltho (Beresford 1987, 74–9). This arrangement is closely comparable to the post-in-trench Structural complex O, which in any one of its 'composite' multi-chambered interpretations, is also a likely contender for a residential building. Whilst lacking evidence for internal partitions, Structures J and K, successive occupants of a prominent site adjacent to the church, might also be interpreted in a similar way. It is impossible to say whether the remainder of the structures with sizeable floor areas (in excess of 30m²) provided domestic accommodation in any one particular phase of the occupation.

There are various functional possibilities for the smaller rectangular buildings represented within the Bishopstone occupation sequence. Late Anglo-Saxon estate memoranda provide a useful reference point for reconstructing the ancillary and service buildings that might be expected at a farm or estate complex of the period: the range includes a kitchen, dairy, bakehouse/brewhouse, pantry, and granary, to which may be added barns and animal sheds (Gardiner 2006).

Service structures

Latrines

The one unequivocal case of a latrine with a timber superstructure (numerous pits with deposits of cess clearly played a similar role) was Structure S, with its distinctive apsidal end enclosing an oval cess pit. This structure joins a small group of later (8th- to 11th-century) Anglo-Saxon timber latrines common to high-status settlements with either royal, episcopal, monastic, or thegnly connotations. With the exception of a late 10th-century example from Goltho (Beresford 1987, 68), these structures were physically detached from the residential building they were designed to serve. The example from Bishopstone is the only one to employ post-in-trench construction (all the others being founded in individual postholes), but otherwise the group displays fairly uniform characteristics: a rectangular roofed superstructure with longest dimensions of between 2–4m with an internal steep-sided cess pit located against the back wall, opposite the entrance. Building 10 from Faccombe Netherton twinned with a contemporary hall (Building 9) dated to the period *c* AD 980–1070 (Fairbrother 1990, 114, fig 4.18), provides arguably the best parallel for the Bishopstone latrine, sharing as it does an apsidal back wall mimicking the contours of an oval latrine pit. The remaining examples subscribe to a rather simpler rectangular plan. Buildings W and X from North Elmham, Norfolk, both dated to the late 9th/10th century, share a four-post design with a sunken cavity, originally spanned by a suspended floor jointed to ground-level sill beams (Wade-Martins 1980, 125–31, figs 113–15). The latrine serving West Halls I and II at Cheddar Palace, dated to the early and late 10th century respectively, was of six-post construction (Rahtz 1979, 156–7, figs 52 and 54), whilst the early 11th-century example associated with the late Anglo-Saxon refoundation of Eynsham Abbey (Oxon) comprised a timber screen and a back wall defined by a row of four postholes (Hardy *et al* 2003, 486, figs 3.16 and 3.17).

More likely than not, Structure S was twinned with a contemporary residential structure. On stratigraphic grounds, the most likely contender is Structure F which was similarly superimposed by Structure C. If this interpretation is accepted, then the latrine was aligned on its attendant hall's long axis but offset slightly from its north-east corner.

A similar functional domain might be tentatively invoked to explain Structure T, the structure with a distinctive U-shaped plan projecting off the southeast corner of the largest of the post-in-trench halls, K. This disposition is shared by the freestanding timber latrine from Faccombe Netherton (Fairbrother 1990, 114, fig 4.18), and the attached example from Goltho (Beresford 1987, 68, fig 68). If this structure did indeed fulfil the function of a latrine, it must have worked on very different principles to the standard version emptying into a sunken pit. If one imagines the pit being replaced by a portable container, then one possible arrangement is a suspended garderobe seat accessed via an internal stair rising from the front entrance of the structure. Similarly designed 'dry toilets' survived in Finland well into the 1950s and 60s in rural locales which remained beyond the reach of municipal sewers (Juuti and Wallenius 2005, 25–31, 49–57).

Cellared structure

Earlier discussion reiterated the view that the cellar should be interpreted as the subterranean component of a timber tower, notwithstanding the fact that some of the structural details of the original published reconstruction have been subsequently revised. Comparative evidence is now brought to bear on this interpretation and on the possible functions which this distinctive design may have served.

There is mounting evidence, both literary and archaeological, to suggest that there was a growing diversity of turriform structures in the late Anglo-Saxon landscape. By the 10th century the addition of towers to stone churches had become established practice, although there is some suggestion that they may have made an appearance on major churches in the preceding century (Fernie 1983, 110, 135; Gem 1995). Existing alongside church towers were turriform structures attached to private fortifications and residences. Evidence for such comes from both physical and textual sources, the latter in the form of the much-discussed *burhgeat* and bell-towers mentioned in an 11th-century text known as the 'Promotion Law' (Williams 1992). The current consensus amongst historians is that the term *burhgeat* should be understood as an 'entrance to a protected enclosure', and thus need not imply a turriform building. Yet a detailed analysis of extant stone towers dating to the late Anglo-Saxon period, most notably Earls Barton, suggests that in certain cases such towers may have been adapted to multi-purpose use, allowing three of the Promotion Law's thegnly attributes – chapel, bell-house, and gateway – to be combined under one roof (Audouy *et al* 1995; Morris 1989, 255). As the showy exteriors of Earls Barton and its counterpart at Barton-upon-Humber testify, towers of this type also provided a powerful architectural statement of lordly wealth and status.

A recent review of the term *burhgeat*, viewed within the wider context of the archaeological significance of 'burh' place-names, observes:

> the gate tower or gatehouse, was an essential and highly important part of an Anglo-Saxon manorial complex, marking its legal threshold and symbolizing the status of its inhabitants. In light of this evidence, we should expect to find many more such structures in the archaeological record at sites of known pre-Conquest manorial status.
>
> (Draper 2008)

The most convincing excavated example of a tower interpretable in terms laid out in the 'Promotion Law' text is the masonry structure (Building S18) of two phases from Portchester Castle which formed part of a possible thegnly complex of late 10th- to 11th-century date established within the circuit of the Roman shore fort (Cunliffe 1976, 49–52, 303). In other cases the evidence is less clear-cut. A further example may be represented by the partially excavated stone foundations associated with a manorial earthwork at Church Norton, Selsey (West Sussex) (Morris 1989, 261, fig 76). Whilst frequently quoted in this context, the stone foundation from Sulgrave (Northants) is no longer considered to represent a tower (Renn 1993, 182, note 28; Audouy *et al* 1995, 89).

Whilst the evidence is admittedly slender, it is almost certain that these masonry towers had counterparts in timber; a building material with which the Anglo-Saxons were of course intimately familiar. Reference has been made to the putative timber tower at Springfield Lyons (Essex), the internal dimensions of which, at 3.5m × 2.5m, are of a similar scale to the Bishopstone structure (Tyler and Major 2005, 127–8, fig 69). Further clues can be found in pictorial, linguistic, and architectural sources. It is not possible to consider the extensive and complex field of visual sources in any detail here, other than to note that Derek Renn, in a persuasive case for the identification of multiple depictions of *burhgeat* in the narrative cycle of the Bayeux Tapestry, has drawn attention to examples with detailing suggestive of timber construction (1993, 178–9). Turning to linguistic evidence, there may be some significance to the fact that one of the words for tower in the Old English lexicon is the compound *stantorr*. From this one might tentatively suggest that a qualifying term was required as a means of distinguishing stone from timber towers, otherwise referred to under the simplex '*torr/tur*' (Biggam 2002, 56–7).

However, arguably the best evidence is enshrined in extant stone towers themselves. As Rodwell (1986) has highlighted, many aspects of the exuberant architectural detailing exhibited by the towers at Barton-upon-Humber and Earls Barton, most particularly the pilaster stripwork, draw directly upon contemporary carpentry techniques. Indeed, his conclusion on the latter structure as much as predicts the existence of our elusive quarry: 'there are many curiosities about the tower at Earls Barton which lead one to believe that the design of its prototype was wholly of timber, where prefabricated framing would be brought on to site ready for erection' (Rodwell 1986, 174, ill 117).

Given a confined floor area of only 8m², domestic accommodation seems like an unlikely function for the above-ground portion of the cellared structure, unless one imagines that this role was provided by the more commodious ground-floor stage proposed in the conjectural reconstruction. On the other hand, it seems far more likely that the residential function was, in the conventional manner, served by one of the flanking rectangular halls. Alternatively, the structural design of the Bishopstone building shares superficial similarities to square post-built structures found at Yarnton (Oxon) and other later Anglo-Saxon settlements interpreted as granaries (Hey 2004; Tipper 2004, 69); certainly on the testimony of *Gerefa* we should expect to find a granary amongst the agricultural buildings of a late Anglo-Saxon estate complex such as this (Gardiner 2006). One would obviously wish to seek backing for this interpretation in the palaeobotanical record, but whilst charred cereal grain was indeed recovered from the burnt layer at the bottom of the cellar, the low yield indicates that its presence was no more than incidental.

Having found these two explanations to be wanting, one is drawn back to the functional domain of towers constructed in thegnly contexts. Indeed, viewing this structure as an architectural embodiment of seigniorial identity brings into focus a possible function for the cellar: a strong-room. This interpretation recalls the use of churches and other securable buildings as treasuries, a practice attested in such early medieval contexts as Irish round towers (Taylor 1974, 167, n 1; O'Keeffe 2004). The theme of security is one that comes across strongly in the impressive range of lock furniture and door fittings represented in the iron hoard buried in the base of the cellar before it was infilled. The imposing proportions of the barrel lock in particular speak of a heavy bolted chest or door, and the hinges, hinge-pivot, and clench-bolts could well have had a similar structural derivation. There is no way of proving a direct link between the contents of the hoard and the cellar which marked its final resting place, but the hypothesis that they were in some way functionally connected in the context of a safe store deserves serious consideration.

Fences/palisades

A number of apparently discrete wall-trenches excavated at Bishopstone (eg Structures Q and R) could represent timber palisades, but the evidence is equivocal and the possibility that they constitute the heavily truncated remnants of buildings cannot be ruled out. A precedent certainly exists for the use of internal palisaded enclosures on later Anglo-Saxon settlements (to define yards, pens, paddocks and the like) and such lend a characteristic appearance to a class of rectilinear manorial settlement exemplified by the Hampshire sites of Chalton, Manor Farm, Brighton Hill, Hatch Warren, and Bishops Waltham (see Reynolds 2003, 125–8). All of these sites and those further afield, such as West Cotton (Northants) (Windell *et al* 1990, 23, fig 13), provide instances of buildings and palisades set on contiguous alignments and this phenomenon is potentially replicated at Bishopstone in the case of Structures Q and R.

Indications of status

What can be inferred about the social status and character of the settlement from the built environment? It is arguably the service structures, over and above the rectangular halls, which impart a distinctive personality to the Bishopstone settlement – one with obvious high-status connotations. As we have seen, Structure S belongs to a select group of later Saxon latrines that were exclusive to royal, episcopal, and manorial residences. We know very little about the typical toilet facilities of the period, but the elaborate apsidal design of the Bishopstone example can scarcely have been a common sight within regular farming communities where communal dung heaps destined for manuring fields may have been the norm. Cellared Structure W, here interpreted as a timber tower with subterranean storage, quite clearly falls outside the standard range of buildings one would expect to find on a late Saxon farmstead. If, as argued, its function was indeed analogous to masonry

turriform structures such as Earls Barton, then it could be regarded, *ipso facto*, as an architectural symbol of lordship.

Aisled buildings U and V may also point in a similar direction, given that most of the parallels for this style of construction in the late Saxon period derive from excavated manorial complexes. Beyond this, the evidence is not so clear-cut for Bishopstone, which lacks a super-sized hall or hall-complex comparable to the 20m+ ranges found at such sites as Cheddar, Goltho, Faccombe Netherton, and Raunds Furnells. Of course, it may be the case that such a structure lies in an unexcavated part of the settlement or, alternatively, it is just possible that the Structural complex O does indeed represent a large east-west range (in excess of 15m in length) echoing a similar building (of 11th- to 12th-century date) excavated at Brighton Hill South (Hants) also occupying an imposing position against the boundary of a contemporary churchyard (Fasham and Keevil 1995, 83–5, fig 44).

Whether such a building existed at Bishopstone or not, it would be simplistic, not to say overly prescriptive, to place too much significance on the size of any one building to determine the status of a settlement (contra Beresford 1987, 29), an argument which has been rehearsed by scholars working on the continental repertoire of early medieval settlements (Hamerow 2002, 89–90). As the evidence from Bishopstone suggests, the social identity of some communities may be evoked more strongly in service structures than in principal dwellings. Site characterisation must therefore proceed from an evaluation of the totality of the built environment and only then in association with other categories of material culture. Indeed, as the dynamic occupation at Flixborough attests, the extent to which these different categories were implicated in expressions of status and social identity could fluctuate over the lifetime of a settlement (Chapter 9.3).

8.2 Scientific dating evidence
by Peter Marshall, Johannes van der Plicht, Gordon T Cook, Pieter M Grootes, Nancy Beavan Athfield, and Mykhailo Buzinny

Introduction

Twenty-four radiocarbon age measurements were obtained from samples of charcoal and both human and animal bone from Bishopstone.

Methods

The two samples (human and animal bone) submitted to the Leibiniz Labor für Altersbestimmung und Isopenforschung, Christian-Albrechts-Universität, Kiel, Germany were processed according to the methods outlined in Grootes *et al* (2004) and measured by AMS according to Nadeau *et al* (1997).

The nine human and animal bones dated at the Centre for Isotope Research, University of Groningen, using Gas Proportional Counting of carbon dioxide were prepared using the method outlined in Longin (1971) and dated as described by Mook and Streurman (1983).

Six animal bones were submitted for dating by Accelerator Mass Spectrometry (AMS) to the Scottish Universities Environmental Research Centre (SUERC), East Kilbride in 2007. The samples were pre-treated using a modified Longin method (Longin 1971) with CO_2 obtained from the pre-treated bone samples by combustion in pre-cleaned sealed quartz tubes (Vandeputte *et al* 1996). Three sub-samples of the purified CO_2 were taken: one 2ml sample was converted to graphite (Slota *et al* 1987), for subsequent AMS analysis; a second sub-sample was collected and sealed in a clean glass vial for subsequent $\delta^{13}C/\delta^{15}N$ analysis, while any remaining sample CO_2 was similarly collected and sealed for possible future analysis. The samples' $^{14}C/^{13}C$ ratios were measured on the SUERC AMS, as described by Xu *et al* (2004).

The three animal bones submitted to the Marzeev Institute of Hygiene and Medical Ecology, Ukraine were converted to benzene and measured by Liquid Scintillation Counting as outlined at http://users.ldc.net/~mbuz/c14.htm.

One charcoal and one human bone sample were dated at Beta Analytic Inc by AMS using methods outlined at http://www.radiocarbon.com/.

The two animal bone samples submitted to Rafter in 2008 were pre-treated and measured by AMS as described by Zondervan and Sparks (1997) and Beavan Athfield *et al* (2001).

All six laboratories maintain continual programmes of quality assurance procedures, in addition to participation in international inter-comparisons (Scott 2003), which indicate no laboratory offsets and demonstrate the validity of the precision quoted.

Results

The radiocarbon results are given in Table 8.3, and are quoted in accordance with the international standard known as the Trondheim convention (Stuiver and Kra 1986). They are conventional radiocarbon ages (Stuiver and Polach 1977).

Calibration

The calibrations of the results, relating the radiocarbon measurements directly to calendar dates, are given in Table 8.3 and in Figures 8.2 and 8.3. All have been calculated using the calibration curve of Reimer *et al* (2004), apart from IHME-1436 that used the calibration curve of Keuppers *et al* (2004) and the computer program OxCal v4.0.5 (Bronk Ramsey 1995; 1998; 2001; 2009). The cali-

brated date ranges cited in the text are those for 95% confidence. They are quoted in the form recommended by Mook (1986), with the end points rounded outwards to ten years if the error term is greater than or equal to 25 radiocarbon years, or to five years if it is less. The ranges quoted in italics are *posterior density estimates* derived from mathematical modelling of archaeological problems (see below). The ranges in plain type in Table 8.3 have been calculated according to the maximum intercept method (Stuiver and Reimer 1986). All other ranges are derived from the probability method (Stuiver and Reimer 1993).

Methodological approach

A Bayesian approach has been adopted for the interpretation of the chronology from this site (Buck *et al* 1996). Although the simple calibrated dates are accurate estimates of the dates of the samples, this is usually not what archaeologists really wish to know. It is the dates of the archaeological events, which are represented by those samples, which are of interest. In the case of Bishopstone, it is the chronology of the settlement and cemetery that is under consideration, not the dates of individual samples. The dates of this activity can be estimated by using not only the absolute dating information from the radiocarbon measurements, but also the stratigraphic relationships between samples.

Fortunately, methodology is now available which allows the combination of these different types of information explicitly, to produce realistic estimates of the dates of interest. It should be emphasised that the posterior density estimates produced by this modelling are not absolute. They are interpretative estimates, which can and will change as further data become available and as other researchers choose to model the existing data from different perspectives.

The technique used is a form of Markov Chain Monte Carlo sampling, and has been applied using the program OxCal v4.0.5 (http://c14.arch.ox.ac.uk/). Details of the algorithms employed by this program are available from the on-line manual or in Bronk Ramsey (1995; 1998; 2001; 2009). The algorithm used in the model described below can be derived from the structures shown in Figure 8.2.

Objectives and sampling strategy

The scientific dating programme was designed to achieve the following objectives, to provide:

- Overall estimates of the start, end, and duration of the activity at Bishopstone
- Precise estimates for the date of the cemetery (start, end, span of use), and its possible spatial development

Table 8.3 Radiocarbon age determinations

Laboratory number	Sample number	Material & context	Radiocarbon age (BP)	δ13C (‰)	δ15N (‰)	C:N ratio	Calibrated date range (95% confidence)	Posterior density estimate (95% probability)
Beta-188373	S87	Human bone	1100±50	−19.7			cal AD 780–1030	cal AD 720–745 (3%) or 765–940 (92%)
GrN-30970	S2573	Human right femur, female, 20-25	1235±20	−19.8	10.7	2.6	cal AD 685–875	cal AD 705–865
GrN-30973	S3122	Human right femur, male, 30-40	1265±20	−19.6	9.7	3.3	cal AD 670–780	cal AD 685–805
GrN-30972	S2720	Human left femur, male, 25-35	1210±20	−19.8	9.7	2.9	cal AD 720–890	cal AD 725–740 (7%) or 765–875 (88%)
GrN-30971	S2686	Human left femur, female, 30-35	1215±20	−20.6	10.9	2.8	cal AD 715–885	cal AD 720–745 (7%) or 765–875 (88%)
GrN-30968	S1171	Human femur & tibia, female adult	1300±25	−19.5	10.4	2.8	cal AD 650–780	cal AD 675–780
GrN-30967	S1105	Human left femur, male 45+	1230±20	−19.7	10.4	2.8	cal AD 690–880	cal AD 710–870
GrN-30969	S2562	Human left femur, female, 35-45	1215±25	−20.3	10.5	2.6	cal AD 690–890	cal AD 715–750 (10%) or 760–875 (85%)
GrN-30966	3055	Cow leg bone	1195±25	−21.4	4.8	3.1	cal AD 720–900	cal AD 770–900
GrN-30965	2255	Cow metapodial	1195±20	−21.5	4.9	2.8	cal AD 770–895	cal AD 775–890
KIA-33897	S280	Human femur fragment	1370±25	−19.7			cal AD 640–680	cal AD 635–690 (85%) or 745–770 (10%)
KIA-33896	1344D	Sheep leg bone	1190±25	−21.8			cal AD 770–940	cal AD 770–900 (94%) or 925–940 (1%)
SUERC-16024	3176	Chicken tibiatartus bone (immature) from articulated disposal	1235±35	−20.0	10.3	3.5	cal AD 670–890	cal AD 680–860
NZA-29964	1344C	Animal bone; cat	1218±35	−17.3	12.1	3.3	cal AD 680–890	cal AD 690–890
NZA-30063	1344D	Animal bone; dog	1123±20	−18.4	10.2	3.4	cal AD 880–990	cal AD 885–975
SUERC-16022	2948	Cat tibia bone from articulated disposal	1235±35	−18.8	10.1	3.5	cal AD 670–890	cal AD 685–885
SUERC-16023	2969	Cat femur bone from articulated disposal	1195±35	−20.5	8.7	3.5	cal AD 710–950	cal AD 710–750 (6%) or 765–900 (85%) or 915–950 (4%)
SUERC-16016	1776	Roe deer radius bone from articulated disposal	1060±35	−24.2	6.7	3.2	cal AD 890–1030	cal AD 890–1010
SUERC-16015	6	Pig humerus (neonate) from articulated disposal	1285±35	−17.9	12.0	3.5	cal AD 650–810	cal AD 655–815
SUERC-16021	2877	Pig leg bone (neonate) from articulated disposal	1260±35	−20.2	7.5	3.5	cal AD 660–880	cal AD 670–870
IHME-1436	141	Sheep, skull fragments	1.13±0.005pmc				AD 1989–1992	–
IHME-1434	376	Sheep, 3 right & left femur + tibia	286±25				cal AD 1510–1670	–
Beta-188374	building 2	wall trench oak	1120±40				cal AD 780–1020	cal AD 780–790 (1%) or 805–990 (94%)
IHME-1435	4015	Cow, metatarsal	50±30				cal AD 1690–1955*	–

- Precise estimates for the dates of key structures and stratigraphic events
- An estimate for the length of time between the abandonment of the cemetery and encroachment of subsequent occupation

The first stage in sample selection was to identify short-lived material, which was demonstrably not residual in the context from which it was recovered. The taphonomic relationship between a sample and its context is the most hazardous link in this process, since the mechanisms by which a sample came to be in its context are a matter of interpretative decision rather than certain knowledge. Material was selected only where there was evidence that a sample had been put fresh into its context. The main

Table 8.4   Radiocarbon result NZA-29964 calibrated using terrestrial and mixed (terrestrial and marine) calibration data

Diet	Calibrated date (95% confidence)
Terrestrial	cal AD 680–890
Marine component 30±5% (Ambrose 1993)	cal AD 810–1020
Marine component 44±5% (Arneborg *et al* 1999)	cal AD 870–1050

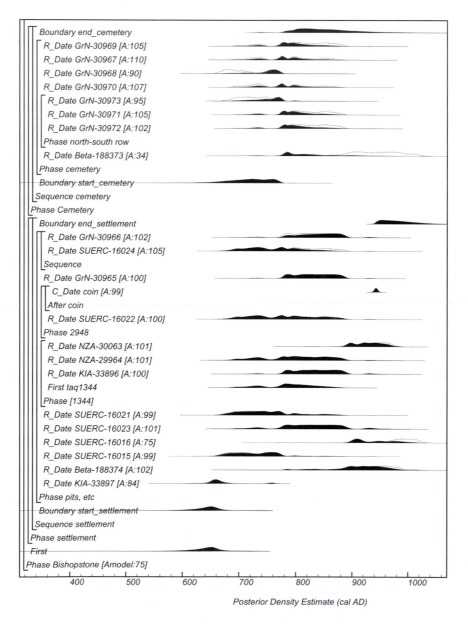

Fig 8.2   Probability distributions of dates from Bishopstone: each distribution represents the relative probability that an event occurs at a particular time. For each of the radiocarbon dates two distributions have been plotted, one in outline, which is the result of simple radiocarbon calibration, and a solid one, which is based on the chronological model used. The large square brackets down the left hand side along with the OxCal keywords define the model exactly

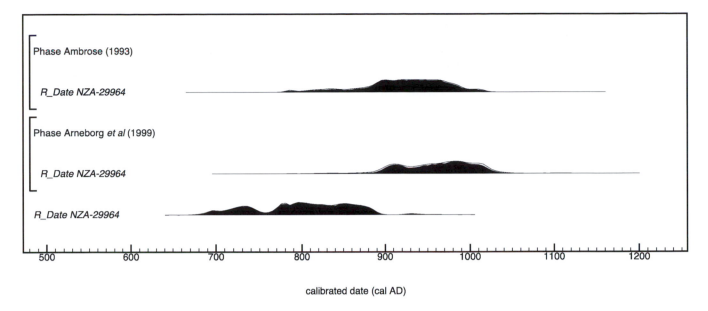

Fig 8.3 Probability distributions of date NZA-29964 (using terrestrial and mixed terrestrial / marine curve calibration data). Each distribution represents the relative probability that an event occurred at a particular time. These distributions are the result of simple radiocarbon calibration (Stuiver and Reimer 1993)

category of materials which met these taphonomic criteria was articulated bone – from inhumations and animal disposals. Articulated bone deposits must have been buried with tendons attached or they would not have remained in articulation, and so were almost certainly less than six months old when buried (Mant 1987, 71).

Once suitable samples had been identified a model was devised, which incorporated the archaeological information along with simulated radiocarbon results. The radiocarbon results were simulated using the R_Simulate function in OxCal, with errors based on the material to be analysed and the type of measurement required (eg single run AMS/high precision). This was used to determine the number of samples that should be submitted in the dating programme.

Stable isotopes

The ratio of carbon isotopes is used to distinguish between a marine protein diet (expected consumer's $\delta^{13}C$ -12‰) and a C3 plant protein diet (mostly vegetables, fruits, and wheat – expected consumer's $\delta^{13}C$ –20‰) (Schwarcz and Schoeninger 1991). Carbon isotope values between –12‰ and –20‰ indicate consumption of a mixture of marine and terrestrial resources.

Nitrogen isotopes are primarily used to determine the input of plant vs animal protein in the diet, although there is some evidence that $\delta^{15}N$ values are also influenced by the nitrogen balance of an organism (Fuller *et al* 2004). In an ecosystem each step up the food train results in consumer tissue, in this case bone collagen being enriched in $\delta^{15}N$ by approx 3–4‰ relative to diet (Schoeninger and

DeNiro 1984). Thus people who eat more animal protein compared to plant protein will display higher $\delta^{15}N$ values (O'Connell and Hedges 1999).

Faunal

The $\delta^{13}C$ values of all faunal bones tested ranged from –24.2‰ to –17.3‰ (Plate 10) with the majority in the range expected for animals in a temperate terrestrial C3 ecosystem, typical of north-west Europe (Katzenberg and Krouse 1989). The herbivore (cow and roe deer) bones yielded $\delta^{15}N$ values of +4.8‰ to +6.7‰.

The $\delta^{13}C$ value of –17.3‰ (NZA-29964; 1344C) indicates that there is a strong marine component in the ultimate source of carbon in the dated cat. Methods of estimating this proportion accurately are not well understood (Chisholm *et al* 1982; Schoeninger *et al* 1983; Bayliss *et al* 2004), but it is likely to be within the range 30–50% marine. For example, using the methodology published by Arneborg *et al* (1999), it can be estimated that 46% of the cat's protein intake was of marine origin, whereas the estimate would decline to only 30% under Ambrose's (1993) system. This proportion is sufficiently large to suggest that it may be necessary to take this into consideration when interpreting the results (Table 8.4).

Most simply this can be done by mixing the atmospheric calibration curve with the marine calibration curve in the proportion suggested by the estimate of marine protein. This is done using the methodology outlined in Bronk Ramsey (1998), calibration data from Hughen *et al* (2004), and a ΔR value of -31±56 for the coastal waters of the English Channel (Reimer and Reimer 2001; http://intcal.qub.ac.uk/

marine/). The results are shown in Figure 8.3 and Table 8.3.

The single sample of chicken (*Gallus gallus*) analysed stands out because it is very enriched in $\delta^{15}N$ relative to the herbivore samples (+10·3‰), clustering with the humans in both carbon and nitrogen isotopic values (Plate 10). This elevated nitrogen isotopic value indicates that the chicken in question benefited from an omnivorous diet, most probably in the form of waste food and scraps which accords with the evidence for on-site husbandry (Poole, Chapter 7.1). Similar isotopic results have been observed for other Anglo-Saxon chicken remains (T O'Connell, pers comm).

Human

The $\delta^{13}C$ of the humans (mean adult $\delta^{13}C$ of −19.9±0.4‰) indicates that they consumed a diet predominantly based upon temperate terrestrial C_3 with a possible small marine component (Schoeninger and DeNiro 1984; Katzenberg and Krouse 1989).

The $\delta^{15}N$ values covered a range of ~1.2‰, from +9.7 to +10.9‰, indicating a reasonably homogenous dietary intake, at least isotopically (Plate 10). All the human $\delta^{15}N$ values were significantly enriched relative to the herbivore $\delta^{15}N$ values, indicating that all consumed a significant amount of animal protein on a regular basis.

The C:N ratio of all the bone samples suggests that bone preservation was sufficiently good for us to have confidence in the accuracy of the radiocarbon determinations (Masters 1987; Tuross *et al* 1988).

The samples and sequence

The following section concentrates on describing the archaeological evidence, which has been incorporated into the chronological models, explaining the reasoning behind the interpretative choices made in producing the models presented. These archaeological decisions fundamentally underpin the choice of statistical model.

Eight inhumations from the cemetery were dated (Fig 5.1), three of these came from one of the north-south rows (S2686, S2720, S3122: GrN-30971–30973), the remaining five were chosen to cover the spatial extent of the excavated part of the cemetery. The remaining inhumation (S280: KIA033897) came from the other side of the church to the main part of the cemetery and seems to represent an earlier episode of burial activity.

The remaining samples, all apart from a single fragment of oak charcoal from wall-trench 93 of Structure D (Beta-188374) were from articulated animal disposals, and came from the fills of rubbish, storage, and latrine pits that were associated with the main occupation area (Table 8.3). The majority of the pits were not stratigraphically related to other features, although samples from two intercutting pits 2821 and 3165 (SUERC-16024 and GrN-30966) were dated, as was a sample from pit 2876 (SUERC-16021) which cut wall-trench 2009 from Structure K. SUERC-16022 came from the same fill as a coin that provides a *terminus post quem* of AD 943.

KIA-33896, NZA-29964 and NZA-30063 all come from the chalk rubble infills of cellared Structure W (context 1344) and provide a *terminus ante quem* for its abandonment.

Results

The model (Fig 8.2) excludes the three measurements obtained from the Marzeev Institute of Hygiene and Medical Ecology, as they all appear to have been contaminated to differing degrees by modern carbon. In addition we have chosen to use the proportion of marine protein estimated using the method described by Ambrose (1993) when calibrating NZA-29964.

The model shown in Figure 8.2 shows good agreement between the radiocarbon results and stratigraphy (A_{model}=75.0%) as presented in the previous section. It provides an estimate for the start of settlement activity of *cal AD 570–755 (95% probability; Boundary_start_settlement;* Fig 8.2) and probably *cal AD 610–670 (68% probability)* and the end of settlement activity of *cal AD 935–1060 (95% probability; Boundary_end_settlement;* Fig 8.2) and probably *cal AD 940–1000 (68% probability)*. The span of settlement activity at Bishopstone is estimated at *195–360 years (95% probability; overall_use;* Fig 8.3) and probably *255–335 years (68% probability)*.

Structure K is estimated to have been constructed in *cal AD 700–860 (95% probability; building;* Fig 8.2) and probably *cal AD 730–820 (68% probability)*. The distribution *first_taq1344* provides a *terminus ante quem* for the destruction of cellared Structure W of *cal AD 690–890 (95% probability; first_taq1344;* Fig 8.2) and probably *cal AD 770–845 (60% probability)*.

The model also provides an estimate for the start of burial in the cemetery of *cal AD 625–780 (95% probability; cemetery_start;* Fig 8.2) and probably *cal AD 690–780 (68% probability)*.

The results show no chronological differentiation between the use of various 'rows' within the main cemetery. The end of use of the cemetery is estimated to be *cal AD 775–990 (95% probability; cemetery_end;* Fig 8.2) and probably *cal AD 790–890 (68% probability)*. The use of the cemetery is estimated to be *1–220 years (95% probability cemetery_use;* Fig 8.4) and probably *30–155 years (68% probability)*.

8.3   Site phasing

Radiocarbon dating has provided some crucial markers for fixing the chronological limits of occu-

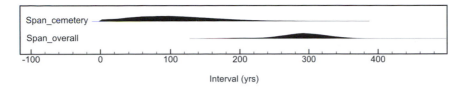

Fig 8.4 Probability distributions showing the number of calendar years during which the main phase of burial activity and overall activity occurred at Bishopstone. The distributions are derived from the model shown in Figure 8.2

pation and burial within pre-Conquest Bishopstone, but the problems involved in attempting to phase the settlement remain considerable. Of course, such difficulties are common to all eroded sites where vertical relationships are few and far between – a characterisation which applies to the overwhelming majority of Anglo-Saxon settlements, as indeed to their counterparts on the early medieval continent (see Hamerow 2002, 80–2; Holst 1997, 97).

Several factors served to exacerbate the problem at Bishopstone. Firstly, many of the smaller features, especially the postholes, were effectively undated and thus could theoretically belong to any period. On the other hand, with the exception of a late Bronze Age burial (Appendix 7), evidence for significant activity or occupation pre- or post-dating the Anglo-Saxon period was absent; on this basis, it is probably safe to conclude that the majority of the undated features belong to the main phase of Anglo-Saxon occupation. Secondly, the level of ground truncation was such that it was often impossible to discern soil distinctions within feature intersections and thus establish a clear sequence of superimposition. Thirdly, the few relationships that could be resolved with certainty were no more than disconnected islands of stratigraphy associated with certain buildings or discrete clusters of pits (for example Structures F, D, and S); it should be noted that Bishopstone lacks the multiplicity of ditched enclosures characterising such settlements as Catholme and Yarnton which can help to tie floating sequences into site-wide stratigraphic frameworks (Losco-Bradley and Kinsley 2002; Hey 2004, 18–21).

Horizontal stratigraphy was useful but only up to a point. As can be seen from Figure 4.1 the orientation of the structures is remarkably uniform. All share alignments which conform to one of two perpendicular site axes, east-west or north-south, the deviation in alignment amongst the buildings being easily accommodated within one or at most two degrees. This level of uniformity suggests that the excavated part of the settlement comprised a planned complex of buildings subject to a high degree of locational stability – ie the timber structures were rebuilt on the same or adjacent footprints, a trend which distinguishes later Anglo-Saxon settlements from their 5th- to 6th-century forebears (Hamerow 2002, 80–2; Loveluck 2007, 70–1; see below).

Such standardised orientations complicate the task of establishing precisely what combination of buildings stood at any one time. It is possible to dismiss certain combinations of adjacent buildings on the basis of coincident wall alignments or else restricted or blocked entrances. The case for Structures E and F being of different phases is clear, but one might equally suggest that Structures K and I were unlikely to be contemporary on the grounds that the end wall of the latter intrudes on the former's northern doorway. This approach has its limitations, however, for it cannot be scaled-up to include a wider array of buildings.

Another spatial dimension that might be expected to provide valuable insights into site phasing is the relationship of structures to surrounding pits since the dating of the latter can be established in more robust terms on the basis of artefacts and radiocarbon assays. This approach relies on the assumption that pits were dug in yards immediately adjacent to buildings. Yet the very uneven distribution of the former, displaying a zoned concentration in the east and north-east sectors of the excavation (Fig 4.39), indicates that this was clearly not a generalised tendency; indeed, precisely the opposite is implied by the notably paucity of pits within the putative domestic compound occupying the western half of the excavation (Chapter 9.1). Too few pits were dated scientifically to allow spatio-temporal shifts within the settlement to be recognised through their distribution. A northwards drift has tentatively been proposed on a possible association between the pit which produced the latest of the radiocarbon date-ranges (pit x = cal AD 890–1030, 95% confidence) and the two adjacent aisled buildings occupying the northern extremity of the excavation, which on constructional grounds have been argued to represent a late phase in the structural sequence (See Section 8.2 above).

Finally, the chronological margins accompanying artefact – chiefly ceramic – typologies and radiocarbon dating are too broad to offer an independent tool for phasing settlement features (Jervis, Chapter 6.1; Marshall *et al*, Chapter 8.2 above). On a more positive note the relationship between the settlement and the adjoining cemetery was marked by considerable stratigraphic clarity: a consistent pattern of six graves intercut by domestic occupation, whether pits or wall-trenches. With the aid of high-precision radiometric dating of human bone, this sequence can be placed on a robust chronological footing with interesting implications for assessing the interplay between spaces of the living and the dead in the spatial development of the pre-Conquest settlement (Chapter 9.2). With regards to the settlement itself, it must be accepted that the evidence available is insufficient to provide a nuanced diachronic picture of its evolution over 200 to 300 years of occupation. Yet how realistic is such a proposition when the average life of an earth-fast timber building of the early medieval period ranged between 25 and 50 years (Loveluck 2007, 50), and when the evidence from Bishopstone (successive rebuilding or replacement of buildings on fixed plots) indicates that the settlement's development was characterised by continuous organic change, as opposed to dramatic transitions in spatial planning? An appreciation of the character and limitations of the archaeology provides a justification for attempting a conjectural snapshot, as will now be attempted in Section 8.4 below.

8.4   Settlement layout and spatial development

Whilst the dynamic model of settlement development generated for a well-stratified site like Flixborough may lie beyond the bounds of the evidence, recent scholarship, fuelled by an expansion in the number of excavations, is transforming our understanding of the morphology of later Anglo-Saxon settlements and this new knowledge can be exploited to illuminate the situation locally at Bishopstone. Through these wider comparisons it is possible to make an estimation of Bishopstone's probable layout and to isolate key elements of the site plan which were likely to have had a long-term influence over the structure of the settlement.

One aspect of the site layout which will by now be familiar is its perpendicularity resulting from the slavish adherence of the buildings to either an east-west or a north-south alignment (Fig 4.1). It can be safely assumed that in any one phase the settlement would have comprised a combination of buildings set out on each of these orientations. This tendency is so common that it can be rightfully regarded as a universal characteristic of Anglo-Saxon settlements (for a selection of sites with perpendicular arrangements of buildings see Reynolds 2003, 125–8). But setting Bishopstone apart from many of these comparanda is the tightly integrated disposition of buildings, remembering that an area measuring less than 45m by 30m produced a sequence of twenty or more structures. This characteristically compact site plan must in part relate to stability in occupation, to a greater or lesser degree imposed by topographical restrictions. But the potential also exists for a relatively intense level of occupation during certain phases, a suggestion which receives further support from the centrality of pit digging to the treatment of

refuse generated within the settlement (Chapter 9.1).

A complex of buildings arranged around a central courtyard makes most sense of the crowded nest of structures represented on the site plan and a likely scenario for the layout of the settlement in its most developed form (Fig 4.1). Occupying the western half of the excavation, this courtyard was enclosed on three sides by rectangular Structures C, W, D, and O, with the putative timber tower (Structure W) at its north-east corner, leaving a gap to the west (Figs 4.1 and 8.5). The extensive evidence for the repair and refurbishment of individual buildings indicates that this suite of buildings formed a relatively stable nucleus within the biography of the settlement; total reconstruction may be responsible for minor locational shifts and the overlapping sequence of footprints seen in the composite plan. The view that this sector of the excavation represents a formal residential compound receives further support from the fact that the internal 'courtyard' and other spaces surrounding the buildings within this supposed range were relatively free of pits. Indeed, the zoned concentration of pits within the eastern portion of the excavation suggests that there was reasonably tight control over segregating the residential/public functions of the complex from more prosaic activities such as waste disposal (see Chapter 9.1; Fig 4.39).

Courtyard ranges analogous to that proposed for Bishopstone represent a common theme on manorial complexes of the 10th to the 12th centuries, the best parallels coming from sites with similarly tightly integrated plans such as Portchester, Goltho, and West Cotton, although more loosely arranged configurations can also be cited including Springfield Lyons and Raunds Furnells (Gardiner 2007, 172; Fig 8.5). Whilst recalling the formally planned, perhaps ritually organised, modules found on an earlier generation of Anglo-Saxon settlements, exemplified by Chalton, Foxley, and Cowdery's Down (Reynolds 2003, 104–10, fig 2), these late Anglo-Saxon cases are clearly proto-typical of the courtyard arrangements epitomising seigneurial domestic planning of the medieval period (Williams 1992; Blair 1993; Grenville 1997, 78–88; Gardiner 2007). An almost identical match for the layout proposed here is replicated in the late Anglo-Saxon (late 10th- to early 11th-century) phase of Portchester Castle (Fig 8.5 A), where a stone tower (Building S18) is similarly located at the angle between two timber halls (Buildings S13 and S16), with a further hall (Building S14) forming the third side of a courtyard range (Cunliffe 1976, fig 99).

Of course, what is currently unknowable is how this focal suite of structures related to the bigger picture, in light of the fact that the excavation failed to recover any limits to the settlement. Indeed, later Anglo-Saxon occupation, again found to encroach upon an earlier phase of burials, was traced in a test pit excavated beyond the western side of the graveyard boundary (see Chapter 10.1). It is a matter

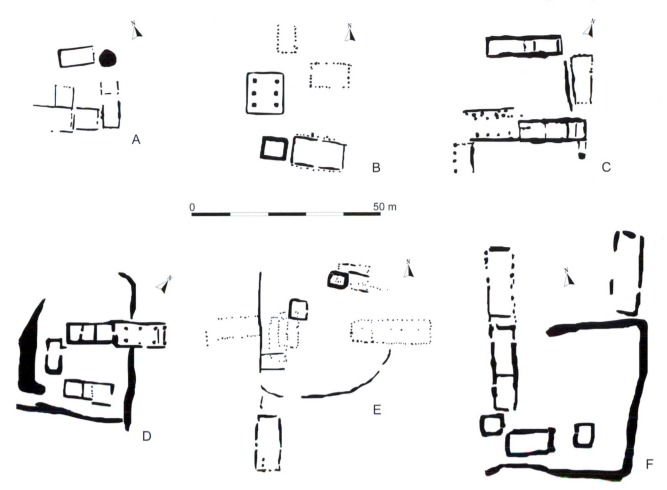

Fig 8.5 Courtyard ranges on later Anglo-Saxon settlements: A) Bishopstone; B) Portchester (after Cunliffe 1976, figs 99 and 100 combined); C) Goltho, Period 4 (after Beresford 1987, fig 59); D) West Cotton (after Windell, Chapman, and Woodiwiss 1990, fig 13); E) Springfield Lyons (after Tyler and Major 2005, fig 68); F) Raunds Furnells (after Audouy and Chapman 2009, fig 5.17)

of speculation whether these latter traces were in any sense peripheral to the settlement remains discovered on the village green or instead formed part of the same complex.

As we have seen, several of the sites offering direct analogies for the courtyard arrangement argued for Bishopstone have been conceptualised in manorial or 'thegnly' terms, or at least this is the identity ascribed to them on the interpretation of associated historical sources. Yet given Bishopstone's attested episcopal links post- AD 800, should we envisage a rather different inspiration?

Relevant to this question is Blair's (1993, 10–12) analysis of the possible ancestry of a group of post-Conquest bishop's residences displaying tightly integrated courtyard plans with corner tower lodgings. In seeking a pre-Conquest pedigree for such planning, Blair draws attention to a close correspondence between the plan of Minster Court, Kent, dated to around *c* AD 1100, and the by now familiar layout of late Anglo-Saxon Portchester, itself a close analogy for the proposed morphology of Bishopstone. Whilst the resemblance between

Minster Court and Portchester is indeed striking, Blair arguably stretches the evidence to breaking point in order to situate the ancestry of the courtyard plan within an explicitly ecclesiastical milieu. In providing the focus for a small cemetery, Portchester's turriform structure (S18) does indeed carry Christian connotations, but it is surely safer to view this activity in proprietorial terms (an estate chapel) rather than envisaging an undocumented religious community, perhaps, as Blair speculates, representative of 'a lost group of eleventh-century establishments on the borderline between secular and monastic, perhaps including the dwellings of unreformed minster clergy and cathedral canons' (1993, 11). A somewhat false religious/secular dichotomy is also established by emphasising the predilection for axial planning displayed by Anglo-Saxon royal palaces such as Cheddar and Yeavering. Yet, as we have seen, the courtyard plan does appear lower down the secular aristocratic spectrum as attested by the complexes excavated at Goltho, Springfield Lyons, and West Cotton (the latter also with evidence for a timber

Fig 8.6   Conjectural reconstruction of Bishopstone courtyard range

tower), evidently built on the estates of minor thegns (Beresford 1987, 123–6; Tyler and Major 2005, 200–02; Windell *et al* 1990, 23–6) (Fig 8.5). On the evidence now at our disposal, then, it is more likely to be the case that the expressions of the courtyard plan examined by Blair represent lineal descendents of a standard form of late Anglo-Saxon seigneurial planning adapted to suit the needs of a post-Conquest ecclesiastical environment.

Overall, the conclusion to be drawn is that whilst there may be compelling *historical* arguments for characterising post-AD 800 Bishopstone as a quasi-monastic community under episcopal sponsorship or even a pre-Conquest bishop's residence in its own right (Chapter 3), this identification cannot

be sustained on the basis of the excavated layout alone. It is difficult to avoid the implications of this argument for a characterisation of Bishopstone, even after an episcopal connection comes into clear historical focus. Notwithstanding this possibility of idealised conceptions governing the layout of a bishop's residence at this early date (and this seems unlikely), the specifications for the construction of the Bishopstone complex may very well have been laid down by a local reeve responsible for the day-to-day administration of the estate. On this quite reasonable assumption, it is perfectly consistent to find overt expressions of thegnly status (as perhaps embodied in the timber tower) in the built environment of a *'biscopes-tūn'*.

9 Bishopstone in context: wider archaeological perspectives

The following chapter attempts to draw together some of the interpretative strands emerging from previous sections in order to evaluate the nature of the occupation excavated at Bishopstone within its local, regional, and national context.

9.1 Waste disposal and settlement character: the significance of pits

It has long been acknowledged that the disposal and storage of perishables, rubbish and/or human excreta has a fundamental influence on site formation processes and the archaeological character of settlements, but more recently archaeologists have also begun to examine how such practices may have been structured by social context and underlying cultural attitudes, some markedly different from our own (eg Hill 1995; Needham and Spence 1997; Brück 1999b; Bradley 2005). Most of this work has been led by prehistorians, but its implications are no less relevant for the interpretation of post-Roman settlements, which remain largely undervalued as an arena for examining the relationship between cultural and cosmological realms and the cycles of daily existence routinely played out in and around domestic spaces. However sceptical one is of these approaches, they should at the very least encourage a more critical enquiry of waste disposal regimes as a source for understanding and appreciating the diversity of lifestyles represented amongst the spectrum of Anglo-Saxon settlements. What follows is no more than a highly preliminary attempt to adopt this type of enquiry for Bishopstone, a settlement whose archaeological personality is, as we shall see, to a considerable extent shaped by a high incidence of pits.

The first point to make in this preliminary analysis is that pit digging for the purposes of controlling waste is not represented uniformly across the corpus of excavated Anglo-Saxon settlements. With the notable exception of the recently excavated settlement of Bloodmoor Hill, Carlton Colville (Suffolk) where the majority of the 200 plus pits appear to have been dug for sand extraction (Lucy *et al* 2009), the practice is poorly attested on sites of the 5th and 6th centuries; it is only from the 7th century that pits began to appear with greater regularity on Anglo-Saxon settlements (Reynolds 2003, 130; 2004, 115). This temporal trend finds clear expression in the settlement sequence at Mucking, Essex, where pits are heavily weighted towards the terminal, later 6th- to 7th-century phases of occupation, but it is also manifested locally in the shifting settlement biography of Bishopstone for only five

such features, four of which were dug as hearths, were represented on the early Anglo-Saxon focus excavated on Rookery Hill (Hamerow 1993, 20; Bell 1977, 226). Between the 8th and 11th centuries, the practice of pit digging expanded to cover a fully differentiated settlement pattern encompassing both rural and proto-urban/urban foci. The high density of pits characterising wics and late Saxon towns is one of the attributes serving to differentiate sharply the archaeological profile of these large and densely occupied centres from contemporary rural settlements (see below).

In a rural context, the increasing incidence of pits during the 8th and 9th centuries can be viewed as a direct expression of a move towards a more stable settlement pattern, also reflected in the increasing use of boundaries to define the parameters of social space and in new technology designed to prolong the life of domestic buildings (Hamerow 2002, 93–9; Reynolds 2003; Gardiner 2003). Properties in fixed locations occupied over successive generations (in contrast to the fluid, short-lived property units of the early Anglo-Saxon era) would have required a more organised, and perhaps in some cases, formally regulated, approach to the daily task of sanitising areas of habitation. Whilst certainly genuine, this temporal pattern belies significant variations in the incidence of pit digging between later Anglo-Saxon settlements; it is precisely this variability which remains to be explored in terms of understanding distinctions in site character.

The first observation prompted by this variability is that some contemporary settlements are evidently completely devoid of pits. One such example is Flixborough, where refuse and presumably cess was discarded in communal middens dumped into a natural hollow occupying the central portion of the excavated area. Similar evidence has been found at other settlements where either natural topography or man-made features (including disused boundary ditches) provided a convenient locale for the dumping of communal middens – Carlton Colville (Suffolk), Whitby (North Yorks), and Sedgeford (Norfolk) (Loveluck 2007, 71–2; 157–59; Dickens *et al* 2006, 73).

Yet it would be wrong to conclude that middening on the one hand and pit digging on the other represent mutually exclusive forms of waste disposal. Studies drawn from several different chronological periods converge to show that the life history of cultural material discovered in pits frequently passes through an intermediary midden stage separating the point of production from final deposition (Hill 1995, 43–4; Buteux and Jackson 2000; Garrow *et al* 2005). A relevant example is

Table 9.1   Pit densities compared across a selection of later Anglo-Saxon settlements

Site	Reference	Area excavated (m²)	Total no. of pits	Pit density per 100m²
Bishopstone, E Sussex		**1700**	**78**	**4.58**
Hamwic, Six Dials	Andrews 1997	5000	500	10
Lundenwic, Exeter Street	Brown & Rackham 2004	233	13	5.58
Thetford, Norfolk, Captain Knocker excavations	Rogerson & Dallas 1984	4315	210	4.87
Thetford, Norfolk, Brandon Rd	Dallas 1993	12140	350	2.88
York, Fishergate	Kemp 1996	2500	67	2.68
Botolphs, W Sussex	Gardiner 1990	800	14	1.75
Portchester Castle, Hants	Cunliffe 1976	3772	57	1.51
Steyning, Market Field, W Sussex	Gardiner 1993	2500	28	1.12
North Elmham, Norfolk	Wade-Martins 1980	12125	87	0.72
West Stow, Suffolk	West 1985	14425	79	0.55
Maxey, Northants	Addyman 1964	11812	55	0.47
Springfield Lyons, Essex	Tyler & Major 2005	9375	33	0.35
Mucking, Essex	Hamerow 1993	18000	52	0.29
Lake End, Dorney	Foreman, Hiller & Petts 2002	55000	123	0.22
Catholme, Staffs*	Losco-Bradley & Kinsley 2002	34000	43	0.13
Yarnton, Oxon	Hey 2004	25000	32	0.13
Bloodmoor Hill, Carlton Colville, Suffolk*	Lucy, Tipper, & Dickens 2009	30000	200	0.6

* These have largely been interpreted as quarry pits on the basis of morphological and depositionary characteristics and thus are not directly comparable to examples from other sites more closely associated with waste management

the mid Saxon occupation excavated at Lake End, Dorney (Bucks), comprising, most unusually, an extensive scatter of pits seemingly devoid of accompanying timber structures which has prompted its characterisation as a seasonally occupied market/meeting-place (Foreman *et al* 2002). Artefact taphonomy, combined with soil micromorphology, showed that the life history of the pits analysed from Dorney modulated between gradual accumulations of primary rubbish and rapid dumps of redeposited midden material (*ibid*, 62–5). Indeed, precisely the same practice is attested at Bishopstone in the case of pit 2039 with its basal layer of dumped destruction debris sealed by alternating horizons of redeposited domestic refuse and cess (see Ballantyne, Chapter 7.3). We should therefore expect sites with pits to have had middens; as superficial deposits, their absence on most Anglo-Saxon settlements undoubtedly relates to post-depositional erosion (Loveluck 2007, 71).

As one moves away from this extreme into a broader class of settlement where pits are represented, then one is immediately confronted with the problem of making statistically reliable comparisons. The fact that very few settlements have been excavated *in toto*, combined with the tendency for pits to cluster in distinct zones, as is clearly apparent at Bishopstone (Chapter 4.2), introduces bias into the equation. Meanwhile, the task of

establishing the total population may be complicated by superficially similar features serving quite different functions (eg structural post-pits), or by undated pits associated with superimposed phases of medieval occupation. Moreover, in an ideal world one would prefer to compare the combined volume of the pits rather than their spatial density. Nevertheless, simple analysis of this kind can at the very least give a crude impression of the range of pit densities found on Anglo-Saxon settlements and, by extension, throw into sharp relief those sites enjoying unusually high totals.

Table 9.1 shows the density of pits (per 100m²) for a selection of Anglo-Saxon settlements. Unsurprisingly, the highest densities are found at mid Saxon wics and later urban centres with Six Dials, Hamwic returning the highest figure of 10, down through Exeter Street, Lundenwic with 5.88 and sites in Thetford ranging from 4.87 to 2.88. In stark contrast, with the exception of Bishopstone, all the rural settlements have totals under 2, with only two sites, Botolphs and Portchester Castle, breaching 1.5. This comparison serves to show that at 4.58, Bishopstone's pit density stands much closer to contemporary urban centres than it does to other rural settlements. Of course this figure may be artificially inflated as a result of the compact size of the excavation and its fortuitous placement over what may very well represent a zoned area of pitting: it must be acknowledged that pit density on all sites is likely to be a function of the area excavated and the part of the site sampled. On the other hand, there is a strong likelihood that this figure would increase appreciably at the Bishopstone site if the opportunity ever arose to excavate to the east of the village green where the concentration of pits was at its highest.

In spite of the many caveats involved with this analysis, it may be tentatively suggested that Bishopstone does indeed have a genuinely high count of pits (particularly latrine pits) for a rural settlement of its period. Indeed, if one's judgement was restricted to pit density alone, one would have little difficulty in classifying Bishopstone's occupation as urban in character. This observation begins to take on additional emphasis when an assessment of the bioarchaeological signatures of the pits is taken into account. For the impression gained from features which appear to have served as formal, incrementally filled cess pits, is that the character of occupation represented at Bishopstone is more redolent of 'proto-urban' than of 'rural' lifestyles (see Ballantyne, Chapter 7.3).

At this point in the discussion, it is of significance to note that Bishopstone combines a more general array of open cess pits of the type discussed above – with one and possibly two latrine structures (S and T) (see Chapter 8.1). The relationship between the two is far from clear, but their very existence at least implies two contrasting pathways for the disposal of faecal waste. If, as has been argued (Chapter 8.1), the latrines were indeed attached to halls serving domestic accommodation, it could be the case that their use was subject to a greater level of exclusivity than open cess pits clustered beyond the residential core of the settlement, the latter perhaps being used communally by servile members of the domestic household. These hypothesised social distinctions, and their implications for daily use of the two classes of toilet, are not immediately obvious from the stratigraphy and bioarchaeology of the relevant pit sequences, but it is worth entertaining the possibility that the enclosed latrines were used less intensively than their open-air counterparts and were conceivably emptied out as and when required.

A final dimension worth considering in light of the parallels exhibited by Bishopstone to contemporary townscapes is the east-west pit alignment found at the eastern extremity of the occupation (Figs 4.43 and 4.44). It could be ventured that other potential alignments exist on the site, for example the north-south row comprising five pits 2101 through to 2931, joined by yet another on the same axis comprising four pits 2506 through to 2830 (Fig 4.39). Yet, whereas the latter could just be fortuitous alignments within larger pit clusters, the regular spacing and distinct morphology of pits 2618, 3016, and 3086 indicates that they were intentionally dug against a boundary or perhaps served as a form of boundary definition in their own right. It is unfor-tunate that only an uncertain length of the totality of this pit alignment was uncovered in the excavation, for it is difficult to reconstruct how it relates to the wider spatial organisation of the settlement. All that can be said for certain is that by adhering to the main site axis, the boundary in question must have been an integral part of a structured layout otherwise expressed very clearly in the standard-ised orientation of the buildings. It is impossible to say whether the boundary was used to define the spatial parameters of a property unit or instead the limits of a functional zone; the latter scenario might be preferred if buildings and their associated yards are conceptualised as composite parts of an inte-grated settlement module, as, for example, in the case of a (proto-) manorial complex.

The marking and maintenance of property bound-aries with alignments of pits and wells is a familiar theme in mid Saxon wics and late Anglo-Saxon towns (Whytehead *et al* 1989, 45, 58; Morton 1992, 47, fig 26; Dallas 1993, 4145; Kemp 1996, 23–5, 67–9; Andrews 1997, 179, fig 80, pl 25; Brown and Rackham 2004). The phenomenon is much rarer in a rural context, as appears to be confirmed by its restriction to only two published case-studies. The first derives from the mid-8th- to 9th-century occupation phase (possibly minster-related), excavated at Eynsham Abbey (Oxon). This comprised nineteen intercutting pits, forming a 10m alignment mimicking one of the main axes of the settlement, which was redefined as a fence line in a subsequent phase (Hardy *et al* 2003, 46–9, fig 3.9, 473). The second example, discov-ered during excavations in the core of the village of Baston (Lincs), again takes the form of an intercut-ting alignment, on this occasion forming part of the structured layout of Saxo-Norman tenement bound-aries (Taylor 2003). Whilst future excavation may well expand the number of rural settlements with pit boundaries, the spaced arrangement of discrete pits found at Bishopstone is only paralleled amongst mid Saxon wics and late Anglo-Saxon towns, an affinity which again draws us back to the seemingly 'proto-urban' character of the occupation.

Some qualification is needed to justify com-parisons between Bishopstone and proto-urban or urban settlements of the 8th to the 11th centuries. The suggestion is certainly not that Bishopstone's population was in any sense 'proto-urban' in size, but rather that a relatively intense level of occupa-tion combined with stability in locale has served to create an archaeological footprint not unlike that recovered from excavated portions of mid Saxon wics and late Saxon towns. Of course it is one thing to make generalised comparisons of this kind and quite another to explain why Bishopstone should stand out in a rural context. In short, why is it that some rural communities of the later Anglo-Saxon period evidently relied more heavily on pit digging as a waste management strategy than others? As discussed previously, it is not simply a matter of the presence/absence of a locale where midden material could be dumped close at hand. Sited on a chalk eminence surrounded by floodplain, such opportunities clearly existed for the Anglo-Saxon community resident at Bishopstone.

A potentially relevant perspective on this problem can be gained by considering the economic value placed upon domestic waste/effluent as a fertiliser for improving arable fields (see Jones 2004). On settlements or parts of settlements where waste management was driven by agricultural needs, one might expect an emphasis on surface middens, which could be actively managed (subject to seasonal requirements) on a day-by-day basis ready for carting out into surrounding fields (Tipper 2004, 158; Lucy *et al* 2009, 432). Such a scenario might explain the low densities of domestic refuse recovered from later Anglo-Saxon agricultural settlements such as Yarnton and Pennyland (Hey 2004, 69–74). Contrastingly, in situations where standards of sanitation may have taken precedence over agricultural necessity, domestic waste may have been regarded less as a resource and more as a contaminant to be concealed from view. One piece of evidence which may point towards the influence of such a distinction at Bishopstone is the fact that the excavated focus was evidently a net consumer of processed cereal grain, implying that the centre of arable operations must have lain elsewhere (see Ballantyne, Chapter 7.3).

One corollary to this speculative hypothesis is that distinctions in status either within or between settlements may have had a role to play in structuring the diversity seen in contemporary waste disposal regimes. It has been suggested that high standards of sanitation may explain the notable paucity of lost or discarded artefacts recovered from the residential compounds of excavated high-status complexes such as Yeavering, Cowdery's Down, and Bloodmoor Hill, Carlton Colville (Millett 1983; Hinton 2005, 71–3; Lucy *et al* 2009, 382, 427; see also Loveluck 2007, 71). From such evidence it is not impossible that the desire to keep such spaces clean stemmed from an idealised perception of the standards to which elite residences should be maintained and presented, bearing in mind that such complexes embodied both public and private spheres. As a waste management regime, the comparatively labour-intensive strategy of digging pits, often within prescribed zones (all too apparent at Bishopstone with its relatively pit-free residential compound), does suggest a level of formality and systematisation that one might expect to find embodied in the culture of elite settlements. On the other hand, this does not explain why pits (beyond garderobe pits attached to individual buildings) are conspicuously absent from the residential areas of high-status/manorial complexes excavated at Raunds Furnells, Goltho, and Faccombe Netherton (Audouy and Chapman 2009; Beresford 1987; Fairbrother 1990).

In the final analysis it is clearly the case that distinctions in the way that waste was managed on later Anglo-Saxon settlements relates to a complex interaction of factors, some no doubt unrecognisable in the archaeological record. Yet on a more positive note, further research could help to lift some of the constraints on interpretation highlighted in the present study. Micromorphology, still rarely used on settlements of historic periods, has the potential to bring tighter definition to the depositionary life history of pits from which factors such as longevity and seasonality of pit usage could be addressed. On a broader scale, if excavated evidence is to be better contextualised, there is a need for comparing the treatment of waste within the domestic sphere of settlements with the 'fields' that surrounded them, by integrating data from field-walking (see Jones 2004).

9.2   Evaluating Bishopstone's pre-Conquest cemetery: spaces of the living and the dead on later Anglo-Saxon settlements

Recent scholarship on the origins of churchyard burial in late Anglo-Saxon England has highlighted an underlying fluidity to the geography of contemporary burial practices, providing a mirror to shifting spatial biographies of contemporary rural settlements. Between the 8th and 10th centuries, before formal consecration was established as the norm, churchyards competed with a range of other burial foci. These included open 'field cemeteries' and, within the confines of settlements themselves, small, short-lived burial plots, some perhaps relating to family units, others socially excluded members of the community including executed felons (Lucy and Reynolds 2002, 12–22; Hadley 2002; 2007; Blair 2005, 241–5, 463–71). In certain settlements, especially those with a monastic focus, as for example Ripon (North Yorks), and Hartlepool (Teesside), multiple cemeteries and satellites might co-exist, some serving distinct sectors of the clerical and/or lay population (Hadley 2002, 213–14). The picture emerging is that of a richly textured mortuary landscape shaped by new attitudes towards expressing social status through burial location, whether in respect of the micro-geography of a single churchyard or within the wider setting of settlements and their surrounding territories (Hadley 2004, 309).

A growing body of archaeological evidence reveals that the spatial framework of churchyards was also subject to dynamic change over the late Anglo-Saxon period. One of the clearest indications of such mutability, other than cases of total abandonment epitomised by the sequence excavated at Raunds Furnells (Boddington 1996), is the growing number of churchyards attesting to a pre-Conquest phase of cemetery shrinkage. The retraction is nearly always followed, usually after a period of disuse, by domestic encroachment of one form or other – the construction of manorial compounds or castles, proto-urban development, or more low-level agricultural activity (Hadley 2007, 195–7). As Bishopstone arguably constitutes one of the best-dated examples of this phenomenon, the opportunity is taken in the following section to make a comparative evaluation of the contraction-encroachment sequences now known and to examine the possible underlying causes.

From the dating evidence available, it would appear that the majority of churchyards attesting to this phenomenon contracted at some point between the later 10th and 12th centuries. Thus at Crayke (North Yorks), North Elmham (Norfolk), and Pontefract (West Yorks), outer burial zones that had been active between the later 9th and 11th centuries were encroached upon, following a period of abandonment, by buildings and other domestic activity in the 12th century (see Hadley 2002, 216–18; Hadley 2007, 195–7; Blair 1994, 66, 72; Blair 2005, 467 for refs). The sequence at Addingham (West Yorks), Aylesbury (Bucks), and Shipton-under-Wychwood (Oxon) is more extended, with a longer period of disuse separating burials dated to between the 8th and 10th centuries and the subsequent encroachment of either the 12th or 13th century. The situation at Wing (Bucks) is somewhat different, for here burial, albeit on an intensity much reduced from pre-Conquest levels, continued as late as the 12th century, by which time domestic activity had infiltrated the churchyard enclosure. Unlike the other examples there was thus no clear break between the cessation of burial and the onset of encroachment (Holmes and Chapman 2008). In spite of some variations, the evidence from these sites points towards a consistent pattern of cemetery shrinkage in the period AD 900–1100; whilst burial may have continued on a reduced level within these peripheral zones, in most cases domestic encroachment was preceded by a period of abandonment and disuse.

Evidence for churchyard contractions predating the 10th century is much harder to come by, although one suspects that this may have something to do with the small sample of sites which have been radiocarbon dated. Two relevant cases include the 7th- to 9th-century burials excavated in the Vicarage Gardens at Brixworth (located some 80m west of All Saints' church and sealed beneath the footprint of a building erected during the 12th century), and burials at Abbey Land's Farm, Whitby (located some 200m south of the medieval abbey church and, in this case, sealed by 13th-century ridge-and-furrow) (Everson 1977, 55–7, 67–73; Hadley 2002, 213). There is a strong suspicion that pre-Conquest burials excavated at Dacre (Cumbria) and Minster, Sheppey (Kent) might produce similarly early date-ranges in the light of supporting stratigraphic evidence and the historic pedigree that these sites share as pre-Viking monastic communities (Youngs *et al* 1986, 127–8; Philp and Chenery 1998).

On the basis of scientific dating, Bishopstone would appear to belong to the latter group of pre-10th-century cemetery contractions. As we have seen, the balance of probability indicates that active interment within the northern and western peripheries of the pre-Conquest cemetery had ceased by AD 900. Of further chronological relevance is the fact that a domestic rubbish pit (6) excavated within the shrunken portion of the cemetery returned one of the earliest radiocarbon date-ranges recovered from the settlement, cal AD 650–810 at 95% confidence (SUERC-16015). Two alternatives can be put forward to explain this anomaly. Either, as seen at a later period at Wing, the sanctity of the churchyard had been breached by some domestic activity before wholesale encroachment took place (perhaps to be expected if the northern limit of the cemetery was not physically defined with a boundary). Or, more controversially, if one prefers to see shrinkage of burial area and domestic encroachment as successive, it could be that burial ceased considerably earlier than AD 900. Whatever the situation with this single pit, occupation on a more intense and sustained level attested by Structure K and other truncating features demonstrates that this zone of burial was soon – on the estimation of available dating evidence no later than the 10th century – permanently engulfed by the expanding margins of the adjacent settlement.

In comparison with many of the other cemetery shrinkages just reviewed, Bishopstone thus stands out for having a particularly early and compressed sequence: there does not appear to have been a significant lapse of time between the latest episode of interment, sometime in the 9th century, and the onset of domestic encroachment in the 10th. This observation has implications for understanding the meaning of Bishopstone's shrunken cemetery (discussed below), but for present purposes it can be noted that some of the best parallels for such dynamic sequences are to be found in mid-Saxon wics where transitory burial grounds established in the 7th century were swallowed up by rapidly expanding proto-urban sprawl laid down in the succeeding century (Scull 2001; Lucy and Reynolds 2002, 13–14) or in the shifting topography of early medieval monastic precincts (see Petts 2002, 30–1).

Three main models have been proposed for the phenomenon under review; whereas the first two are invoked by reference to broad, largely historically derived, conceptualisations of how the church developed over the late Anglo-Saxon period, the third is chiefly inferred from excavated evidence. The first, the reduction in the burial population caused by a change of status to a church, takes its conceptual cue from the minster-inspired view of the Anglo-Saxon church as a socially transforming institution (Blair 2005). According to the model, shrinking cemeteries on the sites of long-established mother churches can be read as a barometer of the minster system's decline at the expense of a proliferating network of local estate churches which gradually eroded the former's monopoly on clerically authorised burial. As their territories and pastoral dominions fragmented, minsters experienced a natural decline in burial population, only to be further depleted by newly founded estate churches recently awarded burial rights of their own (Blair 2005, 463–71).

The second proposed trigger concerns the tighter, more prescribed, spatial definition of churchyards accompanying formal rites of consecration first enacted on a widespread basis by the Church during the 10th century (Gittos 2002b). It is argued that one of the manifestations of this liturgical development (*ibid*, 204) was the use of boundaries to demarcate the limits of ritually consecrated space, a process which may have resulted in the spatial redefinition of churchyards and so to inevitable cases where peripheral burials suffered the indignity of exclusion.

The third explanation for shrinkage stems from the opportunity afforded by total cemetery excavation to track long-term developments in the relationship between spaces of the living and the dead within settlements (Zadora-Rio 2003). One of the key sequences has been derived from the site of Rigny, Touraine, France, where it has been noted that an 11th-century contraction in the area of the burial ground coincided with a greater intensification of burial around the church. The direct implication of this work is that changes in burial topography, perhaps stimulated by evolving perceptions of church community, could lie behind such sequences.

Deciding which of these alternatives might be most appropriate to Bishopstone is fraught with difficulties. As with nearly all sites bearing witness to this phenomenon, extra-mural burials provide only a peripheral view, one which leaves us blind to the kind of internal changes in burial topography observed at Rigny. Compounding the problem further is the fact that we have little or no conception of how the pre-Conquest churchyard relates to a wider mortuary landscape which, on the basis of recent research, we might very well expect to have existed.

Notwithstanding these various caveats, there is arguably a much more formidable obstacle in the way of conceptualising Bishopstone's sequence with reference to these existing models: the early and tightly-defined chronology of the burials. For whether one is talking of minster burial grounds contracting at the expense of those attached to newly founded estate churches, formal rites of consecration, or a growing sense of church community expressed at a localised (?parochial) level, the world evoked is very much confined to the final two centuries of the Anglo-Saxon era. Moreover, Bishopstone does not appear to subscribe to the standard biography of shrinkage followed by disuse followed by encroachment seen at other sites. The implications of this early chronology encourage us to view Bishopstone's sequence in somewhat different terms and perhaps to question the very identity of the excavated burials as a fossilised portion of an early 'churchyard'. Two alternatives can be proposed.

The first, and perhaps more radical of the two, sees Bishopstone in analogous terms to Reynolds' 'Adaptive' model of cemetery development (Lucy and Reynolds 2002, 20). Conceived of thus, the dated burials should not be seen as the remnant of a shrunken churchyard, but instead as part of an entirely separate precursor cemetery only furnished with a church during a later phase, mimicking the sequence attested archaeologically at Barton-upon-Humber. This proposal sheds a rather different light on the spatial proximity between the burials and domestic occupation, bringing Bishopstone into line with a growing number of excavations responsible for exposing unaccompanied burial grounds ('Field Cemeteries'), some transitory, others comparatively long-lived, within or bordering the limits of later Anglo-Saxon settlements (see also Hadley 2007; Astill 2009).

The remaining explanation retains the idea that the dated burials formed part of the original Anglo-Saxon churchyard, but to address the early and compressed sequence, proposes that the process of encroachment involved a direct and relatively swift imposition of domestic occupation. This scenario finds affinities with the dynamic sequences observed at Anglo-Saxon and early medieval monastic institutions such as Monkwearmouth/Jarrow and Whithorn, where parts of existing cemeteries were encroached upon by new ranges of buildings or else industrial activity (Petts 2002, 31; Cramp 2005). An alternative context for similarly dynamic sequences is provided by the expansionist phases of mid Saxon wics (Scull 2001; Lucy and Reynolds 2002, 13–14). Whichever scenario is preferred, Bishopstone's mutable burial topography contributes to the growing impression that the sanctity of cemeteries dating to before the 10th century was not strictly formalised, a situation which only changed with the widespread adoption of consecration rituals somewhat later (Gittos 2002).

To conclude, whilst bearing a superficial resemblance to some of the cemetery contractions seen in late Anglo-Saxon England, on closer scrutiny Bishopstone appears to differ genuinely in respect of its early and compressed chronology. The usual explanations invoked to explain this phenomenon may thus be inappropriate. If the cemetery was indeed accompanied by a church from inception (in the form of a minster churchyard), then it must be the case its periphery was taken out of active service as a place of burial in direct response to the expanding frontiers of the adjacent settlement. A possible context for this scenario may have been the re-establishment or aggrandisement of the adjacent residential complex, perhaps under the instigation of the bishops of Selsey, at some time-point after their acquisition of the estate of Bishopstone *c* AD 800. Alternatively, the burials may belong to an antecedent cemetery established within or immediately beyond the confines of an Anglo-Saxon settlement yet to be anchored to the permanent focus that would emerge as St Andrew's church.

9.3   Archaeology and history: characterising Bishopstone as a later Anglo-Saxon settlement

Introduction

What label should we use to describe the settlement excavated under the core of what is today Bishopstone village: a bishop's residence, a thegnly complex, an Anglo-Saxon minster, or indeed a mutable entity which progressed through all three? This question lies at the heart of a broader interdisciplinary debate concerning the characterisation of high-status settlements in later Anglo-Saxon England which could be argued to have reached something of an impasse (Chapter 1; Loveluck 2001; Pestell 2004; Blair 2005). Rather than attempt to provide a definitive solution to the problem of how to characterise pre-Conquest Bishopstone, the following discussion will focus upon how historical and archaeological approaches can lead to different – and in some cases divergent – projections of the same settlement biography. By laying bare the tensions existing between the two approaches, it is hoped that the reader may gain an informed impression of the complexities and challenges of attempting to understand settlements as embodiments of early medieval society. We may commence by asking the basic question: what archaeological evidence is there to support the conclusion that the excavated complex was a centre of wealth and economic importance?

Socio-economic status

Questions of socio-economic status and site character have been addressed explicitly in the analysis of many of the categories of archaeological evidence excavated from the core of pre-Conquest Bishopstone. A recurring theme arising from these evaluations driven towards social meaning is the high-status nature of the occupation. Yet expressions of superior social status are not signalled in equal intensity amongst the different categories of data, or in ways in which one would necessarily expect. Here we must acknowledge that the visibility of some archaeological 'signatures' will have been obscured by the lack of a tightly phased stratigraphic sequence which means that it is impossible, as attempted at Flixborough (Lincs), to track temporal shifts in the way in which elite identity was expressed through different categories of social behaviour whether it be the built environment, diet, or personal attire (Loveluck 2007, 158–9).

With these caveats in mind, we may commence by reviewing the evidence at its clearest. Positive expressions of the settlement's high-status character are reflected in multiple aspects of the built environment. As we have seen, the courtyard arrangement of buildings forming an established, albeit spatially shifting, component of the settlement sequence, although present in the settlement record from the 7th century, finds its clearest expression in later Anglo-Saxon seigneurial complexes, many argued to be thegnly residences – Portchester Castle, Springfield Lyons, and Goltho (Reynolds 2003; Chapter 8.4). Elevated social status can also be adduced in the spectrum of service structures, particularly the one and possibly two latrines (Structures S and T) and the putative timber tower, cellared Structure W, which in this interpretation can be regarded as nothing but an architectural embodiment of aristocratic prestige (Senecal 2000; Fleming 2001, 11–12). Similar social connotations are less apparent in the repertoire of timber halls, yet the absence of a grand, 20m-scale dwelling as seen at sites such as Goltho and the 'long-ranges' at Raunds Furnells, could simply be the result of partial excavation or regional differences.

Turning to bioarchaeological indicators, Bishopstone meets some, though not necessarily all, of the high-status criteria established by zooarchaeologists working in the early medieval period, most notably in its elevated percentages of pig and marine fish (Poole, Chapter 7.1; Reynolds, Chapter 7.2). The faunal record also indicates that the community at Bishopstone was at least partially sustained by livestock and deadstock provisioned from dependent farms through a tributary system; these external sources probably account for a proportion of the animal bone from the three main domesticates exploited for meat and animal products. Wild species evidently formed an important supplementary strand to the diet throughout the occupation sequence. It is here that some caution is required in the interpretation of zooarchaeological signatures, for the presence of whale bone and a wide range of bird species, dominated by waders, perhaps reflects more directly on the rich resource-base surrounding Bishopstone than it does on the status of its inhabitants (see below).

Whatever the precise role of these wild species, several facets of the faunal record indicate that significant quantities of prime meat and fish were being consumed at Bishopstone, a proportion perhaps in the context of feasting/hospitality rituals. Consumption above a basic subsistence level is also registered powerfully in the charred and mineralised plant biota (Ballantyne, Chapter 7.3). This source demonstrates that the settlement was supplied with clean processed grain ready for storage and/or conversion into foodstuffs. The clear implication is that cereal processing must have been undertaken in an unexcavated unit of the settlement, or the wider settlement-pattern, perhaps associated with a lower-status contingent of the population (Astill and Lobb 1989, 86).

Moving on to portable material culture, it is important that the coinage and metalwork is handled sensitively in order to avoid wayward interpretation. Let us start with the coins. A tally of four late Saxon pennies spread over an occupation sequence of over 200 years seems superficially unimpressive. Yet the time-span represented by the coins – the mid-9th to the mid-10th century – saw a contraction in coin use across southern England to notably depressed levels (Hinton 2005, 115; Blackburn 2003, 31–5, fig 3.6). Site finds from other rural excavations in southern England provide a very similar picture of coin-loss over the late Anglo-Saxon period: Portchester Castle (two site and two antiquarian finds; Pagan 1976); and Faccombe Netherton (six; Archibald 1990). Contrary to first impressions, the numismatic data do provide an indication that there was significant wealth and spending power amongst Bishopstone's Anglo-Saxon population.

Turning to other portable finds, the non-ferrous metalwork can hardly be said to proclaim status, at least not in ostentatious, attention-grabbing terms. Neither gold nor silver is represented in the assemblage, not even in such small quantities as a surface finish to copper-alloy jewellery or dress accessories. The finds that do exist – one disc-brooch, five hooked-tags, two strap-ends, and two rudimentary finger-rings – are fairly mundane in appearance and basic in execution: the work of a jobbing smith as opposed to a master craftsman. How can we reconcile this evidence with other signatures attesting to high-status occupation? In pursuing this question it is impossible to ignore the growing realisation that there were strong regional and chronological variations in attitudes towards the consumption, display, and discard of jewellery and dress accessories in later Anglo-Saxon England.

These patterns are still very dimly perceived and the underlying causes obscure (for preliminary observations see: Ulmschneider 2000, 65, 106–07; Palmer 2003, 58–60), but any socio-economic interpretation of metalwork assemblages must proceed within a contextual framework sensitive to temporal and geographical shifts, as will now be attempted for Bishopstone. First, from a purely quantitative perspective, Bishopstone's total is significant when viewed in its regional context, especially when metal-detected finds from the vicinity of the village are brought into the equation (Appendix 6). With this material included, the total number of 8th- to mid-10th-century coins is expanded to seven, and strap-ends to ten, including examples made of silver or with silver rivets. Significant new finds are added to the repertoire, including a gilt copper-alloy mount bearing zoomorphic interlace decoration in a style reproduced amongst a prestigious range of later 8th-century metalwork, notably such iconic pieces as the Witham Pins (Webster 2001).

These totals pale into insignificance when compared with the richest examples of the so-called 'Productive Sites' of eastern England spread liberally across East Anglia, Lincolnshire, and Eastern Yorkshire – Blair's 'economically precocious zone' (2005, 212). But when evaluated against the Hampshire evidence where the 'productive site' phenomenon has been analysed in detail, Bishopstone emerges firmly within the middle rank of sites producing ten or fewer coins, pins, and strapends (Ulmschneider 2000, 53–65). Whilst similar

analysis remains to be undertaken across Sussex, a preliminary survey indicates that rates of productivity here are broadly comparable to Hampshire, as indeed to other neighbouring parts of 'Greater Wessex' (Thomas 2003b).

A further variable that needs to be taken into consideration in interpreting Bishopstone's metalwork assemblage is a significant downturn in the production and consumption of prestige jewellery and dress accessories from the beginning of the 10th century (Hinton 2005). Both social and economic explanations have been proposed for this decline, but the fact remains that the silver hooked-tags, strapends, and disc-brooches which characterise 8th- to 9th-century assemblages disappear in the following century, to be replaced by a more austere range of base-metal counterparts (Astill and Lobb 1989, 88; Hinton 2005). It would be dangerous to use the presence/absence of certain categories of metalwork as a means of determining the limits of Bishopstone's occupation, but the lack of such classic 9th-century traits as Trewhiddle-style decorated strap-ends and hooked-tags might suggest that activity was at its most intense from the latter half of the 9th and into the 10th centuries.

From this contextual survey there is no need to be unduly dismissive about the modest quantity or quality of the non-ferrous metalwork from Bishopstone: this is not a true reflection of its economic importance. In short, we are working in a temporal and chronological situation where dress accessories and jewellery are unlikely to provide a true measure of a site's wealth; as reviewed above, the built environment and control over economic resources emerge as decidedly more reliable indicators.

Finally, mention should be made of the extensive assemblage of ironwork from Bishopstone in this evaluation. Whilst many of the tools, domestic implements, structural fittings and furnishings are commonplace in this period, the same can not be said of the delicate casket (No. 53) with its decorative iron strapping, nor the elaborate hinges and mounted lock represented in the hoard. These sophisticated expressions of the smith's art can only be regarded as prestige items intended for an elite market.

Changing lifestyles

If it is indeed possible to establish that Bishopstone belonged to the upper echelons of the settlement hierarchy on archaeological grounds, how might we move towards a more nuanced characterisation? One approach, central to the interpretation of the occupation sequence at Flixborough – resolved into a short-lived monastic phase sandwiched between two longer existences as an aristocratic estate centre (Loveluck 2007, 159–63) – is to consider how the character of the settlement may have changed over time. Much as this dynamic view of later Anglo-Saxon settlements may move our understanding forward, it is practically impossible to generate similar, archaeologically derived pictures for poorly stratified chalkland sites such as Bishopstone.

The only, and by no means satisfactory, alternative is to rely upon an historically informed sequence to prop up the archaeological record. The historical synthesis identifying Bishopstone as an Anglo-Saxon minster presented in Chapter 3 certainly lends itself to the construction of a developmental sequence, covering five phases. In what follows, the opportunity is taken to elucidate these different phases, after which the same historical model is placed under critical scrutiny to establish to what extent it can be sustained on archaeological grounds.

1 (*c* AD 650–700): A minster is founded, within an existing agrarian community and selecting a site typical of those favoured at the time. It is dedicated to St Andrew (possibly under Wilfrid's influence) and becomes – either then or rather later – the cult site of a putative virgin martyr of *c* AD 670. A cemetery is established.

2 (*c* AD 750–820): The minster, like most in this period, suffers loss of independence and is brought under direct lordship, first of the Mercian kings and then of the bishops of Selsey.

3 (*c* AD 820–970): The minster continues as a community of priests, perpetuating the cult of Lewinna, but is also pressed into service as an episcopal residence (again following a common pattern at this stage). Buildings on the site are shared between the community and the bishop, and as part of the intensification of occupation the cemetery is overbuilt (presumably being replaced elsewhere). The settlement assumes a character that is not obviously ecclesiastical, with some resemblances to proto-urban sites.

4 (*c* AD 970s): The minster is subject, through its bishop, to influences from the monastic reforms of Winchester, apparent in the decision to translate St Lewinna's relics. The same influences (conceivably extending, at least for a short time, to actual reform as a monastic community) may explain the rebuilding of the church, and the clearing of the complex of buildings on its north side, presumably to be replaced by more regular buildings elsewhere.

5 (*c* AD 1000–50): The minster reverts to being a community of priests, and in this state is encountered by the relic-thief, Balger.

This superficially attractive model presents a trajectory that has been proposed for several other sites conceptualised as Anglo-Saxon minsters (Blair 2005, 279–87). Part of its attraction lies in the construction of an interpretative framework into which historical, archaeological, and – in the case of the pre-Conquest phases of St Andrew's church – architectural threads, can be interwoven. In short, it provides the narrative drive and explanatory depth that could be said to be lacking in a purely archaeologically driven reconstruction. On the other hand, it remains a 'positivist' historical model and for some (this author included) its acceptance reduces the archaeological record to a mere supporting role (Austin and Thomas 1990). When the excavated evidence is scrutinised in more detail and within its own frame of reference, very little can be found that privileges this thesis above alternatives. The following assesses each of the phases in turn and highlights alternative scenarios where appropriate.

The evidence for Phase 1 is extremely exiguous. On the basis of radiocarbon dating, the earliest burials could date to before the 8th century, but this burial ground or portion thereof, need not have been attached to a minster as argued above (Chapter 9.2). In terms of the adjacent settlement, what little evidence there is for this early activity (restricted to a few pits and perhaps Structure A) cannot be resolved into a coherent picture of a minster complex, however one chooses to visualise this arrangement (Blair 1992; Blair 2005, 196–204). The fact remains that it is exceedingly difficult to characterise Bishopstone in any terms at this early date.

Phase 2 cannot be isolated as a distinct stage archaeologically, so is here conflated with Phase 3, thereby encapsulating the *floruit* of the settlement. Taken cumulatively, there is certainly a surplus of evidence for 'direct lordship', embodied in the formal complex of buildings and the various indicators of an aristocratic lifestyle reviewed above. This could relate to a residential complex set aside for the bishop's use, but it is just as likely to have been administered by, and built to the specifications of, a local reeve of thegnly status; the courtyard of buildings with corner tower (perhaps embodying some of the functions associated with structures interpreted as *burhgeat*) is a configuration repeated on many other excavated settlements interpreted as thegnly complexes. It needs stating that St Andrew's origins have been conceptualised in precisely these terms – ie a proprietorial foundation (Gem 1995, 45).

It has not been possible to recognise traces of a distinctly ecclesiastical lifestyle amongst Bishopstone's various archaeological signatures. Evidence for literacy – a traditional but by no means universally accepted criterion for identifying a monastic presence – is conspicuously absent, but then this should occasion little surprise given the rarity of styli in this part of Anglo-Saxon England and the reasons already rehearsed for the paucity of personal accoutrements at Bishopstone (Pestell 2004, 36–48; a distribution map of Anglo-Saxon styli appears as fig 9). Evidence for a monastic diet is similarly elusive, but this silence is again a product of the data – faunal assemblages recovered from documented religious communities of the later Anglo-Saxon period do not present a sharp contrast with settlements of the secular elite (Sykes 2007, 91; Poole, Chapter 7.1). Of course, irrespective of archaeological factors affecting the visibility of a religious community at Bishopstone, the imposition of 'secular' lordship first by the Mercian kings and later by the South Saxon bishopric, as proposed by the historical model, may have effectively drowned out any continuing signs of religious life (Blair and Pickles, Chapter 3.1).

It has previously been argued that one of the attributes which may have set minster complexes apart from contemporary secular communities was a greater density of occupation, a feature apparently shared by Irish and Frankish monasteries (Blair 1992, 259). There are certainly some indications that the complex at Bishopstone was densely occupied, if only for short periods, including the tight disposition of timber buildings and the profusion of pits, the character of which bears some resemblance to proto-urban environments (Blair 1992, 259; Ballantyne, Chapter 7.3). Yet the fact remains that our sample of excavated settlements from the later Anglo-Saxon period is too small to test whether this suggestion really stands up to critical scrutiny; indeed, the existing repertoire of agricultural settlements already includes sites with decidedly crowded plans, Catholme and West Heslerton amongst them (Losco-Bradley and Kinsley 2002; Powlesland 1997, 109–14).

Phase 4 does receive some archaeological backing, for the abandonment of the excavated complex can be dated between the late 10th and early 11th century on scientific grounds. However, the cessation of occupation could have been linked to events other than the hypothesised 'Æthelwoldian' refoundation (for a review of the alternatives see Chapter 10.2); Phase 5 cannot be distinguished within the parameters of archaeological dating.

Conclusion

The aim of this exercise is to make transparent to the reader the assumptions that must be made in order to fit the excavated evidence within a particular historical paradigm. A rather different, but no less finely textured, image emerges when the discoveries made at Bishopstone are projected through a lens more sympathetic to the nature of archaeological evidence and its interpretation: a highly successful estate centre occupying the apex of the local settlement hierarchy in the Lower Ouse valley. It is at this level of resolution that the *modus operandi* of the excavated settlement complex and its occupants becomes apparent. A focal setting where the extraction of natural resources and agrarian surplus was maximised under an integrated system of estate management and where the fruits of that regime were actively invested in statements of aristocratic identity – acts of conspicuous consumption and competitive display that would come to define the codified culture of the late Anglo-Saxon landowning elite (Senecal 2001). Given the chronology of Bishopstone's rise to prominence, it is tempting to suggest that its residents not only drew upon, but perhaps also actively contributed to, the development of that identity within the former borders of the South Saxon kingdom.

9.4   Farmers, fishers and foragers: changing economic strategies

Economic transformations witnessed in Anglo-Saxon England between the 8th and the 11th centuries are often viewed from a macro-perspective informed by broad comparisons of institutions or types of economic activity – towns, coinage, craftworking, agricultural production, marine fishing, and so forth (Hodges 1989; Hinton 1998; Leahy 2003; Barrett *et al* 2004). More rarely are archaeologists afforded the opportunity to track similar developments within the unfolding biographies of single Anglo-Saxon settlements and communities. It was always hoped that discoveries made in Bishopstone village could be held up against the early Anglo-Saxon occupation on Rookery Hill to offer diachronic insights into changing economic circumstances over the second half of the first millennium. The exercise can be attempted, but first it is necessary to confront two serious issues which complicate such comparisons.

First is the fact that the preservation pathways characterising the two settlements are markedly different. Whereas the valley-bottom settlement was superabundant in pits, its hill-top precursor had very few and none were used as receptacles for rubbish and/or human excreta. As a result of these different approaches to managing waste, the latter site produced markedly lower volumes of domestic refuse (most captured by the two sunken-featured buildings) and none of the mineralised plant biota and digested fish remains recovered by the more recent campaign of excavation. For this reason very little economic significance can be attached to, for example, proportional differences in animals associated with animal husbandry (the 139 identified mammal and bird bones from Rookery Hill is hardly a statistically valid sample) or with the respective contribution made by fruit to the diet – a food preserved exclusively through mineralisation (Bell 1977, 283).

The second factor that needs to be borne in mind is that from a social perspective we are not comparing like with like; as argued in Chapter 10.1, there are good reasons to believe that the social composition of the two settlements was rather different. Clearly, we must proceed carefully when attempting to draw inferences from observed distinctions between the two sets of data, as will now be attempted (Table 9.2).

As Gardiner stresses (2003, 153, table 12.1), the domestic economy of Rookery Hill was broad-based and localised in scope. As has been observed, the agricultural mainstays of animal and crop husbandry were both poorly attested in the excavation, although weeds associated with cultivation indicate that, in contrast to its valley-bottom successor, the primary processing of cereals took place within the confines of the settlement (Bell 1977, 239). Wild resources were obtained by hunting (red and roe deer), sea-fishing (limited catches of eel and whiting), and through the exploitation of the foreshore and inter-

Table 9.2   A comparison of the economic profiles of Rookery Hill and Bishopstone village settlements

	Rookery Hill	Bishopstone village
Hunting	Red deer and antler from roe deer	Roe deer, red deer, hare, badger, whale bone
Fishing	Conger eel and whiting (caught from boat)	Herring, eel, mackerel, flatfish, whiting, cod
Sea shell	Mussels, also periwinkle and oysters	Mussel, limpet, oyster, periwinkle, cockle, carpet shell
Pottery	84% of pottery made from Wealden clay	Pottery made from local estuarine clay
Stone	Beach pebbles	Querns: Mayen lava (Germany ?via London), Lower Greensand (Lodsworth, West Sussex), Ashdown sandstone (Hastings area); Hones: Wealden sandstone, Thanet-type sandstone; Spindle-whorls: Ferriginous cement stone, chalk
Non-cereal plant foods	–	Mustard/poppy seed, peas, Celtic beans, wild plums, figs, apple/pear, sloe, wild cherry, elder, hazelnut, and blackberry
Crafts	Textile production and boneworking	Textile production, smithing, non-ferrous metalworking (in lead and copper-alloy), pottery manufacture.

tidal zone (marine molluscs and beach pebbles). Only one category of evidence – pottery – attests to economic penetration beyond the settlement's immediate hinterland, for some 84% of that assemblage was made from clay obtained from the Low Weald. This source may well reflect the seasonal exploitation of Wealden territories, perhaps at this time shared with neighbouring downland communities, but which were subsequently parcelled up to emerge as detached portions of the late Anglo-Saxon and medieval manor of Bishopstone (Haselgrove 1977; for an account of this process elsewhere in Sussex see Gardiner 1984). It is notable that the geological material represented amongst the artefact assemblage was restricted to chalk and beach pebbles obtained within the settlement's immediate locality.

With this basic picture in place, we can begin the comparative analysis by focusing on changes in diet. One distinction between the two settlements, which has some claim to be genuine, is the differential exploitation of fish; in other respects the overall contribution made by wild species to the diet remains broadly the same over the life of the two settlements (Bell 1977, 240). This claim is based on the fact that the small fish assemblage recovered from Rookery Hill's two sunken-featured buildings (both sampled by wet-sieving and flotation) did not contain bones of herring, eel, and mackerel, the most abundant species recovered from the valley-bottom settlement; indeed, those represented on the former, conger eel and whiting, both feature relatively low down the latter's abundance ranking (see Reynolds, Chapter 7.2). This is admittedly slender evidence, but it does indicate that a genuine shift had occurred in the exploitation of fish in the period of transition between the two settlements, a conclusion that is in full accord with national patterns indicating an intensification of marine fishing during the 'long eighth century' (eg Sykes 2007, 57–8, figs 56 and 57). If this activity involved the processing of herring as has been suggested, one might also add here the newly discovered evidence for salt-production in the form of the Saxo-Norman saltern-mounds located in the estuarine levels to the west of Bishopstone.

Clear distinctions also emerge when the mollusc assemblages from the two settlements are compared, a source which is far less prone to preservational bias than other categories of bioarchaeological evidence (Bell 1977, 285–6; Somerville, Chapter 7.4) (Table 9.2). The most pronounced difference relates to the exploitation of limpets; this is the most abundant species at Bishopstone but only accounts for 1% of Rookery Hill's mollusc assemblage, which is dominated by mussel. Similarly the abundance of oyster is nearly ten times greater at Bishopstone than at Rookery Hill. As Somerville notes, exploitation at the former site is broadly spread over a number of common species, whereas at the latter it is focused on mussel. It is very difficult to account for these changes, but it seems unlikely that they were purely determined by the dynamic coastal environment (Chapter 2.2), for irrespective of the precise configuration of the coastline, the full range of species would have been available within a relatively localised spatial compass (Bell 1977, 285). If it is the case that these changes reflect the move to an increasingly marine-orientated diet (as suggested by the fish-bone assemblages), then it is possible that a proportion of Bishopstone's limpet assemblage was used as line-bait, a conclusion not contradicted by the discovery of fish-hooks and a possible line weight from the recent excavation (Ottaway *et al*, Chapter 6.8).

As previously stated, the data are too unreliable to make any firm statements on how food sources were affected by changing farming regimes over the life of the two settlements. On the basis of national patterns, one might expect to find an increased range of cultivars on the valley-bottom settlement dominated by free-threshing wheat, a hypothesis which is certainly not contradicted by the plant biota assemblages analysed from the recent excavations (Fowler 2002, 212–16; Ballantyne, Chapter 7.3). Yet one of the interesting themes to emerge from the analysis of the plant biota (both charred and mineralised) was the exploitation of spelt as an important secondary crop, its grains frequently co-occurring with rye brome seeds, a pairing common in prehistoric assemblages, and one which suggests some continuity in crop ecology, presumably linked to husbandry (Ballantyne, Chapter 7.3). Frustratingly, although abundant in Iron Age and Romano-British levels (Bell 1977, 273), the same crop was not attested directly in the Anglo-Saxon phase of occupation on Rookery Hill, so reintroduction cannot be ruled out. Taking into account the abundant evidence for cereal processing (see querns below) one could argue that the conversion of cereals into foodstuffs, principally bread-flour, proceeded at a much greater level of intensity on the valley-bottom settlement. This conclusion tallies with new evidence confirming that the lower slopes of the Bishopstone spur were being intensively cultivated during the occupation of the excavated settlement (Chapter 2.3).

Moving on to other aspects of the domestic economy, a very sharp contrast emerges in the raw materials exploited for pottery and stone implements (Table 9.2). The former witnessed a radical shift from the dominant use of Weald Clay obtained north of the Downs to locally derived clays and flint-grit temper obtained from the Ouse estuary and the seashore respectively (Bell 1977, 227; Jervis, Chapter 6.1). In this regard Bishopstone conforms to more general ceramic trends in southern England, which document the same transformation in materials during the course of the 8th century (Jervis, Chapter 6.1). In contrast to the greater localisation associated with the production of pottery, the geological material from the recent campaign of excavations shows a new emphasis on external exchange systems as a means of procuring raw materials and finished products. The querns, dominated by German lava probably redistributed in a semi-finished state from London or some other international trading centre, demonstrate the importance of coastal trafficking; this mechanism probably accounts for the presence of stone sourced from regions as distant as Thanet (Kent), a proportion of which could have arrived as ships' ballast (Barber, Chapter 6.4). Exploitation of territories in the Weald, previously attested through the medium of pottery at Rookery Hill, finds expres-

sion in a different corner of the material culture repertoire in the valley-bottom settlement in the form of sandstone querns and hones, perhaps reflecting the commercialisation of quarries within this stone-rich region (Gardiner 2003, 157).

The expansion in coastal trading networks across southern England between the 8th and the 11th centuries brought about more concealed transformations in the domestic environment of the later Anglo-Saxon settlement (Gardiner 2000a). The dining tables of some of its inhabitants were adorned with decorated ceramic vessels imported from northern France and a southern English centre experimenting in glazed wares (Jervis, Chapter 6.1), and figs were served up as a foreign delicacy very likely within the same household (Ballantyne, Chapter 7.3). Favourably located to exploit passing trade, the valley-bottom community was effectively plugged into a much broader economic hinterland than its hilltop predecessor, a development which was to have direct impacts on the materiality of everyday life.

A further aspect to be considered in this comparison is evidence for craft production. Textile manufacture is the only domestic craft securely identified at Rookery Hill, although there is some circumstantial evidence for boneworking (Bell 1977, 240). The former has a continued presence at the successor settlement, but within a proliferating range of crafts directly and indirectly attested in the archaeological record: smithing, non-ferrous metalworking (in lead and copper-alloy), and pottery production (although the site of the kiln was not determined). It would be dangerous to make too much of these distinctions given the sample bias, but one could argue that the a greater level of specialisation is embodied in the craft profile of the later settlement, a conclusion that would be amplified if it could be proven that the selection of complex and finely crafted door furniture contained in the iron hoard was made by a resident smith, whether attached or freelance. With the exception of pottery manufacture, the range of artisanal activities witnessed at the valley-bottom settlement accords favourably with other excavated estate complexes of the later Anglo-Saxon period which combine limited evidence for specialised production with domestic crafts (Thomas forthcoming).

Overall what arguably sets the valley-bottom settlement apart most from its hilltop predecessor is a more intensive level of exploitation across a broader range of economic resources, whether they be foodstuffs or raw materials. In particular, the later of the two communities had become more adept at extracting resources from its territorial hinterland through an integrated regime that harnessed the full potential of coastal, estuarine, downland, and Wealden environments. The success of this regime can be measured in direct physical terms, for it doubtless paid for the aggrandisements and elite lifestyle that seems to distinguish later Anglo-Saxon Bishopstone as a centre of wealth within the local settlement hierarchy.

10 Conclusions

Having examined some archaeological themes of broader contextual relevance to the excavations, it is only appropriate that we draw this report to a close by returning to the original questions and issues that inspired the Bishopstone project – those left hanging at the end of the Rookery Hill excavations published some 30 years previously.

10.1 The wider settlement context: re-evaluating Bishopstone as an example of an Anglo-Saxon settlement shift

We may commence with the chronological gap between the abandonment of the Rookery Hill settlement and the establishment of its eventual successor on the site of Bishopstone village (Haselgrove 1977, 248; Bell 1978, 44). As we have seen, this breach can be bridged from both directions. On the one hand, the redating of structure 47 from the Rookery Hill excavations (Gardiner 2003, 153), allows the hilltop occupation to be pushed beyond the proposed 6th-century terminus into the 7th or 8th centuries. On the other, independent scientific dating recovered from the core of Bishopstone village allows its inception to be pushed back into the 8th century, certainly as a focus for Christian burial, and probably with attendant occupation from the outset. Within the imprecise parameters of available archaeological dating, the gap has all but disappeared. With the evidence now at our disposal there is no need to invent an intermediary gap-plugging focus, whether located at Denton or any other territorial sub-unit of the Bishopstone estate which, through a process of fragmentation, would emerge with a separate identity at the end of the Anglo-Saxon era as a Domesday vill/parish. On this basis, the settlement shift under scrutiny could be regarded as a genuine one-for-one replacement – once established, the new valley-bottom focus drew off the population formerly ensconced on Rookery Hill.

Whilst the simplicity of this model is superficially attractive it rests upon a series of assumptions which demand closer scrutiny. The first concerns the respective scales of the two settlements. The early Anglo-Saxon occupation on Rookery Hill, with an excavated total of 22 buildings and with an estimated total extent of 7.4 acres (c 3ha), has previously been classified as a 'large nucleated settlement' (Bell 1978, 39). New evidence for an extended Anglo-Saxon occupation sequence, amplified by a more informed understanding of the structure of early medieval settlements, might instead suggest a shifting agglomeration of farmstead units, more appropriately termed a 'hamlet' than a nucleated 'village', served by its own community cemetery (Welch 1985, 15; Hamerow 2002, 52–100; Gardiner 2003, 153). By contrast, at least under the interpretation offered here, the excavated complex within Bishopstone village represents part of a high-status compound comprising formal accommodation accompanied by a suite of subsidiary buildings and service structures approximating to a manorial/ecclesiastical *curia* (Gardiner 2007). In terms of habitation, the excavated portion of the valley-bottom focus – a direct physical expression of the emergence of settlement hierarchy in the later Anglo-Saxon landscape – only embraced the social apex of the community and not its totality. This prompts the question: where did the peasants tied to the *inland* of the Bishopstone estate live (Faith 1997, 15–88)?

Without further excavation we can only speculate, but one possibility that might be entertained is that the lower-status contingent of Bishopstone's population lived on the fringes of the excavated seigneurial compound. Unfortunately, quarrying at the northern end of the Bishopstone spur is likely to have removed all potential traces of this occupation, although the truncated remains of Structural complex X may provide a late hint of its possible character (Chapter 4.1). The problem with the view that the *inland* tenants were accommodated in a planned area on the periphery of the Bishopstone *curia* is that it borrows heavily on work undertaken in the Midlands and other nucleated landscapes of England's so-called 'Central Province' (Roberts and Wrathmell 2002, 1–3, fig 1.1). In sequences of this type, perhaps seen most vividly at Raunds, peasant properties were established on the threshold of manorial compounds as acts of regulated planning, usually as a secondary stage in the drawn-out process of village nucleation (Brown and Foard 1998; Saunders 2000; Page and Jones 2006; Audouy and Chapman 2009).

But is it safe to assume that the incipient phases of medieval settlements in the southern chalklands of England followed a similar path? Rippon (2008) has recently argued a persuasive case that settlement patterns in regions falling outside the 'Central Province' of England followed their own distinct trajectories that do not subscribe to a Midland-centric model. Coastal Sussex and similar chalkland *pays* deserve to be studied from just such an independent perspective, not least because they are characterised by a variegated pattern of nucleated settlements combined with smaller hamlets and outlying farms (Brandon 1974, 86–8; 1998, 49–51; Brandon and Short 1990, 60–2). Fieldwork undertaken at Chalton demonstrates that this hybridity existed early on in the Anglo-Saxon period, for the downland surrounding the nucleated settlement of Church Down was marked by a sprinkling of smaller foci represented by scatters of early and mid Saxon pottery (Cunliffe 1972; Hughes 1984). It is difficult to know how to characterise these smaller entities as none was targeted by excavation, but it is not impossible that they represent the forerunners of the upland farms of dependent status, evidenced in late Saxon charters, engaged in specialised sheep-rearing, a practice that would emerge as a fundamental component of the medieval downland economy (Brandon 1998; Gardiner 2003, 154–6).

Moreover, dispersed settlement in the pre-Conquest landscape was unlikely to have been solely restricted to the downland plateau. Lewis comments in her examination of medieval settlement patterns in Wiltshire that 'these chalk valley settlements, although often classified as "nucleated", were very different to the compact agglomerated villages which characterise much of the nucleated village landscapes of the midlands and the north of England' (Lewis 1994, 176). It would appear that the origins of these medieval row settlements very often lay in expansion and infilling between loosely agglomerated foci strung out along valley bottoms, part of a longer-term dynamic sometimes involving later phases of contraction resulting in a return to the disaggregated pattern (Lewis 1994, 185–8). Draper, working in the same county, has also noted that the pattern of valley-bottom settlement is marked by considerably fluidity up to *c* AD 800, the date by which sites of medieval and modern villages appear to have been finally fixed (Draper 2006, 96–9).

Can we use the Wiltshire evidence to bring new meaning to understanding Bishopstone's pre-Conquest form and development? An alternative view to the one-for-one replacement model is that the hilltop community of Rookery Hill fragmented into multiple foci dispersed along the lower slopes of the Bishopstone valley: in other words the local situation could be conceived in an analogous way to an extended row settlement. This suggestion naturally shifts the spotlight of attention on to other component parts of the medieval settlement pattern existing in the locality, most obviously Norton, located some 1km north of Bishopstone village.

Previous to the Bishopstone project, Norton had attracted a brief episode of archaeological attention in the late 1970s when the Lewes Archaeological Group undertook a geophysical survey followed by a small-scale excavation to test the reputed site of a medieval chapel (Combes 2002, 53). Located at the eastern edge of the hamlet, amongst a broader spread of earthworks interpreted as a shrunken medieval settlement (SMR no. 6066), the site had a visible presence as a spread of flint rubble (Fig 10.1). From interim accounts (the site remains unpublished), it appears that the excavation confirmed the presence of a medieval building of 13th- to 14th-century date but its vernacular style, together with such associated discoveries as a corn-drying oven, combined firmly to repudiate the chapel theory (O'Shea 1978; Mike Allen, pers comm).

Key evidence that the origins of the hamlet extend back into the pre-Conquest period was unearthed during an excavation undertaken in the inaugural year of the Bishopstone project, a short distance away from the site investigated in 1978 (Fig 10.1). The target of this intervention was a middle Iron Age terrace dated by test-pitting the previous year, but otherwise identified as a constituent of the complex of 'medieval' earthworks recorded on the Sites and Monuments Record. Amongst the concentration of later prehistoric features were found two latrines and possibly a third pit of indeterminate function dated to the later Anglo-Saxon period on ceramic grounds (Seager-Thomas 2005b). Perhaps associated with the same focus is a small but significant concentration of metal-detected finds and coins of 8th- to 11th-century date, recovered from a large field fronting on to the Bishopstone road immediately to the south of the 2002 excavations (Appendix 6).

Taken in conjunction, these two pieces of evidence confirm that the medieval origins of Norton and Bishopstone are broadly contemporaneous. Their respective names (and indeed Sutton to the south-west) imply that by the late Anglo-Saxon period Bishopstone had emerged as the focal settlement within the wider Anglo-Saxon estate (Combes 2002, 53–4; Blair and Pickles, Chapter 3.1). However, it is not possible to confirm whether this hierarchical relationship originated from the inception of the valley-bottom settlement in the 8th century. One can only speculate, but it might be the case that Norton was occupied by servile tenants working the *inland* of the Bishopstone estate. Such low-status communities – embedded into the social fabric of Anglo-Saxon multiple estates – gain explicit mention in grants of land, forming the primary endowment of important ecclesiastical institutions, the South Saxon bishopric of Selsey included (Brandon 1974, 87; Faith 1997, 15–88).

What can we take from this discussion? First, the sites of Rookery Hill and what would emerge as present-day Bishopstone shared a direct ancestral relationship, with the latter superseding the former certainly no later than the second half of the 8th century. It is perfectly within the realms of historical probability (though of course unknowable) that the pioneers of the valley-bottom settlement were drawn from the same generation as the final occupants of Rookery Hill. At the same time we have seen that it is necessary to set this site relocation within its wider landscape context. A broader focus reveals that Norton was established (or perhaps

Fig 10.1 (opposite)   Location of excavations in Norton and medieval occupation in Bishopstone

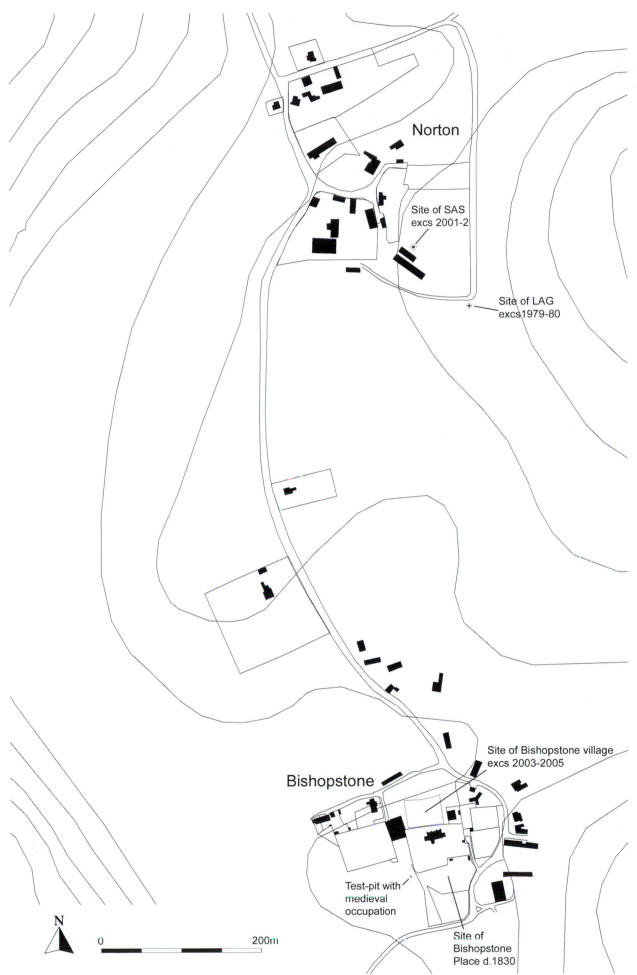

Norton

Site of SAS
excs 2001-2

Site of LAG
excs1979-80

Bishopstone

Site of Bishopstone village
excs 2003-2005

Test-pit with
medieval
occupation

Site of
Bishopstone
Place d.1830

N

0   200m

re-established) at about the same time as Bishopstone, raising the possibility that the population of Rookery Hill fragmented into two or more foci spread along the valley bottom. If such a division did indeed occur, then it raises interesting questions on the social and economic interplay between the respective communities occupying the valley bottom. Acknowledgement of this more complex situation calls into question the view that the high-status complex unearthed at Bishopstone was necessarily the core of an extensive settlement accommodating the full social spectrum.

10.2 The end and afterlife of the pre-Conquest settlement sequence at Bishopstone

The early history of Bishopstone is punctuated by not one but by two phases of discontinuity: the settlement targeted by the current excavations was, like its predecessor on Rookery Hill, subject to total abandonment. In the general scheme of things this is quite unremarkable: it has recently been estimated that roughly half of all England's villages experienced substantial changes to their layouts (whether expansion, contraction, reconfiguration, or a shift of site) down through the medieval and post-medieval periods (Page and Jones 2007). Constrained by the frame of our excavated window, it is impossible to know whether the desertion was balanced by continuity in other parts of the settlement, in other words whether we are seeing the abandonment or replacement of only the manorial centre. Whatever the case, it is one thing to highlight Bishopstone's adherence to this generalising tendency and quite another to provide an explanation and context for the cessation of occupation on the site of the village green. The starting point must be a consideration of the likely completion date for this desertion.

Any such estimation must rely upon the sequence of radiocarbon dates which provide the only reliable means of tying down the chronological limits of the occupation. Statistical modelling generates a probability estimate of cal AD 935–1060 (95% probability) and cal AD 940–1000 (68% probability) for the termination of the settlement (Marshall *et al*, Chapter 8.2). Within these parameters, it is unlikely that occupation within the excavated core of Bishopstone extended much beyond the turn of the 10th century, at least not on the scale/intensity experienced over the preceding two centuries. This proposition is wholly supported by the coins and the typological/stylistic dating of stratified artefacts. This absolute date-range brings into view a series of competing scenarios offering plausible triggers for the abandonment of the excavated complex; the alternatives are reviewed with an open mind.

We may commence with the 'grand-narrative' explanation: that Bishopstone was caught up in the maelstrom of England's second 'Viking age' (Graham-Campbell 1980b, 35). *The Anglo-Saxon Chronicle* leaves one in little doubt that the 990s represented a period of considerable distress and disruption for the people of Sussex, especially those occupying its coastal territories. Following their unsuccessful siege on London in AD 994, a mighty Viking army led by the future English king Swein Forkbeard and his accomplice Olaf Trygvasson (later king of Norway), ravaged the southern coast making inland raiding sorties into Kent, Sussex, and Hampshire. Sussex (along with Berkshire) evidently suffered a similar fate at the hands of the same force in AD 998 (Swanton 1996, 126–8). A decade later (1009), Sussex was to experience further depredations at the hands of a Scandinavian raiding-army, on this occasion under the redoubtable Thorkel the Tall (*ibid*, 138–9).

Was Bishopstone set upon by one of these groups of marauding Vikings? The settlement's visibility from the coast and location beside a riverine artery of major strategic importance would have certainly placed it within the line of fire. There is also plentiful evidence for conflagrations within the settlement – the massive quantities of burnt walling daub perhaps being the most obvious. Yet these accumulations do not suggest that the settlement came to a dramatic end in a single major conflagration. Perhaps most significantly, some of the densest accumulations of daub were buried under layers of cess and domestic rubbish representing extended cycles of deposition: destructive they may have been, but these fires were not responsible for the extinction of the settlement.

Perhaps unsurprisingly, archaeology has failed to project Bishopstone on to the stage of these epoch-defining events. An alternative proposition is that the settlement's demise was linked to environmental factors, specifically the dynamic geomorphology of the coastal reaches of the River Ouse detailed in Chapter 2. As we have seen, it is impossible to gain a precise spatio-temporal handle on eastwards deflection of the river mouth through the process of 'longshore drift', but there is indirect historical evidence that its outfall had been fixed at Seaford by around the time of the Norman Conquest, perhaps superseding an earlier breach in the vicinity of the Bishopstone inlet. The rise of Seaford as the principal port of trade on the River Ouse may have eroded Bishopstone's former economic dominance in the locality, echoing the rise-and-fall dynamics of medieval ports sited on Sussex's other major river outlets (Woodcock 2003).

A rather different perspective can be gained by looking westwards at the fortunes of the South Saxon bishopric in the second half of the 10th century. Although not without considerable complexities of interpretation, forensic analysis of the Anglo-Saxon charters held within the Selsey archive provides a schematic impression of the succession of the South Saxon bishops down until the transferral of the See to Chichester shortly after the Norman Conquest (Kelly 1998, lxxxv–xciv). Of relevance is evidence for a period of destabilisation following a vacancy in the See in *c* AD 953, when an interloping West Saxon bishop, Ælfsige, appears to have dismembered the core of Selsey's endowment (Kelly 1998, 90–1). It should be said that this is only one – albeit a preferred – reading of a notoriously difficult document, but it would provide a context for a hiatus in effective episcopal jurisdiction over more peripheral parts of the endowment, one with direct consequences for the management and upkeep of estate centres such as Bishopstone. It remains only a possibility, but if the episcopal life-line was cut in the 950s, then one might expect knock-on effects not unlike our archaeologically attested abandonment.

Another way of approaching the problem is more directly through the body of interpretation surrounding St Andrew's church presented in Chapter 3. It has been proposed that the construction of the church, as we have it, may have been linked to the translation of Lewinna's relics in the 970s; this date has some architectural arguments to support it, recently strengthened by the discovery that the famous sundial is a secondary insertion. If this revised dating is correct, then it could be the case that the burst of capital investment extended to the construction of a new episcopal complex on a virgin site. There is indeed some archaeological evidence to support the proposition that the centre of operations at Bishopstone had shifted to a new site to the south of the church, if not by the Norman Conquest, then not appreciably later. Test-pitting in 2002 located a rubbish pit, some 15m beyond the south-west corner of the churchyard, containing rich concentrations of domestic refuse including an unabraided assemblage of Ringmer-ware pottery dating to the 12th century (Luke Barber, pers comm) (Fig 10.1). It is worth remembering that no stratified deposits of this date were recovered north of the churchyard. Whilst this is admittedly slender evidence, it does add credence to local tradition that the post-medieval manor house, Bishopstone Place, demolished in 1830, of which only the cellars and fragments of outlying 'designed landscape' survive, stands on the site of a medieval precursor (Farrant 1976, 35–6).

Of course, the final extinction of the excavated complex may have been the result of the combined influence of two or more of the above factors, the reckoning of which must await the scrutiny of future research. Our ability to ask a new set of probing questions concerning Bishopstone's past development will hopefully be taken as a measure of the success with which the current excavations have met their original goal: to harness the archaeological potential locked away in an occupied village core in order to understand its origins and embryonic phases. Whilst open to contrasting interpretations, this window has afforded a glimpse into an intense fluorescence of Anglo-Saxon life hitherto only hinted at in the contested fabric of St Andrew's church. It is hoped that these visualisations, made possible by a spirited programme of research excavation, will provoke new thinking into the *making* of other medieval settlements in southern England and beyond.

Appendix 1: The evidence in Drogo of Saint-Winnoc's *Historia translationis sanctae Lewinnae* by *David Defries*

The *Historia translationis sanctae Lewinnae* [BHL 4902] by the Flemish monk and hagiographer Drogo of Saint-Winnoc (*c* 1030–84) is an entertaining hagiographic text with a great deal to offer scholars of medieval England and Flanders. According to Drogo, in 1058, a monk from the Flemish abbey of Saint-Winnoc stole the relics of the Anglo-Saxon saint Lewinna from an English minster and brought them back to his abbey. In two books, the *Historia* recounts both the *furtum sacrum* (sacred theft) of the relics and Saint-Winnoc's campaign to promote Lewinna's cult in Flanders.[1] Although the text is full of tantalising details about a number of subjects, no other evidence exists to confirm its accuracy. Even the location of the original shrine has been a matter of serious dispute.[2] In this contribution, I will argue that although we may never be certain that the relics were actually stolen (as opposed to bought or given as a gift), we can be reasonably sure that Drogo's descriptions of the minster, its location, and the saint's cult are accurate.

The date of the theft in 1058 provides the *terminus post quem* for the composition of the *Historia*, while its dedication to Rumold, abbot of Saint-Winnoc from 1031 until 1068, provides a *terminus ante quem* of 1068.[3] A date of about 1060 is, however, probable. Three medieval manuscripts preserve the text, which has been printed in three editions that differ very little.[4] The Latin excerpts given below come from the oldest extant manuscript, which is preserved in a lectionary containing texts related to the three patron saints of Saint-Winnoc – Lewinna, Oswald of Northumbria, and Winnoc. Most of the lectionary dates to the second half of the 12th century and was owned by Saint-Winnoc until its dissolution in the 19th century. It is now housed at the municipal library of Bergues (dép. Nord, France), where the abbey was located. Book One (folios 113v–141v) contains the account of the *furtum sacrum* and a description of the saint's virtues. Book Two is a *liber miraculorum* (book of miracles) containing accounts of Lewinna's miracles, most of which she performed when the monks of Saint-Winnoc took her on a tour of coastal Flanders soon after her arrival.

Book One begins with the relic theft. According to Drogo, a monk from Saint-Winnoc named Balger embarked on a ship bound for England with the intention of going to Dover (though the crew wanted to sail to another, unnamed port to sell merchandise). An adverse wind propelled the ship past both ports, and several more in addition, until finally the crew was able to enter a harbour at a place called *Sevordt*. The next morning, discerning a church from the harbour, Balger and a companion walked to the church to celebrate Easter mass. On the way, Balger

suddenly felt sick, and they encountered an old man who informed them that they were approaching the minster of St Andrew in which the body of St. Lewinna lay.[5] Once inside, Balger celebrated mass, then began exploring the building. Finding a shrine around which were parchments bearing writing in English affixed to the walls, Balger asked a priest about them. The priest explained that they were lists of miracles performed by Lewinna, then offered a précis. Balger attempted to negotiate for some of the relics, causing the priest to recoil in horror. The monk explained away his request as a joke, then spent the rest of the day and the following night in vigil before the shrine. During his prayers, he tested the reliquary until he found a way to gain access to the bones. The next day, the sacristan left Balger alone in the church. The monk begged Lewinna to allow him to take her away. He sought to entice her by promising greater veneration in Flanders and by coiling a cord around his neck and laying its ends over the reliquary, the legal process for making himself her serf.[6] At first, she refused and immobilised her reliquary. Eventually, however, after Balger had fallen asleep, she appeared to him and told him to take her to Flanders. He was then able to remove the relics except for some minor bones that Lewinna caused to fall through a hole in the cloth covering her. Drogo explained that the saint caused the bones to fall through the hole three times so that the thief might leave them in the shrine. After several mishaps, Balger returned to Saint-Winnoc with the relics, where they were welcomed in a series of increasingly more dignified rituals. While describing this reception, Drogo revealed that the bones were accompanied by three seals (*sigillae*) and a document (*cartula*) recording some facts about her life, death, and cult.[7]

The *Historia translationis* was one of numerous medieval *furta sacra* accounts.[8] Modern readers might assume that these accounts were so damning to the community that received stolen relics that they must have been true, but modern ideas of theft are misleading here. According to medieval hagiographers, *furta sacra* were not so much thefts in the modern sense as elopements: saints had control over their relics and in order to move them, one had to gain the saint's approval – one had to woo the saint. Drogo incorporated this view into his text when he depicted Lewinna miraculously immobilising the reliquary until Balger offered her blandishments. When the saint allowed her reliquary to be moved, she had been won over. With regard to the veracity of *furta sacra* accounts, the real problem lies in how they obviated the chief question *medieval* people had about relic sales or gifts – who would voluntarily part with the relics of a powerful saint?[9] By claiming that a relic sale or gift had actually been a *furtum sacrum*, a community might hope to avoid doubts about whether a particular jumble of bones really was a saint. Drogo's sensitivity to this issue is evident from the *topoi* he included in his account. For example, Drogo clearly included the exchanges between Balger and local inhabitants like the old man and the priest to testify to Lewinna's status as a saint. The old man informed Balger, 'You see the minster of St. Andrew, to whose honour it is dedicated. Also, St Lewinna, virgin and martyr, rests there corporally, she who is of such great account and for whose merit the heavenly power displays itself through her each day' (*Monasterium sancti Andreæ vides, eius honori habetur quidem dedicatum. Sancta quoque Lewinna virgo et martir ibidem corpore requiescit. Quæ quanti sit, cuius meriti; cælestis virtus per eam omni die ostendit*).[10] The priest gave more detailed witness to the saint's intercessory power:

[Balger and his companion] saw, among other things, sheets of parchment affixed to the wall, and the miracles, which through her holiness the omnipotent Lord had accomplished, were described on these sheets. And, because they were written in English, as is the custom among those people, they were completely unable to read them. Thus, they called a priest of this church to explain these things to them. They asked what the text was, and what its content might be. The priest said, 'The miracles of this holy Virgin are noted here, which things the omnipotent God brought about by her merits, lest they be hidden to posterity and so that she might remain in honor and veneration among the peoples.'

Namque videbant inter cætera; scedas membranarum parieti affixas, et virtutes quas per sanctam suam fecerat omnipotens dominus in eisdem esse descriptas. Et quia Anglicæ uti apud ipsos mos habetur scriptæ erant; minime quidem ab ipsis legi poterant. Ad hæc itaque sibi demonstranda; præsbiterum huius æcclesiæ advocant, quid illud sit, quid huiusce significationis sit sciscitantur. Virtutes huius sanctæ virginis inquit hic sunt notatæ, quas meritis eius patravit omnipotens deus, nequeant latere posteros, et ut hæc ipsa honori et venerationi maneat apud populos.[11]

He then recounted several miraculous cures, further evidence for her status as a saint. The hagiographer also raised the issue of a trade:

The mind of the brother [Balger] was inflamed over these things, he burned with the desire to obtain some of the relics from the holy body of the virgin. Doubtless on account of this, he drew the priest aside by the hand and asked him, 'Take what you will from me and give me relics from this virgin – either a bone or some such thing – which might be able to be held in honor at our place.'

Then, disturbed by the brashness of this request, the priest responded, 'Father! Do you not know what you say? Is it proper that a servant of God wishes this? Fitting that he utters it? Suitable that he do this? Although some fool might wish to permit this crime, you being prudent, you being wise, you, a servant of God, ought to prevent it!'

Igitur super his accensa mens fratris; ardebat aliquid reliquiarum sibi tollere de sancto virginis corpore. Id propter scilicet seorsum manu ducit præsbiterum. Quem etiam ita convenit. Accipe quod vis ait a me, et da michi reliquias de tanta virgine, vel os, vel tale quid, quod nostro loco possit esse honori.

Tunc commotus animo huius insolentia; respondit. Pape, scisne quæ loqueris? An decet servum dei id velle? Convenit dicere? Oportet facere? Quanquam quis fatuus id illicitum vellet admittere; tu prudens, tu providus, tu servus dei deberes tardare.[12]

Balger then retreated. According to the hagiographer, even though the monk had tried to negotiate for the relics, he had been unsuccessful, leaving a *furtum sacrum* as the only way to obtain them.

Given Saint-Winnoc's incentive to disguise a more mundane transaction as a theft, it does not inspire much confidence in Drogo's veracity that he unapologetically shifted from passages testifying to the honour in which the English community held Lewinna to the *topos* of the neglected shrine. He reported that Balger asked the priest if he could celebrate mass before the reliquary, 'for it is apparent that this place is occasionally free of prayer' (*liceat etiam hic interdum orationi vacare*) and that he subsequently pleaded with God and the saint to allow him to take the bones 'to a better location, where her honor would be greater and she, who seemed neglected by all in her current place, would be held in fitting veneration' (*ad meliorem locum … , ubi suus maior honor foret, dignæque haberetur venerationi, quæ eodem in loco uti videbatur ab omnibus esset neglectui*).[13] The purpose of this common *topos* was to explain why a saint was not fickle in withdrawing his or her patronage from one community and to justify the thief's actions. Juxtaposed to the *topoi* of local witnesses to the saint's status, however, it also injects a sense of artificiality.

Despite the issues raised by the *Historia*'s genre and Drogo's use of *topoi*, it is unlikely that the entire account was a fabrication. Flanders was an arena in which ecclesiastical communities competed fiercely for prestige. In particular, Saint-Bertin vied with its sister institution, the chapter of Saint-Omer, in the west of Flanders, and Saint-Pierre competed with Saint-Bavon, its neighbor at Ghent, for primacy in the east. As a result, communities were ready to dispute claims about the patron saints of their rivals. For example, in the 11th century, Saint-Pierre challenged Saint-Bavon's claims about a St Lebuin, whose existence the latter had, in fact, recently fabricated.[14] Local populations may have been receptive to such challenges. For example, the populace of Limoges made Ademar of Chabannes a laughingstock after another ecclesiastic publicly refuted his argument for the apostolicity of St Martial.[15] Though Limoges was quite distant from Flanders, there appears to be no reason that ecclesiastical leaders could not similarly incite Flemish populations. Yet, we have no evidence that anyone challenged Saint-Winnoc's claim that Lewinna was stolen. It is possible that the evidence for such a challenge has not survived, but this absence could also be explained by the steps Drogo took to ward off doubt. First, he made it relatively easy to investigate his account. In addition to Lewinna's name, he specified that Lewinna's shrine was located at the English minster of St Andrew. This is noteworthy because Andrew is the only saint named other than Peter (who is mentioned in reference to a trip to Rome). The hagiographer also noted that Balger had seen the minster from the harbour called *Sevordt*:

> After morning came, the monk [Balger] immediately began to investigate whether there was some church nearby where he might be able to celebrate the divine mysteries. For it was the day of the Lord's resurrection, and full of anxiety, he sought to prevent the possibility that he would not be able to take part in the mysteries of our redemption on such an important day. Thus, from afar, he discerned a minster almost three miles distant from the port. He was made glad by this and, taking only one companion, he set out to complete the journey in haste.

> *Mane vero facto; an æcclesia aliqua esset propter primum monachus cœpit explorare, ubi posset divina misteria celebrare. Dies enim dominicæ resurrectionis erat, et ne expers misteriorum nostræ redemptionis in tanta die foret; sollicitus præcavebat. Cernit itaque a longe monasterium, pæne tribus leugis ab illo portu disparatum. Unde adeo lætus efficitur, et uno tantum comite assumpto; iter accelerare aggreditur.*[16]

Although modern scholars have had difficulties in identifying Lewinna's original shrine based on this information, Drogo's Flemish contemporaries would not have had the same problems. By the 11th century, Flemish relations with the English were both long-standing and frequent.[17] During that century, relations between English and Flemish ecclesiastical institutions were particularly close, with Saint-Bertin at the forefront. For example, in 1055, Bishop Hermann of Ramsbury (1045–55, 1058–78), a native of either Lorraine or Flanders, became a monk at Saint-Bertin. In 1058, he returned to England to occupy the sees of Ramsbury and Sherborne and was accompanied by the monk Goscelin, who later acquired great fame as a hagiographer in England.[18] A trip to the English coast should have turned up local people who could direct inquirers to the original cult site, especially if, as

Drogo carefully noted, some of the relics remained at St Andrew's.[19] It seems, then, almost certain that a cult dedicated to an Anglo-Saxon virgin martyr named Lewinna once existed at a minster on the southern coast of England and that most of her relics were brought to Saint-Winnoc in the 11th century. Whether this translation was the result of a *furtum sacrum* is, however, unclear because the minster community had incentive to cover up the sale or gift of the majority of Lewinna's relics (had it parted with only the 'minor bones' that Balger left in the original shrine, it may have disputed the *furtum* claim).

Plausibility was a second tool that could assuage doubt. The *Historia* is full of details about maritime activity in the Channel. For example, a passage about the return voyage indicates that Flemish traders feared certain parts of the English coast:

> although the middle of the day had passed, [the Flemish] had not eaten. A sailor reminded the others, 'we ought to take food,' he said. 'The [mealtime] hour has now passed.' Another objected, 'truly, we have nothing except loaves of bread, and these are now hard and harmful to the teeth. This place is, however, abounding with fish. Therefore, this monk [Balger] ought to leave the ship to buy enough fish for us. We, however, should sail past this bend of the curved shore. Afterwards we will wait for his return. For no one should cause any injury to him, while the rest of us may perhaps sustain an injury: everywhere, there are men unjustly causing injury.'

> *Sed dum iam transeunte media die adhuc incibati forent; unus alios submonuit, cibum inquit capiamus, iam hora præteriit. Alius huic contra respondit. Nil certe præter panes habemus, et hi quidem iam sunt duri, ad comedendum dentibus iniqui. Est autem locus propter habundans [abundans] piscium, ubi hic monachus navim egrediatur, quantum sufficiat omnibus nobis mercetur. Nos interim legemus flexionem hanc curvi litoris, post simul manebimus adventum revertentis. Huic enim egredienti nemo iniuriam faciet, at alii nostrum exeunti fortassis iniuria fiet. Ubique enim sunt homines iniuste iniuriam facientes.*[20]

The excursion proved disastrous for Balger since the ship was unable to retrieve him: 'the ship was far from land. For it was not able to come to the shore. The sea in that place was dangerous for deep-hulled vessels: it was seen by those approaching to be alternately deep then shallow' (*puppis longe a terra aberat. Non enim litori appropinquare poterat. Iniquum est eo in loco mare altis ratibus, modo altum, modo breve habetur accedentibus*).[21]

Balger hired a small boat for six coins to row him out to the ship, but the wind and the waves proved too strong to overcome. The Flemish crew, presumably fearing the inhabitants or unwilling to risk losing a favorable breeze, sailed off without Balger. Even if these details are fiction, Drogo probably intended them to be plausible fiction, especially in passages, such as this one, that were ancillary to the main narrative. Only about eighty years later, Eadmer of Canterbury wrote a letter to Glastonbury Abbey that reveals the importance of plausibility. In the course of refuting Glastonbury's claim that it had stolen the relics of St Dunstan from Canterbury in 1012, Eadmer excoriated the monks there both for claiming to have stolen the relics and for composing a farcical account of the theft. In particular, he ridiculed them for claiming that monks had carried the body of one of their abbots – whose name was conveniently unknown – 'two hundred miles' in full episcopal regalia and placed it in Dunstan's empty tomb. Eadmer skewered Glastonbury with the obvious question, 'Were there not bones of dead men between Canterbury and Glastonbury?'[22] A few lines later, he also cited the proficiency some hagiographers had developed in composing false accounts: 'Why didn't you consult some foreigner from overseas? They are knowledgeable, very clever and they know how to write fiction; they would have composed some likely lie which you could have bought.'[23] Given the competitive nature of Flemish hagiography, we can treat these details as broadly indicative of maritime activity between England and Flanders.

Drogo's literary style suggests that his account is not only plausible but also trustworthy. The hagiographer was heavily indebted to Vergil's *Aeneid* for the language that he used to describe sailing and the coast of England. Yet, he was also demonstrably concerned with accuracy. This is particularly evident in the passage where he dealt with the harbour at *Sevordt*. He began with a note on its etymology and continued with a description of its physical features:

Indeed, this same port is called *Sevordt* ... Truly, the etymology of the name is fitting: for *Sevordt* is said in Teutonic, in Latin speech it is called 'ford of the sea' [*maris vadum*]. And it is truly a ford: for it was chosen as a ford by those going to the shore. Since I speak to ones unfamiliar, the entrance of this port is so narrow that two ships joined side-to-side would scarcely be able to enter it. On each side, double peaks are raised against the sky, and send down a sloping yoke on which each and every wave is broken when Aeolus' wrath is raised in the turbulent channel. There [in that port], no anchor fetters the ships, no cord restrains the bobbing vessels, but they are content to remain still on their own. They do not fear at all the east wind, nor the north, nor the southwest.

Here, the sailors, tired from their duties, rest their bodies, and the jubilant men rejoice that they have evaded so many and such great perils. But after the feasts [that accompany] such celebrations, night rushes in, and the sky envelops the lands and seas together. One sailor goes to sleep. Then sleep occupies the tired limbs of all.

Vocatur vero idem portus Sevordt ... Verum digna nominis æthymologia. Sevordt enim Teutonice dictum; latino æloquio maris vadum dicitur. Et re vera vadum. Nam vadum fuit venientibus ad litus optatum. Ut nescientibus loquar; isdem portus tam arti introitus est, ut vix binæ carinæ hunc ipsum iuncto latere valeant intrare. Hinc atque hinc bini scopuli versus cælum erecti; declive iugum demittunt, quis omnis unda frangitur, cum eolica [Æolica] rabies turbato freto tollitur. Ibi non anchora puppes alligat, non funis nutantes retentat, verum per se solæ contentæ stare; minime quidem timent Eurum, non Aquilonem, non Affricum.

Hic nautæ fessi rerum corpora recreant, et tot tantaque discrimina læti evasisse exultant. Verum post tanti gaudii epulas nox ruit, ac cælum, terras, maria una involuit. Itur dormitum. Tum sopor fessos omnium artus occupat.[24]

The description owes much to Vergil's depiction of the Libyan harbour near Carthage where Aeneas and his exhausted men took refuge from the stormy sea:

There in a deep inlet lies a spot, where an island forms a harbour with the barrier of its sides, on which every wave from the main is broken, then parts into receding ripples. On either side loom heavenward huge cliffs and twin peaks, beneath whose crest far and wide is the stillness of sheltered water ... Here no fetters imprison weary ships, no anchor holds them fast with hooked bite. Here, with seven ships mustered from all his fleet, Aeneas takes shelter; and disembarking with earnest longing for the land, the Trojans gain the welcome beach and stretch their brine-drenched limbs upon the shore.

insula portum efficit obiectu laterum, quibus omnis ab alto frangitur inque sinus scindit sese unda reductos. Hinc atque hinc vastae rupes geminique minantur in caelum scopuli, quorum sub vertice late aequora tuta silent ... hic fessas non vincula navis ulla tenent, unco non alligat ancora morsu. Huc septem Aeneas collectis navibus omni ex numero subit; ac magno telluris amore egressi optata potiuntur Troes harena, et sale tabentis artus in litore ponunt.[25]

Clearly, Drogo altered the passage from Vergil to fit to what must have been a real harbour. As John Blair argues in his contribution to this volume, there is a high probability that this harbour was located between Seaford and Newhaven head in Sussex.

Allusions to the *Aeneid* form part of a larger theme in the *Historia* in which the hagiographer drew a parallel between Lewinna and Aeneas as heroes destined to find new homelands. The *anagnoresis* occurs on the voyage back to Flanders:

a little while later, sleep from heaven entered all, except this one alone who held the rudder, who ruled the ship. The ship was sailed with great good fortune in the night, so sweetly and so smoothly did the wind fill the curve of the sails that the ship did not even rock – neither this way, nor that; nor, as often happens, did it fall on its side against the water. And thus, it happened, o blessed Virgin, that you held the rudder, you ruled the ship, you managed the cables, you were there filling all offices of the ship. You filled the offices of the sailors, so that those placed in sleep rested quietly. The right course through the sea was well-known to you, equally [well-known] to you was the port of our homeland.

Verum post paululum cælitus somnus omnes invadit, præter hunc solum qui clavum tenebat, qui puppim regebat. Tum autem cum tanta pros-peritate ea in nocte navigatur, tam dulcis tamque suavis aura velorum implet sinus, ut nequidem navis nutaret, non hac non illac uti fit in latus versus aquam caderet. Sic sic eat o beata virgo, tu clavum teneas, tu navim regas, tu amminis-tres rudentes, tu omnibus carinæ officiis assis [adsis] præsens. Fungere vice nautarum, ut illi positi quiescant somno. Tibi optime notus habetur rectus per æquor cursus, tibi æque nostræ patriæ portus.[26]

The passage is reminiscent of an episode in the *Aeneid* in which Aeneas' ship is peacefully sailing along at night under the guidance of the helmsman, Palinurus, the only member of the crew who is not asleep. The god Somnus then causes Palinurus to fall asleep and pitch over the side to his death. Waking up, Aeneas discovers the empty helm and pilots the ship alone the rest of the night.[27] Although it is not clear if the pilot of Lewinna's ship remained awake – Drogo reported that the next morning he chided his crewmates for sleeping while he sailed the ship carelessly – the parallel between Aeneas and Lewinna anticipated by the Vergilian language of Drogo's text is clear. More importantly, the hagi-ographer again seems to have adapted the *Aeneid* to what happened.

The scene in which the saint pilots the ship also stands out because elsewhere in the *Historia,* ships are often at the mercy of the wind and waves. Notably, on the voyage to England, Balger's ship at first enjoyed the aid of a southeasterly wind, but near Dover, 'the North Wind controlled the sails and the waves' (*Aquilo vela undasque sibi vendicavit*) and held the ship in its grasp for three days.[27] During this time, the wind 'battered the ship and its rigging from the side. Therefore, seeing that their labor [to enter a port] was in vain [the crew] retreated. They did not know what they should do, except that they should hold the course that the wind and the waves determined' (*ex latere navim et armamenta navis inpetebat. Frustra igitur suscepto labore deficiunt. Nesciebant quid agerent, nisi si quo ventus et undæ vocabant iter tenerent*).[29]The hagiographer used this opportunity to point out the working of divine provi-dence in the *furtum*. He wrote that in the midst of the storm, Balger urged the ship's crew to pray for God's help. According to the account, 'the words were

scarcely said, when – *mirabile dictu*! – with bulging sails they suddenly entered the port [*Sevordt*], which they were despairing of entering' (*Vix completa oratione; mirabile dictu plenis velis subito portum intrant, quem [cunctis]... diffidebant*).[30]

Drogo's intention to show that God, not the crew, was in control of the ship is evident, but his descriptions of the two ships that carried the relics are also consistent with what is known about a type of medieval ship called a hulk. Although the hagiographer occasionally referred to the ships as 'keels' (*carinae*), this does not seem to have been a reference to the specific type of medieval ship called a keel. Authors, including Vergil, frequently used the word keel as a metonym for the entire ship. And, although Drogo reported that at one point, Balger found the first ship 'standing on the shore' (*in litore stantem*), it does not seem to have been a cog.[31] The flat bottoms of medieval cogs made them useful for sailing in shallow waters and beaching.[32] In the section of the text that describes how Balger was left behind in England, however, the hagiographer noted that the ship could not approach the shore to pick him up because 'the sea in that place was dangerous for deep-hulled vessels' (*Iniquum est eo in loco mare altis ratibus*). Many, if not most, of the ships in which the Flemish sailed back and forth to England were probably hulks, a type of 'reverse clinker' vessel in use throughout the Low Countries and northeastern France.[33] Hulks had rounded hulls and lacked both stem posts and keels with perpen-dicular extensions below the hull.[34] These features helped to reduce both listing (leaning on one side against the water) and leeway (motion lateral to the intended course). Their absence would explain the power the winds had over the ships mentioned in the *Historia*, as well as why it would be notable that the second ship carrying the relics did not 'as often happens, fall on its side against the water.'

It is hard to escape the conclusion that Drogo intended to provide a hagiographic gloss for events that really occurred, or that he thought really occurred. There is little evidence to suggest that he fabricated substantial or important sections of the account. Though we may be properly sceptical of the report of the *furtum sacrum* itself, the *Histo-ria's* description of the English cult and the Flemish activity along the coast seem to represent the state of both in the 11th century.

Notes

1   For a full analysis of the campaign, see Defries, D, 2008 The making of a minor Saint in Drogo of Saint-Winnoc's *Historia translationis sanctae Lewinnae*, *Early Medieval Europe* **16** (4), 423–44

2   Stephens, G, 1959 The burial-place of St Lewinna, *Medieval Stud*, **21**, 303–12; Povey, K, 1928 Saint Lewinna, the Sussex martyr, *The Sussex County Magazine*, **2**, 280–91

3 According to Drogo, 'this translation was accomplished indeed in the year of the Incarnation of our Lord 1058, in the third indiction, on the sixth Sunday, with King Henry [I (r. 1031–60)] holding the royal scepter of the kingdom of the Franks, with, moreover, the exalted count Baldwin [IV (r. 1030/35–67)] governing Flanders, and Drogo, the bishop of Thérouanne [1030–78], living, and indeed the venerable abbot, Rumold, governing the coenobium at Bergues' (*Acta siquidem est hec translatio anno incarnationis domini nostri millesimo quinquagesimo octavo, indictione, III, VI, feria, regente henrico rege sceptrum regni francorum, optimo autem comite Balduino gubernante flandriam, uiuente etiam Drogone episcopo Taruanense, amministrante uero Bergense cenobium Rumoldo uenerando abbate*) (*Historia translationis s. Lewinna* (hereafter *HT*), i.IV.39 (*Acta Sanctorum* (hereafter *AASS*), July V (rpr. http://acta.chadwyck.com/), p 620).

4 Bergues, Bibliothèque municipale, ms. 19, fols. 113v–161v (1150–1200); Saint-Omer, Bibliothèque municipale, 716, fols. 90r–99r (*c* 1200); Paris, Bibliothèque nationale de France, lat. 05296 B, fols. 239–262 (13th century). Mabillon, J, (ed) 1740 *Acta Sanctorum ordinis S. Benedicti*, VI, 2. Venice, 112–26; *Acta Sanctorum*, July V (rpr. http://acta.chadwyck.com/), 613–27; (excerpts) Holder-Egger, O (ed), *Monumenta Germaniae Historica, Scriptores in folio*, XV, 2 (rpr. http://www.dmgh.de/), 782–89. The *Acta Sanctorum* edition is the most easily accessible and complete edition

5 The hagiographer failed to explain, however, how Balger and his companion were able to converse with the old man, since, as would soon become clear, they apparently did not know English

6 Southern, R, 1953 *The making of the Middle Ages*. New Haven, 99–100, 105

7 'Here is the body of the excellent virgin Lewinna, who flourished adorned with many virtues under the king of the Angles called Eubert. Which [virgin] afterwards and during the time of the rule of that same king ended her life in martyrdom, during the lifetime of the archbishop Theodore. Whence after the passing of much time, after God revealed it, her body was raised from the earth by the bishop Edelmo, a great multitude of people being present, and thus with worthy honor was brought inside the minster' (*Hic corpus preclare virginis leuuinne que multis decorata virtutibus floruit sub rege anglorum Euberto nuncupato; que postmodum sub eiusdem regis tempore martirio vitam finivit, archypresule vivente nomine theodoro. Unde post multorum curricula temporum deo revelante corpus eius ab Edelmo antistite a terra est levatum magna populorum astante multitudine, sicque cum digno honore intra monasterium est collocatum*) (*HT*, i.III.38 (*AASS*, p 620))

8 In the introduction to the second edition of his book, Patrick Geary noted that many more than the over one hundred accounts that he had cited in his first edition probably took place (Geary, P, 1990 *Furta Sacra: thefts of relics in the central Middle Ages*, 2nd edn, Princeton, pxii)

9 Abou-el-Haj, B, 1994 *The medieval cult of saints: formations and transformations*. Cambridge, 10

10 *HT*, i.I.12 (*AASS*, p 615)

11 *HT*, i.I.13–14 (*AASS*, p 615)

12 *HT*, i.I.15 (*AASS*, p 615)

13 *HT*, i.I.15 (*AASS*, p 615); *HT*, i.I.16 (*AASS*, p 616)

14 Verhulst, A, & Declercq, G, 1989 Early medieval Ghent between two abbeys and the Counts' castle, 7th–11th centuries, in Decavele, J (ed), *Ghent: in defence of a rebellious city: history, art, culture*. Antwerp, 37–59, at 38

15 Landes, R, 1992 Between aristocracy and heresy: popular participation in the Limousin Peace of God, 994–1033, in T Head & R Landes (eds) *The Peace of God: social violence and religious response in France around the year 1000*. Ithaca, NY, 184–218, at 214–15

16 *HT*, i.I.11 (*AASS*, p 615)

17 Grierson, P, 1941 The relations between England and Flanders before the Norman Conquest, *Trans Royal Hist Soc*, 4th ser **23**, 71–112; Ortenberg, V, 1992 *The English Church and the continent in the tenth and eleventh centuries: cultural, spiritual, and artistic exchanges*. Oxford, 21–9

18 Grierson 1941, 101–02; Ortenberg 1992, 28–9

19 'For when he first raised her from the reliquary, the cover in which she was preserved was disrupted and certain smaller bones fell through a tear. Balger, seeing this happen, picked up the fallen [bones], and restored them to the other bones. Three times he replaced them, three times they fell so that it might be clearly indicated which relics of her body she wished to remain in that place, the place in which she ended her life with the palm of a martyr, where her body was committed to the earth' (*Nam cum primo eam tolleret a loculo; pallium ubi integerrimum habebatur disruptum est, perque scissuram quædam minora ossa cecidere. Cui casui hic ipse invidens; cadentia tollebat, et cæteris ossibus restituebat. Ter reposuit, ter cecidere, ut patenter indicaretur quid sui corporis reliquiarum videlicet ibidem vellet haberi, quo in loco martirii palma finivit vitam, ubi corpusculum terræ mandatum est*) (*HT*, i.II.20 (*AASS*, p 617)

20 *HT*, i.II.25 (*AASS*, p 617)

21 *HT*, i.II.26 (*AASS*, p 618)

22 Sharpe, R, 1991 Eadmer's letter to the monks of Glastonbury concerning St Dunstan's disputed remains, in L Adams & J Carley (ed) *The archaeology and history of Glastonbury Abbey*. Woodbridge: Boydell, 210

23 Van Houts, E (trans), 2006 The Flemish contribution to biographical writing in England in the eleventh century, in D Bates, J Crick, & S Hamilton *Writing medieval biography, 750–1250*. Woodbridge: Boydell, 117

24 *HT,* i.I.101 (*AASS,* p 615)
25 Vergil, *Aeneid,* i.159–73 (Fairclough, H R, (trans) & Goold, G P (ed), 1916, rpr 1998 *Virgil: Eclogues, Georgics, Aeneid 1–6,* Loeb Classical Library **63**. Cambridge, MA, 251–3
26 *HT,* i.III.31 (*AASS,* p 618)
27 Vergil, *Aeneid,* v.835–71 (Fairclough 1916, 501–05)
28 *HT,* i.I.8 (*AASS,* p 614)
29 *HT,* i.I.9 (*AASS,* p 614)
30 *HT,* i.I.10 (*AASS,* p 615)

31 *HT,* i.III.29 (*AASS,* p 618)
32 Unger, R, 1981 Warships and cargo ships in medieval Europe, *Technology and Culture* **22**, 240
33 Ships built in the 'reverse clinker' technique had hulls made by attaching each strake (run of planking) to the inside of the strake below, rather than the outside as was more usual. (Hutchinson, G, 1994 *Medieval ships and shipping.* London, 11)
34 Hutchinson 1994, 10–15

Appendix 2: An unrecognised piece of Anglo-Saxon sculpture from St Andrew's church

The following describes and discusses a hitherto unrecognised piece of Anglo-Saxon sculpture located inside St Andrew's church, Bishopstone (Fig A.2). It is set out according to the conventions established for the series *Corpus of Anglo-Saxon Stone Sculpture* (Cramp 1984, xiii). I would like to thank Dr Andrew Reynolds for bringing the significance of this piece to my attention and to Professor John Potter for assistance with the stone identification.

Grave-marker (Type Bii)

Present location: Now against the west wall of the tower; before 2006 located against the east wall of the porch.
Evidence for discovery: Significance first recognised by Andrew Reynolds in 2002.
H. 520mm, W. 290mm, D. 180mm
Stone Type: Yellow medium-grained (0.3mm quartz grains) glauconitic sandstone. This stone, identical to that appearing in the Anglo-Saxon quoins of the church, has two possible sources. The more local is the Reading Beds Formation (Woolwich Beds facies) at Castle Hill, Newhaven; the alternative is Folkestone Sands, Lower Greensand Group, Lower Cretaceous, the nearest outcrop of which is at Eastbourne, although the closest match for stone-type is at Sellinge, Kent.
Present condition: Intact with moderate to heavy weathering, most severe on the upper right side of the front face (A).
Description: The stone is rectangular with a semicircular head.
A (broad): Decorated with a splayed-armed cross in relief (arm type B6). The arms run up to a grooved outer border.
E (top): Surface broken by an oval socket offset towards the left side with a maximum diameter of 40mm and a depth of 30mm.
Discussion: Grave markers with semicircular heads form an established type within the repertoire of Anglo-Saxon funerary sculpture from southern England having been recorded from a number of sites both north and south of the River Thames (Tweddle *et al* 1995, 22). Few examples carry datable ornament, one of the notable exceptions being the marker from Rochester (Kent) bearing Ringerike-style decoration assigned to the first half of the 11th century (Tweddle *et al* 1995, no. 3, 166–7, illus 147–150). Examples, like Bishopstone, bearing simple crosses carved in relief are generally believed to span the 11th century, and for this reason are grouped under 'Saxo-Norman overlap' sculpture. Bishopstone's closest parallels stylistically and geographically are from Stedham (West Sussex) (Tweddle *et al* 1995, 196–7, nos 7, 10, and 11, illus 243–4, 246, 248).

Fig A.2   Anglo-Saxon grave-marker, faces A and E

Appendix 3: Catalogue of human remains
by Louise C D Schoss and Mary Lewis

This section gives the detailed reports on all the human remains excavated. The literature used for the analysis is given in the main text, Chapter 5. 4.

S86

Sex: Female
Age: 36–45 years
Stature: 157.8cm (femur)

Preservation
This skeleton was in good condition and relatively complete.

Dental pathology
There was one large cavity on the distal surface of the lower right first molar. The lower right second molar was lost ante-mortem.

Skeletal pathology
Degenerative joint disease was present in the tarsals and phalanges of the left foot, and also in the phalanges of both hands. There was also some arthritis in the lumbar, thoracic, and cervical vertebrae. The osteoarthritis of the spine was also visible on the tubercles of the ribs. The left and right ulnae also showed arthritis in the elbow joint.

S87

Sex: Female
Age: 26–35 years
Stature: 160cm (femur)

Preservation
Mostly complete, but fragmentary.

Dental pathology
None. Mandibular dentition only.

Skeletal pathology
The superior surfaces of the lumbar vertebrae 2 and 3 displayed Schmorl's nodes

S1102

Sex: Female
Age: 26–35 years
Stature: 155.5cm (tibia)

Preservation
These remains were fairly complete, though most bones were damaged. The skull was damaged, but fragments of the right parietal, temporal and zygomatic were recovered as were the right halves of the maxilla and mandible.

Dental pathology
The teeth with the most wear were the upper and lower right first molars. Many of the teeth had calculus build-up. In the mandible calculus was visible on the second premolar and all three molars. In the maxilla the second premolar and the first two molars were affected. The lower right third molar also displayed a small cavity.

Skeletal pathology
This woman had a healed Smith's fracture on the right distal radius and suffered from osteoarthritis in her right wrist and elbow. The complete vertebral column showed signs of osteoarthritis and compression of the thoracic vertebrae and L4 and L5. There was no evidence for osteoporosis and so the lesions may be the result of traumatic injury.

S1103

Sex: Male
Age: Adult
Stature: 173.3cm (humerus)

Preservation
This specimen was fragmentary with eroded cortical bone. The long bones were all present but damaged, with exception of the right humerus, which was complete. The vertebral column was missing. More bones were recovered from the grave cut which included the axis and atlas, the left clavicle and scapula, some teeth, and some carpals and tarsals. There were also some remains of a child, including some fragments from the femur and tibia and some epiphyses. But it seems unlikely that this was a double burial. The child remains are more likely to be re-deposited bone fragments.

Dental pathology
No dentition.

Skeletal pathology
The tibiae and fibulae showed profuse bilateral infection (periostitis) that was in the process of healing.

S1104

Sex: Male
Age: Adult
Stature: Not possible

Preservation
This specimen was very fragmentary and weathered.

Dental pathology
No dentition.

Skeletal pathology
This individual had a healed fracture in the right femur, with soft tissue ossification, and a possible fracture and joint disease to the right distal phalanx of the first metatarsal. The femur shows little sign of deformity, which may suggest treatment.

S1105

Sex: Male

Age: 46+ years
Stature: 173.5cm (femur)

Preservation
The remains, the uppermost of a stacked double burial (with S1171), were well preserved.

Dental pathology
Both upper second molars were worn. The teeth showed some dental calculus but no caries.

Skeletal pathology
This individual had a healed oblique fracture of the left fifth metacarpal (little finger), and severe osteoarthritis. The left femoral head and acetabulum had large amounts of bone remodeling, eburnation, and osteophytic lipping. The right acetabulum showed some slight bone remodeling but it was much less severe than the arthritis on the left side. The left patella also showed arthritic lipping on the lateral auricular surface. On the right side the patella, the proximal end of both tibia, and fibula and the distal end of the femur all showed bone remodelling and lipping due to osteoarthritis. Both hands also had osteoarthritis in the carpals, metacarpals, and phalanges. Also the ankle of the right foot showed arthritis in the metatarsals. In the vertebrae osteoarthritis was present throughout the complete column. Osteophytes were also present especially in the lumbar vertebrae.

S1106

Sex: Female
Age: 26–35 years
Stature: 165.7cm (femur)

Preservation
Poor preservation with fragmentary bones. No cranium or foot bones were recovered.

Dental pathology
No dentition.

Skeletal pathology
This individual had a curved, linear defect on the left lower aspect of the sternum. It is most likely that this lesion represents a developmental defect during segment fusion in childhood. However, further research is needed to rule out trauma or post-mortem damage. There was osteoarthritis in both the lumbar and thoracic vertebrae which also showed some slight osteophytes. The right hand also showed signs of osteoarthritis in the carpals. A Schmorl's node was present in the superior surface of the second lumbar vertebra.

S1107

Sex: Male
Age: Adult
Stature: Not possible

Preservation
The remains of this individual were very fragmentary, consisting of one leg, a calcaneus, and fragments of the ilium. Bones listed as 1107B appeared to be mixed and are discussed with the unstratified remains.

Dental pathology
Dentition not present.

Skeletal pathology
No pathology was visible on the bones present.

S1108

Sex: Female
Age: 26–35 years
Stature: 155cm (femur)

Preservation
The skeleton, the uppermost of a stacked double burial (with S1146), was fragmentary and incomplete with most of the upper body missing.

Dental pathology
Dentition not present.

Skeletal pathology
Despite poor preservation leading to the loss of most of the cortical bone, periostitis was evident on the distal aspect of the right tibia, and possibly the left tibia. Both lesions were healed. Degenerative joint disease was present in lumbar vertebrae.

S1109

Sex: Male
Age: Adult
Stature: Not possible

Preservation

Although most elements were present they were very fragmentary. Mandible present.

Dental pathology
None

Skeletal pathology
Fusion of the sternum and manubrium suggest an elderly male. There was some osteophytosis on the first lumbar vertebra, and the left patella also showed some lipping caused by osteoarthritis on the lateral auricular facet. There was also bilateral sacralisation of L5.

S1145

Sex: Non-adult
Age: 1.5 years (dental development)
Stature: Non-adult

Preservation
Skeleton of a non-adult. Cranium, mandible, and long bones present.

Dental pathology
None.

Skeletal pathology
None.

S1146

Sex: Male
Age: 26–35 years
Stature: 166cm (femur)

Preservation
This skeleton, the lowermost of a stacked double burial (with S1108), was in good condition. The skull could be partially reconstructed.

Dental pathology
Apart from the bottom left medial incisor which was lost post-mortem, all teeth were present and in good condition except for the upper left second premolar which had caries on the distal surface which also affected the mesial surface of the first molar. This individual also had a congenital absence of the upper third molars, and had a supernumerary pre-molar in the maxilla. There was also calculus build up on the lingual surface of the lower incisors, canines, pre-molars, and first molar. More calculus was visible on the labial surface of the upper left incisors and canine.

Skeletal pathology
This individual had a completely healed oblique fracture in the right distal femur. Reactive cortical bone on the distal aspect of the femur, above the lesion, and a possible abscess at the site of fracture suggest this was an open fracture, which had resulted in an on-going infection (osteomyelitis). Aside from bowing associated with the infection, there was no evidence of deformity, suggesting that the fracture was confined to the left corner of the knee (medial condyle). There was no sign of trauma or infection on the corresponding tibia.

S1171

Sex: Female
Age: Adult
Stature: Not possible

Preservation
This specimen, the lowermost of a stacked double burial (with S1105), was incomplete and fragmented. Only two cranial fragments were recovered, the left temporal and the right zygomatic.

Dental pathology
Dentition not present.

Skeletal pathology
There was a compression fracture and ankylosis involving two upper thoracic vertebrae, but there was no sign of osteoporosis as the underlying cause. Most of the joints had evidence of osteophytosis, and this was especially severe in the shoulders.

S1211

Sex: not possible
Age: 36–45 years
Stature: not possible

Preservation
The remains of this individual were very fragmentary and incomplete. There were some skull fragments from the parietals, the frontal and occipital bones, and the left half of the mandible.

Dental pathology
Only three maxillary teeth were present (medial incisor, canine and first premolar): none of the teeth showed signs of caries or calculus. The mandible was edentulous and completely healed indicating tooth loss some time before death.

Skeletal pathology
There was some osteophyte formation in the proximal phalanx of the thumb.

S1294

Sex: Female
Age: Adult
Stature: Not possible

Preservation
These remains were recovered from a double burial with 1317. The remains were generally in a poor state of preservation, but most of the skeletal elements were represented. Only two small cranial fragments were recovered.

Dental pathology
No dentition present.

Skeletal pathology
Osteoarthritis with osteophytosis was present in the lumbar vertebrae. Schmorl's nodes were also visible on the superior and inferior surfaces of L5, L4, L2, L1, and T12. Additionally, T12 displayed wedging and bone remodelling on the superior surface. There were also signs of trauma to one of the toes, as one of the distal phalanges was compressed or 'stubbed'. There was severe osteoarthritis, with pitting and eburnation on the right femoral head.

S1317

Sex: Not possible
Age: Adult
Stature: Not possible

Preservation
These remains were from a double burial with individual 1294. The remains were in very poor condition and incomplete.

Dental pathology
No dentition present.

Skeletal pathology
There was some lipping on the anterior surface of the right patella indicating degenerative joint disease.

S1344

Age: 36–37 weeks (perinate)
These remains were recovered from the infilled cellar of Structure W, and comprised a right humerus (49.8mm), a left and right femur (66.5mm and right 65.9mm respectively), suggesting a near full-term perinate.

S1364 A and B

Age: 22–24 weeks (perinates)
These are the remains of two foetuses which were found in the fill of a domestic pit. The bones that were recovered were in very good condition and only two of the bones were damaged. The skeletons consisted of: three humeri, two right and one left; one right ulna and a right scapula; two femora, also a left and a right; and two tibiae, also one of each side. Because of the three humeri and the size difference of the two tibiae and because they were buried together, it was concluded that these remains are those of

twins. Measurements of the bones gave a pre-natal age of 22–24 weeks.

S2004

Sex: Male
Age: 17–25 years
Stature: Not possible

Preservation
This individual is from a double burial with 2019. The remains were fragmentary and consisted mainly of the leg bones and pelvis. The skull comprised a few fragments from the parietal bones, the right temporal, the occipital, and the mandible.

Dental pathology
None.

Skeletal pathology
This adolescent had bilateral osteomyelitis of both tibiae, resulting in severely hypertrophic (enlarged) bones. The whole of the left shaft was enlarged, but the right tibial lesions were mostly confined to the proximal end. The rest of the skeleton was too poorly preserved to track the extent of skeletal involvement, or determine an exact cause of the infection. However, that this infection was of longstanding duration was demonstrated by the distinct channel below the abscess (cloaca) on the anterior aspect of the right tibia, formed by the flow of pus down the bone.

S2019

Sex: Female
Age: 26–35 years
Stature: 157cm (femur)

Preservation
This skeleton was from a double burial with 2004. The skeleton was mostly complete.

Dental pathology
There was severe calculus present on the lingual surface of the lower right second and third molar and lower left canine. There was also calculus on the labial surface of the lower right medial incisor and lower left canine. The upper right second molar displayed a large caries on the distal-lingual surface.

Skeletal pathology
There was some osteoarthritis on the articulation facets of the ribs and in the lumbar vertebrae, which had also developed osteophytosis. The inferior and superior surfaces of L2 and L3 displayed Schmorl's nodes. The right first rib appeared to be atrophied, the cause of this could not be determined as there was no sign of trauma.

S2153

Sex: Non-adult
Age: 9-11 years (dental eruption)
Stature: Non-adult

Preservation
The remains of this child were near complete and in good condition. The skull consisted of the vault which was damaged but could be reconstructed. The mandible was complete.

Dental pathology
None.

Skeletal pathology
None.

S2173 A, B, C, and D

Preservation
These remains were co-mingled and fragmented. It soon became clear that these were mixed remains of adults and children. Because of differences in size among both the mature and immature remains it was concluded that these fragmented remains represent a minimum of four individuals.

S2173 A & D
These are the remains of the two adults, of which one was possibly female and one probably a male. A lumbar vertebra had osteoarthritis with osteophytosis which may indicate that one of the two adults was slightly older. It seems likely that one was a male as one left navicular was larger than the other smaller right navicular. The right proximal ulna present was also large and robust also indicating male sex. The other bones were smaller, but whether they belonged to a female or a less robust male cannot be determined.

S2173 B & C
These were the remains of two children. The younger and most complete was aged 6–8 years old. The older of the two was probably aged between 10–13 years. These age estimates are mainly based on the diaphyseal length of the long bones.

S2232

Sex: Non-adult
Age: 5–6 years (femoral diaphyseal length)
Stature: Non-adult

Preservation
These were the poorly preserved remains of a young child.

Dental pathology
None.

Skeletal pathology
None.

S2233

Sex: Non-adult
Age: 1 year (dental development)
Stature: Non-adult

Preservation
These were the skeletal remains of an infant. The remains consisted mainly of fragments, however the right femur, fragments of the right maxilla and the right half of the mandible were preserved.

Dental pathology
None.

Skeletal pathology
None.

S2556

Sex: Male
Age: 16–17 years
Stature: 177cm (femur)

Preservation
This skeleton was in an excellent state of preservation.

Dental pathology
The teeth were overall in good condition with no cavities and little wear. There was some crowding of the incisors in the mandible.

Skeletal pathology
This individual had a supracondylar process (non-metric trait) on the right humerus and a cortical defect on the distal right femur.

S2559

Sex: Female
Age: 36–45 years
Stature: 162cm (femur)

Preservation
This individual was in a double burial with S2924, some of the hand and feet bones may have therefore been mixed up between the two individuals. This skeleton was fairly complete.

Dental pathology
The teeth of this individual were very worn. There was one case of caries, where a cavity had formed on the occlusal-lingual surface of the lower, right second molar. This tooth also displayed a small abscess at its root.

Skeletal pathology
This woman suffered from osteoarthritis in the lumbar, thoracic, and cervical vertebrae.

There was also arthritis present on the articulation facets of the ribs, in the metacarpals, and some lipping was present on the left patella. There was also some bone growth on the dens of the axis and also on the atlas where the bone was lipping over the dens of the atlas.

S2562

Sex: Female
Age: 36–45 years
Stature: 167cm (ulna)

Preservation
This skeleton was in a poor condition but fairly complete. The right side of the mandible was the only part of the skull recovered.

Dental pathology
Four teeth had been lost ante-mortem (first and second right molars, second right premolar and the second left premolar). The right third molar was present, worn and had caries. The right canine and the left lateral incisor were present and worn.

Skeletal pathology
This woman suffered from osteoarthritis in her lower thoracic and lumbar vertebrae with osteoarthritis of her left hip.

S2565

Sex: Male
Age: 46+ years
Stature: 176cm (femur)

Preservation
The remains of this individual were in good condition. The skull was missing most of the face, and the calvarium was reconstructed.

Dental pathology
There was ante-mortem tooth loss of all four incisors, the left second premolar, the right canine, the right first and second premolar, and the right first molar.

Skeletal pathology
Arthritis was present in the left and right elbow, both patellae, the articular facets of the ribs, in both shoulders on the humeral heads, and in both wrists on the ulna, radius, carpals, and metacarpals. There was also arthritis in the vertebrae, which lead to severe osteophytosis and fusion of T9 to T10, and T12 to L1. The cervical vertebrae showed few signs of arthritis although there was some lipping on the dens of C2.

S2573A

Sex: Female
Age: 17–25 years
Stature: Not possible

Preservation
These remains were damaged by an intercutting feature (Structure T) which extended though the middle of this burial. There were also two foetal bones present – a right radius and a damaged tibia.

Dental pathology
There was calculus on the lingual surfaces of the lower left and lower right first molars and enamel hypoplasias on the lower right second pre-molar.

Skeletal pathology
None.

The foetal bones (SK2573 B)
The measurement of the slightly damaged radius was 26.5mm. This ages the foetus at 23 weeks (Scheuer and Black 2000)

S2645

Age: 36 weeks (perinate)
These foetal remains were represented by the distal half of a humerus and the proximal half of a femur. The width of the distal humerus (14.46mm) gave an age of 36 weeks. This foetus appears to be another near full-term.

S2686

Sex: Female
Age: 26–35 years
Stature: 162cm (femur)

Preservation
This skeleton was in very good condition and nearly complete. The skull was damaged but it was possible to

reconstruct the vault; the face, however, was completely missing. The mandible was complete and a few fragments of the maxilla were also present.

Dental pathology
There was some slight dental crowding of the mandibular incisors. There was also caries in the upper left second premolar.

Skeletal pathology
None.

S2693

Sex: Non-adult
Age: 10–12 years (dental eruption)
Stature: Non-adult.

Preservation
These were the skeletal remains of a child and were in good condition. The skull was almost complete.

Dental pathology
This individual had a diastema (gap between the maxillary central incisors) that would have been noticeable in life.

Skeletal pathology
None.

S2720

Sex: Male
Age: 26-35 years
Stature: 172.5cm (femur)

Preservation
This skeleton was in excellent condition.

Dental pathology
None.

Skeletal pathology
This man suffered an oblique fracture to the distal midshaft of his left tibia. The fracture was well healed with little sign of any deformity. It is possible that the man had sought treatment and that the fracture had been reduced.

S2790

Sex: Female
Age: 36–45 years
Stature: not possible

Preservation
These skeletal remains were fragmentary and in poor condition. The right half of the mandible was recovered.

Dental pathology
Dental calculus was present on the lower right medial incisor and on the labial surface of the lower right canine. The lower right first and second molars had severe dental calculus on the lingual surface. There was caries and an abscess on the lower right first and second molars.

Skeletal pathology
There was some degenerative change on the right transverse processes of the eighth and tenth thoracic vertebrae.

S2791

Sex: Male?
Age: Adult
Stature: Not possible

Preservation
These remains, the uppermost of a stacked double burial (with S2869), were very fragmentary and incomplete. No skull fragments were recovered for this individual.

Dental pathology
Dentition not present.

Skeletal pathology
None.

S2792

Sex: Female
Age: 36–45 years
Stature: 162cm (humerus)

Preservation
This skeleton was well preserved retaining most of the skull and a fairly complete post cranium.

Dental pathology
The teeth of this individual were very worn especially in the maxilla. There was also large caries on the occlusal surface of the upper left second and third molars, causing an abscess.

Skeletal pathology
This individual had a very large occipital bun.

S2869

Sex: Male
Age: Adult
Stature: 174cm (femur)

Preservation
This individual, the lowermost of a stacked double burial (with S2791), was generally in good condition and mostly complete. The skull only consisted of fragments of the occipital, the left parietal, and the left half of the mandible.

Dental pathology
Dentition not present.

Skeletal pathology
Schmorl's nodes were present on the superior surface of T11 and on the inferior surface of T7.

S2924

Sex: Adolescent female
Age: 16 years (epiphyseal fusion)
Stature: Non-adult

Preservation
This teenage individual was in a double burial with S2559 and was in a fairly good state of preservation. However, no skull fragments were recovered for this individual.

Dental pathology
Dentition not present.

Skeletal pathology
None.

S3069

Age: 39–40 weeks
The remains of this foetus consisted only of the proximal end of a femur. Because there was no measurement for estimating age from the proximal femur, it was compared to other foetal remains to give a rough estimate of age. The proximal width of the 3069 femur was 15.59mm and the 1344C proximal femur 14.6mm. This would indicate that the 3069 foetus was older than the others and probably full-term.

S3122

Sex: Male
Age: 36–45 years
Stature: 162cm (femur)

Preservation
These remains came from a grave that was not fully excavated, but preservation was good enough to allow most of the assessments to be carried out.

Dental pathology
Only the right maxilla survived from the canine onwards. The first molar had been lost ante-mortem.

Skeletal pathology
None.

Appendix 4: Petrological analysis of Anglo-Saxon pottery *by Ben Jervis*

Local geology

There are several clay sources in the vicinity of Bishop-tone. All would be easily accessible by land or water. The nearest source is the clay-with-flints deposit on top of the Downs. This a head deposit, containing mixed material. Large, often weathered, nodules of flint are character-istic inclusions in this clay (Gallois 1965, 59). At Castle Hill, Newhaven, there is an outcrop of Eocene London Clay superimposed on a formation of Woolwich Beds. The former is a fine, sandy clay which contains large pieces of flint as well as limestone in small quantities (Gallois 1965, 48). This source is visible when one stands on Rookery Hill which overlooks the site at Bishopstone. The South Downs are bounded to the north by Gault Clay. This contains inclusions of shales, mudstones, sandstones, limestones, and ironstones. Outcrops of this iron rich clay are rare (Gallois 1965, 29).

Finally there is the Lower Greensand. The deposits closest to Bishopstone and therefore those most likely to have been utilised are the Sandgate and Folkestone beds. These run in a band along the northern edge of the South Downs, between the Gault and Weald clays. The Sandgate beds contain sandstone and shales, but in the area around Bishopstone (ie those deposits between Washington in West Sussex and Eastbourne) are char-acterised by glauconitic silts. These deposits are rarely exposed, but become increasingly accessible towards Eastbourne, due to the overlying deposits becoming thinner. The Folkestone beds are the uppermost clays in the stratigraphic sequence and consist of fine-medium grade sands with bands of glauconitic and calcareous sandstone, composed of layers of several clays, generally containing inclusions of glauconitic sandstone and flint with occasional outcrops which are richer in limestone. The upper strata in the area around Bishopstone (the deposits between Washington and Eastbourne) are char-acterised by the presence of limestone and glaucontic silts (Gallois 1965, 38).

Results

Study of hand specimens allowed the fabrics to be divided into four groups; flint tempered wares, sandy wares, chalk or limestone tempered wares and an iron rich fabric.

Flint tempered wares

Fabric 1

In thin section three main inclusions are present; quartz, flint, and iron rich pellets. These inclusions are set into a sparse groundmass of silt-sized quartz grains. The larger pieces of quartz are present in approximately 40% abundance and are moderately sorted. There is a mixture of sub-rounded and angular pieces. The flint fragments are generally angular or sub-angular and are well sorted; they are present in approximately 15% abundance. The iron rich inclusions are large and are present in approxi-mately 5% abundance.

From the clay matrix and the inclusions it might be appropriate to cautiously suggest that the clay source is the London Clay at Newhaven. This is on the basis of the matrix being particularly fine and iron only being present in very small quantities. It is also possible that the clay-with-flints was utilised in the making of this pottery. The angular flints could imply that they were added as temper by the potter.

Fabric 13

A similar fine matrix to Fabric 1 is present. Sub-rounded quartz is less abundant (only 5–10% but is moderately sorted. A higher amount of flint is present (approximately 20% abundance) and it is well sorted and angular sug-gesting at least some may have been added as temper by the potter. Limestone or chalk is also present in a small quantity (5%) and is mostly rounded and is moderately sorted suggesting that this is naturally occurring in the clay. The similarities in the inclusions and matrix could imply a similar source to Fabric 1.

Fabric 14

Inclusions in this fabric were sparse in the thin section making it difficult to define it texturally. There is a different matrix to Fabrics 1 and 13, made up of well-sorted quartz grains. Quartz, limestone, and flint are present in equal proportions (10–20%). The flint is varied between being sub-rounded and sub-angular and is mod-erately sorted, implying that unlike Fabric 13 it may not have been added as temper. The quartz is sub-rounded and is poorly sorted as is the limestone.

The well-sorted quartz matrix and the large inclusions could imply that the clay-with-flints was the clay source.

Fabric 26

The ground mass of this fabric appears coarser than in the local fabrics described above. The flint is angular and the smaller pieces are well sorted. There are however a number of larger pieces. The quartz content makes up only 5%, is sub-angular and is very well sorted. Large pieces of sub-angular limestone and chalk are present. Thin sec-tioning would certainly not be necessary to identify this fabric. This fabric is clearly not local but is difficult to source. The calcareous bands of Gault Clay are a possible source (see Gallois 1965, 36).

Fabric 40

The groundmass is noticeably different to the other flint tempered fabrics being highly micaceous in nature. One piece of limestone is present in the thin section, but the only other inclusion is poorly sorted sub-rounded and sub-angular flint. This is present in approximately 20% abundance. This fabric can be easily distinguished from the hand specimen. It is not possible to confidently source this fabric. The Upper Greensand outcrops do contain some mica (Gallois 1965, 38) so these are one potential source, however one would expect the presence of glau-conite in thin section and flint is not characteristic of this clay. It is possible it was added as temper. A further possibility is that the fabric may originate from a particu-larly micaceous outcrop of the clay-with-flints. This would account for the variability in the shape and sorting of the flint. The mixed nature of the clay-with-flints means that such a local variant may occur somewhere along the downland ridge.

Sandy fabrics

Fabric 2

The main inclusion is quartz. This is sub-rounded and well sorted. Microcline feldspar is present in a similar size but is sparse. Moderately sorted, sub-rounded limestone (chalk) is present in a 5% abundance. Sub-rounded, sub-angular flint is present (10%) and this is well sorted. It is possible this was added as temper. A small number of iron rich pellets are also present. The similarities in the inclusions and matrix could imply a similar source to Fabric 1.

Fabric 3

The clay matrix is similar to Fabrics 1 and 13. Quartz is present in approximately 30% abundance and approximately 33% of this is polycrystalline. The pieces are well sorted and range between being sub-rounded to sub-angular in shape. Limestone is present in approximately 10% abundance, it varies from being sub-rounded to well rounded in shape and is moderately sorted. Sub-angular flint is present in approximately 5% abundance, as with the limestone this is moderately sorted. It may have been added as temper by the potter. Muscovite mica is also present in a very small quantity. The similarities in the inclusions and matrix could imply a similar source to Fabric 1. The presence of mica makes an Upper Greensand source possible, but the presence of limestone counts against this.

Fabric 5

Has a similar groundmass to Fabric 1. The main mineral present is quartz. There is a mixture of sub-angular and sub-rounded pieces which are moderately sorted. They are present in approximately 20% abundance. The other inclusions are not visible in this particular thin section. The similarities in the inclusions and matrix could imply a similar source to Fabric 1.

Chalk tempered fabrics

Fabric 12

The flint is barely noticeable and the pieces small in size. The chalk inclusions are sub-angular and moderately sorted. It is present in 30% abundance. This fabric is clearly has a different source to the flint tempered and sandy wares. A source along the South Downs is the most logical suggestion. The marl associated with the Upper Chalk (Gallois 1965, 43) is perhaps the most likely source. This contains hard, nodular chalk with a small quantity of flint.

Iron rich fabric

Fabric 44

The fabric has a fine grained matrix with sparse inclusions. It is different to any of the other fabrics. Rounded to sub-rounded, moderately sorted quartz is present in an abundance of around 40%. Around a third of the quartz is polycrystalline. Sub-rounded limestone (chalk) of around 0.4mm across is present in an abundance of approximately 10%. The iron rich inclusions are rounded and well sorted, the vast majority of pieces are <0.1mm across, although there are a small number of larger pieces. This inclusion is present in an abundance of approximately 2–5%. The iron rich matrix could imply a source north of the Downs in the Weald or Gault deposits. The absence of glauconite counts against a Greensand source and makes a Weald or Gault source most likely. This is supported by the presence of limestone and the iron rich inclusions. The absence of shale makes a source further north in the Weald unlikely.

Implications

A range of clay sources are represented in the assemblage of Anglo-Saxon pottery from Bishopstone. At least two clay sources in the Bishopstone area seem to have been utilised to make the local flint tempered and sandy fabrics. In addition, it seems that pottery was brought in from the Weald in small amounts. This conclusion is based on the petrology of Fabric 44 and also on the presence of an iron rich black burnished ware which appears similar to a fabric from Sandtun (Kent) and Pevensey (East Sussex). Chalk and limestone tempered wares were imported from further afield, possibly from Chichester, however more localised production, utilising the calcareous Downland clays is likely to have occurred.

Elsewhere in Sussex, thin sectioning has only been carried out on material from two Anglo-Saxon sites – Rookery Hill and Botolphs (West Sussex). Partly on the basis of a lack of shell, it has been argued that the main source for the Rookery Hill pottery assemblage was either the Weald or Gault Clay (Bell 1977, 227). The high flint content of the Bishopstone village assemblage implies a different source of exploitation, either the Eocene deposits at Newhaven or more local exposures of clay-with-flints. This coincides with changes in pottery form including the development of more strongly everted rims, possibly after a hiatus in pottery manufacture at some point in the mid Saxon period (Lyne 2000, 25)

In conclusion, this analysis has identified that the commonest fabrics represented in the Bishopstone pottery assemblage were made of materials derived from the immediate hinterland of the Anglo-Saxon settlement; it has also helped to clarify the existence of a smaller percentage of non-local fabrics attesting to commercial links with other parts of Sussex. In order for stronger conclusions to be drawn more material needs to be examined from this area.

Appendix 5: Methodology and protocol for analysis of faunal remains and plant biota *by Kristopher Poole and Rachel Ballantyne*

Mammal and bird bone
by Kris Poole

The Bishopstone bone was identified using the reference collections of the University of Nottingham, University of Southampton, and the Bird Group of the Natural History Museum at Tring. Attempts were made to identify all bone fragments to element and species, with some exceptions. Mammal ribs, vertebrae, skull fragments, and long bone fragments not identifiable to species, were classed as large-, medium-, or small-sized mammal (except for atlas and axis vertebrae, and frontals, occipitals, maxillae, and horn cores, which were identified to species). Ribs were only counted when the head was present. Apart from the calcaneii and astragali, carpals and tarsals were not recorded. Similarly, for birds, all elements were identified, where possible, to species, apart from vertebrae and ribs, which were classed simply as 'bird'.

Morphological criteria of Boessneck (1969), Payne (1985), and Prummel and Frisch (1986) were utilised to attempt to distinguish between sheep (*Ovis*) and goat (*Capra*). Measurements of pig teeth were taken following Payne and Bull (1988, 31) to try and distinguish between domestic pig and wild boar. Red deer were distinguished from cattle using Prummel (1988), with red and fallow deer differentiated using Lister (1996). Hares and rabbits were separated through Callou's (1997) methods. Attempts to distinguish between chicken and pheasant were made using the pneumatised proximal foramen of the femur and the continuation of the medial calcaneal ridge on the tarso-metatarsus (Cohen and Serjeantson 1996, 63, 79). Geese lack suitable morphological criteria on which to differentiate between individual species, and there is also considerable size overlap between species (Barnes *et al* 2000, 91). Where bones were of a size obviously compatible with domestic goose, they were recorded as such, otherwise they were recorded as *Anser/Branta* sp.

All identified fragments were recorded as individual specimens, with the exception of fresh breaks, which were refitted where possible, and counted as one element. Partial or complete skeletons were recorded as one specimen, with details of the elements present, completeness, measurements etc noted. The most straightforward method of quantification applied was the Number of Identified Specimens (NISP), being merely a count of the identified fragments. In addition, the zoning systems set out by Serjeantson (1996) for mammals and Cohen and Serjeantson (1996) for birds were used to calculate the Minimum Number of Elements (MNE) and Minimum Number of Individuals (MNI) for each species.

Methods used for ageing specimens were dental eruption/attrition and epiphyseal fusion. Grant's methods (1982) were used for recording tooth wear in cattle, sheep and pig, with wear stages assigned using standards set out by Halstead (1985) for cattle, Grant (1982) for pigs, and Payne (1973; 1987) for sheep. Epiphyseal fusion data was calculated using the sequence outlined by Getty (1975) for sheep/goat, cattle, pigs and equids, by Silver (1969) for dogs, and by Smith (1969) for cats. As bird bones lack epiphyses, elements were recorded as either 'fused' or 'unfused.' Where possible, pigs were sexed on the basis of their canines (Schmid 1972, 80). Morphological and metrical traits of the pelvis were used to sex cattle and sheep/goat (Grigson 1982; Hatting 1995; Greenfield 2006). Cattle may be sexed using the metapodials, although other factors also play a part in the dimensions of these elements (eg Albarella 1997). Equids were sexed through the presence of canines and on the pelvis. Presence of the *baculum* was used to identify male dogs in the sample. Presence or absence of tarsometatarsi cockspurs and medullary bone in femora and tibiotarsi was used to differentiate between male and female chickens (Driver 1982).

Measurements were taken following von den Driesch (1976) for mammals and Cohen and Serjeantson (1996) for birds. Withers heights were calculated using the calculation factors given by von den Dreisch and Boessneck (1974). Butchery was recorded in detail, noting the butchery mark type (chop, cut, saw, shave) and its location on the bone. This was achieved using the standards set out by Lauwerier (1988), with additional butchery codes created when necessary. The following non-metric traits were also recorded: congenital absence of P2 and congenital absence of hypoconulid of M3 in cattle and sheep/goats, and location of sheep femoral nutrient foramina.

Plant biota
by Rachel Ballantyne

Introduction

During fieldwork, a total of 195 bulk samples (just over 4000 litres of sediment), were processed by students and volunteers using a Siraf-type flotation tank (Williams 1973). Flots were collected in 250μm sieves and heavy residues washed over 1mm mesh; both fractions were dried before sorting, and no special precautions were taken for the recovery of mineralised remains. Almost all the residues were sorted by students at Nottingham University, with later assessment by The Environmental Archaeology Consultancy (Sleaford, Lincs). The hiatus in processing has meant that it is unclear whether very small mineralised items may have been missed during the initial residue sorting.

The selection of samples for full analysis aimed to maximise the range of identified taxa and allow characterisation of variation both within and between features. Samples were chosen if the assessment (EAC 2008) showed they had abundant well-preserved cereal grain, any cereal chaff, or any mineralised macrofossils; if viewed in isolation, the 92 fully analysed samples thus exaggerate the incidence of cereal chaff and mineralised biota at the settlement. Multiple samples from the fill sequences of large pits were also selected, regardless of composition, to create a dataset capable of addressing intra-feature patterning. The final selection of samples from 39 pits and one wall-trench covered most of the excavation area. Considering the selection criteria and the many unselected samples from graves and wall-trenches, it is evident that pits contained the richest charred plant remains and all the mineralised biota.

All the flots and residue finds submitted to the author were sorted using a x6.3–x40 low-power binocular microscope (Leica MS5). Identifications were made using seed atlases (Anderberg 1994; Berggren 1981; Cappers *et al* 2006) and the reference collections of the Pitt-Rivers Laboratory, Department of Archaeology, University of Cambridge. Mineralised fly puparia were described following observations by Dr Henry Disney (University Museum of Zoology, Cambridge), whose time and advice is gratefully acknowledged. The nomenclature in this report follows the morphological classifications in Zohary and Hopf (2000) for cereals, and Stace (1997) for all other flora (see excavation archive for full tabulated raw data: the counts represent actual items and are not 'multiplied up' for the sub-sampled rich flots).

Items were recorded by 'Minimum Number of Individuals' such as whole seeds, fruits, and puparia – or qualitative estimates where fragmentation rendered quantification untenable. Throughout the text use of the term 'seed' includes items known botanically as achenes, nutlets, and caryopses. Calculations have involved standardisation of the raw data, for example the doubling of spikelet fork counts to give a total number of glume bases. The presence of two wheat types has added complexity to all grain-related analyses. When calculating grain:chaff ratios and the abundance of grain types, counts for ambiguous wheat grains have had to be subdivided in proportion to the pre-existing counts for hulled and free-threshing grains, and then added to those counts. The calculation assumes that both wheat types are equally identifiable when charred and, considering the frequent completely unidentified grains, the calculated values must be treated as approximations.

Preservation pathways

The presence of both charred and mineralised remains in many contexts immediately suggests mixed refuse as the two pathways are essentially independent: charred remains derive from redeposited ash (none of the sampled features are scorched), whereas mineralised remains formed *in situ* from dense organic accumulations, probably including cess.

Integrity of sampled contexts

Although rootlets were common, untransformed plant seeds were rare and only occurred in low numbers, so the assemblage has good integrity. There was no evidence for past waterlogging such as aquatic or semi-aquatic plants, associated microorganisms, or sporadic tough woody seeds (eg elder or brambles). The excavated area was well-drained as features were cut into the underlying chalk bedrock, and so the few untransformed wild seeds were probably modern: buttercups (*Ranunculus acris*/*bulbosus*/*repens*), sickle medick (cf. *Medicago falcata*), cut-leaved crane's bill (*Geranium dissectum*), smooth and prickly sow-thistles (*Sonchus oleraceus* and *S. asper*). These observations are important as, in addition to the wild seeds, there was an untransformed grape pip (*Vitis vinifera*) from pit [2091] and an olive stone (*Olea europaeus*) from pit [2506]. Neither seed showed any sign of mineralisation (the latter is faintly reddish-brown) and they were almost certainly intrusive.

Whilst recent intrusive material was rare, there was good evidence for extensive bioturbation both within and between contexts. Mineralised earthworm cocoons (Lumbricidae) and millipede segments were frequent and widespread. Both creatures could have lived within the pits, especially if filled with decaying plant matter. Piper and O'Connor (2001, 342) have noted that, within refuse pits at Anglo-Scandinavian York, large interstitial spaces could emerge with the decay of freshly deposited organic matter; facilitating the movement of smaller items in-between larger finds and inclusions. Pits with multiple samples at Bishopstone reveal, firstly, that individual bulk samples do not always capture well the heterogeneity of a context; sometimes duplicate samples from a context have quite different compositions. Secondly, richer fills may have 'shed' some small artefacts; contiguous fills sometimes have very similar inclusions, with one rich and the other sparse.

Pathways for charred macrofossils

The quality of charred macrofossils varied greatly across the assemblage. Most samples contained both well preserved items and others that were distorted, abraded, and/or heavily fragmented. It is possible to trace this variability by the proportion of cereal grains identified to genus or beyond in each sample. Survival of fragile charred structures, such as the heteropteran bugs in pits [2039] and [2041], suggests that some pit fill layers formed quite rapidly with only limited exposure to weathering or trampling. Cereal chaff was rare, only occurring in densities above 1 item per litre when grain was also in very good condition. Low density, poorly-preserved grain is likely to be tertiary in origin, and such contexts probably under-represent chaff due to the disproportionate effect that charring and physical processes have upon delicate structures (cf Boardman and Jones 1990).

Pathways for mineralised macrofossils

Yellowish-brown calcium phosphate macrofossils were present in 30 pits, in most cases as very low amounts of arthropod exoskeleton segments, individual seeds, grass/rush stem fragments or amorphous concretions with cereal bran inclusions. Overall fourteen pits had evidence for mineralised cess; defined here as seeds from more than one edible plant taxon in a single context. Identification of mineralised biota has met with variable success as the macrofossils were often irregularly preserved. The process of phosphatisation is affected by a wide range of variables, including the structure and composition of original tissues, their rate of decay, and geochemistry (Green 1979; McCobb *et al* 2001; 2003). Many seeds of corncockle (*Agrostemma githago*) and corn gromwell (*Lithospermum arvense*) survived only as kernels, and probably due to the impermeability of their outer layers (McCobb *et al* 2003; cf Carruthers 2005, 157).

Fly puparia have been identified to Family but no further, due to the irregular preservation of key anatomical features (Disney pers comm; cf Kenward and Girling 1986). Fills (2093) and (2094) of pit [2039] have the same type of puparia preserved by both charring and mineralisation; the juxtaposition, and lack of *in situ* charring, suggests that redeposited surface accumulations were also present. The same two contexts also have wild plum stones and apple/pear seeds preserved both by charring and mineralisation. Other pit fills did not, however, show such a clear overlap in preservation pathways.

Appendix 6: A check-list of Anglo-Saxon metal-detector finds from the parish of Bishopstone

No.	Object/Classification*	Description	Date	Findspot**	Reference	Finder
1	Strap-end; Thomas Class A, Type 1	Cu-alloy with Trewhiddle-style zoomorphic decoration.	9th century	'Few hundred yards north of Bishopstone church'	Graham-Campbell 1989, fig 27	Lee Blackwell
2	Strap-end; Thomas Class A	Cu-alloy, tinned with four empty settings for silver or niello and four silver rivets.	9th century	'Few hundred yards north of Bishopstone church'	Graham-Campbell 1989, fig 27	Lee Blackwell
3	Strap-end; Thomas Class A, Type 4/5	Cu-alloy with a pair of empty longitudinal fields for missing enamel/niello inlays.	9th century	Norton/South Heighton parish boundary	Barbican House Museum, Lewes, 1991.8	Lee Blackwell
4	Strap-end: Thomas Class A, Type 3	Cu-alloy with interlace decoration on a niello ground.	9th century	Norton, South	Unpublished	Peter Sinclair
5	Strap-end; Thomas Class A, Type 1	Silver with Trewhiddle-style zoomorphic decoration on a niello ground.	9th century	Norton, East	Unpublished	Phil Satchell
6	Strap-end; Thomas Class A, Type 4	Cu-alloy with two longitudinal fields decorated with triangular inlays of enamel.	9th century	Norton, East	Unpublished	Phil Satchell
7	Strap-end; Thomas Class B, Type 1	Cu-alloy with incised outer border.	8th–11th century	Bishopstone/Norton boundary	Unpublished	Peter Sinclair
8	Strap-end; Thomas Class B, Type 1	Cu-alloy with incised outer border.	8th–11th century	Norton, South	Unpublished	Peter Sinclair
9	Mount	Gilt cu-alloy. Shield-shaped plate with two projecting attachment lugs and a recessed flange pierced by a pair of rivet holes. The front face bears chip-carved ornament in the form of a looped beast with piercing body elements.	Late 8th century	Bishopstone, West	Unpublished	Peter Sinclair
10	Bridle-fitting	Cu-alloy. Fragment with a central hollow-backed dome surrounded by four projecting arms, only one of which survives, with debased Ringerike-style decoration.	11th century	Bishopstone, West	Unpublished	Peter Sinclair
11	Bridle-fitting	Cu-alloy terminal fragment in the form of a loop with three projecting knops.	11th century	Bishopstone/Norton boundary	Unpublished	Peter Sinclair
Coins						
1		Carolingian dernier of Pepin the Short	AD 751–68	Bishopstone, West	EMC 2001.0900	Peter Sinclair
2		Penny of Offa of Merica, Blunt group 1 (Light Portrait Issue)	c AD 765–92	Norton, East	Unpublished	Peter Sinclair
3		Sceatta, Primary Series	Late 7th century	Bishopstone/Norton boundary	Unpublished	Peter Sinclair

*Strap-end classifications are taken from Thomas 2003 and Thomas 2000 ** Only general locations are given to protect the identity of the individual site foci

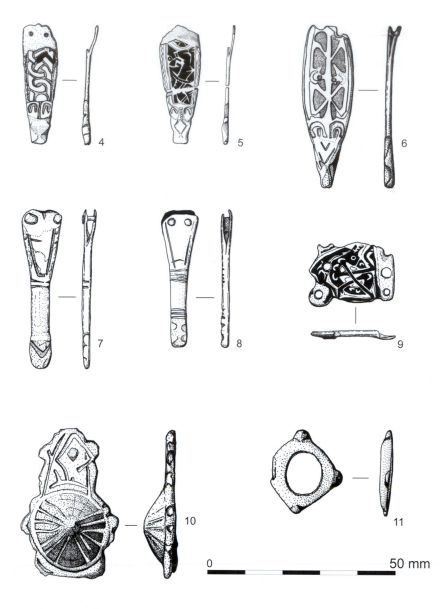

Fig A.6   Metal-detector finds, nos 4–11

Appendix 7: A later Bronze Age burial

During the course of the 2004 excavation season a flexed inhumation burial aligned on a north-south axis was discovered at the southern end of the trench in the narrow gap between Structural complex O and Structure D (Fig A.7). Located some 2m beyond the northernmost limits of the Anglo-Saxon cemetery, this find generated much speculation as a potential deviant burial, perhaps that of an executed felon or some other social outcast excluded from consecrated ground. Speculation along these lines was cut short by the receipt of a radiocarbon determination of cal BC 1260 to 1000 (Beta-198067) which places the burial firmly within the later Bronze Age.

It is impossible to know whether or not this was an isolated prehistoric burial given that it was remarkably fortunate to escape obliteration by Anglo-Saxon and later activity. A potentially related feature was a linear cut which extended from the grave's northern end to a doorway in the eastern wall of the eastern 'annexe' of Structural complex O; the grounds for establishing such an association rest solely on the linear's NNW-SSE alignment which deviated from the principal spatial axes of the Anglo-Saxon settlement. No dated prehistoric features were otherwise located on the excavation.

Fig A.7   A later Bronze Age burial (large scale = 1m)

Bibliography

Abou-el-Haj, B, 1994 *The medieval cult of saints: formations and transformations*. Cambridge: Cambridge University Press

Adams, K A, 1990 Monastery and village at Crayke, N Yorks, *Yorkshire Archaeol J*, **62**, 29–50

Adams, M, 1996 Excavation of a pre-conquest cemetery at Addingham, West Yorkshire, *Medieval Archaeol*, **40**, 151–91

Addyman, P V, 1973 Late Saxon settlements in the St Neots area, 3: the village or township at St Neots, *Proc Cambridge Antiq Soc*, **64**, 45–99

Addyman, P V, & Leigh, D, 1973 The Anglo-Saxon village at Charlton, Hampshire: a second interim report, *Medieval Archaeol*, **17**, 1–25

Albarella, U, 1997 Shape variation of cattle metapodials: age, sex or breed? Some examples from mediaeval and postmediaeval sites, *Anthropozoologica* **25–6**, 37–47

Albarella, U, 2006 Pig husbandry and pork consumption in medieval England, in C M Woolgar, D Serjeantson & T Waldron (eds) *Food in medieval England. Diet and nutrition*. Oxford: Oxford University Press, 72–87

Albarella, U, & Serjeantson, D, 2002 A passion for pork: meat consumption at the British late Neolithic site of Durrington Walls, in P Miracle & N Milner (eds) *Consuming passions and patterns of consumption*. Cambridge: MacDonald Archaeological Institute, 33–50

Albarella, U, & Thomas, R, 2002 They dined on crane: bird consumption, wild fowling and status in medieval England, in *Proceedings of the 4th Meeting of the ICAZ Bird Working Group Kraków, Poland, 11–15 September, 2001. Acta Zoologica Cracoviensa* **45** (special issue), 23–38

Allan, J, 1984 *Medieval and post medieval finds from Exeter*. Exeter: Exeter University Press

Ambrose, S H, 1993 Isotope analysis of palaeodiets: methodological and interpretative considerations, in M K Sandford (ed) *Investigations of ancient human tissue: chemical analyses in anthropology*. Reading: Gordon & Breach Science Publishers, 59–129

Anderberg, A L, 1994 *Atlas of seeds and small fruits of northwest-European plant species. Part 4: Resedaceae–Umbelliferae*. Stockholm: Swedish Museum of Natural History

Andrén, A, 1998 *Between artefacts and texts*. New York: Springer

Andrews, P, (ed) 1997 *Excavations at Hamwic volume 2: excavations at Six Dials*, CBA Res Rep **109**. York: Council for British Archaeology

Andrews, M V, Gilbertson, D D, Kent, M, & Mellars, P A, 1985 Biometric studies of morphological variation in the intertidal gastropod *Nucella lapillus* (L): environmental and palaeoeconomic significance, *J Biogeography*, **12**, 71–87

Archaeology South-East, 2000 An archaeological evaluation of land associated with the Ouse Estuary Project, East Sussex (Stage 2). Unpublished project report 1221

Archibald, M, 1990 The coins, in J R Fairbrother, *Faccombe Netherton: excavations of a Saxon and medieval manorial complex*, Brit Mus Occ Pap **74**. London: British Museum, 436–46

Arneborg, J, Heinemeier, J, Lynnerup, N, Nielsen, H L, Rud, N, & Sveinbjörnsdóttir, Á E, 1999 Change of diet of the Greenland Vikings determined from stable carbon isotope analysis and ^{14}C dating of their bones, *Radiocarbon*, **41**, 157–68

Arnold, C J, & Wardle, P, 1981 Early medieval settlement patterns in England, *Medieval Archaeol*, **25**, 145–9

Ashby, S P, 2006 Time, trade and identity: bone and antler combs in northern Britain *c* AD 700–1400, Unpubl PhD thesis, University of York

Ashby, S P, 2002 The role of zooarchaeology in the interpretation of socioeconomic status: a discussion with reference to medieval Europe, *Archaeol Rev Cambridge* **18**, 37–59

Ashby, S P, 2007 Bone and antler combs, *Finds Research Group AD 700–1700 Datasheet* **40**

Astill, G, 2000 General survey 600–1300, in D Palliser (ed) *The Cambridge urban history of Britain volume 1, 600–1540*. Cambridge: Cambridge University Press, 27–50

Astill, G, 2009 Anglo-Saxon attitudes: how should post-AD 700 burials be interpreted?, in D Sayer & H Williams (eds) *Mortuary practices and social identities in the Middle Ages. Essays in burial archaeology in honour of Heinrich Härke*. Exeter: Exeter University Press, 220–33

Astill, G, & Lobb, S, 1989 Excavation of prehistoric, Roman and Saxon deposits at Wraysbury, Berkshire, *Archaeol J*, **146**, 63–134

Audouy, M, Dix, B, & Parsons, D, 1995 The tower of All Saints' church, Earls Barton, Northamptonshire: its construction and context, *Archaeol J*, **152**, 73–94

Audouy, M, & Chapman, A, 2009 *Raunds: the origins and growth of a Midland village AD 450–1500*. Oxford: Oxbow Books

Austin, D, & Thomas, J, 1990 The 'proper study' of medieval archaeology: a case study, in D Austin & L Alcock (eds) *From the Baltic to the Black Sea: studies in medieval archaeology*. London: Unwin Hyman

Ayres, K, Locker, A & Serjeantson, D, 2003 Phases 2f–4a the medieval abbey: food consumption and production, in A Hardy, A Dodd & G Keevil (eds) *Aelfric's Abbey: excavations at Eynsham Abbey, Oxfordshire 1989–92*. Oxford: Oxford University School of Archaeology, 360–406

Bailey, G N, & Craighead, A S, 2003 Late Pleistocene and Holocene coastal palaeoeconomies: a reconsideration of the molluscan evidence from northern Spain, *Geoarchaeology*, **18**, 175–204

Ballantyne, R M, 2005 Plants and seeds, in R W Mortimer, R Regan & S Lucy (eds) *The Saxon and medieval settlement at West Fen Road, Ely: the Ashwell site*, E Anglian Archaeol Rep **110**. Cambridge: Cambridge Archaeological Unit, 100–12

Barber, L, forthcoming The geological material, in L Barber & G Priestley-Bell, *Medieval adaptation, settlement and economy of a coastal wetland: the evidence from around Lydd, Romney Marsh, Kent*. Oxford: Oxbow

Barber, L, in prep The geological material, in S Stevens *Excavations at the former Baxters printworks*. Lewes

Barclay, K, & Biddle, M, 1974 Winchester ware, in V Evison, H Hodges & J Hurst (eds) *Medieval pottery from excavations: studies presented to Gerald Clough Dunning, with a bibliography of his work*. London: John Baker, 137–66

Barnes, I, Young, J P W, & Dobney, K M, 2000. DNA-based identification of goose species from two archaeological sites in Lincolnshire, *J Archaeol Sci*, **27**, 91–100

Barrett, J H, 1997 Fish trade in Orkney and Caithness: a zooarchaeological approach, *Antiquity*, **71**, 616–38

Barrett, J H, Locker, A M, & Roberts, C M, 2004 'Dark Age economics' revisited: the English fish bone evidence AD 600–1600, *Antiquity*, **78**, 618–36

Barrow, J, 1999 Cathedral clergy, in M Lapidge, J Blair, S Keynes & D Scragg (eds) *The Blackwell encyclopaedia of Anglo-Saxon England*. Oxford: Blackwell, 84–7

Barton, K, 1979 *Medieval Sussex pottery*. Chichester: Philimore

Bartosiewicz, L, van Neer, W, & Lentacker, A, 1997 *Draught cattle: their osteological identification and history*. Tervuren: Royal Museum of Central Africa

Bass, W M, 1987 *Human osteology: a laboratory and field manual*. Columbia: Missouri Archaeological Society Inc

Bassett, S, 1988 *The Wootton Wawen Project: interim report 6*. Birmingham: School of History, University of Birmingham

Bates, M, 1998 Geology and geomorphology of the study area, in Archaeology South-East, *An archaeological assessment (Stage 1) of the proposed Newhaven harbour link road and associated developments, Newhaven, East Sussex*, 27–33

Baxter, S, 2004 Archbishop Wulfstan and the administration of God's property, in M Townend (ed) *Wulfstan, Archbishop of York: the proceedings of the second Alcuin conference*. Turnhout: Brepols, 176–91

Baxter, S, & Blair, J, 2005 Land tenure and royal patronage in the early English Kingdom: a model and a case study, *Anglo-Norman Studies*, **28**, 19–46

Bayliss, A, Shepherd Popescu, E, Beavan-Athfield, N, Bronk Ramsey, C, Cook, G T, & Locker, A, 2004 The potential significance of dietary offsets for the interpretation of radiocarbon dates: an archaeologically significant example from medieval Norwich, *J Archaeol Sci*, **431**, 563–75

Beavan Athfield, N, McFadgen, B D, & Sparks, R J, 2001 Environmental influences on dietary carbon and ^{14}C ages in modern rats and other species, *Radiocarbon*, **43**, 7–41

Bell, M, 1977 Excavations at Bishopstone, *Sussex Arch Collect* **115**

Bell, M, 1978 Saxon settlements and buildings, in P Brandon (ed) *The south Saxons*. Chichester: Phillimore, 36–53

Bell, M, 1983 Valley sediments as evidence of prehistoric land-use on the South Downs, *Proc Prehist Soc*, **49**, 119–50

Bell, M, 1989 Environmental archaeology as an index to continuity and change in the medieval landscape, in M Aston, D Austin & C Dyer (eds) *The rural settlements of medieval England*. Oxford: Basil Blackwell, 269–86

Bell, M, & Walker, M J C, 2005 *Late quaternary environmental change: physical and human perspectives*, 2nd edn. Harlow: Pearson

Beresford, G, 1987 *Goltho: the development of an early medieval manor c 850–1150*, Engl Heritage Archaeol Rep **4**. London: Historic Buildings & Monuments Commission for England

Beresford, G, 2007 The minster church of St Andrew, Bishopstone, and the probable onetime shrine of St Lewinna: a new interpretation following recent conservation. Unpubl report, Bishopstone Parochial Church Council, in East Sussex Record Office PAR 247/16/2/4

Berggren, G, 1981 *Atlas of seeds and small fruits of northwest-European plant species, with morphological descriptions. Part 3: Saliaceae – Cruciferae*. Stockholm: Swedish Museum of Natural History

Biddle, M, 1986 Archaeology, architecture and the cult of saints, in L A S Butler & R K Morris (eds) *The Anglo-Saxon church: papers on history, architecture, and archaeology in honour of Dr H M Taylor*, CBA Res Rep **60**. London: Council for British Archaeology, 1–31

Biddle, M (ed), 1990a *Object and economy in medieval Winchester*, Winchester Studies **7.2** (2 vols). Oxford: Clarendon Press

Biddle, M, 1990b Combs of horn and bone, in M Biddle (ed) 1990a, 678–90

Biddle, M, 1990c Knives used by scribes, in M Biddle (ed) 1990a, 738–41

Biddle, M, 1990d Unidentified bone objects, in M Biddle (ed) 1990a, 1129–45

Biddle, M, & Kjølbye-Biddle, B, 1992 Repton and the Vikings, *Antiquity*, **66**, 36–52

Biggam, C P, 2002 Grund to Hrof: aspects of the Old English semantics of building and architecture, *Architectural History*, **45**, 49–65

Blaauw, W H, 1848 On the translation of St Lewinna from Seaford, in 1058, *Sussex Archaeol Collect*, **1**, 46–54

Blackburn, M, 2003 'Productive' sites and the pattern of coin loss in England, 600–1180, in T Pestell & K Ulmschneider (eds) 2003 *Markets in early medieval Europe: trading and 'productive sites' 650–850*. Macclesfield: Windgather Press, 20–36

Blair, J, 1991 *Early medieval Surrey: landholding, church and settlement before 1300*. Stroud: Sutton

Blair, J, 1992 Anglo-Saxon minsters: a topographical review, in J Blair & R Sharpe (eds) *Pastoral care before the parish*. Leicester: Leicester University Press, 227–66

Blair, J, 1993 Hall and chamber: English domestic planning 1000–1250, in G Meirion-Jones & M Jones (eds) *Manorial domestic buildings in England and northern France*. London: Society of Antiquaries, 1–21

Blair, J, 1994 *Anglo-Saxon Oxfordshire*. Stroud: Sutton

Blair, J, 1997 Saint Cuthman, Steyning and Bosham, *Sussex Archaeol Collect*, **135**, 173–92

Blair, J, 2002 A saint for every minster? Local cults in Anglo-Saxon England, in A Thacker & R Sharpe (eds) *Local saints and local churches in the early medieval west*. Oxford: Oxford University Press, 455–94

Blair, J, 2005 *The church in Anglo-Saxon society*. Oxford: Oxford University Press

Blair, J, & Millard, A, 1992 An Anglo-Saxon landmark rediscovered, *Oxoniensia*, **57**, 342–8

Boardman, S, & Jones, G, 1990 Experiments on the effects of charring on cereal plant components, *J Archaeol Sci*, **17**, 1–11

Boddington, A, 1996 *Raunds Furnells: the Anglo-Saxon church and churchyard*. London: English Heritage

Boessneck, J, 1969 Osteological differences between sheep (*Ovis aries* Linne) and goat (*Capra hircus* Linne), in D Brothwell & S Higgs (eds) *Science in archaeology*. London: Thames & Hudson, 338–55

Booth, J, 1998 Monetary alliance or technical co-operation? The coinage of Berhtwulf of Mercia (840–852), in M A S Blackburn & D N Dumville (eds) *Kings, currency and alliances. History and coinage of Southern England in the ninth century*, Woodbridge: Boydell, 63–103

Bourdillon, J, 2009 Late Saxon animal bone from the northern and eastern suburbs and the city defences, in D Serjeantson & H Rees (eds) *Food, craft and status in Saxon and medieval Winchester: the evidence from the suburbs and city defences*. Archaeol Rep **10**. Winchester: Winchester Museums Service, 55–81

Bradley, R, 1998 *The passage of arms*, 2nd edn. Oxford: Oxbow Books

Bradley, R, 2005 *Ritual and domestic life in prehistoric Europe*. London: Routledge

Brainerd, G, 1951 The place of chronological ordering in archaeological analysis, *American Antiquity*, **16**(4), 301–12

Brandon, P A, 1971 The origins of Newhaven and the drainage of the Lewes and Laughton levels, *Sussex Arch Collect* **109**, 94–106

Brandon, P, 1974 *The Sussex landscape*. London: Hodder & Stoughton

Brandon, P, 1998 *The South Downs*. Chichester: Phillimore

Brandon, P, & Short, B, 1990 *The south east from AD 1000*, Regional History of England. London: Longman

Bronk Ramsey, C, 1995 Radiocarbon calibration and analysis of stratigraphy: the OxCal program, *Radiocarbon*, **37**, 425–30

Bronk Ramsey, C, 1998 Probability and dating, *Radiocarbon*, **40**, 461–74

Bronk Ramsey, C, 2001 Development of the radiocarbon calibration program OxCal, *Radiocarbon*, **43**, 355–63

Bronk Ramsey, C, 2006 New approaches to constructing age models: OxCal4. *PAGES (Past Global Changes) News*, **14**(3), 14–15

Bronk Ramsey, C, 2009 Bayesian analysis of radiocarbon dates, *Radiocarbon*, **51**, 337–60

Brookes, S, & Suchey, J M, 1990 Skeletal age determination based on the os pubis: a comparison of the Acsadi-Nemeskeri & Suchey-Brookes method, *Human Evolution*, **5**, 227–38

Brooks, N, 1984 *The early history of the Church of Canterbury: Christ Church from 597 to 1066*. Leicester: Leicester University Press

Brooks, N, 1988 Romney Marsh in the early Middle Ages, in J Eddison & C Green (eds), *Romney Marsh. Evolution, occupation, reclamation*. Oxford Univ Comm Archaeol Monogr **24**. Oxford: Oxford University Committee for Archaeology, 90–104

Brothwell, D, 1981 *Digging up bones: the excavation, treatment and study of human skeletal remains*, 3rd edn. Ithaca: Cornell University Press

Brown, D, 1994 Pottery and late Saxon Southampton, *Proc Hampshire Fld Club Archaeol Soc*, **50**, 127–52

Brown, D, 2002 *Pottery in medieval Southampton*, CBA Res Rep **133**, Southampton Archaeology Monographs **8**. York: Council for British Archaeology

Brown, T, & Foard, G, 1998 The Saxon landscape: a regional perspective, in P Everson & T Williamson (eds) *The archaeology of landscape*. Manchester: Manchester University Press, 67–94

Brown, L, & Mepham, L, 2007 The Broughton to Timsbury pipeline, part 1: a late Saxon pottery kiln and the production centre at Michelmersh,

Hampshire, *Proc Hampshire Fld Club Archaeol Soc*, **62**, 59–61

Brown, G, & Rackham, J, 2004 Pits, bones and foodstuffs: Excavations at the Lyceum Theatre, Exeter Street, in J Leary *Tatberht's Lundenwic: archaeological excavations in middle Saxon London*, Pre-Construct Archaeology Monograph **2**. London: Pre-Construct Archaeology, 41–65

Brück, J, 1999a Houses, lifecycles and deposition on middle Bronze Age settlements in southern England, *Proc Prehist Soc*, **65**, 145–66

Brück, J, 1999b Ritual and rationality: some problems of interpretation in European archaeology, *European J Archaeology*, **2**(3), 313–44

Buck, C E, Cavanagh, W G, & Litton, C D, 1996 *Bayesian approach to interpreting archaeological data*. Chichester: Wiley

Buckland, P C, Holdsworth, P, & Monk, P, 1976 The interpretation of a group of Saxon pits in Southampton, *J Archaeol Sci*, **3**, 61–9

Burghart, M A, 2007 The Mercian polity, 716–918, Unpubl PhD thesis, King's College London

Burrin, P J, & Jones, D K C, 1991 Environmental processes and fluvial responses in a small temperate zone catchment: a case study of the Sussex Ouse Valley, south east England', in L Starkel, K J Gregory & J B Thornes (eds) *Temperate palaeohydrology*. Chichester: John Wiley, 217–52

Buteux, V, & Jackson, R, 2000 Rethinking the 'rubbish pit' in medieval Worcester, in S Roskams (ed) *Interpreting stratigraphy: site evaluation, recording procedures and stratigraphic analysis*, BAR Int Ser **910**. Oxford: Archeopress, 193–6

Callou, C, 1997 *Diagnose différentielle des principaux elements squelettiques du lapin (genre* Oryctolagus*) et du lièvre (genre* Lepus*) en Europe occidentale*, Série B, Mammifères, n° 8 APDCA. Valbonne-Sophia Antipolis: Fiches d'Ostéologie Animale pour l'Archéologie

Cameron, K, 1977 *English place-names*. 3rd edn. London: BT Batsford

Campbell, G, & Robinson, M, 2009 Plant and invertebrate remains, in M Audouy & A Chapman *Raunds: the origin and growth of a midland village AD450–1500. Excavations in north Raunds, Northamptonshire 1977–87*. Oxford: Oxbow Books, 230–49

Campbell, J, 1986 England, Flanders, France and Germany in the reign of Ethelred II, in J Campbell *Essays in Anglo-Saxon history*. London: Hambledon Press, 191–207

Campbell, J, 1986 Some twelfth-century views of the Anglo-Saxon past, repr in J Campbell *Essays in Anglo-Saxon history*. London: Hambledon Press, 209–28

Campbell, J, 2002 Domesday herrings, in C Harper-Bill, C Rawcliffe, & R G Wilson (eds) *East Anglia's history. Studies in honour of Norman Scarfe*. Woodbridge: Boydell, 5–17

Caple, C, 1991 The detection and definition of an industry: the English medieval and post-medieval pin industry, *Archaeol J*, **148**, 241–55

Cappers, R T J, Bekker, R M, & Jans, J E A, 2006 *Digitale zadenatlas van Nederland*. Groningen: Barkhuis Publishing and Groningen University Library

Carruthers, W, 1991 The plant remains, in P J Fasham & R J B Whinney *Archaeology and the M3. The watching brief, the Anglo-Saxon settlement at Abbots Worthy and retrospective sections*, Hampshire Fld Club Archaeol Soc Monogr **7**. Winchester: Hampshire Field Club, 67–75

Carruthers, W J, 2005 Mineralised plant remains, in V Birbeck, R J C Smith, P Andrews, & N Stoodley *The origins of mid-Saxon Southampton; excavation of the Friends Provident St Mary's Stadium 1998–2000*. Salisbury: Wessex Archaeology, 157–63

Carruthers, W, 2008 Charred, mineralised and waterlogged plant remains, in Framework Archaeology *From Hunter-Gatherers to Huntsmen: A History of the Stansted Landscape*. Salisbury: Wessex Archaeology, 34.1–34.8

Carter, R J, 2006 A method to estimate the ages at death of red deer (*Cervus elaphus*) and roe deer (*Capreolus capreolus*) from developing mandibular dentition and its application to Mesolithic NW Europe, in D Ruscillo (ed) *Recent advances in ageing and sexing animal bones*. Oxford: Oxbow, 40–61

Cartwright, C R, 1982 Aspects of the economy and environment, in P Drewett, *The archaeology of Bullock Down, Eastbourne: the development of a landscape*. Sussex Archaeol Soc Monogr **1**. Lewes: Sussex Archaeological Society, 8–38

Carver, M O H, 1994 Environment and commodity in Anglo-Saxon England, in D J Rackham (ed) *Environment and economy in Anglo-Saxon England*, CBA Res Rep **89**. York: Council for British Archaeology, 1–6

Carver, M O H (ed), 2003 *The cross goes north: processes of conversion in northern Europe, AD 300–1300*. University of York: York Medieval Press

Castleden, R, 1996 *Classic landforms of the Sussex coast*. Sheffield: The Geographical Association

Chamberlain, A C, 2000 Problems and prospects in palaeodemography, in M Cox & S Mays (eds) *Human osteology in archaeology and forensic science*. London: Greenwich Medical Media Ltd, 101–16

Cherry, J, 1978 Computer analyses of the Hamwih pit associations, in R Hodges, *The Hamwih pottery: the local and imported wares from 30 years' excavations at Middle Saxon Southampton and their European context*, CBA Res Rep **37**, Southampton Archaeol Res Comm Rep **2**. London: Council for British Archaeology, 47–50

Chisholm, B S, Nelson, D E, & Schwarcz, H P, 1982 Stable carbon isotope ratios as a measure of marine versus terrestrial protein in ancient diets, *Science*, **216**, 1131–2

Claassen, C, 1998 *Shells*. Cambridge: Cambridge University Press

Clapham, A J, 2005 Waterlogged plant remains, in V Birbeck, R J C Smith, P Andrews, & N Stoodley *The origins of mid-Saxon Southampton; excavation of the Friends Provident St Mary's Stadium 1998–2000*. Salisbury: Wessex Archaeology, 157–63

Clark, K M, 1998 An Anglo-Saxon dog from Salter Street, Stafford. *Int J Osteoarchaeology*, **8**, 61–5

Claussen, M, 2004 *The reform of the Frankish Church: Chrodegang of Metz and the 'Regula Canonicorum' in the eighth century*. Cambridge: Cambridge University Press

Cohen, A, & Serjeantson, D, 1996 *A manual for the identification of bird bones from archaeological sites*. London: Archetype publications

Cole, H A, 1956 *Oyster cultivation in Britain*. London: HMSO

Colgrave, B, (ed) 1927 *The life of Bishop Wilfrid*. Cambridge: Cambridge University Press

Colgrave, B, & Mynors, R A B, (eds) 1969 *Bede's ecclesiastical history of the English people*. Oxford: Clarendon Press

Combes, P, 2002 Bishopstone: a pre-Conquest minster church, *Sussex Archaeol Collect*, **140**, 49–56

Cowen, J D, 1934 A catalogue of objects of the Viking period in the Tullie House Museum, Carlisle, *Trans Cumberland Westmorland Antiq Archaeol Soc* new ser **34**, 166–87

Cowgill, J, 2009 The lead vessels housing the tool hoard, in D H Evans & C Loveluck (eds), 2009, 267–77

Cowgill, J, de Neergaard, M & Griffith, N, 1987 *Knives and scabbards*, Medieval Finds Excav London **1**. London: HMSO

Crabtree, P, 1996 Production and consumption in an early complex society: animal use in middle Saxon East Anglia, *World Archaeol*, **28**, 58–75

Cramp, R, 1984 *Grammar of Anglo-Saxon ornament*. Oxford: British Academy

Cramp, R, 2005 *Wearmouth and Jarrow monastic sites volume 1*. Swindon: English Heritage

Cramp, R (ed), 2007 *Corpus of Anglo-Saxon stone sculpture, VII, south-west England*. Oxford: Published for the British Academy by Oxford University Press

Crawford, S, 2007 Companions, co-incidences or chattels? Children in the early Anglo-Saxon multiple burial ritual, in S Crawford & G Shepherd (eds) *Children, childhood and society*. BAR Int Ser **1696**. Oxford: Archaeopress, 83–92

Cunliffe, B, 1972 Saxon and medieval settlement-pattern in the region of Chalton, Hampshire, *Medieval Archaeol*, **16**, 1–12

Cunliffe, B, 1974 Some late Saxon stamped pottery from southern England, in V Evison, H Hodges & J Hurst (eds) *Medieval pottery from excavations: studies presented to Gerald Clough Dunning, with a bibliography of his work*. London: John Baker, 127–36

Cunliffe, B, 1976 *Excavations at Portchester Castle: II Saxon*. London: Thames & Hudson for the Society of the Antiquaries

Dallas, C, 1993 *Excavations in Thetford by B K Davison between 1964 and 1970*, East Anglian Archaeology **62**. Gressenhall: Norfolk Museums Service

Davidson, P, 1976 Oyster fisheries of England and Wales. Laboratory leaflet no. **31**, Fisheries Laboratory, Lowestoft, Suffolk

Davis, A, 2003 The plant remains, in G Malcolm, D Bowsher & R Cowie *Middle Saxon London: excavations at the Royal Opera House 1989–99*, Museum of London Archaeol Stud Ser **15**. London: Museum of London, 289–302

Davis, A, & de Moulins, D, 1988 The plant remains, in R Cowie, R L Whytehead, & L Blackmore, Two middle Saxon occupation sites: excavations at Jubilee Hall and 21–2 Maiden Lane, *Trans London Middlesex Archaeol Soc*, **39**, 47–163, at 139–47

DeFrance, S D, 2009 Zooarchaeology in complex societies: political economy, status and ideology, *J Archaeol Res*, **17**, 105–68

Defries, D, 2008 The making of a minor Saint in Drogo of Saint-Winnoc's *Historia translationis s. Lewinnae*, *Early Medieval Europe* **16** (4), 423–44

Devoy, R J, 1982 Analysis of the geological evidence for Holocene sea-level movements in south east England, *Proc Geol Ass*, **93:1**, 65–90

Dickens, A, Mortimer, R, & Tipper, J, 2006 The early Anglo-Saxon settlement and cemetery at Bloodmoor Hill, Carlton Colville, Suffolk: A preliminary report, in S Semple (ed) *Anglo-Saxon Stud Archaeol Hist*, **13**, 63–79

Dickson, J H, & Dickson, C, 1996 Ancient and modern occurrences of common fig (*Ficus carica* L.) in the British Isles, *Quat Sci Rev*, **15**, 623–33

Dixon, P, 2002 The reconstruction of the buildings, in S Losco-Bradley & G Kinsley *Catholme: An Anglo-Saxon settlement on the Trent gravels in Staffordshire*. Nottingham: Trent and Peak Archaeological Unit, 89–99

Dobney, K, & Jacques, D, 2002 Avian signatures for identity and status in Anglo-Saxon England. *Acta Zoologica Cracoviensia*, **45**, 7–21

Dobney, K, Jacques, D, Barrett, J, & Johnstone, C, 2007 *Farmers, monks and aristocrats: the environmental archaeology of Anglo-Saxon Flixborough*, Excavations at Flixborough **3**. Oxford: Oxbow Books

Down, A, 1978 *Chichester excavations 3*. Chichester: Phillimore

Down, A, 1981 *Chichester excavations 5*. Chichester: Philimore

Draper, S, 2006 *Landscape, settlement and society in Roman and early medieval Wiltshire*. BAR Brit Ser **419**. Oxford: Archaeopress

Draper, S, 2008 The significance of Old English *Burh* in Anglo-Saxon England, *Anglo-Saxon Stud Archaeol Hist*, **15**, 240–53

Drewett, P, & Freke, D, 1982 The medieval farm on Bullock Down *c* 1250–1550, in P L Drewett, *The archaeology of Bullock Down, Eastbourne, East Sussex: the development of a landscape*. Sussex Archaeol Soc Monogr **1**, 143–91

Driver, J C, 1982 Medullary bone as an indicator of sex in bird remains from archaeological sites, in B Wilson, C Grigson & S Payne (eds) *Ageing and sexing animal bones from archaeological sites*. BAR Brit Ser **109**. Oxford: British Archaeological Reports, 251–68

Dunning, G & Wilson, A, 1953 Late Saxon and early medieval pottery from selected sites in Chichester, *Sussex Archaeol Collect*, **93**, 140–63

Dunning, G, Hurst, J, Myres, J, & Tischler, F, 1959 *Anglo-Saxon pottery: a symposium*, CBA Res Rep **4**. London: Council for British Archaeology

EAC 2008 Bishopstone, Sussex – BH03, B04 and B05, Unpubl Botanical Assessment Report. Environmental Archaeology Consultancy, nr Sleaford, Lincs

Edwards, B J N, 1992 The Vikings in north-west England: the archaeological evidence, in J Graham-Campbell (ed) *Viking treasure from the north-west: the Cuerdale Hoard in its context*, National Museums and Galleries on Merseyside Occas Pap **5**. Liverpool: Liverpool Museum, 43–62

Edwards, B J N, 2002 A group of pre-Conquest metalwork from Asby Winderwath Common, *Trans Cumberland Westmorland Antiq Archaeol Soc* 3rd Ser, **2**, 111–43

Egan, G, 1998 *The medieval household: daily living c 1150 – c 1450*, Medieval Finds Excav London **6**. London: HMSO

Egan, G, & Pritchard, F, 1990 *Dress accessories: c 1150 – c 1450*, Medieval Finds Excav London **3**. London: HMSO

Erlandson, J M, Rick, T C, Vellanoweth, R L, & Kennett, D J, 1999 Maritime subsistence at a 9300 year old shell midden on Sanat Rosa Island, California, *J Field Archaeol*, **26**, 255–65

Ervynck, A, 1997 Following the rule? Fish and meat consumption in monastic communities in Flanders (Belgium), in G de Boe & F Verhaeghe (eds) *Environment and subsistence in medieval Europe. Papers from the 'Medieval Europe Brugge 1997' conference volume 9*. I A P Rapporten **9**. Zelik: Instituut voor het Archaeologisch Patrimonium, 67–81

Ervynck, A, 2004 *Orant, pugnant, laborant*. The diet of the three orders within the feudal society of medieval Europe, in S Jones O'Day, W van Neer, & A Ervynck (eds) *Behaviour behind bones*. Oxford: Oxbow Books, 215–23

Evans, J G, 1983 Mollusca and other invertebrates from Ardnave, Islay, in G Ritchie & H Welfare, Excavations at Ardnave, Islay, *Proc Soc Antiq Scot*, **113**, 302–66 at 350–8

Evans, D H, & Loveluck, C, 2009 (eds) *Life and economy in early medieval Flixborough c AD 600–1000: the artefact evidence*, Excavations at Flixborough vol **2**. Oxford: Oxbow Books

Everson, P, 1977 Excavations in the vicarage garden at Brixworth, 1972, *J Brit Archaeol Ass*, **130**, 55–122

Fairbrother, J R, 1990 *Faccombe Netherton: excavations of a Saxon and medieval manorial complex*, Brit Mus Occ Pap **74**. London: British Museum

Fairclough, H R, (trans) & Goold, G P (ed), 1916, rpr 1998 *Virgil: Eclogues, Georgics, Aeneid 1–6*, Loeb Classical Library **63**. Cambridge, MA: Harvard University Press

Faith, R, 1997 *The English peasantry and the growth of lordship*. Leicester: Leicester University Press

Farrant, S, 1976 Farm formation in eighteenth-century Bishopstone, *Sussex Archaeol Collect*, **114**, 335–6

Fasham, P, Farwell, D E, & Whinney, R J B, 1989 *The Archaeological Site at Easton Lane, Winchester*, Hants Field Club and Arch Soc Mono **6**. Gloucester: Alan Sutton

Fasham, P, & Keevil, G, 1995 *Brighton Hill South (Hatch Warren). An Iron Age farmstead and deserted medieval village in Hampshire*, Wessex Arch Rep **7**. Salisbury: Trust for Wessex Archaeology

Fenwick, V, 1984 Insula de Burgh: excavations at Burrow Hill, Butley, Suffolk 1978–81, *Anglo-Saxon Stud Archaeol Hist*, **3**, 34–54

Fernie, E, 1983 *The architecture of the Anglo-Saxons*. London: BT Batsford

Fish, J D, & Fish, S, 1989 *A student's guide to the seashore*. London: Unwin Hyman

Fleming, R, 2001 The new wealth, the new rich and the new political style in Late Anglo-Saxon England, *Anglo-Norman Stud*, **23**, 1–22

Foreman, S, Hiller, J, & Petts, D, 2002 *Gathering the people, settling the land: the archaeology of a middle Thames landscape, Anglo-Saxon to post-medieval*. Oxford: Oxford Archaeological Unit

Fowler, P, 2002 *Farming in the first millennium AD. British agriculture between Julius Caesar and William the Conqueror*. Cambridge: Cambridge University Press

Fox, C, 1923 *Archaeology in the Cambridge region*. London: Cambridge University Press

Freeth, C, 2000 Dental health in British antiquity, in M Cox & S Mays (eds) *Human osteology in archaeology and forensic science*. London: Greenwich Medical Media Ltd, 227–38

Freshwater, T, 1996 A lava quern workshop in late Saxon London, *London Archaeol*, **8**(2), 39–45

Fuller, B T, Fuller, J L, Sage, N E, Harris, D A, O'Connell, T C, & Hedges, R E M, 2004 Nitrogen balance and $\delta^{15}N$: why you're not what you eat during pregnancy, *Rapid Communications in Mass Spectrometry* **18**, 2889–96

Gallois, R, 1965 *British regional geology: the Wealden district*, 4th edn. London: HMSO

Gardiner, M F, 1984 Saxon settlement and land division in the western Weald, *Sussex Archaeol Collect*, **122**, 75–84

Gardiner, M F, 1990 An Anglo-Saxon and medieval settlement at Botolphs, Bramber, West Sussex, *Archaeol J*, **147**, 216–75

Gardiner, M F, 1993 The excavation of a late Anglo-Saxon settlement at Market Field, Steyning 1988–9, *Sussex Archaeol Collect*, **131**, 1–67

Gardiner, M F, 1995 Aspects of the history and archaeology of medieval Seaford, *Sussex Archaeol Collect*, **133**, 212–24

Gardiner, M F, 1997 The exploitation of sea-mammals in medieval England: bones and their social context, *Archaeol J*, **154**, 173–95

Gardiner, M F, 2000a Shipping and trade between England and the continent during the eleventh century, *Anglo-Norman Stud*, **22**, 71–93

Gardiner, M F, 2000b Vernacular buildings and the development of the later medieval Domestic Plan in England, *Medieval Archaeol*, **44**, 159–80

Gardiner, M F, 2003 Economy and landscape change in post-Roman and early medieval Sussex, 450–1175, in D R Rudling (ed) *The archaeology of Sussex to AD 2000*. King's Lynn: Heritage, 151–60

Gardiner, M F, 2004 Timber buildings without earth-fast footings in Viking-age Britain, in J Hines, A Lane, & M Redknap (eds) *Land, sea and home: proceedings of a conference on Viking-period settlement at Cardiff, July 2001*, Soc Medieval Archaeol Monogr Ser **20**, 345–58

Gardiner, M F, 2006 Implements and utensils in *Gerefa* and the organization of seigneurial farmsteads in the high Middle Ages, *Medieval Archaeol*, **50**, 260–7

Gardiner, M F, 2007 The origins and persistence of manor houses in England, in M F Gardiner & S Rippon (eds) *Medieval landscapes*. Landscape History after Hoskins **2**. Macclesfield: Windgather Press, 170–84

Gardiner, M F, forthcoming. *Structural and social aspects of timber buildings, 900–1200.*

Gardiner, M, Cross, R, Macpherson-Grant, N, & Riddler, I, 2001 Continental trade and non urban ports in mid-Anglo-Saxon England: Excavations at Sandtun, West Hythe, Kent, *Archaeol J*, **158**, 161–290

Garrow, D, Beadsmoore, E, & Knight, M, 2005 Pit clusters and the temporality of occupation: an earlier Neolithic site at Kilverstone, Thetford, Norfolk, *Proc Prehist Soc*, **71**, 139–57

Geary, P J, 1990 *Furta Sacra: thefts of relics in the central Middle Ages*, 2nd edn. Princeton: Princeton University Press

Geddes, J, 1982 The construction of medieval doors, in S McGrail (ed) *Woodworking techniques before AD 1500*, Brit Archaeol Rep Int Ser **129**. Oxford: British Archaeological Reports, 313–26

Gelling, M, 1978 *Signposts to the past: place-names and the history of England*. London: Dent

Gelling, M, & Cole, A, 2000 *The landscape of place-names*. Stamford: Shaun Tyas

Gem, R, 1993 Architecture of the Anglo-Saxon church, 735 to 870, *J Brit Archaeol Ass*, **146**, 29–66

Gem, R, 1995 Staged timber spires in Carolingian north-east France and late Anglo-Saxon England, *J Brit Archaeol Ass*, **148**, 29–54

Gerrard, C & Aston, M, 2007 *The Shapwick Project: a rural landscape explored*. Soc Medieval Archaeol Monogr **25**. Leeds: Society for Medieval Archaeology

Getty, R, 1975 *Sisson and Grossman's the anatomy of domestic animals*. Philadelphia: W B Saunders & Co

Gittos, H, 2002a Sacred space in Anglo-Saxon England: liturgy, architecture and place, Unpubl DPhil thesis, Oxford University

Gittos, H, 2002b Creating the sacred: Anglo-Saxon rites for consecrating cemeteries, in S Lucy & A Reynolds (eds) *Burial in early medieval England & Wales*, Soc Medieval Archaeol Monogr Ser **17**, London: The Society for Medieval Archaeology, 195–208

Godfrey, W H, 1948 The parish church of St Andrew, Bishopstone, *Sussex Archaeol Collect*, **87**, 164–83

Goodall, A R, 1984 Non-ferrous metal objects, in A Rogerson & C Dallas, *Excavations in Thetford 1948–59 and 1973–80*, E Anglian Archaeol Rep **22**. Dereham: Norfolk Archaeological Unit, Norfolk Museums Service, 68–75

Goodall, A R, 1987 Objects of copper alloy and lead, in G Beresford *Goltho: the development of an early medieval manor c 850–1150*, Engl Heritage Archaeol Rep **4**. London: Historic Buildings & Monuments Commission for England, 171–6

Goodall, I H, 1980 The iron objects, in P Wade-Martins *Excavations in North Elmham Park, 1967–72*, E Anglian Archaeol Rep **9**. Gressenhall: Norfolk Archaeological Unit, Norfolk Museums Service, 509–16

Goodall, I H, 1983 The small finds – site XI', in K S Jarvis *Excavations at Christchurch 1969–80*, Dorset Natur Hist Archaeol Soc Monogr Ser **5**. Dorset: DNHAS, 77

Goodall, I H, 1984 Iron objects, in A Rogerson & C Dallas *Excavations in Thetford 1948–59 and 1973–80*, E Anglian Archaeol Rep **22**. Dereham: Norfolk Archaeological Unit, Norfolk Museums Service, 76–106

Goodall, I H, 1987 Objects of iron, in G Beresford *Goltho: the development of an early medieval Manor c 850–1150*. Engl Heritage Archaeol Rep **4**. London: Historic Buildings & Monuments Commission for England, 177–87

Goodall, I H, 1990a Wood-working tools, in M Biddle (ed) 1990a, 273–7

Goodall, I H, 1990b Iron binding strips and mounts, in M Biddle (ed) 1990a, 787–9

Goodall, I H, 1990c Iron fittings from furniture, in M Biddle (ed) 1990a, 971–80

Goodall, I H, 1990d Locks and Keys, in M Biddle (ed) 1990a, 1001–36

Goodall, I H, 1990e Horseshoes, in M Biddle (ed) 1990a, 1054–67

Goodall, I H, Ellis, B, & Oakley, G E, 1979 The iron objects, in J H Williams *St Peter's Street, Northampton: excavations 1973–76*, Northampton Archaeol Monogr **2**. Northampton: Northampton Development Corporation, 268–77

Goodall, I H & Ottaway, P J, 1993 Iron Objects, in C Dallas *Excavations in Thetford by B K Davison between 1964 and 1970*, E Anglian Archaeol Rep **62**. Gressenhall: Field Archaeology Division, Norfolk Museums Service, 96–116

Goodburn, D M, 1992 Woods and woodland: carpenters and carpentry, in G Milne (ed) *Timber building techniques in London c 900–1400*, London Middlesex Archaeol Soc Spec Pap **15**. London: London & Middlesex Archaeological Society, 106–30

Goodburn, D M, 1997 The production of timber for building in England before and after c 1180 AD, in G de Boe & F Verhaeghe (eds) *Material culture in medieval Europe, papers of the medieval Europe Brugge 1997 conference. Vol* **7**. Zellick: Instituut voor het Archeologisch Patrimonium, 155–61

Gough, H, 1992 Eadred's charter of AD 949 and the extent of the monastic estate of Reculver, Kent, in N Ramsay, M Sparks & T Tatton-Brown (eds) *St Dunstan: his life, times and cult*. Woodbridge: Boydell, 89–102

Gover, J E B, Mawer, A, & Stenton, F M, 1936 *The place-names of Warwickshire*. Cambridge: Cambridge University Press

Gover, J E B, Mawer, A, & Stenton, F M, 1939 *The place-names of Wiltshire*. Cambridge: Cambridge University Press

Graham, A & Davies, S, 1993 *Excavations in the town centre of Trowbridge, Wiltshire 1977 and 1986–1988: the prehistoric and Saxon settlements, the Saxo-Norman manorial settlement and the anarchy period castle*, Wessex Archaeology Report **2**. Salisbury: Old Sarum: Trust for Wessex Archaeology

Graham-Campbell, J, 1980a *Viking artefacts: a select catalogue*. London: British Museum Publications

Graham-Campbell, J, 1980b *The Viking world*, London: Book Club Associates

Grant, A, 1976 The animal bone, in B Cunliffe *Excavations at Portchester Castle. Volume II: Saxon*. London: Society of Antiquaries, 262–87

Grant, A, 1982 The use of tooth wear as a guide to the age of domestic ungulates, in B Wilson, C Grigson, & S Payne (eds) *Ageing and sexing animal bones from archaeological sites*. BAR Brit Ser **109**. Oxford: British Archaeological Reports, 91–108

Gravett, K W E, 1975 Brookland belfry, *Archaeologia Cantiana*, **89**, 43–8

Green, F J, 1979 Phosphatic mineralization of seeds from archaeological sites, *J Archaeol Sci*, **6**, 279–84

Green, F J, 1984 The archaeological and documentary evidence for plants from the medieval period in England, in W van Zeist & W A Casparie (eds) *Plants and ancient man*. Rotterdam: A A Balkema, 213–26

Green, F J, 1994 Cereals and plant food: a reassessment of the Saxon economic evidence from Wessex, in J Rackham (ed) *Environment and economy in Anglo-Saxon England*, CBA Res Rep **89**. York: Council for British Archaeology, 83–8

Greenfield, H J, 2006 Sexing fragmentary ungulate acetabulae, in D Ruscillo (ed) *Recent advances in ageing and sexing animal bones*. Oxford: Oxbow Books, 68–86

Greenway, D E, (ed) 1991 *Fasti Ecclesiae Anglicanae 1066–1300: IV*, Salisbury. London: Institute of Historical Research

Gregory, V, 1976 Excavations at Becket's Barn Pagham 1974, *Sussex Archaeol Collect,* **114**, 207–17

Greig, J R A, 1991 The British Isles, in W van Zeist, K Wasylikowa & K Behre (eds) *Progress in Old World palaeoethnobotany*. Rotterdam: Balkema, 299–334

Greig, J R A, 1996 Archaeobotanical and historical records compared – a new look at taphonomy of edible and other useful plants from the 11th to the 18th centuries AD, *Circaea*, **12**, 211–47

Grenville, J, 1997 *Medieval housing*. Leicester: Leicester University Press

Grieg, S, 1940 Viking antiquities in Scotland, in H Shetelig (ed) *Viking antiquities in Great Britain and Ireland,* **2**. Oslo: H. Aschehoug

Grierson, P, 1941 The relations between England and Flanders before the Norman Conquest, *Trans Royal Hist Soc,* 4th ser **23**, 71–112

Grigson, C, 1982 Sex and age determination of some bones and teeth of domestic cattle: a review of the literature, in B Wilson, C Grigson, & S Payne (eds) *Ageing and sexing animal bones from archaeological sites*. BAR Brit Ser **109**. Oxford: British Archaeological Reports, 7–19

Grootes, P M, Nadeau, M-J, & Rieck, A, 2004 ^{14}C-AMS at the Leibniz-Labor: Radiometric dating and isotope research, *Nuclear Instruments and Methods in Physics Research Section B* **223–224**, 55–61

Gumerman, G, 1997 Food and complex societies, *J Archaeol Method and Theory* 4(2), 105–39

Hadley, D M, 2002 Burial practices in northern England in the later Anglo-Saxon period, in S Lucy & A Reynolds (eds) *Burial in early medieval England & Wales*, Soc Medieval Archaeol Monogr Ser **17**. London: The Society for Medieval Archaeology, 209–28

Hadley, D M, 2004 Negotiating gender, family and status in Anglo-Saxon burial practices, c 600–950, in L Brubaker & J M H Smith (eds) *Gender in the early medieval world*. Cambridge: Cambridge University Press, 301–23

Hadley, D M, 2007 The garden gives up its secrets: the developing relationship between rural settlements and cemeteries, *c* 750–1100, *Anglo-Saxon Stud Archaeol Hist*, **14**, 195–203

Hadley, D M, & Buckberry, J, 2005 Caring for the dead in late Anglo-Saxon England, in F Tinti (ed) *Pastoral care in late Anglo-Saxon England*. Woodbridge: Boydell, 121–47

Hagen, A, 1992 *A handbook of Anglo-Saxon food: processing and consumption*. Hockwold cum Wilton: Anglo-Saxon Books

Hagen, A, 1995 *A second handbook of Anglo-Saxon food and drink: production and distribution*. Hockwold cum Wilton: Anglo-Saxon Books

Hagen, A, 2006 *Anglo-Saxon food and drink: production, processing, distribution and consumption*. Hockwold cum Wilton: Anglo-Saxon Books

Hall, A R, 2000 Technical report: plant remains from excavations at Flixborough, N Lincolnshire (site code: FLX89). *Reports from the Environmental Archaeology Unit, York* **2000/56**

Hall, A R, & Kenward, H K, 2000 Technical report: plant and invertebrate remains from Anglo-Scandinavian deposits at 4–7 Parliament Street (Littlewoods Store), York (site code 99.946). *Reports from the Environmental Archaeology Unit, York* **2000/22**

Halsall, G, 2000 The Viking presence in England? The burial evidence reconsidered, in D M Hadley & J D Richards (eds) *Cultures in contact: Scandinavian settlement in England in the ninth and tenth centuries*. Turnhout: Brepols, 259–76

Halstead, P, 1985 A study of the mandibular teeth from Romano-British contexts at Maxey, in F Pryor (ed) *Archaeology and environment of the Lower Welland Valley vol 1*. E Anglian Archaeol Rep **27**. Cambridge: Fenland Project Committee, Cambridge University, 219–82

Hamerow, H, 1991 Settlement mobility and the 'Middle Saxon Shift': rural settlements and settlement patterns in Anglo-Saxon England, *Anglo-Saxon Engl*, **20**, 1–17

Hamerow, H, 1993 *Mucking, volume 2: the Anglo-Saxon settlement*. London: English Heritage

Hamerow, H, 2002 *Early medieval settlements: the archaeology of rural communities in north-west Europe 400–900*. Oxford: Oxford University Press

Hamerow, H, 2006 Special deposits in Anglo-Saxon settlements, *Medieval Archaeol*, **50**, 1–30

Hamilton, S & Waller, M P, 2000 Vegetation history of the English chalklands: a mid-Holocene pollen sequence from the Caburn, East Sussex, *J Quaternary Science*, **15**, 252–72

Hamilton-Dyer, S, 2001 Bird and fish remains, in M Gardiner, R Cross, N Macpherson-Grant & I Riddler, Continental trade and non-urban ports in middle Anglo-Saxon England: excavations at Sandtun, West Hythe, Kent, *Archaeol J*, **158**, 255–61

Hancock, D, & Urquhart, A, 1966 The fisheries for cockles in the Burry Inlet, South Wales, *Fisheries Investigations Series 2*, **25** (3)

Harbison, P, 1999 *The golden age of Irish art: the*

medieval achievement, 600–1200. London: Thames & Hudson

Harcourt, R A, 1974 The dog in prehistoric and early historic Britain. *J Archaeol Sci*, **1**, 151–75

Hardy, A, Dodd, A, & Keevill, G D, 2003 *Aelfric's Abbey: excavations at Eynsham Abbey, Oxfordshire, 1989–1992*, Thames Valley Landscapes Monograph **16**. Oxford: Oxford Archaeology

Harvey, P D A, 1989 Initiative and authority in settlement change, in M Aston, D Austin & C Dyer (eds) *The medieval settlements of England*. Oxford: Blackwell, 31–43

Harvey, B F, 2006 Monastic pittances in the Middle Ages, in C M Woolgar, D Serjeantson & T Waldron (eds) *Food in medieval England. Diet and nutrition*. Oxford: Oxford University Press, 215–27

Harvey, P, 1993 Rectitudines singularum personarum and Gerefa. *English Historical Review*, **108**, 1–22

Haselgrove, D C, 1977 Documentary sources, in M Bell, Excavations at Bishopstone, *Sussex Arch Collect*, **115**, 243–50

Hatting, T, 1995 Sex-related characters in the pelvic bone of domestic sheep (*Ovis aries* L.), *Archaeofauna*, **4**, 71–6

Hedges, R E M, Housley, R A, Bronk-Ramsey, C, & van Klinken, G J, 1991 Radiocarbon dates from the Oxford AMS system: datelist 13. *Archaeometry*, **33**(2), 279–96

Helbaek, H, 1953 Early crops in southern England, *Proc Prehist Soc*, **18**, 194

Helbaek, H, 1964 The Isca grain: a Roman plant introduction in Britain, *New Phytologist*, **63**, 158–64

Hewett, C A, 1978 Anglo-Saxon carpentry, *Anglo-Saxon Engl*, **7**, 204–29

Hey, G, 2004 *Yarnton: Saxon and medieval settlement and landscape*. Oxford: Oxford Archaeology

Higgs, E, & Jarman, M, 1977 Yeavering faunal report, in B Hope-Taylor (ed) *Yeavering: an Anglo-British centre of early Northumbria*, Dept Environment Archaeol Rep **7**. London: HMSO, 325–32

Higham, R, & Barker, P, 1992 *Timber castles*. London: B T Batsford

Higham, T F G, Bronk Ramsey, C, Brock, F, Baker, D, & Ditchfield, P, 2007 Radiocarbon data from the Oxford AMS system: Archaeometry datelist 32, *Archaeometry*, **49** (S1), 1–60

Hill, J D, 1995 *Ritual and rubbish in the Iron Age of Wessex: a study on the formation of a specific archaeological record*, BAR Brit Ser **242**. Oxford: British Archaeological Reports

Hillman, G C, 1981 Reconstructing crop husbandry practices from charred remains of crops, in R Mercer (ed) *Farming practice in British prehistory*. Edinburgh: Edinburgh University Press, 123–62

Hillman, G C, 1984 Interpretation of archaeological plant remains: the application of ethnographic models from Turkey, in W van Zeist & W A Casparie (eds) *Plants and ancient man: studies in palaeoethnobotany*. Rotterdam: A A Balkema, 1–41

Hines, J, 1997 Religion: the limits of knowledge, in J Hines (ed) *The Anglo-Saxons from the migration period to the eighth century: an ethnographic perspective*. Woodbridge: Boydell, 375–410

Hingley, R, 2006 The deposition of iron objects in Britain during the later prehistoric and Roman periods: contextual analysis and the significance of iron, *Britannia* **37**(1), 213–57

Hinton, D A, 1990a Relief-decorated strap-ends, in M Biddle (ed) 1990a, 494–500

Hinton, D A, 1990b Split-end strap-ends, in M Biddle (ed) 1990a, 500–02

Hinton, D A, 1990c Belt-hasps and other belt-fittings, in M Biddle (ed) 1990a, 539–42

Hinton, D A, 1990d Strap-distributors, in M Biddle (ed) 1990a, 546

Hinton, D A, 1990e Disc and rectangular brooches, in M Biddle (ed) 1990a, 636–9

Hinton, P, 1993 Plant remains, in M Gardiner, The excavation of a late Anglo-Saxon settlement at Market Field, Steyning, 1988–89. *Sussex Archaeol Collect*, **131**, 21–67, at 57–64

Hinton, D A, 1996 *The gold, silver and other non-ferrous alloy objects from Hamwic*, Southampton Finds Vol **2**. Southampton: Southampton City Museums

Hinton, D A, 1998 *Archaeology, economy and society: England from the fifth to the fifteenth century*. London: Routledge

Hinton, D A, 2003 Anglo-Saxon smiths and myths, in D Scragg (ed) *Textual and material culture in Anglo-Saxon England*. Cambridge: D S Brewer, 261–82

Hinton, D A, 2005 *Gold and gilt, pots and pins: possessions and people in medieval Britain*. Oxford: Oxford University Press

Hinton, D A, forthcoming, Recent work at the chapel of St Laurence, Bradford-on-Avon, Wiltshire, *Archaeol J*, **166**

Hodges, C C, 1905 Anglo-Saxon remains, in W Page (ed), *Victoria County History, Durham* 1. London: Constable, 211–40

Hodges, R, 1978 A note on a late Saxon and two early medieval imported wares in A Down, 1978, 352–3

Hodges, R, 1981 *The Hamwih pottery: the local and imported wares from 30 years' excavations at middle Saxon Southampton and their European context*, CBA Res Rep **37**, Southampton Archaeol Res Comm Rep **2**. London: Council for British Archaeology

Hodges, R, 1989 *The Anglo-Saxon achievement*. London: Duckworth

Hoffman, R, 2008 Homo et natura, homo in natura. Ecological perspectives on the European Middle Ages, in B A Hanawalt & L J Kiser (eds) *Engaging with nature. Essays on the natural world in medieval and early modern Europe*. Notre Dame: University of Notre Dame Press, 11–38

Holden E W, 1976 Excavations at Old Erringham, Shoreham: part one, a Saxon weaving hut, *Sussex Archaeol Collect*, **114**, 306–21

Hollis, S, 2001 Scientific and medical writings, in P Pulsiano & E Treharne (eds) *A companion to Old English literature*. Oxford: Blackwell, 188–208

Holmes, M, & Chapman, A, 2008 A middle–late Saxon and medieval cemetery at Wing church, Buckinghamshire, *Rec Buckinghamshire*, **48**, 61–123

Holst, M, 1997 The dynamic of the Iron Age village: a technique for the relative-chronological analysis of area-excavated iron age settlements, *J Danish Archaeol*, **13**, 95–119

Hooke, D, 1998 *The landscape of Anglo-Saxon England*. Leicester: Leicester University Press

Hope-Taylor, B, 1977 *Yeavering: an Anglo-British centre of early Northumbria*. London: HMSO

Horsman, V, Milne, C & Milne, G, 1988 *Aspects of Saxo-Norman London: 1, building and street development*, London & Middlesex Archaeol Soc Spec Pap **11**. London: London & Middlesex Archaeological Society

Hubbard, R N L B, & Clapham, A J, 1992 Quantifying macroscopic plant remains, *Review of Palaeobotany and Palynology*, **73**, 117–32

Huggins, P J, 1976 The excavation of an 11th-century Viking hall and 14th-century rooms at Waltham Abbey, Essex, 1969–71, *Medieval Archaeol*, **20**, 75–133

Hughen, K A, Baillie, M G L, Bard, E, Beck, J W, Bertrand, C J H, Blackwell, P G, Buck, C E, Burr, G S, Cutler, K B, Damon, P E, Edwards, R L, Fairbanks, R G, Friedrich, M, Guilderson, T P, Kromer, B, McCormac, G, Manning, S, Bronk Ramsey, C, Reimer, P J, Reimer, R W, Remmele, S, Southon, J R, Stuiver, M, Talamo, S, Taylor, F W, van der Plicht, J, & Weyhenmeyer, C E, 2004, Marine04 marine radiocarbon age calibration, 0–26 cal kyr BP, *Radiocarbon*, **46**, 1059–86

Hughes, M, 1984 Rural settlement and landscape in late Anglo-Saxon Hampshire, in M Faull (ed) *Studies in late Anglo-Saxon settlement*. Oxford: Oxford University Department for External Studies, 65–79

Hughes, R, 2004 Wattle and daub: a technical and experimental study based on materials from the National Portrait Gallery, in J Leary *Tatberht's Lundenwic: archaeological excavations in middle Saxon London*, Pre-Construct Archaeol Monogr **2**. London: Pre-Construct Archaeology, 115–39

Hunter, K L, 2005 Charred plant remains, in V Birbeck, R J C Smith, P Andrews & N Stoodley *The origins of mid-Saxon Southampton; excavation of the Friends Provident St Mary's Stadium 1998–2000*. Salisbury: Wessex Archaeology, 163–73

Huntley, J & Rackham, J, 2007 The environmental setting and provisioning of the Anglo-Saxon monastery, in R Daniels, *Anglo-Saxon Hartle-*

pool and the foundations of English Christianity, Tees Archaeology Monograph Series **3** Hartlepool: Tees Archaeology, 108–23

Hurst, J, 1980 Medieval pottery imports in Sussex, *Sussex Archaeol Collect*, **118**, 119–24

Hutchinson, G, 1994 *Medieval ships and shipping*. London: Leicester University Press

Iscan, M Y, Loth, S R, & Wright, R K, 1984 Age estimation from the rib by phase analysis: white males, *J Forensic Sciences*, **29**, 1094–104

Iscan, M Y, Loth, S R, & Wright, R K, 1985 Age estimation from the rib by phase analysis: white females, *J Forensic Sciences*, **30**, 853–63

Ivens, R J, Busby, P A, Mills, J, Shepherd, N, & Hurman, B, 1995 *Tattenhoe and Westbury: two deserted medieval settlements in Milton Keynes*, Buckinghamshire Archaeol Soc Monogr Ser **8**. Aylesbury: Buckinghamshire Archaeological Society

James, S, Marshall, A, & Millett, M, 1984 An early medieval building tradition, *Archaeol J*, **141**, 182–215

Jarzembowski, E A, 1988 An estuarine mollusc from Bishopstone village, *Sussex Archaeol Collect*, **126**, 229

Jarzembowski, E A, 2003 *The palaeoenvironment of the Ouse Estuary Project (Phase 1)*, privately published

Jennings, S, Orford, J D, Canti, M, Devoy, R J N, & Straker, V, 1998 The role of relative sea-level rise and changing sediment supply on Holocene gravel barrier development: the example of Porlock, Somerset, UK, *Holocene* **8/ii**, 165–81

Jennings, S, & Smyth, C, 1987 Coastal sedimentation in East Sussex during the Holocene, *Progress in Oceanography*, **18**, 205–41

Jennings, S, & Smyth, C, 1990 Holocene evolution of the gravel coastline of East Sussex, *Proc Geol Ass*, **101**, 213–24

Jervis, B, 2005 Pottery and identity in Saxon Sussex, *Medieval Ceram*, **29**, 1–8

Jervis, B, 2008 Late-Saxon handled ceramic vessels from Southern England, *Medieval Archaeol,* **52**, 296–306

Jervis, B, 2009 Pottery from late Saxon Chichester, *Sussex Archaeol Collect* **147**, 61–76

John, E, 1955 The division of the Mensa in early English monasteries, *J Eccles Hist*, **6**, 142–55

Jolly, K, 1985 Anglo-Saxon charms in the context of the Christian world view, *J Medieval Hist*, **11**, 279–93

Jones, A K G, 1977 The fish remains, in M Bell, *Excavations at Bishopstone*. Sussex Archaeol Collect, **115**. Lewes: Sussex Archaeological Society

Jones, G, 1984 Interpretation of archaeological plant remains: ethnographic models from Greece, in W van Zeist & W A Casparie (eds) *Plants and ancient man: studies in palaeoethnobotany. Proceedings of the sixth symposium of the International Work Group for Palaeoethnobotany, Groningen, 30 May–3 June 1983*. Rotterdam: A A Balkema, 43–61

Jones, G, 1998 Wheat grain identification – why bother?, *Environmental Archaeology*, **2**, 29–34

Jones, G, Straker, V, & Davis, A, 1991 Early medieval plant use and ecology in London, in A G Vince (ed) *Aspects of Saxo-Norman London: II. Finds and environmental evidence*, Trans London Middlesex Archaeol Soc Spec Pap **12**. London: London & Middlesex Archaeological Society, 347–85

Jones, M, 2007 *Feast. Why humans share food*. Oxford: Oxford University Press

Jones, R, 2004 Signatures in the soil: the use of pottery in manure scatters in the identification of medieval arable farming regimes, *Archaeol J*, **161**, 159–88

Jones, R, & Page, M, 2006 *Medieval villages in an English landscape*. Macclesfield: Windgather Press

Juuti, P & Wallenius, K, 2005 *A brief history of wells and toilets – the case of Finland*. Tampere University Press, ePublications http://tampub.uta.fi/tulos.php?tiedot=79

Katzenberg, M A, & Krouse, H R, 1989 Application of stable isotopes in human tissues to problems in identification, *Canadian Society of Forensic Science Journal*, **22**, 7–19

Keene, D J, 1982 Rubbish in medieval towns, in A R Hall & H K Kenward (eds) *Environmental archaeology in the urban context*, CBA Res Rep **43**. London: Council for British Archaeology, 26–30

Kelly, S E, (ed) 1998 *Charters of Selsey: Anglo-Saxon charters VI*. Oxford: published for the British Academy by Oxford University Press

Kemp, R L, 1996 *Anglian settlement at 46–54 Fishergate*, The Archaeology of York: Anglian York AY7/1. York: Council for British Archaeology

Kenward, H K, & Hall, A R, 1995 *Biological evidence from Anglo-Scandinavian deposits at 16–22 Coppergate*, The Archaeology of York AY **14**(7). London: Council for British Archaeology

Kenward, H K, & Girling, M A, 1986 Arthropod remains from archaeological sites in Southampton, *AML Report New Series* **46/86**

Kenyon, D, & Watts, M, 2006 An Anglo-Saxon enclosure at Copsehill Road, Lower Slaughter: excavations in 1999, *Trans Bristol Gloucestershire Archaeol Soc* **124**, 73–110

Kershaw, J, 2008 The distribution of the 'Winchester' Style in late Saxon England: metalwork finds from the Danelaw, S Crawford & H Hamerow (eds) *Anglo-Saxon Stud Archaeol Hist* **15**, 254–69

Keuppers, L M, Southon, J, Baer, P, & Harte, J, 2004 Dead wood biomass and turnover time, measured by radiocarbon, along a subalpine elevation gradient *Oecologia*, **141**, 641–51

Kilmurry, K, 1980, *The pottery industry of Stamford, Lincs*, BAR Brit Ser **84**. Oxford: British Archaeological Reports

King, S H, 1962 Sussex, in H C Darby & E M J Campbell (eds) *The Domesday geography of south-east England*. Cambridge: Cambridge University Press, 407–82

Kirby, D P, 1978 The church in Saxon Sussex, in P Brandon (ed) *The south Saxons*. London and Chichester: Phillimore

Kirby, D P, 1991 *The earliest English kings*. London: Unwin Hyman

Landes, R, 1992 Between aristocracy and heresy: popular participation in the Limousin Peace of God, 994–1033, in Head, T, & Landes, R, (eds) *The Peace of God: social violence and religious response in France around the year 1000*. Ithaca, NY: Cornell University Press, 184–218

Landon, D B, 1996 Feeding colonial Boston: a zoo-archaeological study. *Historical Archaeology* **30**(1), 1–155

Lapidge, M, 1999 Flanders, in M Lapidge, J Blair, S Keynes, & D Scragg (eds) *The Blackwell encyclopaedia of Anglo-Saxon England*. Oxford: Blackwell, 186–7

Lapidge, M, & Love, R C, 2001 The Latin hagiography of England and Wales (600–1550), in G Philippart (ed) *Hagiographies, III*. Turnhout: Brepols, 203–325

Larsen, C S, 1997 *Bioarcheology: interpreting behavior from the human skeleton*. Cambridge: Cambridge University Press

Lauwerier, R C G M, 1988 Animals in Roman times in the Dutch eastern river area, *ROB Neaderrlandse Ordheden* **12**

Leahy, K, 2003 *Anglo-Saxon crafts*. Stroud: Tempus

Lewis, E, 1985 Excavations in Bishops Waltham 1967–78, *Proc Hampshire Fld Club Archaeol Soc*, **41**, 81–126

Lewis, C, 1994 Patterns and processes in the medieval settlement of Wiltshire, in M Aston & C Lewis (eds) *The medieval landscape of Wessex*. Oxford: Oxbow Books, 171–93

Lewis M E, 1999 The Impact of Urbanisation and Industrialisation in medieval and post-medieval Britain. An assessment of the morbidity and mortality of non-adult skeletons from the cemeteries of two urban and two rural sites in England (AD 850–1859). Unpubl PhD thesis , University of Bradford

Lewis, M, 2002 *Urbanisation and child health in medieval and post-medieval England: an assessment of the morbidity and mortality of non-adult skeletons from the cemeteries of two urban and two rural sites in England (AD 850–1859)*, BAR Brit Ser **339**. Oxford: Archaeopress

Lewis, M, 2007 *The bioarchaeology of children. Perspectives from biological and forensic anthropology*. Cambridge: Cambridge University Press

Lewis, M, & Gowland, R, 2007 Brief and Precarious Lives: infant mortality in contrasting sites from medieval and post-medieval England (AD 850–1859), *American J Physical Anthropol*, **134**(1), 117–29

Lister, A M, 1996 The morphological distinction between bones and teeth of fallow deer (*Dama dama*) and red deer (*Cervus elaphus*). *Int J Osteoarchaeology* **6**, 119–43

Locker, A, 1984 (n.d. 2) Milk Street, London: the fish bones. Unpubl report

Locker, A, 1987 The fish remains, in B Ayers *Excavations at St Martin-at-Palace Plain, Norwich, 1981*, East Anglian Archaeology, **37**. Norfolk: Norfolk Archaeological Unit, Norfolk Museums Service

Locker, A, 1999 (n.d. 1) The fish bones recovered from excavations of medieval tenements at 76–96 Victoria Street, Bristol. Unpubl report

Long, A, & Roberts, D H, 1997 Sea-level change, in M Fulford, T Champion, & A Long (eds) *England's coastal heritage*, Engl Heritage Archaeol Rep **15**. London: English Heritage, 25–49

Longin, R, 1971 New method of collagen extraction for radiocarbon dating, *Nature*, **230**, 241–2

Losco-Bradley, S, & Kinsley, G, 2002 *Catholme: an Anglo-Saxon settlement on the Trent gravels in Staffordshire*. Nottingham: University of Nottingham

Lovejoy, C O, Meindl, R, Pryzbeck, T, & Mensforth, R P, 1985 Chronological metamorphosis of the auricular surface of the ilium: a new method for the determination of adult skeletal age at death, *American J Physical Anthropoly*, **68**, 15–28

Loveluck, C P, 2001 Wealth, waste and conspicuous consumption: Flixborough and its importance for middle and late Saxon rural settlement studies, in H Hamerow & A MacGregor (eds) *Image and power in the archaeology of early medieval Britain: essays in honour of Rosemary Cramp*. Oxford: Oxbow Books, 78–130

Loveluck, C P, (ed) 2007 *Rural settlement, lifestyles and social change in the late first millennium AD: Anglo-Saxon Flixborough in its wider context*. Excavations at Flixborough **4**, Oxford: Oxbow Books

Loveluck, C, & Atkinson, D, 2007 *The early medieval settlement remains from Flixborough, Lincolnshire: the occupation sequence, c. 600–1000*, Excavations at Flixborough **1**. Oxford: Oxbow Books

Lucas, G, & McGovern, T, 2007 Bloody slaughter: ritual decapitation and display at the Viking settlement of Hofstaðir, Iceland, *European J Archaeol* **10**(1), 7–30

Lucy, S, & Reynolds, A, 2002 *Burial in early medieval England and Wales*, Soc Medieval Archaeol Monogr Ser **17**. London: Society for Medieval Archaeology

Lucy, S, Tipper, J, & Dickens, A, 2009 *The Anglo-Saxon settlement and cemetery at Bloodmoor Hill, Carlton Colville, Suffolk*, E Anglian Archaeol Rep **131**. Cambridge: Cambridge Archaeological Unit

Lyne, M, 2000 The pottery, in C Butler *Saxon settlement and earlier remains at Friars Oak, Hassocks*, BAR Brit Ser **295**. Oxford: British Archaeological Reports, 23–6

Lyne, M, unpub, Excavations at Pevensey Castle, 1936–64. Lewes: Unpublished rep in Barbican House Library

Mabillon, J, (ed) 1740 *Acta Sanctorum ordinis S. Benedicti*, VI, 2. Venice

MacGregor, A, 1985 *Bone, antler, ivory and horn: the technology of skeletal materials since the Roman period*. London: Croom Helm

MacGregor, A, Mainman, A J, & Rogers, N S H, 1999 *Craft, industry and everyday life: bone, antler, ivory and horn from Anglo-Scandinavian and medieval York*, The Archaeology of York **17/2**. York: Council for British Archaeology

MacMillan, J T, 1990 *Mussel stocking density trials*. Sea Fish Report no. 386. Sea Fish Industry Authority, Marine Farming Unit, Crown Estate Commissioners

Magennis, H, 1999 *Anglo-Saxon appetites. Food and drink and their consumption in Old English and related literature*. Dublin: Four Courts Press

Mainman, A J, & Rogers, N S, 2000 *Craft, industry and everyday life: finds from Anglo-Scandinavian York*, The Archaeology of York, The Small Finds **17/14**. York: Council for British Archaeology

Maître-Allain, T, 1991 *La vie en bord de mer*. Paris: Arthaud

Maltby, J M, 1989 The animal bones, in P Fasham, D E Farwell & R J B Whinney *The Archaeological Site at Easton Lane, Winchester*, Hants Field Club and Arch Soc Mono **6**. Gloucester: Alan Sutton, 122–30

Mann, J E, 1982 *Early medieval finds from Flaxengate, 1: objects of antler, bone, stone, horn, ivory, amber, and jet*, The Archaeology of Lincoln XIV-1. Lincoln: Council for British Archaeology for the Lincoln Archaeological Trust

Mant, A K, 1987 Knowledge acquired from post-War exhumations, in A Boddington, A N Garland & R C Janaway (eds) *Death, decay, and reconstruction*. Manchester: Manchester University Press, 65–80

Margeson, S, 1993 *Norwich households: the medieval and post-medieval finds from Norwich survey excavations 1971–1978*, E Anglian Archaeol Rep **58**. Norwich: Norwich Survey/Norfolk Museums Service

Margeson, S, 1995 Iron objects, in A Rogerson *A late Neolithic, Saxon and medieval site at Middle Harling, Norfolk*, E Anglian Archaeol Rep **74**. London: British Museum; Dereham: Field Archaeology Division, Norfolk Museums Service, 69–78

Margeson, S, 1997 *The Vikings in Norfolk*. Gressenhall: Norfolk Museums Service

Marshall, A, & Marshall, G, 1991 A survey and analysis of the buildings of early and middle Anglo-Saxon England, *Medieval Archaeol*, **35**, 29–43

Marzinzik, S, 2003 *Early Anglo-Saxon belt buckles (late 5th to early 8th centuries AD): their classification and context*. BAR Brit Ser **357**. Oxford: British Archaeological Reports

Masters, P M, 1987 Preferential preservation of non-collagenous protein during bone diagenesis: implications for chronometric and stable isotope measurements, *Geochimica et Cosmochimica Acta*, **51**, 3209–14

Mawer, A, Stenton, F M, & Gover, J E B, 1930 *The place-names of Sussex, II*. Cambridge: Cambridge University Press

Mayr-Harting, H, (ed) 1964 *The Acta of the Bishops of Chichester, 1075–1207*, Canterbury and York Society **56**. Torquay: Devonshire Press

Mays, S, 1996 Human skeletal remains, in J Timby (ed) *The Anglo-Saxon cemetery at Empingham II, Rutland*, Oxbow Monogr **70**. Oxford: Oxbow Books, 21–34

Mays, S, Harding, C, & Heighway, C, 2007 *Wharram: the churchyard. A study of settlement on the Yorkshire Wolds, XI*, York Univ Archaeol Publ **13**. York: University of York

McCobb, L M E, Briggs, D E G, Evershed, R P, & Hall, A R, 2001 Preservation of fossil seeds from a 10th-century AD cess pit at Coppergate, York, *J Archaeol Sci*, **28**, 929–40

McCobb, L M E, Briggs, D E G, Carruthers, W J, & Evershed, R P, 2003 Phosphatisation of seeds and roots in a late Bronze Age deposit at Potterne, Wiltshire, UK, *J Archaeol Sci*, **30**, 1269–81

McKitterick, R, 1977 *The Frankish Church and the Carolingian reforms, 789–895*. London: Royal Historical Society

Meadows, I, 1998 Ketton Quarry, *Medieval Settlement Research Group Annual Report*, **13**, 46–7

Meeson, R A, & Welch, C M, 1993 Earthfast posts: the presence of alternative building techniques, *Vernacular Architecture*, **24**: 1–17

Metcalf, D M, 1998 The monetary economy of ninth-century England south of the Humber: a topographical analysis, in M A S Blackburn & D N Dumville (eds) *Kings, currency and alliances. History and coinage of southern England in the ninth century*. Woodbridge: Boydell, 167–97

Miles, D, & Palmer, S, 1986 *Invested in Mother Earth: the Anglo-Saxon cemetery at Lechlade*. Oxford: Oxford Archaeological Unit

Miller, S, (ed) 2000 *Charters of the New Minster, Winchester: Anglo-Saxon charters IX*. Oxford: Oxford University Press

Millett, M, & James, S, 1983 Excavations at Cowdery's Down, Basingstoke, Hampshire, 1978–81, *Archaeol J*, **140**, 151–279

Milne, G, & Milne, C, 1982 *Medieval waterfront development at Trig Lane, London*, London Middlesex Archaeol Soc Spec Pap **5**. London: London & Middlesex Archaeological Society

Moffett, L, 1994 Charred cereals from some ovens/kilns in late Saxon Stafford and the botanical evidence for the pre-burh economy, in J Rackham (ed) *Environment and economy in Anglo-Saxon England*. CBA Res Rep **89**. York: Council for British Archaeology, 55–64

Moffett, L, 2007 Crop economy and other plant

remains, in M Charles & R J Williams *Death and taxes: the archaeology of a middle Saxon centre at Higham Ferrers, Northamptonshire.* Oxford: Oxford Archaeology, 158–81

Molyneux, N A D, Baines, N, & Tyers, I, 2003 The detached bell tower, St Leonard's parish church, Yarpole, Herefordshire, *Vernacular Architecture*, **34**, 68–72

Monk, M, 1981 Post-Roman drying kilns and the problem of function: a preliminary statement, in D Ó Corráin, (ed) *Irish antiquity.* Dublin: Four Courts Press, 216–30

Mook, W G, 1986 Business meeting: recommendations/resolutions adopted by the twelfth international radiocarbon conference, *Radiocarbon* **28**, 799

Mook, W G, & Streurman, H J, 1983 Physical and chemical aspects of radiocarbon dating, in W G Mook & H T Waterbolk (eds) *Proc First International Symposium ¹⁴C and Archaeology*, *PACT*, **8**, 31–55

Moore, H B, 1934 The relation of shell growth to environment, in *Patella vulgate*, *Proc Malacological Society*, **21**, 217–22

Moore, W J, & Corbett, E, 1973 The distribution of dental caries in ancient British populations II. Iron Age, Romano-British and mediaeval periods, *Caries Research*, **7**, 139–53

Moorrees, C F A, Fanning, E A, & Hunt, E E, 1963a Formation and resorption of three deciduous teeth in children, *American J Physical Anthropol*, **21**, 205–13

Moorrees, C F A, Fanning, E A, & Hunt, E E, 1963b Age variation of formation stages for ten permanent teeth, *J Dental Research*, **42**, 1490–502

Moreland, J, 2001 *Archaeology and text.* London: Duckworth

Morgan, O, 1861 Proceedings of the meetings of the Archaeological Institute, Dec 1860, *Archaeol J*, **18**, 66–78

Morris, C A, 1983 A late Anglo-Saxon hoard of iron and copper-alloy artefacts from Nazeing, Essex, *Medieval Archaeol*, **27**, 27–39

Morris, C, 1989 *Churches in the landscape.* London: J M Dent & Sons

Mortimer, R, 2000 Village development and ceramic sequence: the middle to late Saxon village at Lordship Lane, Cottenham, Cambridgeshire, *Proc Cambridge Antiq Soc*, **89**, 5–33

Morton, A D, 1992 *Excavations at Hamwic: volume I, excavations 1946–83, excluding Six Dials and Melbourne Street*, CBA Res Rep **84**. London: Council for British Archaeology

Müldner, G, & Richards, M P, 2006 Diet in medieval England: the evidence from stable isotopes, in C M Woolgar, D Serjeantson, & T Waldron (eds) *Food in medieval England. Diet and nutrition.* Oxford: Oxford University Press, 228–38

Mulville, J, 2003 Phases 2a–2e: Anglo-Saxon occupation, in A Hardy, A Dodd, & G Keevil (eds) *Aelfric's Abbey: excavations at Eynsham Abbey, Oxfordshire 1989–92.* Thames Valley Landscape Volume **16**. Oxford: Oxford University School of Archaeology, 343–60

Murphy, P, 1985 The cereals and crop weeds, in S West, *West Stow: the Anglo-Saxon village. Volume 1, text*, EAA Report **24**. Ipswich: Suffolk County Planning Department, 100–08

Murphy, P, 1997 Environment and economy [rural Anglo-Saxon and medieval], in J Glazebrook (ed) *Research and archaeology: a framework for the eastern counties, 1. Resource assessment*, E Anglian Archaeol Occ Pap **3**. Norwich: Scole Archaeological Committee, 54–5

Nadeau, M-J, Schleicher, M, Grootes, P M, Erlenkeuser, H, Gottdang, A, Mous, D J W, Sarnthein, J M, & Willkomm, H, 1997 The Leibniz-Labor AMS facility at the Christian-Albrechts University, Kiel, Germany, *Nuclear Instruments and Methods in Physics Research Section B* **123**, 22–30

Neal, R, 2008 Beyond the snails: a molluscan and sedimentary analysis of settlement and land use at Bishopstone, East Sussex. Unpubl MSc Geoarchaeology Diss, University of Reading

Needham, S, & Spence, T, 1997 Refuse and the formation of middens, *Antiquity*, **71**, 77–90

Niles, J D, 1991 Pagan survivals and popular belief, in M Godden & M Lapidge (eds) *The Cambridge companion to Old English literature.* Cambridge: Cambridge University Press, 126–41

Noddle, B, 1980 Identification and interpretation of animal bones, in P Wade-Martins (ed) *Excavations in North Elmham Park 1967–1972. Vol II.* E Anglian Archaeol Rep **9**, 375–409

North, J J, 1994 *English hammered coinage 1, early Anglo-Saxon to Henry III, c 600–1272*, 3rd revised edn. London: Spink

O'Connell, T C, & Hedges, R E M, 1999 Investigations into the effects of diet on modern human hair isotopic values, *American J Physical Anthropol* **108**, 409–25

O'Connor, T P, 1982 *Animal bones from Flaxengate, Lincoln, c 870–1500.* London: Council for British Archaeology

O'Connor, T P, 1992 Pets and pests in Roman and medieval Britain, *Mammal Review*, **22**, 107–13

O'Connor, T P, 2001 On the interpretation of animal bone assemblages from *wics*, in D Hill & R Cowie (eds) *Wics: the early mediaeval trading centres of northern Europe.* Sheffield: Sheffield Academic Press, 54–60

O'Connor, T P, 2003 *The analysis of urban animal bone assemblages: a handbook for archaeologists.* The Archaeology of York **19**(2). York: Council for British Archaeology

O'Keeffe, T, 2004 *Ireland's round towers.* Tempus: Stroud

Ortenberg, V, 1992 *The English Church and the continent in the tenth and eleventh centuries: cultural, spiritual, and artistic exchanges.* Oxford: Clarendon Press

Ortner, D J, 1991 Theoretical and methodological issues in paleopathology, in D J Ortner & A C Aufderheide (eds) *Human paleopathology: current syntheses and future options*. Washington DC: Smithsonian Institution Press, 5–11

Ortner, D J, 2003 *Identification of pathological conditions in human skeletal remains*. New York: Academic Press

Orton, J H, 1928 Observations on *Patella vulgata*. Part II Rate of growth of shell, *J Marine Biological Assoc* (UK), **15**, 863–74

Orton, C, Tyers, P, & Vince, A, 1993 *Pottery in archaeology*. Cambridge: Cambridge University Press

O'Shea, E W, 1978. A survey of a Sussex village, *Lewes Archaeological Group Newsletter* **43**

O'Sullivan, A, 2003 Place, memory and identity among estuarine fishing communities: interpreting the archaeology of early medieval fish weirs, *World Archaeol,* **35**, 449–68

Ottaway, P, 1990 Anglo-Scandinavian ironwork from 16–22 Coppergate, York *c* 850–1100, Unpubl DPhil thesis, University of York

Ottaway, P, 1992 *Anglo-Scandinavian ironwork from 16–22 Coppergate*, The Archaeology of York **17/6**. London: Council for British Archaeology for the York Archaeological Trust

Ottaway, P, 1994 The ironwork, in K Steedman, Excavation of a Saxon site at Riby Crossroads, Lincolnshire, *Archaeol J,* **151**, 249–63

Ottaway, P, 2009a Iron domestic fixtures, fittings and implements, in D H Evans & C Loveluck (eds) 2009, 166–187

Ottaway, P, 2009b Agricultural tools, in D H Evans & C Loveluck (eds) 2009, 245

Ottaway, P, 2009c Woodworking tools, in D H Evans & C Loveluck (eds) 2009, 253–56

Ottaway, P, 2009d The Flixborough tool hoard, in D H Evans & C Loveluck (eds) 2009, 256–66

Ottaway, P & Rogers, N, 2002 *Craft, industry, and everyday life: finds from medieval York*, The Archaeology of York **17/15**. York: Council for British Archaeology for the York Archaeological Trust

Owen-Crocker, G R, 2004 *Dress in Anglo-Saxon England*, 2nd edn. Woodbridge: Boydell

Pagan, H E, 1976 The coins, in B Cunliffe, *Excavations at Portchester Castle: II Saxon*. London: Thames & Hudson for the Society of the Antiquaries, 230–1

Page, M, & Jones, R, 2007 Stability and instability in medieval village plans: case-studies in Whittlewood, in M Gardiner & S Rippon (eds) *Medieval landscapes. Landscape history after Hoskins vol 2*. Macclesfield: Windgather Press, 139–52

Palmer, B, 2003 The hinterlands of three southern English *emporia*: some common themes, in T Pestell & K Ulmschneider (eds) 2003 *Markets in early medieval Europe: trading and 'productive sites' 650–850*. Macclesfield: Windgather Press, 48–61

Parker Pearson, M, Smith, H, Mulville, J, & Brennand, M, 2004 Cille Pheadair: the life and times of a Norse-period farmstead *c* 1000–1300, in J Hines, A Lane, & M Redknap (eds) *Land, sea and home: settlement in the Viking period*, Soc Medieval Archaeol Monogr Ser **20**. Leeds: Maney, 235–54

Payne, S, 1969 A metrical distinction between sheep and goat metacarpals, in P J Ucko & G W Dimbleby (eds) *The domestication and exploitation of plants and animals*. London: Duckworth, 295–395

Payne, S, 1973 Kill-off patterns in sheep and goats. The mandibles from Asvan Kale, *Anatolian Stud,* **23**, 281–303

Payne, S, 1985 Morphological distinctions between the mandibular teeth of young sheep, ovis, and goats, capra, *J Archaeol Sci*, **12**(2), 139–47

Payne, S, 1987 Reference codes for wear stages in the mandibular cheek teeth of sheep and goats, *J Archaeol Sci* **14**, 609–14

Payne, S, & Bull, G, 1988 Components of variation in measurements of pig bones and teeth, and the use of measurements to distinguish wild boar from domestic pig remains, *Archaeozoologica*, **2**, 27–66

Peacock, D P S, 1969 A petrological study of certain Iron Age pottery from western England, *Proc Prehist Soc,* **34**, 414–27

Pears, B R R, 2002 A palaeoenvironmental reconstruction of sedimentation in the Bishopstone Valley, East Sussex: a geoarchaeological approach, Unpubl MSc Geoarchaeology Diss, University of Reading

Peers, C, & Radford, C A R, 1943 The Saxon monastery of Whitby, *Archaeologia*, **89**, 27–88

Pelling, R, & Robinson, M, 2000 Saxon emmer wheat from the upper and middle Thames Valley, England, *Environmental Archaeol*, **5**, 117–19

Pestell, T, 2004 *Landscapes of monastic foundation*. Woodbridge: Boydell

Pestell, T, & Ulmschneider, K, (eds) 2003 *Markets in early medieval Europe: trading and 'productive sites' 650–850*. Macclesfield: Windgather Press

Petts, D, 2002 Cemeteries and boundaries in western Britain, in S Lucy & A Reynolds (eds) *Burial in early medieval England and Wales*, Soc Medieval Archaeol Monograph **17**, London: The Society for Medieval Archaeology, 24–46

Petts, D, 2003 Votive deposits and Christian practice in late Roman Britain, in M O H Carver (ed) 2003, 109–18

Philp, B, & Chenery, M, 1998 *Prehistoric and monastic sites at Minster Abbey, Sheppey, Kent*. West Wickham: Kent Archaeological Rescue Unit

Pickles, T, 2009 *Biscopes-tûn, muneca-tūn* and *prēosta-tūn*: dating, significance and distribution, in E Quinton (ed) *The church in English place-names*, English Place-Name Society Extra Series, **IV**. Nottingham: English Place-Name Society, 39–108

Piper, P J, & O'Connor, T P, 2001 Urban small vertebrate taphonomy: a case study from Anglo-

Scandinavian York, *Int J Osteoarchaeol*, **11**, 336–44

Plummer, C, (ed) 1896, reprinted 1946 *Venerabilis Baedae opera historica*. Oxford: Clarendon Press

Pluskowski, A & Patrick, P, 2003 How do you pray to God? Fragmentation and variety in early medieval Christianity, in M O H Carver (ed) 2003, 29–50

Pollington, S, 2003 *The mead-hall: feasting in Anglo-Saxon England*. Frithgard: Anglo-Saxon Books

Poole, C, 1995 Pits and propitiation, in B Cunliffe *Danebury: an Iron Age hillfort in Hampshire. Vol 6: a hillfort community in perspective*. CBA Res Rep **102**. York: Council for British Archaeology, 249–75

Poole, K, forthcoming. Bird introductions, in N J Sykes & T P O'Connor (eds) *Extinctions and invasions: the social history of British fauna*. Oxford: Oxbow Books

Poole, K, in prep The nature of society in Anglo-Saxon England, Unpubl PhD thesis, University of Nottingham

Potter, J F, 2005 No stone unturned – a re-assessment of Anglo-Saxon long-and-short quoins and associated structures, *Archaeol J*, **162**, 177–214

Povey, K, 1928 Saint Lewinna, the Sussex martyr, *The Sussex County Magazine*, **2**, 280–91

Powell, F, 1996 The human remains, in A Boddington (ed), *Raunds Furnells: the Anglo-Saxon church and churchyard*. London: English Heritage, 113–24

Powlesland, D, 1997 Early Anglo-Saxon settlements, stuctures, forms and layouts, in J Hines (ed) *The Anglo-Saxons from the migration period to the eighth century: an ethnographic perspective*. Woodbridge: Boydell, 101–24

Pritchard, F, 1991 The small finds, in A Vince (ed) *Aspects of Saxo-Norman London: 2, finds and environmental evidence*, London & Middlesex Archaeol Soc Spec Pap **12**. London: London & Middlesex Archaeological Society, 120–278

Prummel, W, 1988 *Distinguishing features on postcranial skeletal elements of cattle, Bos primigenus f. Taurus, and red deer, Cervus elaphus*. Kiel: Schriften aus der Archäologisch-Zoologischen Arbeitsgruppe Schleswig-Kiel

Prummel, W, & Frisch, H-J, 1986 A guide for the distinction of species, sex and body side in bones of sheep and goat. *J Archaeol Sci* **13**(6), 567–77

Rackham, J, 1994 Economy and environment in Saxon London, in J Rackham (ed) *Environment and economy in Anglo-Saxon England*, CBA Res Rep **89**. York: Council for British Archaeology, 126–35

Rahtz, P, 1976 Buildings and rural settlement, in D Wilson (ed) *The archaeology of Anglo-Saxon England*. Cambridge: Cambridge University Press, 49–98

Rahtz, P A, 1979 *The Saxon and medieval palaces at Cheddar*, BAR Brit Ser **65**. Oxford: British Archaeological Reports

Rahtz, P, & Meeson, R, 1992 *An Anglo-Saxon watermill at Tamworth*. CBA Res Rep **83**. London: Council for British Archaeology

Rees, H, Crummy, N, Ottaway, P J & Dunn, G, 2008 *Artefacts and Society in Roman and Medieval Winchester: Small finds from the suburbs and defences 1971–86*. Winchester: Winchester Museum Service

Reimer, P J, & Reimer, R W, 2001 A marine reservoir correction database and on-line interface, *Radiocarbon* **43**, 461–3

Reimer, P J, Baillie, M G L, Bard, E, Bayliss, A, Beck, J W, Bertrand, C, Blackwell, P G, Buck, C E, Burr, G, Cutler, K B, Damon, P E, Edwards, R L, Fairbanks, R G, Friedrich, M, Guilderson, T P, Hughen, K A, Kromer, B, McCormac, F G, Manning, S, Bronk Ramsey, C, Reimer, R W, Remmele, S, Southon, J R., Stuiver, M, Talamo, S, Taylor, F W, van der Plicht, J, & Weyhenmeyer, C E, 2004 IntCal04 Terrestrial radiocarbon age calibration, 26–0 ka BP. *Radiocarbon* **46**, 1029–58

Renn, D, 1993 Burhgeat and Gonfanon: two sidelights from the Bayeux Tapestry, *Anglo-Norman Stud*, **16**, 177–98

Resnick, D, (ed) 1995 *Diagnosis of bone and joint disorders*. Philadelphia: WB Saunders Company

Reynolds, A, 1999 *Later Anglo-Saxon England: life and landscape*. Stroud: Tempus

Reynolds, A, 2003 Boundaries and settlements in later sixth to eleventh-century England, in D Griffiths, A Reynolds & S Semple (eds) *Boundaries in early medieval Britain*. Anglo-Saxon Stud Archaeol Hist **12**, 98–139

Reynolds, A, 2005 On farmers, traders and kings: archaeological reflections of social complexity in early medieval north-western Europe, *Early Medieval Europe*, **13**(1), 97–118

Reynolds, R V, 2008 The dynamics of late Anglo-Saxon fish consumption: the evidence from the site of Bishopstone, East Sussex, Unpubl BA diss, University of Nottingham

Riddler, I, 1998 Worked whale vertebrae, *Archaeol Cantiana*, **118**, 205–15

Riddler, I, 2001 The small finds, in M Gardiner *et al* 2001, 228–52

Riddler, I, 2004 Bone and antler, in H Wallis (ed) *Excavations at Mill Lane, Thetford, 1995*, E Anglian Archaeol Rep **108**. Dereham: Archaeology and Environment Division, Norfolk Museums & Archaeology Service, 58–66

Rippon, S, 2000 *The transformation of coastal wetlands*. Oxford: Oxford University Press

Rippon, S, 2007 Emerging regional variation in historic landscape character: the possible significance of the 'Long Eighth Century', in M F Gardiner & S Rippon (eds) *Medieval Landscapes*, Landscape History after Hoskins **2**. Macclesfield: Windgather Press, 105–21

Rippon, S, 2008 *Beyond the medieval village: the diversification of landscape character in southern Britain*. Oxford: Oxford University Press

Roberts, C, & Cox, M, 2003 *Health and disease in Britain: from prehistory to the present day*. Gloucestershire: Sutton Publishing Ltd

Roberts, C, & Manchester, K, 2005 *The archaeology of disease*, 3rd edn. Gloucester: Sutton Publishing Ltd

Roberts, B K, & Wrathmell, S, 2002 *Region and place: a study of English rural settlement*. London: English Heritage

Rodwell, W, 1986 Anglo-Saxon church building: design and construction, in L A S Butler & R K Morris (eds) *The Anglo-Saxon church: papers in honour of H M Taylor*, CBA Res Rep **60**. London: Council for British Archaeology, 156–75

Rodwell, W, 2007 Burial archaeology, in T Waldron *St Peter's Barton-upon-Humber, Lincolnshire: a parish church and its community vol 2: the human remains*. Oxford: Oxbow Books, 15–29

Rogerson, A, 1976 *Excavations on Fuller's Hill, Great Yarmouth*, E Anglian Archaeol Rep **2**. Norfolk: Norfolk Archaeological Unit

Rollason, D W, 1982 *The Mildrith legend: a study in early medieval hagiography in England*. Leicester: Leicester University Press

Rumble, A R, 2002 *Property and piety in early medieval Winchester*, Winchester Studies **IV**.3. Oxford: Clarendon Press

Sabin, R, Bendrey, R, & Riddler, I, 1999 Twelfth-century porpoise remains from Dover and Canterbury, *Archaeol J* **156**, 363–70

Saunders, T, 2000 Class, space and 'feudal' identities in early medieval England, in W Frazer & A Tyrrell (eds) *Social identity in early medieval Britain*. Leicester: Leicester University Press, 209–32

Sawyer, P H, 1968 *Anglo-Saxon charters: an annotated list and bibliography*. London: Royal Historical Society

Scheuer, L, & Black, S, 2000 *Developmental juvenile osteology*. London: Academic Press

Scheuer, J L, Musgrave, J H, & Evans, S P, 1980 The estimation of late fetal and perinatal age from limb bone length by linear and logarithmic regression, *Annals of Human Biology*, **7**, 257–65

Schmid, E, 1972 *Atlas of animal bones*. Amsterdam: Elsevier

Schmidl, A, Jacomet, S, & Oeggl, K, 2007 Distribution patterns of cultivated plants in the Eastern Alps (Central Europe) during the Iron Age, *J Archaeol Sci*, **34**, 243–54

Schoeninger, M J, DeNiro, M J, & Tauber, H, 1983 Stable nitrogen isotope ratios of bone collagen reflect marine and terrestrial components of prehistoric diets, *Science*, **216**, 1381–3

Schoeninger, M J, DeNiro M J, 1984 Nitrogen and carbon isotopic composition of bone collagen from marine and terrestrial animals, *Geochimica et Cosmochimica Acta*, **48**, 625–39

Schwarcz, H P, & Schoeninger M J, 1991 Stable isotopic analyses in human nutritional ecology, *American J Physical Anthropol*, **35**(S13), 283–321

Scott, L, 1951 Corn-drying kilns, *Antiquity*, **25**, 196–208

Scott, E M, 2003 The third international radiocarbon intercomparison (TIRI) and the fourth international radiocarbon intercomparison (FIRI) 1990 – 2002: results, analyses, and conclusions, *Radiocarbon*, **45**, 135–408

Scull, C, 2001 Burials at emporia in England, in D Hill & R Cowie (eds) *Wics: the early mediaeval trading centres of northern Europe*. Sheffield: Sheffield Academic Press, 67–74

Seager Thomas, M, 2005a Understanding Iron Age Norton, *Sussex Archaeol Collect*, **143**, 83–115

Seager Thomas, M, 2005b The excavation of a later Saxon privy at Norton in East Sussex, *Sussex Arch Collect*, **143**, 267–69

Seaward, D R, 1982 *Sea area atlas of the marine molluscs of Britain and Ireland*. Shrewsbury: Nature Conservancy Council

Senecal, C, 2001 Keeping up with the Godwinsons: in pursuit of aristocratic status in late Anglo-Saxon England, *Anglo-Norman Stud*, **23**, 251–66

Serjeantson, D, 1996 The animal bones, in S R Needham & A Spence (eds) *Refuse and disposal at area 16 East Runneymede*. Runneymede Bridge Research Excavations, vol **2**. London: British Museum Press, 194–223

Serjeantson, D, 2006 Birds: food and a mark of status, in C M Woolgar, D Serjeantson, & T Waldron (eds) *Food in medieval England. History and archaeology*, 131–47. Oxford: Oxford University Press

Serjeanston, D, & Woolgar, C M, 2006 Fish consumption in medieval England, in C M Woolgar, D Serjeanston & T Waldron (eds) *Food in medieval England*. Oxford: Oxford University Press, 102–30

Serpell, J, & Paul, E, 1994 Pets and the development of positive attitudes to animals, in A Manning & J Serpell (eds) *Animals and human society: changing perspectives*. London: Routledge, 127–44

Sharpe, R, 1991 Eadmer's letter to the monks of Glastonbury concerning St Dunstan's disputed remains, in L Adams & J Carley (ed) *The archaeology and history of Glastonbury Abbey*. Woodbridge: Boydell

Silver, I A, 1969 The ageing in domestic animals, in D Brothwell & E S Higgs (eds) *Science in Archaeology*. London: Thames and Hudson, 283–302

Slota, Jr P J, Jull, A J T, Linick, T W, & Toolin, L J, 1987 Preparation of small samples for 14C accelerator targets by catalytic reduction of CO, *Radiocarbon*, **29**, 303–06

Smedley, N, & Owles, E, 1965 Some Anglo-Saxon 'animal'-brooches, *Proc Suffolk Inst Archaeol Hist*, **33**(2), 166–74

Smith, A H, 1961 *The place-names of the West Riding of Yorkshire, V*. English Place-Name Society **34**. Cambridge: Cambridge University Press

Smith, R N, 1969 Fusion of ossification centres in the cat, *J Small Animal Practice* **10**, 523–30

Smith, P S, 1987 Marine molluscs, in T Rook, The Roman villa site at Dicket Mead, *Herts Arch*, **9**, 79–175, at 170–2

Smith, B H, 1991 Standards of human tooth formation and dental age assessment, in M A Kelley & C S Larsen (eds) *Advances in dental anthropology*. New York: Wiley-Liss Inc, 143–68

Somerville, E M, 1996 Marine mollusca, in M Gardiner, M Russell & D Gregory, Excavations at Lewes Friary, 1985–6 and 1988–9, *Sussex Archaeol Collect*, **134**, 71–123, at 115–17

Somerville, E M, & Bonell, J K, 2006 The marine shell, in J Manley & D Rudkin, More buildings facing the palace at Fishbourne, *Sussex Archaeol Collect*, **144**, 69–113, at 94–7

Southern, R, 1953 *The making of the Middle Ages*. New Haven: Yale University Press

Spencer, B, 1998 *Pilgrim souvenirs and secular badges*. Medieval Finds Excav London, **7**. London: HMSO

Stephens, G R, 1959 The burial-place of St Lewinna, *Medieval Stud*, **21**, 303–12

Stevens, C, 2004 Charred plant remains, in G Hey *Yarnton: Saxon and medieval settlement and landscape*, Thames Valley Landscapes Monograph **20**. Oxford: Oxford Archaeology, 351–64

Stevens, C, 2006 Charred, mineralised and waterlogged plant remains, in C Ellis & P Andrews, A mid-Saxon site at Anderson's Road, Southampton, *Proc Hampshire Fld Club Archaeol Soc*, **61**, 81–133, at 104–14

Stilke, H, 1995 Shell-tempered ware from the Frisian coastal area, *Medieval Ceram*, **19**, 11–17

Stocker, D, & Everson, P, 2003 The straight and narrow way: fenland causeways and the conversion of the landscape in the Witham Valley, Lincolnshire, in M O H Carver (ed) 2003, 271–88

Stoodley, N, 2002 Multiple burials, multiple meanings? Interpreting the early Anglo-Saxon multiple interment, in S Lucy & A Reynolds (eds) *Burial in early medieval England and Wales*, Soc Medieval Archaeol Monogr Ser **17**. London: Society for Medieval Archaeology, 103–10

Straker, V, 1984 First and second century carbonised cereal grain from Roman London, in W van Zeist & W A Casparie (eds) *Plants and ancient man: studies in palaeoethnobotany. Proceedings of the sixth symposium of the International Work Group for Palaeoethnobotany, Groningen, 30 May–3 June 1983*. Rotterdam: A A Balkema, 323–29

Stuiver, M, & Kra, R S, 1986 Editorial comment, *Radiocarbon*, **28**(2B), ii

Stuiver, M, & Polach, H A, 1977 Reporting of ¹⁴C data, *Radiocarbon*, **19**, 355–63

Stuiver, M, & Reimer, P J, 1986 A computer program for radiocarbon age calculation, *Radiocarbon*, **28**, 1022–30

Stuiver, M, & Reimer, P J, 1993 Extended ¹⁴C data base and revised CALIB 3.0 ¹⁴C age calibration program, *Radiocarbon*, **35**, 215–30

Swanton, M J, (ed) 1996 *The Anglo-Saxon chronicle*. London: J M Dent

Sykes, N J, 2005 The dynamics of status symbols: wildfowl exploitation in England AD 410–1550. *Archaeol J*, **161**, 82–105

Sykes, N J, 2006 From *Cu* and *Sceap* to *Beffe* and *Motton*, in C M Woolgar, D Serjeantson, & T Waldron (eds) *Food in medieval England. Diet and nutrition*. Oxford: Oxford University Press, 56–71

Sykes, N J, 2007 *The Norman Conquest: a zooarchaeological perspective*, BAR Int Ser **1656**. Oxford: Archaeopress

Sykes, N J, forthcoming *Deer, land, knives and halls: social change in early medieval England*

Symonds, L, 2003 *Landscape and social practice: the production and consumption of pottery in 10th century Lincolnshire*, BAR Brit Ser **345**. Oxford: British Archaeological Reports

Taylor, H M, 1974 The architectural interest of Aethelwulf's De Abbatibus, *Anglo-Saxon Engl*, **3**, 163–73

Taylor, G, 2003 Hall Farm, Baston, Lincolnshire: investigation of a late Saxon village and medieval manorial complex, *Lincolnshire Hist Archaeol*, **38**, 5–33

Taylor, H M, & Taylor, J, 1965–78 *Anglo-Saxon architecture, I–III*. Cambridge: Cambridge University Press

Thomas, G, 2000 A survey of late Anglo-Saxon and Viking-age strap-ends, Unpubl PhD thesis, University of London

Thomas, G, 2003a Late Anglo-Saxon and Viking-age strap-ends 750–1100: part 1, *Finds Research Group AD700–1700 Datasheet*, **32**

Thomas, G, 2003b Hamsey, nr Lewes, East Sussex: the implications of recent finds of late Anglo-Saxon metalwork for its importance in the pre-Conquest period, *Sussex Archaeol Collect*, **139**, 123–32

Thomas, G, 2008 The symbolic lives of late Anglo-Saxon settlements: a cellared structure and iron hoard from Bishopstone, East Sussex, *Archaeol J*, **165**, 334–98

Thomas, G, 2009 The hooked-tags, in D H Evans & C Loveluck (eds) 2009, 17–22

Thomas, G, forthcoming, Craft production and Technology, in H Hamerow, S Crawford & D Hinton (eds) *A handbook of Anglo-Saxon archaeology*. Oxford: Oxford University Press

Thomas, R, 1999 Feasting at Worcester Cathedral in the seventeenth century: a zooarchaeological and historical approach. *Archaeol J*, **156**, 342–58

Thomas, R, 2005 Perceptions versus reality: changing attitudes towards pets in medieval and post-medieval England, in A Pluskowski (ed) *Just skin and bones? New perspectives on human-animal relations in the historical past*, BAR Int Ser **1410**. Oxford: Archaeopress, 95–104

Thomas, G, Pears, B, Whittick, C, & Seagar Thomas,

M, 2002 Bishopstone special report, *Sussex Past & Present*, **98**, 4–8

Timby, J, 1988 The middle Saxon pottery, in P Andrews (ed) *The coins and pottery from Hamwic,* Southampton Finds **1,** Southampton Archaeol Monogr **4**. Southampton: Southampton City Museums, 73–122

Tipper, J, 2004 *The grubenhaus in Anglo-Saxon England*. Yedingham: Landscape Research Centre

Tomlinson, P, & Hall, A R, 1996 A review of the archaeological evidence for food plants from the British Isles: an example of the use of the archaeobotanical computer database (ABCD), *Internet Archaeology*, **1**, http://intarch.ac.uk/journal/issue1/tomlinson_toc.html

Trotter, M, 1970 Estimation of stature from intact limb bones, in T Stewert (ed) *Personal identification in mass disasters*. Washington DC: Smithsonian Institution, 71–83

Tuross, N, Fogel, M L, & Hare, P E, 1988 Variability in the preservation of the isotopic composition of collagen from fossil bone, *Geochimica Cosmochimica Acta*, **52**, 929–35

Tweddle, D, Biddle, M, & Kjølbye-Biddle, B, 1995 *Corpus of Anglo-Saxon stone sculpture IV: south-east England*. Oxford: Published for the British Academy by Oxford University Press

Tyler, S, & Major, H, 2005 *The early Anglo-Saxon cemetery and later Saxon settlement at Springfield Lyons, Essex*, E Anglian Archaeol Rep **111**. Chelmsford: Heritage Conservation, Essex County Council

Ubelaker, D H, 1989 *Human skeletal remains. Excavation, analysis, interpretation*. Washington: Taraxacum

Ulmschneider, K, 2000 *Markets, minsters and metal-detectors: the archaeology of middle Saxon Lincolnshire and Hampshire compared*, BAR Brit Ser **307**. Oxford: Archaeopress

Unger, R, 1981 Warships and cargo ships in medieval Europe, *Technology and Culture* **22**, 240

Vandeputte, K, Moens, L, & Dams, R, 1996 Improved sealed-tube combustion of organic samples to CO2 for stable isotopic analysis, radiocarbon dating and percent carbon determinations, *Analytical Letters* **29**, 2761–74

Van der Leeuw, S, 1976 *Studies in the technology of ancient pottery*. Amsterdam: Universieit Amsterdam

Van der Veen, M, 1989 Charred grain assemblages from Roman-period corn driers in Britain. *Archaeol J*, **146**, 302–19

Van der Veen, M, Livarda, A, & Hill, A, 2008 New plant foods in Roman Britain – dispersal and social access, *Environmental Archaeology*, **13**(1), 11–36

Van Houts, E (trans) 2006 The Flemish contribution to biographical writing in England in the eleventh century, in D Bates, J Crick & S Hamilton *Writing medieval biography, 750–1250*. Woodbridge: Boydell, 117

Verhulst, A, & Declercq, G, 1989 Early medieval Ghent between two abbeys and the Counts' castle, 7th–11th centuries, in J Decavele (ed) *Ghent: in defence of a rebellious city: history, art, culture*. Antwerp: Mercatorfonds, 37–59

Vince, A, 2002 Anglo-Saxon pottery, in G Kinsley & S Losco-Bradley (eds) *Catholme: an Anglo-Saxon settlement on the Trent gravels in Staffordshire*, Nottingham Studies in Archaeology **3**. Nottingham: University of Nottingham Press, 102–08

Vince, A, & Jenner, M, 1991 The Saxon and early medieval pottery of London, in A Vince (ed) *Aspects of Saxo-Norman London: II finds and environmental evidence*, London & Middlesex Archaeol Soc Spec Pap **12**. London: London & Middlesex Archaeological Society, 19–119

von den Driesch, A, 1976 *A guide to the measurement of animal bones from archaeological sites*, Peabody Museum Bulletin **1**. Cambridge: Harvard University

von den Dreisch, A, & Boessneck, J, 1974 Kritische Anmerkungen zur Widerristhohen-Berechnung aus langmassen vor-und fruhgeschichtlicher Tierknochen. *Saugetierkundliche Mitteilungen* **22**(4), 325–48

Wade-Martins, P, 1980 *Excavations in North Elmham Park, 1967–72*, E Anglian Archaeol Rep **9**, (2 vols). Gressenhall: Norfolk Archaeological Unit

Waldron, T, 2007 *St Peter's Barton-upon-Humber, Lincolnshire: a parish church and its community vol 2: the human remains*. Oxford: Oxbow Books

Walker, M J C, 2005 *Quaternary dating methods*. Chichester: Wiley

Wallace-Hadrill, J M, 1983 *The Frankish Church*. Oxford: Clarendon Press

Wallenberg, J K, 1934 *The place-names of Kent*. Uppsala: Appelbergs boktryckeriaktiebolag

Walne, P, 1974 *The culture of bivalve molluscs*. West Byfleet: Fishing News (Books) Ltd

Walton Rogers, P, 1997 *Textile production at 16–22 Coppergate*, The Archaeology of York **17/11**. York: Council for British Archaeology

Walton Rogers, P, 2007 *Cloth and clothing in early Anglo-Saxon England, AD 450–700*. CBA Res Rep **145.** York: Council for British Archaeology

Walton Rogers, P, 2009 Textile production, in D H Evans & C Loveluck (eds) 2009, 281–316

Ward-Perkins, J B, 1940 *Medieval catalogue*. London: London Museum

Wastling, L M, 2009 Structural fired clay or daub, in D H Evans & C Loveluck (eds) 2009, 154–9

Waterman, D M, 1959 Late Saxon, Viking and early medieval finds from York, *Archaeologia*, **97**, 59–105

Webster, L E, 2001 Metalwork of the Mercian supremacy, in M P Brown & C A Farr (eds) *Mercia: an Anglo-Saxon kingdom in Europe*. London: Continuum, 263–77

Webster, L E, 2003 Encrypted visions: style and sense

in the Anglo-Saxon minor arts, AD 400–900, in C E Karkov & G H Brown (eds) *Anglo-Saxon styles*. New York: State University of New York, 11–30

Welch, M, 1985 Rural settlement patterns in the early and middle Anglo-Saxon periods, *Landscape Hist*, **7**, 13–25

Whatmore, L E, 1979 *St Lewinna: East Sussex martyr*. Pevensey: privately published

Wheeler, A, 1969 *The fishes of the British Isles and north-west Europe*. London: Macmillan & Co Ltd

Wheeler, A, 1978 *Key to the fishes of northern Europe*. London: Frederick Warne Ltd

Whytehead, R, Cowie, R, & Blackmore, L, 1989 Excavations at the Peabody site, Chandos Place and the National Gallery, *Trans London Middlesex Archaeol Soc*, **40**, 35–176

Williams, A, 1992 A bell-house and a burh-geat: lordly residences in England before the Norman Conquest, in C Harper-Bill & R Harvey (eds) *Medieval knighthood IV: proceedings of the fifth Strawberry Hill conference*. Woodbridge: Boydell, 221–41

Williamson, T, 2003 *Shaping medieval landscapes*. Macclesfield: Windgather Press

Wilson, D M, 1968 Anglo-Saxon carpenters' tools, in M Claus, W Haarnagel, & K Raddatz (eds) *Studien zur Europäischen Vor- und Frühgeschichte*: Neumünster: K Wachholtz, 143–50

Wilson, D M, 1984 *Anglo-Saxon art*. London: Thames & Hudson

Wilson, P, & King, M, 2003 *Arable plants: a field guide*. Old Basing: Wild Guides

Windell, D, Chapman, A, & Woodiwiss, J, 1990 *From barrows to bypass. Excavations at West Cotton, Raunds, Northamptonshire 1985–1989*. Rushden: Northamptonshire County Council

Winder, J, 1980 The marine mollusca, in P Holdsworth, *Excavations at Melbourne Street Southampton 1971–76*. CBA Res Rep **33**, 121–7. London: Council for British Archaeology

Winder, J M, 1992 A study of the variation in oyster shells from archaeological sites and a discussion of oyster exploitation, Unpubl PhD thesis, University of Southampton

Wood, S, 2006 *The proprietary church in the medieval west*. Oxford: Oxford University Press

Woodcock, A, 2003 The archaeological implications of coastal change in Sussex, in D Rudling (ed) *The archaeology of Sussex to AD 2000*. King's Lynn: Heritage, 1–16

Woolgar, C M, Serjeantson, D, & Waldron, T, (eds)

2006 *Food in medieval England. Diet and nutrition*. Oxford: Oxford University Press, 72–87

Wormald, C P, 1985 *Bede and the conversion of England: the charter evidence*. The Jarrow Lecture 1984

Wormald, P, 2001 The strange affair of the Selsey bishopric, 953–63, in R Gameson & H Leyser (eds) *Belief and culture in the Middle Ages: studies presented to Henry Mayr-Harting*. Oxford: Oxford University Press, 128–41

Wormald, C P, 2001 On þa wæþnedhealfe: kingship and royal property from Æthelwulf to Edward the Elder, in N J Higham & D H Hill (eds) *Edward the Elder, 899–924*. London: Routledge, 264–79

Wormald, C P, 2006 *The times of Bede*. Oxford: Blackwell

Worthington, M, 1993 Quentovic: local and imported wares, in D Piton (ed) *La céramique du Vème au Xème siècle dans l'Europe du Nord-Ouest: travaux du groupe de recherches et d'études sur la céramique dans le Nord – Pas-de-Calais, Actes du Colloque d'Outreau (10–12 Avril 1992)*. St-Josse-sur-Mer: GREC, 377–84

Wrathmell, S, 2002 Some general hypotheses on English Medieval peasant house construction from the 7th to the 17th centuries, in J Klápště (ed) *Ruralia IV: The Rural House from the Migration Period to the Oldest Still Standing Buildings*. Prague: Institute of Archaeology, Academy of Sciences of the Czech Republic

Xu, S, Anderson, R, Bryant, C, Cook, G T, Dougans, A, Freeman, S, Naysmith, P, Schnabel, C, & Scott, E M, 2004 Capabilities of the new SUERC 5MV AMS facility for 14C dating, *Radiocarbon*, **46**, 59–64

Youngs, S, Clarke, J, & Barry, T, 1986 Medieval Britain and Ireland in 1985, *Medieval Archaeol*, **30**, 114–98

Zadora-Rio, E, 2003 The making of churchyards and parish territories in the early-medieval landscape of France and England in the 7th–12th centuries: a reconsideration, *Medieval Archaeol*, **47**, 1–19

Zarnecki, G, Holt, J, & Holland, T, 1984 *English Romanesque art 1066–1200*. London: Weidenfeld & Nicholson

Zondervan, A, & Sparks, R J, 1997 Development plans for the AMS facility at the Institute of Geological and Nuclear Sciences, New Zealand, *Nuclear Instruments and Methods in Physics Research* B, **123**, 79–83

Index

Page numbers in **bold** denote illustrations

266